THE AGHRIĀ

A Peasant Caste on a Tribal Frontier

STUDIES IN ORISSAN SOCIETY, CULTURE AND HISTORY

Editors: HERMANN KULKE, GEORG PFEFFER, BURKHARD SCHNEPEL and HEINRICH VON STIETENCRON

Vol. 1: Jagannath Revisited: Studying Society, Religion and the State in Orissa, edited by Hermann Kulke and Burkhard Schnepel

Vol. 2: The Jungle Kings: Ethnohistorical Aspects of Politics and Ritual in Orissa, by Burkhard Schnepel

Vol. 3: Text and Context in the History, Literature and Religion of Orissa, edited by Angelika Malinar, Johannes Beltz and Heiko Frese

Vol. 4: Altar of Power: The Temple and the State in the Land of Jagannatha, by Yaaminey Mubayi

Vol. 5: The Aghriā: A Peasant Caste on a Tribal Frontiers, by Uwe Skoda

THE AGHRIĀ

A Peasant Caste on a Tribal Frontier

UWE SKODA

MANOHAR
2005

First published 2005

ISBN 81-7304-616-6

Published by
Ajay Kumar Jain for
Manohar Publishers & Distributors
4753/23 Ansari Road, Daryaganj
New Delhi 110002

Printed at
Lordson Publishers Pvt. Ltd.
Delhi 110007

Distributed in South Asia by
FOUNDATION BOOKS
4381/4, Ansari Road
Daryaganj, New Delhi 110 002
and its branches at Mumbai, Hyderabad,
Bangalore, Chennai, Kolkata

Für meine Eltern

Dedicated to the memory of

Rabi Narayan Patel,
his wife Satyabati Patel
as well as to Manodari Patel,

who welcomed me in their house,
but passed away during my research

In the final reckoning, I know that the people among whom I have done fieldwork, or about whom I have read, know much more about themselves than I ever will, though I may know things about them that they themselves do not.

T.N. MADAN, 2001: 8

Contents

Acknowledgements

This study, submitted as a Ph.D. thesis at the Institute of Ethnology, Free University of Berlin, was supervised by Professor Dr. Georg Pfeffer and PD Dr. Helene Basu, to whom I am very much indebted for their interest in the project, their support and critical remarks. I first went to Orissa for research in February 2000, for less than three months. I made three more visits—September 2000 to April 2001, October 2001 to January 2002, and July to September 2002—thus spending around 18 months in the field. The idea to stay in the village Mundaloi in a family of influential landlords developed in discussions between G. Pfeffer and D.K. Behera, whose Ph.D.-student Srikant Patel belongs to the very same family—being considered a sister's son (*bhanjā*) there. Thus I was welcomed in a very hospitable family in the village Mundaloi.

I thank all the villagers of Mundaloi and the surrounding villages, and particularly the family of Pramod Kumar Patel, Prasanna Kumar Patel, and Khirod Kumar Patel, my *dadas*, for their incredible hospitality, their time, and the knowledge they shared with me. I also want to express my gratitude to our *mamu* Tularam Nayak, to *sanbapa* Shiva Narayan Patel, to Nabaratna *dada*, Hema *ma*, Sukanti *ma*, Surama *bahu*, to Sarojini *bahu* to Tanaya *nani*, to Meena *nani*, Gita *nani*, to Jyosna *nani*, to Noyna, to my *bhanjās* und *putra* Julu, Tulu and Biju as well as to all the other family members I could not possibly name here. Without their patience and help this book would not have been possible.

To Professors D.K. Behera, P.N. Sahu, and D.C. Naik, all of Sambalpur University, I wish to express my appreciation for their hospitality, encouragement, and practical support. Srikant Patel helped to establish contact with my family in Mundaloi, and was also generous enough to share with me his valuable insights into the Aghriā culture. I also thank late Dr. Binod Chandra Naik, who patiently assisted with earlier drafts of various chapters, Rashmi Pramanic, who translated various Aghriā texts for me, and Montu Pradhan for his help in Sambalpur.

Colleagues and friends in Berlin, helped me formulate my ideas and shape the manuscript. Dr. Lidia Guzy and Jean Berrenberg read the thesis and kindly took the time to comment on it. I also had long discussions with Tina Otten, Peter Berger, Christian Striimpell and Dr. Roland Hardenberg. For their remarks I would also like to thank Chris Gregory of the Australian National University, Arlo Griffiths of Leiden University, and Hans-Joachim Kiderlen for his hospitality in Delhi.

This research has been part of the Orissa Research Project funded by the German Research Council (DFG).

The language was corrected by Brian Boulay and Rachel Herp. However the responsibility for the changes added later, for the content in general, and for the errors, remains mine.

Finally, I want to again thank my parents, to whom this book is dedicated, for all of their help and constant encouragement.

Uwe Skoda

Notes on Transcription

ଅ	a	ଠ	ṭh
ଆ	ā	ଡ	ḍ
ଇ	i	ଢ	ḍh
ଈ	ī	ଣ	ṇ
ଉ	u	ତ	t
ଊ	ū	ଥ	th
ଏ	e	ଦ	d
ଐ	oi	ଧ	dh
ଓ	o	ନ	n
ଔ	au	ପ	p
ଋ	ṛu	ଫ	ph
ୠ	ṛū	ବ	b
କ	k	ଭ	bh
ଖ	kh	ମ	m
ଗ	g	ଯ	j
ଘ	gh	ର	r
ଙ	ṅ	ଳ	ḷ
ଚ	ch	ଲ	l
ଛ	chh	ୟ	y
ଜ	j	ଶ	ś
ଝ	jh	ସ	s
ଞ	ñ	ଷ	ṣ
ଟ	ṭ	ହ	h

* My transcription is based on Hardenberg and Panda (1999).

Notes on Abbreviations

Elaborate descriptions of kinship relationships can be avoided through appropriate abbreviations, whereby I would adhere to the following system as outlined by Trautmann (1995 [1981]: 31):

m.s.	male speaker	f.s.	female speaker		
F	father	M	mother	Ch	children
B	brother	Z	sister	Pa	parents
S	son	D	daughter	Sb	sibling
H	husband	W	wife	Sp	spouse
e	elder	y	younger	os	opposite sex
WT	wife-taker	WG	wife-giver	ss	same sex
+2/+1	grandparent's/ parent's generation	–2/–1	grandchildren's/ children's generation	0	ego's generation

The relationships mentioned above can be combined, to express relationships of second or third degree, for example, FF (father's father), MB (mother's brother), FZH (father's sister's husband), MyB (mother's younger brother), eZDy (elder sister's daughter, younger than ego) or FBSe (father's brother's son, elder than ego).

Glossary

Diacritic marks have been neglected while ordering the list alphabetically according to the English alphabet. For kinship terms see Chapter 5.

All words listed below are common in the local spoken Sambalpuri. Oriya or Laria words are distinguished as (O) and (L) respectively.

Achhuā	'Untouchables'
Ādivāsi/Ādibāsi	aboriginals
aenthā	food remains or garbage
ajā	grandfather
akanda dīpa	continuous and inextinguishable light
aluā (S)	relatively pure variety of *chāul*, not parboiled
amābasyā (O)	new moon
Aṇa-Ādivāsi	Non-Aboriginals (see Ādivāsi)
antyeṣṭikriyā	funeral (specifically 11th day)
apūrṇṇa	unripe
aruā (O)	relatively pure variety of *chāul*, not parboiled
Āṣāḍh	month (mid June-mid July)
Āśbina	month (mid September-mid October)
asubha	inauspicious
asuddha	impure
ātmān	soul
bābā	ascetic
baḍ	big, senior, superior
baḍ baḍiā	very big and powerful people (usually landlord and *baḍ parjā*)
bāḍi	stick

baḍ lok	'big' people, senior people, people of high status
baḍ parjā	senior tenant, tenant of high status
bāer	garden
bāhāl	highest quality of land
bahu	elder brother's wife
Baiśākh	month mid April-mid May
baiṭhak	outer room in a Gauntiā-house for representative purposes
bakharā	room
bal	good, superior
bal lok	good people, people of high status
balkā	lowest variety of *chāul*, parboiled and dried in the sun
Bamra	former feudatory state of north-western Orissa
bandha	type of pond (three artificial walls)
bandha bibāha	'pond marriage'—purification of ponds
bandhu	affines, friends
bansa	clan
bara	day of the week
baraṇ	formal invitation
barāt	groom's party during a wedding
barsika śrāddha	ritual for an ancestor one year after death
barttan	payments within a *jajmāni*-relation
barttaniā	receiver of *barttan*
Bastar	district of Chhattisgarh, former feudatory state
bāṭ	way, street, road
bāṭ chhaḍā	avoidance
bāṭ dekhā	'gift of the way'
bāṭo	elder sister's husband
baula	form of ritual friendship
bedī	altar (especially in the context of marriage)
Beherā	village messenger, village guard
bensāgar	form of ritual friendship
bernā	medium quality of land

beṭh bigāḍi	forced labour
beṭhi	socage
Bhādraba	month (mid August-mid September)
bhāg/bhāga	'share'—payment to the bards of the Aghriā
Bhāi Jiūntiā	annual festival celebrating the brother-sister relationship (in the month of Āśbina)
bhakt	devotee
bhaṇḍār ghar	general store room
Bhandāri	barber
Bhanjā	sister's son (see Kinship)
bhāt	boiled rice
bhāt khiā	affinal gift
bhāt khuā	the first eating/feeding of rice
bheṭi	category of gifts
Bhitriā	confidential, personal assistant (male)
Bhitrien	female *bhitriā*
bhog	food offered for gods
bhogrā	king's land
bhoji	feast
bhuāsen (S)/ *bhūāsuni* (O)	women who have married into one's house (younger to ego)
bhut	category of evil spirits (male)
bidāki	payment for priests
Bidur	or Vidura—mythical figure of the *Mahābharāta*, seen as incarnation of a portion of Dharma
bihā	marriage
bihuḍā	loosening of the soil
Bolangir	district in Orissa, former feudatory state (Patna State)
Brāhmin	highest category within the *varṇa* scheme acting traditionally as priests
brata	ritual vow, also thread bound after performance of certain rituals
buḍ	complete bath
bukā	non-castrated he-goat
bunā	sowing
Butiyā	daily labourer

Chamār	leather workers
chanda-bindu	auspicious symbol (in form of a half circle with a dot)
chāul	pared rice
chaurāsi ghar	84 houses—name used for the Aghriā
Cheitr	month (mid March-mid April)
chhamāsi	funeral ritual to be held six month after death
Chhattisgarh	State of the Indian Union
chheḍ	end
Chhuāti	'touchables'
chipti	category of gifts
chirgin	category of evil spirits (female)
choṭ	small, junior, inferior
choṭ lok	'small' people, junior people, people of low status
chuḍā	flattened rice
chulā	hearth
chun	limestone
dakhinā	payment for priests
dāl	lentils
dām	price
dān	category of gifts
Danḍa Nrutya	'dance of punishment'—see rituals
dānda bāt	outside, outer way
Daśarā	Dossehra, another name for the month of Āśbina, major festival in this month
demul	shrine of the village goddess, sacred grove
Deogarh	District of Orissa, former capital of the Bamra State
dhan	wealth
dhān	paddy
dhān ghar	store room for paddy
dharma	religious and cosmic order
ḍhenki	traditional instrument to grind paddy
Dhobā	washerman
dhoti	traditional white loin cloth for men
dhūpa	incense

Diāli / Dipāvāli	festival of lights
dikhyā	initiation
diku	foreign landlords in Chota Nagpur
dindā pilā /dindā tukel	bachelor/spinster
Disandhrī	bards of the Aghriā
Dongria Kond	community of south Orissa
Dossondhi	bards of the Aghriā
duār	inner yard of a house, also gate
durbar	royal assembly, royal,court
ekoiśiā	ritual of 21st day after birth
gacha bibāha	'tree marriage'—purification of trees
Gadaba	tribal community of south Orissa
gāddī	throne
Gajapati	'Lord of the Elephants'—title of the royal dynasty of Puri
ganjā	cocks
ganja	marihuana
gañji	undershirt
gaunti	land deed of a Gauntiā, headmanship, village kingship
Gauntiā	title of former headmen /'village kings'
Ghanṭuāl	ferryman
ghar	house, room (also 'ritual' in the context of life cycle)
ghar dekhā	inspection of the groom's house by the bride's people prior to marriage
Ghar khiā	maid servant
ghī	clarified butter
ghuḍā	horse
gilti	dishes made of aluminium/steel
go	cow
gochar	land kept for grazing of cattle
godandā/godharsā	paths for animals (usually in the forests)
gotra	clan
grām	village
Grām Śrī	village goddess
guḍ	molasses

guḍā	lowest quality of land
gudri	goat shed
guhāl	cow shed
Guniā	traditional healing expert
Guti	contract labourer
habiṣ	diet kept by the women during *Panchaka* (last 5 days of the month of Kartika)
habiṣyānna	food eaten by the women during *Panchaka*
hāeṇḍ (S)	see *hāṇḍi*
hāṇḍi	pot used to boil rice
hāṇḍi pakā	destroying of the rice pot after death etc.
hantā	altar during Tārinī Brata ritual
hari banś	reading of sacred ṭexts
hari bol	'Say God!'—auspicious utterances particularly of men during rituals
Harijan	'children of God' (euphemism of Mahatma Gandhi applied to 'untouchable' communities, e.g. Gandā in Orissa)
hāṭ	market
hāth lagan	accepting the bride (literally: touching of the hands)
hātī	elephants
hātuā	'people of the market'
homa	fire ritual
hulhuli	auspicious sound of women during ritual performances
ijjāt	prestige, honour
iṣṭā devtā	tutelary deity (god) of royal families
iṣṭā devī	tutelary deity (goddess) of royal families
jagābār (S)/*jageibā* (O)	planting
Jagannāth	most important God of middle India (main temple in Puri)
jāgar	candlestick
jajmān	patron, sacrifier
jalchar	wet land, lands for ponds, land with springs
jami/jamin	land
Jamindār	'land-holder', title for 'little kings'
jāti	'root', 'kind', 'group', caste as empirical

	group, member of one's own community belonging to a different clan, 'witness' during life cycle rituals
jātrā	festival
jātrā dekhā	category of gifts presented on festivals
jhoti	ceremonial drawings on the ground
jiban	life energy, life spirit
jiu	see jiban
jiu dakā	calling of the life spirit back into the house
jiūntiā	thread presented by a sister to her brother on Bhāi jiūntiā
jueḍ	yoke
jutbār (S)	ploughing
Jyeṣṭha	month (mid May-mid June)
Jyotisiā	astrologer
kādo	mud
kām	work, duty, responsibility
kādo karibā	paddling
kālā	black
kālā pithia	'black backs', idiom for tribals
kalas kunḍi	earthen pot
Kālo	sacrificer of the village goddess
kalyānī khunṭ	wooden pole at the centre of Aghriā wedding altars
kām ghar	funeral
Kām karā	female domestic labourers
Kān Guru	Ear Guru
kansā	dishes made of a mixture of copper and tin
kanyā sulka	bridewealth ('bride tax')
kapar	agricultural instrument
Karam	Adina Cardifolia tree
karamdāl	form of ritual friendship
karttā	sacrifier
Kārttika	month (mid October-mid November)
kasi	castrated he-goat
kaṭā	type of pond (one or two artificial walls)
kej-wheels	iron wheels of the tractor used for paddling

Kethria	regional variant for Kshatriya (warrior in the *varṇa*-typology)
khai (O)	rice produced by heating paddy in a pot already filled half with sand
khalā	threshing floor
khali	leaf-plates
Khamāri (Gumāstā)	storeroom keeper, revenue collector, treasurer
khandā	sword
kharāb	bad
kharchā	raw ingredients for a meal
khat kaḍhā	collecting of cow dung (khata) and applying it to the fields
khoel	entrance area of a house
Khumbā	potter
khuṇṭ	wooden post, pole, stump of trees (see Chapter 7)
khuṇṭ kata gaunti	land deed received after clearing the forest
khuṇṭkattidar	clearers of the forest, in the tribal context: original settlers
kirthan-party	group singing devotional songs
Koraput	District of south Orissa
kṣātra-dharma	religious duties and laws for Kshatriya, warrior-ethic
kṣetra	field
Kshatriya	warrior (in the varṇa scheme)
kūāṇ	well
kudāli	hue used to loosen soil around chilli-plants
kural	agricultural instrument
Kurmi	peasant community of Middle India
kusbār	loosening of the soil (after ploughing and transplanting)
lagan dharā	finding/fixing of an auspicious date for a wedding
lāj	shame
Lakṣmī	Goddess of Wealth, Fortune, Rice (see Chapter 7)
Lariā	language of the Aghriā

Leuniā	Aghriā clan
liā (S)	see murhi
litā	food remains having been in contact with the saliva of a person and fallen on the ground, considered to be impure
luhā	iron
Luhurā	blacksmith
lungi	loin cloth for men
maḍiā	mixture of rice powder and boiled rice
maduā	altar, pavilion for rituals, temporary temple, sacred space
Māgha	month (mid January-mid February)
mahāḷayā	ritual for all ancestors at the end of *pitru pakṣ*
Mahābharāt	Indian epic
mahāprasād	form of ritual friendship
māhāpuru ghar	room with the house-shrine, sacred room of the house, 'room of gods'
Mahāsabhā	'great convention', annual meeting of the Aghriā caste organization
Mahuā	tree, Bassia Latifolia
mahuli	alcoholic drink made of *mahuā*
makrā	form of ritual friendship
makuṭ	crown
māl	medium quality of land
māmu	mother's brother
mān	metal pot to measure paddy—roughly ½ kg
mandap	altar, pavilion for rituals, temporary temple, sacred space
mandir	temple
mandli	parties or groups singing, dancing and playing music in a ritual context
mantra	sacred hymns
Mārgaśīrṣa	month (mid November-mid December)
maulā bhār	gifts of a mother's brother to his sister's son
merkhuṇṭ	central post of the threshing floor
mita	form of ritual friendship
muān	*khai* (heated rice) mixed with *guḍ* molasses)

muḍhi (O)	see *murhi*
mukhāgni	lightning of the funeral pyre
mukti	redemption, salvation
muṇḍā	type of pond (four artificial walls)
murhi (S)	*balkā-chāul* instead of paddy heated on sand as described for *khai*
naḍiā phuṭā	ritual breaking of coconuts during the wedding
Naik	title used by Aghriā and by Gaṇḍ-headmen
najar	evil eye
nakhyatra	constellation of stars
Nām Jagya	festival to commemorate Lord Krishna
nāmkaraṇa	name-giving ceremony
Narihā	herdsman
neibedya	food offered to gods
nijer	close
niśā	night
Nuā Khāi	annual festival of eating the new rice
oum	auspicious symbol/sound
pāchen bāḍi	stick to drive the bullocks
paḍā	hamlet
pāen	water
pāendhār	water flow
Pāenti	water carrier
pāikhānā	toilet, bathroom
paitā	sacred thread
pakkā	solid, concrete
pakkā ghar	concrete house
pakhāla	watered rice
palhā ghari	nursery field (for paddy)
palhā jagābār/jageibā	transplanting of rice
panas (S)/*paṇas* (O)	leaves used to offer water for the ancestors
pañchāyāt	village council
pañchāmrut	mixture of five ingredients (milk, honey, curd, molasses, banana)
pāñjji	horoscope
pāp	sin
pāpi	sinner

paralā ḍalā	flat basket, important during wedding rituals
parjā	tenant, subject
patā	land deed
phaklo-lāi (*Lariā*)	paddy heated and moved on sand
phaklo-liā (S)	see *khai*
Phalgun	month (mid February-mid March)
phalśā (S)/*phalās* (O)	leaves used during oblation for the ancestors
phalsiā	sacrificial axe
piṇda	rice balls offered to the manes
piṇḍā	veranda
pindā	cake
pindhā	small wooden stool
piṭha	'seat of mastery'
pithia	back
pitru	ancestor
pitru pakṣ	fortnight of the ancestors
Pouṣ	month (mid December-mid January)
praṇām	respectful greeting
praharī	time unit—three hours
praśād	food left by gods
pratiṣṭhā	purification
pret	potentially harmful spirit of a deceased
pūjā	ritual, worship
Pujāri	temple priest, temple servant
pūni, *pūrnimā*	full moon
puniya	religious merits
Puo Jiūntiā	annual festival
pūrṇṇa	ripe
purohit	family priest
purug	measurement for paddy
puṣkarā	constellation of stars, relevant after death
putrā	elder brother's son
rājā	king
rājādharma	dharma of a king
Rākasbuḍhā	ghost/divine being of the forest
rākhī	thread to be tied around one's wrist by a sister, etc.

Rākhī Pūni	annual festival celebrating the brother-sister-relationship, 'village durbar'
Rakṣā Bandhā	see *Rākhī Pūni*
randhā ghar	kitchen
rāṇḍi	widow
rāstā	road, way, street
rath	chariot
Rath Jātrā	annual car festival of Lord Jagannāth
rupā (S)/*ruā* (O)	transplanting of any plant
saḍak	street, road, way
śāḍhī	*sari*
Sāe	honorific title
sagāi	bridewealth, engagement
sahi	form of ritual friendship
Sāhu	master
sahyā	form of ritual friendship
sajja dān/śajyā dān	gift of a bed during funeral rituals
śakti	female power, potency, creative power
sāl	Shorea robusta tree
śalā	wife's younger brother
śalā bidhā	'groom bashing' by a wife's younger brother at the marriage
samādhi	funeral memorial
samāj	community, society (in the context of caste organization)
samdhen	child's spouse's mother
samdhi	child's spouse's father
samdhi bhet	ceremonial greeting of bride's and groom's father during the wedding
Samlei/Samleshvari	Goddess in north-west Orissa, patron deity of Sambalpur
sān	see *choṭ*
śankar	shell
śānti	peace
Sarliā	'slipped'—Aghriā excluded from the community after having married outside
śāsana	'royal edict', 'duty'—designation for villages offered to Brāhmin
Śibrātrī	festival for Śiva—the 'night of Śiva'

śil	stone used to grind spices and in the context of weddings
śītal	to cool down
Śrāban	month (mid July-mid August)
śrāddha	obituary rites
Suāti	night-guard
Śudra	lowest category within the *varṇa* scheme, considered to be servants
suhāsen	ego's generation set (particularly female relatives)
śuibā ghar	sleeping room
suta	thread
tāmi	unit to measure paddy—roughly 1 kg
tandhei	category of evil spirits (female witches)
tarpan	sacred rice beer offered to ancestors and close family members
teilabhiṣek	anointing of groom and bride with oil and turmeric
tel chaḍa	see *teilabhiṣek* (movement strictly downwards)
tel kām	ritual of the 3rd day after death
Teli	oil-presser
thāḍa ūchchā	general offering of gifts to groom or bride during wedding
thāl	plate
Ṭhikāmuliā	contract/wage-labourer
Tihāri	priests of the Aghriā said to be Brāhmin
ṭikā	dot on the one's forehead
tirtha	place of passage
tithi	day within a fortnight
Tulsī *chaur*	holy shrine with basil plant
uāns	new moon day
uāns (S)	new moon
uḍhni (S)/*oḍhani* (O)	veil
upahār	dowry (voluntarily given)
uṣā	sunrise
uṣnā (S) (*uṣunā* (O))	variety of *chāul*, parboiled and dried in the shadow
varṇa	mythological scheme of caste

Vyāsa	sage, mythical figure of *Mahābhārat*
Yama	God of Death
yathā	turban
yautuka	dowry (designation used in former times)

CHAPTER 1

Initiation into a Converging Tribal and Caste Society

The Aghriā are known for perseverance, and patience of its members and their aptitude for industry. Being self made persons, they believe in the dignity of hard labour. Land is very dear to them and they can turn a barren piece of land into a very fertile one by the very sweat of their brow. . . . They are known for their humble and sober behaviour, it is never in keeping with their nature to be rude and crude. They are also known for their great sense of hospitality.

P.K. Patel, 'The Agharias of Orissa:
A brief synoptic view' (undated manuscript)

1.1. INTRODUCTION

Remarkably little has been written on the Aghriā. In the ethnographic literature they have been almost ignored, which is surprising given their important role in the peasant society of western Orissa and Chhattisgarh. However, it appears that early ethnographers such as S.C. Roy, V. Elwin, and W. Grigson concentrated on traditional tribal communities, but neglected peasants who had migrated into the region.

Nonetheless, there are bits and pieces. First and foremost are cursory accounts by Risley (1981 [1891]) and Russell/Hiralal (1975 [1916]). Apart from very brief summaries of Aghriā mythology and a few social customs, both authors cite an even earlier account of Dalton, describing the Aghriā as 'tall and well-made, with high Aryan features and tawny complexions' (Risley 1981 [1891]: 4; Russell and Hiralal 1975 [1916]: 9). This stereotype—together with their reputation as industrious cultivators also already mentioned in Dalton (in Russell and Hiralal 1975 [1916]: 9)—as well as other parts of these early texts has been copied repeatedly in subsequent Census Reports and Gazetteers.

Short articles on various social and cultural aspects have been published occasionally: for example, by N. Pattanaik (1952) on funerary customs; by S.K. Patel (1995) on Aghriā origin; and by S. Patel and D.K. Behera (1999) on the social construction of womanhood. Additionally, an MA thesis was written by B.B. Nayak (1987–8) on the socio-economic life of the Aghriā, but has not been published. Apart from Pattanaik and Behera the authors are Aghriā themselves, but only S. Patel and D.K. Behera are trained anthropologists. Thus, literary and anthropological sources in English are, to my knowledge, scarce. There is, however, a quite rich descriptive source on Aghriā: their caste organization (or rather caste organizations, since there are three regional organizations). Since the early twentieth century these organizations have published, more or less annually, reports on their proceedings combined with accounts of their origin and the rules of rituals and marriage practice.

1.2. THE SETTING NORTH-WEST ORISSA

Mundaloi is a village situated in Sambalpur district in the north-western part of Orissa (Maps 1–3). Sambalpur, situated on the river Mahanadi, is not only the district headquarters, but also an important commercial centre. Apart from the Sambalpuri style of weaving also known as *ikat*, it is famous for the Hirakud Dam—the longest dam project and water reservoir in India that offers irrigation water for many parts of the region (but not for the village and its immediate vicinity).

The presiding deity of Sambalpur is Samlei or Samleshvari, presumably of tribal origin, who became the tutelary goddess of the Sambalpur kings. Among the Sambalpur kings Veer Surendra Sai (1809–84) is the most venerated and is hailed as a Shivaji of Orissa, since he is said to have led a rebellion against the British. Belonging to the Chauhan dynasty that had ruled Sambalpur since perhaps the sixteenth century, Veer Surendra Sai revolted against the imposition of a ruler by the British after its last Maharaja had died without sons, but was defeated and eventually put in jail. The British occupied

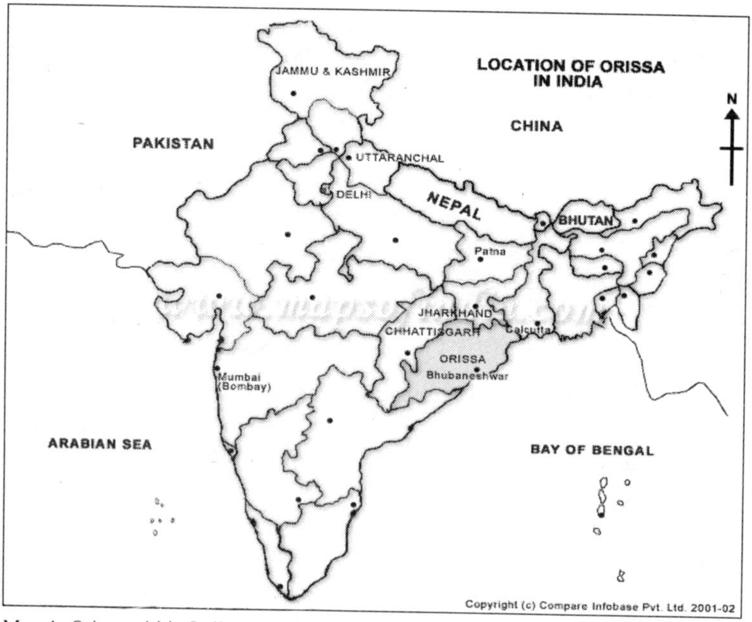

Map 1: Orissa within India.

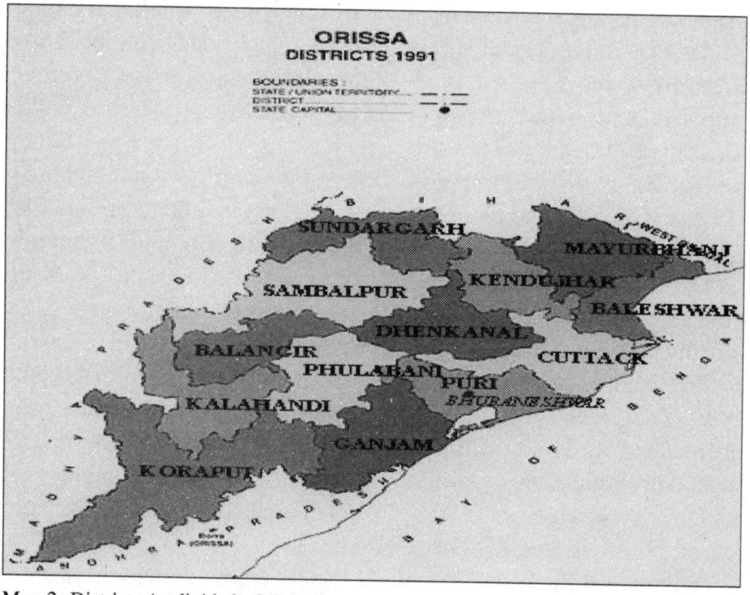

Map 2: Districts (undivided of Orissa).

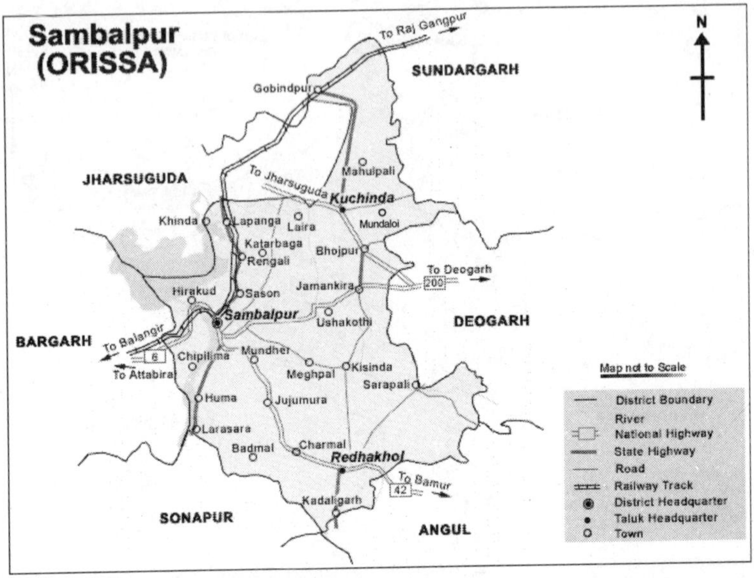

Map 3: Location of Kuchinda in Sambalpur District.

Sambalpur subsequently in order to rule directly. Other feudatory states like Bamra remained, because they had sided with the British from early on. The history of Bamra, which appears to have been subordinated to the Sambalpur kingdom prior to British rule, will be discussed in detail later.

The Sambalpur region forms a part of the north-western upland of Orissa with hills and slopes ranging between heights of around 400 and 800 ft. The northern side of the district—the Kuchinda and Bamra areas—is especially hilly terrain. The climate is extreme. Very dry and very hot summers, in which the temperature may rise up to 51^0 C during unbearable heat waves, are followed by humid monsoon periods and by dry winters with a minimal night temperature of around 5^0 C. The local language is Sambalpuri, which, having been more influenced by Hindi, differs from the Oriya spoken in the coastal belt. Additionally many communities have their own languages, such as Lariā in the case of the Aghriā, which seems to resemble Chhattisgarhi, Hindi dialect, to a large extent.

Mundaloi falls in the Kuchinda Block. Kuchinda is one of three sub-divisional centres of Sambalpur district, about 80 km from

Harvest of rice in Mundaloi.

Sambalpur (Map 3). On the way from Kuchinda—a distance of around 25 km—one has to cross a small river. However, crossing by bus or jeep is impossible during the monsoon. The bus service is interrupted during the monsoon, and bus owners usually tend to search for other routes in the meantime. The 'village highway', as my hosts jokingly called the road, was partly asphalted during my stay and many villagers desperately hope that one day there might be a convenient and all-weather road connecting them to the world.

Though situated right between Kuchinda and Deogarh, the village is accessible by road only from the Kuchinda side, because there is a range of hills on the Deogarh side. Villages in the hills or on the other side—though nearby—may be reached only by foot. Thus the village is remote indeed.

1.3. THE VILLAGE

The villages usually do not appear as continuous settlements, but rather as a collection of hamlets distributed over a certain area divided by fields. Even if an outsider might take a hamlet for a village, for the inhabitants the borders of their village are well marked. It is the village (*grām*)—not the hamlet or *paḍā*—that is traditionally governed by a headman and has a significance as a ritual unit. In most cases

Village road in Mundaloi during monsoon.

gods and goddesses are worshipped on the village but not the hamlet level. However, there may be occasional exceptions.[1]

The village Mundaloi consists of several hamlets (Map 4).

The distance between the Gauntiā's house and Kandh Paḍā may be around 2 km. Nuā Paḍā is situated at the same distance, while Jholdihi Paḍā is slightly farther away. Since most villagers would agree that the Kandh are the first settlers in the village, one may consider Kandh Paḍā as the oldest hamlet. Nuā Paḍā—as the name (*nuā* meaning 'new') indicates—is of rather recent origin, and so is Kutra Wahal. Both parts of the village have been set up by villagers who were forced to move from other hamlets to areas close to the forest after their original house or property was divided among sons. The hamlets around the Gauntiā's house, and the Gauntiā's house itself, were probably established around 1900. Significantly, the Gauntiā's house does not belong to any hamlet, but rather forms the centre of the village. From the perspective of the landlord's house all other houses closer to the hills—and therefore slightly higher (*upar* = high)—are considered as Upar Paḍā, while houses on the other side, but also built along the main road, are classified as Tal Paḍā (*tal* = below). Behind these two paḍās are two more hamlets, Turi Paḍā and Muṇḍā Paḍā. The first is named after a common ancestor

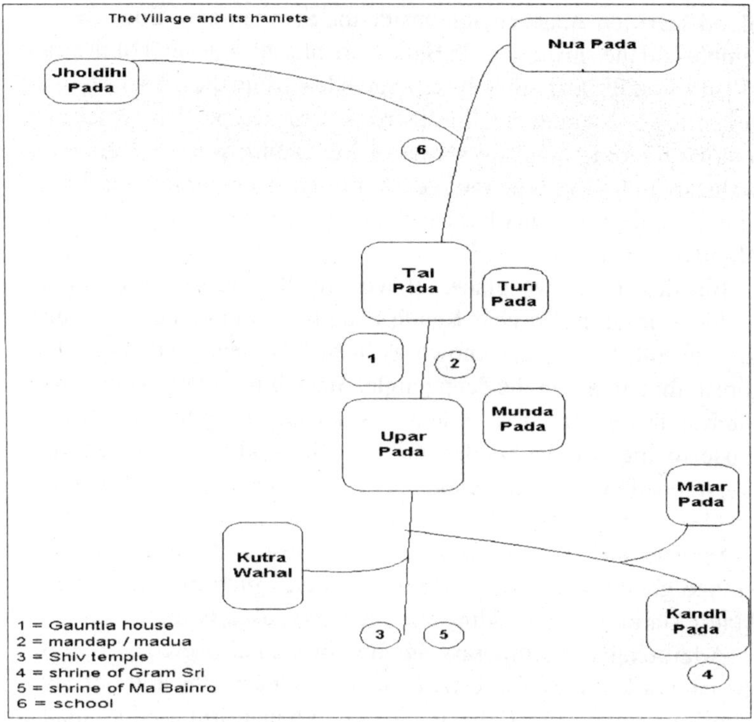

Map 4: Hamlets of the village.

of several Muṇḍā families residing there. In contrast to this, Muṇḍā Paḍā does indeed indicate the community predominantly settling there. It is land ownership rather than membership in a community that is the criterion for settling in a certain hamlet. Thus an Orām family stays in Kandh Paḍā and owns land nearby and there are Kandh living outside Kandh Paḍā. There is no separate hamlet for so-called 'Untouchables', who stay somehow between certain hamlets or on their outskirts, but do not live on the main road. The borders between the hamlets are rather vague and for example there is a Chaṣā house somewhere between the Gauntiā's house and Kandh Paḍā—which does not belong to any *paḍā*.

Outside the hamlets there is a Śiva temple, situated on the outskirts of the village rather close to the hills on the southern side. Directly opposite the temple lies a small shrine consisting of three stones under a tree, erected for Mā Bainro. This shrine is the appropriate place for blood sacrifice, unacceptable inside the Śiva temple. Both the Śiva temple and the shrine for Mā Bainro are placed at the end of the main village road. From here only a footpath leads into the hills. Originally constructed as a mud hut, during my stay the temple was replaced by a stone building, and the shrine of Mā Bainro was surrounded by walls, though there is no roof yet. At present a temple servant (Pūjāri) of the Gauḍ community has been appointed by the village for regular Monday worship.

Besides these two places of worship the shrine of the village goddess or Grām Śrī near Kandh Paḍā is of importance. An empty termite hill, this shrine known as *demul*, is clearly situated in the forest, though not in the deep jungle. Since it is widely accepted that the Kandh were the first settlers, it is not surprising that the shrine is close to the Kandh hamlet and that the goddess is hereditarily worshipped by a Kandh village sacrificer known as Kālo. The village goddess is accompanied by other gods and spirits staying in and around her shrine, for instance in stones close to it. Furthermore, the village goddess as well as other goddesses such as Bauti Mā and Mauli Mā may be worshipped in the fields, usually under trees.

Additionally, a temporary *mandap* or *maduā* is erected opposite the landlord's house for festivals such as *Śibrātrī* (the night of Śiva), *Nām Jagya* and *Rath Jātrā*. It consists of a platform used as an altar on which the respective gods are worshipped. Around the altar there is enough space for singing and playing music while dancing and circling the altar. In his house or on his veranda, close to the makeshift temple, other rituals patronized by the landlord are performed, such as *Durgā Pūjā*, additional *Rath Jātrā* rituals or *Janmāṣṭami*.

The almost 140 households of the village belong to the following communities (see Table 1) and administrative categories (ST = Scheduled Tribe; SC = Scheduled Caste; OBC = Other Backward Class):

Following the administrative categorization one finds that, apart from a small number of Scheduled Caste households (less than 6 per cent of the population)—103 out of 139 households or around 75 per cent of the population belong to the Scheduled Tribes. This corresponds to the very high figure of Scheduled Tribes and Scheduled Castes in Kuchinda *tahsil*,[3] which has been declared part of a Scheduled Area. Within this area of around 2,300 sq. km. and a total

TABLE 1: POPULATION OF MUNDALOI VILLAGE

Community	Administrative Category	Number of households
Gauḍ	General caste, now OBC	8
Gaṇḍ	ST	15
Kandh	ST	12
Aghriā	OBC	11
Chaṣā	OBC	1
Māḷi	OBC	7
Keunṭ	SC, now OBC	1
Kisān	ST	27
Kol/Muṇḍā	ST	30
Luhurā	ST	2
Tūrī	ST[2]	3
Khaḍiā	ST	7
Orām	ST	2
Malār	ST	5
Gandā/Harijan	SC	6
Mochi/Chamār	SC	2
Total: 16 communities		**139**

population of 225,000 people, 125,000 (more than half) are included in the Scheduled Tribes category, while another 27,000 (12 per cent) people are listed as Scheduled Castes.[4] Thus, going by the categories of the government, one can safely conclude that not only the village, but also the Kuchinda region is a numerically tribal dominated area (for a critical analysis of the terms tribe and caste see below).[5] Among the tribal communities of the Sambalpur district the most numerous in 1961 were the Gaṇḍ (93,000); Saora (82,000); Kisān (66,000); Binjhal (46,000); Muṇḍā (35,000); Kandh (23,000); Bhuyān (20,000); Khaḍiā (19,000); Mirdha (16,000) and Orām (12,000) (see Pasayat 1998: 90).[6]

As far as cultivatable land is concerned according to the landlord the village covers around 700 acres (280 hectares) of land, while the whole village comprises around 1300 acres.[7] Of these 600 to 700 acres of cultivatable land 400 acres are *bāhāl*—land of the highest quality, 200 acres *bernā* land, and the rest *māl* and *guḍā* land. Around 150 acres of the total cultivable land are owned by the landlord's extended family, comprising three households. Of these 150 acres, around 100 acres are *bāhāl*. Roughly another 150 acres are owned by the remaining ten Aghriā households. Thus the Aghriā own almost half of the village land—and specifically the high quality land—and can be described as the 'dominant caste' of the village in the sense used by Pocock (1972).[8]

The conditions in Mundaloi appeared favourable for my research project on transitions between tribal and caste society from an Aghriā perspective. Mundaloi is an Aghriā-dominated village predominantly populated by 'Scheduled Tribes'. The village and its structure appear to be very typical for the area and do not differ significantly from neighbouring villages. Similarly beneficial were my living arrangements with the host family, who occupy a socially and geographically central place in the village.

The landlord's house might be best described as a conglomerate of buildings around nine courtyards (*duār*). Initially the complex character of the house—full of corners and with various entrances and passages—appeared to me as a maze. All the yards are grouped around a two-storey stone house—the so-called *pakkā ghar* (concrete house) the heart of the house. It got its name because of its construction material—stones put together with lime, a technology most likely introduced by the Aghriā in the area and standing in contrast to the mud huts by which it is surrounded. Only recently have other villagers started to use bricks to construct their houses, but the vast majority

Part of the Gauntiā's house in Mundaloi (*pakkā ghar* on the left).

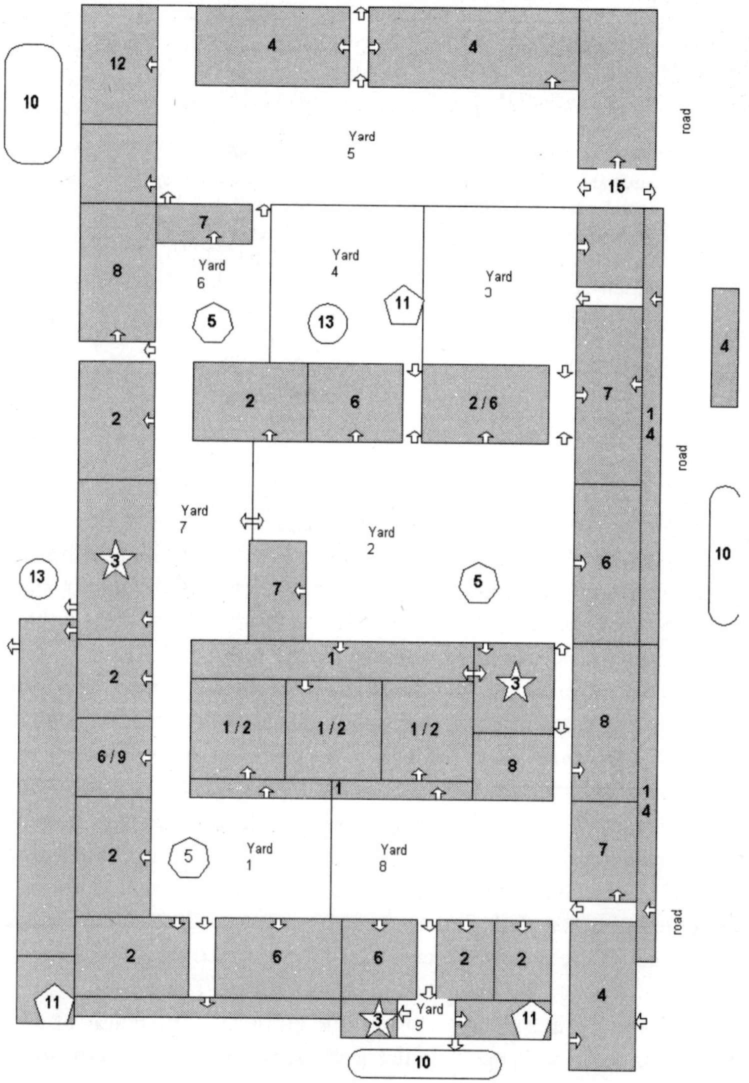

Figure 1: Landlord's house (arrows indicate doors or passageways).

KEY

No.	Part of the house /estate (English)	Part of the house/estate (Sambalpuri)
1	old stone house	*pakkā ghar*
2	sleeping rooms	*śuibā ghar*
3	kitchen and hearth	*randhā ghar* and *chulā*
4	cow shed	*guhāl*
5	shrine with basil plant	*tulsī chaur*
6	general store room	*bhaṇḍār ghar*
7	representative/sitting room	*baiṭhak*
8	store room for paddy	*dhān ghar*
9	sacred room	*māhāpuru ghar*
10	threshing floor	*khalā*
11	toilet/bathroom	*pāikhānā*
12	goat shed	*gudri*
13	well	*kūāṇ*
14	veranda	*piṇḍā*
15	entrance area	*khoel*

are still made of mud and no other building is taller than the *pakkā ghar*. These days of the landlord's compound not only the *pakkā ghar* is made of stone, but almost all parts of the Gauntiā house. However, there is no other building with two floors—though in some cases the roofs or *pāten* are used to dry or to store food, the height is considerably less than in an ordinary living room.

The whole property has been divided among three sons and therefore one finds three kitchens and three threshing floors. Each of these three family parts inherited a room on each floor of the prestigious *pakkā ghar*. One part of the family occupies yards 8 and 9 with direct access to the village road, while another part stays in the rooms around yards 6, 7 and 1 with their entrance via the yards 5 formed by cow sheds belonging to their share. The present landlord's share includes the yards 2 to 4, which also have a direct access to the main road. There are also three sitting rooms, in which official guests such as officers of the king used to be welcomed. These rooms (no. 7 in the diagram) are always close to the entrance. The landlord uses this room for rituals such as the *Rath Jātrā*, which he patronizes. Opposite that room, close to his threshing floor, the already mentioned temporary altar or temple (*mandap/maduā*) is available for festivals of the village. The latter and the landlord's official room are centrally located and ritually central as well.

The whole complex is surrounded by gardens (*bāer*), small fields, and threshing floors, a relatively wide area expanding even beyond the village road. There is quite a distance to the nearest neighbours in contrast to other houses in the village which are quite often next to each other.

The oldest part of the house or estate is grouped around yard 1, which was built in the early twentieth century. A little later, as family members recall, around 1925-30 the old stone house was constructed. At that time it was the only stone house in the village and certainly a sign of prestige, as it continues to be. In the 1960s the house was considerably expanded and buildings around the yards 3 to 6 and 8 were erected in that period, when buildings around the yards 6 and 7 had already been completed. Perhaps the most recent addition is a veranda behind the goat shed built in the 1970s.

1.4. THE GAUNTIĀ FAMILY

The complex structure of the Gauntiā's or landlord's house is matched by the complex family composition. As with the house, it took some time until I comprehended all the relationships. Those who had married into the family, described it as rather complex, given the fact that there was polygyny as well as adoptions in the older generations. The composition of the family is shown in Figure 2.

It was Gopinath—the grandfather of Dharanidhar (A), who took up the headmanship of the village. Dharanidhar had four sons from three wives and divided his property among them. Dharanidhar's youngest son, Shankar (8), inherited another village—the prestigious headmanship of Kuchinda itself. Therefore the Mundaloi property was shared among the three elder sons: Jaya Narayan (B), Rabi Narayan (4) and Shiva Narayan (6). Jaya Narayan (B)—the eldest—became the headman. He passed away around 25 years ago. Having no sons himself, he had adopted the second son (C) of his younger brother, who is the present Gauntiā or Landlord Khirod Kumar. Khirod's son (D)—now around five years old—will inherit this function. Thus the line of Gauntiā is marked from (A) to (D).

At the time of my arrival the house was occupied by around 30 people: the persons 1 to 29 including C and D, but excluding all women marked with (9), who—as married daughters of the house—have settled elsewhere. Due to their service jobs Rabi Narayan's (4)

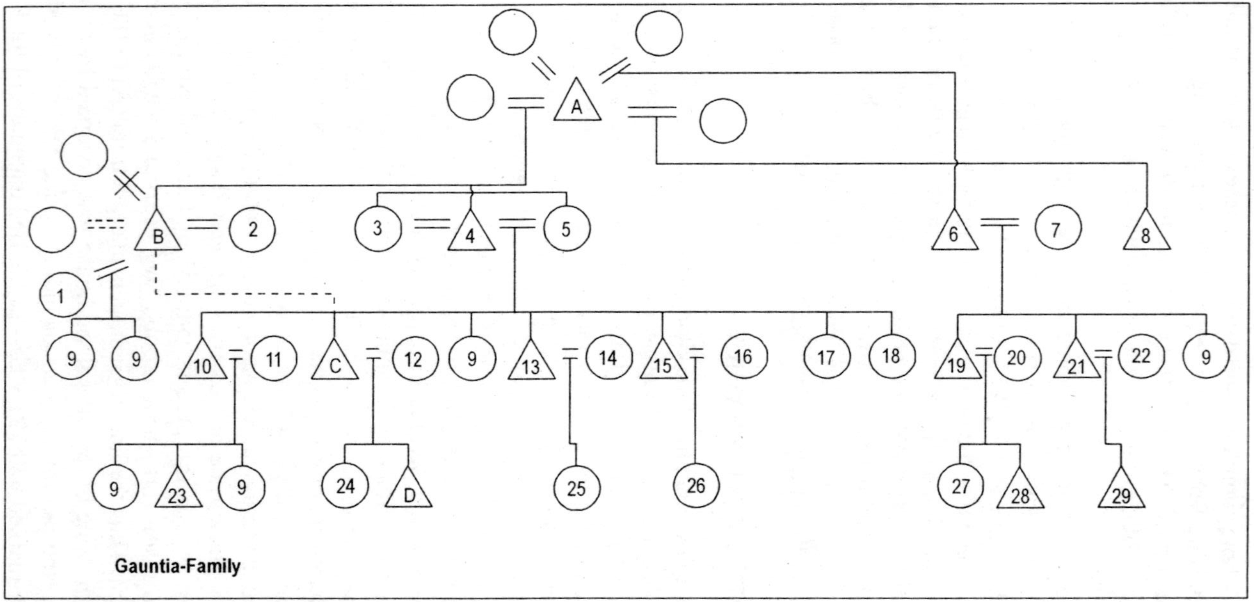

Figure 2: Family of the Landlord, Village Mundaloi.

eldest son (10) and Shiva Narayan's eldest son (19) and their wives and children do not reside permanently in the house, but they are usually present during festivals or on weekends. Rabi Narayan (4), one of his two wives (3), who are sisters, and a wife of Jaya Narayan (B) passed away during my research period.

1.5. ME AMONG THEM

As far as my research methods are concerned, I followed the general paradigm of anthropological research—the participant observation as established by Malinowski (1984 [1922]).[9] Following anthropological standards I concentrated on qualitative methods such as loosely structured interviews instead of quantitative research or fixed questionnaires. Research meant for me what Lindquist (1995) once called 'travelling by the other's cognitive maps'—an attempt to share their life and experiences of others as far as possible and being aware of the process of 'directed writing' that results from participant observation.

Learning the language is a necessary condition to grasping the 'native's point of view', as Malinowski said. Though I progressed in doing so, I was able to read and write the Oriya script and was able to converse, I was not as fluent as I wished to be and I was always grateful for support from my hosts in translating many complicated matters during interviews. Thus I was more or less constantly accompanied by one of them while conducting interviews.

Access to this very large family proved to be rather easy. Staying with the landlord also guaranteed, by and large, easy access to the village and was further helpful in that a landlord is usually well informed. Villagers come to him in order to share their grievances and to ask for the settlement of disputes. Therefore, the landlord himself or, in case of absence, a brother, is a rich source of information. Secondly, the landlord and his family maintain a wide network of relations inside as well as outside the village. In the village many people (particularly labourers) depend on the wealthy landlord, for example on advance payments in times of hardship. True, he also depends on their labour to cultivate his fields, etc. Particularly in the beginning, such relations were highly advantageous for my work. Villagers would rarely deny an interview in the presence of the landlord or his family members with whom I conducted my field research. However, because I was identified with the landlord's family, I had the disadvantage of not being told anything critical. Thirdly, being integrated into the landlord's family was beneficial for me in the sense of not facing any major material hardships. There was plenty of food and instead of staying in a mud hut, as some of my colleagues did, I resided in a kind of village palace.

Around ten days after my arrival—as I was still busy orientating myself in a new culture—the father of my immediate hosts, Rabi Narayan, passed away unexpectedly. It was the biggest family tragedy that I have ever witnessed. The intense mourning was overwhelming and having just arrived I was not at all sure how to behave in such a situation. However—though a catastrophe for the family members—this death helped to integrate me into the family, because it is believed that there was a connection in an earlier life, if you are present at the time of someone's death. During the funeral some sisters of Ràbi Narayan suggested integrating me into the family as a brother of Srikant Patel, because I had come with him initially.

Thus my role within the family network became clearer by being accepted in a fixed kinship category. By extension I became a distant younger brother of my immediate hosts as well—a cousin brother to be precise, because Rabi was a mother's brother of Srikant. Later my relations became even closer to the family, expressed by the fact that I used (and was expected to use) kinship terms as my hosts did. Since I kept the relation to the sisters of Rabi as they had initiated them, my role remained ambiguous and my use of kinship terms was never fully consistent. I termed Rabi's sisters as mother's younger sisters, while addressing Rabi's younger brother at the same time as father's younger brother. Such inconsistencies, however, are not uncommon in wide kinship networks.

My role remained ambivalent in yet another sense. As one of my hosts told me frankly on the day of my departure—before that, I suppose, it would have been against the rules of hospitality—no family of prestige would like to keep an unmarried man in their home, particularly if they have unmarried daughters of marriageable age. And he added that while he was visiting the house of her mother's brother's daughter when they were both unmarried, he did not speak even a single word with her. The behaviour of unmarried daughters and sons is very much restricted in this rather conservative milieu, in which prestige (*ijjat*) and shame (*lāj*) are of utmost importance. Being unmarried myself, an exception certainly in offering accommodation as well as guidance to me, and I am still grateful for this. Naturally, however, contact with the two unmarried daughters of the house (17 and 18 in Figure 2) was truly limited and a conversation beyond the most necessary would have been inappropriate. Thus my sphere of interaction was confined to the men and married women.

1.6. CASTE, TRIBE AND PEASANTRY—ON ESSENTIAL CATEGORIES

The title 'A Peasant Caste on a Tribal Frontier' might easily present difficulties, given the complications concerned with the terms used. The concept of 'tribe' belongs to the most controversial in anthropology—being like caste emotive and having 'moved scholars to "unscholarly anger"' (Bailey 1960: 263). The term 'tribe' or 'tribal' is disputed due to negative or pejorative connotations such terms have particularly in urban India; the terms are identified with primitiveness, backwardness, consumption of alcohol, and promiscuity in addition to the paternalistic notions of tribes as innocent, naïve or closer to nature. Besides—and occasionally even in combination with such connotations, one finds arguments that tribes are distinct because of racial considerations or because tribes speak tribal languages, live far away from civilization, or because they may be characterized by egalitarianism, all of which are superficial—even stereotypical—characteristics, which have all been rightly refuted.[10] Furthermore, the concept of tribe in its long history has been criticized repeatedly. It has been described as a 'problem' (Helm 1968), as an 'illusion' by Southall (1970)[11] and was regarded by Godelier (1977) as being in a crisis—and with it the whole subject 'anthropology', to which the concept of the tribe has been so fundamental. In the African context the concept of 'tribe' has been abandoned in favour of 'ethnic groups' or 'acephalous societies'—terms which are also turn problematic.[12] In India its usage is also controversial, since it is often confused with the administrative category of Scheduled Tribe, which is rather randomly imposed on certain communities and corresponds—at best—very loosely to realities on the ground.

Furthermore, the question concerning the existence of tribes in

India as an entity separate from caste- and Hindu-society is far from irrelevant. It is a highly political question given the present Hindu-nationalist project of constructing a Hindu majority. In Hindu nationalist discourse India is identified as Hindu. Thus, Dubashi, a leading ideologue of the ruling Bharatiya Janata Party (BJP), remarked: 'The key to genuine development is self-assertion—as an Indian, and as a Hindu, for India is nothing if not Hindu' (Dubashi 1992: x).[13] An attempt to 'make India Hindu' (Ludden 1996) would leave no space for deviating tribal ideas and values, as from a Hindu-nationalist perspective diversity would endanger Hindu unity.

Therefore a necessity for explanations, definitions and provisos on the concepts of tribe and caste is self-evident. I shall first introduce some local idioms for tribe and caste as expressed in the regionally relevant literature and by interlocutors, and then summarize the academic debate on the status of tribes before trying to identify differences on the level of ideas and values. It will be proposed here that on this level a distinction between tribe and caste or between tribal society and caste society can indeed be made, and is of analytical value. This does not, however, rule out the possibility of transitions between them in practice. Finally, the concept of peasant society shall be introduced, since the Aghriā are primarily peasants and caste society in its rural dimension appears to represent the peasant mode of production in contrast to the tribal mode.

The foreign origin of the terms 'tribe' and 'caste' and their application to different cultures may have contributed to a confusion and ambiguity concerning their meaning. Tribe is derived from the Latin word *tribus* designating a politico-territorial unit in ancient Rome, while caste is based on the Portuguese *casto/casta*, which may be translated as pure or chaste. None of these terms is of emic origin, but is instead assigned to various indigenous categories—in the case of caste to *varṇa* as mythical groups[14] as well as to *jāti*[15] as empirical groups.

Tribe is not an indigenous category. As Roy (1925) has noted for Orissan tribes—and this is true for many tribes around the world—the name used to designate the group simple means 'man' in the wider sense of mankind. Thus for example Birhor may be translated as 'man of the forest'. Remo, the name the Bondo use to designate themselves, equally means 'human', while other tribes refer to themselves as Bhuyan or 'earth people' (Pfeffer 2002: 215, forthcoming: 13). Contrastingly, from a tribal perspective peasant castes or immigrants in general are *diku* or outsiders (Roy 1970 [1912]: 115).[16]

Additionally, Mahapatra (1987: 26) argued that in north-western Orissa an opposition between tribe and caste is understood in the local idioms *hātuā* versus *kālā pithia*—the former being the 'plainspeople' and the latter 'dark-skinned' tribal communities. I have found that *hātuā* is used for people going to the market frequently or in general for 'people of the market' (*hāt* = local market), but *hātuā* is not used for castes as such. And only in a few cases is the idiom *kālā pithia* used by tribal communities for themselves.[17] Much more widespread and well known is the opposition coined and used by the government, namely *Ādivāsi* or 'aborigines'/'original inhabitants' and *Aṇa-Ādivāsi* (non-*Ādivāsi*). Presently, many villagers included by the government in the category of Scheduled Tribes proudly claim to be Ādivāsi, although it is widely accepted in the village context that only the Kandh were the original settlers and all other communities migrated into the area later.

Not only do some castes like the Aghriā use the term *jāti* (caste) to designate themselves as one among other castes, also communities like the Gaṇḍ (Gond)—considered by the administration to be a Scheduled Tribe—use the term *jāti* to refer to the whole community, for example in publications of their own organization.[18] Furthermore, the Gaṇḍ insist they are Kethria—a local variant of Kshatriya[19]—and thus warriors of high status within the *varṇa* hierarchy. Such a claim may indicate a process of assimilation into the caste hierarchy as Parkin (2000) found among Juang and Bhuiya, two other tribes of the region. However, at the same time Gaṇḍ jamindār (or 'little kings') considered to be Rāj Gaṇḍ, as 'ruling Gaṇḍ' indicating their status as an elite among Gaṇḍ, complain bitterly about not being included in the list of Scheduled Tribes and instead being classified as a separate community. Simultaneously, however, they too leave no doubt about their status as Kshatriya. Similarly Gell (1992: 2) found various designations used among Muria of Bastar depending on the context. The term Gond—which Gell considers, like Muria, to be an invented term—is applied to them in official contexts in correspondence to *jāti* (caste), while Muria meaning 'root' in their own language is rejected by the Muria, who refer to each other as *koitor* or 'humans'. (However, Muria continues to be used by outsiders in non-official contexts.) Therefore, designations similar to *koitor* for tribes as wholes may very well co-exist with caste designations in practice.

In a very similar way as *jāti* is used, the term *samāj* or 'community' is applied by all communities in the village alike to refer to their own as well as to other communities. At the same time, the term *pāṭki* is common to differentiate one's own community from 'others'—*pāṭki* being all others except one's own community. For example it might describe all others in opposition to the Aghriā or Aghriā *samāj*/Aghriā *jāti*. Similarly Gaṇḍ may use it to refer to all non-Gaṇḍ as *pāṭki*, underlining a distinction between 'us' and 'them' irrespective of the status of a community as tribe or caste.

As we have seen, the terms tribe or caste do not fit neatly into the local context and its indigenous categories. Such a multi-valence of terms and designations may have contributed to the debates whether one can speak of distinct tribes at all. One of these debates on the characterization of 'tribals' [*sic*] dates back to the 1940s but is still relevant today. The first and foremost protagonist of this debate was Verrier Elwin—a missionary turned anthropologist and 'philanthropologist'[20] as well as a British turned Indian. He had spent many years among various tribal communities in Middle India at the time of the debate. In a final chapter in his monograph on the Baiga (Elwin 1939) Elwin argues—under the impression of 'psychical apathy and physical decline' among the Baiga's neighbours—that measures should be taken in order to protect them. He proposes a 'National Park'[21] as an area, in which their free access to the forest would be restored. Thus the Baiga may practice their own customs such as shifting cultivation. This park should also be free from missionaries and other 'social uplift' movements causing mischievous effects as well as a place in which Hindus would not be able to despise tribal customs. As he reiterated later, Elwin did not suggest isolation but rather 'planned and controlled contact' (Elwin 1998 [1964]: 291) between culturally distinct entities.[22]

Elwin's ideas were strongly opposed by G.S. Ghurye in *The Aborigines—So-called and Their Future* (1943).[23] Ghurye—a Brahmin and, in sharp contrast to Elwin, a textual scholar and armchair-anthropologist (Guha 2000: 157)—pointed out the similarities between tribes and Hindus, including the existence of 'Hinduized' segments of many tribes and a supposed autochthonism, since there had also been a considerable migration among tribes. He wrote:

> Only very small sections, living in the recesses of hills and the depths of forests, have not been more than touched by Hinduism. Under the circumstances, the only proper description of these people is that they are the imperfectly integrated classes of Hindu society. Though for the sake of convenience they may be designated the tribal classes of Hindu society, suggesting thereby the social fact that they have retained much more of the tribal creeds and organization than many of the castes of Hindu society, yet they are in reality Backward Hindus. (Ghurye 1963: 19)

Leaving aside questions of which and how much protection and development was needed for the tribal population, a central dispute behind the debate appears to be the question how to characterize this part of the Indian population. Are they aboriginals or autochthons as Elwin implies, or are they rather Backward Hindus as Ghurye, a 'nationalist anthropologist' (Béteille 1991: 77) argues? To put it differently: are there separate, cultural—or perhaps ethnic—entities designated either as tribes and castes or as 'animists' and Hindus? Or is such a distinction artificially drawn, since 'so-called aborigines' are in fact Backward Hindus?[24]

The debate initially led by Elwin and Ghurye reappeared, though in a slightly different disguise and on a deeper sociological level, in the late 1950s and early 1960s as controversy between Louis Dumont and David F. Pocock on the one hand and F.G. Bailey on the other.[25] In their programmatic essay 'For a Sociology of India' Dumont and Pocock (1957)—putting themselves into an Indological tradition—declared that 'India is one' on the level of values[26] as their starting point. The tribal population was certainly not their major concern and they argued that others had failed '. . . to recognize that most so-called "primitives" in India are only people who have lost contact' (Dumont/Pocock 1957: 8). According to them the connection had been lost in some cases to '. . . the traditional higher, Sanskritic, civilization [which] demonstrates without question the unity of India' (ibid. 9).

Contrary to Dumont's and Pocock's initial statements Bailey (1959: 88ff), stressing the importance of behaviour in addition to values, argued against an *a priori* assumption of Indian unity. He pointed out that Dumont and Pocock '. . . equate "Indian sociology" with an analysis of the values of Hinduism. Equally, the postulate "India is one" becomes translated into "The ideas of Hinduism form a coherent system"' (Bailey 1959: 91).[27]

Apart from this critique, including the possibility of divergent values in tribal and caste society, Bailey (1961) compares the politico-economic system of a tribal group—the Konds—with that of their Hindu neighbours called Oriyas by him[28] focussing on control over land and rights to its resources. Concluding his study Bailey remarks:

> The Konds of the eastern Kondmals were divided into a number of localized exogamous clans recruited by agnatic descent or by immigration combined with fictions of agnatic descent. Membership of the clan is, under this system, a condition of holding and exploiting land in the clan territory. A right to land is not achieved by subordination to anyone else, but by equality as kinsman. Oriya society is also divided into groups, but the grouping on which we focus is that into castes. These are . . . hierarchically arranged; they are interlinked by economic specialization, by and large within villages; and the village is held together by the concentration of force in the hands of one dominant caste. In this system, there are dependent castes, who achieve a right to a share in the resources of the village land, through a relationship subordinating them to members of the dominant caste. (Bailey 1961: 11–12)

Additionally Bailey (1961: 12) hints at the organic character of Oriya or caste society, while he characterizes Kond or tribal society as segmentary.[29] Besides this, since in practice there are also hierarchically subordinated groups in Kond society, namely Pan, etc., and since a dominant Oriya caste may resemble a dominant Kond clan to some extent, Bailey proposes to view caste and tribe as a continuum rather than disjunctive opposites. And he points out:

> The larger is the proportion of a given society which has direct access to the land, the closer is that society to the tribal end of the continuum. Conversely, the larger is the proportion of people whose right to land is achieved through a dependent relationship, the nearer does that society come to the caste pole. (Bailey 1961: 14)

In rejoinder Dumont and Pocock (1959: 60, n. 2) relativized their assertions as 'too ambitious and too narrow'.[30] Considering the case of the tribal Saora[31] they acknowledged that if 'a certain system of ideas and actions . . . defined as Hindu opposition of pure and impure is fundamental to Hinduism, then the Saoras are not Hindus, for their ideas in the matter are very sketchy.' And, though '. . . Saoras do not ignore the importance attached by Hindus to these things . . . [notion of ceremonial impurity—US]. . . . They do not submit directly to the scheme of Hindu values.' (Dumont/Pocock 1959: 60–1)

Besides, Dumont clarified that tribes and castes did not have 'similar values'; neither were 'tribal ideas and values . . . to be included into the same system [as caste ones]' (Dumont 1962: 121). Dumont further criticized Bailey's reduction of the tribe–caste–continuum to a linear concept relating to the politico-economic sphere, and proposed a multi-dimensional continuum between the extreme positions of caste and tribe in practice.[32] In terms of religion, a continuum between tribal gods and Hindu gods was presented subsequently by Eschmann (1994 [1975]).[33]

However, fundamental differences in the discussion on tribes and castes—as well as on the subject of sociology or anthropology as such[34]—remained insofar as Dumont and Pocock considered ideas and values—often unexpressed—and the whole formed by these value-ideas as of utmost importance, while Bailey concentrated more on observable behaviour and practice.

Ideas and values of the caste system

The concepts of tribe and caste, though not neatly conforming to expressed realities in a particular setting, appear to have some analytic value in the question of social organization as well as on the level of ideas as outlined by Dumont. In an early attempt to characterize caste society and its ideas, Bouglé (1997 [1957]: 65) argued that 'the spirit of caste unites . . . three tendencies, repulsion [*understood as separation in terms of marriage etc.*], hierarchy and hereditary specialization, and all three must be borne in mind if one wishes to give a complete definition of the caste system' (Bouglé 1997 [1957]: 65)

Following this approach Dumont (1980 [1966]) pointed out that the opposition between pure and impure is the fundamental principle of the caste system and its ideology, since it forms the basis not only of hierarchy, but of all these three principles outlined by Bouglé. Hierarchy, perhaps the most crucial among these principles, is characterized by Dumont:

> as the principle by which the elements of a whole are ranked in relation to the whole, it being understood that in the majority of societies it is religion which provides the view of the whole, and that the ranking will thus be religious in nature. (Dumont 1980 [1966]: 66)

Independent of political and economic power as well as natural inequality, hierarchy—essentially religious in nature—can be understood as the order of the relatively ritually pure, in opposition to the relatively ritually impure. Hierarchy as a principle of order sets the elements in relation to the whole; the necessary hierarchical and complementary co-existence of pure and impure is embodied in the extreme by the brahmin and the so-called 'untouchables'. In accordance with Dumont's holistic perspective, which focused—in contrast to modern individualism—on society as a whole, hierarchy is not a linear grading or 'chain of superimposed commands' (Dumont 1980 [1966]: 239), but a relation between the encompassing and the encompassed.[35]

Later, Trautmann (1995 [1981]), Raheja (1988), and Marglin (1989 [1985]) extended this understanding of caste by adding the perspective of the king or kshatriya. Apart from ritual purity, in the king's perspective the role of the universal giver, auspiciousness, as well as female power (*śakti*) are valued.

Tribal ideas and values in India and elsewhere

For an understanding of tribal ideas and values the work of Marshall D. Sahlins (1968) is crucial.[36] He characterized the tribe as

> a body of people of common derivation and custom, in possession and control of their own extensive territory. But if in some degree socially articulated, a tribe is specifically unlike a modern nation in that its several communities are not united under a sovereign governing authority, nor are the boundaries of the whole thus clearly and politically determined. The tribe builds itself up from within, the smaller community segments joined in groups of higher order, yet just where it becomes greatest the structure becomes weakest: the tribe as such is the most tenuous of arrangements, without even a semblance of collective organization. (Sahlins 1968: vii–viii)

Sahlins identified a tribal society as a segmentary society[37] 'not simply because it is built of compounded segments, but also because it is *only* so built: its coherence is not maintained from the above by public political institutions' (ibid.: 15). However, he does not simply oppose tribes and states but hints that tribes in practice represent a range of possible evolutionary developments of progressive intensification of authority, from segmented tribes proper to more complex chiefdoms (ibid.: 20)[38]—and onwards to the state, which itself may have undergone similar change.[39]

As well as arguing that kin-based tribes with a domestic mode of production maintain a 'generalized structure' without distinguishing between an economic, religious, or political sphere as such, Sahlins further relates a distinction between tribe and civilization[40] or state to the contrast between war and peace. War should be understood here in the sense Hobbes had attached to the term 'Warre'—that is, as the absence of an institutionally guaranteed peace. Tribes lack a 'sovereign political and moral authority; the right to use force and do "battell" . . . is held by the people in severalty'. Feuds between local corporate lineages or clans among the Dongria Kondh of South Orissa as described recently by Nayak (1989) exemplify Sahlins' observations. Sahlins (1968: 8f) also pointed at tribal institutions such as exchange systems or kinship, including fictive kinship, which balance 'Warre' and reveal a traditional wisdom in peacemaking. According to Sahlins, the reciprocity which dominates tribal society is a form of 'economic diplomacy' in which exchanges may become peace treaties.

Given the absence of centralized state-like structures as a central criterion of tribal societies according to Sahlins, in his critique Southall (1970: 29) argued that the division of the whole world into sovereign states excludes the existence of tribes as self-contained and politically autonomous units.[41] However, Southall also acknowledges the possibility of remote areas, in which state power appears ineffective and negligible. Apparently parts of Orissa are a case in point, in which the influence of the modern bureaucratic Indian state is rather limited.[42] As Béteille (1991: 67) pointed out, there might be not only a co-existence, but also a certain complementary relationship between tribe and state.[43] Furthermore, Southall (1970: 32) revealed that the colonial influence had led to the 'invention' of certain tribal groups. Colonialists or later national administrations may have misrepresented, substantialized or privileged certain levels—addressing only one level within a segmentary structure as 'tribe' and not the whole structure as such. Such substantialisations could be taken up by the concerned people themselves. In this specific sense tribes may have been 'invented' or might be termed as secondary phenomena and 'a reaction to the formation of complex political structure' as Fried (1968: 15) said. However, such 'crystallizations at the wrong level' (Southall 1970: 32) expressed for example in names of tribes—for which Southall offers various examples—do not contradict the existence of a segmentary 'tribal' structure as such or as proposed by Sahlins.

The topic of tribal communities and their value-ideas in India has been taken up by Pfeffer for Middle India. Pfeffer shares Dumont's structural approach and applies it to Indian tribes without, however, following Dumont's and Pocock's initial assumption regarding tribes. Pfeffer (1982a, 1982b, 2000) recognized as part of the middle Indian tribal design a hierarchical framework of seniority, in which at all levels a senior status is distinguished from a junior status, i.e. differentiating Gadaba from Bondo, a senior Gadaba moiety from a junior one, etc. This goes against general presumptions of an egalitarian ethos among tribes. Apparently the differentiation senior/junior is often, though not necessarily or exclusively, combined with a distinction sacral/secular. In this, middle Indian tribal society ordered by the principle of seniority stands in contrast to the African segmentary system with inherent automatisms for solving conflicts as well as to a more centralized Biblical model ('conical clan'). The pervasiveness of the principle of seniority within tribal society has been demonstrated recently by Berger (2002) for the Gadaba as well as the Desia society in general, by Guzy (2002) in the sphere of religious conversions, and by Otten (forthcoming (a)) in the context of healing.

Taking into consideration not only the presence of groups classified by the administration as Scheduled Tribes, but the Scheduled Castes and Other Backward Classes in predominantly tribal areas, which often share cultural idioms and ideas with their neighbours, Pfeffer (2000: 335; 2002: 212ff) prefers to speak of a symbiotic 'tribal society'[44] instead of tribes.[45] Similarly, for the specific context of Koraput (South Orissa) Berger (2002) stresses that the local category of Desia or 'inhabitants of the land' subsumes and transcends the artificially imposed administrative categories. Thus in the 'Middle Indian' context, the term 'tribe' does not imply fully autonomous and self-contained units.[46]

Comparing tribal society of Middle India to Hindu caste society significant differences have to be noted. One of them is the absence of a *varṇa* model in tribal society (Sinha 1957: 107; Pfeffer 1997: 11, 2000: 342ff). Besides, Pfeffer highlights the difference between status and power. This indicates common ground shared by tribal as well as caste society, even though such an dichotomy is expressed in a divergent manner. While on the one hand in tribal society local lines with sacred functions appear to be differentiated from those having secular duties, in caste society, one finds a disjunction between Brahmin and Kshatriya, priest and king. Additionally complex rules of commensality and marriage are not confined to Hindus but are also practised in tribal society. Tribal and caste society may have influenced each other in this regard. Furthermore, though framed differently, purity seems to be a major concern in both caste society and tribal society, since the tribal population leaves polluting trade and communication with the outside world to their clients.[47] Equally the idea of rebirth and reincarnation appears to be shared by tribal and caste society, although in the latter society alone is it linked to the idea of *karma*. Additionally, both societies may be characterized as holistic—in contrast to hunters and gatherers as well as to a Western, individualistic society.[48]

The distinction between tribe and caste on the level of ideas as proposed by Sahlins and Pfeffer does not contradict transitions and processes of oscillation between these categories in practice—or within the present political process. Thus, in order to gain prestige as well as to see material benefit tribal communities may pursue various strategies such as attempting an assimilation into caste society or an assertion of a distinct tribal identity (Parkin 2000).[49] Even communities classified as castes may try to prove their essential 'tribalness' and indigenous origins in order to benefit from state-sponsored schemes, to stress their land rights, and to exploit modernity in a wider sense (ibid.). Thus, in political discourse agency and ethnicity are decisive factors, which might be constructed and manipulated.

Peasant society

In addition to tribal and caste society, the term 'peasant society' seems to be crucial for an understanding of the context I intend to present. Wolf (1966)[50] located peasant society between a primitive tribal and industrial society.[51] He contrasted the term 'peasant'[52] for the rural cultivator, to 'farmer' as reserved for agricultural and profit-oriented entrepreneurs in industrial society. Peasants run a household rather than a business, and their economy is essentially a family economy. Stressing Wolf's point, Redfield (1956: 18) argued that for peasantry agriculture is a 'livelihood and a way of life, not a business for profit'.[53]

According to Wolf a distinction between peasantry and tribe can be made by the character of outside involvement. While cultivators in a tribal society ideally control the means of production and surpluses are exchanged directly among members or groups, in peasant society a surplus is transferred to a ruling or dominant elite or to non-farming specialists who provide certain services. Thus Wolf (1966: 10–11), corresponding to Sahlins' arguments, remarks:

> peasant denotes no more than an asymmetrical structural relationship between producers of surplus and controllers . . . the crystallization of executive power serves to distinguish the primitive from the civilized. . . . Thus, it is only when a cultivator is integrated into a society with a state—that is, when the cultivator becomes subject to the demands and sanctions of power-holders outside his social stratum—that we can appropriately speak of peasantry.

In this definition Wolf further developed earlier ideas of Kroeber (1948 [1923]: 283ff) and Redfield (1956: 23ff), who had considered peasantry to be in an intermediary position on the axis between rural, tribal, folk and personalized on the one hand and urbanized, state, sophisticated, and depersonalized on the other hand.[54] Kroeber had said:

> Peasants are definitely rural—yet live in relation to market towns; they form a class segment of a larger population which usually contains also urban centers. . . . They constitute part-societies with part-cultures. They lack the isolation, the political autonomy, and the self-sufficiency of tribal populations; but their local units retain much of their old identity, integration, and attachment to soil and cults. (Kroeber 1948: 284)

Kroeber apparently contrasts peasant society to a previous form of holistic or whole society—here tribal society or rather 'primitive society' in the jargon of those days as a whole society[55]—while peasantry had become part of a wider society with urban elites, etc., or a world system in the extreme.[56] However, in the Indian case, the notion of society as a whole or holistic society is certainly more complex than just described. The Aghriā peasants who will be described below are part of a wider market system,[57] and a state, and are in contact with urban centres and 'civilization' in Redfield's and Kroeber's terms, but they are also firmly rooted in caste society as a holistic type of society.

In his argument Wolf might have been influenced by Polyani (1968 [1957]: 128), who had distinguished between various forms of societal integration—reciprocity, redistribution, and market exchange—and related redistribution to centricity or to 'appropriational movements towards a centre and out of it again', while reciprocity had been associated with symmetry. Thus, peasants—parallel to an establishment of state-centred institutions—are involved in redistributive as well as market systems in a way tribes had not been. I will return to this point in my discussion on the Aghriā as representatives of kingship.

Going into more detail than Kroeber, Wolf (1966: 25) noted that swidden cultivators may easily 'step from status of autonomous cultivators to that of dependent peasantry'.[58] Such a situation appears to prevail in the Orissan context as well, where on the one hand tribes still practice shifting or 'slash and burn' cultivation—despite pressure to desist, for example by forest laws. On the other hand, the plough was introduced by brahmins to this tribal frontier (Pfeffer 1978)—apart from peasant castes migrating from other parts of India. The Aghriā, the topic of this analysis, are one of such peasant castes, having migrated into an essentially tribal area.

1.7. TRANSITIONS ON A TRIBAL FRONTIER

The central aim of my research is the analysis of a society on a tribal frontier, in particular of the Aghriā, a peasant caste, in a predominantly tribal area into which castes have migrated. Cultural change or acculturation in this region has so far been viewed predominantly from a tribal angle and not from the standpoint of a peasant caste, and I attempt to fill this gap. In the area of study a transitional or mixed tribal and caste society has emerged, in which tribal as well as caste ideas have been—perhaps uniquely—combined or synthesized. In this converging society, castes and tribes have influenced each other, and, continue to do so.

The Aghriā are classified by the government as an OBC or Other Backward Class, an administrative category which, in contrast to Scheduled Tribes and Scheduled Castes, has received very little attention by social anthropologists.[59] This vaguely defined category might be an appropriate one for communities in a transitional setting, as presented here.

Chapter 2 offers an analysis of Aghriā mythology. Aghriā myths construct relations to the politico-religious centres of Agra (left behind) and Puri (destination), before finally settling down between these two centres. Because of the intervention of Lord Jagannāth the Aghriā took to agriculture—they received a stick to drive plough bullocks instead of the sword that they had been handling as warriors. Other non-Aghriā versions explain that the name Aghriā, instead of being derived from Āgrā, is *a-ghariā* or being 'without house', hinting at social mobility (Kshatriyaization) as seen in other parts of India, in which increasingly wealthy peasants may have constructed a glorious past. Additionally, in their myths Aghriā root themselves firmly in caste society by establishing links to Brahmins and Chamārs at the extreme ends of caste society, while their tribal neighbours do not appear in the myth.

In the Chapter 3, relations that the Aghriā have established within this heterogeneous society will be introduced and analysed. It will be argued that a hierarchy has taken root—resembling to a large extent the known caste hierarchies as described by Pocock (1957) and Dumont (1980 [1966]). However, processes of inclusion and exclusion are expressed in the idiom of senior or good people (*bal lok/baḍ lok*) versus junior people (*choṭ lok*), as is common in tribal society (Pfeffer 2000). Tribal communities have been included in this hierarchy on various higher and lower levels—underlining the artificial character of the administrative category 'Scheduled Tribes' in the analysed context. Apart from known markers of status such as the acceptance of water and boiled rice and the services of Brahmins and barbers relations and hierarchical distinctions are also established and reinforced by the custom of selling endangered and sick children to lower groups in order to fool Yama, the god of death, and in order to help the child to survive. Prior to marriage the children have to be repurchased and their parents pay a considerable amount of money to the low status families. Integration within a mixed tribal and caste society is thus achieved by exchanging material wealth for transcendental protection. In addition, various kinds of ritual friendships—hierarchized in themselves—can be forged between members of different communities only, and identify these members on a personal level. These ritual friendship ties—and to a lesser extent also the selling of children—certainly help to forge relationships between newcomers and earlier settlers; they may reveal mechanisms against 'warre' in the sense of Sahlins (1968) and may also balance a simultaneously established hierarchy.

In Chapter 4 on the Aghriā as village kings, a framework is introduced within which structures of a state—a little kingdom rather than a Western bureaucratic state—have been established and within which a transformation of a tribal, segmentary society has taken place. Aghriā headmen or 'Gauntiā' clearing the forests and becoming revenue collectors and justices of peace for superior kings were influential in turning a tribal, land-owning population into peasants or rather tenants in the sense of a 'peasantization' (MacDougall 1977).[60] The role of migrating peasants like the Aghriā as agents of such a transmission has hitherto been neglected in favour of the Brahmin and Kshatriya/Rajput.[61] Significantly, in this process the Aghriā used the very same cultural idiom for setting up new villages and establishing rulership by styling their headmanship as *khuṇṭ kata gaunti* (headmanship set up by clearing the forest) in comparison with dominant, land-owning tribal clans of the region designated as *khuntkattidar* ('clearers of the forest'), for example among the Munda (Roy 1970 [1912]). Furthermore, the Aghriā—themselves in a process of upward mobility and Kshatriyaization—acted as agents of change not only in a political but also a religious sense by patronizing Hindu festivals such as Śibrātrī; in an economic sense by extensively cultivating rice with the plough, by constructing ponds, etc.; and in an educational sense by setting up schools. However, the presented context is not only an arena of Hinduization, but also of the opposite processes of Tribalization—with the Aghriā participating in festivals of tribal goddesses. In some villages, Aghriā Gauntiā as rulers of the village set up wooden posts—symbols for tribal gods and divine beings—in order to exercise dominance. Furthermore, for an understanding of the character of the state or 'little kingdom' as established on the tribal frontier, it appears more fruitful to characterize Gauntiā as 'village kings' because they have operated and still operate within the same hierarchy (the structural relations to superior rulers and subjects) as other 'little kings'; maintained similar systems of redistribution with the Gauntiā as universal donor at the centre; and claimed similar relations to gods or goddesses to empower and legitimise them.

Yet another kind of transition will be described in the sphere of kinship in Chapter 5. Redfield (1956: 32) had argued that in 'peasant society as in primitive, many links are those of kinship, but the mesh is wider and looser'. Be that as it may, it will be stressed here that a unique regional synthesis has evolved including tribal communities and peasant castes. Comparing the Aghriā kinship terminology to that of their tribal neighbours one realizes how much they have in common—in contrast to kinship systems known from other parts of India. In addition to the principle of seniority, Aghriā clearly share with tribal communities the principle of alternation of generations—a feature atypical for castes. A structural identity of alternate generations is particularly expressed in the context of marriage. There had been a preference among Aghriā to marry girls reaching puberty to distant grandfathers or elder sister's husbands when a suitable groom was not found. Additionally, marriages are to be arranged within one's own generation-set—including grandparents and grandchildren—apart from further preferences concerning matrilateral cross-cousin marriage as well as marriages with sibling's spouse's sibling. Generation-sets, whose importance has been shown by McDougal (1963) for the tribal Juang, are of similar significance and perhaps even more pronounced in practice among the Aghriā. Since the rule of cross-cousin marriage conforms neither to the terminology nor to avoidance rules, the Aghriā case once more exemplifies the necessity of analysing the levels of terminology, rules, and practice separately. Besides, rules of joking and avoidance such as the avoidance of one's husband's mother's brother as found among the Aghriā are, according to my knowledge and going by the standard literature, apparently unknown in caste society elsewhere in India and have only rarely been mentioned for tribal society. If Aghriā have migrated from north India, they must have been influenced to a large extent by their tribal neighbours in the sphere of kinship; and if not been necessary this could have helped establish ties with their neighbours.

The aspect of continuity appears to be of utmost importance within the life cycle, a feature stressed generally in peasant societies (Wolf 1966) and elaborated in Chapter 6. However, in the specific Aghriā context two cycles or two complementary relation-sets dominate life cycle rituals: one connecting mother's brother and sister's son, and another concerning father and son. Without these two kinds of relations an individual cannot become a full social person at the time of marriage and cannot become an ancestor. While in the latter relation a continuity of the household including a relation to the ancestors is stressed, in the first diachronic affinity is stressed—the mother's brother leading the sister's son into the world. Unless a sister's son has been pleased, a mother's brother cannot become an ancestor. Such a vital role for a sister's son, who is also the son-in-law in case of cross-cousin marriage, has so far been documented only for tribal communities of Middle India and the Himalayan region and is perhaps another instance of convergence. Apart from these sets of relationships, two oppositions are prominently expressed in lifecycle rituals: adjacent versus alternate generation, and *jāti* as 'other clan' versus *banśa* as 'own clan'. As already indicated, the Aghriā deviate in this regard from the known north Indian standard; however, even in tribal groups that have terminologies with equations for alternate generations, for which Pfeffer (1983) provided ample examples, generation-sets hardly ever act as a corporate groups during the wedding as they do among the Aghriạ. The opposition contrasting kin (*banśa*) and affines (*jāti*) in abstract terms is expressed only at the subordinated village level and seems to be encompassed on the higher level of caste conceptionalized as *jāti* as well. This stands in contrast to a clear, though not hierarchical, opposition—kin versus affines—found among tribes. Additionally, two major transformative processes—from impurity to purity and from inauspiciousness towards auspiciousness—dominate the Aghriā life cycle. Purity and impurity are a concern during all life cycle rituals including ancestor worship, which appears to be an impure period. Besides this, under certain constellations of stars death may be auspicious for a person, though it may be highly inauspicious for his family—a concept not existing among peasants in north India as documented by Raheja (1988).

In the final chapter, Chapter 7, two cultural symbols will be introduced—Goddess Lakṣmī and the wooden post—in which the ritual, and the agricultural and life cycles are amalgamated. These cycles are not conceived as separate entities, but are rather interwoven and interlinked in various cultural ciphers expressing the 'generalized structure' of society in Sahlins' sense. Lakṣmī appears as goddess of wealth, prosperity and abundance, and of beauty, as well as a model wife of Viṣṇu, but also reveals a more ambivalent character. While a protective and generous mother she may also be a vengeful and even destructive wife, the fruits of the earth and earth itself. Thus Goddess Lakṣmī stands for a whole semantic field presumably wider than traditional Hindu perception has it. Basic values expressed by the goddess, such as fertility and abundance—traditionally exhibited by earth goddesses in tribal society—in combination with her ambivalent inclusive character in relation to her devotees as described in the *Lakṣmī Purāṇa* may have helped to promote her advance in a society on the tribal frontier. Apart from Lakṣmī, the wooden post unites the annual as well as the life cycles, appearing and reappearing on various occasions. Considered a sacred symbol in tribal society—an aniconic manifestation of the divine (Eschmann 1994 [1975])—its proliferation in this transitional society and its prominent place in Aghriā rituals (for example at the centre of wedding altars) hint once again at the inclusion of a tribal idea into the context of a peasant society.

NOTES

1. In one case a wandering Daṇḍa Nrutya group worshipping Kāli and other gods performed their rituals opposite the Landlord's house and a day later in a rather distant *paḍā*. On rare occasions a *paḍā* may share a goat to be sacrificed during the *Grām Śrī Pūjā*.
2. The Tūrī in the village maintained that they have a status as a Scheduled Tribe, but in Census Data of 2001 presented on the internet I found them listed as Scheduled Caste. However, in the village they are not associated with 'Untouchability'.
3. Administrative unit for revenue collection.

4. The figures are cited from the 2001 Census of Orissa, published on the internet, see www.orissagov.nic.in/census (viewed on 12/03/03). Apparently the figures have not changed much. In the 1971 Census of India (Series 16—*Orissa*, Part IX-A, p. 39) out of around 160,000 people staying in the same region 56 per cent belonged to Scheduled Tribes, while another 10 per cent people were counted as Scheduled Castes. For similar figures see also Pasayat (1998: 90ff).
5. The Indian tribal population in general numbers around 100 million people. See Pfeffer (2002: 211).
6. The Saora, Binjhal and Mirdha do not live in Mundaloi.
7. Estimating and measuring land has been rather difficult. Although I did census-work in the beginning of my research, villagers were very explicit about the land they own legally. However, land encroached illegally was hardly mentioned. Therefore I confine myself here to rough figures given by the landlord, which are sufficient for my purpose.

   According to more general data of the Revenue Department, there are 730 acres of cultivable land in the village, for which villagers have land deeds. Another 445 acres are owned by the government, but might be turned into fields at a later stage. It is reserved for government officials, soldiers, etc., but a huge area has already been encroached on illegally. 210 acres are reserved for cattle grazing.
8. With the term 'dominant caste' I do not associate the one being in local numerical majority, but, following Pocock (1972: 26), the caste that controls the political and economical power, especially land and which holds ritual status below the Brahmins. It maintains interdependent relations with a series of specialized service castes. The members of a caste are not in all the villages of a region the dominant caste, and where they are all *patidār* do not have to be necessarily landowners. In this regard it deals merely with a relative concept.
9. Compare also Spradley (1979).
10. For racial classifications see for example Mamoria (1957); for a distinction in biological terms see Sengupta (1997); and for the cliché of a tribal egalitarianism see Pattnaik (1997). Such arguments will not be pursued here, since any causal relation between race, language and culture has already been refuted by Boas (1911, Chap.V). For hierarchical distinctions in tribal society in contrast to a supposed egalitarianism see below.
11. However, Southall (1970: 45) does not fully abandon the concept of tribe and writes: 'We would rather suggest that the concept of tribe, and ethnic unit or ethnic group, will remain useful as preliminary labels for setting the initial framework of communication and discussion.'
12. For critics on and changing usage of the concept of tribe see also Pfeffer (forthcoming b).
13. V. Naidu, BJP president, is reported to have made very similar remarks

during a recent election campaign in Madhya Predesh, where he—according to *The Hindu*, 16.03.03, Online Edition—said: 'Hindutva is the lifeline of this country'. Likewise, he said 'it had no religious connotation and only reflected the identity of this nation' (ibid.).

14. Groups should not be understood here as substantive entities, but rather as relational constructs.
15. The term *jāti* literally means root, but also stock or kind and describes a rather wide semantic field. It may also designate race or even tribe in a very wide sense. Therefore its use is contentious. Compare also Parkin (2000: 50).
16. The term *diku* has been particularly used in Chhotanagpur. Apart from *diku* as a term for outsider generally, the term *sad* seems to have been used for Hindu, though apparently not as frequently as *diku*.
17. I heard this among the Kisān. Perhaps Mahapatra confuses a relation between tribes and castes with one between tribal patrons and their clients as suggested by Pfeffer (1997) for South Orissa.
18. See publication of the 'Gaṇḍ Jāti Samāj', Sambalpur, 1982.
19. In vernacular language the term Khetria is used, while in written sources Kshatriya is preferred. Compare, e.g. publication of the 'Gaṇḍ Jāti Samāj', Sambalpur, 1982.
20. The term is borrowed from his autobiography, in which one of the chapters is titled 'Philanthropology'. It appears appropriate to his endeavour. For a recent appreciation of Elwin's contribution to Anthropology in India see also Pfeffer (2003).
21. Already in the Baiga-monograph Elwin makes it quite clear that he does not intend to create an 'anthropological zoo' (Elwin 1939: 515), but he later regretted this term, since it has 'unfortunate connotations' not intended (Elwin 1998 [1964]: 291).
22. Elwin's tendentially isolationist ideas were applied by Grigson—British administrator of Bastar and amateur anthropologist—see Gell (1992: 6).
23. An extended and revised version was published 1959 and 1963 under the title 'Scheduled Tribes'.
24. For a discussion on this topic see also Sinha (1957: 95ff).
25. For an evaluation of this debate see also Pfeffer (1997: 3ff).
26. In the article explicitly a sociology of values is postulated.
27. For Bailey an analysis focussing on a system of values and ideas only would become a 'straitjacket' (Bailey 1959: 90).
28. The article is also a critic on Ghurye.
29. Apparently the idea of an organic character of society is inspired by Durkheim (1977 [1930]).
30. Compare also Dumont 1962.
31. In a review of Elwin's *The Religion of an Indian Tribe* (Dumont/Pocock 1959: 60ff).
32. For a critic on Bailey's concept see also Nag (1968: 191ff), who rejects

Bailey's focus on landownership and rather postulates the degree of subsistence as a decisive criterion for a distinction between tribe and caste. Thus, dependence on hunting, gathering and shifting cultivation is associated with tribe and intensive agriculture with caste. However, such a differentiation is problematic since some communities like the Gadaba practice both and since it neglects value-ideas completely.

33. Compare also Pasayat (1998: 106ff) offering a very similar argument later.
34. For example Dumont and Pocock (1960: 84, see also Dumont 1962: 121) argued that a politico-economic sphere may not have the same position in every culture as Bailey appears to have assumed. Accordingly comparison—contrary to Bailey's view—should be done on the level of ideas and not on an empirical or behavioural level.
35. This becomes especially clear in the hierarchical relationship between man and woman (Dumont 1980 [1966]: 240), which are identical as man in the sense of a human being on the first, superordinate level, but are opposed (man-woman) to each other as different sexes on a second, subordinate level. The encompassing character becomes recognizable in English through the ambiguous expression man, which denotes a human being as well as a male person, or through the genesis of Bible, in which Eve comes into being out of one of Adam's ribs. While on the primary level, an element becomes included, integrated or 'encompassed' in a whole, a distinction is made on a subordinate level, which is why Dumont speaks of an 'encompassing of the contrary' with regard to hierarchy.
36. Sahlins' work (1968) might be located within a neo-evolutionist framework, indicating possible developments within mankind, but denying a unilinear, irreversible development of peoples or mankind in general passing through fixed stages as early evolutionists did. Contrary to functionalism, in which tribes had also been considered as acephalous groups or as societies without rulers, the question of change and development was more explicitly addressed by neo-evolutionists. For an overview on earlier works on the concept of tribe and attempts to define it see Fried (1968) and Urhahn (1985).
37. On segmentary societies see Middleton/Tait (1970). Evans-Pritchard provided an earlier definition on the concept of tribe too, stressing a common and distinct name; a common sentiment; a common and distinct territory; moral obligation to unite in war; moral obligation to settle feuds and other disputes by arbitration; a segmented structure and opposition of segments; a dominant clan and relation between lineage structure of the dominant clan and the territorial system of the tribe; the tribe as a unit in a system of tribes; and age-sets organized tribally (Evans-Pritchard 1940: 122).
38. The double meaning of tribe—on the one hand a type of society and on the other hand a stage of evolution—has been stressed by Godelier (1977) too. Implied here is a general evolution towards complexity, not historically fixed stages, nor any moral evaluation in the sense of higher developed

societies along an unilateral line of development. It also does not mean that a development towards complexity is irreversible. Godelier also pointed out certain inconsistencies in classifying chiefdoms within Sahlins' evolutionary scheme and apparently Sahlins himself subsumed chiefdoms as part of tribal society (opposed to state society) only at a later stage.

39. As Stein (1975: 68ff) et al. pointed out that medieval states in south India were not centralized and bureaucratic states in the Western sense, and a king as an overlord who had no monopoly in terms of military power 'demanded submission to his claim of superiority, rather than obedience to his orders' (Stein 1975: 77). Thus the state itself developed and Indian medieval states or even little kingdoms at a later stage should not be identified with a Western state in the modern sense. For a discussion on the topic of so-called 'little kingdoms' see Chap. 4.1. Besides, though all tribes have been formally integrated into the Indian Union, the influence of the state might still be very limited in practice and tribes may have retained much of their character.
40. From the present perspective a rather unfortunate term implying that tribes are 'un-civilized', which the author certainly did not intend. The term might be replaced by state here, though this is also problematic. As Béteille (1991: 66) pointed out, for India, Hindu 'civilization' certainly has shown a greater continuity than the state.
41. Southall (1970: 28) defined tribal society as 'a whole society, with a high degree of self-sufficiency at a near subsistence level, based on a relatively simple technology without writing or literature, politically autonomous and with its own distinctive language, culture and sense of identity, tribal religion being also coterminous with tribal society'.
42. See also Hardenberg (2002b: 4). For the Pakhtuns of the north–western part of South Asia a similar argument has been put forward by Béteille (1991: 66).
43. Béteille refers here to the Islamic world rather than to India, but I cannot see, why a similar argument should not be put forward for parts of India as well.
44. See also Hardenberg (2002b). Pfeffer (1982a: 29; 2000: 336) also speaks of a Koraput Complex and a Gond Complex, hinting at similar concepts and ideas shared by various tribal communities within a sub-region of Middle India.
45. As Pfeffer (1997: 7) pointed out, there is no historical hint at a later immigration of Scheduled Caste people into tribal areas.
46. For the same hypothesis for Bastar see also Gell (1992: 3).
47. The term clients is used by Pfeffer for communities such as the Dombo in Koraput, considered by the administration as Scheduled Castes, who engage in petty trade for their patrons or 'lords of the land', the landowning and dominant tribal clans.

48. One may also argue that Western, individualistic society attaching the highest value to the individual might be considered holistic to some extent too.
49. Parkin (2000: 54) refers to processes of 'Santalization' among Santal attempting to constitute themselves as a separate community distinct from caste society. Similar processes have been labelled 'tribalism' by Fried (1968: 17) et al.
50. On peasantry compare also Rothermund (1978), Shanin (1990) and MacDougall (1977).
51. On the question of homogeneity of peasant communities see Roseberry (1989).
52. Peasant may denote two different meanings. It a restricted sense it might be applied to a specialization of labour within caste society (a peasant in contrast to a priest, etc.). In a wider sense, however, denotes a 'way of life' (Redfield 1956: 18) implying evolutionary connotations. My use of the term—explicitly of peasant society—refers to the second meaning.
53. Redfield (1956: 21) also acknowledged significant differences among peasants, e.g. between those residing in a compact village community and those peasants being semi-nomadic or residing in scattered houses.
54. Other approaches to a tribe-caste-continuum such as by Sinha are also discussed in Urhahn (1985).
55. See also Southall (1970).
56. Compare Roseberry (1989).
57. On the importance of markets for peasant society see Redfield (1956: 28ff).
58. Wolf gives several examples for such a development, but also noted that change in the opposite direction, may occur, though rarely.
59. A notable exception is my colleague T. Otten, working currently on the Rona of Koraput district.
60. While thinking about coining the term I realized that MacDougall had already used it in order to analyse movements of resistance among tribal communities of Middle India.
61. See Kulke (2001 [1976]), MacDougall (1977), Pfeffer (1978).

CHAPTER 2

Aghriā Mythology

In this chapter I explore the ways in which the Aghriā locate themselves in the tribal and caste society and how they conceptionalize their origin and status as well as their links to religious and political centres. The Aghriā claim to be descendants of Bidur as a mythological figure of the *Mahābhārata* and to be of Kshatriya origin. Additionally, they locate themselves between Agra, the Muslim centre left behind and Puri, the Hindu centre and their destination of their migration in the past. On the one hand mythological links are constructed to Brahmins, or rather Tihāris as their Brahminical priests, and on the other hand to Chamārs, in other words to both ends of a caste hierarchy, while their tribal neighbours are not mentioned at all. Thus, the Aghriā locate themselves geographically between politico-religious centres and also between the extremes hierarchical antipodes of caste society. In addition, the central, but irresolvable conundrum of caste society, the relation between Brahmin and king appears as a prominent theme in a myth which presents the Aghriā as holders of the plough and the *Disandhrī*[1] as their younger brothers guarding the sacred thread. Similar to kingdoms in western India (Basu 2000: 91), the *Disandhrī* became the bards of the Aghriā, extolling the latter as patrons, thus contributing to their status as village kings.

Since myths are an essential part of a political discourse in which claims and counter-claims are put forward, the myth might well be related to a rise of the Aghriā to the position of 'village kings' in a mixed tribal and caste society as well as to a subsequent process of 'Kshatriyaization'.[2] In this regard, Aghriā myths seem to fulfil a function similar to that of as the *vaṃśāvali* literature or the chronicles of royal families (Kulke 2001 [1987a], 2001 [1987b]; Berkemer 1993; Schnepel 2002).[3] Furthermore, within such a political arena the existence of deviating versions contesting origin and Kshatriya-status is also not surprising. Thus, other explanations of as well as ideas about the origin of the Aghriā and their place in society will be highlighted as well.

These days Aghriā mythology[4] is generally transmitted in two ways. On the one hand myths are passed on by Disandhrīs acting as the Aghriās' bards and reciting mythological stories known as *mandlā*[5] on special occasions. For their performance Disandhrī were entitled to the gift of a cow or buffalo. The relation between Aghriā and Disandhrī is an essential part of the myths and will be discussed below. On the other hand, there are published accounts on the origin of the Aghriā. The Aghriā caste organization or Aghriā Samāj which was founded in 1904[6] has published Aghriā myths from the beginning of the twentieth century and has been particularly influential in propagating certain versions. Thus one finds oral and written accounts not only co-existing (possibly even merging in a process of canonization) but also occasionally deviating in certain details. This double transmission of mythology, written and oral form may lead or may have led to contradictions in the texts, expressing existing conflicts as Goody and Watt (1986 [1968]: 93) have remarked. According to Goody and Watt, the emergence of a literary tradition is often related to the realization of contradictions between various texts, while an oral tradition might be more easily adaptable to changing conditions within society. Various accounts from oral sources as well as written versions have been recorded and shall be presented here in an attempt to discern the core of the Aghriā myth. However, a homogenization and reduction of mythological stories to a singular 'standard version'[7] is not intended, but rather the discursive field described. Subsequently, the myths shall be interpreted by exploring etymologies used by the Aghriā themselves before turning to radically different accounts which may question the status and origin of the Aghriā.

First we shall examine the Aghriā myths. Most accounts distinguish two phases of origin: a very early period and a much later one with dated events, specifically the migration to Orissa.

2.1. EARLY ORIGIN

A Disandhrī narrated the earliest part of the Aghriā myth in the following manner:

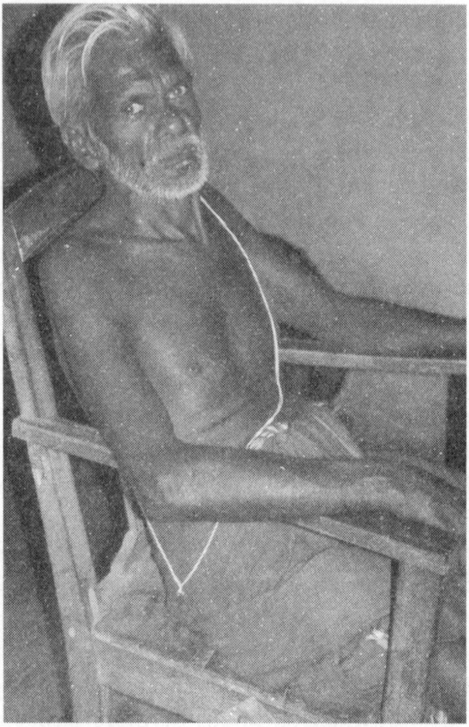

Disandhrī

The wife of Atriya Rushi [a sage] is Anusuyā. The Moon God Chandra had an affair with the Goddess Tārā [star]. The name of the Moon's son is Budha. Puraraba was his son. Puraraba's son is king Prabira. His son was Mata Sananta. His son was born as Raibira. Raibira's son is Dusmanta.

This is to note that Bharata is the son of Dusmanta. The son of Bharta is Abhimanyu and his [Abhimanyu's] son; Biratha—a great hero—is as powerful as Indra. The son of Biratha is king Sambhurana. He has five sons named Kuru. The son of the eldest Kuru is Karaka. The son of Karaka is the king Shantanu Mahadev. The sons of Shantanu were Chitra and Bichitra Birja. They died without sons due to bad blessing. This is the result of sin. Shantanu's wife is Satyabadi and her son is Vyasa Mahajati. The sons of Vyasa Deba, the great Saint (Mahajati), are Pandu and Dhrutarastra. The son of Pandu is the great king Jujesthi.[8]

There was a king named Hath Keshab. His caste was Shudra. His daughter gave king Padmanava children namded Ambhu, Ambhika, Ambalika and Ambabati. The son of Ambhu is Dhrutarastra. The son of Ambhika is king

Pandu. The son of Ambhubati is Bidur. Gandhari got married to Dhrutarastra. King Gainta offered his daughter to king Pandu named Bhojraj.

The marriages of those ancient kings are the same as that of the marriage of the eighty-one kings. His daughter named Punchho has a son Bhanu Chandra. Bhanu is a very powerful miraculous king of the Kuru family. Satyabati, the king's mother, saw the annihilation of the Bhanu Chandra bansa after the death of Bichitra Birja, without any son. . . . The strong desire as per the instruction of king Bhisma. She remembered Vyasa Deba (Mahajati) and requested a remedy for her reproductive capacities and for a son. By obeying the order of his mother Satyabati, Vyasa with his miraculous power arranged the conception of legitimate offspring Dhrutarastra and Pandu and through the servant (*dasi*) Vaishnabi Sanjay of the Sujani caste, Umabati and Bidur are born.

From his childhood Bidur, in the best family tradition, was a prophet of the Bhagbat Gita. He got married to the daughter of the Shudra king Kesab of Hathkesar near Kashi. To his legitimate two sons were born Priya Bhanu and Sura Bhanu.

The status of Bidur's mother and wife are given in the account as Śudra, though in case of his wife a Śudra royal family. In this account Bidur is presented as the son of a maidservant as well as the son of queen Ambhubati which, of course, exhibits an inherent contradiction. Such an ambiguity is also expressed in a variety of other texts. Thus in another Aghriā text[9] it is noted:

The great King Bichitra Birja of the Chandra bansa died without having a son. When his mother Satyabatidevi saw the annihilation of the Soma bansa [*Chandra bansa*], as per the instructions of the magnanimous king Bhisma, she requested the great Saint Vyasadev, who had the ability to see the past and to predict the future, to give her sons. The sage, through his own power, begot Dhrutarashtra and Pandu: from the uterus of Vaishnabi Dāsi Sanjay was born and from the womb of Shudra dāsi, Bidur.

From childhood Bidur was attached to God, and good in behaviour. He was a man of justice and wisdom. The great king Dhrutarastra took advice from him. Bidur got married to the daughter of Keshab Das, the Shudra king of Hatakeshwar near Kashi. The name of the mother of Bidur is in the list of Shudras, but that is not true. She is Ambubati, daughter of king Harikeshwar of the Surya bansa and the second queen of the great king Bichitra Birja.

Thus in the latter version, which is more or less exactly reproduced in more recent publications of the Aghriā Samāj in, for example, 1983, it is emphasized that Bidur was the son of queen Ambhubatī.

In other words, it is asserted that he was apparently of Kshatriya origin, while in the version of the *Disandhrī* as well as in the Gazetteers[10] a Śudra status is proclaimed. This corresponds to the north Indian versions of the *Mahābhārata*, in which Vidura, also called Kshattr and considered an incarnation of a 'portion of Dharma', is described as the son of Vyāsa and a Śudra woman who was the maid of queen Aṁbika (Sörensen 1978 [1904]: 733). However, according to a version of the *Mahābhārata*, that I came across in an Aghriā household and supposedly written by Sarala Das, Bidur married the daughter of a Vaishya king. In this book[11] it is noted (the poetic structure has been maintained as far as possible):

> The king of Harikesh is in the state of Harikesh, He is the king, born in the family of Rudra [Śiva]. His daughter's name is Ambhubatee, The great king Bichitra Birja got married to her. Amba and Ambalika are blessed with sons, but Ambhubatee is deprived of them. You are my son, who is very great in wisdom. You make it to give birth a son through Ambhubatee. The excellent wise person Vyāsa, went by the order of mother, And entered the womb of Ambhubatee. The wife, Ambhubatee, got herself dressed as Amba and Ambalika used to dress themselves. The meeting was emotional with great joy and pleasure. She became fortunate on copulation with Vyāsa. . . . A son fair faced like moon was born at once. The son was born in an auspicious moment of immorality, Vyāsa saw that he was excessively knowledgeable. That son was born from the leg side, Again there were signs of lotus and the conch shells on both legs. He made sounds in the divine speech, in words of the learned. The name Bidur was given by the great ascetic Vyāsa. By holding him on his lap, Vyāsa gave him kisses on his lips, and said 'Let him be very skilled and intelligent'. Be rich in all qualities. Riches and beauty will never break from your shoulder. In enlarged knowledge let all your activities be seen, in wisdom and righteousness let all your days be spent. The excellent ascetic Vyāsa after giving such a boon, handed over the son to the lap of Satyabatee [Vyāsa's mother]. (pp. 32-3)

About Bidur's marriage, the text says, 'A king named Kashe-eshawar was there in the State of Kashee. He has a daughter named Vandanabatee. He has given Vandanabatee as a gift to Bidur, the king of Kasheeshwar who belongs to the Vaishya' (p. 44).

Thus in this version of the *Mahābhārata* Bidur is born to a queen and married to a Vaishya. To sum things up: Bidur's mother and wife are described in the texts either as Śudra, Vaishya, or Kshatriya. Therefore, the Kshatriya origin of Bidur as the ultimate forefather of the Aghriā, on whom a descent model of origin is focused, is somehow ambiguous, although Bidur is closely associated with the royal family of Dhrutarashtra and with a sage called Vyāsa, who is said to have begot Bidur. However, though the Aghriā believe to be descendants of Bidur, to whom Krishna once promised that his descendants would never be poor, Bidur does not play any role in the ritual cycle of the Aghriā.

2.2. MIGRATION

In a second, clearly marked and even more common part of the myth a migration process is described. Once again, the version told by a Disandhrī shall be presented first:

Respect to Shri Vishnu: the Soma-bansa Rajput were inhabitants of Agra. When the emperor (badshah) told them to pay respect, the Aghriā Rajput replied that the Aghriā were heroes (*bīra*) and very strong, and would not bow down to the emperor. Hearing this answer, the emperor was angry. He consulted his courtiers and decided to tie a sword (*karat batā*)[12] in the middle of the court. Those who came to the court with their heads held high would have them cut off. When the Rajputs would hear it, they would be frightened and would bow down their heads. Near the entrance the emperor watched what the Aghriā would do.[13] When the Aghriā came, ten to twenty heads were cut off. Most of the Aghriā died in this way, but they never bowed down their heads. When the Aghriā came to know about this conspiracy they decided to leave Delhi and Agra and even vowed not to take water any more in the absence of a cosmic order (*pani pine ka dharam nahi*). They left Agra and Delhi. They came to the Gajapati Maharaja [Puri] and requested the Maharaja to allow them some occupation. 'If you do not allow us any occupation, what will we do? We have come to the feet of the King [under your jurisdiction].' Gajapati Maharaja replied, 'I will allow you some occupation.'

He constructed sheaths (*dhāl*[14]) for two swords (*khandā*), one of iron, with its handle of silver. Instead of constructing a second sword, he put in the sheath a stick to drive bullocks (*pāchen bāḍi*) with a golden handle. He kept them in front of Parmeshwar [Lord Jagannāth]. The Gajapati told: 'You have to choose one among these two. Whatever is in your fate, that will be your occupation.' After listening to that Uros Raut said [to the Aghriā], 'If you all agree I will lift one sword, otherwise I will not.' All the Aghriā agreed and allowed him to choose one. He lifted the sword with the golden handle, and they pulled out [of from its cover].

Bām and Jatām, two brothers (*bhāi*), handed over their axe (*kaṭār*) to Ram Singh and then they started to take care of the land [started cultivation]. They made 10 shares and one share will go to the Dissondhi. That's the order of the Gajapati.

In a written account[15] the migration of the Aghriā is described in the following manner:

The Bidur Kshatriya continued to live in Agra in Rajputana and in its nearby areas. The Muslim king Adilshah sat on the throne in the year AD 1550 at Delhi. During his reign the Hindu tenants were oppressed. The Kshatriya born in the family of Bidur did not even salute the king by bowing their heads. After having been informed about it the king introduced a new formula to receive salutations. If anyone saluted without bowing his head, while standing on a line drawn by the king on the floor of the house, he would have his throat cut by the very sharp prickly iron saw hung on the top. But even when the Kshatriya born in the family of Bidur got wounded by the saw they did not bow down their heads.

The king announced an order for sending them to the Kandhar war after seeing their determination and moral courage. Those reluctant to go to war would have to accept Islam or else be convicted with capital punishment. When the announcement of this order was known, 44 out of 84 houses (*chaurāsi ghar*) of Kshatriyas, with their families, fled to Orissa. They took refuge there in the year 1550 under the rule of the Gajapati, Maharaja Mukundadeba. The king of Orissa made arrangements for the newcomers (*āgantuka*) of those 84 houses. Two sword sheaths were kept behind the king's throne of Sri Jagannāth—one made of gold with a stick to drive the bullocks (*pāchen bāḍi*) inside and a silver one with an iron sword inside, only the covers being visible while the remaining part were covered with a silk cloth. The Maharaja called the 84 houses and said, 'Let the eldest person among you hold the hilt of any of the two weapons kept under the throne and bring it when lifted up.' Uros Rout, the senior in age, was selected to do that. Tempted, he lifted the weapon hilted with gold. The Maharaja seeing this ordered farming to be their livelihood from that day.

From that day Uros Rout and the rest started cultivating with their own hands after having abandoned the sacred thread. Only the youngest brother of Uros took the Kshatriya sacred thread and axe (*kaṭār*). They were known by the title Disandhrī. The Disandhrī have continued to keep this symbol in successive generations. Like the Brahmin and Kshatriyas they did not till the land with their own hands. They were ordered by Uros in the past to attend to priestly work (*jāchakatā*[16]) in the 84 households as their main livelihood.

Jagannāth worshipped during the *Rath Jātrā*.

The 44 Kshatriya households of Bidur's descendants who had come from Orissa, at first established a colony in Patna State of Routkalā. The contemporary emperor of Patna, after seeing their skills in cultivation, donated large lands and villages to them for the prosperity of the state. A few households from amongst them came out of Patna when the clever Emperor Madhukar Sai of the newly formed Sambalpur State created a colony in the village of Laida. Even now the people of that caste say that the village Laida is the place of inheritance of their family. It is called the place of 'jhāmpi peḍi utra'.[17]

With an increase in the number of families, they started to live in Patna, Phuljhara, Bilaspur, Sambalpur, Gangapur, Bamanda, etc. They are called the Agriha caste as they have come from Āgrā. In due course the word Āgruā changed to Āgriā and further to Agriā. The Āgriā caste (*jāti*) was divided into three parts: Choudhary, Nayak, and Patel. Out of 84 households, 6 are Choudhary, 18 Nayak, and 60 Patel. All are Kshatriya. The Koilikattar [*kattar* = dagger] belongs to Choudhary household, Jama dadha kattar to the Nayak households, and the Meghanada kattar to the Patel households.

Variations of the dominant myth

The myths I have collected differ in some regards, especially the places mentioned: while most people say they left Agra, others say it was Delhi or Rajputana. Secondly, the time period as well as the reigning Mughal emperor is disputed. Some insist it was Akbar together with his minister Birbal, while others believe it was during the reign of Aurangzeb. In a written version of a Disandhrī, a king Dileshwar is mentioned, who, together with his soldier Nagina, conspired against the Aghriā, because they thought too highly of themselves. While most Aghriā favour 'Adil Shah' as ruling at that time, historically he does not seem to fit the context. No Mughal emperor of that name is known to have ruled in Delhi or Agra within the given time frame.[18] The year in which the Aghriā fled is sometimes dated 1556 or 1554, while an elder Disandhrī insisted it was as early as 1440. The latter version claims that Puri was reached in 1447 during the reign of king Jagdish (the throne was subsequently taken over by his youngest brother Narasingh Deda in 1448). However, in most versions, as in the one above, Mukunda Deb is mentioned as ruler of Utkal (Orissa), which perhaps refers to the historical figure Mukunda Harichandana.[19] Furthermore in some versions it is noted that the Aghriā were previously Khare Rajputs. The reasons for flight are also explained differently. Some Aghriā argue that it was the Mughals, their policy of conversion, while others regard the custom of polygamy among the Mughals and, therefore, their constant search for Aghriā women, as the reason. Both lines of argument may well fit into the present political discourse.

Accounts of an Aghriā migration within Orissa subsequent to the decision of Lord Jagannāth also seem to differ. In Bolangir former Patna state the following Aghriā expansion is remembered:

> This caste of newcomers gradually came to Patna in 1565 on the written orders of Gajapati. Knowing them to be a caste adept at cultivation, the contemporary supreme ruler, the widow queen of king Hamir Deb, ordered them to start their livelihood in the neighbourhood of Patnagarh. Tendapadara, Ulba, Bheisha, etc., are the villages populated by Aghria today. One of their branches made habitation at Bolangir and on its neighbouring villages Beherapali, Puinntaba, Gainnala, Malamanda, Bhalora and Kurula. Due to growth in the family they lived in different villages of Bolangir district and became renowned as cultivators. When the king of Patna, Balaram Deb, the brother of Narasingh Deb, established the Sambalpur district separately, some houses of this caste came from Bolangir and started living there (1571). The people of this caste nowadays live in the area of in Raigarha, Phuljara, Chandrapur, Saranggarh, Bilaspur, Bamanda, Bolangir, Kalahandi, Sambalpur, Sundargarh, etc.[20]

Furthermore, in the Bolangir version a leader named Vrosa is mentioned in place of Uros Rout as the eldest among Aghriā in Puri. In Sambalpur district, and more specifically in the area of Kuchinda, the role of the Sambalpur King Madhukara Sye is highlighted. This king is said to have brought the Aghriā from Patna to Sambalpur—Patna being sometimes associated with Bihar instead of present Bolangir, which is a more likely hypothesis.[21]

The mythological link to the Chamār

In some versions of the origin myth, particularly as told by members of the Leuniā clan of the Aghriā, one finds a subsidiary link to the Chamār. They are instrumental in the survival of the Aghriā.[22] Strikingly similar stories are also remembered as well as emphasized by Chamārs.

The most common version told by Leuniā runs in the following manner:

> The Aghriā were called to the Mughal court in order to decide either to bow down their heads or to have their heads cut off by the hanging sword. All Aghriā refused to bow to the emperor, until only two or three were left, who searched for ways to escape. They called some Chamār standing near by for help. The Chamār knew that if they would replace the Aghriā they would die by the hanging sword. They told the Aghriā: 'When we die, who will perform our obituary rites (*śrāddha*)?' The Aghriā promised to perform all necessary rituals for them.

Other versions highlight help of the Chamār in the fight of the Aghriā with the Mughals. For example a Leuniā stated:

> The Chamār fought on the side of the Aghriā. He was severely wounded during the battle. Shortly before his death he asked an Aghriā for water, who for humanitarian reasons poured some drops into his mouth. In remembrance of this incident, *piṇḍa* is offered to the Chamār during the Aghriā *śrāddha*.

In addition, well-educated Aghriā reported that in the eighteenth-century Chhattisgarh was ruled by Rani Dharmati who was an Aghriā widow. When the Pathans reached Chhattisgarh they beat her and killed her. The Aghriā subsequently fled and took shelter in the house of a Chamār. This Chamār feared that he would also be killed if the Pathans found out. As the Chamār had no son, the Aghriā promised to perform all necessary rituals in case he would be killed. The Aghriā kept their promise and offered *piṇda* for the Chamār, but in the back of their dwelling and not inside their house.

In yet another narrative told by an Aghriā of the Leuniā-clan the focus differs slightly. In this account the Chamār voluntarily offers his life in order to save the Aghriā.

When the Aghriā had been called to the Mughal court to bow, a Chamār was the guardian of the gate. Apart from forcing the Aghriā to bow down their heads by hanging a sword, the emperor planned to flay the Aghriā. The Chamār, a fine man, disapproved of that. Having neither a son nor a daughter, he released the Aghriā and said, 'Please, go!' The Aghriā replied, 'The emperor will punish you!' The Chamār replied, 'Only I will die, because I have no children.' He wished that the Aghriā would perform the obituary rites (*śrāddha*) for him, particularly the offering of rice balls (*piṇda*). The Aghriā agreed and escaped.

The father–son or ancestor–descendants link hinted at the offering of *piṇda* is stressed even more explicitly in the following version, this time told by a Chamār.[23]

Most Aghriā were hanged by the Mughal emperor Somnath, but one Aghriā managed to escape. The guards of the emperor followed him. The Aghriā took refuge in the house of an old Chamār, who was hanging pieces of leather on a rope and was pouring some water over them. The Aghriā pleaded to the Chamār, 'Please, save me. Otherwise I will be hanged.' The Chamār replied, 'You will do my work, while I will sit next to the door.' When the emperor's guard arrived at the house of the Chamār and asked, 'Have you seen the Aghriā?' the old Chamār replied. 'Look yourself: only my son is working here, nobody else.' The guard left and the Aghriā had been saved. The Aghriā man made an offering for the Chamār on Nuā Khāi, repeating it every year thereafter.

In some narratives not only is a relation to the Chamār as the lowest in the hierarchy emphasized, but also links between Aghriā and their own Brahmin priests known as the Tihāri are stressed.

Relation to the Tihāri and Brahmin

Significantly, the Aghriā are served by priests who are supposed to work exclusively for them. These ritual specialists are known as Tihāri or Tiwāri[24] and claim to be Kanya Kubja Brahmins, a claim which relates them to the Vedic Brahmins of coastal Orissa.[25] Occasionally they are also called the *kul purohit* of the Aghriā. One of these priests, who resides in Laiḍā where most of the Tihāri are settled, told the following story:

A Muslim king, probably Akbar or Babur, tortured the Aghriā, for example calling Aghriā brides during their wedding nights to his court. Birbal, a minister of the king and wise man, advised the Aghriā to put a tilāk on the forehead of the bride with the blood of goats. If the king asks about the blood they should say it is the blood of pigs. The king was appalled, and the Aghriā had to flee. The refugees were known as the Eighty-four Houses (*chaurāsi ghar*).

The Aghriā are a mixture of castes—though all are Hindus. Therefore Brahmins refused to work for them. In order to hire a priest and to solve their problem the Aghriā went back to Agra to bring the Tihāri, who uses the title 'Tiwāri', but is known as Tihāri. There were two Tihāri brothers in Agra: Adri and Badri. The Aghriā asked Adri to come to Orissa. Adri demanded that he should be the only one permitted to perform all rituals of the Aghriā. They agreed.

An elder Aghriā present on the occasion of this narration did not agree with the content, particularly in the first part of the story. However, a certain tension between Aghriās and Brahmins is also expressed in the following story which is an undated pamphlet, probably an early publication of the Aghriā Samāj entitled 'Why Aghriā do not accept food from a Brahmin'.

In former times Aghriā were Kshatriyas serving the king as warriors. Once there was a war against Kandahar and the Aghriā fought bravely for the king. The Aghriā asked the Brahmins for help in the war, but they refused, saying they did not want to die. Therefore the Aghriā vowed not to accept food from the hands of Brahmins anymore. Due to these difficulties the Aghriā decided to leave the place. On their way to Puri they met a Brahmin from Kānya Kubja, who was a Tiwāri. The Tiwāri saw that the Aghriā did not accept even water from a Brahmin. The Aghriā being happy to have met the Tiwāri, promised that Tiwāris could henceforth perform all their rituals.

Such a statement is also confirmed by various Aghriā publications,[26] for example a description of the Aghriā of 1925 according to which the priestly acts of the Aghriā are conducted by Tihāris. In case there was a scarcity of Tihāri or Kanya Kubja Brahmins, Aghriā would manage with Utkalīya (Oriya) Brahmins or Araṇyaka Brahmin (jungle Brahmins). The same system is currently practised: every Aghriā family should call the Tihāri when a family priest (*purohit*) is needed, but if he is already engaged, any other Brahmin may be called for urgent rituals.[27]

Some Aghriā asserted, however, that they only started accepting food from Brahmins about thirty years ago. Prior to that they used to cook for themselves. Although the rule not to accept food from Brahmin is still maintained during caste feasts (*bhoji*), a Brahmin may be hired to cook for guests at large functions.

2.3. INTERPRETATION

Aghriā origins are remembered in two phases: a very distant and undated mythical past and a more recent historical past conceptionalized with precise dates, for example, the year of leaving Agra (though the dates vary from version to version). The former contains a long list of mythical kings starting from the union between the moon and a star as the 'point of commencement' (Thapar 2002 [1978]: 758). Thus the Aghriā are directly linked to the moon and claim to be of *Chandravanśa* origin (one of the two important lines of Kshatriya-descent)[28] which might also help legitimize their present position as a dominant caste. From there the line of ancestors leads to Bidur—a figure known in the *Mahābhārata* —who is said to be the forefather of all Aghriā. His credentials as a Kshatriya are somewhat ambiguous, however, since in some versions (many of them put forward by Aghriā or Disandhrī themselves) his mother and wife are said to be of Śudra or Vaishya origin.

The second phase relates to a more recent migration and is metaphorically richer in the sense of containing more oppositions. It places the Aghriā somehow in the periphery between two centres and seems to offer an explanation for their place and occupation in Orissa. Apparently there are two centres opposed to each other. On the one hand one finds Agra (or Delhi) as the centre of the Mughal empire ruled by a Muslim dynasty, which the Aghriā leave behind. Agra, as reasoned in the myth, is supposed to be a place where you can neither drink nor eat, implying that it is a place without *dharma* (religious or cosmic duty). Their departure is caused by a trick at the ruler's court to force them to bow down their heads. Such a ploy is obviously incompatible with a *kṣātra dharma*, which prescribes conquest, warfare, and duels on the battlefield instead of tricks.[29] On the other hand Puri in the text is ruled by the Gajapati or a Hindu dynasty and associated with Lord Jagannāth thus signalling it is a place of *dharma*. Thus apparently the migration is based on the following oppositions—the journey or migration itself being a medium of transformation[30] which may also be indicated by the act of decapitation of the Aghriā at the Mughal court:[31]

Agra (Delhi)	Puri
Mughal	Gajapati
west (north–west)	east (south-east)
Muslim	Hindu
absence of Gods/*dharma* (cosmic order)	presence of Gods/*dharma* (cosmic order)
centre left behind	centre of destination
autochthonous	immigrated
revolt against orders	obey orders
negative centre	positive centre

Thus on the one hand one finds Puri, ruled by the Gajapati as Hindu king and situated in the east, the direction generally associated with Hindu gods including Lord Jagannāth. And on the other hand there is Agra, the western centre left behind, where gods and a rightful cosmic order (*dharma*) are non-existing. While Aghriā have to leave their place of origin after having revolted against orders to bow to the ruler, they readily accepted the divine orders of Lord Jagannāth. Keeping in mind that a Muslim population is almost non-existent in north-west Orissa, the construction of Muslim rule in opposition to Hindu kings might come as a surprise, but may implicitly also refer to their tribal neighbours—otherwise conspicuously absent in the myth. As in case of hierarchy, certain relations are hardly verbally expressed, but taken for granted or explained by reference to other communities. Therefore tribal and Muslim people might be implicitly identified as the Others. This, though in a reversed form, may correspond to the opposition of autochthonous *vs.* immigrated—the tribal population imagined in opposition to the Aghriā as newcomers. In contrast to that interpretation, however, a reference to Muslims might also be a replication of family chronicles of royal families in which a victory over Muslims is mentioned at times.[32]

In the final part of their migration the Aghriā follow an order of Lord Jagannāth initiated by the Gajapati King as Hindu king. Similar myths of divine intervention in order to legitimize rulers from outside—or 'intruders'—are also found in other parts of Orissa and the *vaṃśāvalis* or chronicles of the royal family of Jeypore may serve as an example (Schnepel 2002: 148f). Without over-interpreting the myth the Aghriā in this way rationalize their share in consolidating the rule and increasing the revenue of Hindu kings in tribal areas as well as being agents of an on-going Hinduization and peasantization.

It is also significant to note that the Aghriā are placed between two centres. They have to leave Puri too after having been assigned a new occupation. This time, however, they do not escape, but they are ordered by Lord Jagannāth, obeying a divine decision. It is this divine order—combined with their own fault, their greed—which legitimates a decline in status: warriors turn into peasants or a stick replaces the sword (warrior : peasant :: sword : stick).

However, the Aghriā myths are not just the seemingly simple straightforward stories, which reflect only past 'grand events' (Thapar 2002 [1978]: 755) and an explanation for a conceived fall.[33] They are not simply representations of empirical facts, but they are rather characterized by various inversions.[34] In my opinion, a central paradox of the myths concerns the relation between Aghriā and Disandhrī or bards. On the one hand, the Aghriā are presented as elder brothers of the Disandhrī. However, the distinction elder versus younger found here and known from various parts of Orissa and Middle India is not only related to the domain of kinship and biological age, but also to a difference in status, the elder being higher in status (Pfeffer 2000: 342). This seems to be reflected occasionally in local characterizations of the Disandhrī as *sān* (small, 'junior') in relation to and dependent on the Aghriā, who are *baḍ* (big, 'senior') in turn. The superior Aghriā provide their younger brothers with the means to survive, offering one-tenth of their harvest to them as their rightful share (*bhāg*).[35] Hence the name Disandhrī is derived from *dis* (ten).[36] Thus a material dependence is clearly expressed in the myth and related to the elder/younger differentiation. On the other hand, the Disandhrī are ascribed the task of guarding the sacred thread (*paitā*), which the Aghriā had to remove in order to turn to agriculture and to start ploughing. Obviously ploughing cannot be combined with the standards of purity required for wearing the sacred thread, which the Disandhrī wear today. Such a differentiation of status related to the use of the ploughs is found among the Brahmins of Orissa. The Vedic or Śāsana Brahmins engaged in their ritual functions claim superiority over the Oriya or plough Brahmins, who introduced the plough to the 'tribal frontier' (Pfeffer 1978: 425–6). Thus a second conflicting hierarchy of purity is contained within the myth: the Disandhrī as younger brother being relatively purer, but materially dependent as shown below:[37]

higher	*lower*
elder (brother)	younger (brother)
Aghriā (eB)	Disandhrī (yB)
materially independent	materially dependent
lower	*higher*
relatively more polluted	relatively purer
Aghriā	Disandhrī
plough	sacred thread

The ambivalent relation between Aghriā and Disandhrī is expressed in terms of food acceptance. Although the Disandhrī who wear the sacred thread should not, according to their own standards, accept cooked food from Aghriā, in practice they do.[38] The ambiguous position of the Disandhrī in relation to their patrons mirrors the role of the Charan *vis-à-vis* the Rajput to some extent. The Charans as royal bards in western India are conceptionalized as ritual sisters of their Rajput patrons (Basu 2000: 119). This implies on the one hand an inferior status of the Charan within the gender hierarchy, while on the other hand the Charan as sisters are like Brahmin and ascetics recipients of gifts, underlining a higher status (ibid.). Thus, the Disandhrī seem to stand in a similar structural position to their 'patron kin' like Charans in western India—though the ritual idiom to express the relation is completely different.

Without stretching interpretation too far the relation Aghriā: Disandhrī resembles the pair Kshatriya: Brahmin or king: priest in a wider sense.[39] This seems to be confirmed by the fact that priestly functions are assigned to the Disandhrī in the myth—although the latter do not fulfil them in reality—while the Aghriā receive a stick by the order of Lord Jagannāth which itself is a symbol of rule, royalty and ruling in the world.[40] Therefore, the Aghriā appear relatively impure givers in relation to the Disandhrī as purer receivers. Thus, the Aghriā myth seems to deal, like the Asdiwal myth studied by Lévi-Strauss (1992 [1973]: 197ff),[41] with a more general societal paradox, one which Trautmann (1995 [1981]: 285) once called 'the central conundrum of Indian social ideology'.[42] In the myth one finds the contradiction between two conflicting patterns of ordering society, two hierarchies: one from the perspective of the king as universal giver, the other from the perspective of the relatively pure priest. The myth reveals this paradox, though in a disguised form, and thus, following Lévi-Strauss, one might argue that a function of the myth might well be to acknowledge an irresolvable paradox, a practical antinomy (Lévi-Strauss 1992 [1973]: 197ff).[43]

This might be further substantiated by another inversion of the myth. In most versions it is the eldest among the Aghriā, who is described as a greedy person and who commits a serious mistake by choosing the golden sword handle instead of the silver one, a mistake which proves to be so fatal for the Aghriā. Keeping the aforesaid in mind, it seems that the status as Kshatriya is opposed to greed here. In the moment that the eldest Aghriā is tempted and overwhelmed by his greed, the Kshatriya warrior status is lost and a decline sets in. Thus this part of the myth might be a symbolic reminder of a close link between Kshatriya status and generosity instead of greed. Only by generosity, by giving, is Kshatriya status maintained and the *kṣātra dharma* fulfilled, a point which seems to reflect the position of the Aghriā as 'village kings' and givers at the centre of a redistributive system rather than as warriors.

Let us now turn to the peculiar link between Chamārs and Aghriās, mentioned in various versions and stressed by the Chamārs for whom it is certainly prestigious to link themselves to the dominant caste. However, such a relation is also expressed by Aghriā—particularly of the Leuniā clan.[44] One might argue, as some Aghriā do, that the Chamār, who share the same language as the Aghriā—namely Lariā—may have migrated from the same area or at the same time as the Aghriā. One may also explain the rather close relation by the fact that in former times the Chamār used to produce special leather pots known as *puhurā* necessary to pump water and to carry it to the fields. Such pots were essential for agriculture[45] and the Aghriā were, to some extent, dependent on the Chamār for their production.[46] In contrast to that, however, another opposition seems to be expressed here, one related to the relative impurity with which the Chamār are associated throughout India. In their origin myth the Aghriā are endangered by the Mughal, but they are safe in the house of a Chamār. While Chamār are usually associated with death, specifically of cattle, in this myth they appear as protectors of life from the perspective of Aghriā—though they may sacrifice their own lives.

Thus one finds the following oppositions:

Kshatriya	*Chamār*
pure	impure
high	low
needing help	offering help
endangered	safe/surviving
status temporarily given up	status temporarily sought

Being a Chamār or having impure status in a wider sense may offer protection against life-threatening forces. Interestingly this story is remembered specifically in the case of death—some Aghriā acknowledge, that until recently their forefathers had offered a *piṇda* during their *śrāddha*, although nowadays most Aghriā deny such a practice which they probably conceive as degrading.[47] The Aghriā are not the only peasant caste claiming Kshatriya descent who are associated with 'Untouchables' mythologically. In an apparently very similar case of the Noniya of north India (Rowe 1968a)—to which I will turn later—one finds a related myth: escaping warrior–heroes are saved by 'Untouchables', but at the price of eating their defiling food.[48] The very same idea seems to be expressed in the custom of selling sick or endangered children to communities lower in status in hope of their survival. A temporary impure state or an association with Chamār in particular is considered as life protecting.[49]

Finally, in this myth as in other contexts, the Aghriā community is frequently termed *chaurāsi ghar*. Eighty-four (*chaurāsi*), apart from being a sacred number (Schnepel 2002: 94), may hint at a relation to Chhattisgarh, which the Aghriā would have passed through, if they originated from there. According to Babb (1975: 5) the traditional political structure of Chhattisgarh might have been based on so-called *barhon* (or *taluq*) incorporating twelve villages. The next higher political body, including 84 villages or 7 *barhon*, is known as *chaurasi* and forms one *garh* or fort. The strong link to Chhattisgarh, where a considerable number of Aghriā reside, perhaps more than in Orissa, may further substantiate this point as well as the fact that no list of 84 houses could be obtained anywhere—lists of Aghriā–clans contain 48 'houses' at best—indicating the mythical quality of the number 84.

2.4. DEVIATING MYTHS

Though in itself not fully coherent, the mythology presented above, transmitted orally as well as in written form, may be termed the dominant. Apart from these 'official' or 'public' versions—myths circulated by bards or caste organizations—there are various other ideas and deviating legends about the origin of the Aghriā and their name, contesting the dominant myth and putting it into perspective.

For example, B.C. Naik, an eminent Oriya poet and an Aghriā himself, believes that the Aghriā did not come from Agra, an idea not shared by that majority. According to him they have accompanied the Marathas on their way from Maharashtra and Rajputana. The route of migration is said to correspond to the road from Ranchi to Bamra. B.C. Naik also located a Maratha camp in an area known as *podan*—ground near his village Sahaspur in Kuchinda area. As the Marathas did not previously pay money to their mercenaries, but offered landed property, the Aghriā turned to agriculture.

The name 'Aghriā'

The variety of competing versions is demonstrated by explanations of the caste name. According to the myth already mentioned the Aghriā fled from Agra, hence their name Aghriā. However, different spellings and intonations of the caste name leave room for divergent interpretations. In written sources the name is spelled Āgriha, Agria, Agriha, Āgria (see in mythical accounts above), but also Āgrihā and Agharia or Aghariā. A spelling Aghariā, as in publications of the Bolangir Aghriā Samāj,[50] is obviously not fully identical with Agra and exhibits inconsistencies. Spellings such as Aghariā may have led some non-Aghriā, for example, members of the royal family of little kingdoms, to argue that Aghriā is rather derived from *a-ghar-iā* (without house/home) which implies that the Aghriā either had no house after coming to Orissa or they had a low status and were not allowed to enter others' houses. Some Aghriā accept the explanation in the former sense—the Aghriā as immigrants—and state that they used to camp under mahuā trees, which offered some protection and were respected by the community ever since. It is further argued that this special relation is expressed by the fact that Aghriā use mahuā trees at the centre of their wedding altars,[51] and these trees are also very much venerated among tribal communities of the region.[52]

Other explanations exist. Some people apparently confuse the Aghriā with the Aghori or Agnori—a Shaiva sect supposed to 'feed on human corpses' (Russell and Hiralal 1975 [1916]: 13; see also Risley 1981 [1891]: 10). This is, however, very unlikely. In a publication of the Aghriā Samāj in 1983 (Sambalpur) the name is derived from *agra* (front, first row) and *hiya* (chest) which alludes to Aghriā as brave warriors always fighting in the first lines of a battle. Similarly, as an elder Aghriā told me the name is based on *ag* (front) and *rahi* (to march) and that the Aghriā were 'frontrunners' leading the 'Aryans' to central India. Some Aghriā (Patel 1995) are convinced, however, that their forefathers were iron-smelters and their name is logically derived from *āg* (fire), though I tend to believe that they are mixing the peasant community I am talking about with a tribal community of Chhattisgarh (Elwin 1991 [1942])[53] with a similar name.[54]

Still others believe the Aghriā to have been salt makers—the name, according to them, being based on *agar* signifying the salt pan. Such a view is put forward, for example, by Nanda (1994) citing Elwin. These shallow pans, Nanda argues, are used in Rajputana and Punjab.[55] This idea might be substantiated by the fact that some Aghriā or Tihāri argue that the Aghriā caste is in fact a mixture of various castes that migrated to Orissa together. Incidentally, one of the most important clans of the Aghriā, the Leunia, may be related to a caste of traditional salt makers turned peasants called Loniya, Luniya, or Noniya, found not only in Uttar Pradesh, Madhya Pradesh and Bihar (Rowe 1968a, 1968b), but also in Punjab and Sind (Kurin 1990) and perhaps other parts of India as well. As Rowe (1968a: 68ff) says for Loniya residing in UP, these salt makers are in a process of social upward mobility and claim Kshatriya or Chauhān status. There is also a myth which relates the Loniya to the fight against Muslim rulers and 'explains' a subsequent loss of status after their escape from Muslim armies, which is almost identical with the Aghriā.[56] In addition, Kurin (1990: 98ff) describes how the Nunari in Punjab—or Nuniya, Luniya among other spellings—had turned from salt making to agriculture under British influence at the end of the nineteenth century and were, consequently, even included in the category of 'notified' agriculturist castes.[57]

Myths from Chhattisgarh

Caste brethren from neighbouring Chhattisgarh do not share the dominant Aghriā myth of Orissa. During a short survey among the Aghriā of Chhattisgarh (Raigarh and Sarangarh areas) some significant differences, particularly regarding the relation to Puri as the religious centre of Orissa, were noted. The President of the Aghriā Samāj of Raigarh[58] explained the Aghriā origin in the following manner:

> In 1627 the Aghriā Kshatriya were forced to leave Agra by Aurangzeb—a cruel king. They went to Kashi. [Later he corrected himself, stating that the Aghriā came from Rajasthan to Agra in 1627 and stayed there 60 to 70 years before moving on.] In former times they used to wear the sacred thread, did not drink alcohol and did not eat meat. From Kashi they first went to Akaltara—a village near Bilaspur. First they settled down in five villages and nowadays there are about 30 villages around Akaltara still maintaining a traditional Aghriā way of life—wearing the sacred thread, refusing to work with the plough, women being not allowed to wear bangles, prohibiting widow remarriage, etc. This area around Akaltara was a dense forest, in which only Adivasis used to stay. The Aghriā from Akaltara are known as baḍey Aghriā.

Asked whether the Aghriā had gone to Puri, the president, a frequent visitor to meetings of the Aghriā Samāj Sambalpur/ Sundargarh and, therefore, certainly aware of the dominant myth in that area, replied that the Akaltara Aghriā[59] did not go to Puri, but others went. Other Aghriā of the region confirmed the change in perspective, arguing that the Aghriā had come from Agra to Bilaspur and other parts of Chhattisgarh, but had not gone to Puri, while yet others said that the Aghriā had come via Sundargarh to Puri and have spread in Orissa subsequently. Still others argued that there might have been different waves of immigration and some but not all

Aghriā might have gone to Puri. Thus the relation between Aghriā in Chhattisgarh and Puri as centre of the Jagannāth cult—a connection so prominent in Orissa itself—is rather weak in Chhattisgarh. Some Aghriā in Chhattisgarh whom I questioned had no idea whatever of the mythological link between the Aghriā and Puri or Jagannāth, which is not surprising given the distance to the Orissa coast.[60] However, as far as I know there are also no other religious centres figuring in Aghriā myths of Chhattisgarh.

Although no other mythological relations to regional gods or goddesses are established and mentioned in the Chhattisgarh Aghriā mythology, occasionally a link is drawn between them and the Kurmi caste. Some Aghriā say that they fled from Agra together with the Kurmi, who, however, decided to stay in the Gwalior area. Some Aghriā in Chhattisgarh see similarities between Aghriā and Kurmi, who are peasants as well. Furthermore Kurmi seem to have signalled their interest in marriage relations with Aghriā, but so far the Aghriā have refused to comply. According to Aghriā from Chhattisgarh, Kurmi argue that Aghriā and Kurmi are actually one, but the Aghriā disagree. Unfortunately during my research I could not validate this argument from the Kurmi side, but the origin of the Kurmi remains rather obscure in British sources (Risley 1981 [1891]: 528).[61] According to Rowe (1968a: 67), they claim to be Kshatriya while being of Śudra origin.[62]

Contested status of the Tihāri as Brahmin

Finally, the status of the Tihāri is contested. Other Brahmins doubt their Brahmanical credentials very much. Thus one Brahmin told me the word 'Tihāri' is derived from *tijāri* (made of, turned into) implying that the Aghriā just turned someone into their priest, because Brahmins refused to serve the Aghriā at the time of their arrival in Orissa.[63] Another Brahmin[64] argued:

> When the Aghria arrived in Orissa from Agra, Brahmins refused to work for them. The Brahmins said to the Aghria: 'We don't know where you come from and therefore we cannot work for you!' Then the Aghria went to Puri to search for a priest for themselves. In Banki Mahal they asked a man to become their priest. This 'Tihari' was not a Brahmin before. [*But his caste was also not known to the Brahmin, who told this story.*]

Naturally the Tihāri, claiming high status, do not share this opinion, but some of them acknowledge that other Brahmins in Orissa consider them inferior and relate this status differentiation to the fact that they also perform funerals. However, currently all Brahmins serve the Aghriā though they might have initially refused to do so. Some say that they have to earn. Furthermore some Tihāris indirectly support the Brahmins in their opinion by stating that the Aghriā were a very heterogeneous group originally consisting of high and low status castes.

2.5. CONCLUSION

Beginning with the long genealogy given in the first part of a dominant myth, the Aghriā highlight their descent from the moon and later from Bidur, as a figure of the *Mahābhārata*. Subsequently a change in profession is described in the second part—linked to a migration process from one political centre, namely Agra, to another politico-religious centre, namely Puri, the two of which are sharply contrasted. By a divine order from Lord Jagannāth, combined with their own fault, the Aghriā are forced to move into a peripheral region between these centres. However, the myths presented here correspond only very loosely to historical facts as the figure 'Adil Shah' indicates.

The Aghriā perceive their position as in between, not only in a geographical sense, but also in terms of status. The mythical migration as a transformative process expresses a conceived decline of status from warriors to peasants. Similarly the claimed Kshatriya status is not unambiguous in their own stories and contested by others. The Aghriā successfully established themselves as landowners and 'village kings', which shall be discussed later. One might argue that their rise in the late nineteenth and early twentieth century might be related to a concurring myth describing a grand past. The case of the Noniya in north India—as well as that of other communities—has shown that a process of upward mobility is quite often reflected in an elaborated corpus of literature on the 'caste history' published by an influential caste organization (Rowe 1968a). Thus a process of Kshatriyaization might be discovered among the Aghriā, who share many features of the Noniya. In contrast to the Noniya, the Aghriā have not only an influential caste council which certainly tries to enhance the caste status by publishing a 'caste history'. The Aghriā also have their traditional bards narrating mythological stories, who in turn may be considered a status symbol.

Additionally the Aghriā myths, of which written sources exist from the early twentieth century onwards, appear to reflect and perhaps imitate earlier *vaṃśāvalis* or chronicles of the ruling families of the feudatory states of Orissa. These family chronicles and the Aghriā myths have certain features in common: conflict with Muslims or a divine intervention determining the fate of the protagonists. Therefore, the existence of such myths among the Aghriā as peasants-turned-village kings in predominantly tribal areas may indicate an extension of the ideas and structures of kingship on a tribal frontier.

Finally, that which is absent or unexpressed in Aghriā mythology is also telling. In the myths as shown, the Aghriā are linked to Brahmins on the one hand and to Chamārs on the other: to both extreme poles of caste society. However, no direct reference is made to tribal society, to their immediate neighbours. As such a connection is completely absent, the Aghriā firmly perceive their roots in caste society.

NOTES

1. There are various ways of spelling the name of the bards of the Aghriā such as *Disandhrī* (see below), but also *Disondhi*, *Diśondhi* or *Dossondhi* (see, e.g. publication of Bolangir Aghriā Samāj 1993) or even *Bisandhi* in Chhattisgarh area. I use the former version in the text.
2. The term is borrowed from Kulke (2001 [1976]). For further examples of the widespread phenomena of caste mobility and castes aspiring to high status by adopting a Kshatriya model see Rowe (1968a, 1968b). For social mobility in wider perspective see also Dumont (1980 [1966]: 196).
3. *Vaṃśāvalis* or family chronicles gained particular importance during British rule in late eighteenth and early nineteenth century at a time of a routinization of the colonial administration, i.e. the records were consulted by British officers and became a tool of legitimation. Therefore the chronicles of Puri were systematized or even fabricated in the feudatory states of the time (see Kulke 2001: 140ff; Schnepel 2002: 139ff).
4. I use the term mythology in the sense of myths as sacred narratives (Leach 1991: 66), since it is said that the Disandhrī as bard traditionally used to tell these stories only in a ceremonial context and were entitled to gifts afterwards (for the sacred character of oral tradition in orthodox Brahminism see also Gough 1986 [1968]: 135). However, there is no clear-cut distinction between mythology and history—myths may well contain a 'historical core', which

can be cross-checked against independent sources (Leach 1991: 66; for the relation between myth and history see also Basu 2000: 15).

5. On the term *mandlā* and its use in Puri Kulke (2001: 154) states two possible explanations of the term: either as 'beginning'/'first' or as 'king'/'chief'.
6. Compare *Gazetteer of India, Orissa—Sundargarh District*, ed. N. Senapati and D.C. Kuanr, 1971 (1975).
7. Lévi-Strauss (1996 [1980]: 171) had emphasized the importance of retaining a certain heterogeneity of myths while presenting them in order to avoid any imposed homogeneity, but rather to collect various forms of myths to understand their transformation.
8. Apparently identical with Yudhishthira.
9. 'History of the Society of Eighty-four Houses of Agaria and a list of Regulations (copied from the ancient palm-leaf manuscript—true copy).
10. *Gazetteer of India, Orissa—Sundargarh District*, p. 113.
11. *Mahabharat*, by Sudramani Sarala Das, Cuttack, Nimchandi Publishing House, n.d. (believed to be around 40 years old).
12. Also used to cut wood.
13. In the version of another Disandhrī the first part was told as:
    This is the story of the Soma-bansa Rajput. The badshah ordered them to pay respect. But the heroes replied that the Aghriā are brave heroes (*bīra*) and never bow down their heads. They would never bow down their heads in front of the badshah. The courtiers (*nengine*) requested the badshah to tie a sword (*karat batā*) in the middle of the court. After hearing that, the king gave the order to tie that sword in the court (*kacheri*).
14. *Dhāl* literally means shield rather than sword. However, in other versions *ḍhār* is given in this passage indicating cover or sword cover.
15. A translation of *History of the Society of Eighty-four Houses of Agaria* and a list of Regulations (copied from the ancient palm-leaf manuscript—true copy). Original Author: Late Balunkeshwar Pandey, Jharsuguda, compiled by: Sri Rajendra Patel, Village/P.O. Darlipalli, District Sundargarh. An almost identical text has been published by the Aghriā Samāj in their yearly publication 1983.
16. The work for a *jājmān*.
17. *Jhāmpi* designates a basket, while *peīi* signifies a precious box. *Utrā* means 'to get down'. Thus literally it might be translated as: to get down with all one's belongings.
18. Adil Shah neither ruled Agra nor Delhi in the fifteenth or sixteenth century (compare H. Kulke and D. Rothermund, 1999 [1986]). However, one Adil Shah established and ruled the kingdom of Madura from 1356 to 1369 after having been a governor of Muhammad Tughlaq. Secondly, a dynasty known as Adil Shahi is mentioned in Bijapur as one of the Deccan kingdoms of the period. This dynasty was founded by Adil Shah, also known as Yusuf Adil Shah or Yusuf Adil Khan, in 1490, who was succeeded by

Ismael Adil Shah (1510–34), Ibrahim Adil Shah (1534–58), Ali Adil Shah (1558–80) and Ibrahim Adil Shah II. It seems that each of them were involved in constant feuds with Vijayanagara, for which they may have hired and dismissed foreign troops, e.g. Maratha, as well as killed courtiers suspected of conspiring against them. Third, a dynasty founded by Adil Khan (1435–41) and succeeded by Adil Khan II (1457–1501) and Adil Khan III (1501–20) ruled over the Khāndesh kingdom neighbouring Gujarat, whose influence is said to have reached even Jharkhand. Fourth, an Adil Khan is mentioned as Governor of Lahore under Nasir ud din Mahmud in the late fourteenth century. None of these kings has ever ruled in Delhi or Agra.

19. According to Panda (1999: 241ff) King Mukunda Harichandana or Mukunda Deb of Chalukya family is said to have ruled Orissa from 1560 to 1568. He became involved in conflicts between Mughals and Afghans, which ultimately led to the fall of the Orissan kingdom.
20. See *A Brief History of Aghria Caste of Bolangir District: Eighth Great Convention.*
21. According to the *Gazetteer of India, Orissa—Sundargarh District*, p. 114, the Aghriā came to Sambalpur under the rule of Madhuka Sai, the fourth Chauhan King of Sambalpur.
22. See also Russell and Hiralal (1975 [1916]: 8).
23. For the relation Chamār—Aghriā see also Chap. 3.3.
24. I was told that there are twelve common titles used by Tihāri: Sukla, Chaubhaha, Badagayan, Samadariya, Dube, Chaube, Pandey, Upadhyaya, Abathi, Mishra, Gurudwan, and Tiwāri. Marriage among them is possible—always provided they belong to different clans (*gotra*).
25. For the immigration of Vedic Brahmins into Orissa or legends around this migration see Pfeffer (1978: 422ff).
26. See *Description of Aghriā bansa*, published by B. Pandey, Sambalpur, 1925 [the title might be an indicator that the author was an Aghriā himself] or *History of the Society of Eighty-four Houses of Agaria* and a list of Regulations. Late Balunkeshwar Pandey, Jharsuguda, compiled by Sri Rajendra Patel.
27. In some cases Aghriā might also prefer to call a Brahmin for a wedding, since it is known that he charges less than a Tihāri.
28. For the *Mahābhārata* as epic of the Candravaṃśa see Thapar (2002 [1992]: 788). In other myths of India it is also common to claim Kshatriya status (see Thapar 2002 [1978]: 773).
29. For *kṣātra dharma* see, e.g. Zimmermann (1987: 184).
30. In the way that Lévi-Strauss described cooking, etc., as medium of transformation in myths.
31. Decapitation, apart from a common punishment of medieval times, is also a well-known topos of Greek mythology which indicates a transformation

or initiation, e.g. the head of Medusa. However, in the myth the Aghriā escape from having their heads cut off—at least those migrating to Orissa. The decapitation may also be interpreted as human sacrifice which, as in the case of the *meriah*-sacrifices (Padel 1995: 8–9), is believed to be a widely practised tribal custom.

32. For the Jaipur dynasty see Berkemer (1993: 212).
33. The theme of decline in low caste myths is quite frequent, and is occasionally combined with the memory of decisions leading to the fall (see also O'Flaherty (1988 [1976]: 19–21).
34. See Lévi-Strauss (1992 [1973]).
35. Similar traditions of offering 1/10 known as *bhāg* during feasts are found as well among Rona in Koraput indicating that such a tradition might be common in tribal society too (L. Guzy: personal communication).
36. In Chhattisgarh I heard the name Bisandhi indicating a share of 1/20 (bis = 20) for the bards. The name Disandhrī in its 'avatar' *Daśondi* seems to be common in Gujarat as well. Basu (2000: 49, 62) translates it as 'poet' or 'bard'. However, it is apparently not related to the number ten there.
37. For the Brahminical ideal of non-dependence at which the entire ideal life of a Brahmin is aimed, see van der Veen (1973: 47ff).
38. According to some Aghriā they might be allowed to accept food from a Disandhrī, but in practice there is hardly any opportunity, because it is the Disandhrī coming to the Aghriā also seen as his patron, demanding his share (*bhāg*) and not the other way round. Other Aghriā told me that it was strictly forbidden to accept food from a Disandhrī in former times, but a Disandhrī was allowed to enter the kitchen of his Aghriā patrons. Conceptionalized as brothers, every communities practice endogamy, but some cases, Disandhrī might marry Sarliā women, because their own community is too small. To marry a Sarliā woman the Disandhrī needs a permission from the Aghriā *samāj*—the highest caste-council of the Aghriā. A marriage of Disandhrī women with Sarliā men is prohibited.
39. For critical remarks on the structural interpretation of myths see, e.g. Douglas (1988 [1968]: 61ff) who warns particularly of reductions of meanings by imposing binary oppositions, or Burridge (1988 [1968]: 109) additionally advocating a meaningful dialogue between culture and myth.
40. For the stick as royal symbol see Hardenberg (2000: 21).
41. For the thesis, that myths deal with 'deeply troubling' paradoxes see also Doniger (2002: 5). For an earlier functional theory of myths see, e.g. Elwin (1939: 305ff), who saw the authorization of social institutions as their main role.
42. Trautmann related the conundrum to two types of exchange: sacred versus profane and noble versus ignoble. For multiple hierarchies resulting from these overlapping pattern of classification see Basu (2000: 45f).
43. Lévi-Strauss (1985: 239ff) also argued—perhaps in contrast to the rather

pessimistic Asdiwal myth—that myths may express or 'communicate' options, theoretical solutions, or models for certain societal problems out of which one may be chosen by the society.

44. Some Leuniā rationalize the peculiar custom of their clan by stating that they were the leaders of the Aghriā trying to escape, but other Aghriā do not agree.
45. It is not quite clear whether such pots were used for drinking too, but it is likely that they were used in the ancestor rituals (*śrāddha*) of the Chamārs.
46. Pattanaik (1952: 143) argues that some Aghriā worship bellows, which are usually made of leather. That, however, appears rather unlikely to my research.
47. I heard that in some cases children of communities like the Gaṇḍ occasionally teased their Aghriā classmates by calling them Chamār or even beef eater if they were quarrelling. The Aghriā used to explain it as envy.
48. According to Rowe (1968a: 73) a subsidiary element of the Noniya myth describes the escape from a battle against Muslims. Being chased by Muslim armies the Noniya take refuge in the house of an 'Untouchable'. The Muslim officer demands proof that the Noniya Cauhān are indeed kinsmen of the 'Untouchables' as they claim. So the Noniya have to eat the impure food of the 'Untouchables'—being thus saved, but defiled. The similarity to the Aghriā myth is striking.
49. O'Flaherty (1988 [1976]: 21) mentions interesting cases in which some 'untouchable' communities argue that they were Kshatriya pretending to be Untouchables while fighting Muslims, but were later cursed on and, therefore, remained 'untouchable'.
50. See, e.g. a publication of the Bolangir Samāj, 1976. In more recent publications of the same *samāj* the spelling has changed to Āg(a)riā.
51. In one case an elder Aghriā told me that the Aghriā coming from present Madhya Pradesh/Chhattisgarh first settled in a village named Talpatia (close to Jharsuguda). There, they stayed under a *mahuā* tree having no house. Furthermore next to the *mahuā* tree there were some date palms. When the Aghriā had no crown for the groom in a subsequent marriage—as it is a custom among Rajputs to wear a crown during marriages—they used a crown of three date palm leaves. This custom is prevalent today. He had heard this story from elders in Talpatia.
52. For the importance of *mahuā* (*bassia latifolia*) among tribal communities of the region, e.g. among Gaṇḍ see Elwin (2000 [1936]: 13).
53. Elwin (1991 [1942]: 73) considers at least some segments of the Agaria as sub-tribes of the Gond.
54. In one case an Aghriā believed that their name was created under British influence. According to this line Aghriā originally comes from *agrarian*—the British knowing the Aghriā as good peasants or agrarians. In Raigarh I

was told a new way of explaining the name Aghariya: A(gility) G(anga) H(oly) A(ffability) R(egularity) I(ngenious) Y(eomanly) A(uthentic).

55. Apart from that I also heard Aghriā say that there are Agaria saltmakers in Gujarat and that they saw a TV documentary about it. However, I could not gather any further information. Additionally many Aghriā have heard that the title Patel used by most Aghriā is common in Gujarat. Though the title Patel is indeed frequently used in Gujarat, e.g. by *patidār* (see Pocock 1972) there is neither hint at a common origin nor any other common features, the title being most likely only a superficial common characteristic. Apart from that, other titles used by the Aghriā, e.g. Naik, are also widely used by the Gaṇḍ, and no Aghriā sees that as sufficient proof of a common origin.
56. Rowe (1968a: 68ff) analysed the process of upward mobility among the Noniya/Loniya, arguing that they are originally of Śudra descent, but have acquired wealth by doing contract work in late nineteenth and twentieth century and claiming Kshatriya/Cauhān status. Subsequently they started to enhance their status by wearing the sacred thread and by creating 'a body of literature which functionally served as a social charter to authenticitate the claims' (Rowe 1968a: 71). In their myth published by the influential caste organization from early twentieth century onwards, it is said that in the twelfth century under the Hindu king Prithviraj of Delhi they defended the kingdom as brave warriors, but were defeated and had to escape. Now landless they were forced to turn to salt-making. The process paralleled by an improving economic position is conceived as having reclaimed a rightful status. For links between the Noniya and 'Untouchables' see 'Interpretation' in this chapter.
57. Kurin further describes the different developments of Hindu and Muslim segments of the community—the former sticking to their traditional occupation of salt-making, while the latter turned to agriculture using opportunities to acquire land under canal irrigation schemes. In order to be eligible under and to benefit from such schemes Nunari successfully followed a strategy of being included in the Jat category. In addition, Kurin analyses various folk models that Nunari employ to conceptionalize their own community. Though it is highly speculative, one can certainly not exclude the possibility of an Aghriā-origin as salt-makers who turned to agriculture as described by Kurin (1990) or as indicated by Rowe (1968a, 1968b).
58. This caste organization was founded in 1923.
59. Unfortunately I could not meet and communicate with these Akaltara-Aghriā.
60. That does not mean, however, that Jagannath is not worshipped in many parts of Chhattisgarh (see also Babb 1975: 144).
61. E.g. Risley (1981 [1891]: 528) argues that their origin is obscure and some segments might be of Indo-Aryan and Dravidian origin.

62. According to Rowe (1968a: 67; 1968b: 204) the Kurmi tried to add the word Kshatriya to their caste name by sending petitions to census officers.
63. A. Das of Sambalpur University (personal communication) derives the name Tihāri/Tiwāri from Tripathi. According to him *tri* corresponds to 'three', while *pathi* is derived from 'to read'. Thus Tṛipathi denotes someone able to read implying is of course reading the Veda or the sacred books.
64. This Brahmin was considered as a Dānuā Brahmin or a rather low category of Brahmin, which does accept inauspicious *dān*.

CHAPTER 3

Inter-group Relations

Different communities of Mundaloi village are interwoven into various webs of relations—some seem to unite them, while others apparently separate them. The existence of these networks certainly integrates a rather disparate tribal and caste society—even if the network, such as a local hierarchy, is based on distinction. The Aghriā are an integral part of these networks of relationships in the village.

I will argue that a hierarchy has evolved in this mixed society and it resembles, to a large extent, a typical caste hierarchy. As indicated in Chapter 2, Aghriā claim to have brought certain Brahmins into the region in order to serve them. There is also a close connection to the Chamār as the second pole in the caste hierarchy. Therefore, the extremes of the caste hierarchy are clearly marked. The local hierarchy, however, is expressed in the idiom of *bal/baḍ lok* (good, senior people) versus *sān/choṭ lok* (small, junior people), rather typical of tribal society—another fact apparently hinting at the transition between tribe and caste. Furthermore, the local hierarchy is established not only by negotiation and reinforced by transfers and acceptance of various categories of food and other markers of status such as entrance into the kitchen, but also by transferring children in order to save their endangered lives. The latter is a phenomenon that has not yet received much attention but seems to be an important integrative factor.

Significantly, there are also relations that balance established hierarchies. The village community is not only perceived as a family, all villagers having an ascribed kinship position in relation to others, but there are also mythological links and legends describing communities such as Gaṇḍ, Kandh, and Bhuyān as brothers or claiming an equal status between Gaṇḍ and Luhurā. There is also an enormous variety of the forms of ritual friendship, which, I will argue, is aimed to identify friends as far as possible. Such bond friendship cuts across status categories and establishes relations modelled on brotherhood—with the significant difference that no status difference usually existing between elder and younger brother is here implied. These personal relations seem to exhibit a counter-tendency to the hierarchy, but may also be significant in a largely tribal society undergoing transition—i.e. from a tribal society without a central governing body based on the idea of permanent war or rather Warre in the sense of Hobbes (Sahlins 1968: 4ff; Pfeffer unpublished: 5) to caste society, in which governing institutions are or were to be established by the Aghriā as immigrant landlords and headmen (see Chapter 4). The surprising multitude of forms of ritual friendship may hint at a need for allies as well as the importance of integration. This does not mean, however, that the idea of hierarchy is absent in either mythological stories or in ceremonial friendship. On the contrary, the forms of friendship are hierarchized and the choice of friends may to some extent be determined by hierarchical considerations.

3.1. THE VILLAGE HIERARCHY

Hierarchy can be a sensitive topic and should only be discussed personally or privately, not in large groups and certainly not in the presence of people at a lower social rank than to whom you are speaking. If you ask about it in a group discussion, people often say that they do not know when asked these questions in a group format, which appears to be a rather convenient way to avoid these often difficult or awkward questions. The village harmony or peace (*śānti*) is often emphasized, which could potentially be disturbed by an articulation of questions on hierarchy. Hierarchical distinctions are often implicitly made, but are rarely verbally expressed.

Occasionally, however, models may be made explicit if people are asked to rank the communities of the village. For example, an elderly Aghriā once told me of the following model of a village hierarchy—obviously very influenced by administrative categories:

high status	Aghriā
	Other Backward Classes[1]
	Scheduled Tribes
	Scheduled Castes
low status	Mochi (Chamār)

This simplified model, however, does not reflect reality as expressed in transactions, apart from the fact that the SC are placed at the bottom and among them the Mochi are clearly regarded as lowest.

From my observations regarding the acceptance of food, as well as my discussions, quite a different picture of a hierarchy, in terms of purity, has emerged which should not be confused with hierarchical considerations within the framework of kingship (see Chapter 4). A village hierarchy may be represented in Table 3. The names of the communities used in table refer to the names most commonly used in the village. For some communities, older names like Kol may have been replaced by Muṇḍā—though both are still used. Similarly, a community also known as Gandā prefers the name Harijan. Kisān also appears to be an etic name, even though they may refer to themselves also as Kunhar (Mohanty 1963–4: 56).[2]

Classification

Table 3 shows a fourfold classification. The upper category, including communities from the Gauḍ to the Keunṭ, are considered *bal lok* (good people) or *baḍ lok* (big people) in the sense that only they are served by the high status Brahmin as well as barber and washerman. The Kān Guru, who initiates communities by whispering sacred *mantras* into their ears, and the Kālo, as sacrificer to the village goddess without whom one cannot bring soil from the shrine of the village goddess to the wedding altar, both offer their services only to these high status communities. This implies that such services are not offered to the Aghriā as the dominant peasant caste exclusively, but also to communities like the Gaṇḍ or Kandh, traditionally considered tribal communities, but here reflecting a high degree of Hinduization.

Within this category, the highest position in terms of purity is, unambiguously, ascribed to the Gauḍ as former water carriers (*pāenti*)[3] and herdsmen (*narihā*). The latter occupation appears to be common as well among Gauḍ in other parts of Orissa and India.[4] No one in the village will doubt their purity, which is also expressed when the rights of entry to the kitchen are concerned. In Aghriā households, Gauḍ are preferred for work concerning food, e.g. grinding spices, and it is the Gauḍ Narihā who distribute raw food at the end of funerals in

TABLE 3: VILLAGE HIERARCHY (FT = IN FORMER TIMES ONLY)[5]

Group	Administ. Category	Traditional Occupation	Status	Separate Status features
Gauḍ	General Caste, now OBC	Herdsmen, Water-carrier (FT), messenger for ausp. news for *bal lok*	Upper Castes/ Tribal upper castes 'Touchables'/ *Chhuāti*	
Gaṇḍ	ST	Peasants		Sacred thread
Kandh	ST	Peasants, basket maker	*Bal lok/ Baḍ lok*	First settlers of the village
Aghriā	OBC	Peasants, landlords, former revenue collectors	(served by Brahmin, Barber, etc.)	
Chaṣā	OBC	Peasants		No poultry kept inside the house
Māḷi	OBC	Peasants		
Keunṭ	OBC/SC[6]	Fishermen, ferry-men, producers of *murhi/chuḍā* (FT)		
Kisān	ST	Peasants	Tribal lower castes *Choṭ lok*	
Kol[7]/Muṇḍā	ST	Peasants		
Luhurā	ST	Blacksmiths		Contact with leather bellows (FT)
Tūrī	ST	Basket makers		
Khaḍiā	ST	Peasants/producers of *rānu*[8]		Suspected consumption of beef
Orām	ST	Peasants		Suspected consumption of beef —burying strangers/outcasts
Malār	ST	Collecting forest products (honey, incense, roots[9])		No land
Gandā/ Harijan	SC	Beherā, messenger for inausp. news, weavers, midwives, musicians	*Choṭ lok* 'Untouchables'/ *Achhuā*'	No leatherwork, but contact with drums
Mochi/ Chamār	SC	Leatherworkers		

the village. During Aghriā weddings, when parched rice is brought to the house of the bride, a Gauḍ must be hired for this work. These examples display the high status of the Gauḍ who therefore form a separate sub-class within the highest category.

While there is no misunderstanding about the position of the Gauḍ, there is below them room for explanation and discussion. Whereas the Aghriā, though not necessarily wealthy, as landlords and former revenue collectors are the dominant caste and probably the richest community at least in terms of land. The Māḷi also claim a high status by pointing out that they are the only community not keeping poultry inside their houses. Some Aghriā accept this argument, hinting at the fact that the Aghriā had done the same thing in former times. Apparently, a high status is ascribed to the Māḷi in others parts of Middle India as well.[10] However, in contrast to other Middle Indian contexts, the Māḷi are not necessarily the only gardeners as other communities such as the Aghriā or Kisān also keep vegetable gardens. Furthermore, there have been very powerful Gaṇḍ Jamindārs in the region and, in this case, may have contributed to the high status of Gaṇḍ. Jamindārs, as far as the extent of their power is concerned, certainly rank above Gauntiā as village kings. The high status of the Gaṇḍ certainly reflects their position as Jamindārs. In addition, the Gaṇḍ are—apart from Brahmins—the only community to wear a sacred thread (*paitā*)[11] as another feature of high status, while the Kandh traditionally occupy the position of sacrificer of the village goddess (Grām Śrī). Some Kandh insist that their name is derived from the shoulder or *kāndh* from which they were born, according to mythology.[12] The Kandh take pride in the fact they are the original settlers of the village—a claim apparently not disputed by other communities. Gaṇḍ, Kandh and Bhuyān are also considered and consider themselves to be brothers and a therefore very similar status is presumed. It is significant that in nearby villages, apart from the Kandh, the Bhuyān often act as sacrificers to village goddesses. The Keunṭ belong to this category as well. Like Gaṇḍ and Bhuyān, they are closely associated with the Goddess Samlei, acting as temple servants in a Samlei temple not far from the village. Their traditional occupations as fishermen and ferrymen may be a reason for their association with Samlei, whose temples are usually situated on river banks. However, since the Keunṭ have been, until recently, considered a Scheduled Caste, most villagers insist that they occupy a rather low position within this high category, even though by tradition they are also producers of certain food items (like flattened rice) for the village.

The second clearly marked category is formed by the so-called Untouchables (*achhuā*) in contrast to all as *chhuāti*. This category is, however, not homogeneous, rather it is sharply stratified within itself—Harijans consider the Chamār 'Untouchable' themselves. The various restrictions related to untouchability will be described below. The low position of the so-called Untouchables is related to their contact with leather—the Chamār/Mochi as leatherworkers properly disposing of the dead cattle of the village and tanning the leather, while the Gandā/Harijan in a slightly higher category as traditional weavers have only limited contact with leather in their role as musicians playing and producing drums. An occasionally proposed argument that contact with leather automatically places a community in the category of 'Untouchables' is, however, not entirely consistent, as the Luhurā formerly used leather bellows, as they acknowledge, but apparently have not been considered untouchable.

Between these two categories lies a third: communities, which are undoubtedly 'touchable', but nevertheless too low to be served by Brahmins or barbers. Within this category the Kisān certainly rank quite high. They are acknowledged by the Aghriā as diligent peasants like themselves and at least some Kisān try to raise their status by inviting Brahmins to perform their rituals—though these Brahmin are of rather doubtful status. Orām and Khaḍiā are said to rank lower, and many villagers suspect that they regularly consume beef. It is occasionally speculated that the Muṇḍā may also eat beef, though such a suspicion is less pronounced than in the case of the Orām and Khaḍiā.[13] All communities deny a consumption of beef, which seems to indicate a wider phenomenon common in other parts of tribal Middle India, where a progressive change towards Hindu values is visible.[14] Leaving aside the semi-nomadic Birhor, the Orām and Khaḍiā are the only Christian communities in the village, going to a Catholic Church in a neighbouring village. Among these two communities the Khaḍiā may be of a slightly higher status, since only the Orām openly keep pigs, and apparently in two cases in which an outsider and an outcaste had died in the village, the Orām were persuaded to bury them.[15] Finally, the Malār are the only community to not own land in the village—their landlessness relates to the fact that they were the last community to settle in the village long after the land was allocated.

Other groups

Table 3 presents the hierarchy in the village in which I stayed and is incomplete in the sense that other communities that settle in neighbouring villages are also an essential part of a regional culture and may offer services to communities of Mundaloi. For example, no Brahmin family resides in the village itself, but Brahmins do serve the villagers of the higher communities, and there is a clear agreement on the fact that, in terms of purity, they are the highest in status. They rank above the Gauḍ—a fact clearly expressed in terms of the access to kitchens in various communities. The fact that no Brahmin family stays in the village appreciated by villagers who argue that their presence would have negative affects on the village harmony—though there is no straight-forward anti-Brahminical tendency in the village.[16]

Barbers (*bhandāri*), washermen (*dhobā*), potters (*khumbā*) and other service communities stay outside the village, yet serve and interact with villagers. Their position within the hierarchy is much less clear than the position of the Brahmin, and most villagers would place them somewhere in the middle of the hierarchy, below the *bal lok* (the Keunṭ). Some communities, such as the Ghansiā, used to reside in the village, but have since left. In this case the villagers are quite clear about their status as a Scheduled Caste and have a position similar to the Gandā/Harijan with whom they share certain professions (musician or midwife).[17] Aside from these groups, there is a semi-nomadic group called the Makriā (monkey-eaters)[18] by the villagers, but who prefer to call themselves Birhor (*hor* = man).[19] They camp on the outskirts of the village for about four to six weeks each year—collecting bark from the jungle to produce ropes, which are then sold in the village. Their interaction with other villagers is quite limited and their status ambivalent, although not untouchable, it is certainly low.[20]

Internal hierarchies: the Aghriā case

Almost all communities in the village are internally stratified. The Aghriā are no exception. They use an idiom—senior/junior—that is typical for tribal society as recently pointed out by Berger (2002: 69) for Koraput. They distinguish between Aghriā—(*baḍ*)—elder brother (eB), Dossondhi/Disandhrī—(*sān*)—younger brother (yB), and Sarliā—(*choṭ*).[21]

A distinction between 'Bad or superior Agharias and the Chhote, Sarolia or Sarwaria, the inferior or mixed Agharias' was noted by Russell and Hiralal (1916). They considered the latter category to be a mixture of an Aghriā man and a Gaur (Ahir) woman. However, they did not include the Dossondhi in their short description. The Dossondhi, who wear a sacred thread (*paitā*) should not accept food from an Aghriā, but they do in practice. They are considered *sān* in relation to the Aghriā. The relationship is not without ambivalence as the Dossondhi claim a higher status because of the sacred thread, even though they accept cooked food from their 'patrons'.[22] As the younger brother of the Aghriā, a common origin is understood by the Aghriā and the Dossondhi. Nevertheless, every community practices endogamy—which is also true for all the village communities as presented in Table 3. In some cases, a Dossondhi may marry a Sarliā woman, because his own community is too small. In order to marry a Sarliā woman, a Dossondhi must have permission from the highest caste council of the Aghriā. A marriage between Dossondhi women and Sarliā men is prohibited.

According to some Aghriā it is permitted to accept food from a Dossondhi, but in practice there is rarely an opportunity as it is the Dossondhi who comes to his patron demanding his share (*bhāg*) and not the other way round. Other Aghriā would argue that it was strictly forbidden to accept food from a Dossondhi in former times, but a Dossondhi did have permission to enter the kitchen of his Aghriā patrons.

Untouchability

Perhaps the clearest line of separation is drawn between the 'Touchables' and the 'Untouchables', upon which I will expand here. The phenomenon of 'Untouchability' is common to caste and tribal society. It has been frequently described in ethnographic literature as an essential part of caste societies. In tribal societies too the presence of communities such as the Dombo or Pano or other so-called 'Untouchables' considered by the administration as Scheduled Castes has also been noted (Bailey 1960: 127; Berger 2002: 60). However, 'Untouchability' is defined quite differently here. The Dombo and Pano may act as clients of their tribal patrons and engage as petty traders (Pfeffer 1997: 7), but in caste society their position seems to be more defined in relation to cattle and their occupation as leatherworkers. The value-idea of purity, however, may underlie both contexts. 'Untouchable' traders connect tribal society to the outside world and are conceived of as polluting and impure (Pfeffer 1997: 9), while in caste society impurity has a more segregating internal effect. In considering these two positions, 'Untouchability' in the specific context presented here resembles a pattern more from caste than from tribal society—'Untouchables' related to leather[23] rather than petty trade (except a trade in leather perhaps) and as dependant agricultural labourers rather than clients.

The clear separation between 'touchable' and 'untouchable' villagers is articulated in rituals such as *Daśarā*, particularly during the ritual for the Goddess Durgā, when the latter are separated from the other communities on the veranda of the Gauntiā's house, where the ritual is performed. They sit in a corner of the veranda, a little distance from the others. This holds true for other religious ceremonies such as those of the Krishna Guru Party. From daily dance performances between *Nuā Khāi* and *Bhāi Jiuntiā* known as *Huma.* They are excluded, as dancing includes close bodily contact, the dancers forming rows arm in arm. Contrary to this, groups such as the Dombo seem to be included in dances in the tribal 'Desia' society of Koraput (G. Pfeffer: personal communication).

A spatial separation is strictly observed only in village contexts. During other rituals such as the offering of goats on *Daśarā*, in bigger towns, untouchability is not feasible. However, even in the village the separation seems to have been more defined in former times.

Another case of spatial separation pertained to the Beherā—the messenger who called the village meetings. Traditionally a Harijan was appointed as the Beherā. In former times he would sit separately during the meeting of the village council (*pañchāyat*), but today there is no strict separation. Further, many communities did not and to this day continue to not allow Scheduled Caste people to enter their kitchens. The Aghriā extended this rule to the Kisān and Muṇḍā, but labourers are accepted and the rules are slowly loosening. Part of this spatial separation was the prohibition to enter temples—again, still valid in many villages. Compared with other regions there is no spatial separation of SC houses as such as far as the village topography is concerned.

In the past, 'Untouchables' were not permitted to use the ordinary open village wells, but had to use pond water instead. Often they had no separate wells. However, due to the increased use of modern tube-wells introduced in recent years the situation has changed. There is no exclusion anymore—everyone can use tube wells. In the case of open private wells, however, the separation continues. The use of ponds for washing or rituals has never been prohibited for SCs, but they were required to, and still must, use separate *ghāts* (places for washing). However, over the last three to five years these rules too have become less strict.

The worship of gods often does not take place in a temple, because 'Untouchables' are simply not allowed to enter them. In some cases landlords may have been influential in barring them from the temples in their villages. In some villages there are various pavilions (*maduā/ mandap*) for festivals such as *Nām Jagyā*, in which dancing plays a vital part. Apart from a pavilion for the high castes, there may be another for lower communities and still another for 'Untouchables'—built by the Gauntiā or even the government. Entrance to the pavilion for 'Untouchables' may be further restricted to the Harijan. 'Untouchables' are generally excluded from entering the *mandap* of higher communities and—as with the Harijan—may in turn exclude the Chamār from participating in rituals and dancing in their own 'temple'. As other priests refuse to work for them, a special Harijan priest usually performs the rituals there. 'Untouchables' are also not permitted to become a member of a *kirthan*-party (if they do not have separate parties) in order to sing devotional songs (*kirthan*) and to dance for the gods during festivals. During the ritual for Durgā, they can join the festivities, but cannot offer boiled food, only flowers, incense and vermilion.

All communities have to purify themselves if they have any close bodily contact with a so-called 'Untouchable'. Not only historically, but still today a married Aghriā must take a bath and has to wash the clothes that he wears, when he comes in physical contact with an 'Untouchable'. He has to wash his clothes himself in a pond and cannot delegate this job to anyone else. An unmarried Aghriā has only to change his clothes and a bath is not necessary. In the case of a dispute involving physical contact between a Gaṇḍ and an 'Untouchable', the Gaṇḍ must perform various rituals under the guidance of a Barihā—a Gaṇḍ specialist for purification. However, the same ritual has to be performed in the case of a fight between a Gaṇḍ and a person of any other community.

In the context of healing bodily contact does not seem to be as important. An Aghriā healer—a *Sampuā* guru, a healer specializing in snake bites—argued that he can cure 'Untouchables' particularly if their life is endangered and is not excluded from his community for doing so. The offering of *jiban dān*—the gift of life—is not criticized by his caste fellows even if he is asked to touch the person in the process of healing. Similarly, an Aghriā may go to a local Harijan-healer or *Guniā* to be cured. In one case I observed a man suffering from a serious cough and *jhundis*/liver infection. He went to see a Harijan healer who had a reputation for curing these diseases. In the process the healer touched the hands of the patient while circling them in a bowl. However, the medical process had no effects on the relative purity of the patient. Similarly, in the case of children sold to be cured, caste and community boundaries may be more easily transgressible.

Markers of status

In cases such as leatherwork or water carrying, status is clearly related to occupation, but, as already indicated, profession cannot be a sufficient marker of status, as the Kandh rank much higher than the Tūrī, even though both are basket-makers in addition to being peasants. Contact with leather has never been an adequate criterion for status as the case of the Luhurā shows, and most communities, though ranked differently, are peasants anyway. Other occupations are considered to of neutral in status and everyone is free to turn to work such as carpentry. The running of shops or collecting and selling palm wine or *mahuli* may as well be freely chosen as an occupation except for 'Untouchables'. In Mundaloi, Aghriā, Kisān or Muṇḍā act as carpenters, shops are owned by Muṇḍā or Gaṇḍ and a Kisān has chosen the business of producing and selling palm wine. Furthermore, members of various communities such as the Kandh, Gaṇḍ, Gauḍ, Kisān, Muṇḍā, etc., work as day-labourers or contract labourers for others—the landlord in particular. Marriott (1968: 133ff) rejected a primary focus on attributes—not only occupation, but also other features such as the wearing of a sacred thread—in order to understand the caste society of north India. Such attributes may indicate a high or low status, but they are certainly insufficient to explain the position of certain communities within a hierarchy. This means that there are other, probably more important, indicators of status: the giving or accepting of water and rice in various forms; rules of entrance to the kitchen; and the categories of dishes offered to various communities, when meals are being served. Therefore, status in this converging tribal and caste society is to a large extent expressed in transactions between different communities.

Water is an extreme necessity given the climatic conditions. Paddy (*dhān*), as a staple food, is usually given as payment to labourers but also sold and purchased on the market, while *chāul* or peeled rice—apart from being marketed too—is exchanged at funerals within the village community as a whole. That means that not all villagers can be served during feasts such as at the end of funerals and *kharchā* (raw ingredients for a meal including *chāul*, but also raw vegetables, oil etc.) is distributed by the family of a deceased person among all villagers to prepare a meal on their own. Thus, *chāul* is exchanged among villagers more or less regularly. There are usually few occasions to eat boiled rice in another home inside one's own village. However, the necessity may arise in the case of visits to ritual friends or funerals in other villages.

The rules of acceptance for all of these categories of food in the case of the Aghriā are presented in Table 4 (for all other communities of the village see Appendix 3). A few characteristics are apparent. First, there exist more restrictions for married persons than for unmarried people and more for women than for men. While unmarried men may accept food or water from most communities, married women may accept it from the fewest. Thus, the acceptance of water and rice also reflects the importance of marriage and a higher danger of 'pollution' for married persons. Second, this acceptance reflects the three major status categories already presented, e.g. unmarried women may accept water from all communities served by a Brahmin, barber, etc., while unmarried men may accept water from all communities except the 'Untouchables'. Additionally, the very high status of the Gauḍ and Brahmin is confirmed, as married women

TABLE 4: ACCEPTANCE OF WATER AND VARIOUS FORMS OF RICE FROM OTHER COMMUNITIES

AGHRIĀ	Water accepted from				*Dhān* (paddy) accepted from				*Chāul*[24] (pared rice) accepted from				*Bhāt* (boiled rice) accepted from			
	U♂	M♂	U♀	M♀	U♂	M♂	U♀	M♀	U♂	M♂	U♀	M♀	U♂	M♂	U♀	M♀
Brahmin	▒	▒	■	▒	▒	▒	▒	▒	▒	▒	▒	▒	▒	▒	■	▒
Gauḍ	▒	▒	■	▒	▒	▒	▒	▒	▒	▒	▒	▒	▒	▒	■	▒
Aghriā	▒	▒	■	▒	▒	▒	▒	▒	▒	▒	▒	▒	▒	▒	■	▒
Chaṣā	▒	▒	▒		▒	▒	▒	▒	▒	▒	▒	▒	▒		▒	
Gaṇḍ	▒	▒	▒		▒	▒	▒	▒	▒	▒	▒	▒	▒		▒	
Kandh	▒	▒	▒		▒	▒	▒	▒	▒	▒	▒	▒	▒		▒	
Bhuyān	▒	▒	▒		▒	▒	▒	▒	▒	▒	▒	▒	▒		▒	
Māḷi	▒	▒	▒		▒	▒	▒	▒	▒	▒	▒	▒	▒		▒	
Keunṭ	▒	▒	▒		▒	▒	▒	▒	▒	▒	▒	▒	▒		▒	
Kisān	▒		▒		▒	▒	▒	▒	▒	▒	▒	▒	▒		▒	
Muṇḍā	▒		▒		▒	▒	▒	▒	▒	▒	▒	▒	▒		▒	
Luhurā	▒		▒		▒	▒	▒	▒	▒	▒	▒	▒	▒		▒	
Khaḍiā	▒		▒		▒	▒	▒	▒	▒	▒	▒	▒	▒		▒	
Orām	▒		▒		▒	▒	▒	▒	▒	▒	▒	▒	▒		▒	
Tūrī	▒		▒		▒	▒	▒	▒	▒	▒	▒	▒	▒		▒	
Malār	▒		▒		▒	▒	▒	▒	▒	▒	▒	▒	▒		▒	
Harijan	▒		▒		▒	▒	▒	▒	▒	▒	▒	▒				
Chamār					▒	▒	▒	▒	▒	▒	▒	▒				

Legend: U♂= unmarried men; M♂= married men; U♀= unmarried women; M♀= married women; ▒ = accepted in the presence of *jāti* (caste members); ■ = accepted in the presence of *jāti* in former times and nowadays (acceptance in former times more restricted)

may accept water or boiled rice only from these two communities apart from their own.

Another indicator of status is the kind of dishes used or offered to certain people and/or communities. There are basically three types: (1) vessels made of *kansā*—a mixture of copper and tin, considered to pure; (2) ordinary aluminium dishes for daily use and regarded as less pure which means that the risk of contamination is less and (3) banana leaves, which are thrown away after use.[25]

As far as the Aghriā are concerned, *kansā*-dishes should not even be offered to high status communities; ordinary aluminium plates and cups would be used instead (in practice it may be handled differently). In any case, the Aghriā would not use *kansā* plates for non-*bal lok* (in the sense of communities not being served by Brahmin, barber, etc.). Previously, separate dishes were kept or are still kept in some cases for the Scheduled Castes and in some families may also be used for the labourers (*guti*). In other cases a third set is kept for guests of higher status. In some households one could even find two sets of dishes for the family itself: one for vegetarian and a second for non-vegetarian meals, the latter used outside the kitchen. Some people insist that the Aghriā themselves should only use *kansā* dishes, because of their purity.

Most of the communities, particularly the *bal lok*—in the restricted sense of communities being served by Brahmin, barber, etc.,— would not accept boiled food offered by a Muṇḍā or Kisān, regardless of which dish or plate used. The same is true among the *bal lok*—particularly, married people have many restrictions on boiled food from most communities except the Brahmin and Gauḍ. Apart from boiled food, they may easily accept some edibles—again, served in different dishes—and in this context Table 5 gains significance, illustrating the major differences in status between *bal lok* and the rest.

Another indicator of status is the question of who is permitted into the kitchen, a place kept particularly pure. In Aghriā houses the floor is cleaned with cow dung by the women of the house after every meal.[26] Some Aghriā even argue that everyone coming from outside, from *dānda bāṭ* (*dānda* = outer yard, *bāṭ* = way—including the field, which is also not considered to be unambiguously pure) should take a bath before entering the kitchen. However, this rule,

TABLE 5: CATEGORIES OF DISHES AND COMMUNITIES FOR WHOM THEY ARE USED[27]

Community	Dishes offered to the following communities		
	Brass (*kansā*)	Aluminium/Steal (*gilti*)	Leaf plates
Brahmin	None	None	to all guests
Gauḍ	*Bal lok*	Others	to all guests
Gaṇḍ	*Bal lok*	Others	to all guests
Kandh	*Bal lok*	Others	to all guests
Bhuyān	*Bal lok*	Others	to all guests
Aghriā	None/*Bal lok*	All (separate dishes for 'Untouchables')	to all guests
Chaṣā	Brahmin, Gauḍ[28]	Others	to all guests
Māḷi	*Bal lok*	Others	to all guests
Kisān	*Bal lok*	Others	to all guests
Kol/Muṇḍā	*Bal lok*	Others	to all guests
Luhurā	*Bal lok*	Others	to all guests

concerning women in particular, is not strictly practised. In this context it is worth noting which other communities are allowed to enter the kitchen in different communities. A list is supplied in the following Table 6.

Table 6 clearly indicates a higher status of *bal lok*—here once more communities, which are served by the barber and washerman. It signifies that the Gauḍ are slightly higher than the other *bal lok*. However, it also makes clear that some communities ranked middle

TABLE 6: COMMUNITIES ALLOWED TO ENTER THE KITCHEN

Community	Who is allowed to enter the kitchen?	Comment
Brahmin	Gauḍ	not allowed to touch anything
Gauḍ	*Bal lok*	not allowed to touch anything
Gaṇḍ	Gauḍ	might touch the dishes
Kandh	*Bal lok*	
Bhuyān	Brahmin, Gauḍ	for Gauḍ: only to carry water
Aghriā	*Bal lok*	
Chaṣā	Brahmin, Gauḍ	for Gauḍ: only to carry water
Māḷi	Brahmin, Gauḍ	for Gauḍ: only to carry water
Kisān	Disputed: nobody or only *Bal lok*	
Kol/Muṇḍā	Gauḍ/*Bal lok*	
Luhurā	*Bal lok*	
Orām	all communities except 'untouchables'	
Malār	*Bal lok*	

or lower, such as the Kisān or Muṇḍā, in their quest for status, try to be very strict—perhaps even more strict than higher communities. Among the Kisān I did not receive any unambiguous answers to my questions—thus two answers are reproduced in Table 6. Finally, some low status communities such as the Orām allow all higher castes to enter their kitchen, but maintain a border with the 'untouchable' communities.

The handling of dishes used by guests in one's home is another marker of status. The question of who does the dishes is intrinsically related to the status of the person who has used them as a guest. In the case of the Aghriā having guests from a high status community (barber and washerman) except Brahmin/Tihāri, the dishes should be done by an Aghriā man. Aghriā women should not touch these dishes and even the men should bathe afterwards. Lower status communities should wash their dishes themselves. However, not all guests are able to do it and in some contexts it would be very impolite to ask the guests to wash their own dishes. For example, if an 'untouchable' IAS officer visited the house, it would be a borderline case. At times, it seems that the rule of hospitality contradicts the rules of purity and etiquette. If lower status guests are unwilling to wash the dishes, a maidservant (*ghar khiā*) or labourer does the job. Aghriā would be excluded from their community if they washed these dishes. If a *jāti* (another caste member and witness in rituals, checking their proper performance and acting as an instance of social control) came to know about such behaviour deviating from the norms, he would probably demand a punishment for the culprit (usually a feast). An Aghriā excluded from his community must wash his own dishes and clean the place where he was sitting.

In practice it happens occasionally that Aghriā children, not women, do the dishes of low status communities, but rather secretly. Young girls may do so. If there were no children present, unmarried men would be a second preference. If, however, a Brahmin is a guest in an Aghriā house, everyone is allowed to wash the dishes—even Aghriā women. When Aghriā visit a priest, e.g. their *purohit*, they do the dishes themselves and consider it a sin (*pāp*), if they leave the job to the Brahmin family. In practice, the Brahmin may mildly protest against this and may ask his patron to leave the dishes, but this seems to be a way to be polite towards the *jajmān*.

There are other markers of status such as the entrance to cowsheds and the consumption of alcohol. Particularly among the Aghriā—but not only among them as the relation between Muria and Maraar described by Gell (1992: 71) shows[29]—there is a perception that communities that produce and consume alcohol are of low status—even though it is considered a part of the life style practised not only by tribal communities, but also royal families. From an Aghriā perspective drinking is clearly related to poverty and aggression,[30] but this is not a perspective shared by tribal communities, who may relate alcohol to ecstasy. In very limited contexts, Aghriā may produce rice-beer in their houses, e.g. during the Karmā festival, when Aghriā as patrons have to offer it to villagers of other communities, who may participate in a festival that everyone is free to join. However, this production of alcohol leads to an exclusion from the communities, and can be reversed only by offering a feast to all local caste members. Some twenty years ago the Gaṇḍ Samāj—apparently in an attempt to raise the status of the Gaṇḍ—passed laws prohibiting the production of alcohol in Gaṇḍ houses.[31] In practice the rule seems to have been ignored. Though alcohol has been prohibited, the offering of sacred rice beer to the ancestors has not, as some Gaṇḍ related.

An accurate understanding of the context as well as the perspective of the given community is vital for the case of the previously mentioned indicators. Alcohol is valued differently among the communities, among castes and tribes and among higher and lower communities. However, even as a different value can be attached to alcohol and other indicators such as the consumption of beef, the acceptance of water and rice has been and continues to be a common marker of status on which a hierarchy is based largely similar to caste society.

The concept of bal/baḍ lok *(good, 'senior' people)* *vs.* choṭ lok *(small, 'junior' people)*

The hierarchy, resembling a caste hierarchy in many regards, is expressed with the concept of *bal lok* or *baḍ lok*—an idiom of tribal society.[32] This concept has been utilized quite often—though only in its restricted sense as with communities served by a Brahmin, barber, etc.—but its meaning is not limited to this. One must note that it is a relative concept, which means that various meanings can be attached to the phrase *bal lok* depending on the context and the speaker. The primary difference between 'good' and 'small' lies in the services of a Brahmin, barber, washerman, Kān Guru and Kālo (for marriage rituals and Grām Śrī Pūjā), as indicated.

In a more narrow sense this concept can be expressed by the building of various *mandaps*—for festivals like *Nām Jagya*. In some villages there are three *māndāps*. That for the high communities or *bal lok* was erected by the Aghriā–Gauntiā, a second one was built with money from the government for the Kisān excluded from the high caste *mandap*. A third *mandap*—also erected by the Gauntiā—is exclusively for use by the Harijans. Here the Chamār are excluded, as are the Harijan from the Kisān *mandap*. In some cases, however, members of castes without barber and washerman services may be allowed to participate by dancing in the *bal lok-mandap*, if they are members of *kirthan*-parties.[33] Some Brahmins appear to enforce this separation, while others argue that, according to the scriptures, everyone should be allowed to participate.

However, the concept of *bal lok* is a relative one and reflects processes of inclusion and exclusion, which Pocock (1957) described for the caste society of Gujarat. Though such processes of inclusion and exclusion are well known in caste society and in regional configurations of caste societies, in this case they are expressed in an idiom—*baḍ*/senior vs. *sān*, *choṭ*/junior—which is typical of a tribal society (Pfeffer 2000: 342). In this mixed tribal and caste society *bal lok* or *baḍ lok* signify not only high status groups who enjoy the services of Brahmins in opposition to all lower groups, which are *choṭ lok* or small people, but it may also be used by lower communities. Certain services, for example becoming a sacrificer of the village goddess, can only be rendered by *bal lok*—at least in the view of the higher status groups. This does not mean that lower communities would not include themselves in the *bal lok* in certain circumstances, e.g. if asked from whom they might accept water. A Khaḍiā once said 'it is acceptable from all *bal lok*' which indicated that he could drink water from all communities higher than himself including the Kisān and Muṇḍā, while at the same time excluding all communities lower than himself. In this case *bal lok* did not only include all groups served by a Brahmin, etc. Upper communities would likely draw the distinction differently—excluding the Khaḍiā and considering them to be *choṭ lok*. Generally, it would be very impolite to call someone else *choṭ lok* in their presence, but lower communities do use it to describe themselves. For example, a Luhurā, once asked if he would also perform certain rituals that the local landlord performs, replied: 'We are *choṭ lok*, that's why we are not doing such rituals.' Thus, some may apply it to themselves to underline a difference with people of higher status. In a very narrow sense, *choṭ lok* may be applied to the so-called 'Untouchable' communities only, meaning 'smallest'—'smaller' than the Luhurā, who used the phrase for himself in a different context. In the second situation, *choṭ lok* may draw a line of distinction between the so-called 'Touchables' to whom certain services of the Gauḍ, for distributing *kharchā*, etc., are offered that are denied to the so-called 'Untouchables'.

In yet another sense *bal lok* is used to signify all who are neat and clean, that is, all who keep themselves as well as their household spotless. So if one wishes to underline the observation that a certain Chamār is relatively hygienic, one could say that he is a *bal lok* compared to the others. *Baḍ lok* may also denote material wealth, which was perhaps implied in the above-mentioned remarks of the Luhurā, since the performance of rituals—related to status—requires wealth. Most—though not all—high status communities are at the same time relatively rich. Therefore, *bal lok* are to a large extent also *baḍ lok* in terms of material wealth. The richest people in the village—those having the biggest shares of land—are also called *baḍ baḍiā*,[34] which is an expression usually applied to the landlord and to *baḍ parjā* (tenants with an exceptional high share of land), who are important patrons of rituals (see Chap. 4.2.). However, a rich Chamār might be also *baḍ* in the sense of wealth without being *bal* in the sense of status or cleanliness. Newly rich people who aspire to a high status are occasionally disqualified with the proverb 'small people got rich, but remain dirty'.[35]

In another context people who drink alcohol cannot be *bal lok* from the perspective of the Aghriā, who usually do not drink, while drunkards and alcohol addicts are always *choṭ lok* no matter how high their ritual status might be. In some cases drunkards are even called *kharāb lok* or 'bad people', though not in their presence. *Kharāb* has even more negative connotations than *choṭ lok* and is used very rarely. Occasionally, however, the opposition *upār* or 'high' versus *tal* or 'low' is employed to demonstrate differences in status, but it seems to be not as common as *bal/baḍ lok* versus *choṭ lok*.

3.2. THE SELLING OF CHILDREN AS A LINK BETWEEN GROUPS

The title of this chapter may invoke images or thoughts of child bonded labour and the tragic fate of children in the carpet-knotting industry (Gupta/Voll 1999: 113) or elsewhere. Or one may be reminded of children sold to be sacrificed as *meriah*[36] (Padel 1995: 8-9). However, in none of the cases of symbolic selling as well as the throwing away of children described here is any harm done to them. In fact, the opposite is likely more accurate, by selling them or

Aghriā child

throwing them away the parents hope to improve their health and help them to survive.

As far as I am aware the custom of selling children has neither been analysed nor even mentioned in previous literature concerning India[37]. Only in Elwin's diary, written during his stay among the Gond, does he indirectly indicate a selling of children: 'Many of our children bear the names of lower castes—like Bhangi (for what spirit would bother to molest a mere sweeper?) . . .' (Elwin 2000 [1936]: 18). Similarly, the phenomenon of throwing away children has been only touched upon for two tribal cases in the literature—by Grigson (1991 [1938]) for the Gond and Roy (1999 [1928]) for the Oraon in neighbouring regions of Bastar and Chhotanagpur respectively—though only briefly. In the following I will discuss this important sphere of interaction, in which inter-group relations and a hierarchical ranking are constituted by temporary identifying children with other, lower communities.

Selling children

First I will describe a few concrete cases of selling (*bikri* in Sambalpuri/*bikibā* in Oriya) that I came across, before analysing the phenomenon.

THE SELLING OF AN AGHRIĀ CHILD TO A PATHĀN FAMILY—CASE A

A young Aghriā boy at the age of one year—now around 40 years—was sold to a Pathān widow living in the natal village of his mother. The family already had three daughters. An elder brother—the firstborn son—had survived only a few days after birth. The boy himself was rather weak in his early childhood and was suffering from back pain. Under these circumstances the family was worried about his condition. The maternal uncle (*māmu*) arranged to sell the boy to a family of Pathāns, to whom a rather low status is ascribed. The Aghriā family hoped that the boy would survive.

As the father remembered, the act of selling itself was simple. The Pathān lady was invited to the boy's house. She put a copper coin with the picture of Hanuman on the neck of the young boy. The father interpreted this as a symbol of strength, transferred to the boy.

A Brahmin was not necessary. A loose relationship between the selling and buying families continued after the selling. The boy remained with his original family, but visited the Pathān lady occasionally. Now grown up, this Aghriā man suggested that his parents might have been afraid of the wrath of a saint who was treated badly and his elder brother may have died. He also remembers having eaten in the home of the Pathān lady during these visits. The father denies this. The boy received the nickname Pathān.

Before his wedding the boy was repurchased by his family, and the copper coin was returned to the Pathān lady. He had to be purified in a ritual by a Brahmin. Furthermore, a feast had to be given to the *jāti* (caste members of the village) to rejoin his caste (Aghriā) formally.

THE SELLING OF AN AGHRIĀ CHILD TO A KISĀN FAMILY—CASE B

A young Aghriā girl was sold at the age of seven (now she is about 22) to a local Kisān *Guniā*, a traditional healing expert[38] living in her village. This *Guniā* had already been called frequently due to the girl's continuous back pain. Her father's mother suggested selling her to this Kisān family. At the time of sale the *Guniā* spoke a few *mantras* and water was exchanged by the two families. The girl was now seen as the daughter of the *Guniā,* and later after his death as his son's daughter.

She was repurchased immediately before her marriage four years ago. At that time the Kisān family came with their own *jāti* (caste members) and a Kisān priest to offer a coconut in a small ritual. The Kisān then gave some coins to the Aghriā, which was explained as a belated selling price on their side (no money had been paid at the time of sale). Additionally, they offered a *śāḍhi* and a brass pot for the girl. Again, water was exchanged and, subsequently, her father (an Aghriā) paid Rs. 51 and offered cloths to the whole Kisān family in order to repurchase his daughter. The grown girl then sat on the lap of her father as a sign of his parentage and his legal rights over her, as she had done with her 'Kisān father' when she was sold. Her father wanted the child to actually sit on a *purug* (a kind of cask to store rice made of straw ropes—a *purug* can be filled with five bags of 75 kg each or 375 kg) filled with *dhān* (paddy) and should have a basket in her hand to collect gifts for herself. However, in her case, the *purug* was replaced by a smaller basket and she kept a metal plate in her hands. In this manner she collected more than a hundred rupees.

As the Kisān family explained to me, they also demanded the cloths and dishes she had used, as a symbol of their parentage—things they still keep in their home. Furthermore they told me that the girl's illness was not transferred to their family when she was purchased, instead, the child was cured while living in their family.

THE SELLING OF AN AGHRIĀ CHILD TO A CHAMĀR FAMILY—CASE C

In this case, an Aghriā girl (now an old lady of about 65 years) was sold when she was between six months and one year old. Before her birth her elder sister had died at the age of three. She was ill repeatedly and considered weak. Her parents were afraid that she also would die. Subsequently she was sold to a Chamār family in the village of her maternal uncle (*māmu*). She told me about a particular belief that caused her to be sold to a Chamār. As leatherworkers, after tanning, they used to put the leather on a line and would moisten it with water. The salty water dropping from the leather was collected in pots below. Everyone who bathed in that pot would be freed from all illnesses. The Aghriā lady, now around 65, could not remember exactly if she had taken such a bath or not, but said it was likely that she had.

After being sold she received a leather necklace from the Chamār family which she wore until she was repurchased. It was given at the time of sale and was seen as an identification with the Chamār. She called the Chamār mother and father although she continued to live with her Aghriā family. Later, she would visit the Chamār family occasionally and would have light snacks (*murhi*), but no boiled rice. The old lady said that she was treated, to some extent, as though she did not belong to her original caste, e.g. she received less food at feasts (*bhoji*), but she could, in contrast to 'ordinary' Chamār, enter the kitchen and use the same dishes.

Years later she was repurchased immediately before her child marriage. In order to sell her back to her original family, a *purug* filled with parboiled rice (*uṣnā chāul*, not paddy) was prepared and she was made to sit upon it. Her Chamār family had offered a *śāḍhi* which she wore while sitting there. In exchange, the Chamār demanded a new *śāḍhi*, a metal pot, a substantial amount of money

(Rs 5 as silver coins—ten grams each at that time) and the filled *purug*.

THE SELLING OF A KISĀN CHILD TO A HARIJAN FAMILY—CASE D

Last year a very weak Kisān child was sold to a Harijan (Gandā) family in the same village. The parents explained that the child was so weak that it had almost died. The child was sold for Re 1 to the Harijan family, but immediately afterwards the Kisān family gave two chickens—a black and a white one—to the Harijan, who offered them in their home to *dharmadevta*—the Sun God—as witness of the transfer.

According to the Kisān family, the child is considered a Harijan after having been sold—even if only temporarily. However, it can take part in caste feasts. The child can also be identified as a Harijan by a white thread (*suta*) worn as necklace (soaked in some herbal medicine), which the Harijan gave at the time of purchase. The white thread is a symbol for the Harijan as the traditional weaver community. The child got the nickname Gandā—the old caste name of the Harijan.

The Kisān believe that to have a Harijan child in their family excludes or at least reduces the negative effects of the evil eye (*najar*), of evil spirits (*bhut*) or witches (*tandhei*). The Harijan buyer told me that a change of caste, particularly from a higher to a lower one, helps the child to survive. He also added that the rather simple food of the Harijan (less oil, less spices, lower quality of rice, etc.) helps the sold children—or from his perspective, the bought children—to become physically stronger and to have a better chance of survival. Usually he takes the children—he is said to have purchased roughly 50—to his house for one or two days after buying them and feeds them. Contrary to the Kisān, he did not see the evil eye as a reason for the diseases of the children.

The repurchasing of the child has not yet taken place, but the Harijan said that the money he had given for the child must be returned plus interest. In addition, the child would sit on a *purug* filled with paddy—in his opinion roughly 40 kg. Then he would take the white thread off the child's neck and extend the thread with some half-prepared threads (*mudha suta*) so that he can put it seven times around the child's body. This is seen as freeing the child from the Harijan family, who receives the paddy of the *purug* plus four coconuts, seven chickens and money from the Kisān family. The Harijan use the chickens for feasting their *jāti*. The whole procedure must be witnessed by two *jāti* of both sides as witnesses. Also the Kisān must give a feast for their *jāti* in order to reintegrate the child into their group.

EMPIRICAL SITUATION

I came across about 40 cases in which children were temporarily identified with other communities.

Additionally, there is the opportunity to sell children to certain

TABLE 7: SELLING OF CHILDREN[39]

Selling group	Buying group	Number of cases (38)
Tihāri (Brahmin)	Ghansiā	1
Gauḍ	Muṇḍā	1
Gauḍ	Harijan (Dom)	1
Aghriā	Kisān	1
Aghriā	Muṇḍā	1
Aghriā	Harijan	3
Aghriā	Ghansiā	4
Aghriā	Chamār	2
Aghriā	Pathān	1
Aghriā	Gaṇḍ	1
Aghriā	Dhobā	1
Kandh	Māḷi	1
Kandh	Kisān	2
Kandh	Ludha	1
Kandh	Harijan	2
Kandh	Chamār	1
Gaṇḍ	Harijan	2
Gaṇḍ	Chamār	1
Kisān	Harijan	1
Kisān	Chamār	1
Muṇḍā	Gauḍ	1
Muṇḍā	Chamār	1
Khaḍiā	Ghansiā	1
Luhurā	Gaṇḍ	1
Harijān	Orām	1
Harijan	Luhurā	1
Harijān	Chamār	1
Chamār	Luhurā	1
Chamār	Chamār	1

semi-nomadic groups. I met two such groups during my stay: a *gugunādiā* group (in the local vernacular also called 'party') and a *māhuntiā* group. The former is named after a bull of the Śiva-temple the latter received the name because they ride an elephant representing Lakṣmī. Both claim to be able to solve problems like a barrenness and offer medicines for all kinds of problems. According to them, they also purchase children from the Aghriā, Gauḍ, Harijan, and Chamār. In the case of the *māhuntiā* party, the children touch the elephant to get the blessing of the Goddess. Their own claims of high status, e.g. to be Gauḍ, are, however, doubted by locals.

The symbolic act of selling and repurchasing—motives to sell

Despite inherent variations of the four cases introduced here, some features can be generalized. A common feature is the child's weakness, disease or pain before sale. Additionally, elder siblings may have previously died. In any case, the parents feel that the child's life is in danger and hope to improve the odds of its survival by selling the child. However, the strategies pursued for survival varied in the details. Some believed in the healing capacity either of water used by a Chamār in the tanning process (case C), and others trusted a white thread dipped into herbal medicine given by a Harijan (case D). In all cases the children were sold to families with healthy children.

Almost all of the children, except in the case of a Chamār—I will return to this point later—were transferred to another community. With the exception of the Chamār, a sale within one's own community would be impossible. People said that the change of caste or tribe helped the child to survive. Some speculated that the sale of children helped to avoid or to reduce the negative effects of the evil eye, evil spirits, and witches (case D). However, in all cases the transaction and identification remained symbolic—all children continued to stay with their original family.

In many cases the children spent some time in the home of the family who had purchased them and—probably even more importantly—almost all sold children ate in the homes of their new 'families'—even if it was only a symbolical act. Taking Marriott's (1976) transactional theory into consideration, according to which in South Asia a person is seen as a 'dividual' than an 'individual', whose inherent quality is changed depending on the food taken in, the eating in another community, the eating of their food—and food as such—transforms the person and clearly has repercussions on one's own identity. Particularly, the 'bodily substance-codes of [...] low castes are necessarily expected to become the most unselectively heterogeneous, their powers diluted and restricted and their temperaments gross and animal-like. Also, as removers of what the higher castes consider 'pollution', the lowest among them are masters of negative transformations. . . .' (Marriott 1976: 128). As 'dividuals' are always 'composites of the substance-codes they take in'[40] (Marriott 1976: 111) identification with another group, an intended transformation and lowering of the child is achieved primarily by the sharing of food. This corresponds to the argument, occasionally put forward by informants, that the less refined quality of food eaten in these lower status families helps the child to become physically stronger. This line of argument relates to a clichè sometimes found in the upper castes, that the lower castes are physically stronger and therefore hard manual labour or agricultural work is more suitable for them.

The act of selling children is indeed an 'economic' transaction in the sense of a transfer involving money and at least one coin was handed over to the family who sold the child—even if the coin had only a very nominal value or was handed over at a later point in time. Similarly, the money that was paid, when the child was repurchased, was usually a substantial amount compared with the initial sale. At the same time, the sale and much more the repurchase is often accompanied by a gift (*śāḍhi*, paddy, etc.). In many cases the now grown up child sits on a *purug* of rice while it is re-transferred to his original group.

The act of selling is not necessarily accompanied by a ritual performance, but it is noteworthy that in many cases the mother's brother of the child plays a vital role in arranging the sale as often children are sold into his village. Not the sale itself, but rather the repurchase requires the presence of a priest and sometimes the presence of *jāti* members, usually of a different clan—to reintegrate the child into its original group. For a full reintegration, a feast for the members of one's own group is obligatory—a reintegration in turn is unavoidable if one wants to marry. Thus, usually the reintegration takes place immediately before a marriage.[41]

In many cases the child gets visible attributes of its new group at the time of sale in order to be identified with them. 'New Chamār parents' offer a necklace made of leather or the Harijan give white thread as a necklace and symbol of the traditional occupation of weaving. Choudhury (1977: 73) mentions that in similar cases, Lohar (blacksmith) and Ghasi give a strip of goat skin to Muṇḍā children.[42]

As far as I am aware, particularly 'untouchable' castes give these symbols or amulets. These groups are essentialized—in particular by their occupation—and their differences are displayed in public, which, in the long run, has repercussions on the hierarchical order. Scheduled Tribes like Kisān or Muṇḍā rarely give such amulets when they purchase high status children. A Gaṇḍ—locally known as a healer or *Guniā*—who purchased an Aghriā child offered a *daunriā* or small amulet (a little copper box filled with herbs and roots to be worn around the upper arm). In other cases the Chamār also gave some pieces of bullock's horn or some roots as medicine to be worn around the neck. In relation to other Indian contexts[43] one could also argue that groups of rather low or very ambivalent status often seem to have a relatively close link to the divine sphere and could use their proximity for ritual healing.

In addition to amulets, the children usually acquire the name of the 'buyer's' group as a nickname, 'Pathān', 'Gandā'—the old name for Harijan—or as 'Chamāren' (Chamār woman). The use of such nicknames is also known from the Desya-context of Koraput among the Gadaba, where names such as Ghanzi or Dombru are common (G. Pfeffer: personal communication). Thus identification with the new group is not only expressed visibly with amulets, but also verbally. Generally, there is a variety of names used in different contexts: a name fixed in one's horoscope and used in rituals; a name used in official papers such as identification cards; first names used by close family members or nicknames expressing physical attributes, for instance 'the big one', or the order of birth among siblings such as 'the young one'. The nickname one receives after being sold is just one name among many. It is a name particularly used by others, by friends or relatives. While in some contexts it can be considered a serious insult to call someone a Chamār, these nicknames are used to tease the person once sold. Long after being repurchased, the names stick to the persons concerned, are remembered, and may become a permanent part of a multiple identity, even if it was just a temporary identification.

Hierarchy and purity

Another common but important factor that has not yet been sufficiently discussed pertains to the situation that children are predominantly sold to families of lower status. This is deliberate. Thus, one obvious characteristic of the sale is the direction of the transfer. For a clearer understanding of this, it is necessary to remember the local hierarchy introduced at the beginning of this chapter. The act of selling within the local hierarchy is presented in Table 8 in a simplified model.[44]

TABLE 8: SIMPLIFIED MODEL OF LOCAL HIERARCHY AND TRANSFER OF CHILDREN

Caste	Tihāri	Gauḍ	Aghriā	Kandh	Gaṇḍ	Chaṣā	Māḷi	Kisān	Muṇḍā	Luhurā	Khaḍiā	Orām	Harijan	Ghansiā	Chamār
Tihāri															
Gauḍ									1						
Aghriā															
Kandh															
Gaṇḍ			1							1					
Chaṣā															
Māḷi				1											
Kisān			1	2											
Muṇḍā		1	1												
Luhurā													1[45]		1
Khaḍīā															
Orām													1		
Harijan		1	3	2	2			1							
Ghansiā	1		4								1				
Chamār			2	1	1			1	1				1		1

other biological waste, in the latter location natural and sometimes industrial waste such as plastic bags is collected. Although cow dung itself is considered to be pure, both places are regarded as impure and are used accordingly. Afterwards the child usually gets the nickname *kathu* for a male child or *kathi* for a female child. In one case a child was put on the *khat ḍhuḍā* first, but afterwards was sold to a Harijan family showing that these forms are not mutually exclusive and can be combined at will.

A third variety is slightly different: the child is put into the leftovers of a meal. Thus it sits on a plate with some food remains or garbage (*aenthā*) for a short while. Marriott (1968: 142) et al. observed that garbage is regarded as polluted 'by saliva flowing from the mouth of the eater' and it should be handled only by inferiors. As an older Aghriā lady told me, whose late husband was a case in point, this is done to make the child impure (*aśuddha*).[47] He used to be called by his nickname *aenthā* (food remains). The impure child remained in this condition until marriage. A ritual purification and a feast for the *jāti* is obligatory immediately before the wedding.

It seems that Grigson (1991 [1938]: 270) observed a cross-over of the first two ways among the Bison-horn Maria Gond (Gaṇḍ):

> I once witnessed an unusual naming ceremony. A son had been born after three elder brothers had died. It was considered that their deaths had been due to the hostility of some demon or of the familiar spirit of some magician, and on the medium's advice the baby had been suspended in a rough cradle over the rubbish-heap by the fence of the bari garden, and all the men present threw cow-dung and filth all round the cradle, shouting out 'Kacharu' or 'Filth!', which name was given to the child in the hope that thereby the malignant power would be deceived into thinking that the parents set no value on the child.

Similarly, Roy (1999 [1928]: 120) stated for the Oraon (Orām):

> The new-born babe of a woman who has lost one child after another, soon after birth, is [. . .] deposited on the manure-heap by one woman and taken up by another. This is believed to protect the child from the evil attentions of malignant spirits, for it said, that evil spirits do not care for a babe thus thrown into a manure-pit as an useless refuse. Such a boy is named either as Fekuā (cast-away) or as Gūndūrā (belonging to cattle-dung) or as Mādi (pertaining to manure), probably to deceive evil spirits.

Both authors mention the throwing into impure places and emphasize the deception of evil spirits as the main motive, but neither of them, both said to have been keen observers of the local cultures, observed any case of selling children. Roy's case also shows that a transfer of the child is valued, as the child was deposited by one woman and taken up by another.

GIVEN AWAY

Apart from the sale of children and throwing them away there is—at least in some communities like the Aghriā—the possibility of simply transferring them or giving them away within one's own community. This is known as *debā*. Even if some people do not consider it to be as effective as selling it is practised occasionally. In one case among the Aghriā a mother gave her son to her husband's elder brother's wife who had three sons and three daughters. All of them were healthy and strong but her two daughters had passed away. The mother believed that her son would stay alive and remain healthy if she gave him to her sister-in-law. Most importantly here the son was given into another family, she gave him away, because both families had already separated household and property. In another case an astrologer having seen an inauspicious constellation of stars recommended that a mother give away her son, who was in a weak condition at that time. Spontaneously the mother's brother's wife who was present and had no children declared that she would take the child. Until today the child addresses the mother's brother's wife as mother. In a third case a daughter suffered from nosebleed after her birth and was generally weak. Her mother could not give enough milk to feed her. The family decided to give her to her father's younger brother's wife who already had two healthy children. Again, the family had already been divided into separate households. The daughter was returned after six months when her condition had stabilized. To give a child away within your own community does not involve impurity and before marriage no purification is needed.

SELLING YOURSELF TO GOD

Another way to transfer children is by selling them to Krishna or rather to a Krishna Guru Party. Such a Party is established around a throne or *gaddī* of Krishna, which anyone can set up in his house after having been initiated by a guru—quite often recognizable to everybody by a picture of Krishna outside the house. Frequently, the group consists of members of different tribes and castes. The difference here is the aspect of self-sale. While searching for a job in another region a Muṇḍā met a guru who read his palm and told him, that he may die in an accident or would have other serious problems. Later, he survived an accident and subsequently became a follower of the Krishna Guru Party. In order to become a member, he sold himself in a kind of *dikhyā* or initiation and before the *dikhyā,* he had to choose a guru (*guru karibā*). In the small ritual the devotee or *bhakt* gave a brass plate to his guru, on which the latter set his foot, which the *bhakt* washed before drinking some drops of that water. Later, the *bhakt* offered a cloth (*dhoti*) and money to the guru in order to sell himself—'*mui biki hele*'. The act is seen as *śarān paḍibā*—as giving oneself to Lord Krishna, the *śaran guru*—who, from now on, becomes directly responsible for the life.

The elder brother's daughter (*jiāri*) of the same Muṇḍā was also given to Krishna, because an open wound on her leg did not heal. Several doctors had been consulted and different sorts of medicine were applied, but only after joining the Krishna Guru Party did she recover. It is disputed whether or not children can sell themselves or whether this is reserved for adults. Parents can offer their children to Krishna in this manner, but must perform the necessary daily rituals themselves, as it is believed that children are not able to properly observe the ritual routine. This act of selling seems irreversible and impurity is not involved. In any case, the parents hope that the child under the influence of Krishna will be cured, positively influenced and not be taken away by Yama.

Identification of children—transactions and impurity

The converging tribal and caste society in the Sambalpur district is held together, not only by the common worship of Hinduized tribal deities (Eschmann 1994 [1975]: 211ff, Sontheimer 1994: 117ff, Pasayat 1998: 103ff) and by the continuing power structures of the former little kingdoms (Kulke 2001 [1993]: 114ff, Schnepel 2001: 271ff) most notably represented by the still powerful landlords as described in the literature, but also by a subtle network of relationships established, for instance, by selling children. Apart from common rituals, the work of labourers in the landlord's fields or from newly established schools, inter-group relations are established by the giving away of children—however temporary and legally incomplete these relations may be. They form an important sphere of interaction and influence each other.

Considering the larger picture of selling, throwing and giving away there are two overlapping intentions of these transactions. First, the child is transferred—into a family or house not affected by misfortune or illness. Second, the child is made impure in the hope of diverting the evil eye, the attention of Yama, but also to become stronger physically in a lower caste environment. The sale of children, which people see as the most effective method of saving them, obviously combines both aspects: the child is transferred to an impure setting. In being given away to a low status family and becoming impure at the same time, the child has the best chances to survive.

TABLE 9: TRANSFER AND IMPURITY COMPARED

	Child is transferred	Child becomes impure
Giving away	X	
Throwing away		X
Selling	X	X

On one hand, Marriott's transactional theory (1968: 169–70) shows 'rankings established by food transfers' that express the value of avoiding pollution with regard to food as well as of the removal pollution in regard to services.[48] On the other hand, Marriott observed, 'pollution is not dreaded as an absolute evil, instead it may be manipulated or even enjoyed' (1968: 143). A state of self-induced impurity might be a *protected* state. In our case, it is attained deliberately—even though for a restricted purpose and a limited time. Furthermore, not only pollution—prior to marriage—but the act of transfer itself is valued.

One must also note that the child's transfer and temporary identification has no negative effect—either on the high status of the giver at the time of sale or on the receiver by repurchasing the child. The same is true in the reverse direction: the child's receiver of low status cannot improve it, when selling the child. The transaction does not affect the rank of giver or receiver—presumably because it is a market-like transfer. The child is first sold and then eats in the receiver's house. Money is acceptable from everyone and, contrary to Marriott (1968: 144), it seems that money does not even convey 'the slightest degree of subordination'. It rather seems to solidify the transfer of any substance-code.

The temporary identification of children establishes intergroup relationships that reflect a local hierarchy; at the same time, it creates and reinforces a hierarchy in a society with tribal and caste groups. The giving of amulets of leather by the Chamār expresses a process of 'identifying differences' (Jeffrey 2000: 286) as well as essentializing differences between the categories in public and, thus, hierarchically ordering them. Children are sold from groups of relatively higher status—including higher tribal groups like the Gaṇḍ or Kandh—to relatively lower status groups such as the Muṇḍā or Harijan and usually not the other way around. Thus, the sale also shows that tribal groups are not always and exclusively integrated into the lower strata of the hierarchy, as sometimes assumed,[49] but on higher levels as well.

The transactions introduced here are undertaken keeping—more or less explicitly—a third party in mind (see Figure 3). Children are made impure or are transferred to deceive, to distract the attention of or to fool Yama, the God of Death, malignant spirits or anyone having an evil eye, etc. There is nothing wrong with trying to cheat evil

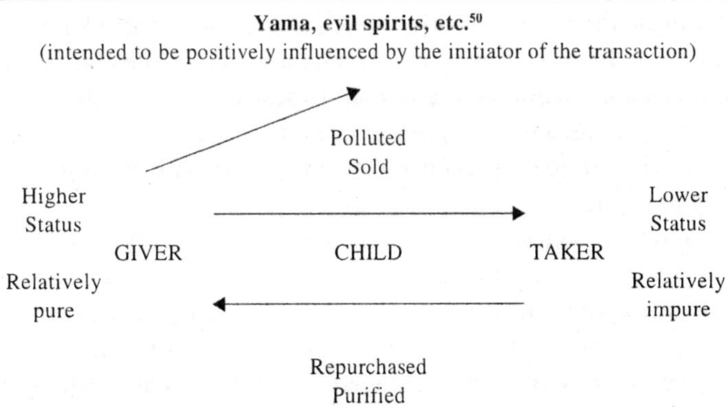

Figure 3: Systemization.

spirits or Yama, etc. Brahmins, too, are occasionally cheated. In times of illness and need a family might offer them gifts known as *dān*, in which a hair or nail of a sick person, etc., may be hidden. In this way one hopes that the disease or negative influence is transferred to the Brahmin, who is also aware of the potential 'poison in the gift' (Raheja 1988). However, in the case of children, there is a fixed time-frame for the transaction and deception. Every child must be repurchased and purified before marriage. In view of the Gods one could also argue that, at the time of marriage Lakṣmī, the Goddess of wealth and happiness comes into one's house—in particular in the form of the bride—which is expected to help checking evil forces endangering family members.

Corresponding time-frame

after birth/prior to marriage ——▸ unripe (*apūrṇṇa*) person
after marriage ——▸ ripe (*pūrṇṇa*) person

Children have to be repurchased and purified after being sold or thrown away in order to be reintegrated into one's own group and in order to marry. On the one hand, this may signify the persistent influence of the caste system in the region, in which the value of purity plays a crucial role (Dumont 1980 [1966]). On the other hand, it may also be a continuity of local—tribal—concepts of ritual purity (Pfeffer 2000: 342). However, the selling and even a temporary breaking of commensality do not endanger the separation of groups according to their relative purity, which is instead reinforced. Essential boundaries, like marriage, are maintained—therefore the identification remains incomplete and mainly restricted to childhood. For women, marriage initiates a new process of identification—the bride becomes integrated and henceforth identified with her husband's family and clan.

Children are sold to communities considered to be physically strong because of their diet. But they are also well equipped or prepared against metaphysical dangers, e.g. the evil eye. By selling children their social status is lowered in order to gain status metaphysically. A temporarily low status is exchanged for material wealth. That which seems to be absurd from a Western 'economic' point of view could be a way to deal with evil forces and at the same time a means of creating and reinforcing the local hierarchy and integrating tribes into it. The temporary identification of children shows that status as identity is not fixed permanently, but rather continuously negotiated and even voluntarily lowered for some time in order to benefit personally within a collectively constructed framework.

3.3. FICTIVE KINSHIP AND THE MYTHOLOGICAL LINKS BETWEEN COMMUNITIES

The hierarchical order is supplemented and perforated by links between different groups, sometimes within hierarchical boundaries and sometimes across them. In the latter case, the links are emphasized by the groups of lower status, for instance by the Luhurā in relation to the Gaṇḍ or by the Chamār in relation to the Aghriā. In contrast, the higher status groups flatly reject the relations—according to them, there are no such mythological relations. In some cases these ties are styled as brotherhoods, such as among the Gaṇḍ, Kandh, and Bhuyān or between the Luhurā and the Gaṇḍ. In the latter case, in some versions brotherhood or a kinship tie is also related to a mythological marriage—as in the case of the Chamār and the Aghriā. The link between the Chamār and the Aghriā is further associated with a story about the origin of the Aghriā. As far as links between the Luhurā and the Gaṇḍ or the Aghriā and the Chamār are concerned, the Aghriā and the Gaṇḍ flatly reject those myths stating a marriage relation. Further, both communities, as the superior groups, would not tolerate the narration of such stories in their presence as that would lower their prestige. However, even if the link or brotherhood as such is not contested—as among Gaṇḍ, Bhuyān, and Kandh—there are disputes about the relative age among brothers and thus implicitly about status differences. Before turning to mythological kinship links, one should note that the village as a whole is conceptualized as a family.

The village as an imagined family

Arriving in the village, one is surprised by the usage of kinship terms, particularly in terms of address. The whole village is linked—no matter to which community one belongs. In the context of the village, it is considered rather impolite—almost an insult—not to use or not to remember the appropriate kin term for fellow villagers. When occasionally it happens that people forget the correct term, they apologise. In every interaction the proper term of address should be used. To address someone—an elder—simply by the name of his caste would be a serious affront.

People think in kinship categories and there is a tendency to include everyone—every outsider provided he stays in the village, e.g. seasonal labourers[51]—into the fictive kinship network. This same tendency was found by Vatuk (1969: 96) in north India, where the universe is conceived in kinship terms. The idea of the village as a family is not only applicable to terms of address, but also to joking relationships.

The system is continued by people simply extending the relations from generation to generation irrespective of biological age. In daily use this may lead to such situations that someone of the same biological age is addressed as grandson, but of primary importance is the social relation already in existence that cannot be ignored. An example: I have to call one who addressed my father as 'elder brother' as my 'father's younger brother'.

GAṆḌ, KANDH AND BHUYĀN AS BROTHERS

An old Kandh man explained that Gaṇḍ, Kandh and Bhuyān were three brothers. He told me that the Kandh had originally worn the sacred thread (*paitā*), but took it off while taking a bath. At that moment, the Gaṇḍ stole it. Occasionally, the story varies in some of the details. Another Kandh told me that his Kandh ancestor, wearing the sacred thread, had taken it off to go for a nature's call and that the Gaṇḍ used the chance to grab it. He criticized the Gaṇḍ for stealing it, but acknowledged that the Kandh could not wear it now.

A similar version was put forward by an old Bhuyān. He related that once the three brothers—Gaṇḍ, Kandh, and Bhuyān—had gone for a bath. The Gaṇḍ was the youngest among them. The eldest—the Bhuyān —used to wear the sacred thread. After his bath he washed the thread, but forgot it near the river and returned home. The Gaṇḍ took it and started to wear it on his way home. The Bhuyān saw his youngest brother with the sacred thread and scolded him. After the dispute the household was divided.

The Kandh, as the middle brother, told his elder brother that he should not scold the Gaṇḍ in this manner and separated from the Bhuyān as well. According to this old Bhuyān, the Gaṇḍ should have returned the sacred thread since it did not belong to him, but he said that it was a mistake to scold the Gaṇḍ in the way the eldest brother did.

In contrast to this, a Gaṇḍ man explained the origin of the sacred thread in a different way. According to them the sacred thread consisted of six single threads representing six gods, Janghā, Lingā, Tamru, Sāl, Karati, and Pāt Gaddi, who once told a Gaṇḍ king that if he wore them in the form of a thread around his shoulder he would be protected and nothing bad could happen to him. Gaṇḍ have worn it ever since.

LINKS BETWEEN THE GAṆḌ AND THE LUHURĀ

According to an elder Luhurā, their community arrived together with the Gaṇḍ in the region, but in the past had a higher status than the Gaṇḍ. The Luhurā wore the sacred thread, which was usually removed while working with the bellows. But one day, a Gaṇḍ stole it from the smithy. From this day onward, the Gaṇḍ wear the sacred thread and are called *baḍ* or 'big' in relation to the Luhurā.[52] Another Luhurā told me a slightly different story. Here, the Luhurā was described as the younger brother of the Gaṇḍ and one day the Luhurā used the sacred thread in order to bind something on his leather-bellows for repairs. When the Gaṇḍ, as the elder brother, came to know about it, he expelled him—apparently, because a combination of sacred thread and leather-bellow had been condemned.

Apart from such stories there is another mythological incident occasionally told by the Luhurā. A Luhurā king once planned to marry off his daughter and opted for the so-called *svayambar*—marriage. In this type of marriage potential grooms or princes are invited to the court and the bride or princess has to choose the groom herself from the assembled candidates. The name *svayambar* is derived from *svayam* 'yourself' and *bar* 'groom' meaning 'to select a groom yourself'. However, in this case the choice of the bride was not completely free, because potential grooms had to meet two conditions. Firstly, the groom had to kill an iron sheep with an axe, which was kept in an iron cage or surrounded by an iron wall. Secondly, the candidate had to eat melted iron. Only a Gaṇḍ prince named Neti was able to fulfil the tasks as demanded and to marry the daughter of the Luhurā king. Their children became the Neti clan of the Gaṇḍ.

The Luhurā say that until today the Luhurā and Neti Gaṇḍ share the same Pargania—a kind of bard and genealogist, responsible for preserving and telling mythological stories.

The following story is told in different versions as well. Another Luhurā recounted that once a king had a daughter of marriageable age and decided to hold a *svayambar*. The daughter was held captive in a fort with iron walls. A Neti Gaṇḍ was able to fulfil all the tasks he was asked to perform in order to marry her, one being to break iron nuts (*luhā chanā*) with his teeth. After the marriage, he asked his younger brother—the Luhurā—to do the ironwork.

Usually, all these versions are rejected by the Gaṇḍ, including the Neti Gaṇḍ—a clan of the Gaṇḍ—who do not see any special relation to the Luhurā. Only one Gaṇḍ I met—although a very prominent one, as the former Vice President of the Gaṇḍ Samaj—verified this link. He mentioned a famous Gaṇḍ king named Byāghra who belonged to the Neti-*bansa* (= clan). This king was so strong that if someone offered peanuts as snacks he demanded iron peanuts and chewed them—grinding them into powder. Some of the Neti Gaṇḍ—although not all of them—became Luhurā later on. Interestingly, there was also marriage in the village between a Gaṇḍ man and a Luhurā woman. In an interview they told me that, although both were excluded from their respective communities, the Gaṇḍ man might now be regarded as a Luhurā—implying the possibility of marriage between Gaṇḍ and Luhurā from the side of the Luhurā.

Earlier, Russell (see Elwin 1991 [1942]: 10) had argued that the Agaria—a community of iron-smelters, whose name is derived from *āg* or fire—are actually an offshoot of the Gond (Gaṇḍ) tribe.[53] If this statement is true and if one takes into consideration the special link between Luhurā and Gaṇḍ just described, it is possible to put forth the hypothesis that the Luhurā are identical with the Agaria as analysed by Elwin. The Agaria may have adopted another, Hindu, name—Luhurā being derived from *luhā* or iron—in this converging tribal and caste society.

THE MYTHOLOGICAL LINK BETWEEN AGHRIĀ AND CHAMĀR

The mythological relationship between the Aghriā and the Chamār has already been discussed. Therefore, we shall only briefly revisit the issue. One Chamār lady narrated the following story, not only hinting at a marriage relation between both communities following the acceptance of an Aghriā boy in a Chamār house, but also, pointing at relations to Brahmin and Gauḍ:

In former times we [the Chamār] had the sacred thread (*paitā*) and then handed it over to Brahmin and Tihāri. That [the sacred thread] was our's. When we handed it over to the Brahmin, then it was their occupation. Usually we appointed the Magda Gauḍ to carry the sedan (*dulā*) [for marriages]. We have given our daughter to you [Aghriā] and hence you are our affines (*bandhu*).[54] We have not come from anywhere. We are the dirt (*mailā*) of God's body. We were having Lord Salegram [Śiva]. When you [Aghriā] were killed [by the King—see Aghriā-mythology], then one little guy [Aghriā] came and requested little bit of help and the little boy requested Lord Salegram to keep him. By that time the old guy [Chamār] told him, to pour little water over there [over the leather]. And then the guy got little water and poured it on the skin. Hence they thought of the little guy as a Chamār-child and left him there. Not being killed the boy grew up in the Chamār-family. Later on the Chamār offered his granddaughter to that guy. He [the Chamār] appointed a washerman and a barber for him and kept him in this family. He [the Chamār] presented Lakṣmī to him. The God had given a golden knife (*sonā churi*) to us. That was also handed over [to the Aghriā].

RITUAL INCLUSION OF THE KISĀN

In addition to these mythological connections there are legends concerning the inclusion of groups into the village community. One such story was put forth by the Kisān. In former times they—as an old Kisān told—led a very nasty life. They did not keep themselves clean and did not take proper baths. Therefore, they were not invited to the *Rath Jātrā* of Lord Jagannāth. Once, however, during a *Rath Jātrā* procession, the carriage of Lord Jagannāth did not move at all. Finally, the people had the idea to ask the Kisān, who had been thus far excluded, as they were known as *kālā piṭhia* (*kālā* = black; *piṭhia* = the back of one's body). They were almost completely black like the Muṇḍā—the Kisān say. Subsequently, an old Kisān, who was called for the procession worshipped Jagannāth and, suddenly, it was possible to move the carriage. Since then the Kisān have always been invited to the *Rath Jātrā*, because Jagannāth does not want them to be excluded.

LINKING COMMUNITIES

Other than these described relationships, there are many examples of such links in the literature, which, however, I could not verify. For example, a mythological relation is described by Roy (1970 [1912]: 333)[55] between Mūndā (Muṇḍā), Urāon/Urain (Orām), and Khāria (Khaḍiā). According to a legend Muṇḍā men accepted Orām wives and the children of these relationships formed a new tribe named the Khāria (Khaḍiā).[56] Roy (1999 [1928]: 19–20) also mentions a link between the Orāon (Orām) and the Māler, who—most likely—are identical with the Malār found in Kuchinda area. According to Roy, the Māler are an 'allied tribe' of the Orāon, while Pfeffer (1997: 15, 2002: 17) considers the Kisān the 'senior' half of the Kurukh tribe—the Oraon (Orām) being the 'junior' half. Pfeffer (1997: 15) further relates the Muṇḍā to the Ho—the two communities forming a pair. However, the links between the Orām and the Malār or between the Muṇḍā, Orām, and the Khaḍiā were not formulated explicitly—one reason behind it may be the conversion of the Orām and Khaḍiā to Christianity.

Additionally, there are symbiotic ties, e.g. between the Aghriā and the Kisān—the latter known to be good peasants, usually found in or near Aghriā settlements and employed by Aghriā landlords. However, I could not find any mythological rationalization or legitimation of this economic link.

One could conclude that the tribal society of Orissa is linked in various ways mythologically—tribes are not fully autonomous or self-contained, but rather integrated or grouped with other tribal communities. In the south of Orissa one may find oppositional pairs such as the Bondo and the Gadaba—the junior Gadaba themselves divided into a junior and a senior half (Berger 2002: 70). In the north-western part the picture appears to be less clear—there are myths linking three groups (Gaṇḍ, Kandh, and Bhuyān or Muṇḍā, Orām and Khaḍiā) and links that may be established by a marriage relationship (Gaṇḍ and Luhurā; Muṇḍā, Orām and Khaḍiā) in addition to brotherhood. However, as indicated in the case of Aghriā mythology, such links are restricted to either tribal communities (Gaṇḍ, Kandh and Bhuyān) or to castes (Aghriā and Chamār), but there are no mythological ties across, e.g. between Aghriā and Kisān. Nevertheless, such links cut across hierarchical categories and may to some extent counter the existing hierarchy.

RITUAL FRIENDSHIPS AS PERSONAL LINKS BETWEEN COMMUNITIES

There is yet another way of establishing or formalizing inter-group relations on a personal level, which I call as ritual friendship. Very close friends, particularly school or college friends, choose this way to create formal and permanent ties. Often also parents arrange the ritual for their young children in order to become friends. Such a relation can only be established between different communities, e.g. between Aghriā and Kisān, or Kisān and Māḷi, but not within one's own group. It will be argued here that such bonds of ritual friendship occur in this converging society particularly on the inter-community level. This stands in contrast to the tribal societies of south Orissa and Chhotanagpur, in which relations of ritual friendship might be forged at the intra-community level connecting various clans, etc. Among the Aghriā the possibility of two men or two women becoming ritual friends is explicitly excluded. To my knowledge the same rule occurs in most communities in the vicinity of the Aghriā (in north-west Orissa). Therefore one may find an adaptation or transformation of ritual friendship between a rather segmentary tribal society in the south on the one hand, and a more complex, transitional society, with hierarchies resembling those of caste society on the other. While in the former society ritual friendship may balance a condition of latent war, or 'Warre' in the sense of Hobbes, which Sahlins characterizes as being typical of tribal society, in the latter type of society it may occur as a counterweight to newly established hierarchies. However, this does not mean that the former type of society should be considered egalitarian, nor does it mean that Aghriā migrating into a tribal region may not have needed allies in a predominantly tribal area. Thus various functions might be attached to the same forms of ritual friendship, which in their turn may also be hierarchized or influenced by hierarchies.

Ritual friendships are mainly arranged between two men or sometimes between two women. In contrast to *dharma* kinship, a tie between a man and a woman is prohibited. Typical of all forms is the complete avoidance of individual names, from which I argue that ritual friendship is aimed at the total identification, even merger, of ritual friends. This particular way of establishing relationships on a personal level has been termed ritual friendship. It seems to me, however, to lie somewhere between our categories of friendship and kinship. It resembles friendship in the sense that friends may choose each other to some extent, although ways of formalizing this are socially determined. It also creates a relationship that does not have any exact equivalent in the kinship sphere. Although people sometimes explain it by saying that it is like the relationship between brothers, they also say that these friends are equal in a way that is not so of brothers, with their differences in age and more importantly status.

This phenomenon bears a resemblance to kinship in the sense that it is extended to other family members: the relationships that are created are not restricted to two individuals, but involve their wider families. In contrast to ordinary friendship, they have a permanent character. Ritual friends are said to support each other and to share everything as, ideally, brothers or sisters do, and some people joke that they would even share their wives, although in practice a ritual friend's wife should be avoided like a younger brother's wife. Obligations to invite each other to festivals resemble those of the kinship network. Ritual friendship appears to be more binding than ordinary friendship because it is sanctioned in front of, and blessed by, various gods. However, even though it does not fit neatly into our categories, for present purposes I have decided to call it ritual friendship. There is an impressive variety of ways to create bonds of ritual friendship. Let me describe these in more detail.

Mahāpraśād

The most sacred way of becoming ritual friends is by eating the *praśād* (leftovers of the gods) of Lord Jagannāth, or *mahāpraśād* (great *praśād*). Although some people decide to create this type of friendship on a pilgrimage to Jagannāth's main temple in Puri, it is not necessary to go on a pilgrimage to obtain *mahāpraśād*: someone else may bring it from Puri. It is not the pilgrimage but the process of eating *praśād* together and the resulting transformation that are decisive, and *mahāpraśād* is regarded as a witness to this transformative process of turning friends into ritual friends. For most villagers a journey to Puri is anyway not easily affordable. With *mahāpraśād* from Puri any Brahmin can perform the necessary ritual. There is no fixed place for the ritual, which can be performed anywhere. Often it is done at a school, because many friends decide to create this ritual bond during their time at high school. This also indicates that most such friends reside outside one's own village, thus creating a network beyond the village.

The new friends address each other as *mahāpraśād* and no longer use their individual names. Friends are not allowed to call one another in any other way except *mahāpraśād. Mahāpraśād*, people say, should never quarrel, for this would be considered a kind of sin. In the other forms described below there is not such a strict taboo against disputes, although friends should not quarrel generally. Furthermore, one Brahmin said that *mahāpraśād* have one and the same life energy or *jiban*, meaning that the separate *jiban* each of them has at the time of birth is merged with their friend's *jiban* in the act of forging the ritual friendship. A *mahāpraśād* bond is unbreakable, and *mahāpraśād* must help one another under all circumstances.

If a *mahāpraśād* friend dies, his partner must conduct a funeral or *kām ghar* in his own house. This includes ritually destroying and replacing the pot used to boil rice; summoning a Brahmin, if the *mahāpraśād* belonged to a high-status community; and, perhaps even more importantly, a feast for his caste fellows or *jāti*, which is a rather expensive affair. However, compared to an ordinary funeral among a high caste like the Aghriā, this funeral is considerably shortened and restricted to the eleventh day (usually it would continue from the ninth to the twelfth day). Nor is it necessary to shave the head. Nowadays, some interlocutors told me, these obligations might not be as strict as they were in former times.

KNOWN CASES OF *MAHĀPRAŚĀD*[57]

Aghriā	Karan
Aghriā	Kultā
Aghriā	Keunṭ
Aghriā	Chasā
Gaṇḍ	Gauḍ

Makrā

A second method is to perform a ritual on *Makar Sankrānti* (see Appendix 2.3.) or January 14 at a place where the festival is observed and altars for Lord Jagannāth and Śiva have been erected. This festival is so popular in the region that in some villages it is even celebrated a few days later in order to avoid clashing with other villages. Compared to *mahāpraśād*, it is therefore easier to become a *makrā*.

There is a legend that Lord Jagannāth and Śiva met on this particular day and became ritual friends or *makrā*. However, other people, in particular a Brahmin performing the *Makar Sankrānti*, merely stated that although the two gods had met on that day, they did not create any ritual friendship. In any case, during the common festival, after initial rituals to invoke both gods, their meeting is remembered by having villagers push two carriages or *raths*, with the idols and priests sitting on top of them, from opposite directions and meeting in front of the temple or altar. Ideally the cars should be pushed around sunset only by those intending to become *makrā*. Then the gods greet each other. After this ritual encounter between the two gods, any couple wishing to become a *makrā* can enter the temple, where they offer a coconut and some money. In return they receive *makrā chāul*, a special kind of *praśād*,[58] with which to feed each other. Then the *makrā* worship each other by placing a sandalwood *ṭikā* on each other's forehead, applying a *ṭikā* of vermilion and kneeling down in front of each other. As in the case of *mahāpraśād*, the aspect of feeding *praśād* plays a crucial role in the transformative process

Makrā-friends

of becoming friends. Commensality, however, is restricted to the ritual context. Though many people are not sure whether a *makrā* can accept food in the house of his ritual friend of a lower community, a high-caste Aghriā *makrā* once told me explicitly that his Kisān *makrā* would arrange a Gauḍ to cook for them if he—the Aghriā—were invited there.

The fathers of two *makrā* call each other *sahayā* or *śarjyā*. Restrictions of avoidance exist between one *sahayā* and the other *sahayā*'s wife, who has to veil her head in the presence of her husband's *sahayā*. A man should not touch the wife of his *sahayā*. The father of one's *makrā* is known as *mita buā* (*mita* = friend; *buā* = father). There is no general agreement whether a funeral has to be performed in a friend's house in the case of *makrā* friendship.

Compared to the *mahāpraśād*, the *makrā* friendship can be dissolved, as a Brahmin who performs the ritual to become *makrā* explained. Although he could reverse the ritual, he said that cancelling a ritual friendship would be bad (*kharāb*) and inauspicious (*asubha*). Neither this Brahmin nor any other person I asked knew a single case where the ritual of becoming friends had actually been reversed. This is also true of all the following kinds of ritual friendship.

KNOWN CASES OF *MAKRĀ* FRIENDSHIP

Gauḍ	Kisān
Aghriā	Tihāri (Brahmin of Aghriā)
Aghriā	Gaṇḍ
Aghriā	Sundhi (wine-seller for *mahuli* wine—OBC)
Aghriā	Kisān
Aghriā	Harijan
Gaṇḍ	Kandh
Gaṇḍ	Keunṭ
Gaṇḍ	Mahāronā (brass-smiths)
Gaṇḍ	Kisān
Gaṇḍ	Luhurā
Māḷi	Kisān
Bhuyān	Kisān
Chasā	Luhurā
Kisān	Orām
Kisān	Khajuriā
Tūrī	Chamār

Bensāgar or Benisāgar

The name of this type of friendship seems to be derived from *beni* 'both' and *sāgar* 'sea', but not everyone agreed with this etymology. Compared to the first two types it appears to be rare. Like *makrā*, this type can be created in a ritual—known as *uṣa*—which is performed by those Gauḍ known as Goṭhiā Gauḍ who herd buffalos in the jungle. Some said that the ritual takes place every Tuesday between *Nuā Khāi* and the full moon of the month of Āśbina, but the Goṭhia Gauḍ I met perform it only four days before the full moon of Āśbina. During the ritual the Gauḍ sit in front of a tree, for example a *sal* tree, and boil rice in a pot or *hāṇḍi* that they turn upside down on a rope made of straw (*bentiā*) lying on the ground. On top of it a winnowing basket is placed, also upside down. Above the basket there is a bow or *dhanu* with several cuts. A bamboo stick known as *jhumkā* with a metal ring on both sides is moved back and forth to make a sound to call goddesses like Manglā, Samlei, or Durgā. Only the Gauḍ family is allowed to touch this sacred instrument if they have taken a bath. The Gauḍ making the music is called *gāhāni*, while a second Gauḍ, usually the eldest, performs the ritual for the gods and enters a trance. At this stage he is called *baruā*, a reference to the goddess in trance. The friendship is sanctioned in front of the *baruā*.

Potential *bensāgar* bring a coconut and *phaklo-liā*, while the Gauḍ who are performing the ritual offer a non-castrated billy goat (*bukā*) and two red cocks. There is a provision here that every year at least two men or two women must become friends. If no one is willing to create a new tie, one of the Gauḍ symbolically creates the friendship with an affine such as his elder sister's husband or wife's sister's husband. This means that Gauḍ can become friends with other Gauḍ provided they belong to other subdivisions (sub-castes), but this seems to be rather exceptional in comparison with other communities and other types of ritual friendship. The tie between affines just mentioned can also be renewed every year if required. But usually there are enough people willing to become friends every year. *Bensāgar* only address each other with this term and usually offer milk to each other if they meet.

KNOWN CASES OF BENSAGAR FRIENDSHIP

Gauḍ (Nangauḍ)	Gaṇḍ
Gauḍ	Aghriā
Gauḍ	Kultā
Gauḍ	Kisān
Gauḍ	Muṇḍā
Gaṇḍ	Luhurā

Sahi

This particular form does not seem to be very common nowadays, though it was certainly more important formerly. In one case I found that an Aghriā girl had become *sahi* to a girl from a Gaṇḍ family. While the Aghriā belonged to a wealthy landlord or Gauntiā family, the Gaṇḍ girl was a daughter of the local *jamindār*, who owned the village of the Aghriā landlord. This tie had been created around fifty years ago after a rumour that a cholera epidemic was imminent and that only families with *sahis* would be saved from it. This story was later confirmed by a case of a Kisān having created a *sahi* friendship with a Bhuyān for the same reason, and by a similar case of an Aghriā man who became the *sahi* friend of a Brahmin after hearing a rumour that 'if you do not become *sahi*, you will be infected by cholera'.

Only families of the same size can create such a bond. For example, in the first case described above the two families each had ten members at that time. However, the families are tied together by just one child or friend each; not all family members have to become *sahi*. Again a Brahmin performs the ritual. *Sahi* feed each other and exchange gifts, usually clothes. The Aghriā and the Brahmin exchanged a coconut and a *dhoti*. The friendship is expressed every year by invitations on the day of *Nuā Khāi*, the eating of the first rice. *Sahi* only call each other *sahi*, never by their individual names. No hierarchical distinction is made between them. Veiling in front of the *sahi*'s husband is not required, unlike *mahāpraśād* and *makrā*.

KNOWN CASES OF *SAHI* FRIENDSHIPS

Brahmin	Aghriā
Aghriā	Gaṇḍ

Gaṇḍ	Kumbhār (potter)
Bhuyān	Kisān
Kisān	Chamār

The *sahi* type is apparently known among the Birhor too, since it is mentioned by Roy (1925: 530). According to him it is only created between married women who have the same number of sons. Roy suggests that the Birhor may have borrowed it from the neighbouring Oraon. The Khaḍiā (Roy and Roy 1937: 161–2) seem to practice it as well.

Karamdāl

The name for this form of ritual friendship may be derived from *karam* 'destiny' and *dāl* 'twig'. On the other hand it may be a reference to the fact that the friendship can only be created during a festival for the goddess Karamsāni, who many are convinced is a form of Durgā. There are actually two festivals for her. One, *bamhān ḳarmā*,[59] is performed in the month of Bhādraba, which is associated with the desire for a good crop.[60] The other, held around *Daśarā* and just known as *karmā*, is combined with *puo jiūntia* and is associated with the desire to have children. It is this one that offers the opportunity to form ritual friendships. Here the ritual is usually patronized by a married but childless couple who celebrate the festival in seven years. While the main part of the ritual takes place in the evening and at night,[61] ritual friendships can be created the following morning. The two friends feed each other *praśād* —offerings left by the goddess, here a small bowl with *phaklo-liā* (parboiled rice heated on sand) and *guḍ* (sugar cane juice)—in front of the altar of Karamsāni, which is represented by a *karam* twig that was brought in procession the day before. Friends call each other *karamdāl* from that time on. In former times *kharcha* (the raw ingredients for a meal) were presented to *karamdāl* friends on *Nuā Khāi* and *Rākhī Pūni* (full moon in the month of Śrābaṇ). However, nowadays this is less strictly observed.

KNOWN CASES OF *KARAMDĀL*

Aghriā	Luhurā
Gandā/Harijan	Chamār

Roy (1925: 29–30; Roy and Roy 1937: 161–2) reported the same type of friendship among the Birhor and Khaḍiā. In these cases two men intending to become friends present each other with a *karam* (*Adina cardifolia*) leaf as well as a piece of cloth, while two women give clothes to each other. *Karam* friends do not use the wood of *karam* trees for firewood. Among the Santal too, according to Troisi (2000 [1979]: 142; also Mukherjea 1962 [1939]: 149), two boys or two girls might enter into a 'life-long friendship' during the *Karam* festival. Troisi notes, 'The alliance . . . is brought about by the parties . . . exchanging *karam* buds and fixing them in each other's hair in the presence of the villagers gathered for the festival. Besides linking two friends who promise each other mutual economic assistance . . . the alliance also puts each one of them into a new relationship with the other's family.'

Sahyā and Baula

A *sahyā* friendship bond may be created by bringing a mango twig (*ām dāl*) to the house of the potential friend, or rather by placing the twig above the entrance of the friend's house. If the friend agrees to the proposal, a day is fixed when the relationship is established formally in the presence of relatives, at which time the friends feed each other with *chuḍā* (flattened rice) and henceforth call themselves *sahyā*. Again a *sahyā* must belong to another community, according to some people a community from whom the friend can accept water. This form is open to women as well as men, that is, men might become the friends of other men, etc. Veiling in front of the *sahyā*'s husband is not obligatory. If the *sahyā* dies, no ritual need be performed at the house of the friend, who should nevertheless attend the funeral in the *sahyā*'s own house. The pot to boil rice is not replaced (no *hāṇḍi pakā*). This form may not be as common as the others. I only found one case of a Khaḍiā man and a Kisān who were *sahyā*. Interestingly the Khaḍiā was a Christian.

Yet another form of friendship, called *baula*, is only possible for women in the month of Phalgun. The friendship, which is symbolized by mango flowers, is not very common in the region, and I found only one case, between a Khaḍiā and a Kisān. A teacher performed a little ritual for which a coconut and some incense were required. Again the friends call each other *baula*. The parents of a *baula* are called *mita-buā* and *mita-mā*. This form is said to be more popular around Cuttack, particularly among *Adivasis* there.

KNOWN CASES OF *SAHYĀ*

Kisān	Khaḍiā

Mita

This form of friendship is generally restricted to people having the same name by birth. People believe that there is a special link between those who share a name. However, the common name is also abandoned in favour of *mita* 'friend'. A Brahmin might perform a little ritual to underline the friendship, but in other cases people regard each other as *mita* just because of their common name . They may also address each other as *mita*, with or without a ritual. As in the other forms *mita* must belong to different communities. The *mita* friendship constitutes a relationship between equals comparable to brothers. However, unlike genealogical brothers difference in age does not matter: there is no distinction between elder and younger brother.

It is not quite clear whether women can become *mita* in the setting I experienced, but in the case of the Birhor (Roy 1925: 530) it is quite explicit that any namesakes may become friends, whether they are women or men. The same friendship was also noted by Roy and Roy (1937: 161–2) among the Khaḍiā.

KNOWN CASES OF *MITA* FRIENDSHIPS

Aghriā	Gaṇḍ
Aghriā	Bandhari (barber)
Aghriā	Kisān
Gaṇḍ	Muṇḍā

Ties of dharma *kinship as intergroup relations*

There is a way of forging ties between men and women who are excluded from ritual friendships. Such *dharma* bonds are, however, clearly based on kinship patterns: that is, the usual terms of address and reference are used, but the word *dharma* may be added. I came across cases of new relationships of this sort not only among the Aghriā, but also between Aghriā and Mawarí or between a Brahmin family and a girl from a Christian family. There seems to be a particular tendency to use this form to adopt daughters or sisters into families in which only sons were born, because the relationship between a brother and sister is particularly significant, for example in rituals such as *Bhāi Jiūntiā* and *Rākhī Pūni*, in which the brother-sister relationship is emphasized, and sisters worship their brothers by praying for their well-being. The *dharma* brother and *dharma* sister relationship can be established on *Rākhī Pūni*. Later these brothers and sisters may celebrate *Bhāi Jiūntiā* too—and in fact a *dharma*-sister should, many people say, be invited to *Bhāi Jiūntiā*—but the relationship cannot be created on *Bhāi Jiūntiā*.

New intragroup and intergroup ties, and even inter-religious bonds, may be established through *dharma* kinship, but the relationship is different from adoption because *dharma* children do not live in the household of their adoptive relatives. The spatial separation continues. On the other hand these relationships also seem to be looser in a legal sense, because in contrast to *posya* adoption there is no formal right to claim a share of the property, and there seems to be no formal recognition by the *jāti*, nor is any ritual required. The relationship with *dharma* children seems to be based first and foremost on personal sympathy and is often seen in a very emotional way. However, this tie is not a purely private matter and has a special status in a society that views itself as a whole kinship network. The relationship is acknowledged by both sides or families, who refer to each other as *dharma* brother and *dharma* sister, or sometimes simply as brother and sister. As my interlocutors pointed out, under certain circumstances *dharma* kin can fulfil the traditional functions of biological or *posya* children, for example by lighting the pyre of the deceased at the time of death. Furthermore, once such a relationship is established, there is an obligation on the partners to invite each other to formal occasions like marriages as a demonstration of the special relationship.

KNOWN INSTANCES OF *DHARMA* KINSHIP

Aghriā	Aghriā
Aghriā boy	Brahmin girl
Brahmin boy	Christian girl

Other forms of ritual friendship in the region

Apart from the examples of ritual friendship just described and slightly different forms in the south of Orissa, which will be considered below, there are several other forms of such ties in the wider region. Roy (1999 [1928]: 140) mentions 'ceremonial friendship' among the Oraon (Oram), marriage between the two families is prohibited if two boys enter into such an 'artificial relationship', even if the families belong to different clans. Among the Birhor, Roy (1925: 29–30) came across another type of friendship known as *ganga jal* (*jal* = water), which can be created among women only by splashing each other with water from a river or drinking water from the same pot (*lotā*). Such friendship is also common among the Santal (Mukherjea 1962 [1936]: 149). Roy (1925: 532) also observed that such friendships, in their various forms, are as real and sacred as actual blood relationships and include the observance of ceremonial pollution after birth, death, etc.

Choudhury (1977: 63–4, 68–9) found a form of ritual friendship among the Muṇḍā known as *sangi* or *sahiya*, which he calls ritual kinship. '*Sangi* relationship exists between two young men of about the same generation and age not necessarily related by blood or marriage. Sometimes, though I have no concrete case, it may be established between a Muṇḍā and a Hindu' (ibid.: 68). This life-long relationship, often created between members of different lineages or 'cousins', is sanctioned by an exchange of clothes and drinking of rice beer in the presence of lineage members. Henceforth the boys use the term *sangi* for each other. The *sangi*'s father is addressed as *sangi-apu*, and *sangi* should invite each other on ceremonial occasions.

Among the Birhor one also finds the *phul* (flower) friendship, arranged by two men putting flowers behind each other's ears, while two women may put the flower into each other's hair. Henceforth friends call each other 'my flower' and swear eternal friendship to each other while mutually feasting and clothing (Roy 1925: 528). This same type is also practised among the Santal. Troisi (2000 [1979]: 142) mentions that *phul* friendships can be created during another festival (*Sibrat Mela*), as can *Baha Phul* friendships[62] among girls and *Jom-nu Gate* among boys, in which there is no obligation to provide economic assistance and no relation of kinship. However, he does not give any further details. Various other forms could be added, for example among the Birhor (Roy 1925: 529) there are *jitia dair*, a type created among boys only, who put a *jitia* leaf behind each others ears, and *jawa dali*, in which girls put a shoot of barley behind each other's ears.

According to Mohanty (1973–4: 132), among the Gadaba a friendship known as a *babu* relationship can be established on a personal level between boys and girls during adolescence. Thus at least among the Gadaba ritual friendship does not appear to be restricted to the same sex. This is again in striking contrast to the converging tribal and caste society I mentioned earlier, in which ritual friendship can only be created between two men or two women, never between a man and a woman. The sexes remain separate, and there is no ritual friendship between them. Only *dharma* kinship can be established between different sexes.[63]

Ritual friendship and the question of levels

As already indicated, there is an astonishing multitude of forms of ritual friendship within this converging tribal and caste society. Roy (1925: 532) argued that the Birhor had borrowed *mahāpraśād* friendship from their Hindu neighbours and *sahi* friendship from their Oraon neighbours. However, I am not in a position to identify the origin of these types of ritual friendship. Tribal communities like the Birhor may have been influenced in this regard by Hindu immigrants or their tribal neighbours, but they could also have had an impact on Hindu peasants.[64] In any case, the sheer variety of forms is significant and constitutes an important arena of interaction contributing to the mutual influence of castes and tribes. Perhaps even more important than the question as to whether Hindu newcomers have influenced an original tribal population[65] or vice versa is the recognizable difference between north-west and southern Orissa in terms of who may create ties of ritual friendship.

Among the Gadaba, according to Mohanty (1973–4), on the one hand there are personal ties of ritual friendship known as *maitar* or *sangat* among men and *baula* among women, which might be created by eating from the same plate during *Pusa Paraba*. In such cases the terms *maitar* or *sangat* are used instead of individual names. Such ties resemble those described already. On the other hand—and perhaps more importantly—there are much more enduring relationships between different clan divisions or lineages in various villages, which are also known as *moitr* (Pfeffer 2001: 137) or *mahāpraśād* (Mohanty 1973–4: 132, 137). Such inter-clan or inter-village links go beyond the rather personal links described above, and seem to be absent in the context of north-west Orissa as I have described it. To stress this point once more, among the Gadaba (also Berger, personal communication), among the Kond (Bailey 1960: 40)[66] and Dongria Kond (Hardenberg 2002a) ties of ritual friendship can be created between clans, while among the Aghriā ties of ritual friendship between different Aghriā clans (*banśa*) are explicitly prohibited. However, this does not mean that Gadaba may not become the ritual friends of other communities, that is, above clan level.

Common to all cases is the fact that ritual friends must belong to different segments. Among the Gadaba and Dongria Kond, but apparently also among the Birhor, Munda, and Oraon, as Roy and Choudhury report, as well as among the Santal or Gaud, such segments might be clans, lineages, local lines or villages. Thus ritual friendship appears to be a way of cutting across existing segments and caste and tribe boundaries, or even religious barriers between Christians, Hindus, and Moslems. Therefore, ritual friendship seems to demonstrate the segmentary structure of tribal society in southern Orissa and Chhotanagpur. In the north-west, however, the lower levels of segmentation such as clans are apparently excluded from forging bonds of ritual friendship, this indicating a transformation of the segmentary structure itself and perhaps a process of substantialization. Only different communities may be related on a personal level through ritual friendship ties. Bonds below this level, like the sorts of collective ties of friendship found among the Gadaba and Dongria Kond, are either completely unknown, as in the case of Aghriā, or may have only a rather residual place in tribal groups in this transitional society.

RITUAL FRIENDSHIP: IDENTIFICATION AND HIERARCHY

Ritual friends are said to help each other and to share everything. Some people even joke that they may share their wives too, which, however, would be in sharp contrast to the rules of avoidance applied to a friend's wife. The creation of a network of mutual reciprocity led Mohanty (1973–4: 131, 151) to argue that the function of these friendship ties lies in achieving integration and resolving conflicts by creating security and mutual love. This appears to correspond to Pfeffer's (2001: 137) observation concerning Gadaba ritual friends (*moitr*):

> If they [moitr or 'co-operative agnates' as Pfeffer has termed them] chance to meet their bond-brothers they bow down deeply in mutual devotion. Love, nothing but pure love, is expected from and given to the moitr. They will never demand a buffalo [during the gotr funeral], but their alter egos will surely provide for them.[67]

Taking into consideration Sahlins' characterization of a tribal society as one in a condition of latent war, one may regard forms of ritual friendship as a kind of peace treaty in addition to, or combined with, other forms of exchange embodying tribal wisdom. Within tribal society there may have been a need for newcomers like the Aghriā to find allies or at least to ensure neutral cohabitants were not hostile towards them, not only within the village, but also in inter-village relations. Certainly such an approach seems plausible, and the successful integration of the Aghriā and other communities into a new mixed tribal and caste society may have been a consequence of their ability to create ties with other communities. However, Nayak (1989: 44)[68] has also pointed out, in relation to the Dongria Kond, that friendship ties between segments such as clans might result in envy in other segments—thus friendship ties might even be counter-productive to harmony. In other words, ritual friendship ties may link certain segments without altering the overall segmentary structure.

Thus, without denying the integrative potential of ritual friendship and the idea of bridging gaps within a segmentary structure, there might be another explanation for the multitude of forms of friendship. Many people like Troisi (2000 [1979]: 142) argue that a tie is created between friends as brothers or sisters respectively. But, as it has been already stressed, in contrast to brothers in the kinship network, in which a difference of biological age is usually translated into a difference of status, such distinctions simply do not matter among ritual friends. Friends, who are often of the same biological age, are equal in status with respect to each other. Their social status or the rank of the community they belong to does not matter in their own affairs. The relationship between brothers might be very similar in many respects, but nevertheless it is not the same. Avoiding a friend's wife may hint at a kinship relationship with a younger brother's wife, who has to be avoided similarly. Such avoidance implies agnatic ties between ritual friends. However, avoidance between ego's father and a friend's mother, or vice versa, rather resembles an affinal kinship relationship between ego's father and wife's mother. Ritual friendship therefore combines elements of affinity and agnation and should be viewed rather as a separate category. Perhaps even more importantly, ignorance or the prohibition of individual names—in all the forms described, friends address each other only according to the type of friendship, for example as *makrā*, etc.—seems to indicate a tendency to equalize and avoid hierarchical connotations. Thus, ritual friendship implies 'total identification' (Pfeffer 2001: 138), a certain 'depersonalization, or the ideal of the merger of friends, as in the case of *mahāprasād*, whose life-spirits (*jiban*) have become one. I therefore argue that ritual friendship—not being expressed as a relationship among brothers—should also be understood as countering the hierarchy established in other fields. Just as hierarchical distinctions are balanced in the kinship sphere, as Dumont (1983: 168) suggested, ritual friendship might play a similar role in village relations.

This, however, should not imply an absence of hierarchy. Firstly, forms of ritual friendship do not embody the same sacred character. Comparing the various types of ritual friendship one notices that some—like *mahāpraśād*, *sahi* or *sahyā*—can be forged on every day while the others like *makrā*, *bensāgar*, or *karamdāl* can be created only during religious festivals usually held once a year. Almost all forms of friendship are sanctioned in front of gods—either present during a festival or invoked in rituals performed by priests. Therefore I agree with Hardenberg (2002a) that all these personal ties of ritual friendships have a sacred character—my choice to term this phenomenon as ritual friendship has been meant to underline this—but sacredness appears to be ranked. There is a clear difference between *mahāpraśād* and all other forms. *Mahāpraśād* is the most sacred and irreversible, since the *jiban* or the life energy of both friends has merged. While a *mahāpraśād*-friendship simply cannot be dissolved, it is unlikely that any other ritual friendship would break up either. Thus, the forms of ritual friendship are hierarchically ranked as shown in Table 10.

TABLE 10: FORMS OF RITUAL FRIENDSHIP AND THEIR SACRED CHARACTER

Type of ritual friendship	Formal/sacred character—hierarchical position
mahāpraśād	most/highest
makrā *bensāgar* *sahi* *karamdāl* *sahyā/baula*	medium
mita	least/lowest

Secondly, in some high castes like the Aghriā the number of friends from lower status communities is rather limited, for status considerations. Though my sample is rather limited (Table 11) it shows that most friendship ties are forged between communities highest in status or *bal lok*[69] in a narrow sense (16 cases) as well as between high communities and lower communities (16 cases), but only rarely between lower communities and 'Untouchables' (2 cases). The Aghriā-figures (in brackets) may show an even more pronounced preference for ritual friends belonging to other high status communities rather than lower status communities—though it is quite possible to become a ritual friend of an 'Untouchable'.

TABLE 11: FRIENDSHIP TIES AMONG VARIOUS STATUS CATEGORIES

Hierarchy/ Status category	Upper communities	Lower communities	'Untouchables'
Upper communities	16 (9)	16 (4)	1 (1)
Lower communities	16 (4)	2	2
'Untouchables'	1 (1)	2	1

Such a finding clearly contradicts Choudhury's argument (1977: 68-9) that friendship should be understood as a concession to the individual in a close-knit, kin-based society. Though there is a degree of personal choice, this is also limited by the culturally determined forms. Although two friends form a new relationship in many cases, this does not mean that an individual decision is necessarily involved. Often the parents might be more interested in arranging a new relationship via their children. Thus ritual friendship is not limited to two individuals, but also includes wider families as expressed in forms of address like *mita ma* (friend's mother) or *mita buā* (friend's father) for the close relatives of the friends. This is perhaps most clear in *sahi* friendship: two families identical in size are connected via one of their respective members.

Moreover, although friends are equal in many respects, this does not mean that restrictions regarding food are no longer valid in inter-community relations. Although ritual friends can feed each other *praśād*—and in fact the bond is created through the sharing of food—they cannot disregard the regulations of the communities they belong to in everyday life. On important occasions like *Nuā Khāi* or *Rākhī Pūni* friends might send each other raw food as a sign of their special bond, but usually they are not allowed to share cooked food. Thus hierarchy invades the sphere of friendship.

Besides, the idea of sharing everything among ritual friends—you give to your ritual friend something of whatever you have—is noteworthy, since it hints at the idea of a pure gift and of generalized reciprocity in Sahlins' terms (1965: 147). Ritual friends are specially cared for, and the greatest hospitality is shown to them. They usually do not demand anything, but they also know that a wish could never be refused. Therefore, apart from the balancing effect of ritual friendship in regard to an evolving hierarchy of ritual purity, ritual friendship may also have a certain counter-effect on, and stand in contrast to, the redistributive systems that have been established in a mixed tribal and caste society.

Summary

In the transitional tribal and caste society of north-west Orissa, a multitude of types of ritual friendship can be found by which castes as well as tribes are linked on a personal level. Various forms like *mahāpraśād* or *makrā* can be created during religious festivals or by eating *praśād*. Compared to kinship and ordinary friendship, these relationships combine elements of both in a unique way and should therefore be considered a separate category. Ritual friends are depersonalized by losing their individual names or merging their life-energies (*jiban*). They are identified with one another and are equal in their own affairs. However, not only are the forms of ritual friendship themselves hierarchized, with *mahāpraśād* being the most sacred, but hierarchy invades the sphere of ritual friendship, first because commensality among ritual friends is restricted to the religious sphere and to food left by the gods, and secondly because hierarchical considerations may determine the selection of ritual friends.

In contrast to the north-west, forms of ritual friendship among the tribal communities of southern Orissa and Chhotanagpur are not limited to personal ties created between communities in the sense of castes or tribes, or even religious communities, but may also exist as collective or personal ties between clans, lineages, and villages. Segments of these lower levels might be combined by ritual friendship corresponding to the segmentary structure of tribal society. However, such structures appear to be quite absent in the converging tribal and caste society of the north-west, suggesting that ritual friendship may have been changed, transformed in a limited way or adapted to personal inter-community links in this context. However, one reason for its immense popularity might be also its balancing effect with respect to evolving hierarchies on the tribal border.

3.5. RELATIONS FORMING A VILLAGE NETWORK

The village seems to be kept together by various relations connecting several categories—not only families, but also tribes and castes as well as religious communities. Some of these relationships, such as the services of the Brahmin and barber seem to separate or hierarchize parts of the village, while other links, such as ritual friendship, seem to equalize or unite otherwise unrelated or particularized categories. However none of the relationships introduced here simply distinguishes or identifies categories—no relation simply hierarchizes or only equalizes. Therefore, in the Figure 4 I speak of tendencies, since in all these networks neither hierarchy nor the aspect of unity or equality is absent.

The equalizing aspects of the ritual friendship such as mutual reciprocity and respect and avoidance of individual names have been underlined and will not be repeated here. It has been noted, however, that rules of commensality and marriage remain. Thus, friends in some respects become equal, in others they do not. In the same way

Hierarchy/ Separating tendencies	- FOOD TRANSFER - SERVICES OF BRAHMINS, ETC. - OCCUPATION	- VILLAGE AS 'FAMILY' - MYTHO-LOGICAL LINKS - SELLING OF CHILDREN	- RITUAL FRIENDSHIP	**Unity/ Equalizing and merging tendencies**

Figure 4: Systemization of village relations.

mythological relations may hint at a brotherhood between certain communities—each one nevertheless insisting on being the elder brother and thus, higher in status. Or a mythological marriage relationship is constructed by one community, but denied by the other community involved. Furthermore, although the village is imagined as a kinship universe or as family within the kinship network, certain relatives have to be respected and avoided, while others are ideal joking partners. The kinship sphere is not free of hierarchical relations either. The sale of children establishes or reinforces a hierarchy of purity in a way, in which higher caste people are temporarily lowered and additional material wealth is redistributed from relatively richer to relatively poorer communities and families. Although there is a close link between occupation and hierarchy, the occupational separation, to some extent also unites the village. For example, the Gauḍ, as cattle herdsmen, enjoy a very high status, but work—at least theoretically—for the whole village insofar as they take care of all cattle and deliver certain messages to all communities. Thus they represent the village community. Finally, even the food transactions—certainly ranking the communities—contribute to the integration of and communication between parts of the village. The raw food distributed at the time of death among all families in the village is a case in point, but, again, certain high status communities must produce and distribute it in order to be accepted by all communities.

Thus, hierarchy is an omnipresent value in this mixed society. The village hierarchy resembles known caste hierarchies, but is, apparently, expressed in a tribal idiom, the opposition of senior and junior, though it is applied in a relative manner showing a synthesis between tribal and caste society. Also, tribal communities are integrated into the hierarchy on various levels—the Gaṇḍ and Kandh on a high level, but the Muṇḍā or Kisān, only on a low level. Thus, the local example exhibits a significant incoherence within the administrative category of Scheduled Tribes.

Finally, food plays a major role in the establishment of relationships and identifications. For example, ritual friends create their special bond by feeding each other *praśād* in a ritual context—an identification of a permanent character. In the case of selling children, they usually eat at least once in the lower status family into which they have been sold. Apart from these attributes, a temporary identification is achieved by sharing the same food, and precisely these possible identifications are avoided by refusing to accept water or various forms of rice from communities of lower rank.

NOTES

1. The Aghriā themselves belong to the category OBC.
2. In the village, however, I have not heard the name Kunhar, translated by Mohanty as 'hill men'.
3. Modern electric water pumps have rendered the service of Gauḍ as water carriers unnecessary in many cases—though in some households they are still used for this purpose. While in the village where I stayed water pumps have replaced Gauḍ for some time already, it could not be clarified if Gauḍ would offer their services during mourning periods or at times of impurity immediately after birth until a household has been purified and reintegrated into the community. I suspect that they either would have rejected this or that wealthy landlords would have paid an extra amount of money to the Gauḍ in case their caste members would have excluded them for continuing their work after death. This money might then have been used for the reintegration of the Gauḍ.
4. On 'Goudo' in Koraput see Berger (2002: 68). They appear to share many features with Gauḍ in Sambalpur district.
5. For the numerical strength of the communities see Chapter 1.3, Table 1.
6. There is some ambiguity concerning the classification of Keunṭ. I was told they had been initially classified as OBC, but changed to SC later, and then recently shifted back to OBC.
7. Kol is used in Sambalpuri, while Kolha is seen as a corresponding Oriya term.
8. A mixture of various herbs essential to produce rice beer (*kusnā*).
9. Such as *patar kandā*—a root that tastes similar to potatoes.
10. Māḷi appear to correspond to the Maraar described by Gell (1992: 70ff) for Bastar, where they live in close proximity to Muria (Gond), but enjoy a higher status than the Muria abstaining, in contrast, from alcohol and beef

consumption. On Māḷi as gardeners in Koraput see also Berger (2002: 65).

11. Apart from the Gaṇḍ, certain schools sponsored by Hindu nationalist organizations are encouraging their students to wear sacred threads—apparently in an attempt to bring them into the Hindu fold. Thus one may occasionally encounter Kisān students of such a school wearing a sacred thread, but this is an exception.
12. This relates to the myth according to which Kshatriyas were born of the shoulder of the first man.
13. In the case of Chamār such a suspicion is almost taken for granted and not worth mentioning for many Aghriā.
14. The consumption of beef—suspected in the case of Orām and Khaḍiā presently and perhaps practised more openly in former times—is known to be or to have been common in many tribal communities. Fürer-Haimendorf (1979: 368ff) describes the sacrifice of a cow as an essential part of a funeral among the Gond of Adilabad in the 1940s. Visiting the same area 30 years later he noted that the cow as a sacrifice had been replaced by a goat indicating an intrusion of Hindu values in a tribal area.
15. As the Orām in the village refused to bury the person, in the more recent case Orām of a neighbouring village were persuaded. They were paid a considerable amount of money from the village fund.
16. On conflicts with Brahmin—specifically between Gond and Brahmin—see Pasayat (1998: 97).
17. There has been no Ghansiā family in the village at the moment after the only family left some years ago. However, the villagers are quite clear about their rank, as this family had done work considered to be that of the Chamār: removing dead cattle. However, they gave up this work, after a Chamār family had arrived in the village. Since then their contact with leather has been restricted to their drums.
18. The English translation was given by my local interlocutors.
19. Roy (1925: 26) translates Birhor as 'jungle men'.
20. They are classified as Scheduled Tribe.
21. Both—*sān* and *choṭ*—mean 'small' or 'junior', but significantly the Aghriā seem to make a distinction here.
22. According to an elder Aghriā in former times the Dossondhi did not use the term *jajmān* for their patrons as they do now. However, this Aghriā did not remember any other term used at that time.
23. Even the Harijan, in attempting to avoid contact and work with leather as far as possible, define themselves indirectly via leather.
24. *Chāul* is produced for the landlords by their Muṇḍā, Kisān and Luhurā labourers. Theoretically, it can be produced by any community except the outcastes. It can be accepted at the time of *kām ghar*/funeral from any community, but is usually returned with some money during the same *kām ghar*.

25. Clay-pots or dishes made of clay are not used.
26. Remains of food boiled in water (*bhāt, dāl*) having been in contact with the saliva of a person and fallen on the ground are considered to be *litā*—impure and polluting. In the same way not only the place where the food remains have fallen, but also a person having food remains on his hand is considered to be *litā* and should not touch anyone else as long as he has not washed his hand.
27. Lower communities like Malār, etc., have been omitted here, since they usually do not have prestigious *kansā*–dishes and most higher communities would not accept anything from them.
28. Additionally the Gosain were mentioned in this category.
29. Maraar base their feeling of superiority on an abstinence from alcohol as well as beef. Similarly one can argue, that devotees of Mahima Dharma, a new religious movement in Orissa, may conceive of their abstinence in a similar way (for the value of abstinence among followers of Mahima Dharma in Koraput see Guzy 2002: 259).
30. While marihuana (*ganja*) is usually related to a peaceful atmosphere, its smoking and addiction to it is considered rather low, despite its being offered to Vishnu, Shiva, and Brahma in the context of a Trinath Mela.
31. See publication of Gaṇḍ Samāj, Sambalpur, 1982.
32. The concept of *bal lok* or good people may be of a wider significance for the whole of Orissa and perhaps beyond. For example Schnepel (2002: 272) cites *Vizagapatam district Gazetteers* of 1907, in which *bollo lok*—translated as courtiers—figure as well.
33. This does not include 'Untouchables'.
34. Outside the village the expression *baḍ baḍiā* can be used for people with connections to politicians, powerful officers, etc.
35. *Chot lok baḍpaḍ pāele, hagari gije gīt gāesan.* My translation is rather liberal. The proverb can be translated directly as 'small people, big promise [in the sense of wealth/power], sing songs without washing their ass'.
36. Coming back to the *meriah* the children are a link between the tribal Kondh offering the sacrifice and the Dom or Pano as 'trading caste' (Padel 1995: 9). The Dom and Pano are an essential part of the regional tribal society interacting with the Kondh for a long time, but are also considered Untouchables and therefore implicitly regarded as a caste. However, there is at present no case known to me where children act as a link between tribes and castes.
37. This phenomenon might be of a wider relevance. Eggan (1950: 27) mentioned an adoption of sick children among American Indians, who transfer endangered children to doctors in the hope that they would bring them back to life. However, in my discussion I am unable yet to include material from other parts of the world.
38. For healing experts in tribal society see Otten (2000).

39. Since I conducted my research primarily among Aghriā, the figures for then are naturally higher. However, I have verified my data among the other communities present and included their cases.
40. Marriott (1976: 109) argued that 'what goes on *between* actors are the same connected processes of mixing and separation that go on *within* actors' and stressed the divisibility of the person.
41. I was told by Khaḍiā that it is necessary to be repurchased in order to start the marriage negotiations.
42. Choudhury (1977: 73) notes: 'When the children of a couple die shortly after birth or if they have only girls and boys die after birth a strip of goat-skin (. . .) is tied around the neck of the next child on the sixth day of his/her birth. This is done by a Lohar or Ghasi man after making an offering of a white chicken to the Sing-bonga [supreme deity of the Munda]. It is believed that it will protect the child from evil spirits and help him to grow into a normal healthy being. . . . it is discarded at the time of marriage of the child. Marriage cannot take place without first ceremonial removing the skin. This ceremony is known as *chamargu*.' This hints at a function of the Chamār in such rituals or the Lohar/Ghansi being equated with the Chamār in the rituals.
43. I am referring here to the example of the Sidi documented by Basu (1994).
44. I have left out the Pathān (or Muslims), who are living in very small numbers in the region, but are usually considered to have an ambivalent status. I do not mention the Ludha and Dhobā as I could not gather sufficient information regarding their status. They are not present in villages I visited personally.
45. This Luhurā lives with a Gaṇḍ and has been expelled from his community.
46. Additionally the Chamār told me that they can sell children to 'Untouchables' like the Pāno and the Ghansiā. However, there was no such empirical case in the families I asked and it might have been a way to claim a higher status for themselves.
47. However, in none of the three ways is a child considered to be inauspicious (*aśubha*).
48. Furthermore, Marriott emphasized the aspect of dominance rather than purity in ranking communities. Thus he stated: 'Gaining dominance over others through feeding them or securing dependence on others through being fed by them appear to be comprehensive goals of actors in the system of transaction. Purity and pollution, among other values, are used as expression of achievement towards these goals' (1968: 169).
49. For example see Kulke (2001 [1978]: 5).
50. In the already mentioned case of the Munda (Choudhury 1977: 73) it is not an evil spirit or Yama to be fooled, but rather Sing-bonga: the supreme deity, who is asked for protection.
51. When the landlord went to bring seasonal labourers to his village for

transplanting, the necessity arose to address them. An old lady among them reminded him of another lady in his *māmu*'s village and he addressed her in the same way as *māi* (mother's brother's wife). All relationships were subsequently ordered along this line.

52. The rather low status of the Luhurā nowadays is often related to the former use of leather bellows, which are today replaced by a construction similar to a bicycle.
53. Elwin (1991 [1942]: 12) relates the Agaria to the ancient Asura of the *Mahābhārata*.
54. There are various meanings of the term *bandhu*. It may be translated as affines, but also as friends.
55. See also Pfeffer (2002: 17).
56. Roy (1999 [1928]: 25) also argues that Orām and Muṇḍā share 'some or most of the village gods and spirits', which, according to him, have been borrowed from the Muṇḍā.
57. There is an interesting custom for new-born babies, who should only see certain mushrooms (*bihiḍen chhati*) and the palm tree and its fruits after some mushrooms and fruits have been put behind their ear. The explanation given for this is that the child and the mushrooms or palm tree and its fruits are *mahāpraśād*.
58. In a village where I witnessed the ritual, this *praśād* consisted of a mixture of rice (*aruā*), til (*māghirāsi*), sugar cane (*ākhu*), sugar cane juice (*guḍ*), honey (*mahu*), ginger (*adā*), coconut (*naḍiā*), cardamom (*ilāchi*), cinnamon (*ḍālchini*), clove (*labanga*), clarified butter (*ghī*) and fruits.
59. It is named after a small insect or *bamhān*, which sucks the liquid out of the growing rice. The ritual is meant as a prayer to the goddess Karamsāni to get rid of this insect and protect the harvest.
60. The festival takes place between transplanting and cutting the rice.
61. After constructing a little pond at the entrance, the couple usually go in a procession known as *ankur* (germination) to the jungle to bring a twig of the *karam* tree to an altar set up on the street in front of the entrance of the house (next to the symbolic pond). Before cutting the twig the patron and his wife circle around it seven times. The twig should not fall on to the ground. The couple must fast during the day. The dancing continues the whole night. Some say that a particular type of drum known as *māndal* (Sambalpuri) or *mādal* (Oriya) is required for the dancing. The patron must offer alcohol to all the participants, including the so-called 'Untouchables'. The next morning the dancers walk in a procession through the village to collect money and rice. In former times it was also common to sacrifice animals—non-castrated billy goats (*bukā*) or cocks (*ganjā*)—in the final year of the ritual cycle. The high cost of the ritual often means that it is interrupted after six years or sometimes never completed at all. At the end of the festival every year the patron and his wife bring the twig to a pond.

If another couple want to continue the festival they must bind a thread around the twig seven times to signal their intention to do so. Afterwards the twig is immersed into a river or pond.

62. In Mukherjea (1962 [1939]: 149), the same type of friendship is apparently known as *phul patao*.
63. The *babu*-relationship mentioned, but not described in detail by Mohanty, might be viewed in the context of dormitories, in which there are fixed relationships between young men and women, e.g. *jor* relations as analysed by Gell (1992: 176ff.).
64. It is often assumed that certain characteristics found in tribal society have been taken over from Hindu neighbours. A case in point is the hypothesis of W. Koppers, according to which a separation of tribal communities into two halves or moieties has been a result of Hinduization—one half of the tribe being more Hinduized adopted endogamy in a way castes do. The hypothesis has been criticised by Pfeffer (1982b), who has related a division into halves to a hierarchical order in tribal society constantly distinguishing between 'senior' and 'junior' segments.
65. This does not mean that there has been no tribal migration, and in some areas tribal groups may be newcomers too.
66. Bailey speaks of 'friends' as well as of 'blood-brotherhood' to characterize the relation *tone* among Kond.
67. During the secondary funeral or *gotr* the *moitr* stand in opposition to the aggressive agnates (*tsorubhai, panjiabhai*) as well as to the affines (*bondhu*).
68. Nayak's observation refers to 'drinking friendship groups', which are not identical with ritual friendship, but might be applied to it as well.
69. Communities are considered as *bal lok*/good people or as upper (see also diagram), if Brahmin, barber, washerman, etc., offer their services to them, which they deny to lower communities and so-called 'Untouchables', to whom in contrast to lower communities entrance to temples is denied and who are excluded in many other regards.

CHAPTER 4

The Aghriā as Village Kings

In this chapter I will investigate first the idea of kingship on the village level and describe the role of the Aghriā headmen or 'Gauntiā' as 'village kings'.[1] These village kings have been influential in establishing state-like structures on a tribal frontier—structures of a little kingdom or pre-modern state rather than a modern, Western bureaucratic state. Aghriā Gauntiā have played a crucial role in integrating and transforming a tribal, segmentary or acephalous society into a peasant society, and this chapter provides an example of the 'superimposition of a feudal state on tribal society' (Thapar and Siddiqi 1997 [1979]: 425)—a process, however, in which not only structures of little kingdoms have been imposed, but the peasants-turned-village kings have been influenced by tribal ideas as well.

The second intention of this chapter is to document and characterize the rise and fall of Aghriā as 'village kings' over the past one hundred years. Despite the abolition of the Gauntiā system, they have kept in many villages a privileged position, particularly in rituals. I will depict the notion of kingship on the village level synchronically as well as diachronically, thus attempting to combine an anthropological with a historical approach.

4.1. THE TRANSITION FROM A SEGMENTARY SOCIETY TO A REDISTRIBUTIVE STATE

Tribal society has been characterized by Sahlins (1965) as a segmentary and acephalous society.

> For the indicative condition of primitive society is the absence of a public and sovereign power: persons and (especially) groups confront each other not merely as distinct interests but with the possible inclination and certain right to physically prosecute these interests. Force is decentralized,

legitimately held in severalty, the social compact has yet to be drawn, the state nonexistent. So peacemaking is not a sporadic intersocietal event, it is a continuous process within society itself. Groups must 'come to terms'—the phrase notably connotes a material exchange satisfactory on both sides (Sahlins 1965: 140).

Significantly, the very same condition was encountered by Hardenberg (2002a, 2002b) among the Dongria Kond of Orissa. Gell (1992: 9) also confirms it for Bastar, a predominantly tribal area without considerable influx of Hindu peasants, as in the Aghriā case. The Bastar kingdom was divided into administrative units (*pargana*) which were headed by so-called Majhi or officials hereditarily appointed by the king representing their respective *parganas,* each *pargana* consisting of around fifty villages. In 1977, the Congress Party tried to sway these Majhi for political gains because: it

> was felt that on account of the formality of their office, a Majhi's words would carry weight and influence among the members of the pargana. (Gell 1992: 9)

However, as Gell points out,

> it is misleading to think that direct service in the king's administration and the duties that it implied would lead automatically to the establishment of a personal basis of power and influence. The authority of the Majhi was mostly an illusion; it was not based on any sanctions that he could bring to command obedience. Most Majhi were relatively poor men who could at most count on a show of compliance at public occasions. The Majhi could not violate the supreme and abiding influence of the village council (*bhumkal*). Whatever his own personal opinion may have been, conflict settlements had to be decided in consultation with the local villagers. Indeed usually the village council decided disputes without inviting his opinion. . . . The office of Majhi may have contributed to a certain measure of personal influence in social relationships, and as a man who could supply gossip on the goings on in other villages his presence at drinking parties would not go ignored. But it did not, by itself, give him any rights of command over other men. (Gell 1992: 9–10)

Thus, Gell effectively highlights the autonomy of the tribal Muria under the traditional system as well as the insignificance of kingship—of a distant 'jungle king' (Schnepel 2002). Gell's account may also indicate that some form of supremacy, exemplified by the post of a Majhi—even though apparently relatively powerless, may have internally evolved prior to the arrival of the Aghriā. However, this characterization stands in sharp contrast to a system centred on the Aghriā village kings or other immigrant headmen (Bailey 1960) who command considerable authority, as I will describe in detail below.[2] The quality of authority certainly changed with the establishment of Aghriā-rulership.[3] This Aghriā rule, in turn, changed after Indian independence and the advent of a bureaucratic state replacing the village kings and centralizing authority, and simultaneously introducing democratic principles. I will confine myself here primarily to the transition from a tribal society to a feudal state, but will also briefly indicate more recent changes.[4]

Apart from the condition of latent war in the absence of a political state in tribal society, Sahlins (1965: 141ff), inspired by Mauss (1994 [1950]), distinguishes between two forms of economic transaction: reciprocity and redistribution. While the former describes a 'vice versa' relationship between the two parties, the latter is applied to a centralized collection of resources from members or groups, the 'pooling', and subsequent 'redistribution'—essentially under 'chiefly aegis' (Sahlins 1965: 141). Sahlins further acknowledges Polanyi's (1968 [1957]) influence. Polanyi had previously argued:

> Reciprocity denotes movements between correlative points of symmetrical groupings; redistribution designates appropriational movements towards a center and out of it again. (Polanyi 1968 [1957]: 128)

Dalton (1968), apart from Polanyi another leading figure in the substantivist tradition[5] of economic anthropology, asserted:

> The integrative patterns which do exist widely in primitive economy are (1) reciprocity, that is material gift and counter-gift-giving induced by social obligation derived, typically, from kinship, as is the case with the Trobriand Islanders; and (2) redistribution, the channelling upward of goods or services to socially determined allocative centers (usually king, chief, or priest), who then redistribute either to the subordinates at large by providing community services, or in specific allotments to individuals in accordance with their political, religious, or military status. Redistribution, [has] often [been] accompanied by reciprocity. . . . (Dalton 1968: 153)

Redistribution, in the sense of Polanyi and Dalton (1968), is not totally alien to tribal society but is clearly subordinated to reciprocity, but becomes a dominant principle in a peasant society like the Aghriā. However, the dominance of redistribution does not exclude forms of reciprocity in a subordinate position.[6]

I have cited these classics here not only to argue that the political sphere is indistinguishable from the economic, but because the transitions and processes just described us appreciate the position of the Aghriā Gauntiā as peasant migrants into tribal areas. By clearing the forests and becoming revenue collectors and dispensing justice on behalf of superior kings, they were influential in turning a tribal, landowning population into peasants—or dependant tenants. Thus, the Aghriā played a major role in the 'peasantization' of a tribal population.[7] They established and reinforced a redistributive system previously absent among tribal communities—with the exception of token payments voluntarily offered to 'jungle kings' (Roy 1970 [1912]: 199; Gell 1992: 4). While there may have been 'big men' (Sahlins 1963) in tribal communities in general or Majhi as in Gell's concrete case, the Aghriā have been, and to some extent still are, 'village kings' with authority, which these 'big men' never had. That fact should be kept in mind in the following sections of the chapter that discuss the collection of revenue; obligations towards the Gauntiā or to superior kings; systems of patronage, for example, in rituals; the redistributive aspect as well as the establishment of a relatively more centralized authority.

The 'little kingdom' as a framework

The kind of state set up and embodied by the Aghriā Gauntiā, with its juridical functions, should not be misunderstood as a bureaucratic state,[8] but rather as a 'little kingdom', which—sharing features with highly stratified chiefdoms (Sahlins 1963). It may be located somehow between tribal society, as described by Sahlins, and a bureaucratic state and may fit particularly well in a converging tribal and caste society.[9]

In recent years, these so-called 'little kingdoms' have received some attention. Cohn (2001 [1959]) coined the term and distinguished several levels of the political system, ranging from the 'local level' as the lowest or most basic administrative stratum consisting of local revenue collectors, indigenous chiefs and lineages, up to the imperial level (Cohn 2001 [1962]: 485–6). Between these strata there is hierarchy of rulers using diverse titles. The distinction between 'raja' and 'maharaja' expresses, paradigmatically, the relationship of a 'little king' to a 'greater king'. As Berkemer (1993: 319) pointed out, the 'little kingdom' has to be understood as a relational construct in which the position of the 'little king' is determined by his relationship to his overlord(s), in which he is subordinate, as well as to his subjects, in which he in turn is the overlord himself.

Berkemer (1993: 22ff) follows Wink in stating that the 'little kingdom' is embedded in a wider network of relationships, in which sovereignty is primarily a question of political alliances and is not expressed in terms of a fixed territory. Territories are overlapping and rather 'discontinuous' (Basu 2000: 15). This implies that the size of the territory is irrelevant, and as Dirks (1979: 172), referring to Hocart, observed, the village community can be thus understood as a microcosm or smaller version of the larger kingdom. Schnepel (1997: 263) points out:

> The attributive 'little' does not, at least not primarily, refer to the size of a kingdom or to other measurable criteria. Rather, it denotes a quality of a politico-ritual kind, which is relational, not absolute in character. Indian kingdoms are thus characterized as 'little' on account of the fact that they were standing in subordinate relations to more powerful and, especially, ritually superior kingdoms. These kingdoms, in turn, count as 'great', though they were not necessarily large.

In 'little kingdoms' the ruler did not enjoy a monopoly of the use of force. Cohn stresses that little kings needed the superior kings' authority. Stein (1975: 77) states that the overlord 'demanded submission to his claim of superiority, rather than obedience to his orders'. Authority was in this way derived from ritual sovereignty which was proven by privileged access to, or a position in, the cults of deities. This access was ranked and could not be automatically translated into political power. The king's authority is expressed through the exchange of gifts, superior kings accepting tribute and transferring honours such as titles. As Dirks (1979: 177) writes, 'As decentralized as the little kingdom appears, the king was the symbolic head of the system of redistribution, which even as it allotted rights to local power configurations, underscored the pre-eminence of the king and the king's rights'. Land—or rather the sharing of the king's right to land—played the major role in this subinfeudation and the redistributive process of the little kingdom.

Although the theories of political relations within and between relatively 'little' kings were developed with regard to medieval and pre-colonial kingdoms, they may also be applied to the relations in the princely states of West Orissa,[10] which by and large remained internally intact until the early twentieth century (Berkemer 1993: 321). Ahuja (forthcoming) observes that the British opted for a policy of very limited interference and in 'administrative practice, the British government often rather preferred to leave the country 'closed'. Furthermore, 'despite all rhetoric, the early colonizers' interest in Orissa consisted not so much in 'opening it up' towards 'civilization', the 'rule of law' and 'commerce', but in getting past it and securing control over this strategic region as cheaply as possible' (ibid.). Thus in many cases, existing power configurations were preserved, even 'frozen'—the British maintained their paramountcy (supremacy) and concentrated on upholding a *pax Britannica*.

Digression: the 'little kingdom' of Bamra

Before turning to the Aghriā 'village kings' it seems worthwhile to consider the state at the next level of reference: the Bamra state.[11] Kesri Gang Deb, distant grandfather of the present king, told me the following history of the royal family of Bamra. This family originated in Patna, where they had ruled until defeated by Chauhān around AD 1300. After this event Prince Saraju Deb was kidnapped by Suna Kondh and Kantar Bhuyan. These names indicate an origin amongst two of the most numerous tribes of the region, Kondh and Bhuyan. A transition from tribe to state is already implied in the founding myth of Bamra state, which states that Bamra had no ruler prior to Saraju Deb. The two tribal men installed the first king under a *sara* (*sāhāḍā*) tree—hence his name, Saraju Deb.

This family ruled for 30 generations until the merger with the Indian Union; the present king is of the thirty-second generation. The family history illustrates not only various tribal rebellions within, but also several conflicts with neighbouring rulers. Under the rule of the tenth king Ramchandra Deb, the new capital—now a district headquarters—was chosen and named Deogarh (Degan). (The eighth raja had earlier shifted his capital from Bamanda to Suguda after an attack by Kondh rebels during his *durbar*.)

The oldest part of Deogarh is now known as 'Purana Gad' or old fort. An essential part of Purana Gad is occupied by the temple of Lord Jagannāth—*iṣṭā devtā* or tutelary god of the royal family—around which are built smaller temples of various gods. The main temple in its present form has been built by the king Prataprudra Deb (probably eighteenth century). Later, Basudev Sudhal Deb, built a new palace nearby. To this ruler are ascribed all major and modern improvements of Bamanda state.

The royal family not only claims to be descendants of the Eastern Gangas, but also takes pride in the fact that Mohini Mohan Deb, a younger brother of the twenty-ninth raja, Dibyashankar Sudhal Deb, was adopted by the then Gajapati Mukunda Deb and subsequently became Gajapati himself—establishing close links between Bamra and Puri. The royal family shares with the Gajapati not only the *iṣṭā devī* or tutelary goddess Kanaka Durgā (sometimes also called *kul devī* or *desh devī*), but also the *iṣṭā devtā* Jagannāth as well as other royal symbols like the *shankar* (shell). The two major festivals of the kingdom—*Daśarā* and *Rath Jātrā*—are related to these two gods. Bamra differs from neighbouring feudatory states, where the patronized *iṣṭā devī* is apparently of tribal origin (like Samlei in Sambalpur state, Patneshwari in Bolangir state, Kumari in Bonai, etc.).

Concerning relations with neighbours, the royal annals emphasize that the king of Bonai had been forced to give his daughter to the eleventh raja, while the neighbouring kingdom Rairakhol had been defeated by his successor. Afterwards the ruler of Rairakhol had to appear at the Bamra *durbar* twice a year. Both hint at a superiority of Bamra over her neighbours. However, the twenty-second raja was murdered by a supposed spy from Rairakhol, conveying a continuing conflict between old enemies. Even if Bamra was able to establish superiority over some of its neighbours, apparently it had to accept the superiority of the Sambalpur kings until the British defeated Sambalpur.

The kings sided with the British from early on—notably during the rebellion of the raja of neighbouring Angul kingdom. For his support the British granted the title 'Raja Bahadur' to the twenty-sixth raja of Bamra. Subsequently followed various titles and status symbols such as elephants and cannons. Bamra as feudatory state was grouped with other princely states into the Chhattisgarh Division of the Central Provinces. Then it became part of Orissa. Under the British Superintendent MacPherson a permanent settlement reforming the land rights was introduced in 1927, when the thirtieth and last raja was still a minor. Prior to that land rights were granted for periods between one and five years. The new law recorded the names and rights of the tenants for all time.

As far as internal affairs are concerned, the royal annals mention various gifts of land, or of whole villages, to Brahmins from the first king onwards—not only to his *purohit* brought from Patna, but also to Kanauji Brahmins. Various temples were built and Brahmins invited. Strained relations with some more or less subordinated Jamindār of the kingdom are mentioned, for example the nineteenth king Hadoo Deb is described as having behaved badly with two named jamindār, who took revenge by kidnapping the king's adopted son and coronating him themselves.

The internal structure of the kingdom seems to have evolved around conflicts and was flexible in the sense that in some areas jamindārs were subordinate to the king, but superior to the Gauntiā, while in other areas the king ruled over the Gauntiā directly. One such dispute between the king and his jamindār around a particular village is narrated in the following story:

> At that time, the Jamindār said: 'This is my village!'. When the Jamidār was appointing a Gauntiā, the men of the King [of Bamra] started some riots in the village and started looting the village and, sometimes, even killed people. If the King appointed someone as Gauntiā, the Jamindār's side killed him. . . . Once the King had appointed a Gauntiā—he was killed by the Jamindār's people, who also took the important people of the village with them [kidnapped them]. They looted the village. When they killed the family members, no one would stop them from plundering. Afterwards, they started cooking on the other side of the river . . ., where the Jamindār had a camp. They killed all of a Teli family [the Gauntiā appointed by the King]. Not all of them—they killed the son, the Gauntiā. The old woman, his mother, also died [seeing this].

In another case the king tried to evict a jamindār who did not pay tribute. The latter fought back violently and the king finally settled the conflict by offering him a Gauntiship thus effectively reducing him *to* the level of a Gauntiā.[12]

The relationship between the king, jamindār and Gauntiā seems to have varied according to circumstances. In Jaipur state, under the jamindār of Kolavira, a Naik, controlling some villages, could appoint village headmen. The jamindār could also offer the headmanship directly, and the present jamindār would argue that only he had the right to do so. In neighbouring Bamra under the king of Deogarh either the king or the regional jamindār[13] of estates consisting of twelve to eighteen villages, could appoint headmen for one or a few villages. An elder Gauntiā informed me that the jamindār was a kind of second king in his territory. Similarly, the revenue was either deposited directly in the king's storeroom or the jamindār took it to the king.

The hierarchical relationship between the king, jamindār and Gauntiā was expressed during the *durbar*, where all met once a year or during royal weddings, funerals, and investitures. While the royal family used to sit on golden chairs, silver chairs were reserved for the jamindārs in the first row, and the Gauntiā sat on simple wooden chairs behind them. For weddings, jamindārs but not the Gauntiā received a *yathā* or turban as an invitation. An elder Gauntiā remembers that his father as Gauntiā used to visit the capital three to

Durbar-Hall, Deogarh.

four times a year, on *Daśarā*, on *Rath Jātrā*, and during royal weddings and other royal ceremonies.

A symbolic hierarchy was also articulated in the possession of prestigious animals such as elephants which only the king and jamindār kept. Gauntiā often used to keep certain breed of horses, while traders used to carry their goods on horses of different breeds. Although there were no restrictions on keeping more valuable breeds of horses, usually only the Gauntiā, the king, and the jamindār could afford them. Today, no one keeps elephants or horses and avoid such expenses.[14] In some cases, the king would present special gifts, such as jackets with embroidered names, elephants, or weapons, to jamindār or Gauntiā with whom he was in close contact.

4.2. THE LOCAL LEVEL

The local level within the structure of little kingdoms has attracted much less attention than royal families and their relationship to their overlords. In the following I look at revenue collectors of the Aghriā community and their position within the 'little kingdom' of Bamra in western Orissa. I will argue that these village headmen, known as Gauntiā, might well be understood as 'village kings', who—standing between the 'little king' and their own subjects—as far as possible replicated and still replicate royal functions in a ritual, political or economic sense on the village level. As 'village kings' Gauntiā operate within the same hierarchy or structural relationship to superiors and subjects and maintain structurally very similar systems of redistribution—with the Gauntiā as universal donor at the centre of the village—as well as relations to the gods or goddesses who empower and legitimize them.

Applying the concept of 'little kingdoms' consistently I will argue that structurally the Gauntiā may well be described as king of the village. This does not mean that differences remain between various levels of kings, for example between a Gauntiā and the king of Bamra, as far as the extent of their power, position in certain cults, etc., are concerned. The idea of kingship is embodied in Gauntiā, the raja of Bamra, and in the Gajapati: it is present on all these levels. Following Galey (1990)[15] and Basu (2000) I emphasize that the idea of kingship is alive, despite abolition of the Gauntiā system after Independence. Essential elements of a royal lifestyle as well as a *rājādharma*, the relations to gods and goddesses and the king's wide networks of intercaste relations on the village level, often labelled *jajmani* relationships will be demonstrated—all showing the presence of kingship and continuous ranking.

4.3. THE EVOLUTION AND SPREAD OF THE GAUNTIĀ SYSTEM

Conquering the wilderness: family histories

The king's conquest of the wilderness is a well-known motif in Hindu scriptures (Falk 1973). The wilderness and its inhabitants are conceptualized as antagonists

> 'to be conquered before a kingship can be established. The king-to-be enters the wilderness, often involuntarily, and there completes the conquest that will herald his new role.' Furthermore, 'encounter with the wilderness is largely a kind of test. It must be passed, and the strong and meritorious man passes it, thus demonstrating his fitness for the throne that he seeks' (Falk 1973: 2).

Thus, clearing the forest is a royal function. Royal annals of Middle India, such as the *Langulesvara Itihasa* record how various kings entered the jungles, built towns and turned wasteland into cultivable land. The acquisition of land was a precondition to being a donor of land to Brahmins or temples, and thus to fulfil one's moral duties as king. The migration of the Aghriā into essentially tribal areas and the subsequent settlement by clearing the jungle follows in the footsteps of earlier kings.

A *gaunti*, or 'kingship of the village', and land rights in general could be acquired in various ways, most commonly by clearing the forest. These rights were termed *khuṇṭ katā gaunti*. *Khuṇṭ* stands for the stumps of the trees, which had to be cut (*katā* = to cut) in order to establish a village as realm of a Gaunṫiā. The superior king acknowledged the rights and formally documented them.

This progressive clearing of the jungle as well the social mobility from tenant to Gauntiā is described in the family history of the Gauntiā family of the village Polamora, probably one of the last villages founded in this manner:

The second son Goberdhan Nayak came to the village Sahajabahal at the age of 18 to 19 years in the year 1918–19 and had been doing the work of cultivation of land at Rupees three (Rs. 3/–) temporarily by cooking and eating in the house of Kalo Gauda. As the village Pohalamora was included in Sahajbahal he occupied 20 acres of land. . . . As per the order of Case No. 302 dated 23.08.1924 . . ., he got permission for 1.3 acres and on 25.08.1930 for 60 acres of land at Poholamara village that were in his occupancy and its land revenue was Rs. 23.95 paisa.

The dense forest of that time has been cleared. After selecting this village as per the order of the government, father had named it Pohalamora. . . . Many people were not staying there as Pohalamora village was getting built up. In those days everybody was afraid to go and come anywhere alone because of the tigers and bears. I and my elder sister used to stay in our house at the root of a Sal tree. We used to play by erecting a cottage like those people who spread reef knots to catch monkeys. Father and mother used to work close by. Always there was fear of tigers. . . .

In other cases, the established rights of former tribal headmen were taken over by Aghriā, for example in auctions, after tribal headmen or any headman was unable to pay their revenue dues. Members of the Aghriā Gauntiā family of the village Bandkaney remember that only Muṇḍā and Pāno had lived in the jungle near the village before the Gauntiā family took over. The family had come from Kirmira (25 km to the west of Bandkaney), where they had been *prajā* or tenants themselves, before bringing Muṇḍā and Pāno into the village as *parjā*. By introducing modern technologies and working hard, the Aghriā–Gauntiā were in a better position to pay the revenue and could, in many cases, replace the Bhuyan or Gaṇḍ headmen.

Sometimes land rights were deliberately offered in exchange for money. The following story of the Gauntiā family of Kuānrmāl of the jamindāri of Kolavirā bordering Bamra is a case in point:

. . . the great-great-grandfather took the headmanship of Pakelpaḍa and Chandlimal. Of the three sons the youngest became a storyteller and went back to Bamra state where he later became famous and the king gifted a village (Vikapali) to him. In Pakelpaḍa the family used to grow til, which was sold in Jhaspur [now in Jharkandh—about 100 km away] or exchanged against cotton. This was spun in the family and given to the weavers to produce dhotis. Once elephants destroyed the harvest. Usually the middle brother sitting on a high stand (machā) watched the fields to protect them. However, in this night he was not present—otherwise he might not have survived. The remains of the harvest were sold for 10 Rs and the elder brother offered the money to the middle brother because he survived. This brother—the great-grandfather—went to visit his wife's brother, with the money rolled in his dhoti. Near a pond he met a Gaṇḍ–Nāik who ruled over a few villages under the Jamindār of Kolāvirā. [A Nāik seemed to been positioned between the Jamindār and the Gauntiā and there is a story that seven Nāik brought the Jamindār to this area as ruler.] The Nāik saw him keeping the money and offered the village Kuānrmāl in exchange for it. At that time that village had about five or six houses. The Aghriā Gauntiā got a document from the Nāik designating him as Gauntiā. Some time later the Naik was unable to pay the revenue anymore and lost his rights. Not only that, but together with the Nāik the Gauntiā lost his rights too. After the *bedakhal*—the loss of rights[16]—the Gauntiā went to Sambalpur not knowing what to do. A British administrator recommended going to court in Nagpur to protest, because he had paid revenue regularly. However, Nagpur was far away and there was no train connection. By coincidence he met the Jamindār of Kolavira in Sambalpur and told him about his problem. The Jamindār then, in 1881, decided to offer the headmanship for five years for a hundred rupees plus the revenue. Before the contract could be renewed, a permanent land settlement was fixed and the rights on the land transferred to the Gauntiā. From this time onward the sons could inherit the land. The great-grandfather thus became the first Gauntiā in Kuānrmāl and subsequently brought an Aghriā, a Kisān, and a Gaṇḍ family into the village.

In this story, we find the element of dispersal—the adventurous Aghriā penetrating essentially tribal regions. A list of villages and their respective Gauntiā is appended below. Often fathers took up several *gaunti* for their sons, or elder brothers for younger, etc., thus reaching a regional dominance in the process. The next two passages from Gauntiā family histories of Kuānrmāl and Mundaloi demonstrate this point:

For his four sons the grandfather then tried to acquire more land. He took the headmanship of the village Pitamāl—a small settlement in the forest with 10 to 15 villagers. Robbers attacked the Gauntiā house to steal paddy. A son was wounded in the attack and the village was given up, being regarded as too dangerous. Land—although not the headmanship—was also purchased in the village Barpān: first 17 acres for 35 Rs., later another 8 acres for 100 Rs. Additionally the [adjoining] village of Pakelkol was acquired. All four sons were expected to settle in separate villages—Kuānrmāl, Barpān, Pākelkol, and Pitamāl—to avoid quarrels regarding the inheritance. However, the grandfather died early in 1942 before deciding the division of property.

The Gauntiā family of Mundaloi comes originally from Loisingh—left behind at least a hundred years ago. At the time of Gopinath, the present Gauntiā's great-great-grandfather, the family took up the headmanship of several villages including Kuchinda, Badamundaloi, Jholdihi, Thaisar, Boromal, and Gabaribhal. The gaunti of Badamundaloi was taken around 1910. According to some people in the village there had been another Aghriā Gauntiā before, named Dosrath, who had left the village due to elephants having destroyed his crops and too much water coming from the hills close to the village. According to others, a Brahmin had been the headman, whose son died after an attack by a tiger.

Gopinath's three younger brothers got a village each, respectively Thainsar, Boromal, and Gabaribhal. The other three gaunti—Kuchinda, Jholdihi and Badamundaloi—were kept by the eldest brother, whose samādhi still stands in Kuchinda. His son and the great-grandfather of the present Gauntiā was a wise man, gratefully remembered for building several ponds in the village. His only son could not manage three villages alone. Therefore Jholdihi—originally part of the gaunti of Badamundaloi—was returned to the King. Lack of communication and the threat of tigers added to the problems in these remote areas. The grandfather had three wives and four sons. He was less wise than his father in the number of marriages. As a precondition of marriage his youngest wife had insisted on her son becoming Gauntiā of the small town of Kuchinda—a very prestigious gaunti. The three elder sons got a share each in Mundaloi, the eldest becoming Gauntiā there. The father had already contemplated giving up the gaunti in this far-off village as well—like Jholdihi—, but was convinced against it by his sister's husband Brundaban from Laḍ—another influential Gauntiā and close friend of the King—to keep it though he could not collect the full revenue and had to pay some of it out of his own pocket.

As a Gauntiā could not cultivate all of the land, many Gauntiā, for example the one from Mundaloi, invited other Aghriā to stay in the village and offered land to other communities, for example, the Chamār, who also took charge of the dead cattle. The new tenants cleared parts of the forest and were required to contribute to the revenue. Mundaloi may serve as an example of how other families, particularly the Aghriā, came into the village. In most of these families the grandparents seem to have been the first generation of settlers:

In one Aghriā family the grandfather (FF) was invited to settle by the Gauntiā Dharaṇnidhar who was interested to have more Aghriā families in the village and offered 18 acres of land to the family from Jamankira—a nearby village.

In another case an elderly lady told me that her grandfather (FF) had died

Gauntiā and his family (around 1900).

very young. Her in-laws treated her grandmother (FM) very badly and she decided to return to her brother to Borowahal. This brother (FMB) offered land to his sister's son that he himself had cleared in Mundaloi. Interestingly, the father's mother's brother had come to know about the possibility of land in Mundaloi from a Gaṇḍ family—friends of the family, who had also cleared some forest in Mundaloi. This Gaṇḍ family is still living in the village as one of the most prosperous families and is considered to be a *baḍ parjā*.

In still another family the grandfather (FF) was the first to come to Mundaloi. Around 80 years ago he cleared some forest (13 acres) with the Gauntiā's permission and started to cultivate it. He had come from Kurgā near Sundargarh, where cholera had broken out. It is not quite clear why he had chosen Mundaloi.

An old man of another Aghriā family reported: his mother's brother had cleared part of the forest with the Gauntiā's permission and started cultivating the land (around 14 acres: 13 acres *bāhāl*, 1 acre *māl*). After the death of the mother's brother's children and the early death of the old man's own parents, his mother's brother brought him to Mundaloi, where he inherited the land after the latter's death.

In the case of an Aghriā widow her father-in-law belonged to a prominent family, being the Gauntiā of several villages. It was planned by her husband's grandfather (the widow's HFF) that her husband would become the Gauntiā in Sahasbahal village. However, due to an affair with a woman from a community of snake charmers the husband was disinherited by his family and, after running away with her, excluded from the community. Living in another village with her he went to court for his share in the family property, without success. After twelve years he came alone to Mundaloi where a distant aunt (FyBW—*kāki*) stayed, who offered him five acres. His Aghriā wife, whom he had left while she was pregnant, returned to him and, after giving a feast, he was reintegrated into the community. The family of this distant aunt belonged to one of the most prosperous families in the village (*baḍ parjā*), owning 70 acres in their best days, which had been cleared on invitation from the Gauntiā.

These cases illustrate that Gauntiā, as soon as they had acquired land rights or rights to clear the jungle, started sharing their rights by inviting other members of their own group as well as others to settle and contribute to the revenue, thus reducing their own share.

In the process of settling, the village forest was not only cleared, but two categories of land were further separated. *Gochar* was reserved for grazing cattle, goats, and other animals. It was forest or some *guḍā* land near the forest. *Godandā/godharsā*—animal paths in the forest—were separated out as well. The herdsmen used them as routes to or within the forest. Both categories were closely related to the cattle from which their name is derived (*go* = cow) and could not be transformed into fields. However, today they are occasionally turned into illegal fields due to the scarcity of land. Decisions about this land were made either by a revenue officer or the Gauntiā. These categories of land may have existed in earlier tribal villages. The Gauntiā became the protectors of this land, responsible for maintaining the structure of the village, and, as some have argued, the Gauntiā was or is still the 'controller' of the village.

4.4. SETTLEMENT PATTERN OF IMMIGRANT PEASANTS AND THE ESTABLISHMENT OF VILLAGE HIERARCHIES

Settling in the region

These fragments of family histories offer some insight into the evolution and spread of the Gauntiā system. There was probably no single wave of settlers, but rather individual families of peasants immigrated and spread over several generations. In accordance with their own mythology it is likely that the Aghriā settlers gradually moved eastwards. In neighbouring Chhotanagpur, originally tribally dominated, Schwerin (1977: 123) found a similar gradual influx of Hindu settlers from surrounding districts, actively supported by the maharaja of Chhotanagpur. Rothermund (1978: 4) did not find evidence of a large-scale transfer of peasants from overpopulated areas to cultivable wasteland, but rather saw a spillover from neighbouring areas. Kings like the maharaja of Chhotanagpur encouraged the clearing of jungles and the immigration of peasants in the hope of increasing revenue. To attract settlers and to increase their own income, they offered initial revenue and tax reductions for newly cleared soil.

In a landlord's deed, or *gaunti patā* of an Aghriā Gauntiā issued by the ruler of Bamra, this is expressed in the following way:

> You or any recorded tenant of your village can occupy any wasteland within the area of your village by taking permission of the State, except the revenue land that is measured and is being utilized for pasture (for cattle). If the tenants of your village cannot or will not occupy it, it can be given to tenants of other villages for occupation in the same system, by taking due permission from the State.
>
> Anyone who has occupied such wasteland will enjoy five years without paying rent. Afterwards, until the next settlement, he will pay half the fixed revenue rent and until then you will be enjoying that rent.

Thus the king and the Gauntiā profited from new settlers. A constant influx of settlers increased the density of the population considerably and, according to Schwerin (1977: 48), the population of the feudatory states of western Orissa almost doubled between the censuses of 1881 and 1931. This did not mean, however, that the tribal population decreased absolutely rather only in relative numbers (Schwerin 1977: 63–6).

As long as there was enough land, there seems to have been a 'symbiosis' (Rothermund 1978: 4) between tribal shifting cultivators and the peasants following them and settling permanently. Although I was informed that peasants either cleared the forest themselves or even hired tribal labours for this work, the 'symbiosis' might be explained by a certain similarity between the tribal society and the society established by the new immigrants. Both have in common a differentiation between original settlers and outsiders. Among the Muṇḍā (Roy 1970 [1912]: 64f, 356f), the first were called Khuntkattidar—being the clan or lineage who cleared the forest and owned the land in the village, in contrast to outsiders or relatives who belonged to different clans—sometimes called *parjā*—who may also have stayed in the village, but did not own the land. Thus Roy (1970 [1912]: 64) writes:

> These outsiders were the eta–haturenko (literally, men of other villages) the parja–horoko of later times as contradistinguished from the hatu–horoko who were the Khuntkattidars—the descendants of the original village–family. These outsiders with the exception of such relatives of the Khuntkattidars as might have been admitted into the village–family by a ceremonial public adoption, had no right to village lands but could only enjoy the crops of such specific plots of land as might have been allotted to them by the Khuntkattidars for their maintenance.[17]

Furthermore, Roy (1970 [1912]: 92) noted that rent or nominal tribute to a superior king or landlord had to be paid—at least initially—by the *parjā*, not the Khuntkattidar as the original clearers of the soil (ibid.: 197). A similar system existed among the Orām, where Bhuinhar (people of the soil) as original settlers were distinguished from non-Bhuinhar or people of other villages, who had affinal relationships to the Bhuinhar (Roy 1999 [1928]: 68, 204–5). The Kond made this distinction between the founding clan and immigrants as well (Bailey 1960: 28ff, 78ff).[18] It is likely that many other tribal groups were differentiated into the real 'lords of the land' on the one hand and those groups belonging to other descent groups on the other hand—even though the presiding goddess may be considered the ultimate landowner (Pfeffer 1997: 9). Thus, one finds the following distinctions:

TABLE 12: THE OPPOSITION BETWEEN KHUNTKATTIDAR/PARJĀ AND GAUNTIĀ/PARJĀ

Tribal society (Muṇḍā case)	*Khuṇṭkattidars* (original clan of the village owning the land—clearers of the forest)	*Parjā* (outsiders—cultivating land particularly of their *khuṇṭkattidar*-relatives—paying rent)
Mixed tribal and caste society	*Gauntiā* (newcomers owning the land—having a *khuṇṭ katā patā* designating them as clearers of the forest)	*Parjā* (cultivating land allotted to them by the Gauntiā or for the Gauntiā to whom they are not related—paying revenue—having no rights to cultivate the land as such)

So long as there was sufficient land, conflicts generally did not arise —the Gauntiā as outsiders clearing the forest acquired land rights in a way very similar to that of the Khuntkattidars, these rights were expressed in the same idiom, *khuṇṭ katā patā*. At least for a part of the tribal population, it was not unusual to stay in villages where they did not own land and were of lower status than the 'lords of the land'. However, disputes most likely started with the scarcity of land and the transfer of whole tribal villages to foreign, exploiting revenue collectors—the hated *diku* or foreign landlords in Chhotanagpur (Roy 1970 [1912]: 193, 198ff, 318; Schwerin 1977: 111). There are numerous accounts of such disputes in Chhotanagpur (Roy 1970 [1912]: 115; Schwerin 1977: 111),[19] and it is likely that the transfer of land rights from tribes to new settlers in the villages was not always peaceful. MacDougall (1977) describes movements against peasantization among the Muṇḍā, Orāon and Santal of Chhotanagpur and the Santal Pargana. Peasant social mobility may have also contributed to this social unrest; tenants were becoming wealthy and influential Gauntiā. However, I did not find sources of any specific anti-Aghriā uprising.

By the 1930s the progress of the Aghriā and similar peasant castes had stopped completely, and no new villages could be founded. Schwerin (1977: 28ff; also Fürer-Haimendorf 1979: 543ff) showed that by that time the British had taken measures to protect the remaining forests, for example by passing a law in 1875 declaring certain forests as reserved. By implementing the new laws the process of clearing forests and penetrating the jungle came to an end. Restricted access to forest limited an essential resource of tribal people and stopped a further spread of the Aghriā. This may have accelerated existing tensions between the original inhabitants and the immigrants. Since migration was no longer an option, it also, however, contributed to a converging tribal and caste society.

The establishing of village hierarchies

The founding of villages included the establishment of hierarchies. Apart from that based on the value of ritual purity with invited Brahmins on the top, another hierarchy was expressed in terms of land ownership, the biggest landowners enjoying the highest prestige (*ijjat*). As already mentioned such a close relationship between prestige, dominance, and landownership is found among tribal communities as well—with the difference that in tribal families it is certain clans, not individual families, that exercise dominance (so too among the Dongria Kondh, R. Hardenberg, personal communication). In the mixed tribal and caste society presented here, however, instead of a dominant clan the Gauntiā as king stands in opposition to all his subjects (*parjā*) and is of a higher rank:

Gauntiā as the village-king ←— opposite —→ *parjā*/tenants

The category of *Parjā* (S)/*Prajā* (O) is further stratified internally into *Baḍ Parjā* (big/senior tenants) opposite the *Sān Parjā* (small/junior *parjā*). 'Big tenants' are characterized by a larger share of land. In the case of the village Mundaloi there are three *Baḍ Parjā* recognized as such: a Māḷi, an Aghriā and a Gaṇḍ, who all—at least at one point in time—had aquired property well above 20 acres. *Baḍ Parjā* are expected to actively participate in village rituals such as the *Rath Jātrā*, offering gifts according to their economic position. A Gauntiā's younger brothers, having received a considerable share of the family property, are, in a strict sense, considered *Baḍ Parjā* as well.

The village hierarchy of wealth (*dhan*) and prestige (*ijjat*) is thus formulated:

TABLE 13: VILLAGE-HIERARCHY IN RELATION TO WEALTH AND PRESTIGE

Hierarchy	Prestige (*ijjāt*)	Wealth (*dhan*)
1. Gauntiā	highest	wealthiest (*dāni lok*/rich people)
2. *Baḍ Parjā*		
3. *Sān Parjā*	lowest	poorest (*gārib lok*/poor people)

Sometimes, however, the Gauntiā and the *Baḍ Parjā* are subsumed under the term *baḍ baḍiā*,[20] for example when service communities like the potter describe for whom they work. Comparing different villages, one could further distinguish between *Baḍ* Gauntiā of the prestigious *gaunti* Kuchinda and the Sān Gauntiā of small villages.

4.5. *KHUṆṬ GAUNTIĀ*—A WOODEN POST AS HEADMAN

In some cases, when village headmen or landlords died, were without issue, were poor, or had any other problem, they used to erect wooden posts. These are called *khuṇṭ* Gauntiā by the Aghriā and *khuṇṭ nāik* by the Gaṇḍ and other tribal communities. Thereafter the Gauntiā ruled on behalf of the *khuṇṭ* Gauntiā as a kind of 'acting Gauntiā'. These *khuṇṭ* would be erected in the mostly tribally dominated villages and this may further exemplify a transition towards state structures.

It has been argued that these posts, in form, essentially represent tribal gods or spirits (Roy 1999 [1928]: 10, 16, 50;[21] Eschmann 1994 [1975]: 214, 221; Kulke 1979: 22ff; Mallebrein 2001b; Jena et al. 2002: 204, 214) or that *khuṇṭ* are synonymous with sub-clans or lineages among the Santal (Troisi 2000 [1979]: 30), Orām (Roy 1999 [1928]: 7, 16, 68ff)[22] or Muṇḍā (Roy 1970 [1912]: 361;[23] Choudhury 1977: 33, 38). Thus, one may find an element of Tribalization[24] here on the part of immigrant Hindus. However, rulership and control seem to be equally important—as ancient Hindu texts (Falk 1973: 10ff) also confirm. Some elder Aghriā remembered that, particularly in the British period, people respected the authority of the *khuṇṭ* Gauntiā. If they had any wish, they first offered garlands to the *khuṇṭ*, before doing the same to the acting Gauntiā. Therefore the *khuṇṭ* may also be related to a rather ancient royal customs. In any case, by setting up *khuṇṭ*, Aghriā village kings were enabled to fulfil their state functions.

I will decribe here three cases in which I found *khuṇṭ* Gauntiā and recorded their story. One of these is situated in the Kusmi village, where an Aghriā Gauntiā—the father of the present Gauntiā who is in his late 60s—erected the post about eighty or ninety years ago. His first wife had died without children and all the children from the second wife of the Gauntiā had either been miscarriages or died shortly after birth. As the present Gauntiā remembers, a *bābā*—a Krishna *bhakt*—recommended that his father transfer the headmanship to a *khuṇṭ* in order to get rid of any negative effect. If he would worship the *khuṇṭ* as a Gauntiā, he would be blessed. The Gauntiā followed that advice and the *khuṇṭ* was seated as the real Gauntiā, as a living being but not as a God. The post was carved out of a *Sāl* tree and a special hut was constructed next to the Jagannāth temple to enshrine it. The *khuṇṭ* was worshipped with lamps and incense on all major rituals and festivals. On *Rākhi Bandhā* a *rākhi* was bound around the *khuṇṭ* by the former Gauntiā— now acting on behalf of the *khuṇṭ* Gauntiā—as well as by villagers asking for his protection. Later, a third wife gave birth to six healthy children, thus apparently fulfilling the Baba's prophecy.

After the father's death the *khuṇṭ* Gauntiā became a part of the property of the third son of the Gauntiā who had erected it and died about 30 years ago. The son brought the *khuṇṭ* into his house after the collapse of the hut in order to worship it, but the daily ritual routine was discontinued. Since the son's death the *khuṇṭ* has stood in a corner of the outer room of the Jagannāth temple. The present Gauntiā—the eldest son of the Gauntiā who erected the *khuṇṭ*—is himself childless and has adopted a son. He contemplates throwing the *khuṇṭ* into a pond, because he does not believe in it, but, his *jāti* are against it.

Another *khuṇṭ* Gauntiā was erected in Betjanan village, sixty to seventy years ago—some say in 1936—after several Gauntiā had died. The *khuṇṭ* stands in a separate mud house about 20 meters from the Gauntiā's house, but still on his property. Apart from the *khuṇṭ* the mud shrine is completely empty. People claim that the acting Gauntiā is protected by the wooden post, because Yama is unable to harm it. It is also believed that King Sudhal Dev—most likely the twenty-seventh raja of Bamra—recommended erecting the posts in times of trouble. Of the first four Gauntiā—a Teli, a Gauḍ and two Aghriā—three died of unnatural causes or became mad. The Gauḍ, in fact, died on the way to Deogarh to get the *gaunti patā* (headmanship record). After erecting the *khuṇṭ* problems disappeared. Villagers as well as the Gauntiā's family visited the *khuṇṭ* for special wishes and to offer sacrifices, though no animals, if the wish was fulfilled. Women are allowed to participate in the rituals in contrast to the *Grām Śrī Pūjā* (ritual for the village goddess). The *khuṇṭ* is worshipped by the Gauntiā on *Rākhī Pūni* by binding a *rākhī* first to the *khuṇṭ*. Later, the binding is repeated by the Kālo or sacrificer of the village goddess (until recently Gauntiā and Kālo were one and the same person). On the days of the *Grām Śrī Pūjā* and *Bihuḍā Pūjā*, the *khuṇṭ* is worshipped as well, and soil is brought from the *khuṇṭ*'s location for wedding altars. In the village, the first *khuṇṭ* is still standing, yet to be replaced.

I saw a third *khuṇṭ* Gauntiā in the village Khandabolonda, where the Aghriā Gauntiā informed me that his father was the first Gauntiā ever to stay permanently in the village. Before that, another Aghriā Gauntiā had attempted this but managed to stay for only a few years, and before him several other Gauntiā—probably Gaṇḍ—had died. King Sudhal Dev then recommended the construction of a wooden post to free himself of the evil eye. According to the Gauntiā, the *khuṇṭ* has existed in the village for 200 years already, although it appears to be younger. The Gauntiā told me about a long and severe drought in 1866 that continued for nine years. Therefore the king was interested in bringing more Aghriā into his kingdom because they were well known as good peasants and were able to act as headmen. According to the Gauntiā, the Gaṇḍ forming the majority in the village were not fit to rule in the same manner as the Aghriā. In August, on *Rākhī Pūni* the Gauntiā binds a thread around the *khuṇṭ* Gauntiā to ask for its help and protection. The *khuṇṭ* was carved out of *Sāl* wood in this case as well. From time to time the *khuṇṭ* is renewed, but there is no name for this process. The renewal is celebrated with a ritual for the King Sudhal Deb. Apart from *Rākhī Pūni* the Gauntiā's family also attends celebrations of the birth of children or weddings, taking soil for the wedding altar from the shrine of the village goddess in other villages. The Gaṇḍ also bring soil for their wedding rituals from the *khuṇṭ nāik*. The place of the *khuṇṭ* Gauntiā is known as the *demul* or as a sacred grove and its divine character thus highlighted.[25]

In all cases the element of protection is obvious, that is the protection of life and procreation. Apart from this very apparent motif there may be another more hidden aspect: a wooden post, as the ruler may be more acceptable to a tribal population than an outsider as the new headman. The collection of revenue could not have been easy in tribal dominated areas as in the second village just mentioned, in which the Aghriā Gauntiā was the only non-Gaṇḍ family. Thus, the Aghriā immigrants may have adopted—perhaps via mediation of a higher king—a tribal ritual idiom. Significantly, Troisi (2000 [1979]: 84), notes that among the Santal, the 'spirit' of the headman is actually worshipped:

> As in all Santal villages, this spirit does not reside in the jaherthan [sacred grove] but has a special place built for him facing the headman's house. This is called manjithan [manji = headman]. Here he is represented by a stone at the foot of the central wooden post. He is believed to act as the spiritual adviser to the current headman. In fact, it is the headman himself who is supposed to propitiate this spirit by offering libations of rice beer and sacrificing two pigeons, which are provided by the headman himself. The heads of the sacrificed pigeons are eaten only by the headman. It is believed that through this ritual communication, the present headman derives his authority from his predecessors. The offering of sacrifices to the dead headman of a particular village is a matter of vital concern to the members of that particular village. (ibid.)[26]

The sacred character of the *khuṇṭ* is exemplified not only by such sacrifices, but also by the villagers' worship of it at times of weddings and harvests. In regard to marriages the *khuṇṭ* also shares qualities with the village goddess, from whose shrine soil for the wedding altar may also be brought. Occasionally, the *khuṇṭ* Gauntiā is also seen in opposition to the land of the village or villagers or even as 'husband' of the villagers, but not in opposition to Grām Śrī or the village goddess, because the latter is regarded higher than the *khuṇṭ* Gauntiā.

In the light of ancient royal customs, another interpretation of the wooden post comes to mind. The idea of the *khuṇṭ* as a tribal phenomenon may not be the sole explanation. As Falk (1973: 10-12) noted:

> It is said that the kings of ancient India would acquire glory and victory and prosperity for their kingdoms if they would observe a certain kind of festival. The focal point of the festival is a log, freshly cut in the forest and brought

into town. . . . There it was raised, and the king and townspeople worshipped it with flowers, perfumes, banners, and ornaments. . . . Asoka paid such zealous attention to the tree that it aroused the jealousy of his queen. So she had the tree destroyed by magic. But she discovered in so doing that she had also ruined her husband; for his life declined with that of the tree. (12)

To summarize, the Aghriā Gauntiā erected or took over wooden posts in times of danger to their lives or their lineage. This means that they deified the headman or his lineage by adopting—or sharing in—a ritual idiom from surrounding tribes or from ancient kings, who may have long ago ventured into the wilderness. In any case, incorporating the idea of the *khuṇṭ*, which also symbolizes wilderness and its domination (the *khuṇṭ* is a culturally transformed tree), also helped them establish themselves as rulers in a tribal area and avoid conflict between immigrating peasants and original tribal settlers. Nowadays however, the worship of *khuṇṭ* Gauntiā—and the Gauntiā system as such—appears to be in a significant process of decline.

4.6. THE GAUNTIĀ AS AN AGENT OF CHANGE AND OF HINDUIZATION

The evolution and spread of the Gauntiā system is not limited to the clearing of forests and subsequent cultivation of land but also includes the setting up of temples, inviting Brahmin and offering land to them, building funeral memorials, introducing new technologies and methods, and opening schools at a later stage, etc. To put it differently, in the perspective of the new settlers it is a process of 'cultivating the land' in a wider sense, that includes not only agriculture, but rather what has been called 'intensive propaganda' (Weber 1988 [1921]: 11) or 'inner colonization' (Pfeffer 1978: 426; Kulke 2001 [1978]: 3). 'Civilizing the wilderness' often means donating land to temples and schools, etc., by a Gauntiā who embodies the king as a universal donor (I will elaborate on this theme later). The Gauntiā—the ideal new peasant/settler—was and still is actively involved in an on-going process of change and may therefore be called 'culture brokers'.[27]

Religious change, the Gauntiā as patron

As far as religion is concerned, this process of change has been termed Hinduization (Kulke 1979: 18f; Thapar/Siddiqi 1997 [1979]).[28] It is intrinsically related to the simultaneous process of tribalization, of which the *khuṇṭ* Gauntiā may be an instance.

There are numerous cases in which the Gauntiā contributed to an institutionalization of religion by financing and building temples in their villages. In most cases Śiva and Jagannāth temples were constructed, which should be understood not only in the context of Hinduization, but also as a community service in a redistributive system. As regards Jagannāth, of course, it is doubtful whether one can speak of pure Hinduization, since in his cult tribal elements are still prominent. However, the Gauntiā offered land for the construction and maintenance of temples as well as priests, who were subsequently given land to live on. Of the motives Pfeffer (1978: 423) observed:

> Any power-holder who founded such a settlement of pious men immortalized his name and expressedly appeased an extremely influential elite of ideologists.

The scale of these offerings among Aghriā-Gauntiā was smaller than in the case of superior kings giving entire villages—*śāsana* villages[29]—to Brahmins. However, this role of the Gauntiā continues even after the formal abolition of the Gauntiā system, and temples continue to be constructed. Here are a few examples:

> The initiative to build a Jagannāth Temple in the village Bankey was taken by Ratni Patel, the Aghriā–Gauntiā's sister, who had returned to her brother's village after her husband's death. Sister and brother, it is told by their descendants, were both interested in the religious merits related to the building of temples. The construction started in 1929.[30] The brother offered three acres as *Jagannāth jamin* and invited a Gosain family to act as temple priest. The priest has to offer food for the gods every day out of the income from these three acres of land. The land is still registered with the Gauntiā who pays revenue for it. The Gauntiā declared that the income from another acre of land should be used for the expenses of the yearly *Rath Jātrā.* This land was registered in the name of his eldest son, who is still performing the ritual. The Gauntiā also financed the building of a smaller Śiva temple, a mud hut, around ten to twelve years ago. He also purchased a *lingā*, a cobra and a rather expensive bull for the temple. All in all the costs of this temple are estimated around 3,000 rupees. A Gauḍ acts as the Pujāri here. He received half an acre of land for cultivation, which is still registered in the Gauntiā's land record, who continues to pay the revenue.
>
> When a new and solid Śiva temple was built in the village Mundaloi in 2001 to replace the older mud temple the Gauntiā family paid for all material

costs. The Gauntiā himself offered the stones, wood and tiles, while a cousin (FyBS) added the cement and the younger brothers managed the transport with their tractor. The villagers built the temple themselves—every villager participating at least a day. During the temple purification the Gauntiā's younger brother and his wife acted as *karttā*/sacrifier and as Gauntiā, because the Gauntiā himself—whose traditional role it would have been—had other important engagements on that day.

Apart from temples—in the case of Jagannāth often erected opposite the Gauntiā house—for dancing at festivals like the *Nām Jagya*, *Śivrātrī*, etc., solid pavilions were constructed. These stand in the vicinity of the temples and Gauntiā houses. These pavilions—having an altar at the centre around which the dancers circle—are known as *mandap* or *maduā*. The importance attached to dance in these festivals is possibly another sign of tribalization, as dancing plays a vital role in tribal society—a role perhaps not matched in Hinduism. The Gauntiā have been influential in erecting these buildings as well. As described in the following case, the temples or pavilions established reflect a hierarchy in this converging tribal and caste society.

In Bankey village next to the temple a *maduā* was erected in 1929 for the Rāhās Jātrā (Rāhās is another name for Krishna) and the Nām Jagya, again on the initiative of the Aghriā Gauntiā's sister. In 2000 the *maduā* was rebuilt by the daughter-in-law of the Gauntiā family (the costs estimated at around 50,000 rupees). Because the so-called Untouchables are not allowed to enter the pavilion the Gauntiā built a separate one in 1987. (For the Kisāns who are also not permitted to enter the *mandap* of the high status groups another one was constructed and financed by the government. All in all there are three *mandaps* now in the village.)

In many cases the Gauntiā did not only build temples, but also *samādhis* or memorials where bones are kept after a funeral until they are ultimately immersed into the river Ganga. It is not clear if it was the Gauntiā who introduced *samādhis* to the region, but frequently the oldest *samādhi* in the villages belong to Gauntiā families. In Kuchinda, the eldest preserved *samādhi* belonged to a Gauntiā who ruled three generations ago.

The landlord's contribution to an architectural manifestation of religion as the construction of not only temples, but also pavilions, and *samādhi* should be understood as another display of his dominance and rule. As Burke (1993) and Assmann (1999: 21) have convincingly argued, temples, memorial stones, and palaces represent and belong to the social and cultural memory. As there is a close association between locality and memory, the landlord's power as well as the glory of a Hindu god is imprinted on them.

The same appears to be true for the Gauntiā acting, or having acted, as patrons of rituals for their own, as well as the village's, well-being by inviting Brahmins and other ritual specialists. Many of the following rituals can be sponsored by other villagers as well, but often it is the headman who is financially capable of hosting it and thus effectively contributing to a Hinduization—though he is also expected to patronize these village festivals in exchange for services villagers offer him.

Janmāṣtami is performed in remembrance of the birthday of Lord Krishna. In Mundaloi the Gauntiā not only opens his outer room known as *baiṭhak* (traditionally reserved for the king, etc.) but also provides all ritual items necessary for the *pūjā*. The reading of the *Haribanś*—a Puranic text—in the morning forms an essential part of the ritual. This text may be read independently of the birthday by invited Brahmins and it is hoped that it helps to fulfil wishes often related to children. The setting appears very similar during a ritual performed for Durgā by the women of the village on *Bhāi Jiūntiā*. In Mundaloi the ritual takes place in front of the Gauntiā's house. The women of the Gauntiā's family traditionally offer a pumpkin stylized as a goat. Other families are free to offer the same, but the Gauntiā family is expected to do so.

In the month of Kārttika the singing of verses from the *Srimad Bhagbad Gita*, popularly known as *Bhagbad* is performed by a *kirthan* party. The Gauntiā or any other sponsor invites the party to read passages and to intone them supported by drums and other instruments. The singing usually lasts for a couple of hours or a night. The patrons as well as the members of the party that everyone can join[31] receive religious merit (*puniya*) for their contribution. For the group some *ganjā* (marijuana), smoked in pipes (*chillum*), has to be offered by the patron in addition to the ritual items (cotton, lamp, flowers, fruit, etc.) for a small *pūjā* for Brundabati in front of the Tulsī shrine.

The Gauntiā, or any interested and well-off party, might act as patron for a *Nām Jagya* in memory of Krishna. The length of the ritual depends on the sponsor. The Gauntiā and his wife act as sacrifiers and have to appear at the *mandap* at least once every *praharī* to earn religious merit. Various groups of dancers are invited, who sing 'Hare Krishna, Hare Rama' continuously supported by drums and brass cymbals. A Brahmin performs the rituals for Krishna, Chaitanya, and his followers. In Mundaloi the Gauntiā sponsors the complete festival including the catering of dancers as well as payments in kind (paddy) for the priest.[32] In other villages the costs may be shared between the Gauntiā and other wealthy families. At the end of the ritual the Gauntiā's wife carries a pot with curd known as *dadhi bhaṇḍa* (*dadhi* = curd; *bhaṇḍa* = big pot) around the altar and smashes it in front of the altar.[33] On this final day dancing parties walk in a procession known as *nagar kirthan* (*nagar* = town) through the village to collect money from households which is then brought to the Gauntiā or patron who counts it and distributes it among the groups.

Nām Jagya are often combined with the celebrations on *Makar Sankrānti*—a festival for Jagannāth and Śiva on January—in which the Gauntiā usually fulfils the same role. During *Śivrātrī,* a festival is sponsored by the Gauntiā—in particular, dancing parties perform at the pavilion. However, the Gauntiā does not act as the public sacrifier in this case; he only worships Śiva in the local temple—as do all other villagers who want to do so.

Apart from these major village festivals, there are other local ones such as for *Ban Durgā*, also known as *Andhāri,* or for the god of Ayurvedic medicine, the so-called *Donantari Pūjā*, which are initiated and/or supported by the Gauntiā and their family members in continuity of their traditional role.

The Gauntiā and his family influence the village community in yet another way: as a role model or as orientation for other villagers—even in their rather private rituals. The *Lakṣmī Pūjā*, is particularly popular among Gauntiā but probably was not an integral part of the ritual cycle before the arrival of the landlord. Significantly, this *pūjā* is performed predominantly by families closely associated with the headman, for example, the family of the sacrificer of the village goddess, and the families of his labourers.

Economic change

Apart from religious changes, new headmen were instrumental in transforming and intensifying agriculture. This is what Cohn (2001 [1962]: 493) once termed the 'developmental function' of 'little kings'. As Thapar and Siddiqi (1997 [1979]: 426) pointed out, a substantial surplus is required for the formation of a state, therefore, economic changes introduced by the Aghriā are certainly related to the establishment of systems of redistribution and kingship. The most important economic modification was presumably a switch from shifting cultivation (*poḍu*), towards intensive agriculture, i.e. plain land agriculture. This process may have occurred in conjunction with a change from millet to rice cultivation.[34] The forest had been systematically cleared in order to grow paddy, and it is likely that on the tribal frontier the Aghriā were influential in spreading plough agriculture and placing more emphasis on transplanting. With the plough, servitude comes into the house, the Prophet Muhammad had noted (Gellner 1993: 1) which seems to hold true for Orissa as well. The Aghriā established their reign simultaneously with the introduction of the plough, which, is worshipped by them but not their tribal neighbours. As far as the introduction of the plough is concerned, the Aghriā appear to resemble Plough–Brahmin, who, through

> their specific technological know-how in plough cultivation and their plough worship seem to have accelerated the introduction of superior methods of agriculture at the cost of the tribal slash-and-burn technique, resulting in a major change of the political landscape. (Pfeffer 1978: 425)

It is not however certain whether the Aghriā introduced the plough (compared to the hoe) or if it was known before. Bailey (1960: 63ff) noted that Konds believe that they were axe-cultivators originally knowing nothing of irrigated rice cultivation, which like the plough was introduced by Oriya from the Mahanadi valley. Taking into consideration also the data collected by Bailey, it appears likely that the Aghriā were influential in transforming agriculture into plough-based wet rice cultivation. Related to intensive agriculture was the building of ponds to supplement rain water in the field. It is also probable that new technologies, such as the use of limestone to construct houses and temples, were introduced.

The construction of ponds is essential for becoming independent of natural rainfall, or at least it as a store of additional water. If possible, land with springs or swamps, so called *jalchar* land, is selected for ponds. There are three different types of ponds constructed in relation to the environmental conditions. For a *bandha* type of pond four walls have to be built, for a *muṇḍā* only three artificial walls and for a *kaṭā*, only one or two walls have to be erected to dam up the water.

In the village Kuanrmāl the first Aghriā headman started to build an enormous pond of around 30 acres size using natural assets. Due to the pond it was possible to irrigate about 150 acres (nowadays increased to 200). Of these roughly 30 acres are irrigated for a second harvest. Apart from this big pond seven smaller ponds were constructed and owned by the Gauntiā family. Six of them had to be given to the Panchayat later, because it was too difficult for the Gauntiā to maintain them. The other small pond is still privately owned. The big pond had to be sold to the Minor Irrigation Department—compensation is still disputed among the family members. In Bankey village, eleven ponds existed before Independence, of which the Aghriā Gauntiā family owned ten. Only one pond was owned by another family—interestingly the family of the former Gauntiā of the village—a Gaṇḍ family.

The ponds show the economic dominance landlord families were able to exercise. Even if the Aghriā were perhaps not always the first to built ponds—as in the case of Bankey suggests—ponds enabled people to produce more. Additionally, if possible, small rivers from the hills were used for irrigation. The water was led into the fields and stopped with small dams, before it flowed into the next field. For adequate watering of wet rice other measures were taken, for example to lower the land level. In this manner *māl* land could be turned into *bāhāl* in which water could be stored longer.

For the construction of the prestigious two storey buildings—the solid houses or *pakkā ghar* so typical for Gauntiā in the region, a kind of village palace—as well as temples or in some cases ponds new building technologies were essential. The Aghriā used limestone or *chun* for this purpose as a binding agent similar to cement. The limestone was collected and burnt. The outflow was used to bind the stones—a method probably not known before in the region, presumably taken over from superior kings, but introduced in the villages only by the Gauntiā. Such two-storey stone buildings, like the *pakkā ghar*, had many advantages: inhabitants were protected against heat and cold in this extreme climate and from attack, and they could spot elephants destroying crops from a distance.

The Aghriā also became famous for the mango trees they planted. In every Aghriā village there is usually at least one mango plantation. That does not mean that other communities like the Gaṇḍ did not do likewise, but the systematic way in which the Aghriā followed this pattern is rather unique. In Mundaloi mango trees were first planted by an Aghriā Gauntiā and only later by a Gaṇḍ *baḍ parjā*.

Educational change

In addition to changes in the religious and economic field the headmen also contributed to educational changes. The village Kuānrmāl may again be an example:

As a young child the present Gauntiā of Kuānrmāl village was sent by his father to his mother's brother's village in Gangpur State for his education. Later his father appointed teachers for his sons and even later he took part in the foundation of a school in Kirmira, a neighbouring village, in 1958.

As Secretary of that school, he was responsible for acquiring donations and funds for the appointment of teachers. He himself supported the school financially. Later on in the 1970s he was instrumental in setting up a Middle School in Aitapali (now upgraded to High School) and became its founder-secretary. After his death the sons were instrumental in the foundation of a High School in Kuānrmāl in 1988. They gave land (part of the land was government owned, part was private property—the private property was exchanged against own land and later on donated to the school) and named the school after their father. His younger son became secretary of the school in Kuānrmāl, a post now held by a grandson. In the future it is planned to turn the school into a government school to receive more funds.

Since the Gauntiā established most of the schools only after the formal abolition of the Gauntiā system it shows how Gauntiā—or at least some of them—continued their royal role as the prime donor in their respective realms preserving their traditional position by adapting to new circumstances. Furthermore, by appointing mostly Brahminic teachers, the influence of Brahminic ideology was increased and consolidated in the—as far as population is concerned—still tribally dominated area.

4.7. EXTERNAL RELATIONS[35]—THE GAUNTIĀ IN RELATION TO HIS OVERLORD

We shall now see how political, economic and ritual relations are constituted in the little kingdom as a system of redistribution. What is accumulated and what is distributed or redistributed?

Revenue collection

The Gauntiā were formally recognized by the king of Bamra, their overlord, in a document known as the *gaunti patā* or land grant. Important Gauntiās or rather jamindārs might have received copper plates as *patā*, but usually they were written on paper.[36]

All obligations and rights of a Gauntiā toward his superior king were fixed in this document. The first Gauntiā received the so-called *khuṇṭ katā patā* after clearing the forest. Prior to getting a *gaunti,* he had to deposit the revenue for one year in advance. A *patā* dated 1942 is cited below in order to illustrate the relationship of ruler to the Gauntiā. The first paragraph says:

> You have been appointed as Landlord (State Employee) within the area of Bamanda of Badbar, village XY from the year 1942–3 until the next settlement as per this agreement (*sartta*). You will have to adhere to the following conditions and any other rule which will be added later while enjoying the possession right as a successor and landlord (*gaunti svatva*).

Today, not many Gauntiā own *patās*, because, as some headmen told me, they had to be returned to the government shortly after Independence at the time of the abolition of the Gauntiā system.

The most important obligation was the collection of revenue, fixed in the *patā* as

> 2. You have to collect revenues from the tenants as per the rent roll or as per the newly made or as per the changed rent roll and you should always give receipts for each collection of revenues and cess from the tenants in the printed receipts books that are brought from the State.
>
> 3. You have to collect the fixed revenue and cess of [your] village as per the calculation of Touzi[37] instalments as given below: 1st instalment Rs. 0–Rs. 40 1st June; 2nd instalment Rs. 0–Rs. 30 1st December; 3rd instalment Rs. 0–Rs. 30 1st March.
>
> After seven years, there will be a revised settlement. In that, the rate of the rent will be fixed in the presently fixed rate of all newly possessed or

occupied land. Accordingly you have to deposit fixed rent collection of the new land of your village.

If . . . the fixed revenue rents are not paid for each instalment, you will have to collect Rs. 6% surcharge (extra) per year. If one arrear of three instalments is not paid up to ten years, you will be deprived of the right of Landlord and the arrears will be collected by selling your movable and immovable property.

The revenue ordinarily had to be brought to the capital or to an office of the king. In some cases the Gauntiā would appoint trustworthy servants, known as *Khamāri*, to collect this revenue for them, but in most cases collected it themselves.[38] Usually the revenue had to be paid in several instalments fixed in the deed.[39] If the Gauntiā were unable to pay the revenue their *gaunti* was auctioned. Landlords immigrating into the region and introducing profitable technologies had advantages in comparison with the more traditional tribal headmen, the latter often losing their office in favour of immigrants. However, in practice there was a certain flexibility in payment. As an old Aghriā Gauntiā told me, 'the Diwan took into consideration the damage caused by elephants and water flowing from the nearby hills after the Gauntiā and villagers had complained. . . . He allowed a reduction of 50 per cent on the revenue.'

Villagers remember that the revenue generally depended on the land quality, Rs. 2.5 to Rs. 0.5 per acre in the 1930s.

Point 4 of the *patā* describes what happens if tenants do not pay their share of the revenue and in point 7 tenants are protected against arbitrary decisions of the Gauntiā.

4. If the tenants fail to deposit fixed revenue in instalments as per the given list you will have to submit a list of instalment. . . .

If your claims are established and your maximum efforts for collection of revenue are convincingly demonstrated, the State will allow collection of arrears through certificates in the name of each tenant. You have to file a rent suit for the rest of the claims that are not included in the list.

7. You cannot remove any tenant from his tenancy without the order of civil or revenue court.

In practice, however, it seems to have been the Gauntiā's privilege to distribute land in the village. The landlord could give forest or pasture tracts to the tenants he chose, they had to first clear the forest and the logs were often taken by the Forest Department to generate extra revenue for the king. Some people remember certain headmen with gratitude who allowed them to stay in their villages and offered them some land to cultivate. Sometimes Gauntiā tried to attract members of their own community or certain service communities like leather workers to settle in their village by offering them land. In many cases the Aghriā Gauntiā invited other Aghriā families to stay with them and to act as witnesses for rituals. To some extent it may have been a necessity to bring tenants into the village to reduce the revenue the headman had to pay—particularly if there was more land than he could cultivate. In some cases, however, the jamindār, king, or British Agent had to agree to land transfers, but merely as a formality. In cases in which the tenants were unable to pay the revenue the Gauntiā had to pay the amount, but could then transfer the land to another tenant. I was told that the Gauntiā had to inform the magistrate and had to wait two years for such a transfer, until then the tenant had the chance to pay. However, in most cases the tenants simply left the village if they were unable to pay and the Gauntiā offered the land to someone else. The protection clause seems to have been of little relevance in practice, as a powerful Gauntiā could simply force some tenants to sell him their land or their best cattle.

Services to the superior king

Apart from collecting revenue, each Gauntiā had to accommodate the king, members of his family, or any government servant on their journeys through the kingdom.

> 6. If the king, agency, British Government and State employee are visiting your area on Government duty, you have to provide cooking utensils and help accordingly as per particular scale and rate during that period.

Usually a special room, the *baiṭhak,* close to the entrance of the Gauntiā's house, was reserved for such occasions. Furthermore, guests had not only to be housed but also served meals.

> 12. You or the tenants of your village have to provide food at the market rate and labour at the reasonable rate for all Government Employees who will be visiting on Government duty. The necessary receipt should be produced. . . .

The meals' ingredients were precisely listed according to the guest's status. Thus, an Agency Officer or a member of the royal family was entitled to

1. Fine raw rice (*aruā chāul*): ½ kg
2. Lentils: 125 g
3. Clarified butter: ½ kg
4. Oil: 60 g
5. Salt, Spices, Vegetables
6. Chicken: 2
7. Eggs: 6
8. Utensils: 4
9. Flour: ½ kg
10. Sugar: 125 g

while a State peon would receive only

1. Rice: ½ kg
2. Pulses: 60 g
3. Oil and Salt: 60 g

However, I have never heard that any such receipt had been sent to the king for refund and it was probably a matter of prestige for a Gauntiā to offer these items voluntarily—in the same way that government officials, such as Revenue Officers, are taken care of today. Apart from food, the guests or government employees had to be provided with carriers or porters to the next village. In addition food had to be provided not only for the royal guests and government servants in the respective village but also for larger ceremonies, such weddings, of the royal family. When the Gauntiā were invited, they had to bring milk, paddy, etc., that was fixed in advance. These gifts, however, are not stated in the land deed.

In some cases headmen were obliged to appear in court as witnesses for certain lawsuits. For their efforts, village Gauntiā were paid Rs. 2.5 while Gauntiā in small towns like Kuchinda received Rs. 5 for the same work.

*Socage/*beṭhi *and gifts/*bheṭi

Although not mentioned in the *paṭā*, Gauntiā and villagers alike remember socage or forced labour they had give the king or Gauntiā. According to some people, *beṭhi,* sometimes called *beṭh bigāḍi*, was abolished two to three years before Independence, and it is difficult to estimate its extent or to describe a system few have themselves experienced. As Gauntiā, and an elder Kandh[40] informed me, *beṭhi* was primarily work for the king—organized, managed, and inspected by the Gauntiā. It included hunting elephants as well as constructing roads and ponds. Some remember that there was neither payment nor food provided for the labourers. Others said that the king paid minimal amounts of money to the Gauntiā for this work. The Gauntiā could distribute the latter among the villagers for their labour or could withhold it. An elderly Gauntiā remembered that the extent of *beṭhi* was calculated according to the revenue of the village: for ten-rupees revenue one labourer or *beṭhiā* (free, unpaid labourer, sometimes called also *butiyā*) had to work until a certain task, for example catching an elephant, was done (the elephants were used or sold by the king later). Elephant hunting was for the villagers a kind of punishment, taking ten to fifteen days. Additionally, certain roads were divided among neighbouring villages, each obliged to maintain its section over the years. In some cases the King and his administration ordered the Gauntiā to provide materials such as firewood, for example for the local jail in Kuchinda—also regarded as *beṭhi* or *bigaḍi*. According to sources found by R. Ahuja (personal communication)[41] it was not unusual that in Bamra state *beṭhi* was forced upon the subjects for up to four months a year. In addition, Ahuja (forthcoming) has shown the importance of corvée labour for the construction and repair of roads. The wages the British paid for such roads was kept by the kings, in whole or in part, for themselves.[42]

In some cases the villagers also had to work for a limited time without wages for the landlord. Some villagers remember that they had to offer their labour in exchange for the costs the Gauntiā used to bear for dancers, meals, etc., at festivals. The Gauntiā used *beṭhi* to dig ponds or wells, and also for urgent works like fire fighting or in his personal fields when additional labourers were needed. In some cases the landlord provided the villagers with meals or paid small wages for their efforts (in some cases this continues today). Some Gauntiā remarked that, in exchange, the villagers were entitled to a gift for their wedding and to a contribution in case of illness.

Schwerin (1977: 96, 117, 269ff) stated that there were similar conditions in neighbouring Chhotanagpur, where a scarcity of labour led to the corveé system. Forced labour varied from village to village, but higher castes—particularly Brahmin—were usually excluded from it. Traditionally, a year could consist of three days ploughing, digging, sowing/transplanting and harvesting each, one or two days threshing, a day for basket-making and seven to fifteen days transport works (ibid.: 271, see also 468). The landlords usually provided food and sometimes also paid for the work, if it exceeded the traditional limit. In 1902 laws were introduced to turn socage into paid labour,[43] although villagers were usually not able to pay any money. Thus, around Ranchi socage continued to exist until the 1940s (ibid.: 470ff). Services—perhaps originally restricted to peasants settled by the landlord under this very condition—had been changed into money rent (Rothermund 1978: 174–5).

Bheṭi, gifts or tribute, should be distinguished from *beṭhi* or socage. In the case of royal weddings or other ceremonies in the capital, the Gauntiā were obliged to offer gifts of food such as milk, paddy, goats, etc., if invited—fixed prior to the function. These gifts, which were also a matter of prestige for the Gauntiā, were known as *bheṭi*. An elder Gauntiā told me that villagers also had to offer as *bheṭi* forest products, such as honey to the Gauntiā.

Schnepel (2002: 272) mentioned that in Jeypore ladies offered *bhet*—probably identical with *bheṭi*—to the Queen attending during *Daśarā*. Hardenberg (2000: 126, 147–8) studying court rituals of the Gajapati, interpreted *bheṭi* offered during the new year's celebration as a tribute constituting an asymmetrical relation between giver and receiver, the receiver who is higher in position, for example the Gajapati, offering titles or other honours in return. These gifts represent the continuous relations between the king and his subjects that pivot on land holding. Following Hardenberg —and contrary to Schwerin—I hold that both *beṭhi* and *bheṭi* express ranked relations from the tenants/*parjā* up to the Gajapati: the *parjā* work for the king of Bamra and the local Gauntiā; the Gauntiā supervises the work of the village and is responsible to the king; the Gauntiā offers gifts to the king of Bamra and—as Hardenberg (2000: 143) notes—the king of Bamra presents *bheṭi* to the Gajapati, who in turn offers it in the context of a transcendental hierarchy to Jagannāth himself. Hence Figure 5:

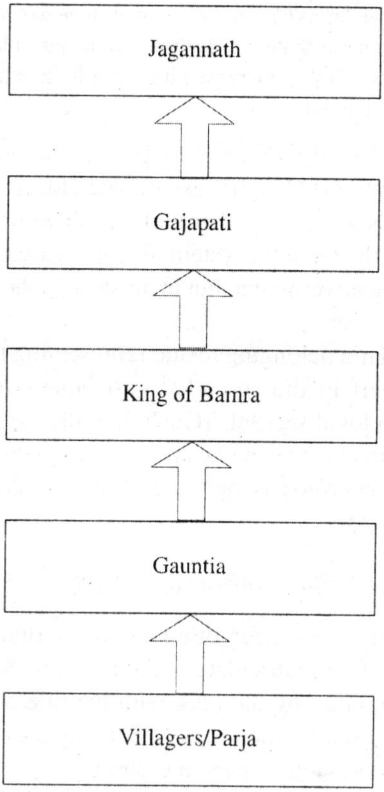

Figure 5: Offering of *beṭhi* and *bheṭi*, socage and gifts

King's land or rent-free land—bhogrā

One of the privileges a Gauntiā enjoyed—directly linked to the *gaunti*—was the right to cultivate land known as *bhogrā* formally belonging to his superior king. In most cases this land was rent-free and of a very high quality. Having *bhogrā* land of about 10 acres was not unusual. In the already mentioned land deed it is stated,

> According to this appointment you will enjoy the free right of land tenancy. If there is no free land . . . , you will get rupees in cash. With this deed (*paṭā*) you will enjoy free land (*bhogrā jami*) as per the tenancy calculation (*touzi*). Free land (*bhogrā*) cannot be transferred, divided, altered, sold, mortgaged or given on loan in any respect. If for any reason there are changes in landlordship (*gaunti*) it will be completely transferred to the successors.

If there is no free land (*bhogrā*) you can arrange new *bhogrā* land or pray for permission from the State. . . . If the Gauntiā has unlawfully taken land, it will be cancelled. If it is increased it cannot be sanctioned and if loan is taken it will be cancelled.

Thus, *bhogrā* land could not be divided among sons, but only transferred to the next Gauntiā, usually the eldest son, who received it as a part of his *gaunti* together with his share of other land. After the abolition of the Gauntiā system, in some cases, *bhogrā* land was taken over by the government, but in most cases the headmen became the registered owners.

The *bhogrā* land belonging to and representing the king of Bamra has a counterpart in the so-called *guti bunā*—rent-free land the Gauntiā gave to loyal servants (Guti), literally for sowing their own land but belonging to the Gauntiā and recorded in the Gauntiā's name. Both may thus be termed as the 'king's land', as they are structurally identical.

Titles, clothes and other symbols of kingship

The overlord used to offer other symbols that represented his supremacy. The first matriculate of the Bolangir State, a matriculate Aghriā was honoured by the king with the title *Sāe*—a prestigious title previously used by the kings of Sambalpur. (The family of the matriculate had previously used the title Patel.)

Occasionally, the king of Bamra would offer clothes to his subjects. One example was a jacket presented by the king to the Gauntiā of Kuchinda, who is said to have been close to the king. The name of the particular Gauntiā was stitched inside this jacket and it is still kept in the Gauntiā family. In the same way clothes—though of a more basic type, such as *lungis*—were offered by the Gauntiā to loyal long-term or contract labourers and house servants. Similarly, the descendants of the jamindār of Bolonda informed me that the king of Bamra had honoured one of their ancestors with an elephant. Additionally, the king used to send turban cloth (*yathā*), to invite the jamindār to all the important functions in the royal family. In this manner the Gauntiā, or jamindār or Guti, are situated relatively higher list in the hierarchy—the turban (or clothes) quite literally mirrors the rite of investiture of the Gajapati, who receives a turban from Jagannāth which is subsequently tied on the king's head.

The Jagannāth cult—sharing the authority of the superior king

Apart from the offering of honours, perhaps the clearest case of sharing the authority of a superior king and deriving legitimacy for one's own rule is the Jagannāth cult practised by kings on all levels. In the village, the *Rath Jātrā* is an important festival traditionally sponsored by the Gauntiā, in which he very explicitly replicates royal functions performed by the king of Bamra as well as the Gajapati in Puri.

In Mundaloi village only a temporary temple for Jagannāth is arranged in the Gauntiā's *baiṭhak.* From here Jagannāth starts in a procession to visit Gundicha, his mother's younger sister (*mausi*), locally placed at the other end of the village. Several jobs like constructing or repairing the carriage or organizing ropes for the procession are distributed among the villagers prior to the festival. Either the house of a wealthy Gaṇḍ, a *Baḍ Parjā*, or a community centre is symbolically turned into Gundicha's temple. Jagannāth's path from here to his carriage is swept with a new broom either by a brother of the Gauntiā or a *Baḍ Parjā* and the Gauntiā sprinkles water simultaneously. Nine days later the God returns in another procession to his temporary temple in the Gauntiā house. Again on this day, *bhog*—food for the Lord—is prepared, for which the Gauntiā offers all ingredients.[44]

By sponsoring the *Rath Jātrā*—most of these festivals on the village level have been introduced after the merger of the princely states with the Indian Union—the Gauntia shares the ritual authority of superior kings. He legitimizes his own rule by styling himself as the first servant of Jagannāth in the same way the Gajapati does (Hardenberg 1999: 153). Thus, it is more than just imitating the overlord and it may also have within it an element of rebellion or challenge: the Gauntia trying to gain ritual sovereignty himself, effectively showing that the performance of the *Rath Jātrā* is not confined to the superior levels of the king of Bamra or the Gajapati.

The 'double-edgedness' of royal symbols displayed during *Daśarā* were also noted by Dirks (1979: 188), who observed that: 'The emblem were symbolic of kingship and while they manifested the chieftain's local authority . . . they could also constitute a serious challenge to the king if displayed without royal permission.' In turn, other villagers or *Baḍ Parjā* may challenge the ritual authority of the Gauntia.[45]

4.8. INTERNAL RELATIONS—THE GAUNTIĀ IN RELATION TO HIS SUBJECTS/VILLAGERS

In former times the headman was entitled to various signs of respect and obedience. Some have been abolished while others simply disappeared and several are still used today.

When the Gauntiā was passing by, a *parjā* had to stop riding his bicycle and had to show his respect by making the *namaskār* greeting. However, it was not necessary to stop the bicycle when the Gauntiā was driving in a car. Often villagers stopped when they met the Gauntiā to ask him about his family or harvest, and many old villagers still follow this tradition, but to a lesser extent. Villagers had to close their umbrella in the presence of the headman or were not even allowed to have one. Usually a labourer held the umbrella for the Gauntiā. An elder Gauntiā explained that, out of fear, no one shouted in front of the Gauntiā. The Gauntiā and his family were the only villagers to wear shoes, trousers and shirts in the modern style. However, due to colleges, etc., where shoes, trousers and shirts were obligatory this has slowly changed and some Gauntiā claim that they encouraged the other villagers to wear modern clothes.[46]

Behind the Gauntiā house in Mundaloi there is pond the villagers use for bathing. Every villager is allowed to bath there even though the Gauntiā actually owns the pond. In former times when the Gauntiā or his family members took their bath other villagers had to wait until they had finished. Today, the Gauntiā family and other villagers can take their bath at the same time, but the Gauntiā family has bathrooms in their house as well.

Royal habitus

For many Gauntiā it was a matter of prestige not be forced to seek work outside the house and to have their own land on which to live. They often ignored other possible sources of income due to their self-image of being a 'landed gentry' for whom it would be a loss of prestige to acknowledge not being able to make a living from their

Gauntiā with his status symbols (around 1950).

own land. Although this has changed considerably, this idea is still present. In accordance with the *kṣātra-dharma* service jobs were not at all valued, since from the king's perspective, all other *varṇas*, not only the Śudras, were in position to be seen dependent servants (Trautmann 1995 [1981]: 284).

One of the privileges of kings, jamindārs and Gauntiā, was the right to keep swords (*khandā*). Other weapons, however, such as a *gupti*,[47] were permitted for all to have. Many Gauntiā still keep guns which are ritually worshipped on *Rākhī Pūni*.

Related to the weapons was hunting, which formed another essential part of the Gauntiā's lifestyle as a local ruler. However, hunting was not an exclusive privilege of the Gauntiā, as licenses for hunting could be obtained from the magistrate by everyone. There were two types of licenses: one for self-protection and another for crop-protection. In the latter case, only male animals were allowed to be killed. However, the hunting of tigers was allowed without restrictions before the 1950s and the administration paid a reward of Rs. 75 for every tiger killed.

While in royal palaces, tigers or bison and other game are displayed as trophies, in Gauntiā houses there are smaller remains of hunting parties such as antlers, sometimes used to build tables. In one case the tooth of a tiger shot by the present Gauntiā's father was added to a golden necklace to be worn for special occasions. Success at the hunt, a reminder of the royal conquest of the wilderness, adds to the prestige of the family, and also imitates the habits of kings.

Old ritual items inherited from forefathers such as a massive brass candlestick (*jāgar*) for *ghī*-lights used for rituals and a high number of *kansā* dishes—often with names like 'Jayanarayan Gauntiā' written on them—indicated wealth. Additionally, wooden doors are often lavishly carved and decorated with elephants, hunting scenes, deities Gods such as Gaṇeṣ or Lakṣmī, or abstract patterns. In one case even the name of the Gauntiā and his title were written on the door.

Apart from these more obvious signs of wealth and prestige, visitors can see subtler things as well. The number of ploughs was usually equivalent to the number of *Guti* (contract labourers) and pairs of bullocks and buffalos, although in some cases more bullocks or buffalos than ploughs were kept and ploughing was done with bullocks during the daytime and with buffalos at the night. In Kuchinda, the Gauntiā owned a maximum of 25 ploughs, while in a village like Mundaloi, the Gauntiā had around 15 ploughs. The number of ploughs and cattle did not only symbolize the land owned by the respective landlord, but indicate also their rank. Today, power tillers and tractors are modern signs of wealth.

Often in a Gauntiā family there would be more than one wife, which may have been necessary in order to manage the whole property and to forge various alliances with other Gauntiā families. Different wives supervised different shares of the land, had different store rooms (*bhandār ghar*) in the house, and were responsible for supplying the essential food stuffs such as oil, rice, spices, etc., from their store rooms for an alternating time period. Wealth was—and is—further displayed by the fact that, compared to other families in the village, the unmarried daughters usually did not work in the fields. In fact, no woman worked in the field and instead, mothers or daughters-in-law supervised the work of the labourers if there was no *Khamāri* or supervisor.

Rākhī Pūni/Rakṣā Bandhā as durbar

The royal assembly or *durbar*—held for example in Bamra in the *durbar* hall on *Daśarā*—formed an essential part of the constitution of kingship in India. Referring to the Mughal court, Cohn (1995 [1983]: 168) saw the act of incorporation as a central part of a *durbar*. Dignitaries seeking or being forced to seek 'incorporation' presented valuables or tributes carefully graded according to their rank and were subsequently honoured or incorporated by means of no less carefully ranked prestations—often clothes—as a sign of higher authority. Cohn (ibid.) noted:

> Under the Mughals and other Indian rulers, these ritual prestations constituted a relationship between the giver and receiver, and were not understood as simply an exchange of goods and valuables. The khelat [prestation offered by the Mughals] was a symbol 'of the idea of continuity or succession . . . and that continuity rests on a physical basis, depending on contact of the body of the recipient with the body of the donor through the medium of clothing'. The recipient was incorporated through the medium of the clothing into the body of the donor. This incorporation, according to F.W. Buckler, rests on the idea that the king stands for a 'system of rule of which he is the incarnation . . . incorporating into his body . . . the persons of whose who share his rule'. Those thus incorporated were not just servants of the king, but part of him. . . .

There is no direct equivalent to this act of incorporation at a *durbar* in the village but once a year all important subjects assemble around the Gauntiā to show their respect and obedience and be honoured for their loyalty in return—both expressed in gifts and tribute as well as a precise seating arrangement. However, very similar processes were exemplified, for example in gifts (*bheṭi*), tribute and the land transfers that have already been mentioned in the relationship between the Gauntiā and his overlord. I will argue that the same notions are expressed on the village level in a festival known as *Rākhī Pūni* in Sambalpuri and *Rakṣā Bandhā* in Oriya, both celebrated on full moon day in Śrābaṇ. On this day villagers present a *rākhī*—a thread tied (*bandhā* = to tie) around the Gauntiā's wrist. Sometimes *rākhīs* are also presented to other members of the Gauntiā's family particularly to his son as the next Gauntiā. *Rākhī* are offered to the Gauntiā as a kind of amulet to show respect and loyalty as well as dependence and a need for protection. I learned that villagers pray for the well-being of the Gauntiā on *Rākhī Pūni*. In exchange for binding a *rākhī,* the villagers at the Gauntiā house receive money and in some cases the raw ingredients for a meal, coconuts, *murhi*, or even cloth.

Since the Gauntiā system is partly in decline, it is not surprising that today fewer villagers come to the Gauntiā on this day than in former times, when the right arm of the Gauntiā—as one of them remembered—was full of *rākhīs*. In 2002, in Mundaloi those who visited were the sacrificer of the village goddess (*Kālo*), a *kirthan* party, the *pujāri* of a nearby Jagannāth temple, the male youngsters of the village, servants, and labourers. However, the return gift in money for the *rākhī* was criticised by a Brahmin of higher status. He argued that he would not go to the Gauntiā, because he is not interested in the money of the Gauntiā as the others are. Thus, the tying of *rākhī* may also have implications on the Brahmin–King relationship, to which I will return at the end of this chapter.

It should be noted that the festival is not exclusively centred on the Gauntiā, but shows various relationships of dependence: sisters fast during the day and bind a *rākhī* to their brothers, who—together with their wives—bind *rākhī* to the ancestors as well as to different representations of gods and goddesses in the house.[48] Various levels of incorporation and superiority are quite literally bound or connected with a *rākhī*.

The Gauntiā as Arbitrator and 'Justice of Peace'

One of the most important royal functions is protection, which is essential for the maintenance of social order. I mentioned the meaning of *Rākhī Pūni* as a 'village *durbar*' in which the villagers show their loyalty and respect and ask for the Gauntiā's protection. The same idea is expressed at weddings. When wedding parties arrive at the village, they first call on the Gauntiā, usually offering a gift of a cloth to him, known as a *gauntiā baraṇ*. The *gauntiā baraṇ* is an invitation as well as a sign of respect and request for security. In the same manner, circus and religious groups wandering around with bulls, coming to the village first visit the house of the Gauntiā, asking for permission to stay and for his protection during their stay.

The Gauntiā's function as judge goes well beyond simply offering protection. He is actively involved in settling disputes and punishing villagers who commit crimes like adultery or theft. In cases of capital crimes, such as murder, the police are called, but there are no such cases on record. To punish defaulters, the Gauntiā would use various types of sticks,—either the stick to drive the bullocks (*pāchen bāḍi*), a tamarind stick, or a stick called *tetel jhānṭ,* on which a hemp rope (*khaunriā*) was fixed. Often the beatings would take place publicly on the village road.

Locals told me that this type of physical punishment was chosen because the villagers had no money to pay a fine and it was usually too far to reach the next police station. However, to call for the police was—and still is—considered a *lāj* or shame for the Gauntiā as well as the village, because it means effectively that the Gauntiā was unable to maintain law and order in his respective area; it means the Gauntiā is somehow incompetent and, ultimately, cannot fulfil his *dharma.*

In this context it is significant that in Aghriā myths the Gajapati, following Lord Jagannāth's divine verdict, gave the Aghriā the most common stick, the *pāchen bāḍi*. This stick, as used by the Gauntiā, is itself an expression of a royal presence. Besides, a major part of the *Mahābhārata* deals with the role of the king and his use of the stick (*daṇḍa*)—as Arjuna tells Yudhiṣṭhira—in the world, because this is in accordance with the *dharma* (Shulman in Hardenberg 2000: 21).

In the following I will describe what happened during my stay.

DISPUTE 1

A Kisān man who had had an affair with a Muṇḍā woman reported it to the Gauntiā accusing her of being a *beji*—a kind of witch.[49] The man, who was married with children, had just ended this affair. The woman was about 45 to 50 years, a widow living with her daughter and daughter's husband, a contract labourer of the Gauntiā. The Kisān now accused her of witchcraft intending to kill him. Shortly afterwards, the Muṇḍā lady consulted the Gauntiā, accusing her former lover of spreading false rumours. The Gauntiā advised the Kisān not to spread these accusations any more, as she could go to the police. The rumours stopped and meanwhile the Kisān started a new affair with another Muṇḍā woman distantly related to the first.

DISPUTE 2

A Gaṇḍ widow married a widower in another village who had promised her some land in case of marriage. Soon she died, some people in her native village suspecting that her husband or his family had a hand in it. After her death, her brother claimed the land promised to her, but all the land was recorded in the husband's name. The Gauntiā of both villages met but could not find a solution. As a result, the case was transferred to the police, but the Gauntiā of the widow's village argued that the brother had no chance to inherit the land, because it was not registered in her name—a mistake made at the time of marriage arrangements.

DISPUTE 3

A woman had beaten her husband's grandfather, a Kisān, with a stick, from which he received a serious wound on his neck. The doctor, after seeing the bleeding cut, sent them to the police. The old man's brother's son consulted the Gauntiā and complained about the behaviour of the grandson's wife. Shortly before this incident, the old man, at a meeting of the village Pañchāyat, had publicly declared that she did not give him enough to eat (his son had already passed away). After this meeting, not much happened, because the old man—almost deaf—did not understand everything being said during the meeting. In any case, the woman was not sent to the police as recommended by the doctor, because it was feared that police sepoys might rape her. Another meeting was arranged and she was sentenced to pay a fine of Rs. 300 to the village treasury. Furthermore, she had to pay for the medical treatment (around Rs. 200) and sign a declaration that she would obey the old Kisān's wishes. The declaration was written by the Gauntiā and signed by the Kisān. Meanwhile the old man recovered.

DISPUTE 4

In a violent dispute, a Kandh tried to stab a Muṇḍā to death with a knife. His attempt failed, most likely because he was drunk. The Muṇḍā had somehow foreseen that something would happen and could step aside—so he was not injured. The cause of the conflict was probably a previous incident, when both had gone to visit their respective fathers-in-law and had walked together for a while. Quite drunk, the Kandh told the Muṇḍā that he would like 'to fuck his wife', because his own wife had just run away. The Muṇḍā man then attacked the Kandh.

A village meeting was called and presided over by the Gauntiā. The Kandh, drunk again, argued he had not forgotten the beating and that he would kill the Muṇḍā if the Pañchāyat would not punish him. He insisted that the Muṇḍā should be punished first and only afterwards would he accept any punishment for himself. However, everyone—including his wife, father and mother—saw him as guilty. The Gauntiā recommended that the Kandh should beg forgiveness and if the Muṇḍā would accept, everything would be well again. If, however, he would not apologize, he would be sent to the police. Everyone knew that there he would have had to pay either as punishment or as bribe. Finally the Kandh publicly apologized.

DISPUTE 5

Two young women around sixteen were working for the landlord threshing paddy. The straw had to be brought to a pile slightly away from the threshing floor. From the pile, the two young women suddenly came crying. Allegedly two young men of about the same age—a Kisān and a Māḷi—had harassed them sexually. After a heated debate on the threshing floor, the women went to the Gauntiā, who then called the men in question. It turned out that the men first had harassed them verbally, and then tried to rape them by force. The women managed to escape. The Gauntiā saw this as a very serious matter. The men had to apologize publicly saying, 'Sister, we have made a mistake'. The parents later decided to leave the matter and did not call the police. However, the Gauntiā threatened to call the police in the case that the men would repeat such attempts, because it was an attack on the prestige and honour of the women as well as of the village.

Usually the verdict of the Gauntiā is accepted. In former times a Gauntiā could probably see that his *parjā*/tenant was put behind bars. Today, however, Gauntiā do not settle disputes in the same manner, but arrange village meetings or Pañchāyats (not identical with the elected political body), in which both sides can give their version. The Gauntiā usually presides over the meeting. Furthermore, I have never heard of any case in which a villager had tried to assault a Gauntiā. Obviously, they fear the Gauntiā and his power, but it was not quite clear, if villagers regarded it as a *pāp* (sin) to beat the Gauntiā.[50] However, with this ability to enforce his verdict the power of Gauntiā goes well beyond that of a tribal headman, who could not achieve this objective in the same way (Sahlins 1968, Gell 1992).

In cases where the verdict of Gauntiā and Pañchāyat is ignored nowadays a villager or family can be ostracized. The family is then separated from the others, it is made *ek ghariā* (*ek* = one; *ghar* = house), 'singled out' of the village, isolated and the services of herdsmen or the sacrificer of the village goddess, etc., are denied. In one case, a Chamār family occupied some government land—an area that had been chosen by the villagers for building a hospital.[51] After the Chamār had started building his house on the disputed land, a village meeting was arranged and the Chamār declared publicly he would leave the land. Then, nothing happened. Later, the Chamār explained that he had a government permit, but it turned out that he had just paid a fine for cutting trees. Another meeting took place—again in front of the Gauntiā's house and under his guidance. Here the Chamār became *ek ghariā*. Finally, the Chamār left the land and occupied some other land—not disputed by anyone—and was readmitted into the community after paying a heavy fine of Rs. 500 to the village treasury.

The Gauntiā as Patron/Jajmān vs. *the Gauntiā as Master/Sāhu*

I turn now to the complex network of relationships between the Gauntiā and service castes as well as between the Gauntiā and his labourers. Since Wiser (1988 [1936]), these relationships—or rather this 'system of interrelatedness' (ibid: xxii)—have been subsumed in the literature under the term *jajmāni* relations.[52] Pocock (1962: 81ff) noted that prior to Wiser's work the term *jajmān* was less accepted and never universally known or used in India—instead the rather neutral term client was in vogue. However, I use the term because it is an emic one.

Wiser (ibid.: x, xix, 1, 56) describing a north Indian setting, stressed the element of reciprocity between the patron or *jajmān* and his servant (or *kamin*)—both sides having rights and responsibilities—but also pointed to the asymmetrical nature of the power relationship and to the redistributive aspect of the whole system.

Later, Pocock (1962: 85ff) distinguished essentially three categories of servants: (1) ritual specialists, 'whose specialization derives from the exigencies of caste system, not from economic needs or from the intricacy of a craft' (91); (2) artisans, who provide a commodity and thus fulfil a mere economic task; and (3) unskilled labourers, whose service is not derived from a 'need for the achievement and maintenance of status, but simply from the permanent and occasional need for labour' (89). Pocock reserves the term *jajmāni* relation only for the first type of service relations (91). The various types of 'religious and secular services only conjunct through the *jajmān*' (89) relations, asserts Pocock.

Particularly in this last point, the society I studied differs from Pocock's case in Gujarat. From the perspective of a Gauntiā there are two significant types of relationships, the relationship to specialists offering ritual services on the one hand and to labourers on the other. The first category, including the Tihāri (*purohit*), Dessondhi (bard), Brahmin, barber, washerman or Ear Guru (Kān Guru), often refer to the Gauntiā as their patron, or *jajmān*, while labourers from the second category refer to him as master/landlord or *sāhu*.[53]

Let me describe the local categories in more detail:

The Gauntiā as Patron/Jajmān—Jajmāni relations

TIHĀRI/BRAHMIN FAMILY PRIEST (*PUROHIT*)

As a family priest (*purohit*), the Tihāri should be called for the performance of all life cycle rituals such as marriages or funerals as well as certain rituals for the well-being of the patron. Traditionally, a small group of Brahmins claiming to have come from Kaṇyakubja and known as Tihāri work exclusively for the Aghriā as *purohits*. However, if the *purohit* is unable to attend a ritual, it is also possible to call another Brahmin, who may doubt the credentials of the Tihāri. In any case, both Tihāri and Brahmin fall into the same category and refer most consistently to their patron as *jajmān*. The priest receives *bidāki* or *dakhinā* as payment usually in form of money, but also receives gifts and particularly auspicious forms of *dān* such as paddy, cloth, or raw food. At times, a distinction is made between *bidāki* as the payment the Brahmin receives if he visits the house of his patron, while *dakhinā* is given in exchange for the performance of rituals. One time a Tihāri's wife explained to me, 'For work (*kām*), *dakhinā* is given, while *bidāki* is what the *jajmān* gives out of happiness.' However, her husband disagreed and denied any difference between *bidāki* and *dakhinā*. The Gauntiā told me the priest is the only servant entitled to receive money—in contrast to many other servants, who increasingly demand money instead of paddy, etc, but have no right to do so.

For death rituals a second, lower category of Brahmin must be invited to accept inauspicious forms of *dān*. They are also known as *Dānuā Brahmin*, as they receive usually no other payment except *dān*.

KĀN GURU—EAR GURU

The Kān Guru, lower Brahmins of the Gosain caste, initiate Aghriā by whispering a *mantra* into their ears at the time of puberty and before marriage. The knowledge of this *mantra* is supposed to be purifying. A Kān Guru receives money as well as cloth, but there is no particular name for these gifts and the relation to the Guru is only ephemeral. He, however, has the right to stay in the house of his patron.[54]

DISANDHRĪ/DOSSONDHI—BARD

On one hand, the Aghriā are the elder brothers of the Dossondhi, but on the other hand, they are their *jajmān*. As the younger brothers and, according to mythology, custodians of the sacred thread that the Aghriā wore before turning to agriculture, the Dossondhi is entitled to one tenth of his patron's harvest as his share. However, in practice he receives much less than that, usually in the form of paddy. At weddings, the Dossondhi should be invited to offer a special blessing (*slaka*) during the *hāth lagan* ceremony, for which additional gifts may be given.

DHOBĀ—WASHERMAN

The washerman, or *Dhobā*, works for all high status groups, but he does this only when called upon and not as regularly at present as in former times. Today he is specifically called at the time of births, deaths, and in cases of reintegration into the community after ritual exclusion. After having completed his work, he receives his payment of *chāul* and money.

However, in former times, when the Dhobā came regularly, he received a fixed payment each year known as *barttan*. Patrons referred to him as *barttaniā*—someone who received *barttan*. However this tradition was discontinued about twenty years ago and there is no name at present for the payment that he receives. The term *jajmān* is no longer used.[55] During festivals he was entitled to receive a gift of money known as *jātrā dekhā* and at the time of *Nuā Khāi*, *Rākhī Pūni* and *Pouṣ Pūni* he used to receive *kharchā* (raw food for a meal).

BANDĀRI—BARBER

The continuation of the barber's services is still considered as essential, which means that he still receives *barttan* as payment—once a year—according to the number of family members he serves. Usually, he comes once a week, but his services are important during the life-cycle rituals as well. As indicated, the barber—as all except the Brahmin—has the right only to demand paddy. However, today it is changing and servants may also receive money, if needed. As one landlord informed me, he gave money to the barber for the first time ever in 2001. Furthermore, he is still entitled to *jātrā dekhā* as well as *kharchā* as the washerman was in former times.

LUHURĀ—BLACKSMITH

As with the washerman, the blacksmith belonged to the category of *barttaniā* in former times, but is now paid only after having completed his work. Formerly he was much in demand during the ploughing season to sharpen the plough and was paid at the time of harvest. However, in richer Gauntiā families tractors have replaced ploughs to a large extent. The blacksmith is also involved in rituals—at least indirectly. If a death occurs in his patron's family under certain constellations of stars known as *puṣkarā* and considered to be inauspicious for the family of the deceased, an additional death ritual is required, for the worship of Yama, and his brother Sama. The latter are represented by iron idols produced by the Luhurā. This task itself is regarded as dangerous and can involve inauspiciousness. Besides, the plough or particularly the ploughshare produced by the smith is also used at weddings for the ceremonial digging of soil needed for the wedding altar. The plough is also worshipped during *Harli Uāns* and *Akshya Trutīyā* among the Aghriā.

TELI—OIL-PRESSER

Traditionally, a Teli was not only obliged to provide oil for the patron's family at the time of weddings—particularly during the *barāt*, the groom's procession—it was his or his family's task to arrange oil for the torches known as *masāl* to illuminate the groom's arrival in procession. For this service, the Teli would receive *barttan.* However, after the arrival of kerosene and gas lamps, this tradition has changed considerably and the service of a Teli is no longer a necessity during weddings. Thus the service relation to the Teli has been disconnected.

KHUMBĀ—POTTER

Traditionally, potters had to supply certain types of pots for an Aghriā wedding, for example 7 pots in every corner of the wedding altar. Five pots known as *ḍibi* were put above each other and on top of these a *kuṇṭi* and a *gubhā* were placed. In all, 28 pots were required for a wedding altar. Seven small pots known as *pāen palṭā* were necessary for the ceremony of *abhihāri pāen utarā.* Additionally, big clay pots to boil rice known as *hāṇḍi* were provided by the potter. The *hāṇḍi* had to be destroyed in the case of a death in a family. A potter too referred to his patron as *jajmān* and received *barttan.* As in the Teli's case, the relation to the potters was terminated about twenty years ago. A Gauntiā told me, that, these days, the potters prefer to sell their products in the market, where they can earn more money than in a *jajmāni* relationship. For their pottery, as commodity, they receive a price or *dām* per piece.

GHANṬUĀL—FERRYMAN

The service of the ferryman falls into the category of *barttaniā* as well. His services are required particularly during the monsoon season and the Gauntiā of nearby villages offer *barttan*. Many Gauntiā have discontinued this regular yearly payment, even though one ferryman told me that he still receives some payment from a local Gauntiā. Nowadays ferrymen have also started to charge for their services. And at present, locals hold the Pañchāyat (not the Gauntiā) responsible for the maintenance of the boats. In any case, many new bridges have rendered the services of the ferrymen unnecessary. I was unable to find any direct involvement of ferrymen in rituals apart from general statements and ideas that a deceased person must cross a river and special restrictions exist for pregnant women, who are prohibited to do so. During funeral ceremonies in the neighbouring Kisān community, a specific funeral priest called *Ghanṭuāl* (ferryman) performs the last rites, before the bones are immersed into a river.

The following model thus emerges (Figure 6):

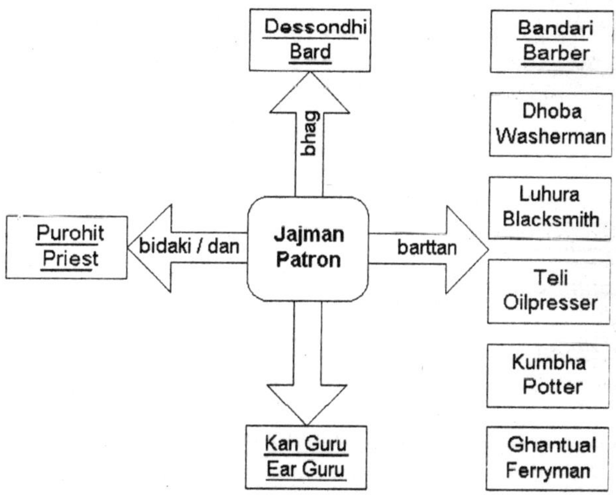

Figure 6: *Jajmāni* relations (present relations are underlined)

It is not necessary that all of these service communities are actually present in the village itself. In fact, even in former times, of all these nine relations, only the Luhurā stayed in Mundaloi—while all others lived elsewhere.

The set of relationships just presented actually falls into at least three sub-categories as far as gifts or payments are concerned. Furthermore, Brahmins are not only a separate category receiving specific gifts, but also privileged in the sense that they receive money—probably the medium of payment that is most easily convertible. Another position singled out is the Dessondhi. He receives *bhāg*, which indicates his relationship as a younger brother (in the separation of a household every brother receives a share or *bhāg*). Finally, apart from the Kān Guru, whose position is not fully clear, all other relations are somehow equated, since all fall into the category of *barttaniā*.

The services of carpenters, gardeners, and astrologers are missing in the scheme presented. If these services are required, a price—*dām*—is paid, for example to the *Jyotisiā* (astrologer), who writes horoscopes after the birth of a child and is consulted about the constellations of stars prior to festivals or life cycle rituals—a work he does occasionally and in addition to agriculture. A Brahmin may also be asked about information on auspicious constellations of stars, but not for a horoscope. In two instances I encountered an Aghriā acting as *Jyotisiā*, which may be one reason why they did not have permanent *jajmāni* relations. As far as carpentry is concerned, every villager is free to follow this profession and would be able to sell his products.

I turn now to the second set of relations:

The Gauntiā as Master/Sāhu[56]

KHAMĀRI AND *GUMĀSTĀ*—STOREROOM KEEPER, REVENUE COLLECTOR, TREASURER

Often rich headmen engaged labourers to take care of the storeroom—the so-called *Khamāri* derived from *Khamār* (godown or storeroom of the king)—and to act as treasurers and revenue collectors the *Gumāstā* (clerk, record keeper). In some cases the same person was responsible for both tasks. A *Khamāri* was also responsible for keeping the records and supervising the cutting of paddy, etc. Almost every Gauntiā had such a supervisor, as the family of the Gauntiā itself did not work in the fields. Naturally, very loyal men were appointed, but in some cases the job was inherited. Nowadays one rarely finds these jobs, which are slowly disappearing with the end of the Gauntiā system. In Mundaloi, for example, a Kandh acted as *Khamāri*, but after his death a few years ago no new *Khamāri* was appointed. Compared to the *Guti,* whose contract had to be renewed every year, the *Khamāri* was engaged permanently. In some cases, land was offered to the *Khamāri* to cultivate it privately. The payment may have differed, but it was certainly not less than a Guti would have received. A Gauntiā told me that his *Khamāri* had refused to accept a higher payment, claiming that he was not doing manual work in the fields, but simply supervising the labourers. Apart from supervising the usually male labourers in the field, sometimes *Khamāri* had other functions in the family. In one case, for example, it was the task of the *Khamāri* to play the gramophone for the Gauntiā's evening entertainment.

BHITRIĀ—PERSONAL ASSISTANT

Sometimes a *Bhitriā* was responsible for domestic affairs. The name literally denotes 'someone allowed inside', hinting at the privilege to enter the inner rooms of the Gauntiā—a right denied to the other servants. A *Bhitriā* must be a *biśvāsi*—a person whom you can trust, as a *Bhitriā* staying in a Gauntiā family often knows all the family secrets. In fact, the *Bhitriā* is usually the most trusted servant and has a higher responsibility for the family than a *Khamāri.*

Some claim that a *Bhitriā* enjoys a higher status than a *Khamāri*, as he is allowed to eat in the kitchen. Others would not make this distinction in status. In some situations the *Khamāri* and the *Bithriā* are the same person.

As a Gauntiā told me, the *Bhitriā* shares the joys and sorrows of his patron's family and is considered almost a family member. He enjoys certain privileges such as the right to allow villagers small quantities of milk in order to perform certain rituals, or he may even allow them to borrow agricultural instruments such as plough shares (*luhā*). He usually does not need the Gauntiā's permission for these favours.

Usually the *Bhitriā* did not work in the fields nor was he engaged in manual labour. In some cases, female labourers might assist the wives of the Gauntiā in the same way and were then known as *Bhitrien*, however in most cases men, particularly younger men, belonging to a high-status community (*bal lok*), preferable Gauḍ, were chosen for this job. There were certain similarities between a *Bhitriā* and a *Ghar khiā* (see below), since both ate in the houses of their patrons. For a trustworthy and long-serving *Bhitriā,* the patron often paid the complete wedding costs and frequently *Bithriā* would leave their patrons after marriage. *Bithriā* or *Bhitrien* might help in the kitchen to wash and cut vegetables and therefore have to belong to high-status communities, but they would not be involved in the cooking process itself. Often the *Bithriā* kept the keys for the storeroom, such as the *dhān ghar* (room to store paddy), when the patron was away. Today these type of servants are rare.[57]

GUTI, HALIĀ, KABĀRI, KAMIHĀN—CONTRACT LABOURERS

There are several terms used to describe contract labourers such as *Guti*, *Haliā*, literally ploughman, and *Kabāri*[58] or *Kamihān*,[59] (literally 'worker' derived from *kām* or work). However, *Guti* seems to be the most common in the region. There is no caste bar on becoming a Guti, who—in this context—ranged from Gauḍ to Chamār. Most *Guti*, however, belong to Scheduled Tribes, notably Muṇḍā, and it may well be true as Roy (1970 [1912]: 131)[60] remarked in the case of the Muṇḍā *Khuntkattidar*—or original 'lords of the soil'—that they were reduced from 'holders of villages' to 'holders of ploughs'. In contrast to an ordinary day labourer, a *Guti* might be called in the middle of the night for a particular job. The contract for the *Guti* is renewed every year on *Pouṣ Purnimā*—the full moon in the month of Pouṣ (around February). [Note that the Bihar and Orissa Kamiauti Act, 1920 limits all such contracts to one year (Schwerin 1977: 477).]

The *Guti* receives the same regular payment as a day labourer (*Butiyā*), but is, in contrast to them, entitled to receive some advance payment, which is known as *nistar*, either in bulk in the form of paddy or saved with the *Sāhu* until the *Guti* is in need. If he cancels the contract before the end he must return the advance payments. Usually the full wage—at the moment roughly five to six *tāmi* or a little less than 5/6 kg—is not given over daily: the landlords keep a portion and the *Guti* can get it at any time. In addition, a *Guti* receives clothes or money particularly at the time of festivals (*jātrā*) such as the *Rath Jātrā*. This gift is known as *jātrā dekhā*. A *Guti* also could, in the past, receive some land from the landlord (0.5 to 1 acre) for cultivation. He was loaned bullocks and ploughs, and even given seeds to sow. The harvest of this land was only for his own private use (in rare cases such land might be given to very loyal *Butiyā* too).

Some *Guti* may also get food in the house of the landlord. In one case, a Gauḍ working as a herdsman for the landlord received a meal in the morning known as *tirpiā* and an evening meal of rice and lentils.

After the complete cutting of the paddy each year the *Guti* gets a gift known as *dājiren*, derived from *dā* 'sickle', symbolizing the end of cutting. Then the landlord gives the ingredients of a full meal, including non-vegetarian food, to all *Guti*, who usually go together to a place on the outskirts of the village or into the jungle to prepare a meal without their families.

In the perception of the government, *Guti* is seen as a type of bonded labour, even slavery, and it is argued that a *Guti* has to work for his patron all day. It is seen as an illegal contract since a *Guti* does not get the minimum wage—around Rs. 50—but insetad around 5 to 6 kg paddy per day, i.e. between Rs. 15 and 30 depending on the price). The latter is also true for day labourers. However, in former times *Guti* were regarded as part of the family and were invited to the landlord's family on *Nuā Khāi*. Often a *Guti* would be addressed as *Guti puo*—'*Guti* son'—by the Sāhu or his wives. In accordance with the principle of equation of alternating generations, a *Guti* was occasionally called *buā* or father, but not *Guti buā*.[61]

GHAR KHIĀ—MAID

Maids are not only entitled to get their food in the house, but also to get everything else they need, such as soap. However, food is clearly the main issue. Therefore, they are called *Ghar khiā* (*ghar* = house; *khiā* = to eat), but usually take their meals outside the kitchen. Often young girls are chosen. They belong to low status communities such as Muṇḍā or Kisān, but are usually not 'Untouchables'. They often come from families with many children. They must clean the house, take care of small children, etc. In one Gauntiā house I learned that, in former times, a *Ghar khiā* used to work a fan fixed on the wall for the wife of the Gauntiā. Their wage was paid in kind and mostly paddy, for example 2 to 3 kg per day. Additionally, the landlord's family is obliged to give clothes, new or used, at the time of festivals. These gifts are known as *jātrā dekhā,* as well. Additional gifts must be presented for a marriage. The landlord is also responsible for the health of the servants and in some cases even their parents. The servants may live in or else return home at night. As in case of a

Guti, a contract is usually made for one year and renewed thereafter, but the child is also allowed to leave at any time.

KĀM KARĀ—FEMALE DOMESTIC LABOURERS

This category of servants is usually hired for certain fixed jobs such as the grinding of spices, herbs or rice or for cleaning the house or cattleshed. Theoretically, there should be at least three *Kāṃ karā* in a house: one for grinding, one for cleaning and sweeping the house, and another for cleaning the cattle shed—work usually to be done in the morning. Theoretically, the woman hired for grinding foodstuff should be a Gauḍen—a woman belonging to the Gauḍ community, but the practice deviates from the theory occasionally. Today, grinding machines have replaced many *Kām karā*.

Kām karā are usually women and constitute an equivalent to the male contract labourers or *Guti*. A contract is settled for the *Kām karā* in the same way that it is done for *Guti* and *Kām karā* ideally work ideally on a daily basis. They also receive *jātrā dekhā*.

PĀENTI/PĀEN DIYĀ/PĀEN BUHĀTI—FEMALE WATER CARRIER

Different names are applied to this type of servant, but *Pāenti* seems to be the most common. A Gauḍen (Gauḍ-lady) used to be employed to fetch water—particularly drinking water—from the well and to bring it into the Aghriā houses. While in most houses water pumps have replaced these servants, in some houses this custom still prevails. It must be a Gāuḍen, because the water of other communities would not be acceptable.

SUĀTI—WATCHMAN

In practice, some servants used to sleep in the Gauntiā's house—defending it against potential robbers. In one case, a Kisān, a Dhobā, a Gauḍ and even an 'untouchable' Gandā were hired at different times as *Suāti*. However, the latter would remain in the outer yard (*guhāl duār*). Often unmarried Guti also acted as *Suāti* and would stay in the Sāhu's house during the night. There was no fixed payment for the *Suāti*, but they were allowed to eat in the patron's house if necessary and would also recieve gifts—in particular clothes—at the time of festivals. Some say there were contracts for the *Suāti*, but others disagree. In one case, female relatives of a Gauḍ—*Suāti* came in the evening to prepare the beds for the Gauntiā family, in other cases, female *Suāti*—*Suāten*—who belonged to the Muṇḍā, Chasā and Gauḍ took care of the wives of the Gauntiā. Some Suāti also gave massages to the Gauntiā and were involved in the evening entertainment programmes in the Gauntiā's house by singing folk songs.

ṬHIKĀMULIĀ—CONTRACT WAGE-LABOURER

This name is derived from *ṭhikā* 'contract' and *muliā* 'labourer for a daily wage'. Thus, a *Ṭhikāmuliā* is somehow a mixture of a *Guti* and a *Butiyā* and this seems to be a rather recent development. He is not obliged to come to the patron's house everyday as does a *Guti*. A *Ṭhikāmuliā* is only called upon if there is work such as the cutting of paddy, the pulling of grass, taking cow dung to the fields, or other major agricultural work. However, in the dry and hot season he is not called upon and is not paid during this period. While a *Guti* must come daily, a *Ṭhikāmuliā* has to be called when his services are needed. A *Ṭhikāmuliā* receives the same payment as a *Butiyā*, but may also receive an advance. The *Ṭhikāmuliā* could get a *kādo chheḍ* (feast after transplanting is over) as well, depending on the landlord.

BUTIYĀ—DAY-LABOURERS

Butiyā are hired for a fixed day (or days). Often the landlord informs them the evening before if there is going to be work. *Butiyā* receive their wages—the same amount as a *Guti*—at the end of each day. Nowadays, more and more often, labourers prefer to work as *Butiyā* rather than *Guti*, as they can choose when to work for the landlord, when in their own fields, and when for contractors who might offer a higher wage for road construction. However, a *Butiyā* has less security of his employment. At the end of the cutting of the paddy a bonus is paid to all day-labourers known as *chheḍ* (end)—sometimes called *dhān duā chheḍ* (*dhān* = paddy; *duā* = cutting) or *ses chheḍ* (*ses* = end). Every labourer usually receives some *khai, chuḍā* and *guḍ* known as *chheḍ liā* or as *chuḍā chitkā*, plus some money, but no *jātrā dekhā*.

Additionally, for transplanting of paddy, seasonal labourers are brought from the outside, who generally stay two to three weeks in the village. The shortage of seasonal labour forces the landlord to bring labourers from other districts such as Bolangir. These seasonal labourers also fall in the category of *Butiyā.* They are paid according to the area cultivated, that is, the acres transplanted, and not according to the hours they have worked. They are entitled to receive a bonus known as a *kādo chheḍ* after their transplanting work is completed, the ingredients of a full meal including meat and wine.

Systemization

The following diagram should help to summarize this set of relations. (The servants presently found in a Gauntiā family in Mundaloi are underlined. *Ṭhikāmuliā* have been neglected here, since they incorporate elements of both *Guti* and *Butiyā.* This also hints at flexibility within the positions, which one should bare in mind—Guti could act as *Suāti* or *Guti* may become *Butiyā.*)

Relationships between Gauntiā and village functionaries

Besides these two networks, there are relations between the Gauntiā and certain villagers who offer services for the whole village.

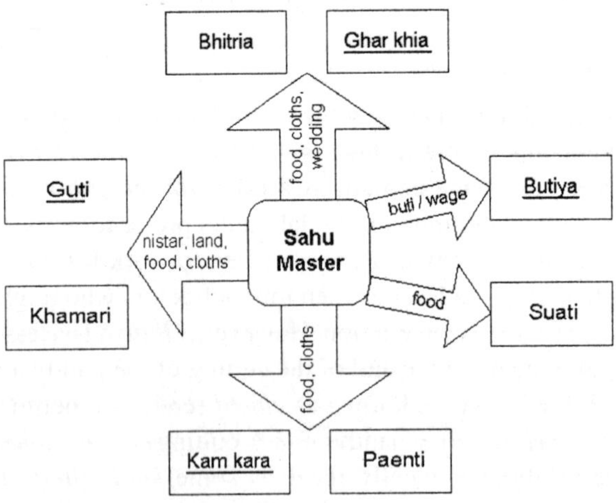

Figure 7: Sāhu-Relations (present relations are underlined)

NARIHĀ—CATTLE HERDSMEN

Usually a Gauḍ acts as the herdsman for the whole village and receives a payment known as *charāni dām* (or sometimes as *buti*). A wealthy Gauntiā with a large herd may hire a Gauḍ as his own personal Narihā, who is then related to the Gauntiā as a *Guti*. In some cases, the Narihā can receive a small portion of land (0.5 to 1 acre) from the Gauntiā, known as *narihā jami*, possibly recorded in the name of the Gauntiā. He is also entitled to receive *jātrā dekhā*, yet the function of a Narihā is a village functionary and not attached to the Gauntiā alone.

In some villages like Muṇḍā or Kisān, men are engaged as herdsmen for the same work. In this case they are called *Charuhā*, not *Narihā*.

KĀLO—SACRIFICER TO THE VILLAGE GODDESS

The relation between Gauntiā and Kālo is characterized by mutual respect. In some villages he may receive land from the Gauntiā known as *jhankar jami* (*jhankar* is another term for Kālo), similar to the *narihā jami*, and is also a receiver of *jātrā dekhā*. The landlord or secular headman offering land and gifts to the sacrificer of the village goddess distinguishes the structure of a Gauntiā village from the traditional tribal villages in which the position of the sacrificer is conceptualized as senior and higher in status to that of a headman, so that latter would probably not offer land to the former.

BEHERĀ—VILLAGE MESSENGER

The British, according to the villagers, created the post of a village messenger. He is appointed by the Gauntiā and village community, although the post can also be hereditary. It is the Beherā's prime function to call the villagers for meetings and to act as a guard during festivals. Traditionally, he is a Harijan. In some villages, the Gauntiā has given the Beherā some land known as *beherā jami*. He also receives *jātrā dekhā*.

PUJĀRI—TEMPLE PRIEST

It has already been mentioned that when a Gauntiā decides to construct a temple land is usually granted to temples as well as to the acting temple priest. This land is considered *mahapru jami* (land of the Lord) and is often recorded in the name of the Gauntiā. In addition to this land grant, the *pujāri* receives a *jātrā dekhā* at the time of *Rākhī Pūni* after he ties a *rākhī* on the wrist of the patron.

CHAMĀR—LEATHERWORKER

Apart from their most important occupation, that of disposing dead cattle and tanning leather, one of the tasks of Chamār is to produce two kinds of leather ropes: *jutā* to fit the yoke (*jueḍ*) to the bullocks, and *nahanā* to connect yoke and plough. These ropes are not sold by the Chamār, but are given every year to all villagers in exchange for their right to take the dead cattle. Thus, all villagers appear as patrons and are called *Sahukār* in relation to the Chamār. However, Chamār do not receive any gift like the *jātrā dekhā*.

Analysis—Categories, relations and hierarchical aspects

Both sets of relationships—of the Gauntiā as Sāhu and as *jajmān*—are compared once more. First, common to both types of relations is the use of the terms 'jajmān' and 'sāhu'. For both *jajmān* and Sāhu, but also for *barttaniā*, the terms are used only as a reference, for example in such sentences as 'Your Sāhu has come, now you can tell him!', 'Your Sāhu is happy with you!', 'He is doing *barttaniā* work for me', etc. They are not used in forms of address. To address someone the fictive kinship terms are always preferred.

Second, while people say that *jajmāni* relations are characterized by intervals—the barber coming once a week, or the priest for certain rituals only—relations to the Sāhu exist on a day-to-day basis. A temporarily limited agreement is reached between a Sāhu and his labourers—usually for a year starting from *Pouṣ Pūni*—but there is no fixed time period for *jajmāni* relations, which are practically permanent.

Third, all communities that are involved in *jajmāni* relations—perhaps excluding the ferrymen – are somehow involved in the rituals performed by the Gauntiā to remove impurity or attain purity. All offer products worshipped in the patron's house, for example the ploughshare and pots used during the weddings. Their higher status may be a result of this involvement. In contrast, the relations with communities that refer to their patrons as Sāhu are usually economic in nature in the sense that no ritual impact could be discovered beyond a participation in *Rākhī Pūni.*

Another important distinction between the two sets of relationships is geographical: communities standing in a *jajmāni* relationship serve their patron exclusively. Neither a *purohit* nor Kān Guru, Dossondhi, barber, washerman, Ghanṭuāl faces any competition within their respective areas. No one else has the right to serve their patron in this area, so long as they are serving their patron properly. Occasionally, there are disputes over these rights, for example, once a potter's family from a different village tried to sell their products in a village considered to be the *jajmāni* of local family and were unable to succeed. The right for this service can—and in fact usually is—inherited by the eldest son or by any other son. In the case that there is more than one son, someone serving a *jajmān* can divide his '*jajmāni area*' among his sons. These two aspects—a geographically fixed area, a certain number of villages, or simply the *jajmāni* on the one hand and the right of sons to inherit the service rights of their fathers—are absent in the relationship between a Sāhu and his labourers.

Fifth, another difference is made as far as status is concerned. Families who refer to the patron as *jajmān* are often ranked higher and receive better treatment than communities served on a daily basis. Thus, *jajmāni* relationships are more valued and of higher status. The barber and washerman are more guests than servants in the strict sense. One is more polite to the barber, and pays less attention to the labourers. However, the treatment of the barber and washerman, is not as good as it is for other patrons in the village. Generally, from the perspective of the Gauntiā, service has been valued very little, although it is changing as far as the bureaucracy and service jobs in the administration are concerned. Therefore, one could likely derive the following hierarchy, which somehow corresponds to concepts of wealth and prestige (these themselves being relative concepts too):

TABLE 14: VILLAGE HIERARCHY

Hierarchy
Gauntiā
Other *Jajmān*/Sāhu (*Baḍ Parjā*/ upper castes)[62]
Barber, Washerman and other *barttaniā* (except Brahmin)
Labourers: Guti/Butiyā

Leaving aside discussions which term the *jajmāni* system as either 'exploitative' or 'integrative',[63] I want to stress the point that the two sets of relationships are hierarchically ordered. In contrast to Wiser's primary focus on reciprocity, Dumont (1980 [1966]: 101–2) had emphasized the hierarchical order behind the *jajmāni* relationships. The barber, for example, serves certain high-status communities only. Communities are not only implicitly evaluated by others in relation to services offered to them or withheld, but the two sets of service relationships are ranked. *Jajmāni* relations are conceptualized as permanent, hereditary and centred on the performance of rituals, for which a certain purity is essential. They are more valued than short-term, contractual labour arrangements with little ritual involvement. Thus the Gauntiā as *jajmān* could be understood as encompassing the Gauntiā as *Sāhu*.[64] That does not imply that we find a complete distinction between a religious level *jajmāni* relationship and a purely economic level. As Parry (1979: 79) argues, there is an ongoing 'extension of the "economic frontier"', which means that even *jajmāni* relationships constructed as permanent could be replaced by, or turned into, market relationships as in the case of potters and oil-presser.

Besides, these categories, *jajmān* and Sāhu relationships, are not only hierarchized, but also connected by particular gifts—receiving *kharchā* (raw food for a complete meal) on *Rākhī* and *Pouṣ Pūni* as well as by receiving gifts during festivals of *Śibrātrī*, *Rath Jātrā* and *Makra Sankrānti*—and/or gifts (usually money or dress material) known as *jātrā dekhā*, the whole of which is systematized below:

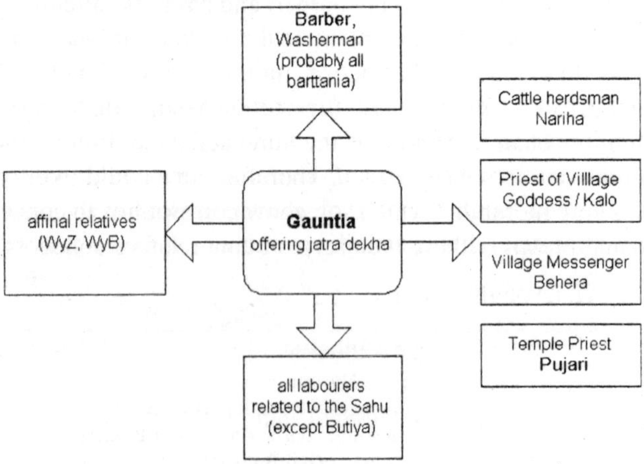

Figure 8: Offering of *jātrā dekhā* by a Gauntiā.

Thus, various sets of relations are not conjunct in the *jajmān* as Pocock found in Gujarat, but are interconnected by a Gauntiā or landlord, who, as king, has conquered the wilderness and thereby gained 'resources' including the services of conquered people (Falk 1973: 3).[65]

In addition to that the Gauntiā incorporates as prime or universal donor almost all categories of the village. Having an essential function as king, he binds all categories to a centre. By offering *jātrā dekhā* and *kharchā* a holistic picture emerges, in which *barttaniā*, Kālo, and lower Brahmin as *pujāri* are equated as receivers of gifts—the only exception being the *purohit,* whose position remains vague. Therefore all receivers, including the wife-giving affines, are in a structurally similar position, which seems to be lower compared to the Gauntiā as donor, who does not take form them.

4.9. THE RELATION TO THE VILLAGE GODDESS

The importance of goddesses—or more specifically of an *iṣṭā devī*— in relation to kings is frequently expressed in royal inscriptions (see, for example, Lāngulesvara Itihasa) and noted by anthropologists and historians working in India (Galey 1990; Tambs-Lyche 1997; Basu 2000) and in Orissa in particular (Kulke 2001 [1978]; Schnepel 1997; Hardenberg 2000; Mallebrein forthcoming). In the following passage I will argue that the relation between the Gauntiā and the village goddess mirrors the link between superior kings and their *iṣṭā devī*. Goddesses (and gods), like kings, are ranked.

The Village Goddess and her sacrificer—Kālo

The village goddess resides in a shrine known as the *demul*[66] (*de* = god/goddess; *mul* = root) meaning a sacred grove or abode of gods in the forest. The village goddess does not live alone, but is joined by other divine beings such as the *Rākasbuḍhā* or *Banaspati* (Lord of the Forest). In most cases her shrine is situated on the outskirts of the village, though not in deep jungle, always surrounded by trees. The goddess is worshipped either in the form of stones, termite hills or, as happened in one case, a half-fallen tree forming a cross with a living tree—all being regarded as her manifestation.

There are three major rituals for the village goddess that correspond to the seasons. The *Grām Śrī Pūjā* after the harvest is completed and before sowing, the *Bihuḍā Pūjā* before the transplanting and loosening the soil (*bihuḍā*) with a special small plough, and finally the *Niśā*-(night) *Pūjā* after the cutting of the paddy. The timing of these three rituals—all related to agricultural work—clearly indicates the quality of the village goddess as an earth goddess. In all the rituals blood sacrifices are offered to the goddess, which have to be male, say billy-goats and cocks. The sacrificer keeps a special axe, known as *phalsiā*, for beheading. Women are generally not allowed to participate in the rituals, nor are they allowed to touch the sacrificial axe on the day of the rituals. Occasionally, the number of participants is further restricted to men of the village or to married men. The rituals can only take place on a Wednesday or Friday, and then only if the village is not polluted by cases of death or birth. The period of pollution varies according to the customs of different communities, but usually does not take more than eleven days in the case of death (at a minimum, the clothes must be washed and the family concerned readmitted into the community) or six to seven days after a birth has taken place (the purification usually follows only after the umbilical cord has fallen).

The sacrificer—not a professional priest like a Brahmin, but a peasant who also worships the village deities in intervals—usually belongs to a high status tribal community such as the Kandh or Bhuyān (see hierarchy) and is chosen by the Gauntiā and the village community, but the post can as well be hereditary. A differentiation between the sacrificer and the headman is common in tribal society, as stated. However, in contrast to a tribal society the relationship between the headman and the sacrificer is not conceived in a senior–junior opposition; there is an additional role for the Brahmin and the role of the Gauntiā is not confined to secular functions.

During rituals, the Kālo does not ordinarily sacrifice the animals himself, but is assisted by another high status group member—often a Gauḍ. Prior to the rituals the Kālo has to fast for at least twelve hours. The evening before the ritual the Gauntiā sends him (via the Narihā) the raw ingredients of a meal known as *kharchā*, that is, he fasts during the day, receives the meal of *aruā chāul* and lentils in the evening, and fasts again until the ritual commences.[67]

In three cases, I observed that the Gauntiā himself or someone from the landlord's lineage acted as the sacrificer of the village goddess. This indicates that here the Kālo did not belong to a tribal community, but to the Aghriā. About a hundred years ago, an Aghriā took over the village as the Gauntiā had left following a mysterious disease. Since the Bhuyān Kālo had left the village, the Aghriā Gauntiā took over the Kālo function as well. Later the Gauntiā's son was not interested in acting as the Kālo, but the function was kept within the local line for a brother's son's son. As in other cases the Aghriā Kālo is normally assisted by a Gauḍ. In yet another case the Gauntiā concentrated on worshipping the Grām Śrī while he left the worship of all other gods and goddesses to his Gauḍ assistant. In such cases the Gauntiā increases his influence on the cult of the goddess being not only the patron, but also as the sacrificer of the goddess concurrently. I turn now to the various rituals, paying specific attention to the Gauntiā's role.

Rituals of the village goddess

In three seasons, the villagers perform a ritual for the village goddess. Before describing these rituals in detail concentrating on the role of the landlord, I have systematized them in a table below:

TABLE 15: SEASONS AND RITUALS OF THE VILLAGE GODDESS

Season[68]	Major Ritual	Activities
Kharā (heat) hot and dry	*Grām Śrī Pūjā* (before sowing) (during the day)	Marriage season—repairing fields and roofs; collecting fire wood; garden work; *Mahuā*—collection; purchase of bullocks
Barṣā (rain) wet	*Bihuḍā Pūjā* (before loosening the soil and transplantation) (during the day)	Start of marriage negotiations—early cutting and threshing—*Rath Jātrā* and *Nuā Khāi*
Jāḍa (winter) cold	*Niśā-Pūjā* (after cutting the paddy) (at night)	Early marriage season—late cutting and threshing of paddy—transplantation of vegetables

GRĀM ŚRĪ PŪJĀ

In Mundaloi, in the morning of the *Grām Śrī Pūjā* a smaller ritual is performed for Lakṣmī in the Gauntiā's house. In front of the *tulsī chaur* a symbolic lotus is drawn with water and rice powder, upon which a pot with white paddy is placed. The Gauntiā's wife offers two garlands made of *mahuā* flowers and mangos, *bel* leaves (resembling a *triśul*), and turmeric. The Narihā carries this paddy together with the other ritual items, such as hibiscus and other flowers, incense, coconuts, *ghī* lamps, and *muān,* to the shrine of the village goddess. All of these items are offered by the Gauntiā.

After cleaning and purifying the shrine with cow dung, the Kālo offers one of the *mahuā* garlands to the Grām Śrī. Apart from the village goddess, Lakṣmī, who is manifested in the white paddy. *Rākasbuḍhā*, and *Banaspati* (Lord of the Forest), are worshipped in front of the termite hill. A slight distance away, Mā Bhainro is worshipped in the form of a stone. For *Rākasbuḍhā* marijuana (*ganja*) is offered. For the goddesses, liquor is also presented. Villagers may offer whatever they are able to afford, for example cocks, but they expect the Gauntiā to offer at least a non-castrated billy-goat each year. These are known as the *baden-bukā.*[69] Before being sacrificed, the goat must be fed some rice, *khai* and *muān* and its eating is regarded as a sign that the Goddess accepts the offer.[70] If the goat does not eat, it cannot be offered. The Gauntiā, or a male member of his family, is usually present during the sacrifice and his physical presence is essential for the proper performance of the ritual. A Gauntiā told me that one particular year he did not attend the *pūjā*, but just sent the ritual items. The goat would not eat anything offered; only after the Gauntiā's appearance did the goat begin to eat. Its body is returned to the donor as *prāsād*, while the Kālo takes the severed head of the animal. The cooking has to take place outside the house—usually close to the shrine. After the *Grām Śrī Pūjā*, the Kālo distributes the white paddy, offered by the Gauntiā to the Grām Śrī, amongst the villagers for the first sowing.

BIHUḌĀ PŪJĀ

The *Bihuḍā Pūjā* occurs at the time of the light ploughing particularly necessary for the late varieties of rice. Before this *pūjā*, *bihuḍā* work and the transplantation is not allowed, but sowing is. In the event that someone begins transplanting or loosening the soil before the ritual, the fine of a billy-goat can be imposed. For the ritual, the Gauntiā offers a non-castrated billy-goat. His presence during the ritual is thereafter obligatory. The ritual procedure is identical with the *Grām Śrī Pūjā* except that no paddy is distributed.

If there is not enough time to perform the *Bihuḍā Pūjā* properly, because the beginning of the monsoon season is the busiest time for peasants, a much smaller ritual known as the *Pāendhār Pūjā* (*pāendhār* = water flow) may be performed in order to start transplanting and loosening the soil. For the *Pāendhār Pūjā,* the Gauntiā offers a black cock to the Goddess. The Kālo sacrifices it, but the Gauntiā's presence is not obligatory.

NIŚĀ-PŪJĀ

After the cutting of paddy, the Kālo performs a *Niśā-Pūjā*, literally a night ritual. The prime deity of this ritual is not Grām Śrī, although she is worshipped as well, but Mauli Mā. The whole pantheon of gods and divine beings is included. Again, the Gauntiā offers all of the ritual items[71] but other villagers are also free to offer the same things individually. The most important offering is a blood sacrifice: in one case a billy-goat for Mauli Mā and two cocks for Grām Śrī; in another case a she-goat for Mauli Mā and two cocks or two coconuts for Bauti Mā. Some locals informed me that this ritual is performed for the well-being of the village and the Gauntiā in particular.

Digression: a note on the goddesses

Basu (1994: 176ff) distinguishes between three ideal types of goddesses in Hinduism: (1) the unambiguous, positively valued mother-goddess, for example Gau Mata; (2) the wife or permanent consort of a male god, such as Sita and Parvati and (3) the terrible, sinister and vindictive goddess represented by Durgā or Kāli. The first is often associated with virginity, while the last is usually linked to infertility, but all three are related to the female cycle of menstruation (Kāli), conception (Parvati), and motherhood (Gau Mātā). There is no clear-cut separation between these ideal types and transitions between them seem to be frequent. Thus, the village goddess appears as a conjunction of the second and third type. Kinsley (1987: 204) notes:

The village goddesses usually avoid both the extreme of the docile, shy, obedient married female and the extreme of the wild, frenzied, dangerous Kālī who is a threat to civilized order. The combination of the village goddesses' power and fierceness with their protectiveness of the well-being, stability, and order of their villages is beneficial. As the protector of the village the goddess must be powerful in view of the dangerous forces that threaten it. No shy, retiring, docile female could successfully protect the village. Although the village goddess may be dangerous because of her great power, for the most part that strength is directed against threatening forces from outside.

In the context described here, the village goddess is also identified with the earth, although Dharti Mātā is known as an earth goddess as such. Apart from her potentially fierce manifestation and the embodiment of female power or *śakti*, the village goddess shares with Durgā, Samlei, and Mauli Mā the acceptance of blood sacrifices and the status of not being 'domesticated' in marriage. In regard to these common features, villagers occasionally recognize Grām Śrī as a local representation or refraction of Durgā of the Great Tradition and the differences between a Grām Śrī and Mauli Mā can be blurred to such an extent that the only remaining difference is the locally bound *śakti* or fixed territory for which every Grām Śrī—in contrast to Mauli Mā or Durgā—is specifically responsible.

The role of the Gauntiā in the cult of Grām Śrī

The Gauntiā has an exalted position in the cult of the village goddess. He is the prime donor for the worship, including the valuable animal sacrifices. Additionally, without his presence, the ritual cannot be performed properly. Having privileged access to the goddess effectively implies having access to the female power (*śakti*) embodied by the goddess. As Marglin (1989 [1985]: 300) noted in relation to the Gajapati: royal power is *śakti* power and every Gajapati is 'symbolically infused with the female procreative powers'.[72] Therefore, not worshipping the goddess in her shrine would mean loosing power, and subsequently the kingdom.[73]

In some cases the Gauntiā even has the additional role of the sacrificer and, thus, becomes the 'patron-servant' (Tanabe 1996: 211) of Grām Śrī. The Gauntiā's role in these rituals resembles the Gajapati's, who according to the pontificial ideology is the king and first servant of the Lord Jagannāth as well; without his presence and involvement as royal sweeper, the *Rath Jātrā* cannot be conducted properly (Hardenberg 1999: 154).

Another important aspect is the site of the shrine, in the forest or in a sacred grove, which means in the wilderness. The fact that the Gauntiā must worship her at her shrine regularly, points to an age-old dilemma of kings. Heesterman (1998: 22–4) argues that the conundrum of kingship lies in the fact that the 'king has to be both part of the community and foreign to it', and that his authority is based on the 'alien, outside sphere of the jungle' (*aranya*), while he has to rule over the 'settled, agricultural community' (*grāma*). Heesterman (1998: 30) understands these facts as a cause for the king's ritual cycle to alternate between these two spheres. Just as the ancient kings, the Gauntiā unites both elements—*bana* and *kshetra* (Sontheimer 1994)—by performing the rituals of the Grām Śrī. The Gauntiā bridges the gap between a caste society often associated with *kshetra/grāma* and a tribal society linked with *bana/aranya* (Heesterman 1998: 24; Sontheimer 1994: 127ff). However, not only the Gauntiā, but the goddess herself unites these different spheres, symbolized in the shrine site: she resides within the village territory, but in a part considered to be bordering on the wilderness. 'As such the shrine is a kind of preserve, a presence of the wilderness in more civilized areas,' Falk (1973: 4) observed. Thus both the Gauntiā and the goddess incorporate aspects of liminality, that is, being placed between tribal and caste society as well as between wilderness and settlement.

4.10. CHANGE AND DECLINE

So far, I have described a rather glorious past of the Aghriā village kings, which is still recognizable today in many villages. However, a considerable economic, political and religious change has taken place in recent decades.

Economic decline

After the abolition of the Gauntiā system, Indian Independence and merger of the States with the Indian Union, headmen lost their former rights to collect revenue, that is, to receive a share of it and/or rent-free land. Most of the Gauntiā had to return their land deeds in the early 1950s and the influential Gauntiā of Kuchinda was replaced by a subcollector in 1963—the last transfer of such privileges of which I am aware. The economic position of the former revenue collectors deteriorated further by several land reforms. However, in many cases the Gauntiā were able to distribute all their land among family members, thus keeping it within the family, or managed to keep hold of their land by prolonged legal battles or were at least able to decide which land to vacate, thus keeping the land of the highest quality. The most decisive factor of decline was—and still is—the continuous division of property due to growing families. Until the 1930s, Gauntiā families took up new villages for their respective sons—acquiring new land every generation by clearing forests, etc. Today, heirs must divide whatever property there is among themselves. Thus there is a sense of decline among headmen even though many of them are still powerful and able to keep a privileged position in the village. Several other examples further illustrate the Gauntiā's deteriorating economic position.

In an extreme case of decline in Tarnmura, the great-grandfather—the first Aghriā Gauntiā in the village—had roughly 80 acres as private property, his eldest son had between 30 and 35 acres, his second 30, the third 9 acres, and the fourth had 18 acres after the division of the family's land. The younger sons later claimed that due to their father's early death they had been cheated. The eldest son died without children, and his wife, who had several disputes with the rest of the family, finally decided to let the land go to the government after her death. Subsequently this land was distributed among poorer villagers. The second son, who has only one son, was able to keep the land undivided and thus is still relatively well off and regarded as a Gauntiā. Yet the living standard of the other two brothers' descendants deteriorated due to further divisions. The fourth brother's two sons inherited 9 acres each. Their two and four sons respectively inherited 4.5 and 2.2 acres each. Not much better off are the three households of the third son's descendants having 3 acres each for cultivation—hardly enough to live on.

A Gauntiā family in Thainsar lost part of its property due to land reforms. The separation of households further diminished the shares considerably. As at Tarnmura, the original estate of more than 150 acres was divided among three sons, 70 acres to the first born, 54 to the second, while the third received a share of only 28 acres. Due to a land ceiling the only son of the first-born was forced to sell 50 of the 70 acres, and now has only 20 acres. The second son's share has not yet been further divided, but with his son having three sons himself, another division is only a matter of time. The two sons of the third shared in equal parts and have 14 acres each.

The first Aghriā Gauntiā in Bankey originally owned about 180 acres of land. This was divided among his two sons, 140 acres and 40 respectively. The elder had no sons and adopted his sister's son. He divided his property into five equal shares of roughly 25 acres each: one for himself, one for his adopted son and the rest for his three nephews. A little more than 10 acres were lost by the ceiling. The specific manner of which could have been influenced by land reforms allowing every family a limited amount property only.[74] The elder son's own share was divided after his death: 19 acres for his eldest nephew (yBS) who became the Gauntiā; 1 acre to manage the costs of the *Rath Jātrā*; the rest of 3.5 acres each distributed among his adopted son and his other two nephews. The Gauntiā's younger brother already divided his share of 40 acres equally among his three sons. The present Gauntiā has four sons and each will receive an equal share of about 14 acres. Thus, after the death of the present Gauntiā, his eldest son as the new Gauntiā will have a property of about 14 acres compared to the 180 acres his great-grandfather (FFF) had (see Figure 9).

Another indicator of economic decline is the loss of ponds, which were sometimes transferred voluntarily to the government in order to save the costs of maintenance. In Bankey, the Gauntiā family

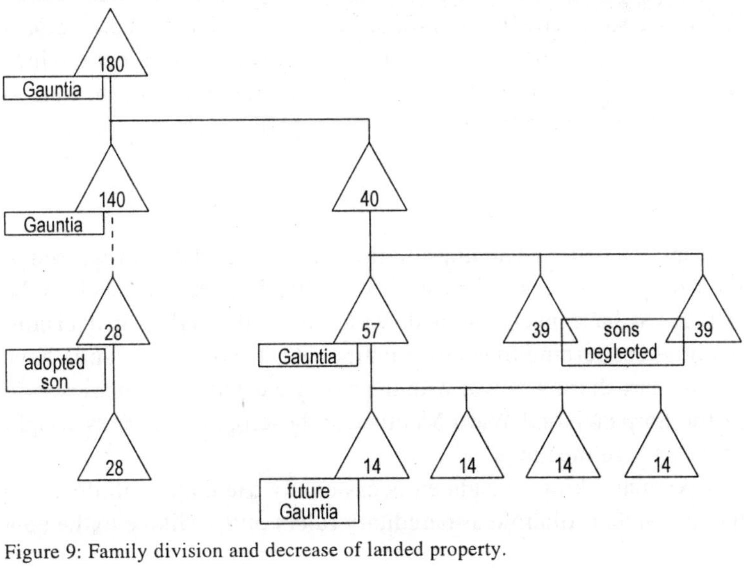

Figure 9: Family division and decrease of landed property.

originally owned ten ponds. All of these have been taken over by the government. At present the family owns only one recently-built pond.

The problem has probably been aggravated not only by decreasing paddy prices, but also by the families' royal *habitus*—any service job was regarded as of low prestige: as a Gauntiā you hired servants, you were not one yourself. Gauntiā families ventured into service-jobs offered by the government and other institutions rather late and, according to my observations, from the 1980s onwards a significant shift took place. Today, salaried jobs are highly valued. Thus, occupation is intrinsically related to the prestige of a Gauntiā. In their transition to new occupations to earn a higher and more stable income independent of agriculture, Gauntiā must keep their prestige in mind. Certain jobs, such as running a hotel, although profitable, would be below their prestige. People would suspect that even the owner would come in contact with the impure food remains of the customers. Thus, a Gauntiā told me that he is afraid of charges like 'You are the Gauntiā, but what are you doing now [in the hotel]?' To sell clothes at weekly markets is also quite profitable, but has low prestige, a semi-nomadic business. It is unlikely that a Gauntiā would turn to such a business. However, to own a shop selling spare parts, or a medical store, would be compatible with their prestige—provided it is a proper, permanent *pakkā* shop and not just a small cabin. Owning a stone crusher or mill, or being a government contractor is also very acceptable today. Other Gauntiā own buses or jeeps, which they can let for rent—both are considered of high prestige as long as they are not driving themselves—although there are exceptions.

Political change

The abolition of the Gauntiā system has also meant the formal end of their role as Justices of Peace. New political institutions such as the Pañchāyat have been initiated, which have the rights of decision-making, concerning road construction, etc. Therefore, Gauntiā have had to start sharing power with the newly elected functionaries such as the Sarpanch and Ward Members, whose opinion carries weight in the village meetings.

Like many kings, headmen occasionally tried, and still do so, to transform their old role as hereditary rulers of the village to the new one as politicians. Often the right to be elected—i.e. passive voting rights—are limited to fixed quotas for Scheduled Tribes, Other Backward Classes, and women, etc. Due to these reservations, there are certain limits of eligibility for the Gauntiā. Some headmen have become secretaries of the Pañchāyat, while others have been elected to other levels of the present political system, for example to the post of a Zilla Parishad member. Political parties offer tickets to influential Gauntiā in the hope that their influence will turn into votes. On the other hand, it is usual that candidates seeking votes before the election consult the Gauntiā and ask for his support. In some cases the local candidates for the post of Sarpanch asked the Gauntiā for advice before their official candidature.

In this way the Gauntiā have managed to keep their hereditary role to some extent and have started to penetrate new institutions, but must still face a loss of formal power in political terms. While in many cases village councils are still chaired by a Gauntiā, much depends not only on their economic ability to maintain their role, but also on their personal interest in participating and in maintaining their traditional role. As village heads, the Gauntiā are invited to inaugurate football tournaments, etc., and to preside over functions. Besides, a certain sharing of power is not absolutely new. In former times respected villagers such as *Baḍ Parjā* appear to have participated in village meetings and voiced their concerns.

Ritual change and decline

There is an observable ritual decline closely related to the economic decline. Some headmen are no longer capable of maintaining the traditional pattern of gifting and, therefore, cannot keep their role as the main sacrifier for the village goddess. Lack the financial assets to offer the necessary items for the rituals, the animals in particular. Therefore, rituals have changed: expensive animal sacrifices have been reduced or replaced by smaller offerings. Buffalos have often been replaced by billy-goats, or billy-goats in turn by coconuts. In some instances these rituals have stopped altogether. In 2001, the Gauntiā of the small town of Kuchinda ceased to offer a billy-goat on *Daśarā*; he promised that he would offer one the next year—thus prolonging the interval of gift giving from one to two years. A considerable shift from blood sacrifices to affordable vegetarian prestations coincides with a widespread Orissan and Indian tendency towards *ahimsa* or non-violence (see also Mallebrein 2001a).

In contrast, there are new festivals. In Mundaloi the Gauntiā has been able to preserve his traditional role to a large extent. He is the sole sponsor of the *Nam Jagya* festival which was introduced only four years ago and, additionally, a *Rath Jātrā* has run in the village for three years. In fact, in many villages, where the *Rath Jātrā* is celebrated, it was not introduced until the late 1950s or 1960s, after the formal abolition of the Gauntiā system. This flexibility is not something new in and of itself. In former times, rituals for Radha and Krishna were popular, or those for Viṣṇu (the *Hari Yajna*) or Rām (*Rām Navami*). These days, however, the *Rath Jātrā*, introduced on the village level only recently, has replaced earlier rituals—most of them belonging to the Vaishnava tradition. Locals say that the higher costs of the older rituals or the villagers' wishes are the main reasons for this change. New village festivals and the growing popularity of the *Rath Jātrā* and *Nām Jagya* enhance the Gauntiā's prestige. This fact may point to the Gauntiā's growing importance in rituals after his loss of economic power. Such a shift appears to resemble the Gajapati's changing role in the cult of Lord Jagannāth: his closeness to Jagannāth is increasingly emphasized as his political power wanes.

To conclude: today, Gauntiā face a considerable change having lost much of their 'kingdoms' in both economic and political terms. Sometimes this also results in a loss of their ritual role, while there may be a simultaneous shift towards an increased ritual role in order to compensate for a loss in other spheres. However, in many cases Gauntiās are still wealthy landowners keeping and, by introducing new and more king-centred rituals, at times even consolidating their traditional position. Though revenue collection has been abolished in its traditional indirect form, there are other modern methods in which dominance is re-enacted, for example the recent introduction of telephones in the region has shown a traditional pattern of power since most of the public phones are installed in Gauntiā's houses, forcing villagers to go to him to make a call. I saw a wealthy Gauntiā refusing to take money from the villagers as that would be below their prestige.[75]

4.11. CONCLUSION: RELATIONS BETWEEN GODS, KINGS AND SUBJECTS

In this chapter, the rise, consolidation, and slow decline of the Gauntiā—the village kings—belonging primarily to the Aghriā community, has been described, as well as their deep embeddedness in the concepts of kingship. Gauntiā were kings following the *kṣātra dharma* while conquering tribal land and cultivating the wilderness—later institutionalizing the king's alternating movement between settlement and forest in the worship of the village goddess. In an arena of Hinduization as well as tribalization, Gauntiā have acted and act as agents of change by building temples, inviting Brahmins and developing the land by using new technologies. They have played a decisive role in the process of 'intensive propaganda' (Weber 1988 [1921]: 11) or 'inner colonization' (Pfeffer 1978: 426; Kulke 2001 [1978]: 3) in relation to tribal communities; at the same time they are influenced by them as well.

Furthermore, the Gauntiā manifested their *kṣātra dharma* by becoming the supreme donors in the village became integrated as subjects into the networks of a superior king, in turn integrating their own subjects at a lower level. Keeping in mind definitions of little kingdoms such as proposed by Berkemer (1993: 13),[76] Gauntiā may well be understood as little kings within their own realm. The relation between a Gauntiā and the Raja of Bamra—between a little king and an overlord—is mirrored strikingly by the relation between a *Guti* and a Gauntiā. Both are bound to their superior by sharing his land as well as by receiving gifts. Gifting and sharing rights establishes the network of relationships between the levels. Cohn (1995 [1983]: 168) points out, in reference to Buckler:

> This incorporation (. . .) rests on the idea that the king stands for a 'system of rule of which he is the incarnation . . . incorporating into his body . . . the persons of those who share his rule'. Those just incorporated were not just servants of the king, but part of him.

Therefore, the king and Gauntiā may represent, what Kantorowicz (1994 [1957]: 31ff) termed a *body politic*: eternal, immortal, invisible, immaterial as well as collective and incorporate not only the actual king in his *body natural*—or present appearance—, but also all subjects as imagined parts. Thus, the *body politic*—the idea of kingship—remains in existence even after the abolition of the kingdom or Gauntiā system and survives the 'absented throne' (Galey 1990: 129), because it represents the whole from the perspective of the king.[77]

There has been much debate about the question of superiority of the king or Brahmin.[78] As Trautmann (1995 [1981]: 278ff), Galey (1990: 169) and Basu (2000: 163) have pointed out, there are different, contextual patterns of classification depending on the perspective, expressed in forms of exchange or rituals in the temple as opposed to rituals in the palace. While the Brahmin stands highest in a hierarchy of ritual purity, it is the king, as supreme donor, who ranks above all in a hierarchy of dependence.

On the village level the statement above is manifested in certain ambivalences. On the one hand, the high status Brahmin remains conspicuously absent during the *Rākhī Pūni* rituals—a kind of village *durbar*—arguing that he is not interested in the money the Gauntiā offers in return for a *rākhī*. However, the lower status Brahmin and temple priest appear at their patron's house in order to tie a *rākhī* and to accept the gifts. The motif of the high status Brahmin trying to avoid the taking of gifts, thus maintaining his independence, seems to be obvious here, although they do take gifts on many other occasions. Significantly, in north India, Marriott (1955: 198) found Brahmin domestic priests tying *rākhīs* on the wrists of their patrons; they were rewarded in cash by the patrons, 'for it is thought impious to accept anything as a free gift from a priest'.

Aghriā-Gauntiā in neighbouring Chhattisgarh (Sarangarh area) told me that Gauntiā—as their superior kings—do not show respect in form of *praṇām* to visiting Brahmins, rather only by offering a privileged sitting position next to the Gauntiā. However, all family members of a Gauntiā—as also the Gauntiā in Kuchinda area—do the *praṇām* greeting.[79] When tea is offered in the *purohit*'s house, it is the Gauntiā who washes the dishes, although the *purohit* (Tihāri or Brahmin) may protest. Not to wash one's own dishes on such an occasion would mean committing a *pāp* (sin) for a Gauntiā, who maintains the respective ritual purity. Thus, the ambivalent relationship between the king and Brahmin reflects that kingship and the royal network of the Gauntiā establish and maintain, for example in offering *jātrā dekhā*, a pattern of ordering society. Such a pattern may become dominant or a subordinate depending on the context.

I turn now to the relationships of kings and gods. Not only the relationships between a Gauntiā and his superior kings as well as subjects within a hierarchy of dependency (Trautmann 1995 [1981]: 278), but also between kings and gods will be systematized here. Galey's (1990) model may help us understand the Gauntiā's position in a wider sacred order. Beginning with kingship in Garhwal, Galey (1990: 166ff) argues that royalty could be defined as a combination of three ritual complexes: (1) the throne or *piṭha* as a seat of mastery to which the king is married and thus spatially rooted and attached to demarked soil (2) the kingdom as ritually conceptualized as an active field or *kṣetra*, animated by female potency (*śakti*) embodied by a goddess to whom blood sacrifices are offered and (3) the king's authority emanting from his special relationship to a sovereign god, in whose cult he has a privileged position. The third element is regarded as the most important for royal legitimacy, as it places the palace within a space governed by the tutelary deity, or *avatār* god, to use Galey's terms, also known as *iṣṭā devtā* or *raṣtra devtā*—Viṣṇu in the form of Badrinath in case of Garhwal. In relation to the *avatār*—god expressed in the place of passage or *tīrtha*, the kingdom becomes a realm of order, a particular universe linked to the general universe, the cosmos. Thus, kingship is manifested by a complementarity of three elements: *piṭha*/mastery, *kṣetra*/potency, and *tīrtha*/universality.

> They associate the king in his palace with a throne, preside over the destiny of a kingdom which takes the form of a sacrificial area, before even inscribing it as a world of earthly limits and illimited potential. (Galey 1990: 171)

Galey (1990) proposed a diversified perspective when speaking of regional configurations of kingship in India. Within this framework, Basu (2000) pointed at a deviating conception of kingship in western India. While the Vaishnava cosmology of Garhwal is dominated by a male god (Viṣṇu), the concept of kingship in Kutch, influenced by Shaiva and Śakti Tantra traditions, an autonomous goddess or *deśdevi,* appears to be at the centre, empowering and authorizing the king.

Returning to the Gauntiā, one could argue that the Vaishnava conception of kingship as described by Galey is applicable to parts of Orissa and at the village level as well, but ritual configurations in Orissa and Garhwal are not identical. Though the concept seems to be similarly Vaishnava-influenced, Lord Jagannāth, in a trinity with his sister Subhadra and his elder brother Balabhadra, as well as in relation to his rather capricious wife Lakṣmī, may differ from Badrinath/Viṣṇu in Garhwal.

At the village level, the Gauntiā is linked directly to the Grām Śrī and through her, a *kṣetra* or 'arena of potency' or an arena of creative power—is established. The Gauntiā derives *śakti* by offering blood sacrifices to the village goddess, who is related to fertility and auspiciousness. As the prime donor in her rituals, the Gauntiā as symbolic head of the village is the direct counterpart of the goddess. He is the one who pours blood on her soil and 'makes it possible for the procreative forces which lie in her womb to find an appropriate soil' (Galey 1990: 168). The *śakti* of Grām Śrī, however, locally or territorially fixed as it is, ranks lower in scale than that of Durgā, or her manifestation as Kanak Durgā, who constitutes an arena of creative power with the Gajapati/Raja of Bamra.

In many cases the Gauntiā have also been able to link themselves to Jagannāth as a form of Viṣṇu and *iṣṭa devtā* of their superior kings such as the king of Bamra as well as the Gajapati. Ultimate legitimacy is derived from Jagannāth as the Lord of the Universe. However, a Gauntiā, as a little king, derives his authority from Jagannāth not directly, but via his overlord(s) and therefore his authority is secondary and indirect—in contrast to the primary *śakti* he derives from the village goddess. Nevertheless, the Gauntiā attempts to derive his authority directly by performing the *Rath Jātrā* himself. Thus, by imitating and, at the same time, challenging his overlords, the Gauntiā tries to style himself as a king, Gajapati or as a 'walking Viṣṇu' (*calanti* Viṣṇu).

The question of the throne remains, and although he has no *gāddī* (throne) as such, the relations of dominance that the throne represents can be found in the village as well. Galey (1990: 171–2) stresses this point:

> The throne thus represents a mere relation than an object. Distinct in that from the tutelary temples, its reference is not one of concrete and permanent geography. Rather, its meaning lies more in the ceremonial display of items and actors than in the items and actors themselves. (ibid. 171)[80]

I have noted that the rituals of *Rākhī Pūni* may well be understood as a royal *durbar* in which the Gauntiā acts as the prime donor, binding loyal subjects to his 'seat of mastery'. Mastery is also expressed in the Gauntiā's role as Sāhu, while the Gauntiā as *jajmān* establishes his place in the cosmology.

The Gauntiā is embedded in the network of relationships just described, which is shown in the following Figure 10 presenting the Gauntiā and his relationships to his ranked overlords, his ranked subjects (*Baḍ Parjā* and *Sān Parjā*) as well as to the gods and goddesses, to the Grām Śrī and ultimately to Jagannāth. Lord Jagannāth, as Lord of the Universe representing the whole, is not bound and therefore not put into a rectangle in the model. To Jagannāth, an indirect link has been established: a Gauntiā used to derive and may still derive authority via his overlords. Furthermore, a Gauntiā may attempt to establish a more direct link by performing the

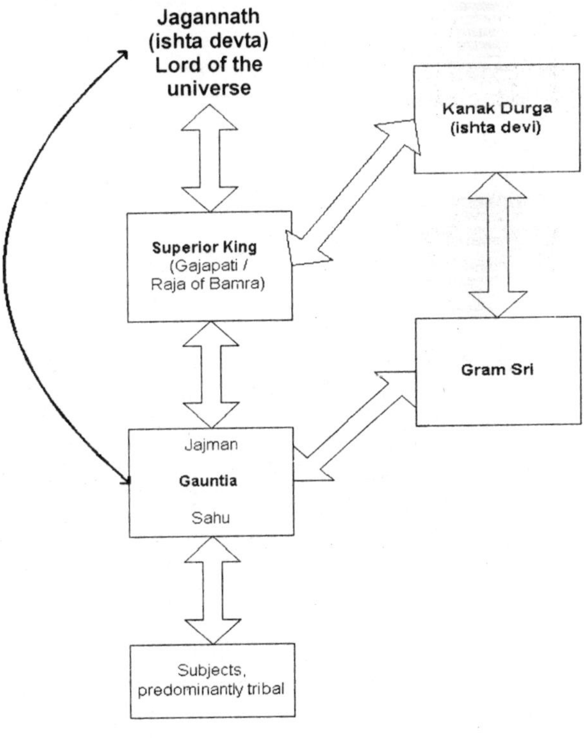

Figure 10: Gauntiā in relation to Gods, Overlords and Subjects

Rath Jātrā. However, links in the diagram are simplified to some extent: for example, a Gauntiā may also try to establish relations to Durgā by performing rituals for her on *Daśarā*. Jagannāth and Kanak Durgā are also related (see Hardenberg 2000).

Our model indicates that a Gauntiā is firmly integrated into state structures of smaller or greater kingdoms and their redistributive systems, into which he, in turn, integrates the predominantly tribal population of his village.

4.12. APPENDIX I: VILLAGES AND GAUNTIĀ WITHIN A RADIUS OF 15 KM FROM BADAMUNDALOI

TABLE 16: VILLAGES AROUND MUNDALOI AND THE COMMUNITY OF THEIR GAUNTIĀ

Village	Community of Gauntiā
1. Badamundaloi	Aghriā
2. Sanmundaloi	Aghriā
3. Rengali	Aghriā
4. Polamora	Aghriā
5. Thainsar	Aghriā
6. Kusmi	Aghriā
7. Lundrudehi	Aghriā
8. Tarnmurha	Aghriā
9. Gosainpada	Aghriā
10. Janda	Aghriā
11. Badawahal	Aghriā
12. Jamankira	Aghriā
13. Lamdurā	Aghriā
14. Salekaman	Aghriā
15. Rangiatikira	Aghriā
16. Kukum	Aghriā
17. Ekagudi	Aghriā
18. Sahasbahal	Aghriā
19. Jharāgogua	Aghriā
20. Jarmal	Aghriā
21. Luḍhar	Aghriā
22. Loimura	Bhuyān
23. Joldihi	Kisān (first Aghriā)
24. Kendukhunti	Dhobā
25. Nuadehi	Gaṇḍ
26. Puḍiakhaman	Māḷi
27. Bamlaikela	Nanda Gauḍ
28. Beniaposi	Kisān?
29. Dimirikuda	Teli
30. Gandam	Nanda Gauḍ (Mahakul)
31. Ledki	Gaṇḍ
32. Purunāpāni	Bhuyān
33. Depāni	Bhuyān
34. Bhālugua	Gaṇḍ
35. Haridābāhāl	Gaṇḍ

This list represents a situation around the time of Independence when the system was about to be abolished. It shows that almost two-thirds of the headmen in this small region were Aghriā, while fewer than a third belonged to tribal communities. The Aghriā dominated almost all of the important villages.[81]

Earlier changes in the headmanship could not be included.

NOTES

1. The term 'village king' has been chosen in order to emphasize the royal role of Gauntiā in contrast to tribal headmen, whose leadership appears to be of a different quality. However, as the Aghriā use the term headman in order to translate the title 'Gauntiā' and, therefore, the terms are used synonymously, they are different from tribal headmen.
2. The role of the Aghriā appears to resemble the role of Oriya Sardars in political units known as *mutha* in Kond areas as described by Bailey (1960: 178ff). However, in contrast to the Aghriā the area was largely dominated by a single tribe, the Kond (residing however together with Pan), while in the north-western region seems to be more diversified in terms of tribal communities settling together (with the Aghriā).
3. On the issue of whether a state was imposed on tribal people by outsiders or whether it emerged internally see also Thapar and Siddiqi, who argue that this is still an open question. The evolution of certain forms of chiefdoms does not contradict the thesis that the Aghriā were influential in setting up the structures of a state, if one considers the development in an evolutionary perspective. It might also be the case that different tribal communities may have had varying forms of authority at the time of a peasant immigration which itself stretched decades, or perhaps longer. However, one may conclude that compared to the system established by the Aghriā in tribal society the absence of a centralized authority was prevalent.
4. Transitions of a different kind, i.e. the establishment of industrial centres in predominantly tribal areas and therefore transitions from tribal society to market or industrial society, are currently under scrutiny by my colleague C. Strümpell (2003).
5. Polanyi (1968 [1957]) as well as Dalton (1968) understood economy in its substantive meaning as 'the general existence of organizational requirements for the sustained provision of material goods which must have been fulfilled in any society.' (Dalton (1968: 149). They argued against the formalist tradition of economic anthropology according to which economic is seen as 'economical' or 'economizing' and 'denotes a special set of rules designed to maximize the achievement of some end or to minimize the expenditure of some means' (ibid.). Thus 'Substantivists' (see also Jensen 1992 [1983]) stressed the embeddedness of economy within cultures and refuted the idea of an application of economic categories to other cultures and against 'the assumption that primitive economic processes and devices are functionally equivalent to their Western counterparts' (Dalton 1968: 160)—as implicitly found, for example in Boas' writings.

6. Compare Polanyi (1968 [1957]: 132), who is not fully consistent in his characterization of tribal society arguing on one hand, that 'tribal societies practice reciprocity and redistribution, while archaic societies are predominantly redistributive . . .', while he also states that 'redistribution, [is] the ruling method in tribal and archaic society'. I regard the first statement to be more appropriate for the context to be described here.

   Besides, none of these two forms or combinations exclude the parallel existence of markets, in an auxiliary and subordinated place. Market exchange has been the third integrative form in substantivist theory in addition to reciprocity and redistribution. However, as Dalton (1968: 157) highlighted, having a local market is not identical with being integrated into a market system 'that is, an economy wide complex of resource and output market integration through which most people acquire their subsistence livelihood'.
7. A similar process has been indicated by MacDougall (1977: 311ff) for Chhotanagpur under British rule. MacDougall also emphasized the limit of peasantization by referring to measures taken by the British or of missionaries in order to preserve tribal society.
8. The definition of the modern Western bureaucratic state follows Weber (1985 [1922]: 122ff, 815ff) who understood it as a legitimate reign based upon rational law apart from a monopoly of force (it includes parties, parliament, etc., in the wider sense). Weber contrasts it with premodern state or traditional rulership based on an order conceived to be of sacred origin, which may be applied in a loose sense also to a little kingdom.
9. In his analysis of a little kingdom in south India Dirks (1979: 170–1) refers to the theories of A. Southall and B. Stein distinguishing between a segmentary state and a unitary state. The former is characterized by: 1. a limited recognition of territorial sovereignty declining from centre to periphery; 2. a coexistence of a centralized government with peripheral quasi-autonomous foci of administration; 3. a pyramidal repetition of administrative structures and functions in the peripheral foci; 4. an absence of an absolute monopoly of legitimate force at the centre; 5. shifting allegiances at the periphery. As Cohn (in ibid.) observed the term 'segmentary' is rather unfortunate, since it implies a focus on descendance. Perhaps a designation 'discordant' may have been more suitable. However, Southall's and Stein's model highlights an important distinction between different forms of the state. Contrary to a unitary state, for example, in a little kingdom ('segmentary' or 'discordant' state) an absolute monopoly of force does not exist, although compared to tribal society there is a centre with a rather 'centralized' authority.
10. They are also known as 'Garjat states', 'feudatory states' or 'tributary *mahals*'.
11. Sometimes written 'Bamanda'. The name of the kingdom was derived from the first capital *Bamanda Garh*.

12. The Gaṇḍ-Gauntiā of Kairawahal claim to be the former Jamindārs of Turei. The family tells the story that after being formally evicted they (the Gaṇḍ) followed Sachidanand Tribnuban Deb (28th Raja of Bamra) on his way up to Calcutta, forcing him to offer the village of Kairawahal as *gaunti*: four ploughs, a large quantity of paddy and 150 acres land.
13. There were five to seven Jamindārs in Bamra State: a Bhuyan in Boxta, a Gond in Bolonda, a Sud in Soodbonda, etc.
14. In the village Mundaloi horses were sold 35 to 40 years ago and replaced by cars. Similarly, the elephants of the Jamindār family of Bolonda were also sold.
15. Galey (1990: 130) argued, 'In short, kingship has survived the eviction of the king . . . [. . .] If radical replacements took place they only changed certain institutionalised aspects of royalty in the political body but left the values of kingship intact.'
16. *Dakhal karibā* = to enjoy the land; right to use the land; *bedhakal* = to loose the land rights after failing to pay the revenue.
17. Compare also Choudhury (1977: 2).
18. Bailey (1960: 28ff) describes the offering of land by a mother's brothers to sister's son. The latter are not counted as 'owners of the earth' originally, but may slowly be integrated into this category.
19. Schwerin (1977: 125) points out that there was a considerable tribal migration as well. Thus, not only did Hindu peasants move into certain tribal areas, but so did tribes.
20. The term *baḍ baḍiā* may be used for people having good connections to politicians, as well. However, for businessmen, rich traders, etc., it is usually not used, as they have no land.
21. Roy (1999 [1928]: 50) speaks particularly of nature spirits. In contrast to that ancestor spirits are represented by stones.
22. Roy (1999 [1928]) uses the term *khūṇṭ* for the sub-clan/lineage and their spirits and the term *khūṇṭā* for pegs (implying wooden post). He also uses the spellings *khunt* or *khūnt* (see footnot below), but I regard the concepts as equivalent.
23. Roy speaks of *khunt* (or *khūnt*) as 'stirpes', but a meaning as local line seems to be implied.
24. I borrow the term from Kulke (1979: 18).
25. At the *khuṇṭ* another ritual for the village goddess is performed known as *narai chidā pūjā* (*narai* = straw; *chidā* = to fall after cutting) or *khal pūjā* (*khal* = straw), which corresponds to the *Niśā-Pūjā* performed in other villages.
26. Roy (1999 [1928]: 69) mentions another story in which a member of a Māhtō *khūṇṭ* (the lineage of the secular village headman) vowed to sacrifice in case his fishing trap in a rice field would be full. Consistent with his fulfilled wish he erected a wooden post (*khuṇṭā*) for the sacrifice. Since

then the members of the headman's lineage perform a sacrifice every three years for the spirit that is supposed to be located there.

27. Concerning this term see Sinha 1966 (cited in Urhahn 1985: 58) and Pfeffer (1997: 13).
28. Thapar and Siddiqi (1997 [1979]: 424) distinguish between Sivaism and Vaishnavism within the process of Hinduization. They further argue that in Chhotanagpur the Sivaism reflects an early period of contact compared to Vaishnavism—in Orissa particularly related to Chaitanya—which, however, should be considered as a more intensive Hinduization.
29. According to Pfeffer (1978: 423) *śāsana* is translated as 'royal edict' or 'duty'.
30. The cost of constructing the temple are difficult to estimate, but the descendants suspect a price of between Rs. 20,000 and 50,000 if one were to pay it again today. A local mistry acted as the architect, and a carpenter created the idols.
31. As usual the so-called untouchables have to sit slightly separated from the rest of the party.
32. The Gauntiā guessed that the festival had cost him around Rs. 2,000.
33. In the euphoric finish of the ritual participants may subsequently roll in the mud. However, in Mundaloi the Gauntiā did not take part in that expression of joy.
34. For a change or perhaps continuum of rice and millet cultivation, see Gregory (2003).
35. The distinction between external relations and internal relations is a matter made for clear analysis—is it not made by interlocutors.
36. In the Sarangarh area these *paṭā* were known as *lāl paṭā* (*lāl* = red) since they were kept in red envelopes.
37. *Touzi* is understood as the process of revenue collection.
38. In Sarangarh a powerful Gauntiā had a representative in every hamlet (*sahi*)—not only to collect the revenue, but also to give his orders. However, in the Kuchinda region it was not the case.
39. A long-term assessment was made for the collection of revenue by officers of the King, who used to revise the settlements after some years. Thus, the system of revenue collection seems to incorporate elements of both, previous Mughal as well as Maratha systems (Rothermund 1978: 36).
40. The Kondh called this kind of work *bheṭ bigāḍi.*
41. Report of the Enquiry Committee, Orissa States, 1939, Cuttack: Orissa Mission Press, n.d.: 1–4 [The Orissa States Enquiry Committee was appointed in 1937 by the Orissa States People's Conference; its enquiries into the conditions of the people of the Garjat states met with non-cooperation and resistance.]
42. Ahuja further argues that *beṭhi* was immensely unpopular among the villagers leading to mass desertion, low work discipline and even resistance.

In addition the use of forced labour for road construction was highly problematic given the fact that is was not sanctioned by British law—particularly after the abolition of slavery. However, in practice the right of the rulers of peripheral Orissa to demand forced labour was not called into question by the British as long as they provided them with cheap labour for their projects. For *beṭhi* among Muṇḍā see also Roy (1970 [1912]: 122ff).

43. Schwerin (1977: 269, 475) notes that the process of Christianization was influential in the abolition of socage, which was a source of frequent uprisings or 'riots' in the second half of the nineteenth century.
44. The ingredients include rice (*aruā chāul*), molasses, milk, clarified butter (*ghī*), lentils (*mugdāl*), coconut, cardamon, cloves, raisins, cashew nuts and rice powder.
45. There are some cases in which the role of a Gauntiā in ritual affairs was usurped by other villagers and there are discussions continuing about the role of the challenged Gauntiā. The *Rath Jātrā* in Jamankirā village is a case in point, which started about thirty years ago. According to some people the idea for this festival was put forward by a trader who donated the veranda of his house to accommodate Lord Jagannāth. In the version of the Gauntiā it was a Brahmin, who came into the village after he had lost his land elsewhere due to a dam project, who initiated the *Rath Jātrā*. However, it is undisputed that it was the Gauntiā family who offered land to invite a priest for the daily worship of the god (later on the Brahmin was replaced by a Gosain Pujāri). Different parts of the wider Gauntiā family offered land. The trader started to sweep the road during the festival—a function assigned to the king of Puri and therefore regarded as a function of the Gauntiā. The Gauntiā, however, only sprinkles some water, while the trader is sweeping. Asked about the reason, the Gauntiā said that at the time when the *Jātrā* started, he was alone in the village, his son studied in Sambalpur and he could not fulfil all tasks—implying that it was his right to do the sweeping. The younger generation of the Gauntiā family shows growing discomfort with their role during the *Jātrā* and they insist that the sweeping is their prestigious task. The Gauntiā should do it himself and should not leave it to someone else, implying that their role has been challenged and they are trying to reverse this.
46. One Gauntiā family told me that the villagers emulate the Gauntiā, for instance in the choice of names for their children.
47. A bamboo stick roughly one and a half metres long fitted to a dagger of half a metre.
48. Concerning *Rākhī Bandhan* and the relationship between brother and sister see Malamoud (1992: 39ff). Malamoud stresses the aspect of protection by an elder brother of a woman after the parent's death—an element very prominent in the context presented here. However, he also argues that a

rākhī marks the boundary of incest in the relation between brother and sisters.

49. Sometimes *beji* is also interpreted as big *guniā* (local healer), but 'witch' is more appropriate here.
50. For a researcher staying in the house of an influential headman, being identified with his family and often walking around with him or family members it is obviously difficult to come across critical remarks about the headman.
51. In other reports people argued that a Chamār house at such a prominent location at the centre of the village was another reason to refuse the settling of the Chamār at this spot.
52. See Rothermund (1978), Pocock (1962) et al.
53. For Sāhu in Chhattisgarh the terms Malik or Kisān are used as well.
54. An ear guru may also give protective amulets known as *kaṇṭhi* that are worn around the neck and to some extent a symbol of initiation by the guru. There is no specific time to give such an amulet.
55. Although his main occupation is washing, he has also some land.
56. In some cases the Gauntiā might have appointed other labourers/service-holders (for example people known as *Daḍhā*) to collect revenue for him, if the village is very big, but in most cases they collected it directly. In Sarangarh, a powerful Gauntiā had a representative in every hamlet (*sahi*)—not only to collect the revenue, but also to convey his orders. The *Daḍhā* resembles a Behera, but with broader functions. However, I did not come across such cases in present Orissa.
57. The category of *Bhitriā* was an important one in the royal palace of the king of Bamra too. Until today there has been a neighbourhood in Deogarh, known as *Bhitriā Sahi*, were descendants of these servants stay. In Puri eunuchs acted as *Bhitriā* (personal communication R. Hardenberg).
58. This term nowadays has a negative connotation and is no longer used (usage stopped about 10 years ago).
59. In Sarangarh *Kamihān* denotes someone sent by the Gauntiā to fetch something, such as oil from the Teli.
60. Roy refers to a report of Rickett.
61. Historically, the relationship between Guti and Sāhu might have been more ranked, the Guti being more a debtor to the Sāhu than today. Schwerin's (1977: 281ff, 475ff) picture shows a much more difficult situation of contract labourers in neighbouring Chhotanagpur at the end of the last century—comparing their lot with slaves, depending on the landlord. But though poor they were described as very loyal to their landlords.
62. In Mundaloi, about 25 families maintained *jajmāni* relations. These families belonged to the Aghriā, Māḷi, Gaṇḍ and Kandh communities.
63. For these discussions see Parry (1979: 76ff).
64. The case of Kangra presented by Parry (1979: 59ff) hints at a similar

situation. The *purohit*—the barber belongs to this category as well—is opposed to or rather tied to the *jajmān* in a 'permanent alliance'. In contrast, the relation of the *Kamin* (craftsmen)—the term itself having 'distinctly derogatory connotations and always applies to inferiors'—to the *Zamindar* it is rather contractual, as the *Kamin* has no right to serve as the *purohit* has a right from ancestral heritage. Furthermore, while the *purohit* receives gifts (*dān*), the *Kamin* receives payments. However, while Parry distinguishes between 'priests' and 'craftsmen', in the case I describe it is a differentiation between 'priests cum artisans' and 'field-labourers cum domestic servants'.

65. Other villagers might be *jajmān* and Sāhu as well, without, however, being necessarily also Gauntiā.
66. An Aghriā man told me that the shrine of the village goddess can be called *mer* and the sacrifice *meriā*, similar to the *mer khunṭ* at the centre of the threshing floor.
67. In addition to rituals at the shrine of the village goddess, it is the responsibility of a Kālo to give *ṣiṣā* before *Nuā Khāi*. *Śiṣā* consisting of a *mahuā* or *bhehuan* leaf with a spike of paddy (*dhān keṇḍā*) rolled in it. The *ṣiṣā* is put in the upper left corner of the door frames of the entrance, kitchen, *pūjā* room or any other important door and is supposed to ward off evil forces. After he offers *ṣiṣā* to all villagers (including Christians), he receives *chher chherā* consisting of paddy or *kharchā* as an extra bonus.
68. Apart from the peasant's categorization of the seasons, there are other systematizations of the seasons in Sambalpuri and Oriya. In the former five seasons summer (*kharā*), rainy (*barṣā*), autumn (*daśarā*), winter (*jāḍa*) and spring (*phagun*) are distinguished, while in Oriya six seasons namely summer (*grīṣma*), rainy (*barṣā*), autumn (*śarat*), early winter (*hemanṭa*), winter (*śiḍh*) and spring (*basanṭa*) are known.
69. All offerings, including vegetarian gifts, are called *baden* (derived from *badibā* = to promise to offer) and animal sacrifices are known as *sahani*. In any case, these offerings are usually sacrificed after the Grām Śrī has granted a wish.
70. Some people say that it is also a sign that the goats 'agrees' to be sacrificed.
71. I obtained a list including: (1) *manda phul* (hibiscus); (2) *aruā chāul*; (3) *agarbatti*; (4) *ghī*; (5) *guḍ*; (6) *sindhur*; (7) *pañchāmrut* (milk, honey, curd, molasses and banana; (8) *solitā* (cotton rope as lamp); (9) a pot with water (*gaḍu pāen*); (10) *jungār* (*muān*).
72. Marglin (1989 [1985]: 300) observed an opposition between the royal power/*śakti* and the power of ascetic heat/*tapas*.
73. See Falk (1973: 4) for examples of this theme in ancient scriptures.
74. According to my informants every family was allowed to keep 33 acres (= 10 standard acres).
75. However, the phone had also some disadvantages for the Gauntiā, because callers asked him to send messages to other villagers.

76. Berkemer (1993: 13) observed: 'Ein politisches System, dessen Herrscher sich innenpolitisch als unabhängig betrachten kann, also zum Beispiel eine eigene Armee hält, Steuern einzieht, Tribute von kleineren Königen und chiefs empfängt und ihnen Titel verleiht, und der zudem eine unabhängige Ritualpolitik im Inneren seines Territoriums betreibt, aber zugleich einen politisch wie rituell |ber ihm stehenden, militärisch überlegenen Oberherrn anerkennen muß, dessen Autorität er teilt und zur Legitimation seiner eigenen Herrschaft nach innen hin benötigt, soll als little kingdom bezeichnet werden.' This definition in a wider sense fits very well to the Gauntiā. Obviously the Gauntiā do not command their own army, nor do they levy their own tax, but as shown, the Gauntiā have the right to keep certain weapons and rightfully receive gifts or tributes, etc.
77. See also Dirks (1979: 200), who argues that particularly the alienation of land symbolized 'the personal authority of the King . . . and . . . represented a part of the whole which was symbolized by the king'. Keeping in mind the holism of the caste system Galey (1990) proposed that the whole represented by the king may stand in a hierarchically lower position to the whole.
78. See Dumont (1980 [1966], Raheja (1988) et al.—Intrinsically related to this question is the point of sacrality of the king. While Hocart (1927: 1, 236–7) argued that kingship is essentially divine, Dumont (1980 [1966]: 293) insisted upon a secularization of kingship, the king having been left only with magico-religious functions.
79. Some people say that Aghriā brides and grooms wearing crowns and symbolizing Lakṣmī and Narayan should not do the *praṇām*, but they usually do.
80. Galey (1990: 172) adds: 'Once united with the throne, the king is no longer the first among equals but "the whole and the parts" ritually acknowledged by all clans.'
81. The former royal family of the Sarangarh area and local Gauntiā stated that 90 per cent of the headmen were Aghriā, although the majority of the population belongs to the administrative category of Scheduled Tribes.

CHAPTER 5

The Aghriā Kinship System

In this chapter on the Aghriā kinship system I will try to include comparative material on neighbouring tribal and non-tribal communities, in order to detect certain structural principles. The central question is not only what kind of structure the kinship system has, but also to what extent such a structure is shared.

In analysing a kinship system, three levels must be distinguished (Needham 1973: 171; Trautmann 1995 [1981]: 21ff, 29; Barnard/Good 1984: 9, 12ff). The terminology or categories in which relationship is conceived or the cognitive aspect is the first of these. The second level represents the rules, ideals or the normative domain and the third is the level of practice, behaviour, or the empirical-statistical situation. While the first two levels refer to the community and are thus socio-centred, the behaviour or conduct refers to small groups and is ego-centred. According to Good (1991: 55, 95 ff), the relationship between the three levels includes several inconsistencies. On one hand, they possess a kind of autonomy and need not be congruent—for instance an association of a symmetrical terminology with an asymmetrical rule is common. Yet they are not supposed to remain in direct contradiction to one another: the rules cannot contradict the native categories and the social practice seems to be meaningful only in relation to the concepts and rules that form the social system.

5.1. TERMINOLOGY

The Aghriā terminology presented in this chapter demonstrates not only some characteristics of north Indian systems, but also features typical of south Indian kinship. This is not surprising as the region is a part of the frontier zone between the two Indian kinship systems just mentioned—the 'Indo-Aryan' in the north and the 'Dravidian' in the south as Karve (1998 [1953]: 50–1), Trautmann (1995 [1981]: xvi) and Skoda (2002) have already pointed out. There are also parts of another kinship system, which Karve (1998 [1953]: 72) has already hinted at in analogy to the regional Muṇḍā-language family. The work of Pfeffer (1983) and Parkin (1992) confirms this, without sharing the hypothesis that a language family necessarily correlates to a kinship system.[1] For a thorough analysis, all three kinship systems must be described briefly.

South Indian or 'Dravidian' terminologies (the Tamil example)

It was Dumont who in the 1950s pioneered the research on 'Dravidian' kinship. He was inspired by Lévi-Strauss (in particular his alliance theory as described in the book *The Elementary Structures of Kinship*, 1949), and incorporated it into his own work on India, and developed it further. Dumont based his analysis on his field research on several castes in Tamil Nadu (*Pramalai Kallar* among others) and their Tamil field terminology. He identified 16 clearly distinguishable categories, which form the semantic scope for ego. Every member of the subcaste is assigned one—and only one—category. Accordingly, the structure of the semantic sphere was based on four fundamental distinctions: (1) according to the generations; (2) sex; (3) age (only in generation 0) and (4) a division of the relatives within the generations −1–+1, which Dumont recognized as the categories 'affines' and 'kin',[2] because special affinal terms were conspicuously missing. The category *maman*, for instance, also stands for SpF and FZH, along with the relation MB.

Dumont (1983 [1953]: 10ff) argues, in accordance with these oppositions, that ego and his F (in Table 17 as category B), though connected by kinship, are terminologically separated by the principle of the generation gap. But F and MB are united through this principle (as a part of one generation) and are separated through the contrast between 'kin' and 'affines'. The MB is the immediate affinal relative of the F (ego, F, MB, stand for the respective classes of relatives and not only for the genealogical relationships). The typical fundamental structure of the 'Dravidian' terminology is therefore essentially based on the relationship's ego—F and F—MB. In accordance with the

TABLE 17: TAMIL–TERMINOLOGY

Generation	male (II)	female (II)	female (X)	male (X)
grandfather		A (+ fem. A')		
father	B			E
		C	D	
ego: > ego	F	G	H	I
ego: < ego	J			M
		K	L	
son	N (+ fem. N')		O [= k + N]* (+ fem. O')	
grandson		P (+ fem. P')		

Notes:* This line gives the disposition in Tamil, where K probably means 'marriage'. Strictly in this case alone, N and O form a single category.

A are the 'grandfathers' (A the 'grandmothers'), B the 'fathers', C the 'mothers', D the 'father's sisters' and 'mothers-in-law', E the 'mother's brothers' and 'fathers-in-law', F the 'brothers' older than ego, J the younger 'brothers', I and M the 'male cross-cousins' older and younger than ego, G and K the 'sisters' (older and younger) and H/L the 'female cross-cousins' (older and younger respectively), N the 'parallel sons' (fem. for the 'daughters', O the 'cross sons' (fem. for 'cross daughters) and P the 'grandsons' (fem. for 'granddaughters'). Ego, male and female, are only indirectly located in the figure.

Source: Dumont 1983 [1953]: 10, slightly adapted by the author.

native point of view, Dumont has derived the relationship between ego and MB derives through the F. This means that the MB is conceptualized as FWB and is not derived through the M, as, according to Dumont, the misleading term MB generally suggests, which is descriptive and originates in our own culture and therefore expresses a certain ethnocentrism. In the generation –2/+2 Dumont (1983 [1953]: 8–15) verifies the 'merging' of the categories of 'kin' and 'affines' for his case study. He explains this with the fact that on one side ego is related to both grandparents through F and M, who are both kin for ego, but on the other side both grandfathers enjoy an affinal relationship with one another (this is similar for the grandchildren).

The relationship of affinity between F and MB, which has arisen through marriage, has expanded itself in the terminology in successive generations. Thus, ego's cross-relatives are, at the same time, ego's affinal relatives. This implies that, in this case, affinity possesses a vertical, diachronic dimension, which is embedded in the terminology and for which Dumont uses the term 'alliance'. Dumont argues that a marriage prescription—namely cross-cousin marriage—is inherent in the terminology, as only this rule presents an appropriate formula for the maintenance of the system, above all of the cross–parallel differentiation and therefore, of the alliance (Dumont 1983 [1953]: 17).

North Indian or 'Indo-Aryan' terminologies (the Hindi example)

If we consider the 'Indo-Aryan' terminologies—I will restrict myself to Hindi as a well documented example—what immediately attracts the attention is the great variety of terms, and with them the common semantic distinctions in comparison to 'Dravidian' terminologies. The most significant difference to Tamil is that the opposition between the cross and parallel category is missing in Hindi terminology. There exists a greater differentiation in Hindi in the generations –1 and +1 in comparison with Tamil in regard to the distinction between F, FeB and FyB, which are separated in Tamil only by prefixes. Other than this, there does not exist any such differentiation between M, MeZ or MyZ, SpF, FZH and MB are strictly separated in Hindi, in contrast to Tamil, where these relationships coincide with each other terminologically. In Tamil, ego's Ch can be commonly classified with SbCh of the same sex and can be distinguished from the SbCh of another sex (therefore men and women classify the Ch complementarily). However, in Hindi SbCh are summed up without any reference to the relative sex of ego and his/her siblings (men and women classify the Ch equally—see Table 18).

One can find a greater number of semantic differentiations in generation 0, as with Tamil. The only example in which Hindi is considered to be more 'synthesizing' than Tamil, is the division according to the age relative to the ego, which split the entire generation in Tamil but does not exist in Hindi. Ego's generation (0) is remarkable particularly for its abundance of affinal terms and a comparative lack of consanguine categories. Thus, all cousins (MBS/D, FBS/D, MZS/D, FZS/D) are classified as B or Z (*bhai* or *bahin*)—a distinction in cross—and parallel—relatives is henceforth not recognizable. However, a terminological differentiation between WT (e.g. ZH = *jija*), consanguines (e.g. B = *bhai*) and WG (e.g. WB =

TABLE 18: COMPARISON OF THE SEMANTIC DISTINCTIONS IN TAMIL AND IN HINDI IN THE GENERATIONS –1 AND +1,

Hindi and Tamil kinship terms, parents' generation

Hindi									
phupha FZH	*mama* MB	*mausa* MZH	*caca* FB	*bap* F	*ma* M	*mausi* MZ	*caci* FBW	*bua* FZ	*mami* MBW
FZH	MB	MZH	FB	F	M	MZ	FBW	FZ	MBW
maman		*(periya–, cinna–) appa*			*(periya–, cinna–) amma*			*attai*	
Tamil									

Hindi and Tamil kinship terms, children's generation

Hindi									
bhanja ZS		*bhatija* BS		*beta* S	*beti* D		*bhatiji* BD		*bhanji* ZD
BS(f.s.)	ZS(m.s.)	ZS(f.s.)	BS(m.s.)	S	D	BD(m.s.)	ZD(f.s.)	ZD(m.s.)	BD(f.s.)
marumakan		makan			makal			marumakal	
Tamil									

Source: Trautmann 1995 [1981]: 97, slightly adapted by the author.

sala) is apparent, whereby this clear distinction can be made only in ego's generation (0) and not in previous and following generations (Vatuk 1969: 106; Trautmann 1995 [1981]: 91–103)—a distinction (WT *vs.* WG) which befits a central significance particularly because of the status difference associated with it.

Another important characteristic of the Hindi terminology is the extension of the terminology and the tendency to include all persons in the kinship sphere by using kinship terms and capturing the universe in the various kinship categories (Vatuk 1969: 96). An example the category of *bhai* or B (as well as *bahin*/Z), which is fundamental to the understanding of the terminology. In using the term *bhai* various meanings can be implied, ranging from the 'genealogical B' to a 'man—roughly of the same age as ego' (the most inclusive meaning), whereby a reference is always implied to the common forefathers (from F to the distant ancestors). The term *bhai,* in a restricted sense, can stand opposite to the term *sala* (WB). However, if we look from another angle *bhai* (in its most inclusive sense) can also encompass *sala*. Since *bhai* is not opposed to any other comparable category, Dumont considers this term to be purely descriptive. However, the category *bhai* is pivotal above all for its quasi-infinite repercussions on the other categories, for instance *mama*, the 'brother' of the mother. An exact specification of the relationship between close relatives (e.g. a genealogical MB) and the more distant relatives (e.g. a man from the mother's village, who can also be considered as a distant *mama*) is possible by adding certain words to the existing term (e.g. in the sense of 'near' MB). (Dumont 1966: 99–100; Vatuk 1969: 96–7)

The thorough analysis of the Hindi terminology by Dumont was substantially complemented by Vatuk (1969), who discovered that the terms for the WT or the WG are extended to their WT or WG, which means that the same term, used for the WG, can be used for the WG of the WG and vice versa. On the other hand, consanguine terms are used by persons or groups who have given to certain WT or have received women from the same WG. This was termed 'quasi–consanguinity' by Vatuk (1969: 101–4, see also Trautmann 1995 [1981]: 97–102). R. Jamous was the next to expand the analysis. He discovered that even in the case of a married couple, the Z of the H and the B of the W use consanguine terms for each other (the relation BWB and ZHZ as *bhai* and *bahin*), which he describes as 'metasiblingship' (Jamous 1992: 97; also Trautmann 1995 [1981]: xvii). Vatuk and Jamous indicate that even affinal relatives (e.g. WZH or BWB) fall in the category of *bhai* (or *bahin*) and can be regarded as consanguines. This means that the terminological tripartition (WT—consanguines—WG), which was mentioned at the beginning, must be extended to WT (including wife-takers' wife-taker)—consanguines (including quasi-consanguines, metasiblings, wife-takers' wife-giver and wife-givers' wife-taker)—WG (including wife-givers' wife-giver).

The characteristic features, briefly summarized here, have already made it clear, that the Hindi terminology, unlike the 'Dravidian' terminologies, is not reducible to a system of binary oppositions. This is the reason why Dumont does not speak of a structure in a narrow sense, but refers to a configuration of categories (just as he prefers to call the Hindi terminology a 'vocabulary', as opposed to the 'Dravidian' 'terminologies'). Following L.H. Morgan, Dumont sees the Tamil terminology is classificatory with a universal division of relatives according to certain oppositions. On the other hand, he describes the Hindi 'vocabulary' as descriptive, because the elementary relations are based on the ego (Dumont 1966: 96).

Middle Indian or 'Mundaic' terminologies

In comparison to the others, this kinship system is limited in its geographical distribution, and less well known. In recent years, however, more features of the system have been discovered by Pfeffer (1983) and Parkin (1992). While Pfeffer considered Middle Indian tribal society[3] as a whole, Parkin concentrated on groups with Mundaic languages.

Both Pfeffer (1983: 100) and Parkin (1992: 123, 142) have argued that the principle of alternation is a fundamental feature of the system. The terminology of the Ho (Pfeffer 1983: 110–11), a tribe in the Singhbhum district and in Chhotanagpur, decribes an equivalence of the generations –3 and +3, for which the common term *gungu* is used. In addition, the same term denotes FeB (MeZ), BCh (m.s.) and ZCh (f.s.), which indicates relatives of the parents' and children's generation. This means that *gungu* is used alternately in every other generation. Similar terminological identifications between alternating generations are known among the Juang (Pfeffer 1983: 104–5) of Keonjhar district of Orissa. In their case, MB and DH—relatives of the generation +1 and –1—are terminologically equated. Further examples could be cited from Juang[4] and other terminologies of the region.[5] There is a tendency to classify, on the one hand, the relatives of one's own generation with relatives of alternating generations and, on the other hand, to equate the relatives of adjacent or uneven generations. Both categories and 'generation–sets' (McDougal 1963: 153; Pfeffer 1983, 1996) stand in opposition to each other.

Both authors agree that in Middle Indian terminologies the distinction by relative age is of the utmost importance (Pfeffer 1983: 100; Parkin 1992: 138), but Parkin argues that this principle is restricted to generation 0 and to the parallel kin of the parents' and children's generation. Both agree again on the symmetrical character of the terminologies (Pfeffer 1983: 103; Parkin 1992: 137). In addition, Parkin (1992: 138), comparing various terminologies, abstracts a typical north and central 'Mundaic' pattern—reproduced as Table 19.

TABLE 19: TERMINOLOGY AMONG GROUPS SPEAKING NORTH AND CENTRAL MUNDA LANGUAGES

	parallel		cross		affines
Gen.	male	female	male	female	
+2	Pa		Pa		Composita
+1	FFB	FZMBW	MBFZH	MMZ	SpPa
0	ego; B PaSbS SpSbSp/SbSpSbSp	(ego) Z PaSbD / SpSbSpSb	Sp/SpSb/SbSp /ChSpPa/ SbSpSb (various terms)		<<
−1	S BS SpZS	D BD SpZD	ZS SpBS	ZD SpBD	ChSp
−2	Ch		Ch		Composita

Source: Parkin (1992: 138), adapted by the author.

According to this ideal type, the following features can be stated: (1) equations MB = FZH; FZ = MBW are seen as characteristic, but these relations are strictly separated from SpF or SpM respectively, which are classified by Parkin as 'affines'; (2) a terminological identification B = PaSbS and Z = PaSbD is predominant (except in the Koraput region); (3) there are separate terms for SpSb, SbSp, SbSpSb, ChSpPa, Sp, etc., in ego's generation and (4) in generation −1 parallel relatives are distinguished from cross relatives, which are, again, not identical with affines. This implies that the Ch of a male ego are equated with BCh (m.s.) and WZCh, but neither with ZCh (m.s.) nor with WBCh or ChSp. Additionally, Parkin (1992: 128, 140) considers the category SbSpSb to be pivotal, because, according to him, SbSpSb is the preferred marriage partner in many north and central Mundaic groups.

Reconsidering the first and last points of Parkin's model, the content or character of the cross category is not exactly clear, as Parkin separates it from the category of affines. Henceforth, is not FZH = MB an affinal relative of the ego? Perhaps the distinction between FZH = MB, on one hand, and SpF, on the other hand, could also be considered a north Indian tendency, as MB, FZH and SpF are strictly separated there. Even more problematic seems to be Parkin's separation between cross relatives and affines in generation 0. Particularly, the category of 'affines' in the ego's generation causes confusion. The model does not reflect the principle of alternation considered by the author to be essential.

In contrast to Parkin's abstract model, the high number of communities in the Middle Indian region distinguishing between FF and MF is striking. Let us use the Gond as an example, as they are an essential part of the regional culture even though they speak a Dravidian language. They do not only separate MF from FF, but they also equate yB with SS (yZ with SD) and MF with DS (Grigson 1991 [1938]: 308–9).[6] Thus such a differentiation may indicate a cross-parallel separation in the grandparent's and grandchildren's generation. The same idea is also found in the Halbi kinship system (C. Gregory: personal communication). Gregory relates such a pattern to marriage rules and accordingly coins the terms 'cross grandparents' and 'parallel grandparents', who are identified with cross-cousins on the one hand and parallel grandparents and siblings on the other—the former being marriageable. Pfeffer (1999: 24), in his analysis of Gutob (Gadaba) terminology,[7] shows not only a separation of MF from FF, but also mentions the equations MF = FMB and FF = MMB that clearly indicate a cross–parallel differentiation usually known in a typical Dravidian pattern—though not for the grandparents. Additionally, an equation eZH = MF and eB = FF indicates a cross–parallel distinction in alternate generations, which, however, remains incomplete as, for example, eZH is not equated with WeB. A similar pattern is also reported for the neighbouring Parenga, who have equations such as FM = eBW or FF = eB (Pfeffer 1999: 42).[8] For the Munda-speaking Juang, McDougal (1963: 447) mentions a differentiation in the grandparents' generation and also noted an equation eZ = FFZ, which hints at a cross–parallel differentiation in the grandparent's generation as well, but his material remains insufficient in this regard.

In summary, all four characteristics mentioned by Parkin could also be a result of a synthesis of northern and southern elements. That means that the principle of alternation and opposition between junior and senior, combined with a symmetrical terminology, represented first and foremost by the equation HF = WF, has to be seen as typically 'Mundaic' or Middle Indian, even though a Mundaic system remains a vague concept. In a Middle Indian or 'mundaic' pattern—or at least in one of its subtypes—a combination of equated alternate generations and a cross-parallel distinction seems to be central, and is closely related to a marriage rule that allows a grandparent's marriage or, more specifically, a cross-grandparent's marriage.

I turn now to the Aghriā pattern:

The Aghriā terminology[9]

TERMS OF REFERENCE

TABLE 20: TERMS OF REFERENCE AMONG THE AGHRIĀ

Terms of reference	Relation
Generation +4	
paenajā	all men (FFFF, FMFF, etc.)
paenāī	all women (MMMM, FMMM, etc.)
Generation +3	
baḍu	all men (FFF, FMF, MFF, MMF, etc.)
baḍi	all women (MMM, MFM, FFM, FMM, etc.)
Generation +2	
ajā, dadā	all men (FF, MF, etc.)
āī, āimā, bāi	all women (MM, FM, etc.)
ajāśaśur	WFF, WMF (possible specification)
āīśāś	WMM, WFM (possible specification)
Generation +1	
bāpā, buā	F
mā	M
babā, baḍkā bāpā	FeB, MeZH, MeZHB, (HBWF)e>F, (HZHF)e>F, (WBWF)e>F, (eSbSpF)[10]
baḍi	FeBW
munubāpā/sānbāpā	FyB, MyZH
munumān/sānmān	FyBW, MyZ
kakā	FyB, BWFyB, (HBWF)y<F, (HZHF)y<F, (WBWF)y<F, (ySbSpF)
kāki	FyBW, (ySbSpM)
phuphu	FZ, FZHZ, MZHZ
phuphā	FZH, FZHB
mamā, māmun (MeB: *boromamo*; MyB: *sanmamo*)	MB, MBWB, FBWB, MBSWF, MBDHF
māmi, māin	MBW
munumān, māusī (old form: *musi-bāi*)	MyZ, (MBWZ)e>M, MyZHZ, FyBWZ
baramā, baḍkāmā	MeZ, (MBWZ)y<M, FeBW, FeBWZ (eSbSpM)

(contd.)

TABLE 20 (contd.)

munubāpā, mausā (old form: *mausiā*)	MyZH, MyZHB
śaśur	WF, HF, ZHF, SbSpF
śāś	WM, HM, ZHM, SbSpM
babāśaśur	WFeB, HFeB
kakaśaśur	WFyB, HFyB
phuphuśāś, baramāśāś	WFZ, HFZ
mamośaśur	WMB, HMB
māinśāś	WMBW, HMBW
māusiśāś	WMZ, HMZ
Generation 0	
barabhāi, dadā	eB, (FBS)e, (MBS)e, (FZS)e, (MZS)e, (BWB)e, (HeBWeB)e, (HeBWeB)y, (HeBWyB)e
majlābhāi	mB
sānbhāi, bhāi	yB, (FBS)y, (MBS)y, (FZS)y, (MZS)y, eZHB, (BWB)y, (HeBWyB)y
barabahen, bāi, nāni	eZ, (FBD)e, (MBD)e, (FZD)e, (MZD)e, eZHZ, (HW)e, (ZHZ)e/eZHZ (usage varying), eZHSWM, eZHDHM, (HeBWyZ)e, HeBWeZ
majlābahen	mZ
sānbahen, bahen	yZ, (FBD)y, (MBD)y, (FZD)y, (MZD)y, (ZHZ)y/yZHZ (usage varying), (HW)y, (HeBWyZ)y
bāṭo	eZH, eZHB (if eZHB much older than ego, if not: sangī), eZHZH, eZHSWF, eZHDHF
bahenjuien	yZH, yZHB (sec eZHB), yZHZH
sangī	BWB, ZHB (old: bāṭo/bahenjuien)
sangāt	ZHZ (m.s.), BWZ (m.s.)
guiyān	ZHZ (f.s.), BWZ (f.s.) (old form)
bahu	eBW, WeBW, BWBW
bhāibahu, bahariā	yBW, WyBW
bar, swāmī	H
kaniān, strī	W
deḍśāś	HeZ, WeZ
bhaṭuā-śaśur	HeZH
nanand	HyZ
nandiā (*nandiā-diār*)	HyZH
deḍśaśur	HeB
diar	HyB
jeṭhen	HeBW
deenren, debarānī	HyBW
śalā (WeB: *baḍśalā*, WyB: *san-śalā*)	WB, DHMyB + SWMyB + (WBWB)y<W as śalā, DHMeB + SWMeB + (WBWB)e>W as baḍśalā
śālī	WyZ, WBW, WBWZ
śaḍhu (reciprocal)	WZH
samdhi, samudhi	SWF, DHF
samdhen	SWM, DHM
Generation 1	
baḍā po, baḍa beṭā, baḍkā beṭā	eS

(contd.)

TABLE 20 (contd.)

majlā po, majlā beṭā	mS
sān po, sān beṭā, chuṭe beṭā	yS
baḍa ji, baḍa beṭī, baḍkā beṭī	eD
majlā ji, majlā beṭī	mD
sān ji, sān beṭī, chuṭe beṭī	yD
baha, baharia (old usage)	SW, yBW
juen	DH [DHB, BDH (m.s.), HBDH]
putrā	eBS (m.s.), ZS (f.s.), eZHZS (f.s.), HeBS, SWB, BWBS (f.s.), ZHBS (fs)
jhiārī	eBD (m.s.), ZD (f.s.), DHZ, HeBD, eZHZD (f.s.), BWBD (f.s.), ZHBD (f.s.)
bhatijā	BS (f.s.), WBS (Aghriā), BWBS (m.s.)
bhatiji	BD (f.s.), WBD (Aghriā), BWBD (m.s.)
bhanjā	ZS (m.s.), BS (f.s.), WBS,[11] HZS, ZHBS (m.s.), ZHZS (m.s.), BWBS (m.s.)
bhānjī	ZD (m.s.), BD (f.s.), WBD,[12] HZD, ZHBD (m.s.), ZHZD (m.s.), BWBD (m.s.)
baḍu	yBS (m.s.), HyBS, WyZS, BWyZS (m.s.)
baḍi	yBD (m.s.), HyBD, WyZD, BWyZD (m.s.)
mausā po	WeZS, BWeZS (m.s.)
mausi ji	WeZD, BWeZD (m.s.)
putrābaha (*baha*)	eBSW (m.s.), HeBSW
putrājuen	eBDH (m.s.), HeBDH
bhanjājuen	ZDH (m.s.), HZDH, WBDH, eBDH (f.s.)
bhānjībaha (*bhānjī*)	ZSW (m.s.), HZSW, WBSW, eBSW (f.s.)
baḍijuen	yBDH (m.s.), HyBDH
baḍibaha	yBSW (m.s.), HyBSW
Generation 2	
nāti	all men (SS, DS, WBSS, HZDS, etc.)
nāten	all women (SD, DD, HZDD, WBSD, etc.)
Generation 3	
baḍu	all men (SSS, SDS, DDS, etc.)
baḍi	all women (DDD, SSD, DSD, etc.)
Generation 4	
nāti, ajā, paenbaḍu	all men (SSSS, etc.)
nāten, āi, paenbaḍi	all women (DDDD, etc.)

TERMS OF ADDRESS—FORMAL/INFORMAL ADDRESS

TABLE 21: TERMS OF ADDRESS AMONG THE AGHRIĀ

Terms of reference	Term of address	Formal *vs.* informal address (aso *vs.* a)[13]
Generation +4		
paenajā	*ajā, dadā*	a
paenāī	*āī, bāi, āimā*	a

(contd.)

TABLE 21 (contd.)

Generation +3		
baḍu	*baḍu, baḍkā bāpā, babā, baḍkā buā*	aso (a)
baḍi	*baḍi, baḍkāmā, baramā*	a
Generation +2		
ajā, dadā	*ajā, dadā*	a
āī, āimā, bāi	*āī, āīmā, bāi, bohu* (for MM, not FM)	a
ajāśaśur	see *ajā*	a/aso
āīśāś	see *āī* (but not *bahu*)	a/aso
Generation +1		
bāpā, buā	*bāpā, buā, bapā* (*beṭā*)	a/aso
mā	*mā* (*beṭi*)	a/aso
babā, baḍkā bāpā	*babā, baḍabāpā*	a/aso
baḍi	*baḍi*	a
munubāpā/sanbāpā	*sānbāpā, beṭa*	a/aso
munumā/sānmā	*munamā, beṭi*	a
kakā	*sānbāpā, kakā, beṭā*	a/aso
kāki	*kāki, sānmā, munumān*	aso (some exceptions: a)
phuphu	*phuphu, beṭi*	a
phuphā	*phuphā, juen*	aso
māmun (MeB: *baḍamamo*; MyB: *sānmamo*)	*māmun, māmā, bhanja*	aso
māmi, māin	*māmi, māi*	aso
munumān, māusi	*munamā, māusi*	a
baḍamā, baḍkāmā	*baḍamā, baḍkāmā*	a
munubāpā, mausā	*munubāpā, mausā*	aso
śaśur	*bāpā, buā, bapā*	aso
śāś	*mā*	aso
babāśaśur	see *babā*	aso
kakaśaśur	see *kakā*	aso
phuphuśāś, baramāśāś	see *phuphu*	aso
mamośaśur	see *mamo*	aso
māinśāś	see *māin*	aso
māusiśāś	see *māusi*	aso
Generation 0		
baḍabhāi, dadā	*dadā*	a
majlābhāi		a
sānbhāi, bhāi	*bābu*, by name	a
baḍabahen, bāi, nāni	*nāni, bāi*	a
majlābahen		a
sānbahen, bahen	*nani*, by name	a
bāṭo	*bāṭo*	a
bhaṭuā-śaśur	*bāṭo*	aso
bahenjuen	by name	aso
sangī	(BWB)e/(ZHB)e as *dadā*, (BWB)y/(ZHB)y by name	aso
sangāt	(ZHZ)e as *nāni*, (ZHZ)y by name	aso

(contd.)

TABLE 21 (contd.)

guiyān	*guiyan*	aso
bahu	*bahu (bhābi)*	aso
bhāibahu	*bahariā* (old usage), by name (except HyB)	aso
bar, swāmī	by teknonymy or sounds like "eh"	a/aso
kaniān, strī	by name	
deḍśāś	*nāni, bāi*	aso
nanand	by name (old usage: not by name, only *nani* [not *nāni*])	aso
nandiā (nandiā-diār)	by name (old usage: not by name, only *bābu*)	aso
deḍśaśur	by teknonymy (adressed as F of his Ch) or *baḍa* (old) or *nandiā-diār*	aso (only in rare cases)
diar	by name (see *nandiā*), *bābu* (old usage: only *bābu*[14])	aso
jeṭhen	*bāi*	a/aso
deenren, debarānī	by name	a
śalā (WeB: *baḍsala*, WyB: *sānśalā*)	*baḍśalā* as *dadā – śalā* by name	aso (WeB) a (WyB)
śālī	*śāli*	a
śaḍhu (reciprocal)	*saḍhu* (*dadā* by name)	aso
samdhi, samudhi	*samdhi*	aso
samdhen	*samdhen*	aso
Generation 1		
baḍā po, baḍa beṭā, baḍkā beṭā	*beṭā, buā, bāpā, bābu*, by name	a
majlā po, majlā beṭā		a
sān po, sān beṭā, chuṭe beṭā	(see *baḍa po*)	a
baḍa jhi, baḍa beṭī, baḍkā beṭī	*beṭī, beṭā, mā*, by name	a
majlā jhi, majlā beṭī		a
sān jhi, sān beṭī, chuṭe beṭī	(see *baḍa jhi*)	a
baha, baharia (older usage)	by name, *mā, baharia* (old usage)	a/aso (aso as old form)
juen	by name, *buā, bābu, bāpā*	a
putrā	*putrā, bābu*, by name, *beṭā* (for *kāki* only *bābu*, not *putrā*]	a (♂)/aso (♀)
jhiārī	*nani* [not *nāni*], *jiārī, beṭī, mā*, by name	a (♂)/aso (♀)
bhatijā (older usage)	by name	a
bhatiji (older usage)	by name	a
bhanjā (m.s.)	*bhanjā, bāpā, māmun, māmā*, by name (in former times also: *bhachhā*) [not *bābu*]	aso
bhānjī (m.s.)	*bhānjī, mā*, by name (not *nani*– in former times also: *bhachhi*)	aso
bhanjā (f.s. or BWBS m.s.)	*bhanjā, phuphā*	a
bhanjī (f.s. or BWBD m.s.)	*bhanjī, phuphu*	a

(contd.)

TABLE 21 (Contd.)

baḍu	*baḍabāpā, babā, baḍu, baḍkābāpā*	a/aso (aso as older form)
baḍi	*baḍamā, baḍi, baḍkāmā*	a/aso (aso as older form)
mausā po		a
mausi jhi		a
putrābaha (*baha*)	by name, *mā, baharia*	a
putrājuen	by name, *bābu* (not *putrā*)	aso (some ♀: a)
bhanjājuen	*bhanjā, māmo,* name (not *bābu*)	aso
bhānjībaha (*bhānjī*)	*bhanji, mā,* name (mostly *bhanji* – former times: *bhāji*)	aso
baḍujuen	by name, *bābu*	aso (♂), a (♀)
baḍibaha	by name	aso (♂), a (♀)
Generation – 2		
nāti	*bhāi, dadā, dādā, ajā* (rarely), *nātiyā,* by name	a
nāten	*bāi, nāni, bahen, naten* (not *āi*), by name	a
Generation – 3		
baḍu	*baḍu, baḍkā bāpā, babā, baḍkā buā*	aso
baḍi	*baḍi, baḍkāmā, baramā*	a
Generation – 4		
nāti, ajā, paenbaḍu	*nāti, dadā*	a
nāten, āi, paenbaḍi	*nāten, bāi*	a

Note: All elder relatives of the wife's side are formally addressed, e.g. as āso.

Considering the Aghriā terminology, a synthesis three kinship systems is fairly distinct. Starting with the parents' generation the equations FeB = MeZH or MeZ = FeBW are striking. These are reminiscent of the Dravidian pattern (compare Table 17). However, in contrast a distinction according to the relative age is added here that does not exist in Tamil. The terminological identifications FeB = MeZH and MyZ = FyBWZ or MB = FBWB point to a cross–parallel dichotomy less clearly marked than in Tamil. The existence of separate terms for SpPa contradicts a clear-cut opposition of kin and affines. On the one hand, the separation of SpF, MB and FZH is typical for Indo-Aryan terminologies as shown in Table 18, on the other hand, the equations mentioned are in opposition to the known Indo-Aryan pattern. Yet these equations are quite common in Middle Indian terminologies. The identification of SpF = ZHF and SpM = ZHM seems to be significant, as it supports Parkin's hypothesis that ZHZ, more generally osSbSpSb, is a preferred marriage partner.

Other than a few exceptions, one's own generation—as the parallel kin in the parent's generation—is divided according to the relative age of ego (or ego's parents). One of these exceptions is WZH, but one could argue here that this division is disappearing on the fringe. As the separate term for WZH shows, there is no metasiblingship among the Aghriā. The principle of seniority is atypical for Indo-Aryan terminologies, but is well known in the Dravidian (Tables 17 and 22). In contrast to those a classification of middle siblings is possible among the Aghriā. All 'cousins' fall into the category 'brother' and 'sister' or 'elder brother' and 'younger brother' in relation to ego—a pattern somewhat typical for Middle India and very much so in the north, if we avoid the distinction of relative age. A cross–parallel opposition is completely missing in generation 0. The extension of the terms from ZH to ZHZH (for eZH to eZHZH, etc.) or for WyB to (WBWB)y>W, which was prevalent in the north, would also contradict such an opposition. However, a differentiation between eZH and yZH has not yet been found in north India, even though it conforms to the common opposition of junior/senior prevalent in tribal society. A possible combination of elements of the north and south is represented in Table 22.

TABLE 22: CLASSIFICATION OF GENERATION 0—
A COMPARISON OF SOME RELATIVES

WB	FBS MZS B MBS FZS	ZH

Indo-Aryan system

(FBS)e (MZS)e eB	(FZS)e (MBS)e (WB)e (ZH)e
(FBS)y (MZS)y yB	(FZS)y (MBS)y (WB)y (ZH)y

Dravidian system (parallel/cross relatives)

WeB	(FBS)e (MBS)e (MZS)e (FZS)e eB	eZH
WyB	(FBS)y (MBS)y (MZS)y (FZS)y yB	yZH

Aghriā system

In ego's generation, a north Indian pattern seems to be predominant; but analysis of the terms of the children's generation shows an entirely different situation. Sibling's children are classified according to the sex of ego—a similarity to Dravidian features and unknown in the north. A pure Dravidian pattern is, however, contradicted by the existence of separate terms for ChSp—another feature of Mundaic systems. The different ways of classifying children—'Dravidian' *vs.* 'Indo-Aryan' terminology—are also shown in Table 18. In the case of the Aghriā, the prevalent Hindi lexic is significant. The terms *bhanjā* or *bhatijā* are a case in point. Neither, however, is used in the same way as in Hindi—this means that spouses apply the terms complementarily (and not equally as in Hindi). Even if the Aghriā terminology resembles the Dravidian pattern in the classification of children, an obvious difference remains: the distinction of nephews/nieces in relation to the relative age between the ego and his siblings. For example, eBS is separated from yBS, but there is no complete division of this generation, as ZCh are excluded. Furthermore, a differentiation of one's own children according to their age is possible, but only with prefixes. Again, a middle position can be identified.

In the generations of grandparents and grandchildren only two terms are applied to all persons within. Some relationships may be additionally specified by composites, e.g. WFF as *ajāśaśur*. The existence of only two terms in both generations shows another parallel to the Tamil terminology, whereas Indo-Aryan terminologies usually have four terms in these generations. At least in some cases Dravidian terminologies with a four-fold division in the generations +2/–2 have been documented (Trautmann 1995 [1981]: 232; Good 1991: 59–60) and a two-fold classification plus composites seems common in Mundaic systems as well.

A distinction between elder and younger in the generations 0, –1 and +1 and the pattern of classification for the generations of the great-grandchildren, great-grandparents and beyond exists neither in Dumont's analysis of the Tamil terminology nor in most works on Indo-Aryan terminologies (Vatuk 1969; Pocock 1972; Conzelmann 1996),[15] except in Mundaic or tribal contexts. The identical classification of the generations +3 and –3 among the Aghriā is particularly significant. Even in a region like Gujarat, where syntheses of Indo-

Aryan and Dravidian systems do occur (compare Trivedi 1969 [1961] in the Mer example; Basu 2000: 264), the classification of relatives always ends in the generations –2/+2.

Apart from the above-mentioned equation of the generations –3/+3, in which all men are classified as *baḍu* and all women as *baḍi*, the term *baḍi* is used as well for FeBW and MeZ. Furthermore, FeB is referred to as *baḍkā bāpā/babā*—terms used in address for *baḍu*, e.g. in Gen +3. Equally striking is the classification of yBCh (m.s.), HyBCh and WyZCh as *baḍu* and *baḍi* respectively. I hold that the category *baḍu/baḍi* among Aghriā clearly points to the principle of alternation as represented in Table 23.

Similar terminologies are known from the Kondh of Baudh-Kondhmal district and the Kurukh or Oraon from Chhotanagpur and Raigarh district in Chhattisgarh. The terminologies of both groups, which are part and parcel of the tribal society in the wider sense, have been analysed by Trautmann (1995 [1981]: 140 ff, 142 ff). They show a surprising number of common features—structural as well as lexical—with the Aghriā terminology. In the Kondh terminology the term *boḍu* denotes FeB = MeZH and *boḍai* is applied to FeBW = MeZ. However, these terms are not only used in the parents' generation, as *boḍu* also denotes yBS (m.s.), HyBS and WyZS, *boḍai* stands also for yBD (m.s.), and HyBD and WyZD in the children's generation. For the generations +3/–3 no information is available about the Kondh, but there is plenty on the Kurukh/Oraon. They use the term *baras* (if one neglects the prefix *eng–* which is part of all terms) for all men (great-grandfather, etc.), while women (great-granddaughter, etc.) are classified as *bari*. And *baras* also denotes FeB = MeZH = yBS (m.s.) = eZS (f.s.) and *bari* MeZ = FeBW = yBD (m.s.) = eZD (f.s.). Both terms structurally and lexically classify relatives in the generations –1 and +1 very similar to the Kondh, however here the generations –3/+3 are likewise included. The Aghriā

TABLE 23: ALTERNATION OF TERMS IN THE AGHRIĀ TERMINOLOGY

Generations	Terms	Relations
Gen. +3	*baḍu/baḍi*	PaPaPa
Gen. +1	*baḍu/baḍi*	FeB/MeZH, FeBW/MeZ
Gen. –1	*baḍu/baḍi*	yBCh (m.s.)/HyBCh/WyZCh
Gen. –3	*baḍu/baḍi*	ChChCh

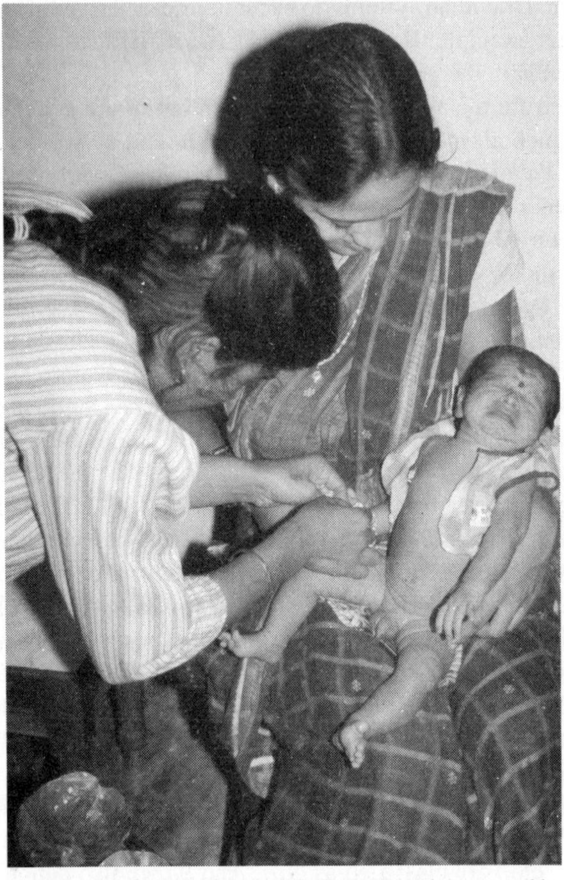

A *rākhī* is bound by a mother's father's younger sister to an elder brother's daughter's son, i.e. to classificatory younger brother

terminology resembles these two cases and the category *baḍi/baḍu* has a very similar semantic scope when compared with the categories *boḍu/boḍai* among the Kondh and *baras/bari* among the Kurukh/ Oraon. The semantic field of the Ho category *gungu* (Pfeffer 1983: 110–11)—is apparently identical with *baḍu/baḍi* as already introduced above. Similarly, Roy (1925: 128–33) mentioned for the Birhor of Chhotanagpur the following equations:

1. MyZH = WeZS and
2. MeZH = FeB = yZS (f.s.) = WyZS = yBS (m.s.) = HyBS.

This classification is almost identical with the Aghriā case, in which, yZS (f.s.) falls into a different category and the generations +3/–3 are also included.

Further examples such as the Ho and Juang that share similar structural features have already been mentioned. These striking characteristics are also common in the terminologies collected from tribal communities such as the Gaṇḍ, Khaḍiā or Muṇḍā in the area immediately surrounding the Aghriā.

This means that apart from 'Dravidian' or 'Indo–Aryan' influences, the principal of alternation comes to light in the Aghriā terminology. This hypothesis is supported by the generations +4/–4, despite most interlocutors having been somehow unsure of the proper terms for these generations. It happened occasionally that four generations in one family live together and usually terms for relatives within these generations were clear to everybody. However, in a rare exception during a festival, family members of five successive generations gathered and it was much less clear how the generations on the fringe (great-great-grandparent and great-great-grandchild) should address each other. Nevertheless, interlocutors' statements are significant, as the principle of alternation did emerge. In the generation +4, the terms *ajā/āī* are used as in generation +2, but a prefix *pain–* is added. In a similar way the terms *nāti/nāten* applied to grandchildren reappear in generation –4. In contrast, other interlocutors also state that the terms *ajā/āī* are used for the generation –4, which implies that this generation is identified with generation +2, another even generation.

The point made by analysing the terms of reference becomes clearer yet, if we also take the terms of address into consideration. Here we find the equations eB = FF = MF or eZ = FM = MM, which are denoted as *dadā* or *bāi* and addressed in the same way. Furthermore, in address—though not in reference—not only FZH and DH, but also MB and ZS (m.s.) are identified. There is also an indirect equation between MB and FZH since the FZ refers to her BS as *bhanjā* as well. Moreover, eBS is equated with S in the address term *beṭā* and with F as well as with FyB, who could also be addressed as *beṭā*. Therefore, these relationships may be subsumed in one category and MyZH and WeZCh are equally identified. As MyZH is equated with FyB, we could include WeZCh in this category. A WeB/WyB

TABLE 24: SIMPLIFIED AGHRIĀ TERMINOLOGY

(male categories only)

Gen.	Parallel	Cross			
+3/– 3	**baḍu**				
+2/–2	dadā (ajā) – eB				
(+4/–4)	bhāi (nāten) – yB				
+1/–1	**baḍu** (FeB, MeZH, yBS (ms), HyBS, WyZS) F/FyB MyZH S/eBS (m.s.) WeZS	MB, ZS (m.s.), BS (f.s.)	FZH DH	SpF (SbSpF)	
0	dadā – eB (BWBe/ZHBe/WeB/WZH)			ChSpF	eZH
	bhāi – yB (BWBy/ZHBy/WyB)			WZH	yZH

may be addressed as *dadā/bhāi* respectively and occasionally a WZHe can be included in the category eB/*dadā* as well (although I never came across the opposite form for WZHy). Thus the terminologies can be presented in a simplified version as shown in Table 24.

The principle of alternation as presented in Table 24 as a common feature shared by tribal groups and castes in the same region, and shown in their terminologies, is clearly visible between the generations 0, +2, +4, –2, –4 and between +1, +3, –1, –3, although these equations are far from complete. It is likely that there exist generational super-categories that underlie the terminologies: *baḍu*/adjacent generation as opposed to *dadā* or *bhāi*/alternating generation. The principle of seniority interferes in the generations –1 to +1 with the alternating principle. The alternation of generations finds expression in life-cycle rituals particularly during Aghriā wedding ceremonies and those ceremonies connected with the brother–sister relationship. Some ritual functions can only be fulfilled by representatives of the bride's or groom's generation and the generations of the grandparents/grand-children, but not by members of the generations of the parents or children. That means that, in practice, the principle of alternation tends to dominate the principle of seniority within a generation. I will return to this point in the next chapter.

I suggest that the Aghriā terminology is not only a synthesis of Dravidian and Indo-Aryan elements, but within the context of the tribal society of Orissa and adjacent areas of Chhattisgarh and in relation to peculiar Middle Indian Mundaic kinship features. Aghriā terminology is fully comprehensible only within the context of tribal society. The following principles order this type of terminology:

1. Alternation
2. Kin—Affines Distinction (partly as B—Wife-Taker/Wife-Giver—Differentiation)
3. Seniority/Relative Age
4. Sex/Gender
5. Tendency to merge adjacent categories (e.g. HeB/HF; yBW/SW or *baḍu/pāinbaḍu*)
6. Tendency to differentiate categories in terms of reference and to merge them in terms of address

These principles seem to interfere frequently. Thus a clearly ordered whole is not recognizable. In Dumont's terms, the Aghriā use a 'vocabulary' rather than a 'terminology', which may be the result of the influence of the neighbouring communities that use these terms in everyday interactions in villages conceived as fictive kinship groups.

5.2. RULES AND PRACTICE

Endogamy

The first rule I will consider is endogamy, by which marriage (and sexual relations) should be restricted to the Aghriā caste. A breach automatically leads to exclusion from the community.[16] For women, an affair or marriage outside the community, brings excommunication, final and irreversible. Any Aghriā having arranged a marriage outside the caste loses status as an Aghriā and is regarded as a *Sarliā*; an inferior category, which, according to interlocutors, has come into being as a result of mixed marriages.[17] The lower status of these mixed marriages is expressed by the word *sarliā* itself, which means 'slipped'. Any marriage between an Aghriā and a *Sarliā*, who still call themselves Aghriā, is forbidden. A distinction between '*Bad* or superior Agharias and the Chhote, Sarolia or Sarwaria, the inferior or mixed Agharias' has been noted by Russell and Hiralal (1975 [1916]: 9), who explain the latter category as a mixture between an Aghriā man and a Gaur (Ahir) woman.

Some Aghriā from Orissa claim that marriage should be arranged within the former undivided districts of Sambalpur, Bolangir and Sundargarh and should not include Aghriā from Chhattisgarh, who are regarded as having inferior status. Some Aghriā from Bolangir district believe that in Chhattisgarh Aghriā have ST-status, while Aghriā in Bolangir, Sambalpur and Sundargarh are considered to be OBC. However, according to my own survey, Aghriā are OBC in both regions. The Aghriā from Chhattisgarh[18] regard the Aghriā of Orissa to be lower in status, because they claim that the Aghriā in Orissa eat the meat of castrated goats (*kasi*) and practice (or have practised) marriage with the elder brother's wife (*bahu*). In Chhattisgarh such a marriage is strictly prohibited, as a *bahu* is seen as a mother. Yet many Aghriā from Sambalpur/Sundargarh districts refer to the strict taboos in their region on the meat of castrated goats,[19] onion and garlic and the maintenance of poultry inside the house. In any case, a distinction in status is expressed on both sides, but these opinions are not shared by all Aghriā. In the last four to five years some marriage relationships between Orissa and Chhattisgarh have been arranged—some Aghriā from Chhattisgarh claim that it is because Orissan Aghriā have stopped their degrading customs. However, there is no hypergamous hierarchy between the three major regions of the Aghriā population in Orissa and Chhattisgarh.

The breaking of caste endogamy can be tolerated, as shown by the case of an influential Aghriā landlord and revenue collector, who, in addition to three other marriages with Aghriā women, had a relationship with a Chasā without officially marrying her. This caused a scandal among the Aghriā, for the landlord had brought her into his house without being expelled from his caste.[20] A married Aghriā woman, however, was excluded from the community for having an affair with her Gaṇḍ neighbour. In a third case, an Aghriā woman married a man from another high caste and was expelled. I heard that her father was also excluded temporarily, but later readmitted into the caste after having given a feast. A reintegration into one's own caste—visible by the participation in feasts and rituals—is possible after some time, as the above case shows, but it depends very much on the families concerned.

During my stay in Orissa, the family of an Aghriā man, who married outside the community visibly distanced themselves from the relationship: they boycotted the wedding.[21] The elder relatives thus showed their disagreement, which was further evident by the fact that the invitation had been written in the name of the groom himself and not in the name of elder relatives, as is usual. If the family had supported the relationship, they would have been questioned by their *jāti*, who would have demanded a feast. However, the Aghriā husband and the new daughter-in-law/sister-in-law were privately accepted into the family, even though they still remained excluded from the community. In a sample of 373 marriages I came across only three cases of intercaste marriages (less than 1 per cent)—two of them in an urban milieu. In most cases these were 'love marriages'. It seems that marriages with members of castes of a similar status, e.g. Aghriā and Chasā, are more frequent, while marriages implying a bigger status difference, such as between an Aghriā and a so-called 'Untouchable', are extremely rare. In another case, the bride's parents, who belonged to the Chasā community (Kandayat), supported their daughter, and the wedding was celebrated in their house mixing the customs of both communities, but there was no reception on the groom's side.

We must distinguish here between marriage and affairs. While both are theoretically considered to be a breach of the rule of endogamy, the former is not tolerated at all in practice. Affairs can be ignored if the person involved is influential and powerful. However, in most cases—particularly those, in which Aghriā women are involved—any breach of the rule of endogamy is sanctioned.

There have been attempts to reintegrate the *Sarliā* into the Aghriā fold. Some Aghriā remembered this example. Once, at a caste meeting an influential Aghriā—the father of a former minister of the Orissan Government, president of a local caste council and an important member of the community—argued for marriages between the Aghriā proper and the children of *Sarliā* by claiming that the children were not responsible for their parents' mistakes. However, elder Aghriā present interrupted his speech shouting, 'Stop it!'

The Aghriā Samāj (caste organization) of Bolangir district has set up rules to avoid the marriages of their sons—particularly literate/ educated sons—with women of the Sambalpur and Sundargarh regions that belong to a separate Aghriā caste organization. Five to ten years ago, a rule was initiated that every groom marrying an Aghriā girl from the formerly undivided Sambalpur and Sundargarh districts must pay a fine of Rs. 10,000; if not, the family would be excommunicated. However, a caste feast is not required in order to be reintegrated, once the fine has been paid. The usual argument for the rule's defence is that a higher dowry is given in Sambalpur and Sundargarh. Thus the much sought-after grooms holding jobs often decide to marry a woman from these districts in order to receive the higher dowry including luxury goods. A fine had to be imposed as hindrance.

Despite this 'rule', marriage relationships are arranged in practice. The current president of the Bolangir caste organization estimates that the number of such marriages is 57, while he knows of six in the opposite direction. Of 57 marriages, 25 have been arranged in the past 10 years. In all cases a fine has been paid, or is in the process of being paid (a fine may also be paid in several instalments). Paying the fine appears to be a sign of prestige.[22] No fine has to be paid if the families can arrange an exchange of brides between the two regions/ caste organizations.

A rule of endogamy restricts marriage to one's own generation: that means it is a form of intra-generational endogamy or an endogamy of generation sets, marriage between persons of adjacent generations should be avoided. Persons who belong to the grandparent's or grandchildren's generation—in fact to any alternating generation—may be married provided they belong to a different clan (for exogamy see below). This rule is quite consistent with the principle of alternation found in the terminology. Such a provision has been mentioned by Grigson (1991 [1938]: 245) for the Gonds of Bastar too[23] and is found as well among many village neighbours of the Aghriā such as the Kisān, Malār or Tūrī.

In former times there was the custom of grandfather-marriage (*ajā-bihā*), which meant that a girl reaching puberty might have been married to a distant grandfather, if a suitable groom for the girl had not yet been found. To give the daughter in marriage to a distant grandfather or *ajā* was an opportunity to marry a daughter off at an early age. Although close grandfathers (FF, MF) were not eligible, it was possible to marry one's mother's mother's brother (MMB) or one's father's mother's brother (FMB) and more distant grandfathers. Apart from the grandfathers, an elder sister's husband (*bāṭo*) was a possible marriage partner as well, underlining the equation of alternate generations. Usually the girl had been divorced from her 'grandfather husband' subsequently and married to her 'proper' husband, whenever a suitable match could be arranged. The girl never stayed in the house of her grandfather as a wife. For the first marriage with the grandfather most of the rituals, in particular the anointing with oil and turmeric, the *teilabhiṣek/tel chaḍā* and the circling around the fire were performed. Later, the grandfather had to sign the divorce papers. For the second marriage another *teilabhiṣek* was not necessary, but the circling was repeated before the bride was brought to the groom's household. This custom clearly demonstrates the endogamy of 'generation-sets'. No 'uncle' or relative of the father's generation would have been a possible match. The Aghriā I asked agreed that a marriage with a distant grandfather is more acceptable than marrying a distant niece or nephew such as a brother's daughter or a distant uncle or aunt like a father's sister or mother's sister, etc. However, as early as 1921 the Aghriā Samāj started to prohibit and thus to eradicate this custom—possibly considering it to be degrading.[24]

I came across several cases of symbolic marriage with a grandfather, e.g. an elder lady had married her father's father's younger sister's husband's younger brother (FFyZHyB). This Aghriā woman married her classificatory grandfather at the age of four or five (around 1930) before marrying again, thirteen years later (around 1943). Another woman remembered that her father's sister's daughter had married her distant grandfather as well. The groom was her mother's father's younger brother (MFyB). However, this custom seems to have been in decline by the 1930s. One reason may be the caste organization's attempts to abolish the tradition. Nevertheless, there are still cases of marriages arranged with a distant grandfather—although they are indeed rare. In 1996, an Aghriā woman married her mother's father's mother's brother's son (MFMBS). According to my data, 6 out of 373 marriages, including the last were arranged in this manner, but the figures must have been higher in previous days. Most Aghriā I spoke with vaguely remembered that some family members were married to a grandfather, without being able to specify the exact relationship.

The rule demanding the avoidance of marriage to persons of adjacent generations can be evaded in practice if the marriage partners are very distantly related. For example, one man married the daughter of a distant, classificatory sister. In my sample, 13 out of 373 marriages (3.5 per cent) were arranged with a partner from an adjacent generation. None of these involved close relatives.

Exogamy

The Aghriā are divided into exogamous, patrilineal clans known as *bansa* (*bana*) and *gotra* (*barga*), and marriage within one's own clan is strictly prohibited. *Bansa* and *gotra* seem to be structurally identical, which means that each person belongs to one *bansa* and one *gotra* and every *bansa* corresponds to one and only one *gotra*. An overlap between *bansa* and *gotra* is excluded—it is impossible for persons of the same *gotra* but different *bansa* or vice versa. Therefore, *bansa* and *gotra* express the same rule of exogamy, but it is impossible to find an explanation for the double formulation of this rule. *Gotras*, as patrilineal clans, are well documented. They are found in north India (e.g. Karve 1998 [1953]: 52) among castes of all status categories, but particularly among Brahmins and Kshatriyas. The importance of this rule is highlighted when *bansa* and *gotra* of potential spouses are compared repeatedly to avoid the breaking of the rule. Only after the necessary confirmation can marriage arrangements proceed.

The Aghriā are also known as *chaurāśi ghar* or '84 houses', because it is said that the Aghriā originally consisted of 84 *bansa* and *gotra*. They believe that of these 84 clans only 44 have come to Orissa. Each of the 84 had acquired one of three titles, so that 60 clans now bear the title Patel, 18 the title Nayak and another 6 the title Chaudarī. For marriage, however, these titles play no decisive role, which indicates that marriages can be arranged in both directions between all three categories. A list is given below. It is significant to note that this list is not fully consistent in the sense that some *gotras* (Kouśik, Bedbyās) appear twice in the list, though different *bansa* are mentioned.

BANSAS AND *GOTRAS* OF THE AGHRIĀ[25]

TABLE 25: LIST OF AGHRIĀ-CLANS

Bansa (*bāna*)	Gotra (*barga*)	Title (*śreṇī*) and Symbol
Khīchi	Komaṇḍal	Chaudarī/Kauli Katar Sword
Kumbha Kalas	Nārad	— do —
Nāhān	Baṭuśyām	— do —
Kuṭhī	Atreya	— do —
Hansā	Augirā	— do —
Thelā[26]	Kapil	— do —
Leunia	Kumbhaj (Agasti)	Nāyak/Jamadhada Katar
Kalihārī	Bedbyās	— do —
Jhiṭorī[27]	Sāgar	— do —
Śirsanṭ	Kāśyap	— do —
Sanchirā	Jamadar	— do —
Chitā	Śankar	— do —
Gonā	Jamunā	— do —
Alkarā	Gajakeśar	— do —
Sinduriā	Jantrikā	— do —
Chaupaṭṭā	Bhujbal (Jagyabal)	— do —
Rājkeśar	Kouśik (Kouśal)	— do —
Birihabarāg	Maheśvar	— do —
Chandramā	Ahalyā	— do —
Karāyat	Gayāghāṭ	— do —
Bankā	Karchuli	— do —
Dibrā	Jagadhar	— do —
Gokulkān	Gayādhar	— do —
Kalyā	Bedbyās	— do —
Tihuriā (Tihiria)	Narmadā	Paṭel/Meghanad Katar Sword
Panoriā (Pandiria)	Aśīl	Paṭel
Khanḍriā	Kāśī	— do —
Geruāṇ	Gāeghāṭ	— do —
Madhughāghar	Gayāpiṇḍ	— do —
Ghīsāgar	Ahal	— do —
Haṭnāngar	Baṭuśyām	— do —
Ṭhusar	Saṇḍil	— do —
Sanāhī	Brahmā	— do —
Rāut	Mahilāgar (Mahilapar)	— do —
Phalāhā	Deostān	— do — (Sāe)
Dāans[28]	Kouśik [see rajkeshar bansa]	— do —
Barāh[29]	Goutam	do
Nahilā	Jagachillī	— do —
Bhainsā	Karsāyel	— do —
Balrām	Bharadvāj	— do —
Agni Kumār	Ghoghar	— do —

(contd.)

TABLE 25 (contd.)

Aṇḍilbāg	Nīldhar	— do —
Ṭeksinjhariā (Tekasiharia)	Jamadagni	— do —
Sonbarṣā	Phalāgar	— do —

Note: The transcription is based on a list from 1925[30]—deviating versions given in brackets.

In practice, other titles are also used. In the Bolangir district, the title *Sāe* had been conferred on the family of the first matriculate[31] of the former princely state. The family had belonged to the *Phalhā* clan using the title Patel, but now calls itself *Sāe*—a title used, e.g. by the king of Sambalpur, in former times. Other Aghriā remember that formerly additional titles such as Singh, Kalihāri, Rāut, Mājhi or Rām were also used. However, these titles are not common today. One additional title not listed, but common in the Jharsuguda district is 'Pandey'. Some Aghriā suggest that the Pandey originally formed a separate clan—the 85th—but are now included in the Aghriā fold. Thus, the position of Pandey Aghriā remains ambiguous.

Village exogamy as a preference/tendency is recognizable, but it is not as strong as the *bansa-/gotra*-rule. If the Aghriā wish to evade the *banśa-/gotra*-rule of exogamy, they can try adoption. This means that if bride and groom are of the same clan, one of them must be adopted before marriage by someone from another clan, so that the rule is not formally broken.

Marriage preferences: cross-cousins and others

The rule of cross-cousin marriage seems to have been previously wide-spread, with a preference for the matrilateral cross-cousin (MBD)—a custom the Aghriā share with many tribal communities in their immediate vicinity such as the Kandh and Malār.[32] It is significant that according to some Aghriā, apart from the *bhanjā dān* the biggest gift a mother's brother can give to his sister's son is *kanyā dān*, the gift of his daughter. By offering a daughter, a mother's brother earns not the common religious merits (*puniya*), but the biggest merit possible—*māhāpuniya*. Earning this highest merit is a means to *mukti* or salvation, the ultimate goal of leaving the cycle of birth and rebirth.

Marriage with the patrilateral cross-cousin (FZD) is possible as well, but practised only rarely. Nowadays, the rule of cross-cousin marriage or marriage with close relatives generally seems to have lost its importance, due to the occurrence of the sickle cell anemia—a relatively frequent genetic defect, through which the red blood corpuscles are unable to bind enough oxygen. This can cause anaemia, disturbances of the blood circulation or a blocking of the capillaries, which leads to damage to the heart, lungs and the brain, and even the potential breakdown of these organs (Dey 1997: 1–3). Sickle cell anemia is a sensitive topic, because it reduces people's marriage chances. Therefore only very limited information can be gathered about this subject so far.

Many Aghriā try to avoid cross-cousin marriages and prefer structurally and spatially distance marriages, because doctors recommend marriage with non-kin. Thus, K. Sāe, an Aghriā from Bolangir, writes in a leaflet[33] in 2002, 'distance [*sic*] Marriages should be encouraged' to avoid sickle cell anemia. Therefore, I hold that the process of social change is imminent, from cross-cousin marriage as a rule or MBD-marriage as a preference, towards completely new kinship ties. This does not mean that no more cross-cousin marriages are arranged, but only that they are no longer as preferred as they used to be in the past. But cross-cousin marriages are still possible and in no way prohibited as they are in north India.

My own data on the frequency of certain types of marriages are shown in Table 26.

In my sample 92 marriages were arranged within one's own circle of relatives, a little less than 25 per cent. The figure without the village Mundaloi is a bit above 23 per cent, while the figure for Mundaloi

TABLE 26: STATISTICAL FREQUENCY OF MARRIAGE TYPES

Villages	No.	Close				Distant				Other distant relatives
		MBD	FZD	*sangāt*	*śālī*	MBD	FZD	*sangāt*	*śālī*	
Mundaloi	49	2			1	4	2	4		5 (1 MyZD, 1 FBD, 1 BD, 1 ZD)[34]
Other villages	324	12		6	5	7	5	7	1	33 (11 FBD, 5 BD, 4 FZ, 1 MyZ, 4 *ajā*, 6 MZD[35]
Total	373	14		6	6	11	7	11	1	36

with 35 per cent is significantly higher. As I spent most of the time in Mundaloi, this figure should be more precise, even though the sample is small. However, careful research in the other villages could reveal a high percentage of marriages among relatives, as in Mundaloi.

The research conducted by Dey (1997: 68) documents the frequency of cross-cousin marriages among the Aghriā in two different regions the undivided districts Sambalpur and Sundargarh in the north of Orissa and part of the undivided Bolangir district in the south. The results are briefly presented in Table 27.

In the northern region the frequency of cross-cousin marriages is roughly 10 per cent, in a sample of 876 marriages. The higher percentage of marriages with the matrilateral cross-cousin compared to the patrilateral cross-cousin is significant. In the southern region there is only a 5 per cent frequency of cross-cousin marriages, however, here the sample is far more limited in numbers. Therefore, I take the data of the northern region to be more reliable. It is significant, though that the percentage of MBD-marriages in both regions is around 5 per cent, while the share of FZD-marriages amounts to only 1 per cent (for close relatives). Comparing several case studies of cross cousin marriage, Trautmann (1991 [1985]: 218 ff) considered an actual frequency of cross-cousin marriages of between 10 and 30 per cent to be usual,[36] which means that a figure of altogether around 10 per cent for the Aghriā appears quite likely, especially if the additional factor, sickle cell anemia, is taken into consideration.

Apart from matrilateral cross-cousin marriage, the data show two other types of relations occurring frequently in marriage: *sangāt* (ZHZ/BWZ) and *śālī* (WyZ). Marriages have been arranged with

TABLE 27: STATISTICAL FREQUENCY OF MARRIAGES AMONG AGHRIĀ

Type of Marriage	Northern Region		Southern Region	
Marriage with cross-cousin of 1 degree:		percentage		percentage
matrilateral cross-cousin	41	4.68	14	4.49
patrilateral cross-cousin	12	1.37	3	0.96
Marriage with classificatory cross-cousin[37]	43	4.91	1	0.32
Percentage of cross-cousin marriage	96	10.69	18	5.77
Number of marriages	876	100	312	100

Source: Dey 1997: 68, adapted by the author.

these two categories of close relatives only—at least in my sample. In contrast to matrilateral cross-cousins, there is a certain preference for these categories, but it is not formulated as a rule in the sense that someone can earn *mahāpuniya* such as a *māmu* (MB) giving his daughter.

That means that marriage relations are not only repeated diachronically in subsequent generations as with cross-cousin marriage, but in one's own generation, or synchronically, as well. Furthermore, marrying a *sangāt* or BWZ might imply a repetition of the marriage direction—accepting a wife from a family, who has already given a daughter as in the case of the mother's brother's daughter marriage or wife's younger sister marriage—but it can also mean a reciprocal exchange, in case a *sangāt* or ZHZ is married. Significantly, among the Juang the category of *saliray,* including eBWyZ, eZHyZ and WyZ, is prescribed and most marriages (54 per cent) are arranged with brides belonging to it as the sample, though rather small, of McDougal (1963: 162) shows. In contrast, only 18 per cent matrilateral and another 6 per cent patrilateral cross-cousin marriages had been arranged among the Juang (ibid.). Thus, the cases of the Aghriā and the Juang indicate that repetition of marriage relations within the same generation is valued and a category of relatives, which corresponds roughly to the German category of *Schwippschwägerin* (ZHZ/BWZ) appears to be preferred in Middle India, although the category *saliray* is framed slightly differently than the category *sangāt* among the Aghriā.

In all cases of cross-cousin, *sangāt* and *śālī* marriages, successful marriage relations are repeated, even though the direction may be reversed. It demonstrates that affinity is valued indeed—to use Dumont's famous phrase. This is substantiated by the fact that there is a considerable number of marriages among distant relatives, e.g. FBD, provided she belongs to a different clan.

During my stay I came to understand that cross-cousin marriages or more generally marriages within one's own network of relatives are increasingly avoided, condemned and currently declining because of sickle cell anemia. There is a predominant feeling among those affected that the problem can be avoided by choosing more distant relatives or, better yet, by marrying into families with whom one is not related at all. Thus, it seems that, apart from valuing and repeating

TABLE 28: MARRIAGES AMONG RELATIVES OVER THE LAST DECADES

Year	No.	Close			Distant				Other dist. relatives
		MBD	*sangāt*	*śālī*	MBD	FZD	*sangāt*	*śālī*	
1921–30	2								
1931–40	2								
1941–50	2								
1951–60	5			1					
1961–70	3					1			
1971–80	8				1		1		
1981–90	9	2		1			1		
1991–2000	8								
2001–	1				1				
Total	40	2		2	2	1	2		

existing affinal ties, there is also the opposite tendency. The Mundaloi sample presented below in Table 28 is, however, too small for any verification of this hypothesis.

Fortunately Dey (1997: 70) provides data for the northern region, which I reproduce in Table 29.

Dey's data too are insufficient to clarify this point. Although the number of cross-cousin marriages has decreased in his data by roughly 5 per cent for the decade 1975–85, this is not sufficient proof of my hypothesis, as the numbers for the previous decades were rather low (around 10 per cent). By supporting my hypothesis, one necessarily opposes Dey's (1997: 69) opinion, as he considers the number of

TABLE 29: CROSS COUSIN MARRIAGES OVER THE LAST DECADES

Year of marriage	Number of marriages	Cross-cousin marriages	
		Absolute	percentage
1916–25	4	0	0
1926–35	35	6	14.71
1936–45	91	8	8.79
1946–55	175	16	9.14
1956–65	212	20	9.43
1966–75	225	32	14.22
1976–85	134	14	10.45
Total	876	96	10.96

Source: Dey 1997: 70; adapted by the author.

cross-cousin marriages to be relatively stable. More data for the last fifteen years would be necessary to confirm this.

It is also necessary to collect more data in order to obtain a better idea of the relationship between the rules and ideals on the one hand, and the practice on the other. It would be important to understand whether or not a cross-cousin of a marriageable age was available or not. Only with such data at hand could the adherence to the ideal be clarified. Apart from demographic factors that essentially determine cross-cousin marriages, individual strategies and aims are equally important on a practical level. In a case I observed, a cross-cousin marriage (MBD-marriage) was arranged and people insisted, that by means of this marriage the maintenance of the relationship was secured. However, in the same family another cross-cousin marriage could have been arranged between the younger siblings of the spouses. This did not happen because new marriages with other families were considered a priority.

In practice, a contradiction appears between cross-cousin marriage on one side and the kinship terminology on the other. As shown above there is no distinction between cross and parallel cousins in the Aghriā terminology, which indicates that all cousins can be classified as brothers or sisters. Therefore, in the case of a cross-cousin marriage, a classificatory sister is married. This can cause considerable confusion among the relatives especially with regard to the form of address. The younger brother of the man, who has married his cross-cousin, calls the wife of his elder brother 'sister', just as before the marriage, although she now stands in the relation of a *bahu* or eBW to him. In contrast to other ethnographic contexts (e.g. Trivedi 1969 [1961]: 58 ff) in this case, there is no adjustment of the categories after marriage—the older relation and form of address remains the most important.

Wife-takers and Wife-givers—affinal gifts and the distinction of status

It has been argued many times that the status distinction between wife-givers and wife-takers is crucial for an understanding of north Indian kinship. According to the ideal, the relationship between them should be irreversible and strictly asymmetrical or hierarchical, the higher status ascribed to wife-takers. Such an asymmetry may be a reflection of a hypergamous hierarchy, but may also be constituted by a unilateral gift exchange—gifts ideally being given non-reciprocally to wife-takers (Dumont 1980 [1966]; Vatuk 1969; Conzelmann 1996, Skoda 2002).

The same ideal was significant among the Aghriā. No Aghriā should accept anything in the house of wife-takers unless he offers a gift of money known as *bhāt khiā* (*bhāt* = boiled rice; *khiā* = to eat) when visiting the wife-taker's house for the first time after marriage. Though the name of the gift refers to rice and once more indicates the importance of rice to the Aghriā, water too should not be accepted if *bhāt khiā* has not been given. This rule is limited to the houses of married younger female relatives, i.e. the houses of younger sisters, daughters, brother's daughters, sister's daughters, son's daughters or daughter's daughters. Apparently this rule corresponds to the category of *dhyani* (Vatuk 1975)—though, to my knowledge, the category is not named among the Aghriā. The category of receivers of *bhāt khiā* stands in contrast to the category of *bhuāsen* (Sambalpuri)/*bhūāsuni* (Oriya) including all women, who have married into the house and who are younger than the ego. Thus, daughters-in-law, brother's son's wife, son's son's wife or even elder brother's wife (younger than ego) fall into this category, only one's own wife is excluded.

The ideal can be further confirmed by the giving of *maulā bhār* or gifts of a mother's brother to his sister's son, given on several occasions until the sister's son's marriage, while even at the time of death of a mother's brother a gift known as *bhanjā dān* (*bhanjā* = sister's son) is given in the same direction. On the other hand, the ideal could be substantiated by the gift of a dowry or *upahār* from the wife-givers to the wife-takers at the time of marriage. As the Aghriā stress, it is *upahār* or a completely voluntary giving instead of *yautuka* as the dowry demanded in former times—though it seems to be more a change of labels than a substantive change. In contrast, previously bridewealth was given as well. In the early scriptures of the Aghriā Samāj it was known as *sagāi* or *kanyā sulka* (*kanyā* = bride; *śulka* = tax) and it clearly contradicted the ideal of non-reciprocity. Also, both prestations—dowry and bridewealth—seem to have co existed. While the former consisted of household goods, the latter—since abolished—was a payment of money.

A difference of status between the wife-takers and the wife-givers could also be expressed by the so-called *śalā bidhā* at the time of the wedding. During the *hāth lagan* ceremony the hands of bride and groom are tied with a thread by a priest. It is the responsibility of the *śalā* or bride's younger brother to tear this thread apart. At this very moment a *śalā* may hit the groom and this beating is viewed as a kind of revenge for taking his sister. Though practised only rarely today, it is still well known. If one interprets this act of 'groom bashing' as a form of rebellion, as the ritual resistance of a wife-giver and as an inversion of roles, it may indicate a superior role of the wife-takers.[38]

However, contrary to the ideal of a strict unilaterality and in return to *bhāt khiā,* a gift is presented known as *māen*—usually cloths. *Māen* is also offered after a *ghar dekhā* (inspection of the groom's house by the bride's people prior to marriage) to the bride's people at the time of departure and appears to be a category of gifts from wife-takers or potential wife-takers to wife-givers. Some Aghriā explain that the name may be derived from *mānya* or 'good behaviour'. There are two more general categories of gifts that contradict a unilateral gift-exchange: on one hand, *bāṭ dekhā* or 'gift of the way' as a gift of sweets or vegetables should be given when visiting any relative—regardless of their positions as wife-takers or wife-givers. It is particularly the responsibility (*kām*) of couples to bring this, as forgetting this gift would be considered a shame (*lāj*). On the other hand chipti—again a gift of sweets—is offered to all guests at the end of a wedding function, after *naḍiā phuṭā*, after Daśarā or after *ekoiśiā* (ritual on 21st day after birth though on *ekoiśiā* it is not obligatory). The name of the gift literally means a big leaf bowl, in which the sweets used to be offered in former times. Again *chipti* is given to the wife-takers and wife-givers, if present on the occasion.[39]

Finally, there is another category of gifts known as *jātrā dekhā*, which are offered to younger wife-giving relatives, e.g. WyB (or WyZ), to wife-taking relatives such as BD or BDH as well as to relatives such as ZS/ZD, whose position is not unambiguous given the rule of cross-cousin marriage. *Jātrā dekhā* is given to these relatives, if they are present at the time of festivals such as *Rath Jātrā,* but it is also offered to contract labourers, service castes or village functionaries at the same time. Therefore, I argue that *jātrā dekhā* is no prestation solely from wife-givers to superior wife-takers, but a form of prestation from a king, the universal donor during the festival.

Thus, two patterns of gift exchange found by Trautmann (1995 [1981]: 277ff) in the Dharmashastra literature appear to be practised among the Aghriā as well.

In practice, the gifting pattern may again be contradicted by the rules of marriage or may contradict other levels of the kinship system. Thus, in cases of *sangāt*-marriage (ZHZ-marriage) it is very difficult to draw a line between wife-givers and wife-takers, since a marriage relationship has been reversed and therefore stands in direct opposition to an ideal of strict unilaterality. Further, though matrilateral cross-cousin marriage can be combined with a hypergamous tendency as well as a non-reciprocal gift exchange, in practice, however, it is not. For example, in a case of the closest matrilateral cross-cousin marriage an elder brother wanted to pay *bhāt khiā* when visiting his married younger sister for the first time after her marriage. However, the mother-in-law of his sister—due to cross-cousin marriage also his father's sister—did not accept it, explaining that the house of his married sister is primarily the house of his father's sister. In that case he is a *bhanjā* in the house of a father's sister and should not pay anything for eating there. This example clearly demonstrates again that the levels of a kinship system do not have to be necessarily consistent and adaptation may well be found in practice.

Considering gift-exchange, there are gifts such as *bhāt khiā* or *māulā bhār* that indicate a distinction in status between wife-givers and wife-takers—the latter being higher in status and nothing should be accepted from them after a daughter has been given. And if they do accept something, they must pay for it. Unilaterality is, however, not a strict rule—gifts such as *māen* are given from wife-takers to wife-givers, though only in return. *Māen* itself does not initiate an exchange, and such a differentiation in status is blurred by exchange-marriages such as the common *sangāt*—marriages and this distinction is neither made in reference to parents of a married couple (both fathers greet and feed each other during the *samdhi bhet*, when the processions of the groom's people as well as the bride's folk meet ceremonially nor do people make any terminological difference. In addition to a Brahmanical pattern of gifting expressed in such sacred gifts as *kanya dān,* forms of a *kshatriya* or royal pattern of giving also appear as gifts such as *jātrā dekhā* and are given to as many recipients as possible.

Rules of avoidance and respect

One essential part of the kinship system on the normative level pertains to the rules of avoidance. They do not only determine behaviour and limit the contact between certain relatives, but they also indicate taboos regarding sexual relations and marriage and symbolize a status difference. Avoidance is expressed in the local language as 'to give way' (*bāṭ chhaḍā*).

1. HeB and yBW should avoid each other. It is expected that an yBW be veiled (*uḍhni*)[40] in the presence of her HeB. At the time of marriage, the HeB is to offer a symbolic veil (*uḍhni*) to the bride, which from then on she has to wear in front of him. HeB and yBW should not stay in a room together and should not eat together—particularly if alone. An yBW is not allowed to eat the food remains of her HeB.
2. HMB and ZSW should also avoid each other. Formerly, this rule seems to have been significantly stronger, however, today both may be in the same room and may also talk to each other. The structural similarity between HeB and HMB is expressed by the fact, that it is the HMB to offer a veil to the bride during the wedding, if there is no HeB. Some elderly Aghriā say that the HMB is preferred for this task.

To welcome elder relatives after a long absence and to show one's respect, the feet are usually touched as *namaskār*. To the relatives to be avoided—HeB, HMB—women kneel down at a distance of at least a meter in order to avoid any physical contact and touch the ground with their forehead.

3. The relationship between WeZ and yZH is subject to similar restrictions, but a veil is not required.
4. *Samdhi* (ChSposPa) and *samdhen* (ChSposPa) are subjected to the same restrictions, but are allowed to stay in the same room.

In all four cases of avoidance the relatives concerned should not sit together on a bed or scooter, and, while driving in a car, a certain distance must be kept. In former times the female relatives left the room when the person to be avoided entered. Nowadays this custom is not followed as strictly, but some Aghriā say that they do not feel comfortable in the same room, particularly with their HeB. In the ritual context, relatives who must avoid each other cannot act as *suhāsen* during the wedding and cannot eat the food offered for an ancestor they were required to avoid while alive (e.g. *pani* served during the *barṣika śrāddha*). Thus rules of avoidance do not cease even after death.

5. Another rule practised in the past, but well remembered is the veiling of the MBW opposite her HZS. However, veiling did not exclude the touching of the husband's *bhanjā*'s feet; a MBW was expected to show her respect. Some Aghriā say that the rule of avoidance of HZS by the MBW is different from the rule concerning the HeB, because the HZS belongs to a younger generation and therefore avoidance is less strict. The same may hold true in comparison to the avoidance of the HeB to HMB—the latter is less strict.[41]
6. FyBW had to veil herself in the presence of her HeBS in former times—a rule no longer practised. Like a MBW, she was expected to touch the feet of her HeBW (*putrā*). Another sign of avoidance was the use of formal terms of address only. Thus, a FyBW could address her HeBS as *putrā* or *bābu*, but never by name (some say the usage was restricted to *bābu* and even *putrā* as a term of address was prohibited). Likewise a FyBW could not use the term *jhiārī* as a form of address for her HeBD and a HeBD had to be addressed simply as *nani*. Also, a *putrā* was not allowed to join the marriage ceremonies, in particular the *barāt* of his FyB, because he was—and still is—seen as the son and should not see the marriage of his 'father'.[42] Again the Aghriā Samāj might have been influential in eradicating this custom. Already by 1921 it threatened caste members with exclusion should they continue the practice.[43]
7. Some Aghriā claim that in the past the *māin* (WMBW) had to be veiled in front of a *bhanjājuen* (HZDH), but nowadays it is practised only rarely.

In addition to the rules of avoidance, special respect to all persons of the parents' generation is expected, not only the father and mother, but also FB, SpF, FZ, MZ and SpM, etc. As Parkin (1992: 190–1) argues, this is a basic Middle Indian pattern. However, a significant change is observed in relation to MBW and FyBW as well as to the MB. While an MB used to pay respect to his ZS, the relation is almost reversed now, although he does not receive the same sort of respect as, for example, a FeB. The relation to an MB is much more familiar, and seems to resemble a common north Indian pattern in which the MB shows a latent deference toward ego corresponding to the role of a wife-giver as lower in status to the wife-takers (Madan 1998 [1975]: 296–7). In contrast, the MB may appear as an authority figure in the context of the tribal society of Middle India, as the example of the Juang documents (Pfeffer 1983: 101).

Practically, the rules of avoidance between HeB and yBW prohibit all forms of contact, which means that they are almost 'untouchable' to each other. For example, an yBW cannot give directly tea to her HeB; she puts it on the ground in front of him. In many cases the presence of her HeB is a reason for her to leave the room, if the presence of the HeB cannot be avoided in advance. In cases of emergency such as illness, these rules can be broken and HeB and yBW may stay in one room together. In the presence of her HeB or HMB, the yBW or ZSW usually veils her head, particularly the back of her head and the hair, but not the face. In all these cases physical contact should be strictly avoided. If it happens, for example, in a crowd, the man—or the person who touches first—must offer a coconut in a temple as a kind of penitence.

The rule of avoidance between HeB and yBW appears to be the strongest in practice, while, as interlocutors confirmed, it is weaker for the WeZ and yZH relationship. In one case there was even an affair between a WeZ and an yZH, which did not lead to any formal sanctions, but the WeZ, belonging to an influential Gauntiā family, was criticized. Occasionally, 'modern-minded' people even break the rules in the case of their WeZ deliberately and sit together on one bed, but I have not come across such cases in regard to an yBW.

All rules of avoidance stand in conflict with the rules of cross-cousin marriage in practice. Considering the second rule—avoidance between HMB and ZSW—and a case of matrilateral cross-cousin marriage, we see that the father must avoid his daughter (or an FB his BD) which contradicts my own observation. In a combination of the third rule of avoidance and a cross-cousin marriage, a brother should avoid his older sister, which again is not confirmed in actual social practice. However, the rule of avoidance between HeB and yBW is strictly observed even in cases of cross-cousin marriage, which, in this case, is avoidance between an elder classificatory brother (eB) and a younger classificatory sister (yZ).

Joking relationships

Ritualized, public, and partly obligatory joking is practised in several 'joking relationships'. In many cases a special intimacy is attached to, or expected from, those with whom people have joking relationships. In opposition to the rules of avoidance and respect, joking relationships can hint at a familiar relationship and to possible sexual relations or later marriages, e.g. in levirate relations (Kolenda 1990: 144; Parkin 1992: 188). Correspondingly, among the Aghriā, relatives with whom one can joke, such as a husband's younger brother and a wife's younger sister are allowed to marry, while relatives one must avoid—here the husband's elder brother or the wife's elder sister—are not matches for a remarriage. A junior levirate, i.e. a marriage with the husband's younger brother after the husband's death, seems to have been frequent in former times, although people rarely remember any cases. As previously mentioned, the Aghriā in Chhattisgarh say that the status of the Orissan Aghriā is comparatively low, because they practise this custom frequently. However, according to my interlocutors it is still possible to marry a *bahu*.[44] In contrast, no case of senior levirate—marriage with the husband's elder brother after death of one's husband—was known. Similarly, a junior sororate—marriage with the wife's younger sister after the wife's death—is quite possible and indeed practised. In opposition, marriage with a wife's elder sister—a senior sororate—is not allowed.

Generally, joking can have an anti-structural or anti-hierarchical effect and can represent a limited symmetry in a relationship (as far as symmetrical joking is meant). Among the Aghriā there are several such joking relationships, but the jokes and the intensity of joking vary. Women are generally expected to joke more mildly or with more reserve. Differences are shown in the following Table 30.

No joking is practised with relatives of the parents' or children's

TABLE 30: JOKING RELATIONSHIPS

Joking relation	Characteristics
1. *śalā* and *bāṭo* (WyB and eZH)[45]	Strongest joking (including physical jokes)
2. *bāṭo* and *śālī* (eZH and WyZ)	
3. *diar* and *bahu* (HyB and eBW)	
4. *sangāt* and *sangī* (BWB and ZHZ)	
5. *bahu* and *nanand* (eBW and HyZ)	
6. *bhaṭuā-śaśur* and *bhāibohu* (HeZH and WyBW)	
7. *nati/naten*[46] and *ajā/āī*[47] (ChCh and PaPa—sexual allusions only with *ajāśaśur*—WFF, WMF)	Mildest joking (limited to verbal jokes)

generation (including the generations of great-grandparents and great-grandchildren). Relatives who joke with each other can usually also accept food leftovers from each other, e.g. a WyZ could accept the food remains of her eZH or vice versa. However, it is disputed whether or not a HyB should accept food from a *bahu* (eBW).

There are some joking relationships limited to specific contexts—first and foremost with persons of one's own generation, for example, between brothers and sisters, between brothers or between sisters in the wider sense. These are of central importance during weddings and occasionally include persons of the grandparents' or grandchildren's generation. In comparison to the explicit joking relationships already described, these relationships, limited more or less to the context of marriages, do not play any part in daily life and therefore can be characterized as weak joking.

In general, joking takes place within one's own generation or between persons of alternating generations, but never with relatives of the parent's generation, because they are entitled to respect. Additionally, one also does not joke with persons of the children's generation, particularly if these 'children' are older. Joking with persons of the generations +3/–3 seems also to be considered inappropriate. Thus, joking is restricted to one's own generation set.

Generally, the intensity of joking decreases with age and people over forty (roughly) only rarely or mildly joke with others of a similar age or older, but still joke with joking partners if they are much younger. Joking is also lessened after a marriage and comparatively much stronger beforehand. A few examples are given below.

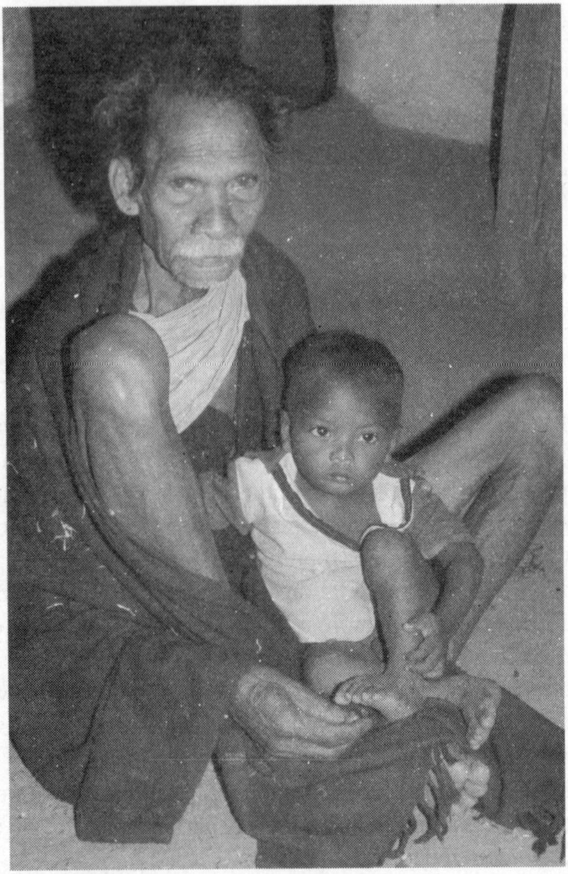

Grandfather and grandchild.

Strong joking includes physical contact and goes beyond verbal exchanges. One may put a pot of water on a door in such a way that it falls down as soon as the joking partner enters the room. Or one may pull a joking partner's ear. In one case a *bahu* (eBW) cracked jokes with her new, but distant *diar* (HyB). During his first visit to the *bahu*'s house she offered a cot to sit on—as is usually done for guests. However, in this case the wooden rack of the cot had been prepared—without any ropes, but covered with a bed sheet in order to appear perfectly normal. Of course, the *diar* fell down through the bed. Later the *bahu* served tea to her *diar*—an important part of the local hospitality. This tea, however, was special, as the *bahu* had added a large quantity of chilli. Both cases exemplify strong joking, though the case described above was certainly extreme, even for the given joking relationship.

In practice, jokes between eBW and HyB may be related to a marriage arranged for the HyB. In one case an eBW cracked jokes about the potential bride of her HyB, e.g. that the family had already chosen a bride for him and only he, the potential groom, was unaware. As far as cross-cousin marriage is concerned, various relationships can overlap, e.g. HyB and eBW can be classificatory siblings. Nevertheless, joking is practised in this way. An eBW or classificatory sister told her HyB or yB jokingly that he could have married her younger sister and added that he should finally admit that he does not like her. Or she told him teasingly, that she had found him another bride.

Joking with grandparents is slowly declining, because the grandparents are seen more and more as persons entitled to respect. However, often jokes including sexual allusions are shared with an *ajāśaśur* (WFF, WMF) who is the appropriate partner for these kinds of jokes. Joking with small children is also generally accepted, although these relations are not institutionalized. For instance, an MB may crack jokes with his ZS or a FB with his BS, but in these cases the ZS or BS have to be very young and the joking is always one-sided from the MB to the ZS and not vice versa.

In the context of marriage, joking is related to the bride and groom, with whom a unilateral joking is practised by the ritual functionaries, the so-called *suhāsen*, for whom joking is a part of their role. During the wedding ceremonies the *suhāsen*, who may come from the bride's or groom's generation, or the generation of the grandparents or grandchildren have, for example, the task of anointing certain parts of the body of the bride and groom with turmeric and oil. Their faces do not have to be included but many *suhāsen* anoint the face thoroughly as a form of joking particularly disliked by the bridal couple.

Joking between brother and sister in the context of marriage also includes the blocking of the main entrance or kitchen door when the groom returns with his wife.[48] Additional jokes are cracked even after the marriage. In one case classificatory sisters of a groom cracked jokes with him during the dance performances known as *huma* (usually between *Nuā Khāi* and *Daśarā*). The sisters sang: 'Our elder brother got married, and he did not ask us, and now the *bahu* (elder brother's wife) is in her home as guest (*kunuān*), and we will beat her with a heavy stick (*bāḍi*)!' Thus joking also expresses tensions that exist between sisters being replaced by brother's wives in their native villages. At the same, time joking is a way of maintaining relations, which change after marriage.

Analysis: joking and avoidance

Since Radcliffe-Brown's (1952 [1940]) pioneering work on joking and avoidance, the structural implications of these relationships have been revealed and they have become a part of every analysis on kinship.[49] In north Indian settings, avoidance rules and joking relationships are well known and documented. Karve (1998 [1953]: 61) and Vatuk (1975: 182–3) both described how older male affinal relatives of their husbands (especially HeB) are avoided by the wives, which is somehow balanced by the joking relationships they have with the younger male affinal relatives (e.g. HyB). This close relationship between avoidance and joking is confirmed by Kolenda (1990: 118, 140) for her area of research in UP, in which three joking relationships were institutionalized: (1) between HyB and eBW, (2) between WZ and ZH and (3) between WM and HF.[50]

Two of the three rules found by Kolenda exist among the Aghriā as well, although the joking relationship WZ/ZH is limited to WyZ/eZH. As far as avoidance is concerned, Grigson (1991 [1938]: 245) notes that such a relation between WeZ and yZH and indicates a similar relationship between HeB and yBW, insofar as a senior levirate is prohibited, while a junior levirate is quite common.[51] The same rules exist among the Munda of Chhotanagpur (Choudhury 1977: 66–7), who also joke between BWZ/ZHZ and ZHB/BWB like the relation between the *sangāt* and *sangi* among the Aghriā. Furthermore, among the Munda HyB/eBW,[52] WyB/eZH and WyZ/eZH also act as joking partners and Choudhury (1977: 63, 67–8) notes 'mild joking' between grandparents and grandchildren as well. The pattern of joking and avoidance among the Aghriā and the Munda in neighbouring regions is almost identical.

Thus in the mixed tribal and caste society of which the Aghriā are part, the rules of joking and avoidance should not be considered specifically Aghriā, but are shared by most communities. According to my enquiries in the village, tribal groups such as the Gaṇḍ, Kandh, Kisān, Muṇḍā, Malār, and also Christian tribal people like the Khaḍiā and Orām and non-tribal peasants such as the Chasā all practise a similar pattern of joking and avoidance. According to preliminary data I have collected Chasā, Kandh, Gaṇḍ, Khaḍiā, Malār, the Orām, Turī, Kisān and Muṇḍā share the same joking patterns as the Aghriā except for the relationships between eBW/HyZ and HeZH/WyBW. I came across these two relationships among the Aghriā at a later stage of my research, after an initial survey among other communities had been completed. However, it seems likely that these relationships exist not only among the Aghriā and Munda, but also among many neighbouring communities.

I also noticed minor differences, for example, in the joking between grandparents and grandchildren, and among the Kisān only distant grandparents were true joking partners—a restriction also found among the Aghriā. In one case among the Kisān a joking relationship with ChSpF was mentioned, but I could not confirm this in other cases. As far as avoidance is concerned, all the aforementioned communities practised avoidance of HeB/yBW and WeZ/yZH. The Khaḍiā stressed the avoidance of (WMBD)e, but it might have been a special variant of the WeZ rule. An avoidance of HMB/ZSW, however, could be confirmed only for the Kandh, Chasā, Tūrī, and Malār.

The assumption that the Aghriā pattern of joking and avoidance resembles, to a large extent, a Middle Indian or tribal model is confirmed by the literature. Thus, Roy (1937: 159ff) mentions the following rules:

1. a man may joke with his WyZ, WyB, BWZ, BWB and grandparents
2. a woman may joke with her HyB, HyZ, ZHyB, ZHyZ and grandparents
3. a man has to avoid WeZ (WMBD)e and WeB
4. a woman has to avoid HeB and yZH.

Additionally, a rule of avoidance between HMB and ZSW is

TABLE 31: JOKING- AND AVOIDANCE RELATIONS AMONG SANTAL

Joking	Avoidance
PaPa/ChCh	HeB/yBW
WyZ/eZH	yZH/WeZ
eBW/HyB	HeZH/WyBW
yBWZ (m.s.)/ZHeB (f.s.)	HyZH/WeBW
eBW/HyZ	ChSpPa (os)/ChSpPa (os)
eBWZ (m.s.)/ZHyB (f.s.)	MB/ZCh
eZHyZ (m.s.)/eBWyB (f.s.)	
WyB/eZH	

mentioned by Parkin (1992: 191) for the Kharia. And, for the Santal, Kochar (1970: 72ff) notes the following rules—though they are followed 'in greater or lesser degree' (Kochar 1970: 72).

Additionally Mukherjea (1962 [1939]: 148) argued that there is a joking relationship between BWZ and BWB on one hand and ZHZ and ZHB on the other.

Finally, for the Juang, McDougal (1963: 102ff, 133ff) describes the following joking relationships:

TABLE 32: JOKING RELATIONSHIPS AMONG JUANG

Joking	
WeB/yZH	lesser extent
WyB/eZH	great extent
WyZ/eZH	great extent
BWyZ, ZHyZ/eZHB, eBWB	great extent
ChSpF/ChSpF	lesser extent
ChSposPa/ChSposPa	lesser extent[53]
PaPa (ms)/ChCh (ms)	
osPaPa/osChCh (bondhu)[54]	
eB/yBt; eZ/yZ	mild
eBW/HySb	great extent
yBW/HeSb	lesser extent

Although the lists—Roy's, McDougal's as well as Kochar's—are neither identical nor consistent in themselves,[55] they resemble each other as well as the Aghriā pattern to a larger extent than the rules known from north or south India. To my knowledge, joking within one's own generation set or 'intra-generational' joking as well as joking between the categories ZHZ/ZHB and BWB/BWZ—obviously common in the tribal setting of Middle India (Pfeffer 1983: 100)—has not been mentioned in the case of any caste. As in the tribal cases just described, but also among the Aghriā joking with grandparents/grandchildren, joking between ZHZ/BWZ and BWB/ZHB and joking between WyZ and HyB implies the possibility of marriage, and in the former cases points to categories of possible and even preferred marriage partners.

However, it is important to note that there is no formalized joking between cross-cousins among the Aghriā or other groups. Cross-cousins keep a social distance from each other, without, however, avoiding each other. This is expressed by non-conversation during adolescence and prior to marriage and contradicts a simple equation joking relationship and possible marriage partner, because cross-cousins are potential marriage partners with whom one does not joke. Probably, joking is rather necessarily related to the existence of clear-cut categories. As far as cross-cousins among the Aghriā are concerned, a separate category does not exist—cross-cousins are subsumed as siblings among the Aghriā. Thus, inconsistencies between the levels—cross-cousins are preferred marriage partners, though not categorically distinguished—may have resulted in a form of social distance rather than joking between cross–cousins.

5.3. COMPARATIVE ANALYSIS OF THE LEVELS—CONCLUSION

The kinship system of the Aghriā shows the impressive autonomy of the different levels, categories, rules, and practice. Therefore, all three levels have to be analysed separately and contradictions between them levels are possible to a certain extent. For example, the categories do not correspond to a pattern, which would be expected in relation to cross-cousin marriage, which itself seems to be in the process of change. In addition to that, the preferred form of cross-cousin marriage—the matrilateral form—stands in a kind of contradiction to the recognizable principal of alternation in the terminology, whereas in a matrilateral cross-cousin marriage the marriage of one's father is structurally repeated. However, as I have shown, certain inconsistencies between the levels are tolerable in practice, indicating that the functioning of the whole system is not in doubt, even though a confusion may exist in some contexts, of which the Aghriā themselves are well aware.

The lack of congruence of the levels could be the result of the influences of various kinship systems. On one hand, the classification of generation 0, in particular the categorical distinction between the wife-taker (ZH) and the wife-giver (WB), to a large extent the lexic, the existence of *gotra*, but also, in part, the avoidance and joking relationships (especially towards HeB and HyB) can be considered typical of north India. On the other hand, cross-cousin marriage does characterize the south Indian system. The cross and parallel distinctions in the parents and children's generation, although incomplete, also point to a similarity with the south and to the symmetrical prescriptive terminologies there.

The principle of alternation is recognizable not only in the terminology, but also in the patterns of avoidance and joking relationships and in the ritual functions. The principle of alternating generations or at least the partially existing distinction between even and uneven generations and their opposition is not known in northern or southern systems. This is also true of the predominant separation of the generations –1 to +1 in 'elder' and 'younger' or in 'senior' and 'junior', in which the 'senior' is of superior status. All this, plus specific avoidance relationships (HMB) and marriage preferences (ZHZ/BWZ), points to a Middle Indian pattern. Similar patterns are described for the tribal societies of Orissa and Chhattisgarh. Therefore, the Aghriā system is not only a synthesis of northern and southern elements, but also tribal. The Aghriā share with their tribal as well as non–tribal neighbours major features of terminology, rules as well as practice, even though differences in detail may exist. Thus there is no recognizable gap that separates the Aghriā from neighbouring communities—at least as far as the kinship system is concerned. Sharing these structural characteristics must have helped establish relationships with other communities in a village conceptualized as a fictive kinship group and integrated themselves into local networks.

In summary, the Aghriā kinship system cannot be assigned unambiguously to any of the three kinship systems introduced in the beginning, but combines various elements of these to their own unique regional syncretism. Considering the terminology, marriage preferences as well as patterns of joking and avoidance a very significant Middle Indian influence must also be acknowledged. Thus, in the sphere of kinship the Aghriã do not differ radically from their tribal neighbours, but rather share most features with them.

NOTES

1. In an analogy to the three big Indian or South Asian language families Karve (1998 [1953]: 50) and Trautmann (1995 [1981]: 19) recognized different kinship systems, for which they used the same terms: (1) the Indo-Aryan, (2) the Dravidian and (3) the Mundaic kinship system (the assumption for the Munda-system is also shared by Parkin 1992: ix). In my opinion it is possible that the speakers of a particular language family might share the same or a similar kinship system, but this cannot be an *a priori* conclusion about the kinship system from the language family and vice versa as Boas (1911: 133) has shown in his comparative work. Also Karve (1998 [1953]: 51), Trautmann (1995 [1981]: 19, 122) and Parkin (1992: ix) accepted that, considering many exceptions from the formulated analogy, and indirectly opposed any form of linguistic determinism. The situation in Orissa is particularly complex, because several groups are bilingual or different parts of a group speak various languages. According to Elwin (1991 [1942]: xxix) parts of the Agaria tribe speak Hindi, an Indo-Aryan language, while other groups speak a Munda language. A correlation between language and kinship system seems unlikely in this case. In general, a common classification of language families and kinship systems under the same term rather contributes to the confusion, which Barnard/Good (1984: 59) tried to avoid by using the term 'Dravidian system' with and without quotation marks. New terms could help to express the distinction—language family vs. kinship system. I prefer to use geographical terms instead—north Indian (Indo-Aryan'), south Indian ('Dravidian') and Middle Indian ('Mundaic') to denote the kinship systems. Although these terms are not totally free of a geographic determinism, it is not my intention to convey this. Like Barnard/Good, I use the terms for the language families in quotation marks if they refer to kinship systems.
2. Trautmann prefers the term 'consanguine' instead of 'kin'. Both can be understood as 'blood relatives' only inadequately, as this would suggest biological ties ana would not include the social dimension of kinship. In the following I have used 'kin' synonymously with 'consanguine'. The more neutral terms of 'parallel' and 'cross' have gained acceptance in the literature (Trautmann 1995 [1981]: 47; Good 1991: 58) to signify Dumont's categories 'kin' ('parallel') and 'affines' ('cross'). I use these synonymously as well.
3. Pfeffer (1983: 118ff) does not explicitly postulate a Middle Indian kinship system, but seems to recognize it implicitly.

4. For a comprehensive study of the dualistic culture of the Juang see Pfeffer (1994).
5. See e.g. Grigson for the Gond, who equate yB and SS, MF and DS or MB and WBS; Roy (1925: 128–33) for the Birhor, who identify WeZS = MyZH or MeZH = FeB = yZS (fs) = WyZS = yBS (ms) = HyBS or Kochar (1970: 68) for the Santal, who equate for example FZH and WBS.
6. Grigson also noted an equation between WBS and MB.
7. The Gadaba speak Gutob, a Dravidian language, but again language should not be a decisive criterion here.
8. Pfeffer (1999: 42) acknowledges that his Parenga material may include several mistakes and an equation FF = FMB or MF = MMB may be one of them. Furthermore, the terminologies of the Bondo (Remo) or Didaye (Gitare) differ considerably from the pattern presented here. The Gutob pattern presented by Pfeffer seems to be confirmed by the neighbouring Rona as well (T. Otten: personal communication).
9. The terminology has been collected in the Kuchinda area. It differs to some extent from the terms in Chhattisgarh, e.g. *kakā* (Kuchinda) = *kākā*, *cāca* (Chhattisgarh); *baḍi* (Kuchinda) = *bāḍe bāi*, *bāḍi* (Chhattisgarh), etc.
10. For the relationship eSbSpF the term *śaśur* is used as well. The Term *babā/ baḍkā bāpā* may also be used primarily in forms of address, although some insisted that *śaśur* is the proper term of reference. The same is true for eSbSpM, ySbSpF etc.
11. Traditionally used in other communities.
12. See previous footnote.
13. Apart from a very formal imperative in the verb forms used as address only for officials and persons much higher in status two forms of address-imperatives are common—a formal one and an informal one. Thus, for certain relatives the more formal mode is chosen, e.g. *aso* = come, while others are called more informally, e.g. a = come.
14. Not by name, as, formerly, HyB was treated like a H.
15. Conzelmann (1996: 381) mentions the existence of terms for the generation of the great-grandparents.
16. Some marriages outside the community are even regarded as a sin (*pāp*), e.g. marriages with Brahmin girls, as every Brahmin woman is considered to be a mother.
17. It seems that the rule is slightly different in Chhattisgarh, where I was informed about one case in which an Aghriā man married a woman from Punjab. He himself was not excluded after the marriage, but his wife and his children remained outside the community.
18. I include the Aghriā from the Bhukta region of Orissa in Chhattisgarh, because they belong to the Raigarh Aghriā Samāj (Chhattisgarh) and not to the two Aghriā Samāj in Orissa (Sambalpur/Sundargarh and Bolangir) and this border region between Orissa and Chhattisgarh (a part of Bargarh

district) has traditionally closer contact with the Chhattisgarh due to a mountain range, which somehow disconnects it from the rest of Orissa.

19. The former Vice-Chancellor of Sambalpur University, Prof. D.C. Naik, told me that in his childhood he once had brought a piece of meat from a castrated goat into the house and was punished. His family threw this meat away.
20. Some people say that they did not share a bedroom, at least in the beginning. Others say that the lady was officially considered a servant, at least for some time.
21. Only an elder sister staying in a metro city was present at the wedding.
22. A former President of the Aghriā Samāj from Bolangir told me proudly that he was able to offer the Rs. 10,000 immediately. The money of fines thus collected is presently kept by the president of the caste organization and there are controversies on how to spent it properly. The president wants to spent it on medicine.
23. Grigson (1991 [1938]: 245) notes 'A man may not marry his mother-in-law or her co-widow or any woman related to them as a "sister", or any of his aunts or nieces, even though of an *akomama* or wife-clan.' Although there are considerable terminological differences between the Maria Gond and the Aghriā, the rule seems to be identical—even though there are no brother and wife clans among the Aghriā. Grigson found, however, only one marriage relationship with a granddaughter. Also, Choudhury (1977: 67) mentions the possibility of marriages with grandparents/grandchildren, even though they rarely occur.
24. See Aghriā Samāj publication, e.g. *Great Convention* (*Mahāsabhā*) *of Laida, Dt. 27.03.1921*; A list of rules for women: rules 27 and 48.
25. A short survey in Chhattisgarh confirmed the following *bansa*: Nahan, Jhitori, Shirsanta, Alkara (but with the title Patel instead of Nayak), Panoria and Madhugugar.
26. *Thelā* also designates a tiny basket made of bark.
27. *Jhiṭorī* means also a woman with open hair.
28. Dāns is also the name of an insect or big mosquito.
29. Barāh also means boar.
30. The manuscript, including the list, is titled *Āgriā bans bibaraṇ* and was written by Balukeshwar Pandey.
31. Ravi Chandrā Sāe was the first matriculate from Patna State (the former princely state around the capital Bolangir). His descendants—now around 100 people—still use this title.
32. As far as I could inquire, the Orām and Khaḍiā are the only communities that have a rule prohibiting at least a cross-cousin marriage with close relatives. However, marriages with their ZHZ/BWZ is not prohibited.
33. Titled '*Samajār samāstyā au samādhān*' discussing certain problems of the Aghriā community.

34. Another very distant relative, who could not be specified exactly.
35. Out of these 6 cases: 4 MyZD, 1 MeZD and 1 case is not specified.
36. Grigson (1991 [1938]: 247) found 54 per cent cross-cousin marriages among the Maria Gond.
37. The author distinguishes between 'First cousin once removed', 'First cousin twice removed', 'Second cousin' and 'Beyond second cousin'—a specification which remains rather vague. I have included all these categories under the label 'Classificatory Cross Cousin'—as sufficient for the purpose.
38. For similar acts of rebellion and exchanges of roles during marriage ceremonies in north India see Pocock (1972: 112) and Kolenda (1990: 135ff).
39. *Chipti* is also offered to cattle and bullocks on *Harli Uāns*.
40. Veiling in former times meant the head as well as the face. However, today covering the back of the head is obligatory, particularly the knot of the hair known as *khupā* should be covered.
41. The rule of avoidance of a mother's brother's wife gains significance when compared to some African communities like the Ashanti (Fortes 1987 [1950]: 271) or the Tallensi (Fortes 1969b: 277), which practice a rule of widow inheritance. A sister's son may under certain circumstances inherit a mother's brother's wife. However, no such marriage relationships to widows have ever been mentioned among the Aghriā and a relationship of avoidance—e.g. to husband's elder brother—seems to exclude any marriage relationship, even after the husband's death.
42. In the same way, children of a first marriage should not participate in the marriage of their father in the case that he marries a second time.
43. See Aghriā Samāj publication, *Great Convention* (*Mahāsabhā*) *of Laida, Dt. 27.03.1921*; A list of fixed rules for women: rule 42.
44. Recently, the husband of a young pregnant Aghriā died in a tragic accident. Since the deceased husband has a younger brother, people say it is possible for her to marry him, but it is up to her. In another case, a widow refused to marry her *diar,* explaining that she regarded him as a brother.
45. Sometimes extended to WeB, yZH, WBWB and ZHZH.
46. All persons of the grandchildren's generation—perhaps including generation –4.
47. All persons of the grandparents' generation—perhaps including the generation +4.
48. Roy (1999 [1928]: 166) mentions the same among Oraon.
49. Joking relationships were defined by Radcliffe Brown as 'a relation between two persons, in which one is by custom permitted, and in some instances required, to tease or make fun of the other, who in turn is required to take no offence' (1952 [1940]: 90). He further argued that it is a combination of friendliness and antagonism—a form of permitted disrespect—which would arouse hostility in other contexts. In contrast, avoidance was considered

by him not as hostility, but as a mode of friendship avoiding conflict and as an extreme form of respect. Both—joking and avoidance—were viewed as responses to social disjunction or descendence as well as to social conjunction or marriage. Thus, Radcliffe Brown argued that a social function of joking and avoidance lies in the maintainence of a stable system of social behaviour, in which conjunction and disjunction are combined.

50. I could not gather sufficient information on joking in south India. It may not have the same importance in there as in the north. Many authors do not mention them explicitly or, apparently, do not devote attention to them (see Dumont 2000 [1986]; Trawick 1992; Kapadia 1996). However, according to my colleague C. Strümpell among Telugu groups of northern Andhra Pradesh and South Orissa joking is common between cross-cousins, while with a husband's elder brother it is generally avoided. Thus, I may tentatively conclude that joking relationships differ from north India to some extent, but perhaps more radically from Middle India with an apparent proliferation of such relationships.
51. For the same customs among Santal see Troisi (2000 [1979]: 229).
52. The same is mentioned among Oraon by Roy (1999 [1928]: 167).
53. Social distance shall also be maintained (McDougal 1963: 138).
54. The *bondhu* group incorporates all affines.
55. In Roy's data the question remains as to why a differentiation between ZHyB/ZHyZ versus ZHeB/ZHeZ is considered important, when he also mentions that ZHB, as such, is marriageable as well BWZ, etc., and as far as marriage is concerned obviously no differentiation is made between elder and younger. The mentioning of two rules of avoidance HeZH/WyBW and HyZH/WeBW seems to be doubtful in Kochar's list and, considering the Aghriā pattern, only the latter can be a relationship of avoidance.

CHAPTER 6

The Life Cycle

6.1. BIRTH, MARRIAGE, DEATH AND THE CONTINUITY OF LIFE

In this chapter I will analyse life cycle rituals of the Aghriā. Since the entire life cycle consists of a long and complicated series of rituals one has to focus on certain elements and important relations between them, which might help to understand the whole. However, a detailed description of all life cycle rituals as far as they could be observed is added in Appendix 1.

I hold that continuity is especially emphasized within the life cycle in various ways. For instance, an essential link between relatives and ancestors is stressed; and the unity of generation-sets, their re-generation as well as the continuity of the clan in opposition to all others are given importance. Complementary and cyclic relation-sets are accentuated between mother's brother and sister's son on the one hand and between father and son on the other, between those who depend on each other for continuity within their own life cycle and beyond. Wolf (1966) has pointed out that in all peasant societies there is an emphasis on continuity within the life cycle and that of the household, yet I argue that the Aghriā, though conforming to Wolf's contention, share many characteristics with their tribal neighbours as well.

6.2. COMPLEMENTARY RELATION SETS

Diachronic affinity—mother's brother and sister's son

The role of the *māmu* (mother's brother) in relation to his *bhanjā* (sister's son) starts a few days after the latter's birth with the rituals of *ṣaṭhi* (the sixth day).[1] Apart from the aspect of purity, prestations stand at the centre of these rituals. The baby's mother's brother should provide the new cloth that the mother and the baby wear on this day.[2] The mother's brother washes the feet of the baby with milk—a custom known as *goḍ dhuā* (*goḍ* = foot; *ḍhuā* = to wash). The gift of the mother's brother, money or a gold necklace, is essential to show his responsibility of the mother's brother's house to care for the child. During *ekoīśiā* (the 21st day) and *nāmkaraṇa* (the name-giving ceremony) the mother's brother presents gifts such as a golden ring known as *maulā bhār* after he has applied some sandalwood paste on the forehead of his sister's child and has put a garland around his neck.

The role of the *māmu* during *bhāt khuā*—the first eating or feeding of rice—might be even more important. The child should first eat rice around six months after birth. It is considered auspicious to feed the first rice on the day of the *Rath Jātrā* or on *Nuā Khāi*. Only then can the child be brought before the gods, particularly Jagannāth. Some Aghriā stated that the child gets his soul (*ātmān*) by eating the first rice given by his mother's brother. If possible, the closest mother's brother (*nijer māmu*), who is personally invited, should be present on this occasion and the child should sit on his lap while he feeds the child. The *māmu* is expected to give some gifts on this day such as

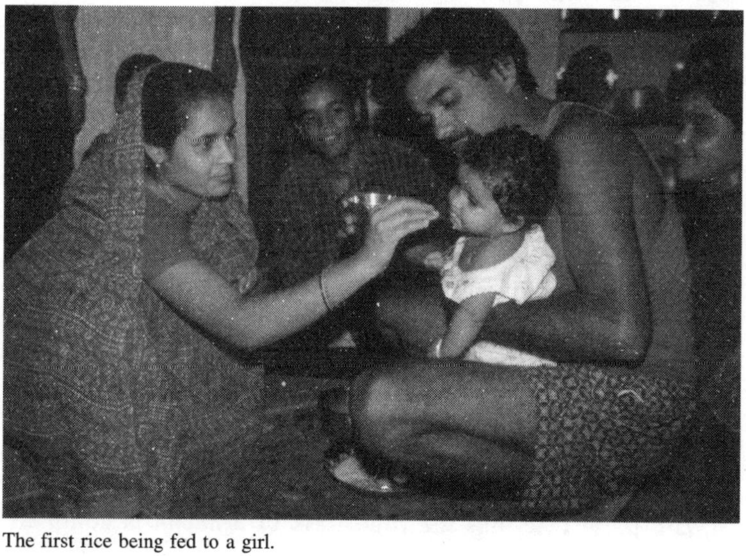

The first rice being fed to a girl.

sweets, some money, and possibly a gold ornament. In any case he has to offer a plate usually made of brass (*kaṇsā*), but in rare cases of silver or gold. Some Aghriā call these gifts '*maulā bhār*'. While feeding the child the *māmu* should say, 'Everyday you should get that much nectar (*amruta*). Everyday five fingers shall go to your mouth (implicit: you should always have enough to eat). My *bhanjā/ bhānji* should get everyday sweet rice like this.' Other relatives may repeat the feeding and might offer some money.

The mother's brother may be invited for the first haircut (*bāl pakā*). although it seems not to be as obligatory as the *bhāt khuā*. In one case, the mother's brother brought all necessary items for the haircut, i.e. a new towel for his sister's son, a mirror, razorblades and a cloth for the barber, who afterwards received all the other items as well. Previously the ear piercing (*kān bedhā*) was also an important step in the life cycle. In one case, the maternal grandmother (MM) offered an earring representing the mother's brother's house.

The presence of a *māmu* is also of utmost importance during the wedding ceremonies. He should be invited (personally) immediately after the Grām Śrī (village goddess) has been invited, and before all the other relatives. In any case the wedding ceremonies cannot start before a *māmu* of both bride and groom has arrived and has been ritually welcomed. Arriving at the outskirts of the sister's child's village, he stops to send a message. Accompanied by drummers and a small procession he is led to the house. In front of the house he is asked to stand on a small stool (*pindhā*), where his sister washes his feet; he then enters her house.

On the second day of the wedding the *māmu* appears again as prime donor for his sister's child. While the groom and bride stand at the wedding altar together with the parents, it is the responsibility or privilege (*kām*) of the groom's or bride's *māmu* to offer the first gift, called *maulā bhār*, usually money, sweets and some jewellery such as a golden ring placed on a brass plate (*kansā thāl*). The giving is also known as *thāl dharā* (*thāl* = plate; *dharā* = to give). Without this gift and a *māmu*'s[3] presence a wedding cannot take place. It is also the mother's brother who feeds some sweets to his sister's child and who has previously offered the clothes that are worn by bride or groom and their parents on this occasion.

With these offerings the ritual task of a *māmu* is complete.

However, he is still generally responsible for the well-being of his sister's children and he should be present during the formal division of the family known as *bhāgbaṇṭā* in order to ensure a sufficient share of property for all sister's sons. Furthermore, the mother's brother plays a role at the time of death of his sister or her husband (rather, his sister's son's father or mother). On the tenth day of the funeral the sister's sons get new white *dhotis*, *gañjis* and towels. If one is married, these are given by the father-in-law.

At the time of the *māmu*'s death, the *māmu-bhanjā* relationship is somehow reversed. The presence of a *bhanjā* is essential at the *māmu*'s funeral. On the eleventh day—the main day of the funeral a special gift is given to the sister's son of the deceased (or in the case of a woman, the sister's son of her husband). The *bhanjā* and sometimes also the *bhanjā*'s wife are worshipped and fed by the family, for example the widow, and receive some money and cloth. Without an offering for the *bhanjā*, without his presence during the funeral rituals, the *ātmān* of the deceased *māmu* cannot find peace (*śānti*).

Comparing the Aghriā to other north as well as south Indian cases (Bennett 1983, Conzelmann 1996, Kapadia 1996, Madan 1989 [1965], Parry 1994, Randeria 1999 et al.) we find many common features in connection with the role of a mother's brother in early life cycle rituals and in marriage. However, the role of the sister's son in funeral rituals does not feature in any of these comparable cases. As explained above, among the Aghriā the *māmu's* presence is obligatory on the eleventh day.[4] Therefore let us first examine this, the sister's son's role first. Within the region—and in contrast to north India—the role of the *bhanjā* seems to be not as unique as it may appear at first glance. I was told that the same custom of *bhanjā dān* is common among Chasā, another peasant caste of the region which is structurally similar to the Aghriā. Here the *bhanjā* not only receives his *bhanjā dān*, but also has the right to demand his share of all gifts of the category *dān* that are considered auspicious for a receiver. His share should be equal to that of the family priest.

Elwin (1945) mentions in his description of funerary rites in Bastar the necessary presence of a *bhanjā* among the Bison–Horn Maria Gond. Apart from a ritual specialist the sister's son is the 'chief actor' (Elwin 1945: 95) who 'climbs up to the roof and makes a hole which is intended symbolically to allow the message of death to spread out through the world'; he beats on the drums and finally—and probably most importantly—'he sits on the *uraskal* [memorial menhir] while it is being carried to its hole; he makes the appointed offerings before the stone; he kills the sacrificial and festal cow' (Elwin 1945: 95). In bringing the menhir for the ultimate peace of the deceased it is the sister's son 'who plays a leading part' and 'touches the stone and addresses the dead man. 'In your name,' he says, 'we are bringing this stone. . .' (ibid.: 113). Elwin's material was later confirmed by Fuchs (1960: 337) for the tribal Gond and Bhumia in a neighbouring area, where it is the responsibility of a sister's son to immerse the bones or ashes of a person into a river.[5] Furthermore, Fuchs (1960: 327) mentions that a *nat*—an affinal relative—is required for all ceremonies related to death, for example bathing the deceased and carrying him to the cremation or burial ground; but unfortunately he does not specify the category *nat*.[6] In the same manner Fürer-Haimendorf (1979: 370ff) remarks that among the Gond of Andhra Pradesh—apart from agnate—the role of an affine known as *soira* is obligatory for all funeral rituals and it is the *soira* who sets up a wooden post as an ancestral memorial for the deceased. However, this affine or *soira* is not further specified, though it is clear that at least in some cases a son-in-law acts in this role, and he may be a sister's son, given the preference for cross-cousin marriage.

Similar examples of a prominent role for a *bhanjā* in funeral rites are found among tribal groups in Nepal. Oppitz's research on the Magar in north-west Nepal is a case in point. I will briefly summarize Oppitz' (1991: 413–35) description of the *bhanjā's* role: the *bhanjā* is to a large extent responsible for the safe passage of the deceased on his way, which includes firing a gun at certain critical points of the procession. Thus the role of the sister's son could be understood as a guide for the dead. Furthermore, the *bhanjā* acts as a barber for the sons of the deceased who are of higher status. More importantly it is the *bhanjā*'s exclusive right to guide the dead symbolically into the other world at a later stage by leading an ox through the village and by crossing the separating river together. Only by holding the tail of that ox is the deceased able to cross the river. This service of the *bhanjā* is highly valued among the Magar; the family of the deceased present him with an ox and copper dishes, gold, silver, or clothes. The next day the *bhanjā* once more escorts the deceased to the world beyond by guiding a sheep out of the village, which is seen as a companion of the deceased on his way. Apart from other tasks during ritual feasts, he is the one to erect the memorial stone, where the deceased finds a permanent resting place as an ancestor. Again the role of the *bhanjā* is essential in transforming the deceased into an ancestor.

The role of the *bhanjā* in death rituals of the tribal Mewahang Rai in East Nepal does not differ considerably from the Magar. In his account Gaenszle (1999: 49ff) describes the sister's son or son-in-law as main actor of the ritual, who plays 'a significant role at all the important stages of the funeral' (ibid. 62), in particular the procession—a 'journey to the beyond' (ibid.: 56), in which the deceased is 'guided away'. 'The procession is headed by men who fall into the category of *makcha* (CM. 'DH, yZH' [DH = daughter's husband/yZH = younger sister's husband]) or—if none is available—a *bhānij* (N. 'ZS' [sister's son] in relation to the deceased. These 'sons-in-law' . . . open the way to the beyond . . .' (Gaenszle 1999: 52).

The cases just described, and others may be found as well,[7] show striking similarities. Obviously the sister's son plays an important role in death rituals in two peripheral regions of the Indian subcontinent—the hill region or hinterland of Middle India (Orissa and Chhattisgarh) and parts of the Himalaya. The common feature is that the sister's son (or son-in-law) guides and escorts the deceased into the world beyond. He ensures the safe passage into the next world. I argue that the role of the *bhanjā* among the Aghriā has to be understood in the same way because interlocutors explained that the soul of the deceased could not find peace so long as the *bhanjā* is not satisfied.

Another possible explanation for the *bhanjā dān* could be a compensation of the mother's brother to the sister's son for not giving him his daughter as a bride as expected in a society with a traditional ideal of matrilateral cross-cousin marriage. However, none of my interlocutors among Aghriā or Chasā confirmed that, and I do not see how this could fully explain the ritual role described above.

Let us turn to the mother's brother. In cases of cross-cousin marriage he is ego's father-in-law and thus of crucial importance. Even in cases in which families are not closely related, one always tries to find a relation in which the father-in-law appears as *māmu* and is subsequently addressed as such.[8] In Aghriā society the role of a mother's brother is required during life cycle rituals until the marriage of his sister's son (or sister's daughter). Without his presence and before the arrival of his gifts, these life cycle rituals would be incomplete or could not even start.[9] This means that the *māmu* is deeply involved in the transformation of his newly born *bhanjā* into a complete social person—a concept common among most of the local communities and perhaps even more pronounced among Brahmin communities.[10] In a wider sense a *māmu* is responsible for the well-being of his *bhanjā*—particularly in his childhood and early life.[11] Thus it is not surprising that the *māmu* or *māmu ghar* often has a hand in cases of seriously sick *bhanjā* being transferred, and, significantly, in many cases ill *bhanjā* are sold into the *māmu*'s village. Healing in general is sought within kinship structures involving the *māmu* prominently (see also Otten 2000).[12] Furthermore, a *māmu* is expected to help his ZS as far as his profession and financial future is concerned. In one case a MB offered a loan to his ZS to purchase a tractor as a way of earning money and to establish a financially sound basis for his life. There are several cases in which a *bhanjā* inherited from his *māmu*, particularly if the *māmu* died without male issue. It is also the *māmu* who is expected to protect the rights of every *bhanjā* in the case of the partition of a household among brothers. Apart from his father's or father's brother's house a *bhanjā* may stay as long as he wishes in his *māmu ghar.*[13]

However, the *māmu's* responsibility is terminated at the time of his *bhanjā's* marriage. According to the Brahmanical literature (Pandey 1993 [1969]: 153–4) and confirmed by ethnographic reports (Dumont 2000 [1957]: 277)—it is precisely at this moment that a person, in particular a male,[14] becomes socially complete and entitled to perform rituals in which, quite often, his wife has an important part as well. It is marriage (and to a lesser extent the inheritance of a share of property), which turns an 'unripe' (*apūrṇṇa*) youth into a 'ripe' (*pūrṇṇa*) person.

To summarize, the *māmu* guides the *bhanjā* into the world and is to a large extent responsible for the *bhanjā* becoming a social person. After marriage, however, it is the *bhanjā* whose responsibility it is to lead his *māmu* into the world beyond. In some cases the presence of a *bhanjā* was already required earlier: at the time of the death of his *māi*. When a man's wife dies, the presence of his *bhanjā*, not the wife's *bhanjā* is imperative. This means that the role of a *bhanjā* starts precisely when the *māmu* begins to lose his full ritual status—without his wife he is no longer able to perform certain rituals and is thus a ritually incomplete person.[15] I have tried to systematize the two opposite, yet complementary ritual roles in Figure 11.

***māmu* = mother's brother**
guidance into the world
transformation into a social person (householder)

→

ego

←

transformation into an ancestor
guidance into the world beyond
***bhanjā* = sister's son**

Figure 11: MB-ZS Relationship.

Figure 11 shows that your father's closest affine guides you into the world, while the closest affinal relative in the children's generation, your son-in-law (or sister's son in the case of cross-cousin marriage), escorts you into the other world. This complementarity characterizing the life cycle is further substantiated by the fact that according to my interlocutors a mother's brother and a sister's son should never sit in the same boat (dug-out) while crossing a river[16] and should not stay together in a house during lightning. It looks as if they should avoid any danger to die at the same time, which would pose a serious threat to the lifecycle's continuity.

In addition, Aghriā, and possibly among Gond[17] too, equate *māmu* and *bhanjā* in terms of address. In an ideal formula of bilateral cross-cousin marriage, *māmu* and *bhanjā* of ego would be related as father's father (FF) and son's son (SS). That would simplify Figure 11, because there would be two generations only. And this means: the closest affinal relative of an adjacent generation forms and transforms the social person, as shown in Figure 12.

This formula might also accommodate the funeral customs of the tribal Gadaba of Koraput and to some extent the tribal Juang of Keonjhar. According to Berger (2001), among the Gadaba there are

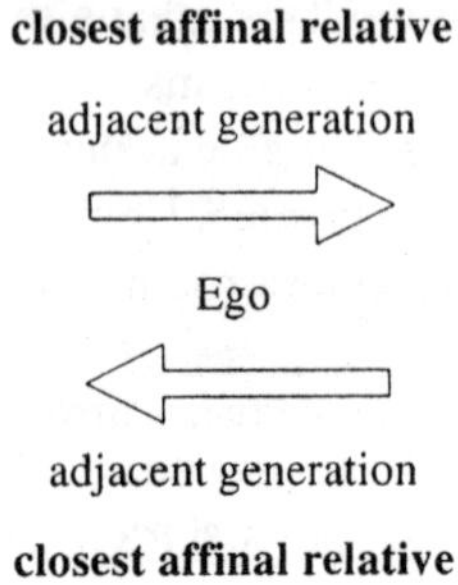

Figure 12: Affinal Kin.

two main actors figuring prominently in rituals prior to the final *gotr*-ceremony: an agnate (*tsorubai*) acting as a funeral priest and the mother's brother (*māmu*) of the deceased. Together with the *tsorubai* the *māmu* leads the procession to the cremation ground and later offers drinks to his *bhanjā*. He gives and receives gifts—just to mention a few significant details. As it is unlikely that the genealogical *māmu* will be present at the funeral of his sister's son or *bhanjā* due to the age difference, quite often he is replaced by his son or son's son. In any case, the role of the *māmu* is stressed among Gadaba. Contrary to other cases cited here, the *māmu* does not only participate in the development of the social person as expressed by his prominent role in marriage rituals, but also in transforming it. Here, as in Figure 12, the closest affinal relative of an adjacent generation performs both tasks: to bring the relative into the world and to guide him into another. Thus the *māmu* combines both functions directly and does not contradict my general hypothesis.[18]

The case of the Juang is similar. Although the mother's brother (or an equivalent in his role) is not directly involved in the funeral, it has to be an unmarried man from the mother's brother's village who is responsible for the ritual purification of the deceased and his family (McDougal 1963: 131). Furthermore, though the mother's brother has no specific role in the marriage of his *bhanjā* and is generally treated more like a father, there is still an exchange between the mother's brother and the sister's son. The *bhanjā* offers a share of his game meat to his *mama* in exchange for bow and arrows (ibid.). Thus the *mama* has to be involved in transforming his *bhanjā* into a successful hunter in this world. In addition, McDougal (1963: 155ff) shows that the principle of alternating generations is prominent among the Juang, particularly in relation to marriage rules.

Such patterns do not only exist in India. Radcliffe Brown (1978 [1924]) analysis of the role of a mother's brother provides data from tribes of South Africa and Oceania.[19] The mother's brother takes special care of his growing sister's child, who enjoys the liberty of demanding food or even property, for example, that which is needed for the bridewealth. The mother's brother is said to have the power of life and death over his nephew and he is also the one who would conduct sacrifices in case his sister's son is seriously ill. Radcliffe Brown points out the sister's son's important role during the funeral of his mother's brother. He burns his hut, kills sacrificial animals and brings the prayers to a close. However, all the societies analysed so far do have patrilineal and patrilocal features, and the picture might differ in matrilineal and matrilocal groups, as analysed by Eggan (1950).[20]

Another feature expressed in the life cycle rituals is hierarchy. A *bhanjā* is held in highest esteem among the Aghriā. As the proverb says: 'To feed a Brahmin is more valuable than feeding 100 cows. But to feed a *bhanjā* is more valuable than feeding 100 Brahmin.' This indicates a status difference among *māmu* and *bhanjā*—the latter being elevated to a position even higher than a Brahmin. Such an elevation of the sister's son may hint at another synthesis between tribal and caste society. A sister's son having a priest-like function in a social context in which a Brahmin representing caste-society have not been fully established. This transitional society may well be characterized by the co-existence of Brahmin and *bhanjā*.

This position of the *bhanjā* correlates with the custom of showing respect to him (sister's son, m.s./husband's sister's son) in former times. The mother's brother and his wife were obliged to touch the feet of their *bhanjā*.[21] Nowadays this rule is subject to change, respect being shown more and more to the mother's brother and his wife as 'elders' like the father's brothers and other relatives of the father's generation. Often young *bhanjā* feel uncomfortable being publicly given signs of respect by their mother's brother and his wife, and sometimes even run away. Yet, occasionally elders still want a *māmu* or even more a *māi* (MBW) to show their respect for the *bhanjā*, for example, during funerals at the time of giving *bhanjā dān*. A hierarchical distinction is further demonstrated when auspicious *dān* usually given at the end of the fortnight of the ancestors (*pitru pakṣ*) to a Brahmin is, in case no Brahmin is present, offered to a *bhanjā* instead. The change in this relationship is conveyed in the change of address. In former times a sister's son was always formally addressed as *bhanjā*, never in an informal manner using personal names as is acceptable today. A mother's brother (and his wife) should not accept any food or even water from a *bhanjā*. Elder Aghriā said, *dān* given away—and accepted by a *bhanjā* as described above—should not be returned to the giver. Accepting something from a *bhanjā* in his house would imply such a return, but if you cannot avoid accepting something you have to pay for it. Additionally, no leftover food should be accepted from MB and MBW. In a similar way leftovers of food from SpF and SpM should not be eaten (SpF and SpM stand in a structural relation to MB and MBW). People believe that MB and MBW would be pauperized if boiled food left by them were to be eaten by their nephews and nieces (ZS m.s., HZS, etc.). Only dry food or biscuits do not fall under these restrictions.

Today this relationship is thus characterized by ambivalence. On the one hand *māmu* and *māi* may still show respect to their *bhanjā* publicly, though this is quite rare. On the other hand, the relation to a *māmu* is very close, physically much closer than to the father or other relatives of the father's generation, who are also entitled to signs of respect. That does not mean, however, that a MB is not respected and wishes articulated by the MB are not fulfilled immediately by their ZS, but in a way different and less strict compared to his father. The relation between *bhanjā* and *māmu* is more characterized by familiarity than that between father and son. Both *māmu* and father, however, are loved. Nowadays the situation resembles Madan's (1998 [1975]: 295ff) characterization of a latent deference shown by a *māmu* towards his *bhanjā*[22] which has changed from a position of explicit superiority of a *bhanjā*. In any case a *bhanjā* still is in a hierarchically higher position than his *māmu*. I will return below to this point.

Semi-diachronic affinity: wife's younger brother—elder sister's husband

Another diachronic affinal link expressed during wedding rituals is the wife's younger brother—elder sister's husband. This affinal tie has a synchronic dimension as both relatives belong to one generation.

Yet, because the principle of seniority is decisive here, it is diachronic rather than synchronic. This relationship appears to have only a subordinate position within life cycle rituals, but after the hands of bride and groom have been tied together during the *hāth lagan* ceremony, a younger brother of the bride (or *śalā* of the groom) has to tear the thread apart. Traditionally the wife's younger brother has the right to beat his elder sister's husband afterwards—a custom known as *śalā bidhā*. The *śalā* has to be younger than the groom and the hitting is seen as a kind of revenge for taking his sister. Though it is rarely practised today, it is still well known. In any case, the groom has to present a gift, either money or some cloth, to the *śalā* for opening the thread. Complementarily the *bāṭo*'s (eZH) is expected to be actively involved in the wedding of his *śalā* (*śāli*), i.e. anointing him with turmeric and oil, carrying him to the pond for bathing, etc., but it is not obligatory and a brother may fulfil the same function.

The *śalā bidhā* indicates the wife-giving family's and specifically the younger brother's ritual resistance against the wife-taking groom. A *śalā* may also resist his prospective status lower than his sister's sons. Similar phenomena have been observed in north India and explained as an exchange of roles between wife-takers having a higher status versus the wife-givers (see Pocock 1972: 112; Kolenda 1990: 135–44). As Turner (1995 [1969]: 94–6) has shown, a temporary inversion of status works anti-structurally. In other words, hierarchies cease to be in force for a given time and *communitas* may be created, which means that an unstructured or rudimentarily structured community is established for the liminal phase of transition.

The only truly synchronic affinal link expressed during the coming together of the groom's and bride's processions in the bride's village is called *samdhi bheṭ*. The potential affinal relatives (HF and WF) heading the processions meet in a formal way and a new relation, in which no hierarchical distinction is made, is ritually enacted in their meeting. However, in most cases the fathers offer precedence to their brothers—often younger brothers—during this ceremonial welcome in order to tie the relation among brothers more closely. The *samdhi* honour each other by giving *ṭikā*. They feed each other with sweets, smoke a cigarette together or share some betel nuts (*pān*), offer a cloth (*dhoti*) and hug or lift each other up.

Diachronic affinity: mother's father—daughter's son

In funeral rituals members of one's own generation play only a subordinate role. However, during the procession to the cremation ground or graveyard a lamp is carried in front of the bed on which the deceased is laid out. If possible a daughter's son performs this duty. In case there is no daughter's son, it may be any grandson, but a daughter's son is clearly preferred. On the twelfth day the *śrāddha* is observed in the kitchen of his house and is conducted by the eldest son. A big leaf plate for the deceased is placed in the middle with some smaller plates for other ancestors surrounding it.[23] After raw food has been offered, boiled food is given. This is eaten by the family members, although some Aghriā say that the food on the main leaf should be eaten by the daughter's sons of the deceased or by other grandchildren. A similar *pūjā* is repeated exactly one year after the death (*barṣika śrāddha*).

Madan (1989 [1965]: 190) reported a similar role for a daughter's son during funerary rites among Kashmiri Pundits. During the funeral (specifically on the twelfth day after death) as well as for the *śrāddha,* the presence of a daughter's son is regarded as highly desirable.[24] At that time a daughter's son may pour libations for his mother's parents. He may also offer *piṇḍa* for them at pilgrimage centres on auspicious occasions. Elwin (1945: 95–7) mentions an unspecified granddaughter playing a prominent role in the already mentioned funeral customs of the Bison–Horn Gond. The granddaughter is, together with the wife of the funeral priest, responsible for ensuring that the deceased in case of rebirth returns to his house. She offers water to the deceased and is involved in the preparation of food.

Madan (1989 [1965]: 190) argues that the role of a daughter's son has to be seen as an obligation to the mother's brother's house. Thus, an affinal link is extended into another generation. We might also argue that the daughter's son is the *bhanjā* of the next generation helping his mother's brother as chief mourner to progress in life cycle by fulfilling these ritual obligations. Therefore, the pronounced complementarity of *māmu* and *bhanjā* within the life cycle is indicated at the time of death for the subsequent pair of *māmu* and *bhanjā* as well. Following the principle of equation of alternating generations just illustrated and common to Middle Indian tribal society (Pfeffer

1983), the daughter's son is, of course, the younger brother of the deceased. Thus, a continuity of one's generation–set might be suggested as well. Since the daughter's son might be replaced by any grandchild one might argue that alternating generations share a special commensality[25] on certain occasions (*śrāddha*), but further research is necessary in this regard.[26] I will return to the principle of alternation below.

Diachronic consanguinity—father and son

During the early stages of the life cycle the father's ritual role is pronounced in his position as sacrifier during the rituals of the twelfth and twenty-first day—contrary to the role of the mother's brother as giver of certain gifts and 'feeder' of the child. However, the father is conspicuously absent in the rituals of the sixth day. During the wedding his role is rather limited as well. Together with his wife and child he performs a ritual for the ancestors, feeding them and asking for their blessings after they have been invited to the marriage altar. In front of the *mahuā* branches seven wicks (*soltā*) soaked in *ghī* are lit in remembrance of seven generations from the father's side—sometimes also described as *bāli piṇda* (*bāli* = sand; *piṇda* = offerings to the ancestors). The number of ancestors worshipped may differ from family to family. In one case the groom's father, the father's elder brother, the father's father, great-grandfather (FFF) and great-great-grandfather (FFFF) were included, together with their wives. Later some of the cakes offered were distributed among family members and some people say it should be given only to one's own clan. While the groom (or bride) stands at the wedding altar during *thāḍa ūchchā*—the general offering of gifts—the father joins him to the left and the mother to the right. In case of a daughter's marriage, father and mother offer her to the groom during the *hāth lagan* ceremony—probably the most central part during the wedding.

As far as death is concerned the son or eldest son as chief mourner and sacrifier (*karttā*) is of the utmost importance. He—together with other sons or sons-in-law—is expected to carry the deceased to the cremation ground or graveyard. He lights the pyre. Some say that the eldest son should leave the pyre afterwards without looking back. The following day the eldest son collects seven small bones for the tomb (*samādhi*) and for immersion in the Ganga. Additionally, there are restrictions for the eldest son (or sons) and the whole family regarding oil, fish, meat or eggs or any non-vegetarian food. These restrictions are to be observed until the end of the eleventh day. In addition, the eldest son is expected to sleep on the ground instead of using a bed for the same period.

On the tenth day the eldest son offers food in the form of ten balls (*piṇda*) to the *pret* of the deceased. The number ten is related to the tenth day, but it is also seen as recreating a body.[27] Afterwards everything is put in one large pot and immersed in the pond, and then the hut is burnt down. Subsequently, the head of the eldest son is completely shaved. Additionally, a small *pūjā* may take place inside the house called *ghar sanskār* in order to purify it. After this the eldest son leads a procession to the *samādhi* which has already been erected. The eldest son carries the seven bones and places a red flag on top of the *samādhi* before the bones are put inside.

On the eleventh day—*kām ghar/antyeṣṭikriyā*—the eldest son acts again as sacrifier. He puts offerings of cloth (*dhoti*) and food (*piṇḍa*) into a large bowl which he then holds on his right shoulder for a few minutes while promising to bring the bones to the Ganga. Various gifts are then offered to several Brahmin. On the twelfth day or the ritual of six months—*chhamāsi*—an almost identical *pūjā* is performed. Additionally, a ritual for the ancestors is conducted in the kitchen by the eldest son and his wife. In the ritual, raw as well as boiled food is offered to the ancestors whom the deceased has now joined. This *pūjā* is repeated a year after the death (*barṣika śrāddha*).

Analysis

A continuity of the local line is emphasized in rituals through the life cycle. Ceremonies in which father and son are involved also include, in most cases, the ancestors or clan (ideally based on a common ancestor) who underline the aspect of lineality and clan-membership. The ancestors are fed by father and son together during marriage, this being the first time a son, as groom, is allowed to worship the ancestors. Besides, a kind of hierarchical commensality is established in the *pitru pūjā*—the clan and nobody else will share the food first offered to the ancestors.[28] The line of ancestors is also symbolized by the *pinda* being held on the shoulders of the eldest son who promises to bring the bones to the river Ganga. Of equal importance is the construction of a tomb for every deceased person, on family land. This tomb, erected usually next to other tombs of patrilineal ancestors and sometimes in a walled compound, is a reminder of the local line. In relation to non-Hindus, the tombs, as observed by Bloch and Parry (1982: 34), are erected here 'as a symbol of the property holding kinship group'.[29]

Just as the father, together with his wife, or any married couple replacing them (e.g. FyB/FyBW), acts as sacrifier in early rituals so will the son act later in the same role during his father's funeral. Thus the roles of father and son are complementary, in a similar way to a mother's brother and sister's son. Still, the function of father and son as sacrifier establishes a sacrificial community with their ancestors which stands in opposition to the role of the *māmu* and *bhanjā*. The latter is clearly related to gifts—the *māmu* being the prime donor, while the *bhanjā* is the valued receiver of gifts at the time of death.

The two complementary relation-sets just presented bear some resemblance to Fortes' concept (Fortes 1969a, 1970; see also Barnard/Good 1984) of 'complementary filiation'. This means that in unilineal societies not only is the line of descent stressed—here the Aghriā patriline—but also the opposite side through which descent is not traced in terms of clan membership. Thus, Fortes (1969a: 98) pointed out, 'The descent principle is normally, probably invariably, counterbalanced by the principle of complementary filiation.'[30] However, contrary to cases described by Fortes, among the Aghriā the cyclical element appears to be dominant. The role of a sister's son in relation to his mother's brothers or of a son in relation to his father is combined with their terminological equation.

In addition, one may also consider the gifts offered unilaterally by the mother's brother to his sister's son as well as the transfer of property from father to son as a 'double transmission of property' in the sense of Dumont (1957: 29) highlighting the distinction between kin and affines. While in the former case moveable goods in the form of gifts are handed over, in the latter case immoveable possession is transferred. However, some of the gifts of a mother's brother, such as offering the first rice, have only limited material value. A focus on affinal gifts as transmission of property would neglect the meanings attached to these gifts as far as the formation of a social person is concerned—a point I have tried to highlight here.

If one takes synchronic affinity into consideration, which, however, is not stressed as prominently within the life cycle as the other two complementary relation-sets, a quadripartite model emerges as presented in Figure 13. This model, an elaboration of Figure 12, has been inspired by to the formula of a tetradic society as developed by Allen (1986, 2000), and by Dumont's (1983 [1970]: 184) analysis of the Australian Kariera system. Such a quadripartite model (Figure 13 left) as 'the simplest structuring of society' (Allen 2000: 82) is based on the opposition between even and odd generations (horizontal separation—dividing A1 and B1 from A2 and B2; 1 signifying odd and 2 designating even generations) and between two moieties exchanging marriage partners: agnates versus affines (vertical separation—dividing A1 and A2 from B1 and B2; A and B signifying moieties or kin/affines). The distinction of the sexes has been taken for granted. A tetradic society would consist of only four sections or categories, a tetradic terminology of four terms respectively.[31] Both distinctions are already implicit in Figure 12.

In life cycle rituals of the Aghriā, and probably in structurally similar cases as well, the diagonal relation (mother's brother/sister's son) as shown in Figure 13 (middle) is of the utmost importance. If we abstract the formula even further then for every ego it is the closest affine of the adjacent generation who guides him into the world and beyond—for A1 it would be B2 and vice versa, while for B1 it would be A2 and vice versa.

In summary, there seem to be two essential relations symbolizing a continuity of life during the life cycle. The aforementioned relation between father and son aims at a continuity of the local line and at lineality, while the relation to the *bhanjā* or sister's son/son-in-law shows a continuity in affinal relations,[32] obviously valued. These two

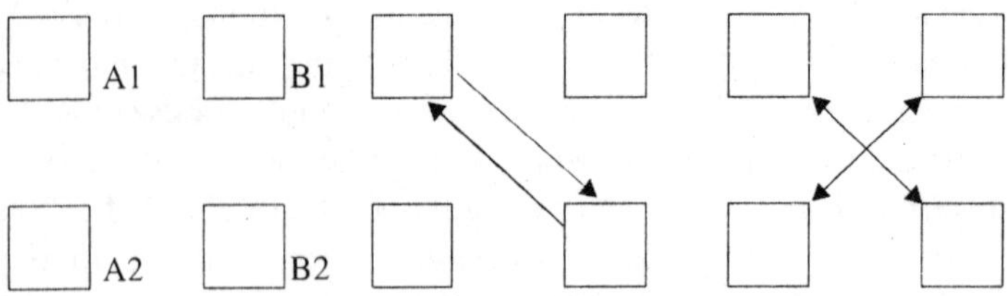

Figure 13: Tetradic Model with Diachronic Links.

diachronic and complementary relation sets dominate life cycle rituals. Besides, a third link is ritually marked: the relation to a *samdhi* (DHF/SWF) as the only synchronic affinal tie. Thus, affinal ties of ego's generation are presented rather weakly within ego's life cycle. Perhaps the relation to a wife's younger brother (characterized as semi-diachronic) and the link to a daughter's son might, in a wider sense, both belong to the same category, if the alternation of generations is taken into consideration. All three relations are represented in Figure 14 in a genealogical and descriptive way.

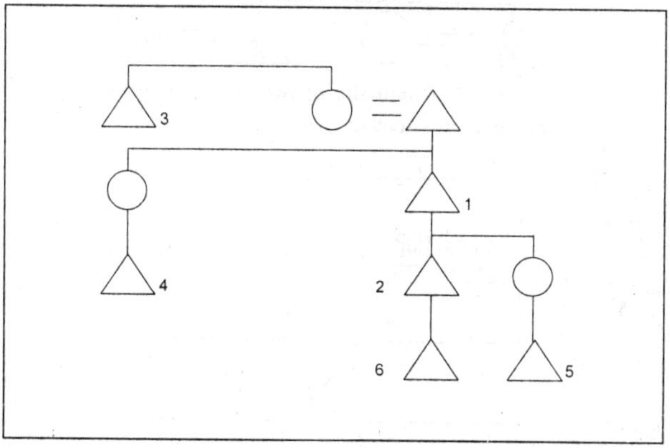

Figure 14: Three lines of continuity presented in a genealogical manner—starting from ego (1) to a son (2) to a sister's son (4) or mother's brother (3) and to a daughter's son (5) or son's son (6)

In the ideal-type of a society which practises bilateral cross-cousin marriage, the roles and relation sets aforementioned would belong to two lines only (as represented in Figure 15.)

With regard to equations found in the Aghriā terminology, however, it seems that two—or perhaps three—lines of continuity correspond to a tetradic, quadripartite model, i.e. to the three other sections apart from ego's own. This is because, according to the principles formulated in the earlier category, A1 would include the sister's son equated with the mother's brother; B1 the son again in terms of address equated with the father; and A2 the daughter's son and wife's younger brother, though they are not equated terminologically. All four sections are once more represented in Figure 16. Female roles within the life cycle might be represented in a similar fashion.[33] Thus, kinship roles

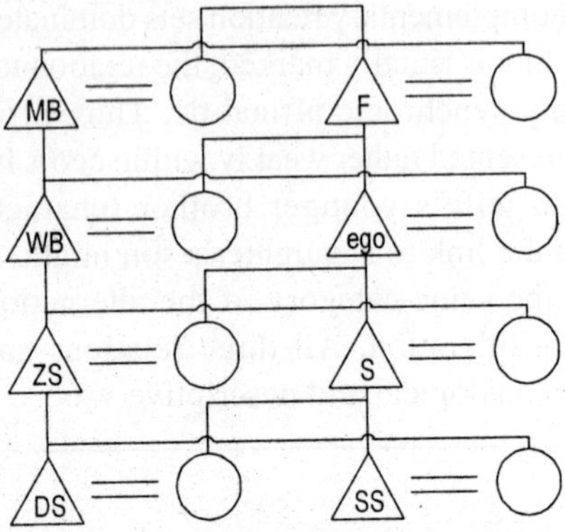

Figure 15: Continuity of two lines practising bilateral cross-cousin marriage

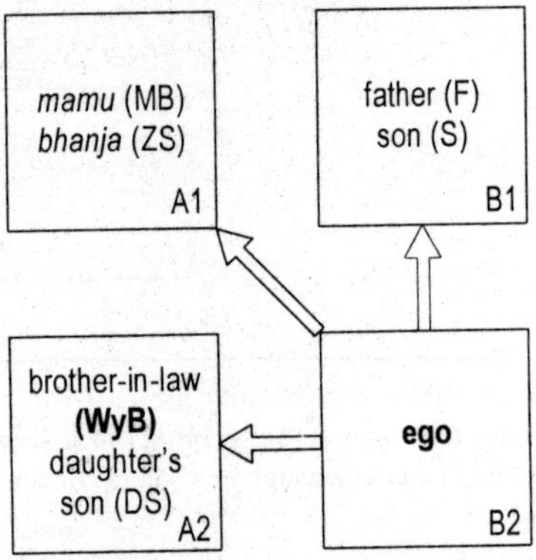

Figure 16: Lines of continuity presented in a tetradic way—starting from ego (B2) to the son/father (B1), to the sister's son or mother's brother (A1) and to wife's younger brother/daughter's son (A2).

within the Aghriā life cycle resemble the tetradic model, though not fully, since the principle of seniority interferes with this basic structure.

6.3. COMPLEMENTARY OPPOSITION SETS

There are two very basic oppositions found within one's life cycle: the opposition between generation sets as well as between 'own clan' and 'other clan'. In the first opposition, one generation-set is manifested in the wedding rituals. This highlights the generational difference, uniting ego with his wife's younger brother or daughter's son, while contrasting them to the mother's brother and father. In the second opposition, clan membership is the central criterion and ego's own clan is opposed to all other local clans, which are, in turn, potential affines.

Re-generation—alternate generations

Although grandparents may offer presents during the early stages of their grandchild's life cycle, such as *ekoīśiā* or *bhāt khuā*, the role of generation sets is most pronounced during wedding rituals in which the role of the so-called *suhāsen*[34] is essential. *Suhāsen* are women of one's own generation and alternating generations (grandparents and grandchildren), provided they are neither widowed nor standing in an avoidance relation to the groom. Similarly, their male counterparts—not explicitly named as in case of the *suhāsen*—are involved in the rituals. Their role is, however, not as prominent as that of the women.

On the first day of a wedding the *suhāsen* are bring *mahuā* sticks for the wedding altar. Two *suhāsen* carry a *kalas kuṇḍi* each (an earthen pot either filled with paddy (*dhān*) symbolizing Lakṣmī, or filled with water symbolizing Narayan). Together with the Kālo they dig out soil to be placed under three *mahuā* branches. This soil symbolizes the village goddess. One of the most important rituals performed by the *suhāsen*—the *teilābhiṣek*—takes place on the evening of the first day in both houses. Groom and bride are guided to the wedding altar by a *suhāsen.* Quite often it is a sister-in-law (eBW) who takes the role[35] of guiding the groom, although in one case I observed a bride being led by her maternal grandmother (MM). Afterwards, at least seven male *suhāsen*, followed by at least seven female *suhāsen,* are required for the ritual. After a Brahmin[36] has started the ceremony, every *suhāsen* applies a mixture of turmeric and castor oil not only to the whole body of the groom, but, towards the end of the ceremony, also to all other persons present. This practice is another form of joking during the wedding. The bringing of soil as well as the *teilābhiṣek* are repeated the following day.

Later the *suhāsen* are ritually bathe the bride or groom. Neither groom nor bride should touch the ground before returning to their house. Ideally a *bāṭo*, an elder sister's husband, should carry bride or

Suhāsen holding a basket while the sacrificer of the village goddess throws some soil into it.

groom[37]—also on his way to the bride's house. The *suhāsen* carry two *kalas* and an umbrella for the bride or groom in a procession. The groom or bride sits in the basket (*paralā ḍalā*) near a pond while the female *suhāsen* draw seven circles with different coloured powders between the basket and the water before they start another *teilābhiṣek*. Finally, seven *suhāsen* collectively pull the basket towards the water.

After the *thāḍa ūchchā*, the groom and bride are required to sit in the basket (*paralā ḍalā*) once more. Seven female *suhāsen* carry him/her around the *mahuā* branches, seven times counter-clockwise. Later seven *suhāsen* stand in a circle with their backs to the groom or bride who is still sitting in the basket next to the *mahuā* branches. One of the *suhāsen* then ties a white thread seven times around the other *suhāsen* standing in the circle. The thread, called *kankan moer*, is soaked in turmeric. In the end, it is knotted ten times around the right wrist of the bride and groom where it remains until the arrival of the couple in the groom's house. These ten knots are a reference to Lakṣmī (her number is ten). Before leaving his house the groom, guided by a *suhāsen*, worships the *kalyānī khuṇṭ*, the Goddess Gauri and the four *kalas* in each corner of the altar by offering a *ṭikā*.

During the subsequent rituals of *bibāhā pāni grahana* (acceptance of the bride), the bride is continuously accompanied by the *suhāsen* and is often addressed only indirectly, via the *suhāsen*. In addition, a gift of money has to be given to the bride's *suhāsen* by the groom's side. Sometimes this gift is demanded before the couple is allowed to leave the bride's village, but often it has already been paid at the wedding altar. This gift, the *sanga chhaḍāni* (*sanga* = friends)—is essential because without the *suhāsen*'s consent a bride is not allowed to leave the wedding altar. A bride cannot go anywhere without the *suhāsen*'s consent. In exchange for the money the *suhāsen* hand over their rights to the groom, thus terminating their role.

Apart from general participation, members of ego's generation or any alternate generation do not have specific roles during the funeral rituals. The exception, however, is the preference for a daughter's son to carry a light during the procession to the cremation grounds. He is preferred over any other grandson. This may indicate the importance of affinity beyond death, since the daughter's son must belong to a different clan and thus is a potential future affine—though of an alternating generation.

Abstract affinity—jāti as potential affines

During all major life cycle rituals the *jāti*—Aghriā of a different clan, but living in the same or neighbouring village—act as witnesses to insure that the rituals are properly performed. Among the Aghriā, the *jāti*'s participation is imperative. Considering the rule of clan exogamy, I see *jāti* as potential affines. However, since there is a tendency towards village exogamy it is rather an abstract affinity—*jāti* denoting 'others' from the perspective of ego's own clan.

Jāti may demand a feast on the sixth day after a birth. They should, however, at least be fed on the twelfth and twenty-first day. Furthermore, a *jāti* has to be present during *lagan dharā* (the fixing of the wedding date), during *nadiā phuṭā* (the breaking of coconuts) and on all subsequent days of a wedding. They also help to bring the *mahuā* sticks for the wedding altar and—significantly—provide the *kalyāṇī khuṇṭ* at the centre of the altar. In the same way, the small stool (*pindhā*) on which the bride and groom sit at the altar is offered by a *jāti*. Separate meals are offered for the *jāti* later on in the groom's and bride's village respectively (in the groom's village meals are offerered to them for three days.

During funeral rituals the role of a *jāti* may be of even higher importance. A *jāti* carries the big pot used by the family of the deceased to boil rice during the procession. This pot is then destroyed at the pyre. After the cremation, and before leaving the pond, all the men stand in a row. The first man, sometimes a *jāti*, takes a stone and hands it over his shoulder to the man behind him. This action is then repeated until the last man finally throws the stone into the pond. Some Aghriā think that this is a precaution so that death may not occur again. On the third day after death certain food restrictions, for example those regarding oil, are lifted. This is symbolized by a *jāti* of the family cooking a simple meal for all caste members in the village. A *jāti* also observes the rituals on the tenth day and may even assist the family in preparing food for the ancestors. Another feast for the *jāti* is offered on the eleventh day, which is again prepared by the *jāti* themselves.

Analysis

In addition to the two relation sets dominating the life cycle, these two oppositions seem to be of equal importance. The generation-sets are most marked at the time of weddings, specifically between women of one's own generation-set and the bride or groom. These women as *suhāsen* are much more involved in the life cycle rituals than their male counterparts, who only act as such during the first anointing of the bride and groom. Within the generation-set relative age is played down or even neglected: any sister or brother's wife, may act as *suhāsen*, no matter whether he or she is older or younger. Besides, affinal or kin ties are no criterion within the set: a sister may act in the same way as a mother's brother's daughter on the occasion. Only for the guiding of groom or bride to the wedding altar do some Aghriā prefer an elder brother's wife to any other *suhāsen*, though any sister, etc., might perform the task as well. However, on other occasions during the ritual cycle, notably on *Bhāi Jiūntiā* and *Rākhī Pūni,* the sister-brother-relation—grandmothers and granddaughters being classified as elder and younger sisters respectively—is emphasized.

This phenomenon has not been well documented in the literature.[38] Only Fuchs (1960: 271ff) mentions a male *suasa* and a female *suasin* as main attendants of both the groom and bride during the wedding among Gond and Bhumia.[39] Among the Baiga, Elwin (1939: 273ff) notes two *suāsin* as young, unmarried girls—either sisters or 'cousins' (mother's brother's daughters)—who perform similar duties as *suhāsen* among the Aghriā. Additionally, a male *suāsa* is brought up as guardian of the groom. Still, in both cases no reference is made to the principle of alternation.[40] Attendants of bride and groom are common, for example, in north India (Mayer 1960: 231)[41] as well as south India (Dumont 2000 [1957]: 249)—though they are not recruited on the basis of generation-sets. The phenomenon of generation sets acting as corporate groups during wedding rituals, at least in the regional culture of north-west Orissa, seems to be a widespread one. In interviews with members of other communities living in Aghriā villages (Gaṇḍ, Kandh, Bhuyān, Māḷi, Keunṭ, Kisān, Gauḍ, Malār, Luhurā, Chamār, Harijan and Brahmin), I was told that *suhāsen* play a role in their wedding rituals. That means in virtually all communities except the Chasā this custom was prevalent—though with minor differences, e.g. regarding the necessity to be married in order to act as *suhāsen.*[42] As far as the rituals performed by the *suhāsen* are concerned, the following aspects appear to be important: 1. fertility, for example, in the digging and bringing of soil; 2. purity, for example, in the anointing (with turmeric) and bathing of the bride or groom; 3. transcendental protection, for example, by tying a thread around the bride's and groom's wrist; and 4. transformation, for example, through emptying the 'unmarried water' or increasing the heat by anointing the groom with a certain oil—heat being usually required for transformation.[43] To summarize, I wish to argue that the idea of unity as well as renewal of the generation-set—a re-generation—stands at the centre of the life cycle.[44]

Apart from the binary opposition of two generation-sets which may be abstracted as 0 and 1, the distinction *jāti* versus *banśa* is prevalent during all life cycle rituals. Someone belonging to a clan other than ego's own, but from the same or a neighbouring village—a *jāti*—witnesses and thus controls the performance of all rituals of the life cycle, but has no role in rituals related to agriculture, etc. A *jāti*, however, has a role in legal matters, for example, the transfer of land or an adoption. Every member of ego's own clan (*banśa*) is excluded from acting as a *jāti*.[45] The principles of age or generational distinctions are of no importance within ego's own clan or the *jāti*.

The central criterion for eligibility as a *jāti* is formulated in the rule of exogamy: a *jāti* has to belong to another clan and all other clans except one's own are potential affines. A residential rule is expressed: *jāti* should belong to one's own village. Since there is a preference for village exogamy, the *jāti* of one's own village are usually not preferred marriage partners, though there are exceptions. Therefore, I have coined the term 'abstract affines' to describe the *jāti*: they are theoretically marriageable, though there are hardly such marital relations in practice. Such a general distinction between a marriageable category of agnates and a non-marriageable category of affines is common among tribal communities of Middle India (Pfeffer 1999: 17ff) where *bondhu* as hereditary affines are usually allowed to reside in the village as a minority opposed to a dominant land-holding clan. Such a distinction is typical for the tribal Gadaba of Koraput (Berger 2000: 20–1) as well. They differentiate between non-marriageable 'brothers' (*bhai*) of a dominant clan and affinal *bondhu* residing in the same village. It is significant that for many life cycle rituals, a witness known as *sakibhai* is required. This witness usually happens to be a *bondhu*. In contrast to the practice among the Aghriā, it is not just one clan consisting of brothers in a wider sense opposed to all other marriageable clans—within as well as outside one's village—but among Gadaba certain clans are also seen as being related as 'brothers' and, therefore, non-marriageable. All these brother clans are collectively opposed to all *bondhu* clans as affines. In addition, all Gadaba are conceptionalized as *bhaibondhu*—apparently as the sum of all brother clans and all affinal *bondhu* clans (P. Berger: personal communication; for the neighbouring Rona also T. Otten: personal communication).[46]

Thus, there is a striking similarity as far as the opposition of marriageable category versus non-marriageable category is concerned. We have to keep in mind that such a clear opposition does not exist in north India, where rules such as the three or four *gotra* rule[47] temporarily prohibit marriages within certain clans where a marriage had already been arranged in order to avoid the repetition of marriage for a certain period. Among the Aghriā there is no such rule and marriages with any clan—except one's own—can be arranged continuously. However, compared to the Gadaba there are some important differences as well.

On the village level, one's own clan or *banśa* is opposed to all other clans (*jāti*) as far as life cycle rituals are concerned. However, on the level of caste—also termed *jāti*—*jāti* encompasses *banśa* in the sense of Dumont's paradigm of encompassing the contrary. *Jāti* (in the sense of all Aghriā) includes all clans and thus transcends the opposition on the village level—as represented in Figure 18 (including the generation-sets) or in a Dumontian way in Figure 19. Contrary to the Gadaba, who may resolve the opposition between marriageable *bondhu* and non-marriageable *bhai* by simply combining them into a single category *bhaibondhu* (Figure 17), the Aghriā seem to conceptionalize the same opposition in a more complex, hierarchical manner. For the Aghriā the opposition is framed in a caste-like way. The idea of caste—as Dumont (1983: 168) had pointed out—does penetrate the domain of kinship (though he conceded that some 'islands of equality' might be left). In the case presented here, however, caste does to some extent encompass the sphere of kinship. Not only are there hierarchical distinctions among relatives—as it has already been shown in the case of the relationship between a mother's brother and a sister's son—but apparently clan and caste are hierarchically ranked as well with *jāti* being considered superior.

Figure 18 shows a similarity to features of the tetradic model.

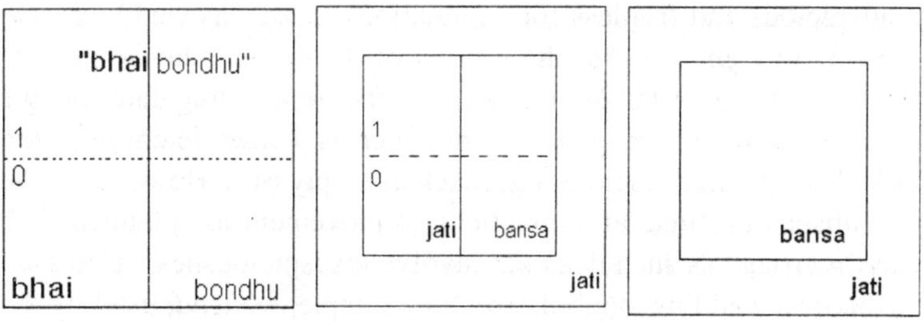

Figures 17-19 (Figure 17, left: Gadaba-model;[48] Figure 18, middle: Aghriā-model; Figure 19, right: Aghriā-model).

One finds the same basic ideas—marriageable *vs.* non-marriageable and generation 0 *vs.* generation 1—among the Aghriā and their life cycle rituals. However, compared to the Gadaba (or cases like the Kariera) the idea of moieties is absent or at least formulated in a very different way.

TRANSFORMATIONS

Auspiciousness/inauspiciousness

There are various restrictions for pregnant women in order to avoid inauspicious circumstances, for example, they should not start a journey on Sankrānti.[49] Some people say the movement of a woman should be in harmony with the movement of the Yogini, who should always be in the back and never in front of her. The movement of the Yogini is found in a *pāñjji* and should be taken into consideration for all auspicious events.

Although birth as such is conceived as auspicious, certain times, in particular the new moon days (*uāns* in Sambalpuri; *amābāsyā* in Oriya) are considered inauspicious. In former times people believed that girls born on a new moon day were unfit for marriage. Such girls were known as *uānsi kaniā* (new moon brides) and some people were convinced that their husbands would die. In opposition to that, the day of Sankrānti is a favourable time to give birth to a son. Inauspiciousness appears to be relevant for choosing a name for the child. For example, horoscope names beginning with the letter P are considered inauspicious and are avoided.

The time of marriage is selected in regard to auspiciousness. For example, the month of Pouṣ (around December/January) is considered inauspicious and fruitless for negotiations as well as weddings. On the way to a *ghar dekhā* (the visiting of the groom's house prior to the wedding) or to the *lagan dharā* (to fix the wedding date) people carefully watch for auspicious signs, such as women fetching water, as well as any inauspicious sign, such as empty pots. However, if the circumstances, time, and directions of movement are planned with care, marriage as such does not involve inauspiciousness. Common auspicious wedding symbols are, for example, *mehendi* used by the bride, threads tied by the *suhāsen* around the groom's/bride's wrist as well as sounds produced by the drummers in order to ensure a successful wedding and long-lasting marriage. While leaving the groom's house there should be no smoke in the kitchen, which is considered inauspicious. The same also holds true for any bad odour emanating from the house on the way out. During the *barāt* or wedding procession the groom should not pass the house of the bride. It is equally inauspicious for a groom to see another *barāt* in the village of the bride. Immediately after returning to the groom's house the bride and groom are seated on a bed next to the altar where sweets have been placed—again a very auspicious symbol.

Death is generally considered inauspicious (*aśubha*), but only rather vaguely. It is, however, accompanied by auspicious and inauspicious symbols. There are elements regarded as highly inauspicious for the living, but auspicious for the deceased. To some extent life and death are symbolically inverted. A case in point is the position in which the deceased is laid out in the house. His head points towards the north and his feet towards the south—a direction associated with death. Nobody in the house would lie down in such an inauspicious direction, but it is auspicious for the dead. In any case, the family tries to secure auspiciousness by giving certain gifts (*dān*) that are regarded as auspicious for the giver. On the eleventh day the giving of ten gifts—known also from Brahmin castes of north India (Kaushik 1976: 277)—is considered auspicious for the giver as well as for the receiver. The bed of death (*mrutya sajja dān*), however, is an exception. If, however, the death occurs at a time called *puṣkarā* it is explicitly auspicious for the deceased, but very inauspicious for his family. *Puṣkarā* is identified by the day of the week (*bara*), for example, every Tuesday, by the day within a fortnight (*tithi*), for example, every second day, and by a certain constellation of stars (*nakhyatra*). In such a case additional rituals are necessary to remove the potential dangers and possible negative effects or simply the inauspiciousness. This inauspiciousness is even stronger if two or three of these conditions (*pada*) come together: for example, the death occurs on a Tuesday which is also the second day within a fortnight.

In the case of *puṣkarā,* a special ritual is performed during the night, in which a *dān* is given to a lower Brahmin in the name of *Yama* and his brother *Sama*. Once again it is considered auspicious for the giver, but, in this case, highly inauspicious for the receiver. A higher family priest (*purohit*) would not accept this *dān* of a pot filled with raw rice, to which every family member has given one handful, thus symbolically removing the inauspiciousness. The lower Brahmin has to leave the house.

This Brahmin of lower status is sometimes called Dānuā Brahmin because of his acceptance of certain *dān*. He is considered as an appropriate receiver of the bed of death (*mrutya sajja dān*) and of the *puṣkarā dān*. Two out of three Dānuā Brahmin I asked acknowledged the inauspiciousness they are receiving and one told me that due to the potential danger he would never sleep on a *mrutya sajja dān*, but would give it away.

Purity/impurity

After a birth, the household is considered impure (*aśuddha*). The impurity is subsequently removed in a series of different rituals performed on the sixth, twelfth and twenty-first day. Some Aghriā believe that this impurity is even stronger than that in the case of death. Usually the Aghriā do not take water—not to mention food—into a house where there has has been a birth until after the sixth day. People say that in former times nobody was allowed to touch the mother until *ṣaṭhi* (sixth day ritual) had been performed. Nowadays this is confined to other pregnant women who should not touch the mother, her baby, or any women who have assisted during the birth. Aghriā visiting a house before the *ṣaṭhi* should change their clothes after returning to their own house—for women an additional bath is advisable, but for men a change of clothes is sufficient. The house is purified in various ways. The mother is not allowed to enter the kitchen for six days and, furthermore, is prohibited to cook until the twenty-first day. Apart from that, the pot used to boil rice should be destroyed. However, this rule is not as strict as in the case of death, when it must be destroyed. Later the first haircut and—even more importantly—the initiation by a Kān Guru, who whispers a *mantra* into the ear of a child, are performed in order to purify the child.

Contrary to birth and death, marriage does not generate impurity. However, that does not mean that purity and impurity is negligible during wedding procedures. The wedding should be understood as consisting of various sequences leading to the highest possible purification within the life cycle. Particularly the ceremonies of *teilā-*

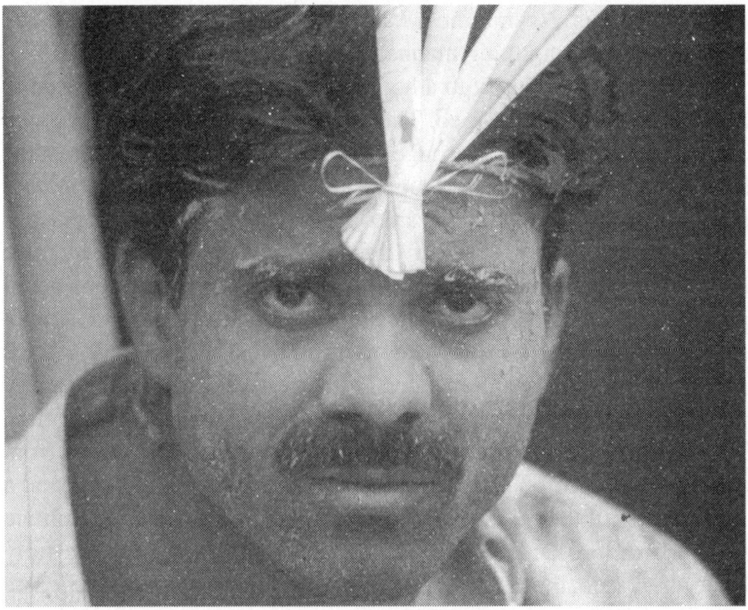

Aghriā-groom anointed with turmeric and oil.

bhiṣek, the anointing of the whole body of the bride and groom with oil and turmeric three times, lead to purer stages of being. Both bride and groom keep the oil and turmeric mixture on their body for at least a day, after which they are given a ritual bath. Higher purity correlates to a higher ritual status: After the second *teilābhiṣek,* groom and bride wear a crown (*makuṭ*) of palm leaves symbolising their higher status. Afterwards they do not have to show their respect to any elder relative, but only to the priest (some Aghriā said the groom is considered king). The purity is further increased by a subsequent ritual bath. In order to avoid contamination neither groom nor bride should touch the ground before they return to the house. Later the barber shaves the groom and cuts the nails of both the bride and groom. It is considered a privilege for the barber to demand the clothes the groom has worn up to this stage, which some Aghriā regard as rather impure. After having taken another bath and receiving new clothes, the groom may proceed to the bride's village in order to get married. However, at the wedding altar, a priest (Tihāri) may try to increase his purity once again by handing over a mango leaf for the groom to bite on. This is a symbolic cleansing or purification of his teeth, although done in a joking manner.

Death brings impurity to a household. Due to this the pot used to boil rice has to be destroyed. The family is excluded from all social activities, for example, marriages, and from worshipping gods in the house or in their temples. Some Aghriā explained that afterwards they are to some extent temporarily 'Untouchable'. These restrictions should be observed not only by the nuclear or joint family, and also by the whole patrilineal clan (*banśa*), whose members are considered polluted. In addition, rituals for the village goddess (Grām Śrī) cannot take place until eleven days after a death, because the whole village is regarded as impure. Separated from the social realm, the family members have to purify themselves according to their contamination. This contamination affects the eldest son in particular. Apart from the destruction of polluted articles, a series of purifying baths and a strict diet until the *tel kām*, barber, washerman and *purohit* facilitate the purification. Only on the eleventh day will the family be fully integrated into the caste again symbolized by sharing the caste commensality.

Apparently a rather mild form of impurity is associated with the ancestors too. During the fortnight of the ancestors (*pitru pakṣ*) family members neither shave nor cut their nails and the house is cleaned only in the most superficial way—if at all. Similarly, it was observed by Pattanaik (1952: 145) that within this fortnight cropping the hair is strictly prohibited and clothes are never sent out for washing. This indicates that this period is clearly not a time of purity. However, at the end of this period no elaborate purifying measures comparable to rituals after birth or death are required.

Purity and auspiciousness within the life cycle

There are a lot of features Aghriā life cycle rituals have in common with other north Indian cases (Bennett 1983, Conzelmann 1996, Parry 1994, Randeria 1999 et al.), particularly in the idea of impurity after birth and death described above. Still, there are certain characteristics in Aghriā life cycle rituals which have not yet received proper attention.

Contrary to Das' (1997 [1982]: 143) findings, impurity goes well beyond death: it is a permanent concern in relation to the ancestors—

ancestor worship involves impurity. Though marriage is the only major life cycle ritual not generating any impurity as birth and death do (see also Dumont and Pocock 1959: 33), ritual purity is of utmost importance during marriage as well. I wish to suggest that the life cycle rituals from birth to marriage should be understood as a continuously progressing purification, which leads to the highest stage of purity a person can reach within a conventional life cycle.[50] Almost all early life cycle rituals from birth onwards—in particular the ritual haircut, initiation by an Ear Guru,—increase one's purity, which reaches its climax at the wedding. A person is passing through subsequent steps of purification. This is symbolized by the fact that items or clothes used during the first haircut as well as clothes worn by the groom during the early part of his wedding should be given to a barber and should not be used again by the married person who has in the meantime attained a higher purity. This rule is formulated most strictly at the time of death when the clothes of the chief mourner or sons of the deceased have to be left at the pond and cannot be brought into the house again. Once more it is the privilege of a barber to take these clothes. The clothes left at the pond after death are never touched again by anyone in the family. This is not the case after the marriage rituals when everyone might still touch the old clothes of the groom. The degree of a purification is clearly different: in the case of death, the old clothes would be a form of pollution for all family members, in the case of a wedding, there is little risk of contamination of family members.

Thus, a person reaches the highest relative purity at the time of marriage. Therefore, it should not surprise us that among the Aghriā marriage is closely associated with purification and that ultimately marriage stands as a ritual idiom for the highest stage of purity. The purification of a pond or mango trees is essentially expressed as a kind of marriage—as *bihā* or *bibāha*.[51] A pond marriage or *bandha bibāha* is essential in order to use a pond for any ritual purposes.

Before the marriage ritual, which usually lasts three days, a basil shrine or *tulsī chaur* has to be erected next to the pond. Additionally, a pillar known as *tilśiri* is built in the middle of the pond with a crown (*makuṭ*) or *triśul* on top. On the second day a Brahmin supervises the construction of an altar (*bed*) resembling a wedding altar. The *tulsī chaur* is usually included in the altar where the gods—

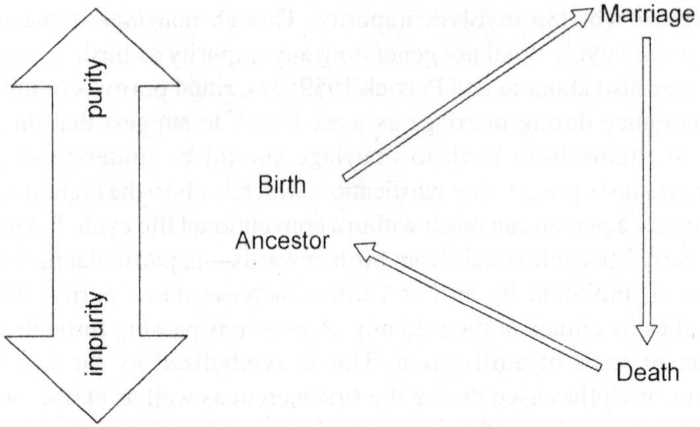

Figure 20: Transformation of a person in relation to his relative purity

most Aghriā say Krishna, some others say Lakṣmī are worshipped. A married couple, in most cases the owners of the pond, act as *karttā* or sacrificer in the fire ritual (*homa*), that the Brahmin then performs at the altar, reciting sacred texts. Afterwards the married couple set a boat into the pond and worship the gods. They then circle the pond seven times, clockwise. A feast usually completes the ceremony. The performance of a tree marriage or *gacha bibāha* may even have more resemblance to a proper marriage. Some interlocutors said that even *suhāsen* used to perform the *teilabhiṣek* ritual and tied a white thread around the trunk of the mango tree(s), and that 'Untouchable' musicians as well as the *jāti* used to join in.[52] S.C. Roy (1999 [1928]: 90ff) and Griffith (1993 [1946]: 201) describe very similar rituals for the Orām and Kol respectively. In addition, Roy (ibid.) mentions a marriage with early rice shoots among the Orām. He also indicates that purity and marriage might be similarly related in tribal society.

Figure 20 indicates the major developments in the life cycle related to relative purity. The child being born in a condition of relative impurity is gradually purified, until getting married, when purity reaches the maximum. After marriage, this high purity can apparently not be maintained. This is due to sexual intercourse, involvement in ancestor rituals, and ceremonies for the village goddess. Some Aghriā said that marriage is essential for proper participation in the rituals for the village deity. Such rituals, specifically the eating of sacrificial meat, are considered impure: the meat has to be eaten outside one's house. Thus, the degree of relative purity seems to decrease to some extent after marriage. At the time of death maximal impurity is reached, which is transformed towards purity by means of the rituals. However, ancestor worship still involves some impurity. Thus, as far as purity is concerned, marriage and death are clearly opposed to each other:

marriage/maximal purity ⟷ death/maximal impurity

Furthermore, the life cycle, in particular for men, consists of two major transformations from relative impurity to purity: 1. from birth to marriage and 2. from death until transformation into an ancestor. Theoretically, death is the most polluting event that occurs after marriage. The figure, however, is not meant to imply that the impurity occurring during the *pitru pakṣ* (fortnight of the ancestors) is identical with birth pollution. The duration of the pollution and the measures required for a purification are clearly divergent. For example, the impure period of *pitru pakṣ* though longer than after birth, does not necessitate the services of a washerman. However, since there are very obvious links between birth and death or, rather, between birth and the ancestors, there might also be a connection as far as purity is concerned. Though birth itself certainly generates impurity, there are also hints at prenatal impurity.

Apart from transformations towards higher purity, the opposition between the auspicious and the inauspicious, and a striving towards the former characterizes the life cycle. The importance of the concept of auspiciousness has been demonstrated by Das (1997 [1982]), Madan (1985), Marglin (1985) or Raheja (1988) for north India and coastal Orissa, but again the Aghriā case might provide some new insights. Contrary to Dumont and Pocock (1959: 33), I wish to argue that it is not possible to trace this opposition back to the ultimate opposition of pure against impure, but rather—as Madan (1985: 17) has pointed out—that 'Auspiciousness . . . is an absolute value, which manifests as a quality of events in the lives of human actors (*pātra*) and involves the dimension of time (*kāla*) and space (*sthāna*).'

As Marglin (1985: 68) indicates, the opposition auspicious *vs.* inauspicious is not exclusively binary. Instead, auspicious or inauspicious symbols and times play a role during one's entire life, and can occur together. For example, during a death procession the position of the bed in which the deceased is carried is turned upside down—unambiguously interpreted as an inauspicious symbol—while the very same bed is decorated with banana leaves, considered auspicious. Thus, Das's statement (1997 [1982]: 143–4) that auspicious events are associated with life and the future, inauspicious events with death, might be true for the Aghriā in only a vague sense. On the contrary, to see a dead person or death procession is considered very auspicious, and to be present while someone is dying is not inauspicious but rather indicates that there has been a connection between the person present and the departing in an earlier life. Birth might occur at an inauspicious time or one may find inauspicious symbols or indicators at the time of marriage, for example, certain smells being inauspicious for the groom and to some extent to the family as a whole. Apart from time and space, the perspective of the actor has to be taken into consideration. Death under a certain constellation of stars, locally known as *puṣkarā*, may be highly auspicious for the deceased, but highly inauspicious for his family. An association between auspiciousness and death has—to my knowledge—so far only been mentioned by Narayanan (1985: 58).[53]

However, the Aghriā do not only recognize inauspicious signs. They are actively involved in removing inauspiciousness from the house and family. Raheja points to such transfers of inauspiciousness via gifts, in particular *dān*, as an ordering principle in a peasant caste of UP. In her work she particularly links *dān* to the transfer of inauspiciousness, concluding that 'the significance of *dān* . . . was focused on the transfer of inauspiciousness from donor to recipient.' (Raheja 1988: 31). In the Aghriā life cycle such transfers via certain types of *dān*, for example, the *puṣkarā dān*, exist as well, but are limited in extent. During funeral rituals, *puṣkarā dān* may be transferred to a lower Brahmin to ensure auspiciousness for the family of the deceased. The Brahmin has to leave the house immediately afterwards—indicating a transfer. The same is true for the bed of death or *mrutyu śajyā dān/mrutyu sajja dān* (also known as the bed of the ghost or *preta śajyā dān*). Contrary to Raheja's case, the Aghriā know many other forms of *dān*, such as the *bhanjā dān*, or *go dān* given on the same occasion, clearly auspicious for the donor as well as the receiver (a *bhanjā* and a higher Brahmin or *purohit* respectively, who would not accept any *dān* involving inauspiciousness). *Dān* as a category of gifts has the potential to transfer inauspiciousness, but not every *dān* does so.

To sum up, the life cycle apparently revolves around two transformative processes based on the fundamental opposition of pure and impure, and auspicious and inauspicious. The latter is not an exclusive opposition, but rather—as Marglin (1985: 79) observed in the context of *devadasis* in Puri, the 'coexistence of both auspiciousness and inauspiciousness has a transformative effect of renewal'. The two oppositions cannot simply be linked to each other. Furthermore, the opposition pure vs. impure seems to be more socio-centric, not only affecting the whole household or kin group, though to a varying degree, but being a matter of caste as well (*jāti* demand a feast after death, etc.). Inauspiciousness is, in contrast, a rather private or domestic affair and other caste fellows will not force you to do any *puṣkarā* ritual even if a Brahmin tells you it is required.[54]

6.4. BIRTH, REBIRTH, AND THE CIRCLE OF LIFE

In this final part of the chapter the period between death and birth will be considered. Contrary to Raheja's (1988: 147) emphasis on the cutting of ties being central to funerary rites among Gujar, I wish to argue that among the Aghriā, the cyclic element is of major importance. This means a limited communication with ancestors in rituals and in dreams is possible, though not to the same extent as among many tribal communities (see Vitebsky 1993). Ancestors ultimately return, though not always to their own house. Thus, among the Aghriā death might be highly auspicious for the deceased and is—contrary to Das' (1997 [1982]) findings in north India—an event in which a future is envisaged. Of equal importance, birth is an event in which the past is clearly envisaged and recaptured.

Transforming a spirit—ghost (pret) *into an ancestor* (pitru)

The main objective of the funeral is to turn the *pret*,[55] who has dangerous potential, into an ancestor or *pitru*, who is seen rather as a protective force whose blessings are sought for agricultural production, weddings, etc. Such a transformation from *pret* to *pitru* is a main characteristic of death rituals in the northern part of the subcontinent (Bennett 1983, Conzelmann 1996, Gaenszle 1999, Kaushik 1976, Parry 1994 et al.). Many of the rituals already described resemble a general north Indian Hindu pattern. In all these cases, the transformation is a gradual process, aimed to pacify the *pret* and to gratify his needs in order to facilitate his transition and, finally, his merging with the ancestors.

Among the Aghriā as well as 'in Brahmanically influenced Hindu contexts the status or place of a departed person is not well defined' (Michaels 1999: 116). As a *pret* he wanders around in complete darkness. Lights either carried by a daughter's son in the death procession or the continuous and inextinguishable light (*akhanda dīpa*) on the ninth day are therefore offered in honour of the *pret*. Immediately after the cremation and bath, a little mango plant is set near a pond or river, to offer some shade to him. People place some stones next to it to offer a temporary house or shelter for him until his tomb has been erected.

The *pret* stays thirsty and hungry. The mango plant is watered (*pāen diyā*) regularly to ease his thirst. On the ninth day a pot with water is placed inside the house. This pot is not just a seat for the *pret*. Droplets fall onto the ground through holes in the pot. People either say that this is done to quench the thirst or that the *pret* leaves the house in the same way as the drops fall to the ground.

On the tenth day the eldest son, supervised by the family priest, prepares half boiled rice (*darsijha bhāt*) as a favourite dish for a *pret* and offers water and ten rice balls (*piṇda*) to him—one for each day. This offering of the tenth *piṇda* on the tenth day is common in north India where it is described as *piṇḍadān* and is seen as the 'symbolic recreation of the dead man's body' (Kaushik 1976: 274). The half boiled rice obviously symbolizes the liminal state of the *pret* who has not yet reached the state of a *pitru* to whom fully-boiled rice is offered during the following rituals. Then the *piṇda* are immersed in water. One family priest told me that life would develop in the mother's womb in the water during the tenth month. Similarly, the *pret* would need ten days to leave the house and he leaves it through the water.

On the eleventh day *antyeṣṭikriyā* rites boiled rice mixed and fruits is offered to the ancestors by the eldest son. This offering is in the shape of three rice balls (*piṇda*) representing the last three generations. An extra *piṇda* is given to the deceased. Finally, everything is merged. This part shows similarities to rituals known as *sapiṇdikarana* (Kaushik 1976: 279), or *sapinda sraddha* (Bennett 1983: 105), that are seen as decisive steps in the transformation. Although the *pūjā* is repeated on the next day, only three rice balls for the last three generations are prepared. It seems by now that the *pret* has already been transformed into an ancestor.

However, in the case of the Aghriā the transition is marked in yet another way by the offering of the gift of a bed or *sajja dān*. This custom is also quite common amongst north Indian Brahmins (Dumont 1998 [1966]: 96) and the 'Untouchables' (Randeria 1999: 103–4). But, there one *sajja dān* is usually given to a Brahmin,[56] while there are two different kinds of *sajja dān* among the Aghriā. Apart from all other kinds of gifts given to the deceased on the eleventh day, a *mrutya sajja dān* (the bed of death) or *preta sajja dān* (the bed of the ghost), is imperative. It is given to a lower Brahmin who, on this occasion, represents the *pret*. The eldest son before handing over the gift, says, 'I give you, *pret*, this gift. Please accept it happily.' On the twelfth day the *pūjā* is repeated but no 'bed of death' or 'bed of the ghost' is given. Instead a bed known as *sukha sajja dān* (happy bed) or *pitru sajja dān* (bed of the ancestor) is given away and now accepted by the family priest himself, who is thus identified with the *pitru*. The necessity of giving two *sajja dān* is probably not only related to the transformation from *pret* to *pitru*, but also to the transformation from inauspiciousness to auspiciousness.

Marriage and merits: who becomes an ancestor?

Not every Aghriā becomes an ancestor. Most Aghriā believe that one has to be married in order to become a 'forefather'.[57] The complete funeral ceremonies are performed only for married Aghriā. Unmarried Aghriā are not even allowed to worship the ancestors. It is only as brides or grooms that they can first perform a ritual for the ancestors. Some Aghriā explicitly state that the *tel chaḍā* is the most important among all the rituals in order to be able to become an ancestor. Furthermore, there is the idea that if unmarried adult women remain in the house, the ancestors will get nothing to eat. Therefore, early marriages, in particular child marriages or other forms of symbolic marriages had formerly to be arranged in order to satisfy the ancestors. Some people believe that bachelors and old spinsters—*dindā pilā* and *dindā tukel* respectively—turn into evil spirits or *bhut*, or remain in the state of a *pret,* since they are considered to be *apūrṇṇa* or *apurba*, not ripe.

Even married Aghriā do not become ancestors automatically: not people who have committed suicide, or women who die during pregnancy or confinement until the sixth day after birth. These persons become spirits or ghosts instead of ancestors—in case of suicide a *bhut*, in the latter case a *chirgin.* Some people take the growth of nails and hair after death as a clear indicator that the deceased turns into a *chirgin.* Women who have passed away during pregnancy or confinement are not burned, but buried, like small children. In these cases no *samādhi* is erected. In former times a *guniā* or local healer was consulted in the case of death during confinement. This healer then performed a special ritual to lock the evil soul in the cemetery. These Aghriā are never remembered in rituals for the ancestors. In some cases, however, it seems that *piṇḍa* is offered for all those dead—one *piṇḍa* is later thrown away and not eaten by relatives like the others.

Among the Aghriā there is no clear concept of a good one opposed to a bad one as found among tribal communities like the Kisān, where a good death is essential to become an ancestor. However, there are certain notions and ideas about a good death. Certain days (such as Thursdays in the month of Mārgaśīrṣa, the day of *Nuā Khāi*, *Pañchaka* or *Gaṇeś Pūjā*) are considered auspicious and people believed that if one dies on such a day the soul goes to heaven directly. One who dies on such an auspicious day is regarded as *bhāgyabān*—a lucky person. Furthermore, a good time to die is after the conclusion of individual duties such as the marriages of one's children, who should be secure financially. Contrarywise, an untimely death, for example, by accident, is a bad one. If a father witnesses the death of his son or a grandfather that of his grandson, the elders are considered as *pāpi*, being punished. Suffering, for example, by becoming or being paralysed, means to be a *pāpi* too, as well as being a *hatabhāgā*, or an unlucky person. Such strong punishments are related to one's *karma* and the merits or sins in an earlier life. Still, the idea of *karma* seems to be rather vague.

Worshipping the ancestors

The main rituals for the ancestors, apart from rituals for those who have recently died, take place during the dark side of the moon in the month of Āśbinā or *Daśarā* (September–October) when the ancestors return to their families. During this period, the 'fortnight of the ancestors', peculiar rules have to be observed. Aghriā are neither allowed to cut their hair and nails, nor to shave. The house is not cleaned properly—only a broom may be used. The ancestors are constantly worshipped during this period. Every morning a daughter-in-law of the house offers flowers, ground rice, milk as well as green gram, and circles a *ghī* lamp together with some incense. The offering is made under the eaves of the house, usually the eaves of an inner courtyard on a spot precisely between the veranda and the place where the rain falls from the roof. This place has been selected for the ancestors and a small stool with cigarettes and tobacco are placed there, with small twigs serving as toothbrushes.

Additionally, there are rituals for ancestors whose bones have not been taken to the Ganga. A ritual should be performed for them within this fortnight, on the lunar day (*tithi*) of their death. This means that when a relative died on the sixth day no matter which month, he should be worshipped on the very same day during the *pitru pakṣ*. For all female ancestors a collective ritual should be performed on the ninth day, while all male forefathers are remembered on the tenth day. On the ninth and tenth neither ploughing nor the use of bullocks is allowed. In particular, the use of ploughs is strictly prohibited and no agricultural instruments worshipped on Harli Uāns should be used—anyone caught ignoring these rules would be an outcaste. On the last day of the fortnight—known as *mahāḷayā*—food is offered to all ancestors.[58] Subsequently, gifts (*dān*) such as sweets, cloths, and paddy should be given to a Brahmin, but not to the family priest (*purohit*) who would not accept them. In case there is no Brahmin, *dan* may be offered to a sister's son (ZS).[59] Finally a daughter-in-law brings a *ghī* lamp into the field and requests the ancestors to protect the fields.

Another important occasion of ancestor worship is at the time of marriage when the bride and groom together with their parents first perform a ritual for the ancestors—the so-called *pitru pūjā* mentioned in a previous chapter.

Rebirth and communication with the ancestors

Even if ancestors are not considered to be present in the house, communication is possible. If an ancestor appears in dreams, it shows concern for his family. Ancestors can ensure that the harvest is successful—the most essential thing in a rural society—or that guests are served properly. Or else they may complain about being treated badly by their family or may announce their wish to return to them.

An Aghriā lady once dreamed of her late father-in-law who recommended contacting a friend of the family for help, since she and her husband alone were not able to take care of the fields in a proper way. At that time boars frequently destroyed the paddy fields. The next morning that very friend of the family appeared at their house. It turned out that he himself had also dreamt of the father-in-law the previous night. In his dream, the father-in-law had asked the man to help his family to save the harvest. They went to the field together, saw the damage the boars had already caused, and started cutting the paddy. In this way further damage was avoided. The very same father-in-law appeared once more in a dream to the same woman and complained that she had forgotten to offer him tobacco during the rituals for all ancestors in Āśbinā. She replied in the dream that he would find the tobacco in a box on top of the cupboard. The next morning she found the box, which had been full the evening before, half empty. Other Aghriā remembered that their ancestors had told them in dreams about the mistakes they had made in some ritual so that they could correct it and perform it properly the next time round.

Women often dream about ancestors during pregnancy. A pregnant woman had dreamt of her grandfather (her father's father) several times before giving birth to a child in 2002. Family members recalled that the grandfather had been particularly fond of this granddaughter. In one dream the grandfather asked for a glass of water mixed with *bel* pulp. A little later the pregnant granddaughter woke up and was thirsty for *bel* drink, but could not find any. The mother's father's younger brother became angry after hearing about this dream. In his opinion, his father should come back to his own house and should not be reborn in the house of his son's daughter in another village. He cracked jokes with his pregnant elder brother's daughter, saying it would be better if she would not come into his house. A little later the woman had a dream in which the grandfather complained about the behaviour of his son (the mother's uncle), who wished to bar him from coming into his own house. However, the father's younger brother of the mother acknowledged that his father had had some problems in the later stage of his life and was not interested in agriculture anymore. Instead his father as an ancestor had now decided to join the family of his granddaughter, for whom agriculture was not the main source of income.

After a baby is born, family members are always keen to find some similarities with departed ancestors. In one such case, in which prior to the birth a father's mother had already appeared in a dream of her daughter-in-law, an uncle (FeB) of the child told me that in his opinion the mouth of the newborn girl resembled that of his mother. He said that it was quite possible that his mother was reborn into the family as his niece (yBD), but that one can never be sure. When similarities are found, the children are often seen as rebirths of these relatives. Children are addressed the same way as the departed ancestors they are believed to be. The new born girl is, therefore, addressed as 'mother' by the sisters of the baby's father. Similarily, another child in the family is called 'father's elder brother' (*baḍa bāpā*) by his father's sisters, because he is considered to be a rebirth of his grandfather.

If a newly-born baby refuses to eat or drink it is believed that the reborn ancestor is unhappy and must be appeased. A case in point is the birth of the late Binod Chandra Naik—popular poet and writer,—who was born in the house of his mother's brother. The family was convinced that Binod, considered the reincarnation of his father's father, refused to drink milk because he was not born into his 'own' house, the house of his father. This reincarnated father's father was unhappy that he was born in the mother's brother's house. A proof that Binod is the rebirth of his father's father was seen in the fact that an old horse bowed its head in front of the child. The British had presented the horse to his grandfather. It is believed animals can see the soul (*ātmān*) and, therefore, the horse obviously recognized his old owner—now reborn. The father's elder brother arrived accordingly in the mother's brother's house to beg pardon that the baby was born there and not in his own village. Additionally, the baby's mother's father welcomed the baby as the reincarnation of his *samdhi* or affinal relative (daughter's husband's father—DHF). Therefore, Binod got the nickname *ajā*—grandfather.

In a similar case a girl—now around 26 years old—who was born in the village of her mother and not in her father's house refused to drink the milk of her mother. This continued for a couple of days. A relative dreamt of the girl as rebirth of her father's father, who said 'I'm going to your family once more in the stomach of my daughter-in-law'. When the girl still refused to drink, the mother's mother asked the baby: '*Samdhi* (DHF), why are you angry with us?' She worshipped the girl by washing her feet with milk. Afterwards the girl no longer refused to be breastfed by her mother.

Although it is quite often assumed that a grandparent is reborn into the family, in some cases it might also be a rebirth of another child in the family, for instance, a brother. A landlord's child nicknamed Ghansiā had passed away at the age of one and a half. The child's aunt (the father's younger brother's wife) loved him very much and criticised the mother for not having cared enough for the child. During the funeral this aunt sat crying in a corner. Her own son—at that time around four years old—saw her and asked 'Why are you crying?' and the mother replied 'I had hoped that you and Ghansiā would grow up together and that both of you would go to school together, but now you are alone.' The son replied: 'Why are you crying? He will come back!' In the same month the aunt became pregnant again and gave birth to another son who showed similarities with Ghansiā, for example, in the form of his ears. During the ritual of the sixth day the mother of Ghansiā saw the newborn baby, held him in her arms, and looked into his eyes for a long time. Then she said: 'Perhaps I have not loved you enough. I have beaten you. Your aunt loved you so much and now you have gone to her.' Another of the landlord's wives, considered equally as mother (although not a mother in biological terms) had dreamt of a Baba after the death of Ghansiā. This Baba offered the child again to her (or her family) and said: 'You don't have to worry. The child will return to your family.' Later this mother recognized the particular form of the newborn child's neck as characteristic of Ghansiā. The similarities found between Ghansiā and the newborn aunt's son might have been an important reason why Ghansiā's father later adopted the son of his younger brother. In other cases, however, great grandparents, or even persons staying in a family although not related to them, might be reborn into a family.[60]

The keen interest in rebirth is obvious. In former times a way of identifying rebirths was to reckon up the names of ancestors when babies were crying a lot. If the child fell silent after hearing a particular name, it was believed that the child was his or her reincarnation. There is an underlying assumption that, as one Aghriā has expressed it, 'Ancestors wait in heaven for a rebirth. They are worshipped to come back to their family.' Although most ancestors seem to be reborn in an alternating generation—as grandchildren—this is no fixed rule. A forefather might appear in the same generation again, as in case of death of a child, or an ancestor might be reborn as a great grandchild. Additionally, a male forefather might reappear in the family as a girl. Compared to other communities in the village there is, however, no standardized way to prove a rebirth.

Continuity within the life cycle

Apart from marriage and death, various stages of the life cycle are interwoven. By such links—by the 'synchronization of events' (Iteanu 1999: 276) the cyclic character of life is underlined. A case in point is the period of transition between different stages within the cycle. After marriage the wedding altar has to remain in the house and cannot be dismantled for a year. One would risk the failure of the marriage in question. Similarly, only after a transitory period of a year can one fully become an ancestor. This is symbolized by the performance of a *barṣika śrāddha*—the ancestor ritual—exactly one year after death. In addition, a child should be brought before Jagannāth within the first year. In all these cases a transformation, or at least stable relationships, seem to have been completed or been established within this period. However, there are other interlinked time-frames: while a new-born is delivered within ten months—birth taking place in the tenth month, after nine months of pregnancy—the dead are transformed to on the tenth day after death, a day on which ten *piṇḍa* are offered to the departed and later immersed in water. Occasionally this immersion is explicitly related to birth. It is stated that in the tenth month a baby leaves the womb of its mother, in other words, leaves the water, while the deceased return into the water. Such time frames not only reveal certain inversions between life and death, but also indicate a synchronization of life cycle events.

Besides this, birth and death are linked in many other ways. Pregnant women are strictly prohibited to cross river. They should particularly refrain from crossing it by boat, but also in a jeep. A bridge is, however, seen as less dangerous. A deceased person however, has to cross the river Baitarani in order to join the ancestors. In addition, his relatives are required to provide the gift of a cow to facilitate his journey. Thus, life and death are directionally opposed—also indicated by the sleeping position of the living who face northwards in contrast to the position of the deceased, who is laid out on a bed facing south. Furthermore, tattoos, painfully applied during childhood, particularly on girls, are said to help reduce the punishment of Yama, who one has to face at the time of death. If people suffer during their lifetime, Yama's verdict will be less harsh. Therefore, suffering prior to death is linked and contrasted to post-mortem pain.

If death is seen as immanent and if the Aghriā are afraid that their relative might not survive the next night, some Ganga water mixed with sacred (*tulsī*) leaves is put into the mouth of the dying person. After this offering, known as *dān deba*, the person is—*ipso facto*—considered dead. However, if the person survives and recovers—some say a kind of mistake made by Yama—it is seen as a birth. Thus, this person cannot eat boiled rice (*bhāt*) before a Brahmin has performed a small ritual and some gifts (*dān* such as paddy) have been given to the priest.[61] After such a *de facto* death, the cycle starts again: personhood seems to be closely linked to the eating of rice. This might be further substantiated by the fact that the Aghriā in Bargarh offer rice as a last dish to the deceased. Not eating rice actually means to be dead!

Comparative digression: the concept of the Aghriā and of their neighbours

The Aghriā share many features with their neighbours. 1. A decision for either burial or cremation is made on economic grounds, though a cremation is clearly preferred. 2. The rituals of all high status tribal communities are performed by Brahmins and thus resemble each other to a large extent. Lower status communities like the Muṇḍā or Kisān deviate from the Brahmanical pattern as far as the giving of *sajja dān* or *puṣkarā* is concerned. Nevertheless, wealthy Muṇḍā may build a *samādhi* for their ancestors as well and they may also worship Dharam Devtā—the supreme god of the Muṇḍā and other related communities—on the same occasion. Apart from the necessity to hire a Brahmin for their rituals, the time-frame within communities is much more flexible. Among the Muṇḍā or Kisān, for example, the main funeral may be performed after ten days as among the Aghriā. It may also, however, be arranged a year after the time of death. 3. The tribal neighbours seem to have a much sharper concept of a good and bad death. For example, death due to an accident—a bad death—will bar someone from becoming an ancestor among the Kisān, but not among the Aghriā. 4. Some tribal communities have more clearly marked mechanisms to discover and determine a rebirth. After announcing the name of an ancestor, the Kisān throw two grains of rice into a bowl with turmeric water. A rebirth is considered verified if the rice grains collide in the bowl. 5. All tribal communities offer a specially prepared and sacred rice-beer (*tarpan*)[62] to their ancestors, while the Aghriā do not. 6. Many tribal communities do not observe the fortnight of the ancestors, but rather combine this ritual with *Nuā Khāi*, etc. 7. Another important difference between tribal communities and the Aghriā is the so-called *jiu dakā*–ceremony or 'calling of the life-energy' (*jiu* = life-energy/life-spirit;[63] *dakā* = to call), which is mentioned in the literature on the Birhor (Roy 1925: 276–7), the Khāṛiā/Khaḍiā (Roy and Roy 1937: 297–8), the Oraon/Orām (Roy 1999 [1928]: 178) and the Muṇḍā (Roy 1970 [1912]: 264). This ceremony seems to be surprisingly common among all tribal communities of the region, e.g. Kisān and Muṇḍā. However, in some communities like, for example, the Kandh it has, at least by some members, been recently discontinued. A hut is usually erected in the courtyard of the house and relatives making noise with, for example, iron sickles go to the outskirts of the village. This noise making is performed in order to call the *jiu*—sometimes also translated as 'shade'. Often the hut is also burnt in order to attract the attention of the *jiu*. However, the Aghriā in Kuchinda block do not perform this ceremony. Finally, in all local communities marriage is the essential provision to join the ancestors. For example, the full funerary rites are not performed for unmarried Aghriā, while in many tribal communities a *jiu dakā* is not added, when the deceased had never been married.

6.5. CONCLUSION

The life cycle among the Aghriā is, to a large extent, dominated by two relation sets: father and son as well as mother's brother and sister's son. Both relations are complementary. I have tried to highlight the role of the sister's son (*bhanjā*) or potential son-in-law during the funerary rites among the Aghriā because here the Aghriā seem to deviate from the general north Indian caste pattern. However, I have shown that among the Gond of the region (Elwin 1945), in which a *bhanjā* rides on the dead man's memorial stone, or among tribal Rai (Gaenszle 1999) and Magar (Oppitz 1991) of Nepal, the sister's son plays an important role as among the Aghriā. The *bhanjā* guides the deceased into the world beyond and transforms the mother's brother into an ancestor. The role of the *bhanjā* in funerary rites is complementary to the role of his mother's brother in helping him into the world or to become a complete social person. Generalizing this result and combining it with the basic tetradic model suggested by Allen, the diagonal link within the four sections or the relation to the closest affinal of the adjacent generation is certainly of the utmost importance in life cycle rituals not only among Aghriā. In this regard, the Aghriā might have adapted a pattern found in their predominantly tribal surroundings. However, significant differences with their Middle Indian tribal neighbours remain, for example, to Sora described by Vitebsky (1993; for south Indian hunters and gatherers see also Demmer 1999), who may communicate verbally with their ancestors via shamans.

The importance of a sister's son's presence in all these cases seems to stand in contrast to cases cited by Parry and Bloch (1982) in which 'the avoidance of exchange constructs the image of permanence' (ibid.: 32) and in which eternity seems to be symbolized by the 'end of affinity' (ibid.: 27). Here the *bhanjā*—or the presence of a close affinal relative of an adjacent generation in the wider sense—may hint at a continuity of kinship ties or affinal links beyond death. This is because, as it can be argued with Elwin and Gaenszle, the *bhanjā*'s role is connected with the practice of cross-cousin marriage in which the sister's son ideally is the daughter's husband and son-in-law as well.

Apart from the continuity of affinal ties highlighted in the role of the *bhanjā,* a continuity of the local line—lineality—is prominent in the role of the eldest son as chief mourner. The last point seems to be illustrated by the *samādhi* of the deceased being built next to the other tombs of the family on their land, symbolizing the descent group. The *samādhi* built for each ancestor separately stands in contrast to the postulated 'lack of individuality in Brahmanical conceptions of the after-life' (Michaels 1999: 127–8) or the destruction of the individual after death in Hinduism, 'where nothing of the individual is preserved which could provide a focal symbol of group continuity' (Bloch and Parry 1982: 36). By retaining an individual *samādhi* the deceased might keep a limited individuality, which is comparable to some tribal groups where 'shape and size of the memory stones are selected according to certain calculations on the basis of male/female and social status considerations' (Nayak 2001: 44). Thus, the dead may keep individual aspects after the final burial, as well as after they have become ancestors.

Apart from these central relation sets, two oppositions are prominently expressed in life cycle rituals: adjacent versus alternate generations and *jāti* as 'other clan' *vs. banśa* as 'own clan'. As far as the former is concerned the Aghriā again deviate from the well-known north Indian standard. The principle of generation-sets explicitly expressed among the Aghriā during wedding customs and in kinship terminology and also typical for Middle Indian tribes, is found here as well. In this regard the Aghriā might have been influenced by the tribal groups of the region. The latter opposition contrasting kin and affines in abstract terms is expressed only on a subordinated village level, but is also encompassed on the higher level of caste understood as *jāti*.

Additionally, two major transformative processes dominate the life cycle. Purity and impurity are a concern during all life cycle rituals, including ancestor worship. Central parts of the life cycle, in particular between birth and marriage as well as from death to ancestry, are characterized by a striving for higher purity, which reaches its climax at the time of marriage. Contrary to impurity, which is a caste-related concern, we have said, auspiciousness or inauspiciousness is a domestic affair. Life cycle rituals are performed to ensure auspiciousness for the family, but in practice these rituals are characterized by auspicious as well as inauspicious symbols and conditions, the combination perhaps essential for a renewal within the cycle.

Finally, continuity is stressed from death to birth. Compared to north Indian peasant castes such as the Gujar observed by Raheja (1988: 147) no complete breaking of the relations with the ancestors is intended among the Aghriā, but rather a transition from one state to another. In the view of American Indians death is 'merely a change in residence' (Eggan 1950: 59-60). The same seems to be true among the Aghriā. Ancestors waiting to be reborn reside in their abode (*pitrlok, yamlok*) provided, of course, that the Aghriā are 'ripe' enough to become an ancestor and, therefore, may not have the fortune to leave the cycle of birth and rebirth. The time from birth to marriage is considered an essential process of ripening, brought to completion by the wedding. Thus, the life cycle is interlinked and synchronized in various ways and continuity is not only stressed at the time of death, the continuity of life as well as of the household is also emphasized throughout the life cycle—perhaps typical for peasant society.

NOTES

1. I omit presentations prior to a child's birth.
2. In one case I observed, it was the mother's mother who was present and offered gifts on behalf of her son.
3. The *māmu* may be a widower.
4. If there is no close *bhanjā* a distant, classificatory *bhanjā* will replace him.
5. Fuchs (1960: 337) noted that the obligations and role of a sister's son are more elaborate among Gond than Bhumia.
6. Fuchs (1960: 327ff) mentions sister's husband and father's sister's children as *nat*, but in his own kinship terminology (1960: 158ff) he distinguishes between elder sister's husband and younger sister's husband (the younger sister's husband being equated with sister's son, but somehow also with son and husband) and mentions a terminological equation between father's sister's children and mother's brother's children. Thus his terminology remains unsatisfactory the affinal content of the category *nat* becomes apparent.
7. Probably other cases could be cited, in which the *bhanjā* plays an important part in funeral rites as well, e.g. among Byansi from north-east Uttarakhand (N. Allen: personal communication).
8. Not by the son-in-law himself, who is always addressing him as *bāpā*/father, but by the brothers of the son-in-laws.
9. Kapadia (1996: 23) observes for non-Brahmin Tamils a girl having no close *māmu* may face immense difficulties to marry, since there is nobody to present the necessary gifts and to act in this central role.

10. Among Oriya Brahmin as well as among Gosain (considered to be Brahmin, acting as temple priests, but not as family priests) I heard very similar stories about a *boru* (initiation rituals and investment of the sacred thread). During the rituals the young Brahmin to be initiated is dressed like a beggar (*mangtāri*), who walks in a small procession along a road onto which his family priest has drawn three lines, which are known as *Lakṣman rekhā*. Near the line the mother's brother of the boy is waiting and has to stop him, before he crosses it. Usually the mother's brother asks his sister's son approaching the lines: 'Where are you going?' The sister's son then replies: 'My parents kicked me out. They have not arranged my marriage. I am becoming a *brahmachari*.' Subsequently the mother's brother promises to arrange a marriage for him and to bear the expenses. Thus marriage—probably the most decisive step in order to become a full social person and implicitly an ancestor—is conceptionalized as a responsibility of one's mother's brother.
11. Often in the earliest childhood the mothers sing songs to their children, in which her brother—or the *māmu-ghar* in general—figures prominently and is described as a person or place where the child will get good food. Thus these songs already indicate a caring *māmu*. However, in these songs the mother may also be expressing a yearning for her own family.
12. Otten (2000: 351) noted that among the Desia (or tribal) population in Koraput in cases of illness it is often healing experts in the village of the mother's brother who are consulted.
13. And in the father's sister's house provided she is living alone, because this does not hold true for the father's sister's husband's house. However, I came across a case where a father's sister stayed alone after her divorce.
14. I have not taken into consideration the social transformation of women by motherhood here.
15. Cases of remarriage have not been taken into consideration here.
16. The same is true for avoidance relationships.
17. Among the Magar there is no such an equation. Instead the categories *mama* and *bhanjā* extent over three generations each, but nevertheless there is the reciprocal set *mama*/*bhanjā*, which as such is comparable to the Middle Indian cases. And it is the *mama* who among Magar plays an essential role during weddings, he gives his daughter to his sister's son and helps to complete the transformation of his *bhanjā* into a full social person in a most direct way (the mother's brother is the wife's father according to the traditional Magar alliance system). See Oppitz (1991: 45ff, 76ff, 327ff).
18. There are other cases in north and south India in which a MB plays a vital role in relation to his ZS as chief mourner—often tying a turban on the latter's head in funeral rituals. See Galey (1990: 165) for Garhwal, Dumont (2000 [1957]: 276) for the Pramalai Kallar of Tamil Nadu, Raheja (1988: 155). However, in contrast to the cases mentioned here, the MB does not act in relation to his ZS as chief mourner, but in relation to the deceased as

his sister's son. Thus, the role of the mother's brother seems to be more related to the life cycle of the deceased, while in the other cases (Dumont, Raheja, Galey) the reintegration of the chief mourner and his life cycle are the central aspects.

19. I do not share Radcliffe Brown's view that the mother's brother is a 'male mother' (Radcliffe Brown 1978 [1924]: 87).
20. Eggan's (1950) data on the various matrilineal and matrilocal groups of the Western Pueblos of Arizona and New Mexico show a different picture. The mother's brother is the head of the household and the one most entitled to respect. His role in life cycle rituals of his sister's son is more or less confined to the wedding. In contrast, the father's sister plays a vital role being involved in all rituals from birth to death. Contrary to Indian terminologies among the Pueblos having Crow-type terminologies, the category father's sister is not organized on a principle of generation as one might expect (Eggan 1950: 22). In almost all groups described it is also the father's sister who fulfils the important task of washing the head of the deceased brother's son. An exception from the pattern just described are the Laguna (Eggan 1950: 259ff), among which the mother's brother plays a decisive role. He is not only the guardian of his but also the digger of his grave (in addition to the father's sister's role). A possible explanation for the deviation might be the prolonged Christian influence (Eggan 1950: 265). Among matrilineal and matrilocal groups the sister may fulfil the role of the closest affinal relative forming, as well as transforming, the social persona of her brother's son.
21. It is not quite clear if the *bhānji* had to be respected in the same way.
22. Contrary to Madan's (1998 [1975]: 295ff) opinion, the *māmu*'s role among the Aghriā does not appear to be an extension of his earlier role as wife's brother, since at least the wife's younger brother and elder sister's husband have a joking relationship.
23. Another small one is offered to Vishma Deb, slightly separated from the others.
24. For the exchange of gifts between grandparents and grandchildren in the context of death among Muslims in Pakistani Punjab see also Alvi (1999: 75)
25. Here commensality shifted in time.
26. One might also argue that the daughter's son of the deceased as *bhanjā* of the son of the deceased helps his *mama* who is the chief mourner to attain his new status—namely that of the head of the family after his father has passed away. Dumont (2000 [1957]: 275ff, 284–92) documented a similar case in south India. Among Pramalai Kallar the mother's brother (or his son in the role of the mother's brother) of the chief mourner plays a leading part in the funeral. It is the mother's brother who ties a turban on the head of his sister's son symbolically reintegrating him into society. However, such an explanation alone does not take into consideration that, according

to my interlocutors, the daughter's son helps his grandfather (mother's father) to reach heaven. He should eat the grandfather's cooked food at the *śrāddha*.

27. The ten *pinda* are meant for: for the head/forehead; nose; eyes; neck; chest; arms; legs; navel; hair and for the life or for everything (*sabu*).
28. However, after food has been served to the ancestors at the *śrāddha*, the son does not eat any share of it, since it is considered to be *dān*—a gift, which is given strictly in one direction.
29. In relation to Hinduism Bloch and Parry (1982: 37) speak of 'a total destruction of the physical body', but do not mention tombs. However they mention the clear influence of ascetic ideals in funerary customs of Hindus, which might be applied to the *samādhi* as well. *Samādhi* in some yoga traditions means ecstasy or a kind of trance in which the ascetic (*yogi*) does not realize any more that he is meditating. He becomes one with the object of his meditation and his individual consciousness becomes part of the cosmic self (Waterstone 1995: 87). But for the *yogi*, *samādhi* is also a way of departure from this world by 'burying himself alive' (Sharma 1988: 82). On the one hand the building of a *samādhi* known in the region only for the last decades and representing a rather recent change might by influenced by this ascetic ideal. On the other hand, memorial stones are common among tribal groups of the region, already in a process of change at the time of Elwin's research (1945: 109) when he noted a 'Hinduization' of tombs.
30. Fortes (1970: 89) observes: 'It appears that there is a tendency for interests, rights and loyalties to be divided on broadly complementary lines, into those that have the sanction of law or other public institutions for the enforcement of good conduct, and those that rely on religion, morality, conscience and sentiment for due observance. Where corporate descent groups exist the former seem to be generally tied to the descent group, the latter to the complementary line of filiation.' One might argue that within the life-cycle the complementary line may even be more important than the descent line, which seems to be related to cross-cousin marriage.
31. Applied to Figure 13 (left) in a simplified way these categories include the following relations starting from ego as **B2** being identical with brother = father's father = son's son; **A1:** mother's brother = wife's father = sister's son, etc.; **B1:** father = father's brother = son, etc. and **A2:** wife's brother = sister's husband = mother's father = daughter's son, etc. The tetradic model implying cross-cousin marriage resembles to or is abstracted from the Kariera of Australia having very similar kinship structures (see Radcliffe Brown 1931: 7ff, 15ff, 108).
32. The presence of a *jāti*, who is always a potential affine as well, might suggest the same idea.
33. The following roles might be mentioned here in relation to Figure 16: in

category B1: mother and daughter; in category A1: father's sister and in category A2: elder brother's wife.

34. According to some Aghriā the word *suhāsen* is derived from the Sanskrit word *suhāsini* 'always happy'. Similarly A. Das of Sambalpur University derives the word from *su* 'good' as also the root in *subha* 'auspicious' and *hasen* 'to laugh'—*suhāsen* thus meaning 'someone with good laughter'. Thus the word might indicate the joking relations existing between bride and groom on the one hand and *suhāsen* on the other. Some Aghriā simply translate it as bride's or groom's 'maids'.
35. It is also the elder brother's wife who should instruct the groom as far as the first night after the wedding is concerned.
36. Not the *purohit*.
37. Some Aghriā speculated that this custom might be a legacy of child marriages.
38. Otten (personal communication) presumes that among Rona of Koraput district a similar phenomenon is observable during high status weddings.
39. Fuchs usually speaks of a singular *suasa* and *suasin* though in some passages a plural is indicated. No such role is mentioned in Elwin's work on the Baiga.
40. The *suāsin* are involved in bringing soil from an anthill, carrying a *kalas* or lead bride or groom around the pole of the wedding altar. Elwin mentions two *dosi* who accompany the *suāsin* to an anthill to bring soil. We might speculate that the *dosi* (old man belonging to an adjacent generation) are opposed to the *suāsin* (young sisters, etc., belonging to groom's or bride's generation), but this must remain a speculation since Elwin—apparently not so much interested in kinship and kinship roles—does not provide detailed data on the matter. (Elwin 1939: 273ff).
41. In Malwa the male and female attendants of bride or groom—known as *khvansa* and *khvansi* respectively—are real, classificatory or ritual sisters (mother's or father's sister). See Mayer (1960: 231).
42. In some communities like the Māḷi only married persons can act as *suhāsen* —thus unmarried grandchildren or widows are excluded. I was told that among Chamār *suhāsen* must have passed an initiation (*boru*) in order to be able to become *suhāsen*, while a Tūrī told me, that *suhāsen* have to be unmarried. In other communities like the Aghriā or Gauḍ marriage is not essential to act as *suhāsen*, i.e. unmarried granddaughters may fulfil this role, though widows seem to be generally excluded.

    In general sometimes people, e.g. Malār being asked about the custom of *suhāsen* just answered: 'we are doing it like the Aghriā'. In such cases people might consider it a question of prestige for them and may intend to claim the performance of high status rituals. However, since I tried to cross-check it with as many interlocutors as possible and since my interview partners did indicate differences to the Aghriā customs—e.g. regarding the question if *suhāsen* have to be married or not—I think it is quite safe to conclude, that the custom is indeed widespread and not only a phenomenon of the Aghriā. Nevertheless, a considerable change might have occurred as far as wedding rituals are concerned and some Muṇḍā and Kisān interlocutors told me that the *teilabhiṣek*—the custom of anointing bride and groom—has been a recent innovation (as the *barāt* etc.). However, they also argued that in former times there have been *suhāsen*, who used to accompany bride and groom.

43. Babb (1975: 83–4) argues that apart from a beautification the anointing of groom and bride should be understood as a worship of god and goddess, which might be another aspect of the ritual.
44. Some of these ideas such as fertility, protection and transformation might also be expressed in the role of the mother hinting at the opposition male versus female found in wedding rituals as well.
45. Once I asked my interlocutors, whether a mother's brother (MB) belonging to a different clan (other than ego) could act as a *jāti* and my interlocutors denied that. However, they also pointed out, that close mother's brothers in almost all cases do not reside in one's own village and therefore the question does not arise.
46. For a similar opposition *bondhu—kutumb* see also McDougal (1963: 151ff).
47. For the *gotra*-rule see Skoda (2002: 28–9).
48. The Gadaba model is simplified in the sense that only the marriage categories—marriageable *bondhu* versus non-marriageable *bhai*—are considered here. Other categories more important for funerals such as *moitr* are neglected.
49. Pregnant women should not start any journey on *Sankrānti, Uāns* or *Prati Padā*, but if they have to, they should take a leaf of the *jām* tree while passing it and keep it during the journey.
50. I term the life cycle as conventional here, in opposition to the ideal life-cycle as formulated in the *Brahmanas*, which includes the stage of world-renouncer. I concentrate on life cycles in practice, during which Aghriā predominantly remain within the domestic group. One's purity might also be increased temporarily by fasting or by a vegetarian diet, but such individual factors are not my concern here.
51. If a temple is purified and consecrated it is called *pratiṣṭhā* and I have never heard any Aghriā calling it a marriage, although central elements such as the necessity of a married couple circling around the temple are identical. Another case in point is the inauguration or purification (*pratiṣṭhā*) of a *samādhi* after death, when the son circles it seven times. At the moment I can only speculate why these cases are not described as marriage—perhaps the gods or ancestors are involved in a more direct way.
52. The custom is certainly in decline and there are not many Aghriā left who have actually seen a mango tree marriage themselves. In case of mango

tree marriage rituals might have been mixed with another type of tree marriage for widowers, but it seems clear that purification stands at the centre of both rituals—either for the fruits or the pond.

53. Narayanan considers Śrīvaiṣṇava ritual and literature apparently based on Tamil sources.
54. During my stay in the village an elder Kandh passed away.,According to the Brahmin the time of death would have required a *puṣkarā* ritual, but the son decided against it—presumably for financial reasons. Even weeks later his mother/wife of the deceased told me, how much she regretted the decision of her son and she was still trying to convince him to perform the necessary rituals—though without success.
55. Among the Aghriã there is no clear-cut distinction between the soul (*atmān*) and the ghost (*pret*). Sometimes both are combined in the term *pret-ātmān*, which people use to describe the fate of the deceased. In contrast to that the term *bhut-pret* is sometimes coined when evil forces attack people. *Bhut* stands for evil spirits in general.
56. Sometimes the *sajja dān* is given to a high status Brahmin (Bennett 1983: 104), sometimes to a funeral Brahmin, who is lower in status (Conzelmann 1996: 367) and sometimes, in case of Brahmins highest in status, to a wife-taker (Dumont (1998 [1966]: 96).
57. Not all priests of the Aghriã shared this opinion and in one case an Aghriã argued that unmarried Aghriã also became ancestor (*pitru*) but are not remembered during the rituals for the ancestors and so do not become full ancestors.
58. In all rituals ancestors get served special food such as cakes prepared of *khuda*—small pieces of ground rice. It is believed that the cake known as *khuda piṭha* offered once a year during the dark side of Aswinã remains in the stomach of an ancestor for a year. However, unlike tribal customs, no alcohol is served to the ancestors.
59. In a landlord family I observed this tradition was discontinued in the 1980s.
60. The family of a wealthy landlord patronized the religious movement of Mahima Dharma at one point of time and invited male or female ascetics—known as Baba and Mata respectively—to stay in the family. Thus, for several years a Baba and a Mata used to live together with this family. A daughter of the landlord was particularly fond of the Baba—and vice versa. Thus they played and spent much time together. In contrast, the daughter rather annoyed the Mata. Later the daughter had a son—known to be very patient, calm, and supportive to his mother. Her family is convinced that the Baba is reborn in this son. A daughter was born to the landlord's daughter, who is slightly mentally disturbed and demands her mother's attention. Some people say that she is the rebirth of the Mata, now disturbing the landlord's daughter.
61. The first rice in this case should not be given by any specific person (like

the *māmu* in case of a child), but it should be a close relative or *ātmiya lok* —a person who is related to the soul, sharing all joy and pain, for example, the eldest son. If there is no Brahmin to perform the ritual one can also mix Ganga–water and parboiled rice (*chāul*) in a pot and hold it towards the sky thus giving it symbolically to a Brahmin and Dharma Devtā. This gift (*dān*) is considered as rather inauspicious and impure and should be given to a lower Brahmin (*dānuā* Brahmin). The family priest or *purohit* would refuse to accept it. It should not be given to a *bhanjā* (ZS) either, because it resembles the *mrutyu sajja dān*.

62. For *tarpan* among the Muṇḍā see also Roy (1970 [1912]: 218) and Choudhury (1977: 41). Among the Pandits of Kashmir *tarpan* seems to symbolize water offered for the ancestors (Madan 2001 [1987]: 24, 35, 136).
63. The Sambalpuri term and concept *jiu* (Oriya: *jiban*) can be translated, e.g. as life-energy, as life-spirit, as soul or shade. However, I consider the first two translations to be the most appropriate.

CHAPTER 7

Amalgamation of Cycles: Lakṣmī and Khuṇṭ as Cultural Symbols

7.1. AGRICULTURAL CYCLE, RITUAL CYCLE, AND LIFE CYCLE INTERWOVEN

When Aghriā meet on the streets or elsewhere quite often reflect the cycles—in particular the agricultural and life cycles. If they meet coincidentally in January and the following months, they talk about weddings, as the marriage season is about to start. Friends and relatives then might exchange the latest news about arranged marriages, about relations newly established and so on. In the time prior to that—beginning around October—matters relating to the harvest dominate small talk. How much rice has been harvested? Has the process of threshing already been completed? How high is the paddy price? And even earlier in the year—in August/September—the transplanting and the damages caused by insects and fungus figure prominently in discussions, and a distressed farmer might claim 'My field is totally gone!' indicating expected losses. Before transplanting sowing and the rain are some of the most important things on a peasant's mind and figure highly on the public agenda.

In this chapter I am going to examine how the ritual, agriculture and the life cycle as such are linked, interwoven, and amalgamated. As indicated above, marriages are celebrated in the hot season after the harvest—a period without major agricultural work, when peasants are free to solemnize weddings. Thus the marriage season as a major life cycle ritual and the paddy harvest as perhaps the most crucial period of the agricultural year are synchronized in the sense of Iteanu (1999) within a single time frame. In addition, all cycles are amalgamated in a certain cultural symbol which appears and reappears in various disguises throughout the cycles and brings the generalized structure of this converging tribal and caste society to light. In the following pages, I would like to present two of the numerous amalgamating symbols: on the one hand the goddess Lakṣmī and on the other the *khuṇṭ* or wooden posts. Other symbols like the ancestors being welcomed during one fortnight, taking care of fields, and being reborn within the same family—may be added as well.

SYMBOLIC DIMENSIONS OF LAKṢMĪ—THE GODDESS WITHIN THE CYCLES

Lakṣmī—Goddess of wealth, prosperity, abundance, but also of beauty appears as bride within the life cycle and as rice within the agricultural cycle as well as being worshipped together with her consort Viṣṇu or Jagannāth. Because of her ambivalent character—a protective and generous mother as well as a vindictive and even destructive wife, fruits of the earth and earth itself—she stands for a semantic field rather than a single idea. The basic values expressed by the goddess, such as fertility and property but also her ambivalent and inclusive nature may help to promote her advance within a society on a tribal frontier.

Worshipping the goddess

Among the Aghria no goddess is worshipped as intensely as Lakṣmī. Though Manglā is also worshipped once a week for the entire month of Chaitra, preparations for Lakṣmī are clearly more elaborate. Moreover, Lakṣmī is worshipped not only every Thursday in the month of Mārgaśīrṣa, but also throughout the year whenever a Thursday falls on a tenth day of a fortnight. Such a combination—her day of the week coinciding with her very special number 'ten'—is known as *Su Dasā Brata*. Additionally, a *Lakṣmī Pūjā* is performed on Akshya Trutīyā and on Nuā Khāi, before the first rice—the new rice—is eaten, and on the day of the *Grām Śrī Pūjā*. On the latter occasion, however, not all Aghriā families perform the ritual; it is done only by the wife of an Aghriā-Gauntiā or headman in the yard (*duār*) of her house before some white paddy, already worshipped, is brought to the shrine of the village goddess (Grām Śrī). Apart from this, Lakṣmī and Viṣṇu are worshipped in a ritual known as *Ām Gundi Pūjā*—performed prior to the eating of the first mangos. The essential elements of worshipping Lakṣmī are usually the same, but *Lakṣmī Pūjā* is most lavishly performed during the month of Mārgaśīrṣa. Hence an account of such a ritual in a wealthy Gauntiā house will now be described.

LAKṢMĪ PŪJĀ

Women begin preparations for the *Lakṣmī Pūjā* on every Thursday of Mārgaśīrṣa, on the previous day. Flower garlands are bound, and water lilies (*kain*) are arranged (no lotus flowers are found in this area). Above every door or entrance gate ten mango-leaves are hung. Not only is the throne of Lakṣmī—the Lakṣmī-*khatli*—as part of a house shrine cleaned, but also the *tulsī chaur*, the shrine of the sacred Goddess Tulsī[1]—and the house in general. The house is whitewashed. All places for rituals, including the entrance of and the threshing floor, are plastered with cow dung.

In the evenings of those Wednesdays pictures known as *jhoti* are drawn. These auspicious symbols are found particularly on the threshing floor (*khalā*), at the entrance of the house (*khoel*), and inside the house including the *pūjā* room. The motives are: lotus, shells, fish, footprints of cattle, and footprints of the goddess herself. The Goddess' footprints lead into the house. Inside, abstract patterns dominate as *jhoti*, drawn by women. Sometimes in front of the altar a *jhoti* with sixteen footprints—known as *solā kathi* is drawn. Additionally the goddess should be worshipped with *chāul* (*aruā*) of the present harvest, which should be ground the day before the ritual. For the ritual a bunch of white paddy ears (*saru* or *atisaru*) called *meṇṭa* is prepared and occasionally covered in a red cloth. The bunch—looking like a broom—is placed at the altar and worshipped as Lakṣmī.[2] It is made solely for the ritual purpose. In one case, I observed that it was made by a daughter-in-law of the house. The *meṇṭa* is set in a *mān* (metal pot to measure paddy) filled with white paddy. Sometimes a second *mān* is used on which three ears (*kheḍ*) of paddy and ten blades *duba* grass are placed.

Dietary restrictions have to be observed before and during the ritual. On Wednesday *ghī* should be eaten instead of oil. In addition, only *aruā-chāul* is allowed. Non-vegetarian food is forbidden. Furthermore, a particular mixture known as *gandhā anlā* is prepared by women and used to anoint themselves on a Thursday before the ritual. Nothing should be prepared in the fire like sweet corn or *khai* on a Thursday. No *murhi* should be eaten. However, it is proper to prepare the food in water. The rules for brides and newly married women are particularly strict on this day: they should eat after their families and husbands. It is not tolerable to eat before one's husband on this day, as on others. Cotton is not cut on this day. Women do not use combs and their hair is bound only with a loose knot, having been washed on the Wednesday. Parents should avoid beating their children. Nobody should quarrel.

On Thursday the women take a bath well before sunrise and the first cockcrow, and wear white clothes because Lakṣmī is said to like white. However, the clothes are not completely white like the clothes of widows, but have small patterns on them such as blue flowers. Then they—most importantly the daughters-in-law—perform a first little ritual at the entrance of the house (*khoel*). There is a belief that on this night Lakṣmī moves around on the road. Accordingly, in the first ritual a *namaskār* is made to the Goddess. She is invited to bring wealth into the house. Contrary to the worship of other goddesses, one finds a clearly marked movement from the *khoel*—the main entrance and liminal place between outside and inside—into the home. At the entrance *dhūpa* and *dīpa*, a *kalaś* and flowers are offered on the *jhoti* that has been drawn before it. Auspicious sounds are produced with a gong and a shell. Occasionally the women sing *hulhuli* and footprints of Lakṣmī leading into the house are offered *ṭikā*, rice and flowers.

A first ritual is then performed inside the *pūjā* room. A daughter-in-law acting as main functionary reads from the *Mārgaśīrṣa Māsa Mātā Mahālakṣmīnka Gurubār Brata.*[3] In the text first the goddess is invoked by various names and epithets mother of the world (*lokmātā*), Ṭhākurāṇī —a title frequently used for village and earth goddesses—Mahāmāyā (a name associated with Goddess Durgā), and as Mahālakṣmī. Subsequently a seat (*āsana*) is offered her and she is bathed. Additionally, *pañchāmrut*—a mixture of curd, milk, clarified butter, honey and molasses—is presented with symbolic dress material, flower garlands (*puśpamālā*), a symbolic ornament of lotus flower, and sandal paste. Lamps are lit, including a candlestick with ten lights. *Dhūpa*, a gong, and a shell are used and the *hulhuli* sound is produced. Two radish and two sugarcane plants are offered as prescribed in the text. In front of an altar or house shrine on a banana leaf, ten kinds of fruits such as custard apple, bananas, guava, pomegranate, sweet potato, papaya, apple, mosambi, sugar cane, and coconut are given. The fruits may vary, but ten kinds should be offered. They are eaten as *praśād* later.

After this ritual, sweets and food are prepared for the goddess in the kitchen. Sweets known as *mandā*—dough filled with coconut and fried in *ghī*—are very popular on this occasion. Ten sweets or *neibedya* are offered to the Goddess in another ritual with *dhūpa*, *dīpa*, and auspicious sounds. Subsequently the Tulsī shrine is worshipped with the same ritual items just mentioned. Sweets and fruits are offered here as well. A *kalaś* is placed in front of the shrine. *Oum*- and *chanda-bindu* symbols are drawn and *ṭikā* is given to the basil plant before the women circle the shrine seven times.

Another small ritual is performed at the threshing floor—again on the *jhoti* drawn there. Water is sprinkled before flowers, *duba* grass, *buro* leaves, *anlā* leaves and *dhān* are placed there. *Dīpa* and *dhūpa* are circled. Then the piles of rice are worshipped with flowers, milk, *chāul* and *pañchāmrut*. *Ṭikā* and *chanda-bindu* are drawn with vermilion on the piles. The rice is regarded as Lakṣmī. Additional *ṭikā* are put on the footprints of the goddess, bringing her into the house again.

Back in the house food prepared in the meantime is brought to the altar and offered to the goddess. Every kind of food should be offered ten times, for example ten times *kiri*, ten times *dāl*, etc. However, it is not obligatory to offer ten different kinds of food. Once more the arrival of the Goddess is praised; flowers are offered; the goddess is saluted (*praṇām*), and a prayer of forgiveness the *Mārgaśīrṣa Māsa Mātā Mahālakṣmīnka Gurubār Brata* text is read out. Afterwards the sacred *Lakṣmī Purāṇ* is read.

SU DASĀ BRATA

The ritual is celebrated if the tenth day of the light side (*ujwala pakṣ*) happens to fall on a Thursday. This combination usually occurs up to three times a year. On this day a strict vegetarian diet should be kept. Furthermore people should not cut their hair or shave. In the morning a ritual for Lakṣmī is performed at the house shrine by a

Lākṣmī Pūjā at a house shrine

daughter-in-law—as in the *Lakṣmī Pūjā* already described. On the altar are placed a *kalaś*; ten types of fruits, lamps, five types of white and five kinds of red flowers, but not hibiscus; *duba* grass; *buro* leaves; sandalwood paste; *supāri; pañchāmrut* (see above); a special cake (*mandā pithā*—10 pieces); *chāul*; *brata;* and also the book, *Su Dasā Brata*. Additionally, the shell and gong produce auspicious sounds, while the women may add their own *hulhuli*. A daughter-in-law binds a saffron-coloured thread around her right upper arm with some *duba* grass wrapped in a mango leaf with eight rice corns. She fasts the entire day. The *praśād* is given only to close family members, i.e. not to cousin-brothers (FBS, etc.), to any uncles (FB), to married daughters or married sisters. The latter may perform a separate ritual in the house if they are present.

At the end of the ritual the already mentioned *Su Dasā Brata* is read. Since family members told me the story from memory, I decided to present this shortened account here:[4] King Vikrami Ditya had several ministers. Among them the prime minister, whose wife performed the *brata*. Once the wife of the prime minister accidentally lost her *brata*, and was disappointed. She stopped eating and drinking. Her husband asked her what had happened. His wife explained. Her husband was worried and asked where he could get the *brata* for her. At the same time the queen was performing the *brata*. She had the *brata* tied around her arm and the wife of the prime minister told her husband that he should get the *brata* from her. The prime minister went to king and asked for the *brata* and told him that he would step down if he would not get it. The king promised to give him the *brata* and went to the queen. She refused to give it but he took it forcibly and gave it to the prime minister. Afterwards the king lost everything including his wealth and kingdom; his son went mad. He became an ordinary labourer, the queen a servant in a family of Brahmins. Once the Brahmin family performed the *brata* and the queen, who had been turned into a servant, was very interested in performing it too. They allowed her to do it and subsequently she managed to get back everything she had lost. The people in the kingdom started to search for their king with the help of an elephant loaded with gold and water. The person over whom the water was poured whould become king. The elephant poured the water over the old king after the queen had performed the *brata*. The king got back his kingdom. Now all women perform the *brata*.

AKSHYA TRUTĪYĀ (THE FIRST SOWING OF RICE) AND *NABĀNNA/NUĀ KHĀI* (EATING THE NEW RICE)

The ritual has to be celebrated on the third day of the light side of the month of Baisākha. *Akshya* means 'never ending', hinting at the permanent character of the ritual and the agricultural cycle renewed by the first sowing every year. The seeds—given by the Gauntiā and blessed by the village goddess in the earlier ritual are brought to the field before sunrise. Ideally nobody should see this happen. An astrologer is consulted to decide the exact time and direction for the walk to the fields. He also decides which family member should perform the ritual. The ritual is also known as *Dhān Muthi* or throwing of seeds (*dhān* = paddy, *muthi* = fist—hinting at the seven handful of paddy in the fist in the act of throwing).

In the evening before the first sowing a ritual is performed inside the house, in an inner yard or inside the kitchen facing eastward. During the ritual a plough with *luhā* (iron rod), *jueḍ* (yoke), *koeḍ* (hoe) and *mān* (unit to measure paddy), a *tāmi* and a new *burni* basket for sowing are worshipped. Additionally, a *kalas*, flowers, *aruā chāul*; milk; *pañchāmrut*; *soltā* (long cotton lamps); *dhūp*; sandalwood paste; vermilion and fire are required. The *mān* and *tāmi* are filled with paddy and regarded as Lakṣmī. They are decorated with flowers painted with rice powder paste. Additionally *hantā* is needed, and *aruā chāul* is ground for the seven handprints, which are applied to the eastern wall inside the kitchen. Afterwards the paddy is brought into the field.

Nabānna—the Sambalpuri name and Oriya *Nuā Khāi* refer to the first rice of the season. Usually the house is newly painted or at least cleaned before the festival and all family members should wear new clothes. It is the time when the harvest begins and the first, earliest variety is ripe. *Nabānna* is celebrated on the fifth day of the light side of the month Bhādraba—a day after *Gaṇeś Pūjā*. It can be performed only after the *Bihuḍā Pūjā* for the village goddess has been completed. Invitations should be sent to the family members even if the day is fixed and well known. Two to three days before *Nuā Khāi*, the rice is collected. The first rice—the earliest variety eaten on this occasion known as *sariā dhān*—should be ground in a manually worked grinder known as *ḍhenki* (not in a electric mill, etc.), which should be cleaned with cow dung before using it. The *sariā dhān* is only peeled, not parboiled. It is mixed with curd, sugar, honey, *ghī* and milk—a mixture also known as *nabānna*.

Before eating the rice, the women perform a ritual for Lakṣmī believed to be present in the new rice. In the same ritual, however, Brahma, Viṣṇu, Śiva, Samlei, a banyan-tree, a *pipal*-tree, the rice fields, the *tulsī chaur* and the cattle-shed are also worshipped.[5] The entire family should be present on this day—including the servants (in particular the *Guti*). If someone is unable to come, the ritual eating of the first rice might be delayed until *Daśarā*. Before starting to eat, everyone gives himself a *ṭikā* with the rice mixture. After eating the new rice, juniors ask for the blessings of the elders of the entire village.

Goddess Lakṣmī as bride and wife

In the context of marriage Lakṣmī is permanently present, and the central aspects of fertility as well as Lakṣmī's relation to her husband Nārāyaṇ (Viṣṇu) are highlighted. At the wedding altar Lakṣmī appears together with her husband in the form of two earthen pots known as *kalas kuṇḍi*. One of these, filled with paddy, symbolizes Lakṣmī, while a pot full of water denotes Nārāyaṇ. The outer part of Lakṣmī's pot is additionally smeared with cow dung, onto which single paddy corns are pinned—both are considered auspicious. Cow dung itself is frequently linked to Lakṣmī (Zimmer 1947: 91). Both pots are carried by the *suhāsen* in all processions in the respective villages of bride and groom, for example the bringing of soil from the shrine of the village goddess. While other gods such the *kalyāṇī khuṇṭ* remain at the altar, the ceremonies are dominated by the divine couple of Lakṣmī and Nārāyaṇ. The opposition Nārāyaṇ and water versus Lakṣmī and paddy/corn/fruits at the altar hints at a common theme in the mythology of Lakṣmī. In an early association of Lakṣmī with Indra (Kinsley 1987: 25), the female earth goddess is opposed to, but also simultaneously united with, a male sky and rain god. In this symbiotic relationship the rain is said to fertilize the earth—an aspect further stressed by Indra's phallic connotations and his identification with the plough (ibid.).[6] Apart from a rather abstract presence of the goddess in the form of rice, the bride and groom are also identified with Lakṣmī and Nārāyaṇ—or Janaki (Sitā) and Rām—respectively in the words a Brahmin recites during the circumambulation of the fire.[7]

An analogy between water, Indra/Nārāyaṇ, and husband on the one hand, and rice, Lakṣmī, and wife on the other may be expressed in another peculiar belief. According to this, while boiling rice, married women are not allowed to add water. If additional water is required to boil the rice properly, an Aghriā man or an unmarried woman has to be called to do so. If the married women added the water themselves, it is believed, they would become widows. Though it is not expressed as such by the Aghriā, perhaps it is intended to keep the male aspect in the form of water or rain separated from the female aspect in the form of rice.

Furthermore, in another vital step of the wedding ceremonies bride and groom exchange garlands. The garland for the groom should be made of *mālti*-flowers (a symbol of Viṣṇu) and basil (*tulsī*), a manifestation of Lakṣmī. It is also associated with Brundābāti.[8]

Lakṣmī is not only represented by the earthen pot of paddy at the altar, the bride herself signifies Lakṣmī. During the wedding ritual bride and groom—being continuously purified—are elevated to a divine as well as royal status, expressed by a crown (*makuṭ*) made of at least three leaves of a date palm tree which is offered to them and the pots standing for Lakṣmī and Nārāyaṇ, Kalyāṇī khuṇṭ, the *mahuā* trees, and other gods believed to be present at the altar. The crown symbolizes high status: and bride and groom do not have to show their respect to any elder relative, only to the priest. A fusion of royal and divine status may be inherent in the goddess, since Lakṣmī herself as goddess of wealth symbolizes not only prosperity and property as such, but also ruling power and majesty. The royal tie is to be seen specifically in her name Śrī applied to kings, an in the elephant as her essential attribute figuring in royal titles such as Gajapati (Lord of the elephants).

A very clear analogy between bride, rice, and Lakṣmī is also found among the Gadaba in Koraput (personal communication, P. Berger) and communities in Bastar (Gregory 2003: 7). In these cases rice, conceived as bride, is brought in a procession from the fields to the threshing floor or house. The same, however, is not ritually enacted among the Aghriā or any other community in the immediate vicinity.

While Lakṣmī may be vindictive she is also a protective mother. The element of protection is perhaps best documented at the time of marriage, when the *suhāsen* bind a thread consisting of seven single threads around the wrist of the bride and groom prior to their first meeting. The thread called *kankan moer*[11] is soaked in turmeric and is knotted ten times in honour of Lakṣmī—the number ten is specifically related to her. Such a thread has associations with *rākhī* or *jiūntiā*—threads bound most importantly by sisters to their brothers offering a transcendental protection after having fasted. The thread remains around the wrist during all ceremonies from the *barāt* (procession of the groom's wedding party) until the arrival of the couple in the groom's house later on—that is, during the whole transitional and transformational period.

The idea that the bride and Lakṣmī are connected continues after the wedding in the specific meaning of *lakṣmī* as auspicious. In contrast to *subha* which is understood as auspicious in general, *lakṣmī* is applied to auspicious persons only. A bride is expected to embody auspiciousness and to bring luck to her husband's family. She is also supposed to be obedient and inaudible. If a bride in her new family walks noisily, runs around, speaks too loudly, or even shouts, people say she is *lakṣmī chaḍā* (without *lakṣmī*) or *alakṣmīen* (a woman unlike Lakṣmī). To eat noisily, or too much—-particularly as a guest —is also considered *alakṣmīen* (for women) or *alakṣmīā* (for men). In addition, bringing bad luck to a family in the sense of starting to quarrel, is *alakṣmī*—corresponding to early accounts of Lakṣmī, in which her sister Alakṣmī is said to embody misfortune and inauspiciousness expressed in poverty and hunger (Zimmer 1947).

Goddess Lakṣmī as rice

Lakṣmī is identified with rice in all its forms: paddy, peeled rice, boiled rice, etc. She thus embodies fertility and abundance in addition to her relation to the earth. The importance of rice is perhaps best exemplified by the multitude of its categories and by the fact that rice—usually in form of *aruā chāul*, but also in form of paddy—is used in all rituals. An identification of Lakṣmī with rice is symbolized on the one hand by ritual activities in which paddy, placed at the house altar in form of a *meṇṭa,* is said to represent Lakṣmī, and on the other hand by applying her attributes to utensils to measure rice. *Mān*, a paddy measure is decorated with elephants. In a wider sense Lakṣmī offers everything necessary for life; and everything required to survive is Lakṣmī. In this sense Lakṣmī is not only rice as staple food, but also land. She provides for the continuity of life. Even a modern tractor may appear as Lakṣmī, since it guarantees wealth. Additionally an equation of rice and abundance with daughters and potential brides may be expressed by adding the names of daughters of the house to baskets in which all kinds of food are stored and paddy is measured.

Certain restrictions are observed at work in the rice field. Some Aghriā maintain that one should not go into the fields wearing shoes, which would be an insult to Lakṣmī. Menstruating women do not work in the fields, but many people also acknowledge that most people do not care about such rules in practice—to the extent that people even defecate in the fields. Therefore, a field is not considered a pure place. Fertility and purity are not necessarily connected.[9] Similarly paddy on the threshing floor should not be cleaned with an ordinary broom (*baḍhun*) which would be considered inauspicious and a serious insult to the Goddess. However, while sweeping the threshing floor as such may be inauspicious and a broom impure, certain specific brooms made of *biren* grass, known as *biren baḍhun*, are allowed.[10]

An identification between Lakṣmī and rice is also demonstrated by the common idea that all rice which has grown in the field has to be brought into the house. You simply cannot leave Lakṣmī outside, you have to bring her into your home. If due to insects or fungus the harvest is reduced, the rice should nevertheless be cut—even if in the end the wages for the labourers are higher than the profit of the landlord. In practice, however, not all Aghriā can do so being forced to calculate harder by a falling rice price. But even these businessmen know that to leave Lakṣmī in the field is disrespectful. In the same way, the smallest quantity of rice that falls on the road during transport to the house is collected.

While ideally Lakṣmī should be always brought into the house and should never leave it, in practice paddy has to be sold. However, not all is sold since Lakṣmī should never fully leave. Thus, in one incident a new daughter-in-law of a Gauntiā family rushed to sweep the ground and to hand over the paddy to a trader. But he and the family members immediately reminded her that Lakṣmī should not leave the house and therefore she should sweep only after the trader has left. The remaining paddy—though formally owned by the trader—should be kept in the house until the trader comes around for the next purchase. Also, paddy sold to a trader is never carried via the threshing floor—even if it would be a short-cut to the waiting lorry—that would mean selling Lakṣmī.

An identification of Lakṣmī as rice and as bride is obvious in her day of the week: Thursday (*Gurubār*). On a Thursday a bride should never leave her house after marriage. Thus dates for a marriage are carefully arranged. A newly married couple may leave the house of the bride, where the wedding takes place, on any day except Thursday. Lakṣmī—the bride—should never leave her house on her very own day. Even after marriage a daughter or married couple should avoid leaving the house on Thursdays. Similarly rice or paddy is never sold on a Thursday. Even less religious-minded Aghriā keep these restrictions in Lakṣmī's month Mārgaśīrṣa. Additionally, on certain auspicious days such as Sankrānti and specifically Makar Sankrānti it is inappropriate to sell paddy.

The ambivalence of Lakṣmī

Lakṣmī stands or sits on a lotus. According to Kinsley (1987: 21) the lotus symbolizes on the one hand 'vegetative growth that has distilled the life-giving power of the waters into embodied life'. On the other hand it represents purity and spiritual power. However, one also has to note that the lotus—though it blossoms above the water—is nevertheless rooted in mud. While Kinsley (ibid.) argues that Lakṣmī remains 'completely uncontaminated by the mud', Zimmer (1947: 90–1) pointed out that mud (*kardama*) is in fact one of her two sons, and the lotus may also be considered as the gate to the womb of the universe. Thus Lakṣmī on the lotus may stay somehow aloof and pure, but her muddy roots remain dubious. Such ambivalence is reflected in attitudes towards rice fields, as we have seen.

Iconographical considerations aside, Lakṣmī is usually characterized as a benevolent and benign goddess. Thus, Kinsley (1987: 28) noted, 'As Viṣṇu's wife, Lakṣmī loses her fickle nature. As the great cosmic king's queen she is depicted as a model Hindu wife, loyal and submissive to her husband.'

And Khanna pointed out:

> Although there are innumerable goddesses worshipped in India, the mythologies of the epic heroines Parvati, Sita, Lakshmi and Savitri provide the prime examples of the ideal women. These goddesses have been referred to as Shaktis of their male partners and are cast as mortal and divine figures. They are married to a God. As wives they are solely dependent on their husbands and never break away from the bonds of control imposed by them. They have no special stories attributed to them nor any sovereign authority to call their own. They are partial Shaktis. In later Hinduism, these goddesses emerge as classical stereotypes and provide the feminine ideals of womanhood. (Khanna 1999: 87)

Contrary to this I argue that protective and benevolent aspects are certainly incorporated, but Lakṣmī may also be angry and vindictive, taking revenge, or even being destructive—features not related to ideal wives. These aspects are found in the *Lakṣmī Purāṇ*.

LAKṢMĪ–PURĀṆ (*MĀṆABASĀ*)

As the final part of the *Lakṣmī Pūjā*, the *Lakṣmī Purāṇ* is read by the women of the house. The reading usually takes around an hour. Central elements of the Lakṣmī cult are found in this sacred text.[11]

Lakṣmī is praised as Mother in the text, as guardian of all property and fortune, as worshipped by all women.[12] With the consent of Jagannāth, she visits the earth in the early morning of Thursday, prior to boiling food for her husband. She comes to see the house, which is not cleaned properly and she tells the Brahmin lady how to perform her worship. The rules she gives include among many other things the worship of rice, the avoidance of meat and fish, a taboo on ploughing on Sankrānti, the wearing of white clothes during the *pūjā*, an avoidance of beating the children, as well as an avoidance of sleeping naked. During her visit to several houses she finds women still asleep: in none of these houses is her worship being performed properly except in the house of a Chaṇḍāla lady, who properly fulfils all the prescribed rules. Impressed by this 'Untouchable' woman, Lakṣmī enters her house and promises her a happy life without worries and hardships. Balaram, elder brother of Jagannāth, comes to know about Lakṣmī's visit and convinces his brother to leave his wife. When she returns in the morning to boil rice. Jagannāth sends her away—considering her an 'Untouchable'. Subsequently Lakṣmī predicts that Jagannāth will not get any rice for twelve years; he will be poor, without rice, water, or clothes. Viśwakarma constructs a new palace for Lakṣmī, who—supported by her servants—removes all food and items from Jagannāth's house including his bed. Without rice, Jagannāth and Balaram are forced to beg, but Lakṣmī with the help of Saraswati influences the tongue of the people, and they refuse to give anything to them. Both are scolded as thieves instead. Later, an old lady recognizes both as Brahmins and boils some rice for them, but the pot miraculously disappears and she realizes that both men are against Lakṣmī. Therefore she throws them out of her home. Balaram tells Jagannāth that he should not care about caste, since they will die if they do not get food. Still later they meet an ascetic, whom they ask for rice. The ascetic sends them to the sea for rice and water, but Lakṣmī heats the sand, so that they cannot walk on the beach. Finally they reach Lakṣmī's palace as beggars. Via some servants Lakṣmī inquires if they, as Brahmins, would accept something from her. In their reply Jagannāth and Balaram ask for separate dishes in order to prepare their own food. Lakṣmī contemplates and realizes that if the men cook for themselves, they do not need women any longer. Therefore she asks Agni, the fire god, to prevent a lighting of the fire at the hearth. Thus Jagannāth and Balaram have to eat Lakṣmī's food in her house—regardless of her caste. Balaram—though surprised not to find any man in the house and fearing for his life—decides to eat, and likes the food. The goddess—via a servant—inquires about the marriage of both brothers and Jagannāth starts telling his story. The servant replies that Jagannāth has gone mad throwing his wife out of his home, since without a wife a man is poor. Jagannāth and Balaram realize their mistake. Jagannāth enters Lakṣmī's room where she waits for him to wash his feet. He tells his wife that he now clearly sees Lakṣmī as mother of the world and promises to her that Brahmins and low communities will eat together. After this promise Lakṣmī returns to Jagannāth. Together with her wealth, fortune, and happiness return as well.

Thus the *Lakṣmī Purāṇ* demonstrates the power of the goddess. Her husband Jagannāth or Viṣṇu/Govinda and his brother Balaram are reduced to the status of starving beggars and thieves—totally powerless without his wife/brother's wife, upon whom they utterly depend. Finally Jagannāth has to agree to Lakṣmī's visit on earth including all houses and consents once more at the end of the Purāṇ. Thus, Lakṣmī's revenge by removing food and everything else from the palace, is successful. Without her there is no prosperity: as Marglin (1989: 182) remarks, Lakṣmī robs the supreme sovereign Jagannāth of his sovereignty. Thus, Lakṣmī is certainly bound in marriage and is presented in the text as an ideal wife too—washing Jagannāth's feet after their reconciliation—, but it is Jagannāth, who first has to promise that Lakṣmī can continue visiting all houses including those of 'Untouchables'. Thus, apparently in the story it is Lakṣmī who teaches a lesson to her husband and even curses him.

LAKṢMĪ AND THE *RATH JĀTRĀ*

Lakṣmī's anger also comes to the fore during the *Rath Jātrā*, more specifically during the return journey, the *Bāhuḍā Jātrā*. On this day Jagannāth, Lakṣmī's husband, returns from the house of his *Mausi*

Guṇḍicā, where he had spent some days, to his own temple. Before Jagannāth is actually allowed into his temple, he has to pacify his wife Lakṣmī, who is sulking due to his long absence (nine days) and because she had been left behind. The argument between Lakṣmī and Jagannāth is symbolically re-enacted by reading a text known as *Lakṣmī Jagannāth Khotap Kathan* (*khotap kathan* = conversation) or *Lakṣmī Jagannāth Bachchanikā* (*bachchanikā* = argument). On one occasion the text was read by a *pujāri* as Lakṣmī sitting in the temple, while another man outside took the role of Jagannāth. Lakṣmī closes the door at the arrival of her husband, leaving him outside. Jagannāth has to appease her by offering her a *sāḍhi* and is finally allowed inside, before the *jātrā* is completed. Again Lakṣmī is showing her power and the only thing Jagannāth can do is to pacify and appease her.

Such an outburst is not exactly the behaviour expected from an ideal wife. In addition, Marglin (1989 [1985]: 256) has noted another example of Lakṣmī's temper, ritually enacted during the *Rath Jātrā* in Puri, which had not been performed on the village level. On the fifth day of the Puri *Rath Jātrā*—while Jagannāth stays at the house of Guṇḍicā—Lakṣmī having been left behind follows her husband in anger. Her outrage is expressed in songs sung by *devadasis*: 'The Daughter of the Sea came out in a fighting mood. This mother will punish everyone and smash the three cars. From there the goddess sallied forth. She entered the palace of Guṇḍicā. She broke the car and beat the black backs [the builders of the cars]. The mother tore the garment of the Gajapati. Having broken the car she went to meet Lord Jagannātha' (Marglin 1989 [1985]: 257). Additionally, at the end of this episode Lakṣmī throws some magic powder in Jagannāth's face in order to bring him back to her.

In all three events Lakṣmī not only shows her immense power—described as even greater than Jagannāth's—but also indicates what she is able to do if due attention is not paid her. Left—even though only temporarily—by her husband she does not hesitate to destroy the cars used for the *Rath Jātrā*. In this manner Lakṣmī seems to differ quite considerably from Sitā, with whom she is linked via her husband Viṣṇu.[17] Sitā as an ideal wife seems to remain steadfast in her devotion and loyalty to her husband, continually faithful to him regardless of his character, while Lakṣmī, especially during the *Rath Jātrā*, even suspects her husband of having an incestuous affair with his sister, with whom Jagannāth had spent his time in Guṇḍicā's house. In considering these incidents, a rather ambiguous picture of the goddess emerges, which in my opinion is also reflected in an ambivalent relationship to elephants in the region.

LAKṢMĪ AND THE ELEPHANTS

Generally in Indian iconography Lakṣmī is closely related to elephants (*hātī*), which are considered to be her carrier as well as a royal symbol. Groups of wandering elephants—usually belonging to temple and to some extent trained by their guides known as Mahuntiā—visit villages after the harvest and collect gifts meant for the goddess. Villagers worship these elephants as Lakṣmī by washing their legs with water mixed with turmeric, applying vermilion to their trunks (*chhur*), and offering paddy and rice to them—though most of the rice is collected by the Mahuntiā and not fed directly to the elephant. In addition, villagers bow down to them, and trained elephants may roar in turn, regarded as a blessing of the Goddess.

However, elephants are not only benevolent. When paddy is ripe, wild elephants sometimes visit the village at night and eat it—either in the fields or already cut and collected near the threshing floor. A herd of elephants may damage and destroy fields worth thousands of rupees. Apparently elephants are increasingly forced to search for food in villages, since their natural habitat, the jungle, has been progressively reduced by illegal clearings. This is not a totally new phenomenon. Thus the elephant as Lakṣmī may also reveal a darker element. Villagers have tried to avert damages caused by elephants by using fire crackers in order to frighten the animals. But terrified elephants can be an even bigger danger, and there have been several cases of villagers being trodden to death by elephants running wild. Knowing very well the threat elephants embody, villagers may worship Lakṣmī and her trained carriers not in spite of the wild elephants, but because of them.

Goddess Lakṣmī in a mixed tribal and caste society

Lakṣmī may fit particularly well into a context on a tribal frontier in which caste Hindus as well as tribes interact closely. On the one hand Lakṣmī appears in the ritual cycle as the benevolent and obedient consort of Viṣṇu/Jagannāth, on the other hand she is also as a jealous wife seeking revenge. In the *Mārgaśirṣa Māsa Mātā Mahālakṣmīnka Gurubār Brata* Lakṣmī is addressed as Mahāmāyā and as Jayeśvarī or goddess of victory, as Māheśvārī (wife of Māheśvār—Śiva) and as Ādyā—all names of Durgā also. Such a link between various traditions of Hinduism has also been noticed by Mallebrein (1993: 202) in Maharashtra, where Mahālakṣmī appears in the guise of Durgā: Mahālakṣmī is worshipped in the context of *Daśarā* (*Vijayādaśami*), etc. The multi-facetted role of Mahālakṣmī—being simultaneously a virgin as well as a warrior—has been noted by Biardeau as well (1994 [1981]: 138). However, in the Aghriā context, Lakṣmī appears to be more mild than wild (Michaels 1998: 247); she does not accept blood sacrifices, is married, belongs to a *bhakti* tradition. A supposed opposition between mild and wild goddesses may help us understand various traditions within Hinduism, but it remains an ideal—typical distinction not necessarily corresponding neatly to realities on the ground. In the village context I am presenting here, even Durgā does not receive blood sacrifices, but instead pumpkins indicating animals. However, Lakṣmī—though bound in marriage—apparently does not lose her power in contrast to her husband Jagannāth as told in the *Lakṣmī Purāṇ*. Additionally, among the Gonds of Andhra Pradesh Lakṣmī receives blood sacrifices and is worshipped at *Daśarā* as well Fürer-Haimendorf (1979: 413, 471–2).

Besides, by referring to Lakṣmī as Ṭhakurānī—a name commonly applied to village goddesses—an implicit link to Durgā is drawn, since a Grām Śrī is often believed to be a local manifestation of Durgā. Such an association may also reveal the character of Lakṣmī as an earth goddess. Such a quality as Mother Earth was also ascribed to Lakṣmī in the *Rig Veda* period (Zimmer 1947: 92). Her connotations as an earth goddess perhaps predestine her to become a major goddess in a tribal and caste society.[13] This observation is substantiated by Fürer-Haimendorf (1979: 413ff), who describes the worship of Lakṣmī as Bhui Lachmi, as earth goddess, in addition to her role as Ana Lachmi or grain goddess among tribal Gonds of Andhra Pradesh.[14] Eschmann (1994 [1975]: 220) argued that Durgā fits particularly well into a tribal context as local tribal goddesses are often associated with her in her form as Ban (forest) Durgā. Being not so distant from Durgā may help Lakṣmī to appear as an appropriate goddess in a mixed tribal and caste society, in which additionally there are striking similarities between the cults of village and tribal goddesses (Eschmann (1994 [1975]: 218–19).

Thus it is surprising that *Lakṣmī Pūjā* is becoming more and more popular in this converging tribal and caste society. Not only Hindu caste families perform *Lakṣmī Pūjā* during the month of Mārgaśīra, but also many families belonging to Scheduled Tribes.[15] It is, however, significant that most of these tribal families are linked rather closely to their Hindu landlord—either as labourers or as sacrificer to the village goddess. In the latter case the Kālo visits the house of the landlord frequently and arranges with him all rituals for the village goddess.

I have observed the performance of *Lakṣmī Pūjā* among Kandh, Kisān, Gaṇḍ, Muṇḍā, and Māḷi families—though this list may not be exhaustive. There is certainly the tendency that high status families—non-tribal or tribal—are more likely to perform the ritual. However, while all twelve Aghriā families of the village performed the ritual, but not all Gand, and relatively few Kandh did so. So too with the Muṇḍā. Thus the importance of Lakṣmī appears to be higher among the Aghriā than among other communities and the Aghriā may have influenced other communities in this regard.

Generally, the *Lakṣmī Pūjā* in the aforementioned communities is less elaborate in comparison to the Aghriā. This may correspond to differences in wealth ánd education, but perhaps also to differences attached to the importance of the ritual. Usually fewer offerings were made and less significance was attached to the number ten. In the cases I observed or discussed, I found that among communities other than the Aghriā the *Lakṣmī Purāṇ* was not read or recited. However, in most cases *jhoti* had been painted a day before and was worshipped, and there was a clear identification between Lakṣmī and rice. Additionally, the *merkhuṇṭ* as central post of the threshing floor is usually included in the ritual and *ṭikā* (red spot) of vermilion is offered. Often one also finds Lakṣmī *khatli* showing Lakṣmī with elephants, which are worshipped by offering flowers and rice.

Even though the Aghriā may have promoted the cult of Lakṣmī and influenced their neighbours in the performance of *Lakṣmī Pūjā*, it does not mean that similar traditions did not exist prior to the Aghriā-immigration. In neighbouring Bastar, Lakṣmī is worshipped by tribal communities such as the Bhatra (Tandon 1966: 96ff), who perform very elaborate and partly corresponding rituals for her in the month Kārttika known as *Lakṣmī Jagar*. The inclusive character of Lakṣmī, vigorously expressed in the *Lakṣmī Purāṇ* depicting her ambition to be worshipped and to be accessible by all devotees, plus the personal devotion or *bhakti* may have helped to incorporate regional traditions.[16] Bastar with its own tradition of Lakṣmī worship might be a case in point and might also have influenced, in turn, the Lakṣmī cult.

Thus, as far as I could note during wedding ceremonies of tribal communities, the pair Lakṣmī and Nārāyaṇ appears to be less prominent at the altar than among the Aghriā. However, among some tribal communities a close connection seems to exist or has existed between the plough and yoke on the one hand and marriage on the other—a link which may express a very similar idea. Thus among the Kandh and Muṇḍā, but perhaps among other communities as well, one used to find and perhaps in some cases still finds agricultural instruments at the wedding altar. Among the Kandh—I was told—a plough and a yoke, unconnected, were placed at the centre of the wedding altar enclosing a *śil* (a stone used to grind spices, etc.).[17] The plough and yoke are clearly identified as male categories and women are not allowed to touch them—except on the occasion of marriage, when bride and groom may even stand on the plough.[18] In contrast to this a *śil*, which a bride touches during the wedding, appears to be considered as female forming a pair with the male pestle, which is missing during the wedding. Thus a combination of the *śil*, representing the earth–bound, female aspect, with a plough and yoke as its male counterpart resembles to some extent the divine couple Lakṣmī and Indra and may be easily related to it.

7.3. CYCLES AMALGAMATED IN THE RITUAL IDIOM OF THE *KHUṆṬ*

The wooden post or *khuṇṭ* is another central and amalgamating symbol in this mixed tribal and caste society. The *khuṇṭ* is basically a wooden post, pole, or log. Every post erected as part of a fence of a field is known as *khuṇṭ*. Also small posts erected to tie bullocks or buffalos to are known simply as *khuṇṭ*. Furthermore, poles used in house construction are known as *khuṇṭ*. Apparently *khuṇṭ* means 'to sustain something'. As interlocutors told me, the Sambalpuri word *khuṇṭ* is related to the Oriya word *khambā*.

I would like to argue that a *khuṇṭ* in the form of *merkhuṇṭ* dominates the threshing floor, while at the same time it is a crucial object of the wedding altar in the disguise of a *kalyāṇī khuṇṭ* and the *mahuā* sticks. The *khuṇṭ* figures in the rituals of various gods and goddesses such as Samlei, who is represented not only in form of her *mūrti* (idol) inside her temple, but also as a wooden post or *bali khuṇṭ* in front of the temple entrance. Given the fact that gods or spirits in many tribal communities are represented in the form of wooden posts (Eschmann 1994 [1975]: 214ff; Grigson 1991 [1938]: 193); Jena et al. 2002: 204, 214; Roy 1999 [1928]: 10, 16, 50;[19] Kulke 1979: 22 ff) the exalted position of *khuṇṭ* may be a tribal element.

Merkhuṇṭ *at the centre of the threshing floor and head of the family*

Wherever tractors are not used, the threshing floor is dominated by a wooden post known as the *merkhuṇṭ*. *Mer* stands for 'main' or 'centre', but some people also regard the place of the village goddess as *mer* and the sacrifice for the village goddess as *meriā*.[20] *Khuṇṭ* simply denotes a wooden post, which in the case of a *merkhuṇṭ* should be made of *mahuā* wood. Thus *merkhuṇṭ* is the 'main post' or 'post at the centre'. Practically the bullocks or buffalo used for threshing are tied to the *merkhuṇṭ*—usually there is a cut in the upper part of the post for the ropes—and they circle it in the process of threshing. Apart from this—as the usage in relation to the village goddess hints at already—the *merkhuṇṭ* plays a ritual role and displays once more the intrinsic relationship between ritual and the agricultural cycle. The *merkhuṇṭ* is worshipped during the *Lakṣmī Pūjā* in particular. Flowers and rice are placed on top as well as in front of the *merkhuṇṭ*; *dīpa* and *dhūpa* are moved around it, and some milk is poured on the *khalā* just in front of the *merkhuṇṭ* clearly indicating the aspect of fertility. Both words—*mer* as well as *khuṇṭ*—are seen, like the plough, as male in opposition to the threshing floor or *khalā*, paddy the land, and water, which are all female. Moreover, some Aghriā believe that the *merkhuṇṭ* is the 'owner' or 'guardian' of the threshing place. In the same manner the head of the family (even occasionally a woman) is sometimes the *merkhuṇṭ*. However, the usage of the term *merkhuṇṭ* for the head of the family seems to have declined in recent years and is now only rarely used.

A new *merkhuṇṭ* is ritually erected. In one case, the owner after having taken a bath dug a hole to place in it some *aruā chāul*, *haridā*, and a copper coin (all pure items). In front of the standing *khuṇṭ* he performed a little ritual for Lakṣmī and Nārāyaṇ using *dīpa* and *dhūpa*.

Additionally Gothiā Gauḍ herdsmen who travel with the animals in the jungle erect ritually a wooden post to tie the animals to before setting up a new camp. This *khuṇṭ*—also known as *merkhuṇṭ*—is not driven in by using stones, but a hole is dug to place the *khuṇṭ* in. According to some Gauḍ this ritual is performed for Rakasbuddha—believed to be the god of the forest—while others say it is done for Mainśāsur (*main* = female buffalo; *asur* = giant) as God of the buffalos. In any case not only in the *merkhuṇṭ* is set up, but incense and *aruā chāul* are offered. Furthermore, the owner of the buffalos sacrifices a male goat in front of this *merkhuṇṭ* at the time of *Daśarā*.

Khuṇṭ Gauntiā/*khuṇṭ Naik* as headman

The *khuṇṭ* Gauntiā or *khuṇṭ Naik* heads the village the way in which a *merkhuṇṭ* dominates the threshing floor and the family. *Khuṇṭ* Gauntiā is the name used by the Aghriā, while Gaṇḍ or Bhuyān call it *khuṇṭ Naik*. However, compared to a *merkhuṇṭ* of *mahuā* wood, for a *khuṇṭ* Gauntiā *sāl* wood is preferred. The *khuṇṭ* Gauntiā is also worshipped by the sacrificer of the village goddess on the same days as the village goddess and additionally on *Nuā Khāi* and on *Rākhī Pūni*.

A *khuṇṭ* Gauntiā was usually erected when village headmen or landlords died, did not have children, were poor, or had any other problems, in mostly tribal villages. The headmen then ruled on behalf of the *khuṇṭ* Gauntiā as a kind of 'acting Gauntiā'. Here the aspect of control and rulership seems to be important as well as the element of protection—protection of the lineage through offspring, the protection of the physical life of the Gauntiā, etc. Apart from this very apparent motif there might be another hidden aspect not explicitly expressed: a wooden post, a *khuṇṭ*, as ruler might be more acceptable for a predominantly tribal population than an outsider as new headman. Ruling and collecting revenue, for example in a village in which an

A Gauntiā binding a *rākhī* to the *khuṇṭ* Gauntiā.

Aghriā Gauntiā was the only non-*Gaṇḍ* family, must have been far from easy. Thus, Aghriā immigrants might have adopted—perhaps via mediation of a higher king—a tribal ritual idiom: the *khuṇṭ*, whose supernatural quality representing deities or spirits has already been indicated.

An example of the existence of such wooden posts in tribal communities embodying the quality of rulership is presented by Fürer-Haimendorf (1979: 432) for the case of the Gonds of Andhra Pradesh. He noted that the divine village guardian known as Aki Pen 'is represented by a square pointed post (*munda*) which is carved from teakwood and usually bears the symbols of sun and moon. Such a post is put up at the time of the foundation of a village, and may be renewed when the wood begins to decay'.

About the role of Aki Pen among other divine beings present in the village Fürer-Haimendorf observed, 'His position among the village gods is compared to that of the headman among the villagers, and when Aki appears to a seer in his dreams he assumes invariably the outward form of a village headman' (Fürer-Haimendorf 1979: 433).[21]

In addition, Bodding (1935: 747) noted that among Santal the term *khuṇṭut* does not only designate a wooden post, but is also associated with the headman. Furthermore, Gausdal (1960: 28) reproduces a picture of the 'spirit of the headman, who founded the village—and his wife' represented by carved wooden heads apparently standing on wooden poles.[22]

The Aghriā Gauntiā either established or took over wooden posts or *khuṇṭ* in villages, in which their personal life or their lineage was endangered. Thus it seems that they deified the headman (his lineage in actuality) by adopting—or sharing with—a ritual idiom from their tribal neighbours. Ancient kings who may have ventured into the wilderness long ago may have also employed the very same idiom. In any case the *khuṇṭ* represents wilderness as well as divine rulership and dominance. Identifying themselves with such a tradition obviously helped to establish themselves as rulers in a predominantly tribal area, and to avoid conflicts between immigrating peasants and original tribal settlers. Presently, however, the worship of *khuṇṭ Gauntiā*—as the Gauntiā system as such—is in a significant process of decline.

Khuṇṭ *in the context of marriage and lineage*

During Aghriā weddings a small wooden stick, around 50 cm long and with seven cuts, is of utmost significance. It is called *kalyāṇī khuṇṭ* or *kalihāri khuṇṭ*. Either it is believed to be Kalyāṇī, the goddess of blessing, or is translated as *kalihāri*, 'not to be disputed' indicating a sign of unity. As Marriott (1955: 212) noted, in north India *kalyāṇī* may also mean 'auspicious'. Some people further explain this feature as denoting seven stars or seven divine (represented by the seven cuts) witnesses at a wedding. In any case, a *kalyāṇī khuṇṭ* has to be manufactured and offered by a *jāti*—a caste member from a different clan—who is named in a meeting of all *jāti* in the village before the wedding. The *kalyāṇī khuṇṭ* is placed in front of three *mahuā* branches known as *mahul ḍāl* which are also installed at the centre of the wedding altar. They are placed on soil brought in a procession from the shrine of the village goddess by the mother and the *suhāsen*—women belonging to the bride's or groom's generation or an alternate generation. In subsequent wedding rituals all these wooden posts are worshipped as divine beings[23] and crowns (*makuṭ*) are presented to them as well as to bride and groom.

Such wooden posts significantly dominate the wedding altars not only of Aghriā, but also of all communities in the village except the Chasā. However, the number of the *mahul ḍāl* may vary from one to three. Sometimes only *mahuā* posts are used, sometimes *mahuā*, *sāl* and even *jām* trees. While Aghriā use three *mahuā* branches, the Gaṇḍ place two *mahuā* branches and one *sāl.* Among the Kisān, three such wooden posts are erected, *mahuā*, *sāl* and *jām.*[24] Among tribal communities beyond the north-western part of Orissa such posts may also be an important symbol of the wedding altar. Fürer-Haimendorf (1979: 320) describes the erection of a wooden post at the centre of the marriage booth as a vital part of the ceremonies:

> . . . the groom's kinsmen with a man skilled in wood carving set out for the forest, where they select a tree, they salute it in ceremonial fashion and two young men fell it. The wood carver then carves from the central part of the bole a munda four or five feet high; he shapes the top into a pointed cone, carves a crescent moon and full sun on the face and, wrapping it up in a new cloth, brings it with drums and trumpets in procession to the village boundary where the womenfolk of the groom's house anoint it with turmeric. The munda is then taken to the marriage booth; the post is washed with water . . . and it is then placed into a hole made in the centre of the booth, and the earth is filled in.

Thus the Gond wooden post is termed *munda*, not *khuṇṭ*. However, it seems to be significant that *munda* describes a similar semantic space, because the post of the divine village guardian (mentioned above) is named in the very same way. Further examples from tribal Middle India could be cited (for the Baiga see Elwin 1939). Among the Bhumia and Gond, Fuchs (1960: 271) underlines the importance of posts at wedding altars. 'The wedding post which is called by the Bhumia and mangrohen or mangroli by the Gond plays an essential role in the wedding ceremonial of these tribes. It is by walking around this post that the marriage is contracted.'

Such posts seem to be common among some Hindu castes in Chhattisgarh as well (see Babb 1975), but Chhattisgarh may well represent a transitional region to north-western Orissa. Contrarily, in other parts of India, for example Gujarat,[25] wedding altars appear to be centred around a sacred fire, not a post.

In some tribal communities like the Muṇḍā, Orām, and Santal—but not the Aghriā—the *khuṇṭ* apparently also stands for the sub-clan, lineage, or local line (for the Santal see Gausdal 1960 and Troisi 2000 [1979]: 30; for the Orām see Roy 1999 [1928]: 7, 16, 68ff; for the Muṇḍā see Roy 1970 [1912]: 361, Schwerin 1977: 80ff[26] and Choudhury 1977: 33, 38). Perhaps most pronounced (or best documented) are *khuṇṭ* or *khuṭs* in Gausdal's spelling among the Santal, where they appear to designate clan divisions. In some cases *nij khunt* seem to be opposed to *sada khunt*—the former being conceptualized as older than the latter (Gausdal 1960: 54, 139).[27] Since both terms are presumably of Hindi origin—*nij* means 'own', while *sādā* stands for 'simple' in Hindi—one might argue, as Pfeffer (1997: 19; 2002: 224) did, that the former designates lines of 'real' or original settlers in contrast to everyone else or the latter. Such a distinction may also demonstrate the attachment of the first settlers to the wooden post set up at the time of founding the village and to the village guardian as already depicted by Fürer-Haimendorf and Gausdal. Referring to such distinctions, Pfeffer (1982a: 22) recognized the *khuṇṭ* as a form of differentiation between senior lines of sacred specialists versus junior lines of secular leaders on the village level; for example among the Santal an opposition is made between *naike khūnt* (village sacrificer) and *manjhi khūnt* (secular headman).

However, in my research area only the term *merkhuṇṭ* in the sense of 'head of a family' is common among the Muṇḍā and Orām and is also used by Aghriā. The usage of the term seems to imply the notion of *khuṇṭ*. Implicitly a meaning of *khuṇṭ* as lineage or even local line may exist in yet another way. Among the Gaṇḍ, as part of the marriage rituals, one used to find a custom known as the *khuṇṭ tarpani*. *Tarpan* usually denotes a sacred rice beer offered to the ancestors and consumed by close family members. It is produced while observing strict rules of purity. Following this custom—recalled for me, though the Gaṇḍ Samāj tries to eradicate it[28]—the kin of the groom have to offer money to the kin of bride before taking her away from her village. This money is intended to be spent on wine—usually *mahuli* (made of *mahuā* flowers). Thus the Gaṇḍ tradition of *khuṇṭ tarpani* may imply an imagined community or rather line on the bride's side including the ancestors—though more research is needed in this regard. If one, however, reconsiders the *kalyāṇī khuṇṭ* in this perspective, it may well be possible that the aspect of a local line or lineage is expressed too—even if it is not expressed by the Aghriā.

Khuṇṭ *as representations of gods and goddesses*

In the ritual cycle various *khuṇṭ* figure prominently on several occasions. To start with, in the cult of the goddess Samlei *khuṇṭ* play a crucial role. In front of the temple—outside, but within the larger walled temple compound—two *khuṇṭ* are erected, the *bali khuṇṭ* (sacrifice) and the *joḍa* (together)[29] *khumba*. These two sacrificial posts are the place where male animals, he-goats and cocks, are offered during the *Boil* festival (on full moon after *Daśarā*). Usually both *khuṇṭ* stand next to each other and a red cloth might be tied around them, but sometimes there is also a gap of about 30 cm between them. This gap, people say, hints at the former custom of sacrificing buffalo. The neck of a buffalo was tied between the *khuṇṭ* in order to make sacrifice easier. Usually the *bali khuṇṭ* are made of *sāl* wood and people believe the goddess to be present in the *khuṇṭ*.

A *khuṇṭ* also plays a vital role in the so-called *Danḍa Nrutya*. Every year groups of temporary ascetics move around carrying the pictures of Śiva, Kali, and Parvati. In between the annual journeys these pictures in the form of standards are usually placed in a Śiva Temple. Next to a temple I visited, these standards stood under a simple wooden roof (without walls). In front a wooden post had been erected—known as *merukhuṇṭ* (*meru* = pole[30]). It is in front of this wooden post that a he-goat is sacrificed at the end of *Danīa Nrutya* on Panā Sankrānti—an act known as *meru bhangā* (*bhangā* = breaking). Next to it there are small stones and another smaller wooden post in between. The pūjāri of the temple calls these stones and the wooden post *danḍa ghar*.

A *merkhuṇṭ* is also worshipped by the Gothiā Gauḍ on *Daśarā* in a ritual called *uṣā* (sunrise). The wooden post standing next to their camp in the jungle is called *khuṇṭ naiken*—*naiken* as a female form of *naik*/headman—on this specific day.[31] A small stool is put in front of the post and *bel* leaves are placed there. The head of the family—known as *merkhuṇṭ*—offers a red he-goat and red or black roosters. His wife, also called *naiken* or *nariyen*, has no role in the ritual apart from arranging the ritual items. On top of the *khuṇṭ naiken* milk is poured, while blood from the sacrificed animals is offered on the soil around the post—obviously symbolizing different aspects of fertility. According to the Gauḍ the milk is presented to Nakul and Sahadev—two Pandavas, the latter seen as the cattle-keeper, while the blood is offered to female goddesses, Mā Bhainra and Samlei. As already indicated a *merkhuṇṭ* at the centre of the threshing floor is also worshipped during *Lakṣmī Pūjā.*

The *Jangā lingā* as the main gods of the Gand also appear in the form of wooden posts, but hanging on ropes. They are worshipped by other communities of the village including the Aghriā. Furthermore, there are small shrines in which a wooden post or *khuṇṭ* is erected such as a Hanuman shrine in Aitāpali village, where a *khuṇṭ* and a small idol of Hanuman with a club are placed in a shrine inscribed *bajrang bali.* Similarly, on the outskirts of Tilemani village, opposite a Durgā or Kāli shrine there are three *khuṇṭ*—two of them under a temporary roof. The shrine with these three *khuṇṭ* is known as Asurkol indicating an association with the Asura demons.

There are numerous other examples of wooden posts as divine beings worshipped in tribal communities. Eschmann (1986a) provides ample material on this, for example on Khambeśvari or the 'lady of the post', a Kond deity later turned tutelary goddess of feudatory states. Apart from stones and earthen pots, according to Eschmann wooden posts belong to the prime uniconical symbols of tribal religion.[32] Such symbols might be closely or else loosely associated with Hindu gods or goddesses such as Ban Durgā. Thus Eschmann (1986a: 85):

> In many Kondh villages, for instance, there is no apparent Hinduization whatsoever, except for the fact, that when the post which represents the goddess . . . , is renewed—which happens perhaps every thirty years—a Brahmin is called to impart the *prāṇa pratiṣṭhā-mantra* of Vana Durgā (the 'Durgā of the woods') and thus theoretically acknowledges the post as a mūrti.

Eschmann further argues that wooden posts representing tribal gods may have turned into movable images (*calantī pratimā*) of these gods in a process of Hinduization, which may co-exist with the main image inside the temple. Apart from Samalāī in Sonepur—apparently identical with Samlei in Sambalpur and elsewhere—Eschmann

(1986a: 89) cites instances of Khilamuṇḍa and Bhagavatīkāṭhi. A link to Jagannāth and his sister Subhadrā and their images is evident too. In addition to Eschmann's findings, the presence of gods symbolized by wooden poles among the Gaṇḍ/Gond, who worship these posts at fixed times around the year or in cases of calamities and who relate them to the soil over which the gods rule or which they guard, has been mentioned frequently (Grigson 1991 [1938]: 193 for the Maria Gond, speaks of 'log gods'; Fürer-Haimendorf 1979: 432ff for the Gonds of Andhra Pradesh; for the Dongria Kondh Jena et al. 2002: 204, 214; for Santal Gausdal 1960: 107 describes festivals in which a post is erected for Jom Sim Bongas associated with the sun).

7.4. CONCLUSION

The agriculture cycle centring on rice as well as the ritual cycle, and the life cycle are not conceived as separate entities. They are interwoven, interlinked, or amalgamated in various cultural symbols demonstrating a generalized structure of society in the sense of Sahlins. Figure 21 is meant to demonstrate this point.

On the one hand, I introduced Lakṣmī as one of two symbols, related to the earth and fertility, to rice, and marriage. She appears as a central female aspect. On the other hand, wooden posts or *khuṇṭ* appear and reappear within the cycles and seem to embody a

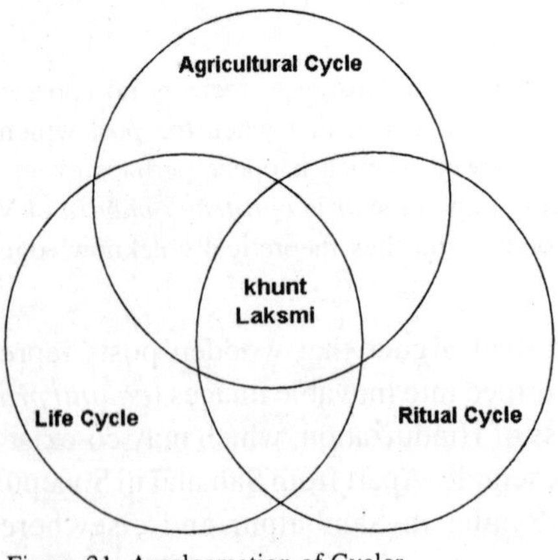

Figure 21: Amalgamation of Cycles.

predominantly male aspect. At the centre of the wedding altar, at the threshing floor, or as headman of the village a *khuṇṭ* gives the impression of rulership of a fixed entity or bound territory. Thus it appears as lord of the sacred wedding altar, the threshing floor, or the village as fixed and dominated territories or may appear as the head of a family or male line.

Apparently both idioms—in which the cycles converge—are linked as well, for example in the sense that the *merkhuṇṭ*, the phallic symbol at the centre of the threshing floor, is seen in opposition to the threshing floor (*khalā*), which also represents the earth, an important aspect of Lakṣmī. Thus, they may be opposed to each other, but nevertheless they are united in relation to rice. To both a sacred character is ascribed. Given Lakṣmī's obvious Hindu background—though several traditions may have merged in her figure—one might argue that a tendency towards Hinduization[33] is recognizable. Simultaneously, however, the wooden post as a major aniconic representation of the divine in tribal society may hint at an opposite tendency towards a Tribalization. Moving away from the Hinduization—Tribalization dichotomy one may further recognize wider processes of 'Universalization' and 'Parochialization', which Marriott (1955: 197ff) has described for north India. According to him, local goddesses are linked to a 'great tradition' (universalization) and vice versa; there is a process of downward transmission 'from great to little tradition', and Marriott (1955: 195f) himself provides an example of a 'parochial Lakṣmī' and a universalized local goddess. Similarly one may argue that a *khuṇṭ* Gauntiā might be understood as a parochial or localized form of a wider idea of *khuṇṭ* as a local line. However, such statements remain highly speculative. In any case the symbols presented here—which both describe a semantic field rather than a single idea—reveal an essential interrelatedness of agriculture, religion, and one's own life.

NOTES

1. Tulsī is also identified with to Goddess Lakṣmī.
2. A ritual bringing of rice from the field dressed as Lakṣmī and as bride with earrings, bangles, etc., and a subsequent marriage is mentioned and described by Gregory (2003) for Bastar as well as by Berger (personal communication) for Koraput. Among Aghriā no such ritual of bringing the

rice is performed, but a small red cloth around the *meṇṭa* may indicate a similar idea.

3. In the case I observed a hand–written text is used, which seems to have been copied from somewhere else, but I could not identify any original source.
4. A similar version, is published in Tripathi (1972 [1936]: 161ff).
5. The temple servant performs a ritual in the Śiva Temple and the Kālo of the village goddess at the Grām Śrī Shrine.
6. The *kalyāṇī khunṭ* at the wedding altar may also have phallic connotations, though it is said to be a goddess. Besides, one has to note that water as such is conceptionalized as female and in Hindu tradition Lakṣmī is associated with water via her father—Varuṇa, the god of the ocean—as well. In tribal traditions of neighbouring Bastar she is conceived in a similar position as daughter of Megha Raja, the king of clouds (Tandon 1966: 98) or Meng, the 'cloud' or god of the monsoon rain (Gregory 2003: 7).
7. A Brahmin may recite, 'The divine Rām and Janaki appeared, then Lakṣmī and Nārāyaṇ are seen to be so beautiful.'
8. For an association Tulsi Mata and Lakṣmī see also Parry (1979: 61, 64).
9. Similarly, birth is considered impure—though it is a life-giving act and an expression *per se* of fertility.
10. Interestingly a broom—even a new one made in the house of the parents—should never be given to a married daughter amongst the various things for her new home.
11. An edition of the *Lakṣmī Purāṇ* is planned. A longer or perhaps complete account of the text – though deviating in some details—is given by Tripathi (1972 [1936]). Unfortunately he does not contextualize the account in the sense of which communities may read the text or where he found the manuscript. An edition of the full *Lakṣmī Purāṇ* is intended at a later stage. Since the text is still in a process of translation, I omit diacritical signs here. The central part of the story is also found in Marglin (1989 [1985]). Significantly, the same myth is also part of a much longer story known as Lachmi Jagār and recited in neighbouring Bastar in order to worship Lakṣmī among tribal communities too (Gregory 2003).
12. Chanḍāla are known as guardians of the cremation ground.
13. The close connection between Lakṣmī and the earth is expressed in Sitā—born in a furrow and found while her father was ploughing. Also, in some iconographical representations of the goddess Lakṣmī is doubled and Bhu-Devi as earth-goddess is highlighted as one of her central aspects (Mitchell 1995 [1982]: plate 8/9).
14. Fürer-Haimendorf mentions her role as cattle goddess additionally, which may perhaps indicate also a more generalized pantheon. Besides, instead of rice apparently millet is offered to Lachmi among Gond and the goddess is more related to millet that to rice.

15. As my colleague L. Guzy noted *Lakṣmī Pūjā* is getting more and more popular in Koraput district too.
16. The Goddess Lahi as a rice goddess—or *lahi penu*—among the Dongria Kondh may be a case in point (Hardenberg: personal communication; Jena et al. 2002).
17. I was told that among Luhurā and Gaṇḍ similar rituals are performed or had been performed in the past. Similarly among the Kisān I witnessed an engagement ceremony and a couple demonstrated an older form of engagement/marriage, in which the couple stood on a yoke.
18. I noted that accounts differ to some extent—probably because the marriage ceremonies have changed considerably.
19. Roy (1999 [1928]: 50) speaks particularly of nature spirits except ancestor spirits represented by stones.
20. As Fürer-Haimendorf (1979: 413) mentions, among the Gonds of Andhra Pradesh the post at the centre is simply known as *meri*.
21. The clan god, Persa Pen, is said to reside in a *mahuā* tree and is described as king or raja of the *sanalir* or of the 'departed'. It is Persa Pen symbolized by a tree who settles disputes among the *sanalir*. See Fürer-Haimendorf (1979: 393, 526).
22. They seem to stand next to a bigger wooden post, which, however, is not explained by Gausdal, who also notes that the spirits of headmen are often also represented by stones.
23. This corresponds with data from Chhattisgarh, where a wooden stake described as 'god of the wedding' had been noted by Babb (1975: 83).
24. As far as I could verify, the Gauḍ place two *mahuā* branches; Luhurā two *mahuā* and one *sāl*; the Māḷi two *mahuā* sticks; Keunṭ two *mahuā* and one *sāl*; the Malar one *mahuā* and one *sāl*, and the Harijan one *mahuā* at the centre of their wedding altars. Since no other communities uses three *mahuā* branches—as the Aghriā as dominant caste do—this may also imply hierarchical considerations.
25. For Gujarat, see e.g. Skoda (2002).
26. Schwerin cites J. Hoffmann (in Encyclopaedia Mundarica) as a source.
27. Generally Gausdal data are presented in a rather confusing order—almost in a postmodern fashion. The exact meaning of *khuṇṭ/khũts* remains rather vague and its relation to other categories such as *khil* is not clarified.
28. Compare publications of Gaṇḍ Samāj 1982.
29. *Khumba* seems also to designate a post or pole as in Khamheśvarī, the 'lady of the post' (see Eschmann 1986a: 86)
30. Used for example in regard to north or south Pole, but also backbone.
31. Others say that the *merkhuṇṭ* is the representation of the goddess *Khuṇṭ Naiken*.
32. Eschmann (1986a: 86) implicitly acknowledges the possibility that wooden posts may turn into more permanent stone images of the gods or goddesses in order to avoid complicated rituals to renew the wooden images.

33. On the term Hinduization see Eschmann (1986a, 1986b), who not only locates Hinduization 'between the two poles of tribal religion and codified or "High" Hinduism' (1986a: 82), but distinguishes various typologies of Hinduization (*śākta*, *śaiva* and *vaiṣṇava*).

CHAPTER 8

Conclusion

I would like to summarize my major findings concerning the Aghriā and their place at the interface of tribal and caste society. Peasant castes like the Aghriā which migrated into tribal areas experienced a social ascent and decisively shaped a developing mixed society, have been neglected in research. Cultural change and the problem of the transitions between tribal and caste societies were predominantly discussed from the view of single tribes, Brahmin migrations, or on the level of little kingdoms, but hardly in the perspective of the peasantry. My work tries to fill this research gap tentatively and to fathom ideas and values of the tribal and caste society in a probably unique regional synthesis. My emphasis lay particularly on the following themes: mythology, social relations with the local groups, kingship, kinship, life cycles as well as the amalgamating of the cycles, on the basis of cultural symbols.

On the one hand the Aghriā claim descent from Bidur—a mythical figure of the *Mahābhārata* a wise advisor of the king, but with a disputed social origin. On the other hand the Aghriā in Orissa locate their recent origin in Agra, the Mughal political and economic capital, for which they served as warriors according to their own myth. In these origin traditions, essentially maintained by their own bards, the Aghriā disobeyed and opposed the Muslim rulers and fled to Puri, and asked the Hindu king there for protection. In Puri, the religious centre of middle India and the Jagannāth cult, agriculture is assigned to the Aghriā as their future occupation. Obeying the verdict of Jagannāth and, thus, subordinating to a Hindu order of *dharma*, they establish themselves in north-west Orissa as peasants in a predominantly tribal area on the periphery of the Mughal realm and the Gajapati kingdom. In supplementary versions of the myth the relations with the Tihāri as their own Brahmins and with the Chamār are stressed. The latter helped the Aghriā with their escape in many myths. Thus relations with the extreme antipodes of caste hierarchy are emphasized, while tribal society is not mentioned explicitly.

The dominant myth of the Aghriā, however, is disputed. Non-Aghriā often refer to the etymology 'a-ghariā' implying the Aghriā as newcomers had originally no house or were not allowed to enter the house of someone else and had experienced a social ascent only recently. Thus, the Aghriā as rich peasants may have been subjected to a process of the Kshatriyaization combined with and expressed in a glorification of their past.

Social integration in this transitional society is structured by a hierarchy of relative ritual purity, which resembles the caste system. Processes of inclusion and exclusion are expressed within the hierarchy in the idiom of 'big and/or good people' versus 'small people', typical of tribal society in Orissa. The former is considered higher in status and/ older than the latter. However, this distinction is not bound to the value of purity. Within the mixed society, tribal groups are integrated into the hierarchy at different levels. This casts doubts on classifications of the government—particularly the category Scheduled Tribes. Hierarchical differences between the tribal groups on the one hand and common features between certain tribal groups and immigratnt peasants on the other hand are not the issue in the administrative classification. Difference in status is primarily determined by the acceptance of water and of different food categories, as well as by services of Brahmins, barbers, etc., and is manifested in actions, but hardly publicly verbalized.

Hierarchical distinctions are established and renewed by the so far hardly considered phenomenon of symbolic sale of ill or threatened children, who are transferred from higher to lower groups in hope of recovery and as an attempt to escape the attention of the death god Yama. An identification with the buyers' low status becomes is usually achieved by commensality—the child eats at least once in the buyer family. Before their marriage the children are redeemed against the payment of substantial amounts and are ritually cleansed. Thus, re-integration into society is reached by an exchange of material wealth against a desired transcendental protection.

Beside mythologically justified connections between certain groups and categories, relations in the form of ritual friendships are forged between persons of different groups. Such formalized relationships differ from family relations and friendships, and form a separate category. As in the case of the sold children, a desired identification with a ritual friend is reached by sharing the same food, here *praśād* in the ritual context. The hierarchy of purity, and the rules concerning the acceptance of different categories of rice and water aim at avoiding unwanted identifications. Ritual friendships, however, establish an equality among the friends and also a depersonalization of them, which is stressed for example by ignoring individual names. However this does not mean that the initially presented hierarchy does not affect the ritual friend. The forms of ritual friendship in its multiplicity are actually hierarchized, and the choice of becoming ritual friends may be affected by hierarchical considerations.

Contrary to neighbouring regions in which ritual friendships exist also between different clans, I assume a substantialization of the levels in the context presented by me—also in the sense of a change of segmentary structures within tribal society, since the possibility of ritual friendships is explicitly negated for instance between Aghriā clans. While within the mixed society individual categories are thus separated hierarchically, on the level of the families and/or certain persons they can nevertheless be connected and united by temporarily sold children or by more permanent ritual friendships. The Aghriā are a firm component of these developed networks.

The structures of kingship form a further, probably still more important, framework for the transformation of a segmentary tribal society, which is characterized by the absence of a central authority. A state order, although of a little kingdom rather than a bureaucratic, Western state, was established by the Aghriā as Gauntiā, i.e. as village headmen or 'village kings'. As such they secured rights to clear the forests and on appropriate property, became justices of the peace and revenue collectors for superior kings. In this role they contributed to a 'peasantization' of the tribal population and the creation of asymmetrical and redistributive systems with executive power. These were and still are partially embodied by the Gauntiā at the village level. The importance of immigrant peasant castes in the process of transformation has not been sufficiently appreciated.

During the establishment of its rule and the founding of new villages, the Aghriā used a cultural idiom of tribal society. In this society the landowning clan of the village founders is distinguished from affinal relatives or members of other clans who moved into the village at a later stage. Thus the Muṇḍā differentiate between *khuṇṭkattidar* (those, who cleared the forest) and *parjā* (tenants). Similarly Aghriā Gauntiā styled their rule as *khuṇṭ katā gaunti* (village rule by clearing of the forests) as against the other tenants (*parjā*) in the village, who could belong to different castes or tribes.

The Aghriā shaped the developing society not only by a political change, but also in an economic sense by the introduction or extensive cultivation of wet rice with the plough, building ponds for irrigation. Besides, the Aghriā did act and do act as 'culture brokers' in the sense of the patronage of religious Hindu festivals, as for Śivrātri (the night of the God Śiva), or the building of temples. This contributed to Hinduization and to an institutionalization of religion in particular. Simultaneously the Aghriā were influenced and were subjected to a parallel process of a tribalization. In my opinion the phenomenon of the *khuṇṭ Gauntiā*, the village headman in form of a wooden post, underlines this last point. This aniconic symbol of the wooden post—representing rule, control, but above all also divineness—prevalent in the tribal society of the region, has been reinterpreted by the Aghriā as a symbol of their dominance.

Furthermore, a characterization of the Gauntiā as 'village kings' is based on the fact that they acted within the same hierarchy and the same structural relations as the little kings above them. The Gauntiā did maintain similar systems of the redistribution, for example the little king used to oblige the Gauntiā with rent-free land while the Gauntiā in turn obliged the contract workers (Guti), but offering rent-free land on a long-term basis. Within the village the Gauntiā had and often still has the role of a universal giver and stands on the top of a hierarchy of giving in which the subjects are either *Sān Parjā,* (small tenants) and *Baḍ Parjā* (large tenants). This hierarchy is expressed on *Rākhī Pūni*, which in the village context is a kind of *durbar*. In addition, the Gauntiā has a privileged access to, and position in, the cult of the village goddess, who bestows creative power (*śākti*). His royal credentials are also underlined by his role in the *Rath Jātrā*, thereby either indirectly or directly acquiring the authority of Jagannāth as the ultimate ruler of the cosmos. With the eradication of the tax privileges, however, the position of the Gauntiā has changed.

Another transition is revealed in the sphere of kinship. If one compares the kinship system of the Aghriā with that of their neighbours, many common features are noticeable, while at the same time there are enormous differences from the north Indian and the south Indian systems. A mutual influence and synthesis between the tribal population and immigrants like the Aghriā can be documented particularly well in the sphere of kinship. In the analysis of the Aghriā terminology the principle of alternating generations and generation-sets has been shown. This is a well-known feature of Middle Indian tribal society, but, to my knowledge, hitherto unknown among a caste of the region. It is amazing when one considers an immigration of the Aghriā from a northern direction. A structural equating of alternating generations is expressed in the context of the marriage, i.e. marriage must be arranged within the generation-set. Thus, the rule of endogamy does not only refer to the Aghriā altogether, but to the generation set in particular. This thesis is also confirmed by the fact that up to the 1950s, when girls used to be married before puberty, a marriage could be arranged with a distant grandfather or brother-in-law.

Additionally the Aghriā system is characterized by a high autonomy of the levels—categories, rules and practice are less consistent than contradictory. The rule of cross-cousin marriage does not fit the given categories, since non-marriagable sisters are summarized in a category with cross cousins. Similarly, the rules of avoidance and joking have many parallels to neighbouring tribal groups. Many of these rules have only been found among the tribal neighbours. A case in point is the avoidance of the mother's brother of the married man. Such a rule contradicts the principle of cross-cousin marriage. However in practice such inconsistencies are not insurmountable. Altogether the clarity of Dravidian systems is missing in the structure of Aghriā kinship, while it does not appear as fragmented, however, as Indo-Aryan configurations.

In the Aghriā life cycle continuity is the dominant motive. Two complementary and cyclic relations appear to be of central importance: on the one hand the relationship between mother's brother and sister's son and on the other hand that between father and son. Without these relations one cannot attain the status of a complete social person and potential ancestor. While in the father–son relationship the continuity of the household and the male line is particularly stressed, in the second cycle, the relationship between mother's brother and sister's son, the leading into the world, for example by feeding the first rice, and the transition to the ancestor is emphasized. One cannot become an ancestor if the son of the sister is not satisfied. The outstanding role of the son of the sister—at the same time preferred son-in-law among the Aghriā—appears to me a further indication of a converging society, since this role of the sister's son has parallels in Middle Indian and Himalayan tribal society. However, the high status of a *bhanjā* (son of the sister), to whom in former times and partially still today priestly functions as a gift receiver were assigned, is in a process of change. The increasing role of the Brahmin seems to be related to the change of the evaluation of a *bhanjā*.

Apart from these two cycles, which are also expressed in equating the relations in address terms, two oppositions play a central role within the life cycle: the opposition of the generation sets and the opposition of *jāti* (as abstract marriage partners) versus *bansa* (clan). The first opposition dominates the rituals of the wedding and the example of the Aghriā is a rare case in which a generation set—here the *suhāsen*—act as a group.

The second opposition, contrasting non-marriagable (*banśa*) and potentially marriagable (*jāti*), superficially resembles dichotomies in tribal society. However in contrast to it, *jāti* refers only to the abstract affines of the village, which attend all larger life cycle rituals as witnesses. While *jāti* on a subordinated level opposes one's own clan (*banśa*), *jāti* understood as the entire Aghriā caste encompasses one's own clan. Thus the opposition *jāti* and *banśa* is expressed in the idiom of caste society.

In addition two transformations determine the life cycle: from impurity to the purity and from inauspiciousness to auspiciousness, or in reverse. Questions of purity and auspiciousness come to the fore from birth to the worship of the ancestors, whereby the period of ancestor worship appears to be impure. Death under certain constellations of stars can be very auspicious for the dead, but may also bring calamity for the family concerned at the same time, which must be turned away by additional rituals. With regard to purity, auspiciousness and rebirth, in which the continuity of the life and not the terminating of a relationship are emphasized, the Aghriā again differ considerably from peasant castes of northern India, but partially also from other groups in tribal society, in which for example a rebirth can be determined by means of certain tests.

In the end the generalized structure of the mixed society shall be emphasized here, again expressing the synthesis between tribal and caste society. Ritual and agricultural cycle as well as the life cycle are connected and interwoven. This becomes particularly clear with the symbols Lakṣmī and *khuṇṭ*. Lakṣmī is not only the goddess of the wealth and prosperity, but is also identified with the rice and with the bride. In the ritual cycle she appears as a protecting mother, as the vindictive or capricious wife of Jagannāth, as fruit of the earth and as earth itself. Altogether Lakṣmī is a semantic field more than a singular idea. On the frontier of tribal society, Lakṣmī seems to have more ambivalent characteristics and resembles rather Durga or tribal deities, not Sita. This ambivalence may lead to her rising popularity in tribal areas of Orissa or to her increasing association with local goddesses. Contrary to Lakṣmī the cultural cipher *khuṇṭ* seems to originate, at least in a synchronic perspective, in tribal society, but has however in the cycles of the Aghriā a prominent position comparable to Lakṣmī. A *khuṇṭ* is an indispensable component of the wedding altar, stands at the centre of the threshing floor, is a manifestation of regional divinities such as Samlei, and the head of a family, which indicates the similar concept of local lines of the same name among tribes of the region. Besides, the role of the *khuṇṭ* and *khuṇṭ Gauntiā* in legitimizing the rule of the Aghriā has to be emphasized again, since it points to the inclusion of ideas of tribal society in peasant culture.

On the interface between tribal and caste society in north-west Orissa the Aghriā as an immigrant peasant caste have substantially contributed to the development of a mixed or a transitional society, in which ideas and values from both social contexts are combined and synthesized.

APPENDICES

APPENDIX 1

The Life Cycle—A Description

1.1. BIRTH (*JANMA*), BIRTH RITUALS AND THE BEGINNING OF THE LIFE CYCLE

Conception[1] *and pregnancy*

Quite often the parents turn to local or regional gods and goddesses, if their wish to have children—specifically sons—is not fulfilled. Usually they vow to offer certain sacrifices or gifts if their wish is granted, e.g. to donate a brass cobra to the local Śiva temple. However, parents in many cases also wish to have a daughter as a first child followed later by a son. In one case a woman went to a Śiva temple with just that wish, promising to offer seven coconuts, if it were fulfilled. Her wish was granted and she sacrificed the coconuts.

The fourth day after menstruation is considered a good day for conception some men argued. In addition to that, just after midnight is also seen as a favourable time.

There are certain rules applied to pregnant women (*dehen achhe*) and sometimes to their husbands as well. Neither should see any deceased nor should they kill any animal, especially snakes. Additionally, both should avoid visiting Śiva temples, which are often situated on the outskirts of a village near a forest or jungle. Śiva is the lord of evil spirits (*bhut*), which often stay close to the temple and could have a negative influence on the couple. For the same reason—the presence of *bhut*—pregnant women should keep away from cemeteries and should not leave the house around sunset, a time at which *bhut* are particularly active. At this time there is also a higher risk of attracting the evil eye. A husband with a pregnant wife should not eat any *praśād* of the village goddess, i.e. the meat of animals sacrificed for her; however, both are allowed to eat meat during pregnancy in general.

A pregnant woman should not cross a river, and she should particularly refrain from crossing it by boat or by jeep. A bridge is seen as less dangerous. If it cannot be avoided, she must throw a coin into the river. Often also a coin is given to newly born children to be thrown into the river, when crossing a river for the first time.

Also, pregnant women should not visit their parents on a Saturday, which is believed to be inauspicious, and after their arrival there they should not leave their parent's house on the sixth, ninth or twelfth day nor on a Sankrānti or Prati Padā (a day after Sankrānti and new moon). The movement of the women—as some say—should be according to the movement of the yogini (female attendants of Goddess Durgā), who should always be behind one, never in front. The movement of the yogini is found in a *pāñjji* (astrological calendar) and should be taken into consideration for all auspicious events. Generally, pregnant women should not start a journey on Sankrānti, Uāns, or Prati Padā, but if they must, they should take a leaf of the *jām* tree when passing one and keep it until their arrival.

During the fourth or fifth month of pregnancy a child moves in the womb of his mother for the first time. This moving is known as *chhuā khelibā* (*chhuā* = child; *khelibā* = to play). It indicates that a child, although still in the womb (*pet* = stomach, womb), has *jiban* or 'life energy'/'breath' from now on—like all other living beings. However, the womb is also imagined as hell (*narka*), but not as the kingdom of Yama (Yamlok). Sexual intercourse usually ends at that time and some believe that the child would suffer seriously if continued, e.g. the child would loose the hair.

In the seventh month, the parents of a pregnant woman are supposed to offer a special gift known as *sadhāli bhār* (*sadhāli* = wish of a pregnant woman to eat various flavours; *bhār* = wooden stick used to carry goods on the shoulder). This consists essentially of typical Aghriā sweets. Apart from that, a *sadhāli pithā* (*pithā* = cake) is also an essential item.

There is a dreaded disease of pregnant women in the seventh month of pregnancy known as *alti* or ulcer, which can affect the skin or the stomach. Different types of medicine must be taken by a potential mother. Together with the aforementioned sweets, parents should send *manturā ghī*—*ghī* powered by *mantra*—for the pregnant woman. Additionally, some local women, often belonging to other communities, offer a medicine against *alti* named *alti uso* (*uso* = medicine), which the pregnant woman has to take under the eaves of the house or *ulchhā tal* (*ulchhā* = eaves; *tal* = under)—at the same place where the umbilical cord is later buried and where the ancestors are worshipped every year.

During the eighth month, pregnant women should not go anywhere, not even to their parent's house. However, in the ninth month pregnant women particularly if they are giving birth for the first time, return to their parent's house in order to spend the remaining time prior to birth with them (often also some time afterwards). After the labour pains or *aṇṭā dukhā* (*aṇṭā* = abdomen;[2] *dukhā* = pain) have started, the husband and all the other relatives are informed immediately.

Birth

For a birth a new moon day (*uāns* in Sambalpuri; *amābāsyā* in Oriya) is not favourable, even inauspicious. In former times there was the belief that girls born on a new moon day were unfit for marriage. These girls were known as *uānsi kaniā* and some people were convinced that their husbands would die. In contrast the day of Sankrānti is considered a favourable time for the birth of a son.

Nowadays, many births take place in local hospitals or nursing homes, while in former times all births took place at home. A room for confinement is chosen which is slightly off the main part of the house and less frequented. The mother does not leave this room for six days. The father is not permitted to enter the confinement room. However, other women including women without children or unmarried women are allowed to assist at birth. No particular importance is attached to the position of the woman during confinement. Furthermore, a midwife (*dāi*) is essential, who traditionally belongs to so-called 'untouchable' communities such as the Harijan (*Gandā*) or Ghansiā. She is also called *sutrien*—literally 'impure'. The midwife cuts the umbilical cord by using a knife or a broken tile (*kapri*). Her work also includes the washing of clothes before the sixth day. She is not allowed to wash clothes in a pond used by villagers for their own baths. Therefore, she must wash everything in a nearby river. She is entitled to some clothing after the birth. It is the obligation of the mother's parents to pay for the first birth of a daughter.

In former times, after birth the placenta or *phul*—the same word used for flower—would be buried under the bed in the confinement room. On the very same spot a fire was kept burning for six days, which some saw as protection against animals. Nowadays, in the case of a birth in a hospital there is no fixed place for the placenta. Either midwives in the hospital dispose of it or it is buried in the garden of the house.

Historically, the birth of a son would be publicly announced by beating a brass-plate—brass (*pithal*) symbolizing gold—, while in the case of a daughter, a *kansā*-plate—*kansā* symbolizing silver—was beaten by a midwife outside the confinement room. Others say two firecrackers would be burst after the birth of a son and just one after the birth of a daughter. In the case of a landlord, sometimes rifle shots were fired. Later the child could be fed at the breast of any woman able to do so. If another woman fed the child with her breast milk, she would be considered a mother as well.

If the child has a tooth at the time of birth, it is believed that the child is a *rākas* (giant) and there is the belief that if the firstborn child is a daughter it will extend the life of the father. Birth is always seen as a kind of rebirth—not only for the child, but to some extent also for the mother, who receives a *śaḍhi* (*sari*) from her in-laws after the birth. In the same way people who survive a serious illness receive a new cloth after their recovery, because it is considered to be a form of rebirth.

Birth and impurity

After birth the mother, the child and the whole family are considered impure (*aśuddha*). In different steps on the sixth and twenty-first day, the impurity is removed. Usually up to the sixth day after birth, the Aghriā do not take water in an Aghriā house where a birth has taken place. A child should not leave the house before the sixth day—or, some say, not even before the twenty-first day but can leave the confinement room and can move around inside the house. However, with modern hospitals this rule cannot be strictly observed.

People say that in former times no one was allowed to touch the mother until *ṣaṭhi*. Nowadays, before the sixth day other pregnant women should not touch the mother, baby, or women who assisted at the birth. Other Aghriā visiting a house before *ṣaṭhi* has been performed should change their clothes after returning to their own houses—for women, a bath would additionally be advisable, but for men a change of clothes is sufficient. The house is purified in various ways prior to *ṣaṭhi*. A mother is not allowed to enter the kitchen for six days and is prohibited to cook until the twenty-first. Apart from that, the pot used to boil rice should be destroyed, but this rule is not as strict as in the case of death.

Senkā—massage

After birth a child must be massaged (*sekibā*). Traditionally til (*rāsi-tel*) and castor oil (*jaḍā-tel*) are used, but nowadays modern cosmetics such as baby oils are becoming more and more fashionable. Til is preferred for the body to get stronger, while a cooling effect is ascribed to the castor oil, which helps digestion, it is believed. Particularly the stomach should be massaged intensively. A massage is also a way of trying to bring the body into a beautiful shape, i.e. to try to form a round-shaped head, to form a beautiful nose, etc. Additionally, olive oil is used in some cases because people believe it helps to bring fair skin.

Massaging a child for the first six months belongs to the traditional work of the midwife, who is entitled to receive a garment every three or six months, some money per month, and some food. In recent times, however, often the mother or other relatives rub the child.

Part of the daily hygiene of a baby is also mouth washing with honey, known as *muhun puchhā* (*muhun* = mouth; *puchhā* = to clean[3]). It is done until the age when a child can brush his teeth himself. When a child is brought to a pond for bathing for the first time, some *aruā chāul*, flowers and coins are offered for the water god, Bāruṇ.

Crying

If a baby cries a lot or moves too much, negative influences of evil spirits (*bhut* or *chhum*) are suspected and feared. In such cases a mixture of leather, lentils, turmeric, hair, mustard, rubber and salt is burned and the ash is disposed of at a crossroads later on. If the condition does not improve, a local healer or Guniā may be contacted. In former times, however, as some mother's remember vividly, opium was given to babies in order to keep them quiet. Some Aghriā also believe that, if a baby cries in the night without being fully awake, Yama—the God of Death— tells the child that his father has died. If the child, however, smiles or laughs in the same situation, it is believed, that Yama tells the baby that his mother has passed away. The child then laughs because, having been breastfed a little while ago, he does not believe it. Yama is said to crack bad jokes with the babies.

Ṣaṭhi/Ṣaṣṭhi—the sixth day

If birth has taken place at a hospital, the baby is ceremonially welcomed in the house. For that day the house is already cleaned, parts are newly plastered with cow dung, others parts may be painted or otherwise cleaned, and the whole decorated with flowers and mango leaf torans. The family awaits the child at the door keeping a pot (*gaḍu*) with water, a light, and milk next to a kalas. The child is washed—particularly the feet—and fed with milk.

A first ritual takes place on the sixth day after birth known as *ṣaṭhi* (= sixth in Sambalpuri) or as *ṣaṣṭhi* (= sixth in Oriya). It should be performed in the house of the couple (the husband's house), but in some cases, if the mother still stays in her parent's house, it may be done there. In the case of an illness of the mother, it must be delayed. In the morning the young mother takes a bath in water mixed with *nīm* leaves and *nirgun* leaves, which are said to help against germs. The other women in the house take a deep bath on this day—including a complete dip in the water and the washing of the hair.

On this day, the barber and washerman are called upon. The first one—apart from cutting the hair if necessary—shaves the men and cuts the nails of the women; the latter takes at least one cloth of all Aghriā houses in the village for washing. In addition, the house is to be purified with cow dung and water mixed with turmeric. The mother's brother of the baby should provide the new clothing that the mother and the baby wear on this day, but in a case I observed, it was actually the mother's mother who was present and offered it on behalf of her son.

Later on the same day, the umbilical cord, which usually falls within six days after birth, is buried either by the mother, still in the new clothes, or in some cases by her midwife. The burial is performed under the eaves of the house—a place known as *ulchhā tal* (*ulchhā* = eaves; *tal* = under) exactly between the spot where rain drops fall and the veranda. This is the very same place where the ancestors arrive once a year in the dark side of the month of Āśbina and where they are worshipped. Together with the umbilical cord some *haldi chāul* (grinded raw *aruā* rice with turmeric) and *haridā* (a local fruit) are buried. The mother digs a small hole for it with a sickle (*dā*). Some Aghriā say that the burial formerly took place secretly. In contrast to other rituals, it is not necessary to have a *jāti* as a witness on this day.

Later the baby is bathed and receives new clothes. Both grandmothers of the baby (FM, MM), if alive, may wash the baby's feet with milk. The elder women of the house may follow. The women also present gifts to the child, known as *goḍ dhuā*. The gift of the mother's brother is particularly essential in showing the responsibility of the mother's brother's home to care for the child.

The cooking should not begin before the barber and the washerman have arrived and have completed their work. Later in the evening the house is once more sprinkled with Ganga-water for purification. Often in the evening meat is served for the family and guests or a *jāti* feast can also be offered.

Bāra Rāta—the twelfth night and protection of the child against the evil eye

On Bāra Rāta a simple fire ritual or *homa* is performed by a priest, to which the following gods and goddesses are invited: Ganesh, Nārāyaṇ, Rudra/Śiva and Ambika/Durgā. The following ritual items as listed by a priest are required for the ritual: (1) *kalaś*; (2) coconut; (3) flowers; (4) *duba* grass; (5) *chokni*/leaf-bowl with sand; (6) *sāl* wood; (7) *jāgar* (light filled with *ghī* during ritual); (8) *gobar* (cow dung); (9) *ghī*; (10) *dhup kāthi* (incense sticks); (11) milk; (12) *dakhinā* (payment for the priest); (13) *pātri* (small copper bowl with *chāul, haridā, kusa* grass in it); (14) *kharchā* for the priest (*chāul*, salt, veg, lentils, tomatoes, potato) and (15) *chāul* and *haridā* in *sāl chokni*.) To purify the family, Ganga-water is sprinkled over the mother—or both parents if present—and over the child. *Ghī* is offered to the mother and child, who additionally receive a *ṭikā* of *ghī* and a black one of ash. Additionally, the priest recites the blessings. According to some Aghriā the ritual on the twelfth day is particularly for *ṣaṣṭhi*, the goddess of fate, who writes the fate of the new born child on his forehead on this day. At least one *jāti* should be fed on the same day. Sometimes the barber and washerman are called in again.

The baby should get a small black thread known as an *aṇṭā dor* (*dor* = thread) or sometimes simply as a *sūtā* (thread) with a little piece of gold to wear around his hip on this day. This is particularly necessary for girls. In former times young women would wear it during their first menstruation as well. If a family could afford it, a black thread might be replaced by a silver chain known as *gūnchi*. The black thread, like the black *ṭikā* on the forehead, wards off the evil eye while gold is auspicious and pure. This black spot or *ṭikā* on the forehead is applied to a child for at least one or two years and is renewed everyday after the washing. Traditionally, the black substance used is produced either by burning some cotton cloth with castor oil or by using *kajal* mixed in the house to combine with black substance under the cooking pots, castor oil and malam (cye-anointment from a medical store). The applied ash is said to keep away the evil eye known as *ainkh parbā* (*ainkh* = eye; *parbā* = to apply) in Lariā or as *buri najar* (*buri* = bad, inauspicious; *najar* = sight), *najar lāgibā* (*lāgibā* = to apply) or *najar parbā* in Hindi. The black *ṭikā* should be applied on the day of birth, but more importantly when the child leaves the house. *Kajal* is also applied to the eyes of the children. As in the case of pregnant women, small children should not leave the house around sunset until they can walk to avoid any negative influence of evil spirits.[4]

Sometimes an amulet is given to children to wear around the neck. Made of five metals, a combination of iron, gold, silver, copper and tin. It is worn on a black thread similar to the north Indian *tawiz*, but known here as *ḍeunriā*. It may be filled with roots or leaves of medical plants known as *jari būṭi*. These amulets are said to help protect the child against the evil eye, but also against the negative effects of the planets. Some children are said to have a hard shadow (*kar chhāyā*) and are less vulnerable to evil spirits (*bhut*) or the evil eye. Others, however, are said to have a soft shadow (*mrudu chhāyā* or *siar chhāyā*) and are easily affected by these evil forces.[5] In the latter cases or if the child is generally weak and parents are afraid that he may not survive, the child may also be sold to lower communities.

Ekoīśiā—the twenty-first day and nāmkaraṇa—the name-giving ceremony

Often the rituals of the twenty-first day and name-giving are combined. For every child, the twenty-first day ceremony should be done before marriage, if it is impossible on the twenty-first day itself. However, nowadays this rule is not strictly kept. In some cases there are children already around ten years of age and still an *ekoīśiā* has not yet been performed.

The *ekoīśiā* is usually a *Satyanārāyaṇ Pūjā*—a ritual for five gods, Nārāyaṇ, Śiva, Gaṇeś, Suryā and Durgā. For them a small platform is erected and is surrounded by four small bowls with rice. In each of them a wooden stick is placed in order they form a pyramid together. On top of this pyramid some flowers and a red cloth is kept. For every god, a betel leaf is kept on the stool as seat (*padmāsan*) and another *mandala* for the nine planets is prepared. The parents of the child sit as sacrifiers or *karttā* next to the priest. After inviting and worshipping the gods, the clothes of the parents are tied by a sister of the father who wraps rice and a betel nut within it. Later, a fire ritual (*homa*) is performed by a priest. Finally the mother's brother of the child appears and, after showing his respect to the invoked, applies some sandal on the forehead of his sister's child, puts a garland around his neck and then offers gifts such as a golden ring. The gifts of the mother's brother are known as *maulā bhār*—as in the case of marriage later as well. Other relatives, such as the mother's younger sister, the father's sister, the father's brother, follow who also wash the feet of the child with milk and *pañchāmrut* and feed the child with them before offering gifts—usually jewellery, cloths or money. Another fire ritual is performed subsequently, in which the parents circle around the fire seven times clockwise (*bedhā bulā* = circling), followed by an *ārthi* before the father's sister opens the knot of the parents again.

Usually children have more then one name, that is, different names are used in different contexts. One name is fixed in the horoscope prepared by an astrologer or a priest. He decides, for example, the first letter of the name during the ritual just described and the parents must then find a suitable name—a name that is relevant to the rituals later. According to some Aghriā, this name should be uttered into the ear of the child, before it is announced publicly and a coconut is broken. Another name, rather a kind of nickname, is selected for daily use, while often yet another is used on official papers such as identity cards. Relatives, such as the elder brothers of the father, are often involved in choosing names while any relative may suggest a name. These names may also hint at rebirths.[6] Names beginning with the letter P are considered to be inauspicious and are avoided in ritual contexts. Additionally, a child may take on even more nicknames later, e.g. by being sold.

Some Aghriā argue that the main purpose of the *ekoīśiā* is to feed the *jāti*. At the end of the ceremony all relatives on the mother's side receive a gift known as māen. It is not obligatory to give that gift to the relatives of the father's side, but it is often done.

Jātak—horoscope

After birth, an astrologer or *Jyotisiā* writes the horoscope of the child by observing the constellation of stars at the moment of birth and predicting future influences on the life of a child by observing constellations of stars. Negative as well as positive effects of certain planets may result in the loss of all wealth, in illnesses, but also in bright prospects for a marriage, for example, as singled out by an astrologer.

At the time of death the *jātak* should be burnt on the pyre or should be immersed in a river or pond together with the ash of the deceased. However, it is not inauspicious to keep it.

Bhāt khuā—the first eating of rice

The child should eat his first serving of rice roughly six months after birth and usually less than a year after birth. It is considered very auspicious to feed the first serving of rice on the day of a *Rath Jātrā* or on *Nuā Khāi*, when the new rice is eaten as an essential part of the agricultural cycle in the month of Aśbina. However, this is not obligatory for all children. In this case a priest or astrologer would fix an auspicious date.

Some Aghriā argue that a baby gets his soul by eating the first serving of rice given by his mother's brother. Before a child has eaten rice, it should not touch any elder, while they are eating. Furthermore, before eating rice the child should not be brought in front of the gods, particularly not Jagannāth. However, it is very popular to bring small children during the *Rath Jātrā* to the carriage of Jagannāth in order to receive the Lord's blessing by touching his car known as the *rath chhiān* (*rath* = car; *chhiān* = to touch)—of course after the children have eaten their first meal of rice.

If possible, the closest mother's brother (*nijer māmu*), who is specially invited, should be present on the occasion of the first rice feeding and the child should sit on his lap while he feeds the child with *khiri*—a mixture of boiled rice (*aruā-chāul*), sugar and milk. This means that the mother's brother offers the first meal of rice to the child. However, sweets and *mahāpraśād* may also be offered to the child in the case that the feeding of rice takes place during the *Rath Jātrā*. In one case, however, the father's father also did it, but that situation seems to be an exception. The *māmu* is also supposed to give some gifts on this day such as sweets, some money and if his family is financially sound, a gold ornament. In any case he has to give a plate usually made of brass (*kansā*), but in rare cases of silver or gold. Some Aghriā name these gifts *maulā bhār* (like during *ekoīśiā* and during the wedding), while others disagree with this custom. However, a *māmu* should state, while feeding the child first: 'Everyday you should get that much nectar (*amruta*). Everyday five fingers shall go to your mouth (implicit: you should always have enough to eat). My *bhanjā/bhānjī* should get sweet rice like this everyday.' Other relatives, like the mother's mother, father's mother, father's sister, father's father's younger brother, etc., who are present, should repeat this feeding and may also offer some money.

Bāl pakā—the first ritual haircut

The first haircut—or *bāl pakā* (*bāl* = hair; *pakā* derived from *pakeibā* = to throw)—considered to be auspicious is usually done within the first two years after birth. It seems that more importance is placed on the haircuts of sons, although some Aghriā also perform the first ritual haircut of their daughter. A day is usually fixed by a priest, who then performs a small ritual before a barber finally not only cuts the hair, but shaves the head of the child completely. The mother's brother may be invited to this ceremony. In one case, the mother's brother brought all the necessary items for the haircut, i.e. a new towel for his sister's son, a mirror, razorblades and a cloth for the barber. Everything was later given to the barber. Before cutting, some milk was rubbed into the hair of the child. The hair was kept in a towel subsequently until someone from the family was able to throw it into the sea in Puri.[7]

In some cases, the Aghriā also combine the first haircut of their child with a pilgrimage to Puri or another holy centre, where the hair is cut within the temple premises and then thrown into the sea.

Kān Guru—initiation

The child is initiated by a so-called Kān Guru (*kān* = ear), who whispers a *mantra*—a sacred hymn—into the ear of a child at about the age of ten. The mantra is not only sacred, but also secret and the child is not allowed to tell it to anyone else. Nevertheless, it is known that a Guru uses the same mantra for all clients—male and female—who are at the same time his *jajmān*. For the initiation a Baruṇ Pūjā is performed, in which the Kān Guru also presents a garland made of *tulsi* leaves. In the region a Kān Guru usually belongs to the Gosain-community[8] and the Guru is seen and addressed as a father by his clients—no matter how old they are. Additionally, the wife of the Guru is also seen as a mother or as *guru-mā*.

Every child should be initiated in this manner before marriage in order to be purified. However, nowadays it is not done in all cases or sometimes even after marriage.

Following steps

Some Aghriā also say that a mother should not eat meat or fish until the child is around one or one and a half years old. The milk teeth of a child are thrown on the roof of the house (on the tiles) after having fallen out, as no one should walk over them. The weekday of the birth, which is remembered, keeps some significance in the sense that some Aghriā refrain from cutting their nails or their hair on this day, e.g. a Saturday. This rule is, however, not strictly observed by everyone.

There is no fixed rule for the length of breastfeeding among the Aghriā. In some cases it may continue for several years. To wean a child women can apply use the paste of the *nīm* leaves.

In former times, around the age of six, the piercing of the ear for earrings was considered an important step known as *kān bedhā* (*kān* = ear; *bedhā* = to pierce). This was done also in the case of boys. As one Aghriā remembered, children received big sweets and a *bhāgbād* (religious singing) was performed before the barber finally pierced their ears. In this case the maternal grandmother (MM) offered an earring, which should be given by the mother's brother's house if possible.

Banā gudhā—tattoos

Formerly, at the age of ten or twelve, but usually before their marriage, girls were tattooed. Some people said that without tattoos, known as *banā gudhā*, women were not allowed to marry. In most cases arms, lower legs and feet were decorated by specialists called Guḍiā by using needles and turmeric. Nowadays these tattoos, which were also seen as a present of the girl's parents to their daughter, can be seen only among elder women. Young women often have only a very small tattoo in form of a lizard, scorpion or abstract pattern of two lines and a point on their hand, which are applied by other girls.

Tattoos, painfully applied, are said to help reduce the punishment of Yama that one must face at the time of death; if one has already suffered during one's lifetime, Yama's verdict will be less harsh. Or older women may also argue that their decoration—often flowers oı an abstract pattern—will remain even after death on the way to Yamlok, while family members keep the other jewellery. This change of custom is either explained by the fact that the Guḍiā do not visit the villages anymore or by a changing fashion—that women or even men do not like these tattoos any longer.

1.2. MARRIAGE AND WEDDING CUSTOMS

The marriage season starts at the end of January, after the harvest and threshing of paddy have been completed, and it lasts until the beginning of the monsoon when the agricultural work starts again. Negotiations can be initiated the whole year round except during the month of Pouṣ (around December/January) which is considered to be inauspicious, fruitless and without merits as far as rituals and such negotiations are concerned.

Kanyā dekhā—seeing the bride

The first step to arranging a marriage is to see the bride—or *kanyā dekhā* (*kanyā* = bride; *dekhā* = to see). It should take place after *De Uthā*. The groom, accompanied by some male or female relatives—quite often elder brothers, elder sister's husbands, elder sisters and elder brother's wives—or sometimes even some relatives without the groom visit the house of a potential bride without necessarily informing them in advance. After having reached the bride's house, first brass pots with water are placed at the disposal of the guests. They are then offered a snack and, during the course of the visit, the bride usually serves some tea to the guests. Before leaving the house the groom's side is expected to make certain statements such as 'please, tell us the date, when you would like to visit our house' or 'we like the bride and will send our parents' or 'we will send a message for a *ghar dekhā*', etc. Or they just ask for the date and time of birth of the bride in order to see if the horoscopes match (*sujhabār*, *bal sujhabār*). The horoscopes should be compared prior to marriage. In any case at this stage nothing binding is formulated.

Between the *kanyā dekhā* and the actual wedding, the groom is not supposed to visit the house of his prospective father-in-law. In some cases relatives known to both sides act as go-betweens, but there are no formal mediators. To inquire about the opinion of the potential bride in regard to the groom, often a *bahu*, a married sister or a grandmother (FM, MM) will act as a mediator, because a daughter is not expected to criticise her father, mother or brother—or their suggestions or decisions —in their presence, but would rather show them her respect. A critic is expressed via a mediator then.

Ghar dekhā—inspection of the groom's house

If both sides are satisfied with the *kanyā dekhā* and interested in this new relationship, some time later a visit to the house of the groom is arranged. This time, however, the bride's side informs the groom's family about the date of their visit. During this visit older relatives—preferably in an odd number—such as the father, father's brothers, mother's brother, grandfather, father's sister's husband, as well as relatives of the groom's and bride's generation are included. Before their departure, sometimes the bride's people will put a small brass pot (*gaḍu*) filled with water, flowers, basil, curd and small fishes (such as *pitā jhuri*) at the entrance of the house to symbolize an auspicious beginning or *subha lagna*. The bride's side has the right to inspect the potential in-laws house of their daughter thoroughly during the *ghar dekhā* (*ghar* = house; *dekhā* = to see). This may include a look at the threshing floor—from the straw the harvest and, thus, the wealth of the family can be estimated—the well, the stable, and the kitchen.

After offering a meal both sides sit together and discuss marriage plans. Often an elder or the eldest members of the of the bride's side begin—on behalf of the group—to state their impression of the house by saying, 'We are happy to see your property and we would like to give our daughter. Tell us if you have any demands or problems' or the groom's side may begin by saying, 'You have seen the house, you have seen the boy, so please tell us your opinion!' In this manner both sides convey their impressions and if both agree they may even proceed to fix a marriage date after consulting an astrologer. The groom usually keeps a low profile during the gathering but may be called upon in order to be interviewed by the bride's people. Before leaving the house, all relatives of the bride's side receive some gifts consisting of sweets known as *chipṭi* and a cloth. The gift of a cloth is called *māen* and returned if the relationship breaks up before marriage.

In the case of marriage with a cross-cousin or other close relatives, there is no necessity for a *kanyā dekhā* or a *ghar dekhā*, because the families are already closely related and 'familiar' with each other. However, even in these cases it is done sometimes as a mere formality.

Pindhen/Pindhānī ghar—engagement

Occasionally, although not necessarily, before the actual wedding an engagement ceremony is celebrated. This is done in cases where there is a longer time period between the negotiations and the planned wedding. It is then seen as a confirmation of the wedding to be observed later. In one case an engagement was celebrated in April for a marriage planned for January the following year. However, engagement ceremonies seem to be a recent innovation adopted from other castes.

The word *pindhānī ghar* is derived from *pindhibā* or to wear—here in the special sense of wearing jewellery, which the groom's side is obliged to give as part of their gifts to be handed over on the occasion. Ideally some of the jewellery of the potential groom's mother should be given.

In a concrete case observed which I observed in an urban setting, the groom's party, including the groom himself, visited the house of the bride for the engagement. There, a small fire ritual was performed by a Brahmin. The groom appeared and worshipped the gods. After he left, the bride did the same. A sister of the groom offered a *śāḍhi* (*sari*) and different cosmetic articles to the bride. Usually, however, the mother or father's brother's wife would offer some gold ornaments on this occasion to show their prestige and wealth. Later, the groom and bride appeared together and exchanged golden rings before accepting the blessing of their older relatives, including the *māmu* of the bride.

The engagement is not seen as legally binding, but there is also no known case in which the wedding did not follow an engagement.

Lagan dharā—finding of an auspicious date and invitations

For a wedding, the determination of an auspicious date called *lagan dharā* (*lagna* = auspicious date; *dharā* = to give) is of the utmost importance. A Brahmin or astrologer is consulted. Seven days before a wedding, the date should be fixed and during a meeting of both sides in the house of the bride a formal invitation called *lagna patri* should be exchanged. Usually an auspicious *ṭikā* of turmeric is added to this invitation card, which has sometimes already been printed for this particular day. A *jāti,* as the witness, should be present during the final negotiations. On the way to the *lagan dharā* meeting people carefully watch for any omen or auspicious or inauspicious signs. In the case that there are both auspicious signs (women fetching water) as well as inauspicious signs (empty pots) the auspicious signs are considered more important.

Thereafter the movement of the bride and groom should be restricted and they should not leave the house unnecessarily. Nowadays, invitation cards (*nimantraṇa patrā*) are sent, while previously an invitation consisted of turmeric wrapped in a mango leaf together with *guḍ* and *chuḍā*. This should still be sent at least to the 'daughters of the house' (FZ, Z, D, BD) for whom the mixture of *guḍ* and *chuḍā* is traditionally meant to be food for the journey. This older form of invititation is also known as *gundā debā* or 'to give powder' here in the sense of giving turmeric powder.

The first invitation should always be sent to the village goddess, whose blessings are sought. In some cases the sacrificer performs a small ritual in front of her shrine and in the presence of the groom to invite her formally. After the *Grām Śrī*, the *māmu* should be invited next, and a brother of the groom or bride should bring an invitation to him personally. Furthermore, all sisters should be invited by their brothers personally. To the *jāti*, *haldi chāul* is brought and thrown in front of the kitchen—a process also known as *neutā*.[9] The other villagers are invited by a Gauḍ Narihā in his function as messenger of auspicious news.

In former times the wedding ceremony took up to seven days, this has slowly been shortened over the years to the three days celebrated nowadays. The programme of the last two days has not changed, but prior to that, up to five days were filled with a process of anointment with oil known as *tel chadā* feasts, and songs depending on the financial conditions of the families. The women used to wail the entire length of the days.

First day

NAḌIĀ PHUṬĀ—BREAKING OF COCONUTS

Traditionally, on the evening of the first day some men of the groom's side visit the bride's side. It should be an odd number of men and among them should be a *jāti* and a Gauḍ (member of a caste, which is responsible for cattle herding and in former times also water carrying in the village). The latter is supposed to carry a *bhār* (a wooden stick carried on the shoulder with two baskets fitted to it—the traditional method of carrying goods) with food. In one case, apart from these two men, an elder brother, two elder sister's husbands, an elder brother's daughter's husband and an elder brother's daughter's husband's father went on this occasion. The groom himself does not go. Their departure from the groom's village is often celebrated with firecrackers and the car they take is blessed. They should take 21 coconuts, three *śaḍhis* (one for the bride, called *antil*, one for the bride's mother, called *dasami* plus an additional one named *chagna* or *sagei*), jewellery for the bride, and some *chuḍā*. All of these items are usually carried in a big basket named *jhāmpi*.

After the arrival of the groom's people in the bride's village, they are led to the house of a bride's *jāti*, but not directly to the bride's house. Here some food is served to them. Later, a member of the groom's party is sent to the bride's house with a coconut and a cloth, which iṣ known as *raibārī chalā*, which is derived from *raibārī* either as Sunday or as farce and from *chalā* 'to walk'. The combination *raibārī chalā* also means 'to walk slowly'. Quite often people of the bride's village give the wrong directions to the groom's envoy who is often not familiar to the bride's village. Ideally, the envoy should walk the way seven times—though it is hardly done in practice. Both misleading the groom's men and sending them away after their initial visit is seen as a form of joking. In former times and occasionally still today, the bride's party used to give or gives a condition to the messenger such as 'We are a big family. Will you agree to that?' Subsequently, the envoy returns to his party and must come again with an affirmative answer.

Later, after finding the bride's house and after the initial gifts have been accepted, the groom's entire party goes to the bride's house, where they explain the reason of their visit. An elder member of the groom's party says, for instance, 'We have heard that there is a daughter about to get married in this village and we would like to marry her to our son.' Formerly the groom's side would ask the following sentence at the beginning of the *raibārī chalā*: 'Our son is flowing in the river. Will you help rescue him?' Afterwards, the clans (*banśa* and *gotra*) are publicly compared to avoid any violation of exogamy rules. The negotiations are then continued inside the house and again the clans are compared. Finally, an elder member of the bride's party agrees to the proposal. This is followed by the handing over of the coconuts and other gifts by groom's people. All gifts, particularly the jewellery, are displayed in front of all guests and commented upon. The bride's side also offers at least seven coconuts. Two potential relatives—a member from each side—break the first coconut together and simultaneously, before all the other coconuts are broken. However, one coconut of the groom's side will be kept for the bride in order to be carried by her during the following rituals of *tel chaḍā*. Pieces of the broken coconuts are mixed with the *chuḍā* and *guḍ* and offered by the groom's side. They are regarded as *prāśād*, as the coconuts are broken in the name of Jagannāth and Viṣṇu. The father of the bride usually remains in the background and is not actively involved in the discussions and proceedings.

The *naḍiā phuṭā* is seen as an initial important step for the wedding and it is said that a marriage cannot be stopped after the *naḍiā phuṭā* has been performed. All the members of the groom's party who have gone to the bride's village on this occasion, are entitled to receive a cloth and some sweets known as *chipṭi* from the bride's side.

In many of the following rituals of marriage, the mother, father or both parents of the bride or groom have to enact important roles. However, if the mother is a widow or somehow excluded from the caste, she is not allowed to perform these rituals. For the entire ceremony a married couple fulfilling the roles of mother and father is of the utmost importance. If the mother or father of the bride or groom has already passed away, another married couple, for instance an uncle or aunt (e.g. FyB/FyBW, etc.) can act as 'parents' in these auspicious rituals including the ritual for the ancestors and the acceptance of gifts, etc.

At roughly the same time similar rituals take place in the bride's and groom's villages until the groom's party finally heads to the bride's village. Therefore, in the description provided below I have summarized activities occurring in both villages simultaneously under the same heading.

THE COLLECTION OF *MAHUĀ* BRANCHES AND *GRĀM ŚRĪ PŪJĀ* (OR *DEVGANASAN*)

The ceremonies cannot start before the mother's brothers (*māmu*) of the bride and groom have arrived and have been ritually welcomed. The *māmu*'s stops on the outskirts of the sister's daughter's or sister's son's village. He then sends a message to their house and the drummers are sent with a pot full of water in order to bring him to the house in a small procession. He is then made to stand on a small platform where his sister washes his feet before he enters the house.

While some male members of the groom's side have gone to the bride's village for the *naḍiā phuṭā* in the groom's village, the mother of the groom together with some *suhāsen*[10] walk in a procession to the outskirts of the village. The same is also usually done in the bride's village while the groom's people there are sitting in the *jāti*'s house, although it should be done only after the *naḍiā phuṭā* has been performed. In this procession the mother carries a big basket called a *paralā ḍalā* on her head, which contains a coconut partly wrapped in a white cloth with some grinded rice, oil (*tel*), *chāul*, *soltā* (*ghī*-lamps), a cloth and seven kinds of powder sometimes formed in small balls. If balls have already been formed, seven of them are required. The powders consist of: (1) white *pithau,* a mixture between *chunā* (rice powder) and water; (2) red *itāgunda* or brick powder; (3) yellow *haldigunda*/turmeric powder; (4) black *koilāgunda*/coal powder; (5) crème-coloured *kasārgunda* or *murhigunda* as a powder made of *murhi* (a form of *chāul* heated on hot sand); (6) brown *khata* or dried cow dung; and (7) green *phagugunda* or coloured powder. Additionally, some cow dung, symbolizing Gauri, which some believe is a form of Durgā, is carried in the *paralā ḍalā*. Two female *suhāsen* carry a *kalas kunḍi* each—an earthen pot either filled with paddy (*dhān*) symbolizing Goddess Lakṣmī or filled with water symbolizing Nārāyaṇ (Viṣṇu). On top of each pot, a lamp is placed.

The procession, led by drummers, halts in front of a bullock cart, where some *mahuā* branches are placed and considered to be pure and auspicious. Seven circles are drawn by the mother using one of the coloured powders each before she touches the *mahuā* branches seven times with a paste of *chunā* (rice powder) and water in her hands leaving seven handprints on the *mahul ḍāl*. As in the case of the village goddess later, this is understood to be an invitation to the gods and goddesses to act as witnesses for the wedding. The *mahuā* branches on the cart are then carried to the wedding altar by some male *jāti*, member while the mother carries the *paralā ḍalā* and the *suhāsen* the *kunḍi* back. The procession is welcomed back in the house by some older women of the house, who have placed auspicious *kalas* on some drawings of rice powder and sprinkle water over the participants of the procession seven times.

Afterwards, another little procession follows and a second ritual is performed near a tree to dig some soil, which is later put beneath the three *mahuā* branches at the wedding altar. The digging is done by the Kālo, assisted by the Narihā. Initially, the Grām Śrī, but also other local gods and goddesses such as Mā Bhainro, Rākasbuddhā, etc., are invoked and worshipped. An abstract pattern with the various coloured powders is drawn for the gods and a little *teilābhiṣek* may be performed. Then the Kālo digs some earth with a ploughshare, around which he ties a white thread seven times. The ploughshare is touched by seven *suhāsen* while he is digging. The soil, symbolizing the village goddess, is then thrown by the Kālo over his right shoulder into the *paralā ḍalā* behind him, as it is said to be disrespectful for a sacrificer of the village goddess to show her his back. This digging of the soil is also explained as a promise to go to the proper shrine of the village goddess the following day. Some Aghriā say this small procession in the evening or perhaps even during night is led to the outskirts only, because—keeping in mind the wild animals—it would be too dangerous to visit the village goddess in the forest. The ceremonial welcome in the house is the same as the collecting of the *mahuā* branches.

TEILABHIṢEK OR *TEL CHAḌĀ*—ANOINTING OF BRIDE AND GROOM WITH OIL AND TURMERIC

The *mahuā* branches are brought to the wedding altar, a square wooden construction with wooden posts and an earthen pot in each corner representing the four directions. In former times seven pots would be placed: five big pots (*ḍibi*), a medium size pot (*kuṇḍhi*) and finally a small one (*guḍā*) on top. On the roof some *jaṃ* branches and leaves are placed which people believe have a cooling effect. Some male *jāti* members now climb up to the roof of the altar in order to pass the three *mahuā* branches from the roof down to the middle of the *bedī*. The three branches that have been brought in the procession are sometimes referred to as Viṣṇu, Śiva and Brahma. It is the responsibility of the female *suhāsen* to pull the *mahuā* branches down from the roof after the *jāti* have put them slightly through the roof—just enough for the *suhāsen* to grasp them. As a part of a joke the *jāti* usually pour water from the roof over the *suhāsen* below while they are trying to pull down the *mahuā* branches.

Once the three *mahuā* branches have been installed at the centre of the wedding altar, the mother sits in front of it with the lower part of the *paralā ḍalā* on her head. While she looks downwards under her veil, seven female *suhāsen* hold the basket circling and pulling it back and forth over her head before they finally place the soil in the basket under the three *mahuā* branches. Next to the *mahuā* branches are the two *kalas kundi*, which have already figured in the procession. Additionally, a small wooden stick with seven cuts is of the utmost significance. Kept in front of the *mahul ḍāl*, this so-called *kalyāṇī khuṇṭ* or *kalihāri khuṇṭ* is said either to symbolize the Goddess of Blessing (Kalyāṇī) or *kalihāri* is translated to 'not to be disputed'—as a sign of unity. Some people further explain this feature as symbolic of seven stars or seven sages (*rishi*) invited as witnesses for the wedding. The *kalyāṇī khuṇṭ* must be produced and given by a *jāti*, who is named in a meeting of all *jāti* in the village prior to the wedding. In the same way, the small stool on which bride and groom sit during the subsequent rituals is offered by a *jāti*. The *paralā ḍlā* is also kept in the middle of the altar, which is usually decorated with some abstract pattern called *jhoti*, made of rice powder. Another addition is a small ball made of cow dung, essentially representing the Goddess Gauri. Apart from the necessary arrangement for the altar, a group of drummers, usually belonging to the so-called 'untouchable' caste of Ghansiā or Harijan/Gandā, is essential to produce the auspicious sounds.

In both the houses, the *teilābhiṣek* takes place on the evening of the first day of the wedding rituals, and the groom or the bride is guided to the *bedī* by a *suhāsen*. It can only begin after the mother's brother or at least his gifts, called *maulā bhār* have arrived some turmeric, oil, vegetables, *chāul*, a cloth, plus the gifts he will later present to his sister's son. Quite often a sister-in-law takes the role[10] of guiding the groom, although in one case I observed the bride was led by her maternal grandmother (MM). The groom and the bride, with their hands folded, each carry a coconut to the *bedī*. Their hands are decorated with *mehendi* a day before. The *suhāsen,* walking in front of the bride or groom, holds a pot of water (made of brass) and drops some on the ground as she goes. After this first clockwise round at the altar and after the groom or bride has put some paddy in all four corners and at the centre of the stool as well as after he has thrown paddy in all six directions (north, east, west, south as well as, up and down), the bride or groom sits down on a small stool. Bride and groom face eastwards during this and all the other rituals that follow.

Now the *teilābhiṣek* begins, which should be performed first by a Brahmin (not necessarily the *purohit*). Subsequently, at least seven male *suhāsen* followed by at least seven female *suhāsen*—each belonging to the generation of bride and groom or to an alternate generation (such as grandparent's and grandchildren's generation)—are required for the ritual (widows and widowers are excluded).[11]

Each of the *suhāsen* takes two mango leaves, dips them into a mixture of turmeric and clarified butter or sometimes oil and then anoints first and foremost the *kalyāṇi khuṇṭ*, the two *kalaś*, the *paralā ḍalā* and then the groom or bride. *Ghī* is considered to have a heating capacity, while turmeric is believed to have a cooling effect apart from being purifying. The anointing of the bride and groom commences with touching their feet with the same mango leaves followed by the knee, the hips, the shoulders and finally the head. All this should be done seven times. The movement with the mango leaves in this particular *teilābhiṣek* is strictly upwards and is therefore also called *tel chaḍā* (*chaḍā* = to climb up). At the end each *suhāsen* takes some extra turmeric oil mixture in his or her hand to anoint the face of the groom or bride, a ritual which the *suhāsen* usually enjoy more than the bride or the groom, and which again is seen as a joke between the *suhāsen* and the bride or groom. After the seven male *suhāsen* have completed the *tel chaḍā*, the bride or groom are once again led around the *mahuā* branches, before the seven female *suhāsen* follow. A final round in the same manner completes the ritual.

After the *teilābhiṣek,* the bride and groom should not take any baths until before the wedding party (*barāt*) leaves on the next day, but there is no such strict rule nowadays. For relatives and separately for the *jāti* of the village, a feast (*bhoji*) is served, but groom and bride should not eat any non-vegetarian food.

Second day

GRĀM ŚRĪ PŪJĀ (OR *DEGANSAN)*— RITUAL FOR THE VILLAGE GODDESS

In the morning of the following day, another procession is led to the shrine of the village goddess (*demul*). Usually the evening before, a nearby tree is worshipped as place of the Grām Śrī because her main shrine is too far away in the jungle and the place is seen as too dangerous to be visited after sunset. However on the second day the proper shrine of the village goddess is approached. Once more the mother, carrying the *paralā ḍalā*, the *suhāsen* and the drummers join the procession and the same digging ritual is performed by the Kālo. Again, the Kālo asks the Grām Śrī if he is allowed to remove some soil, which is then brought to the altar.

TEL UTARĀ

Later in the morning or around noontime the *teilābhiṣek* ceremony is repeated, but with a few significant differences from the first day. The groom (or bride) appears in the same clothes worn during the first ritual and not washed since. After the bride and groom have arrived at the altar in their respective villages they circle around the *mahuā* branches as described earlier. Afterwards, only female *suhāsen* anoint the bride and groom in the same way as before, but now they use a mixture of turmeric and castor oil. Furthermore, on this day the anointing is done not only upwards, but also downwards—from the head to the knees. Instead of *tel chaḍā,* it is now called *tel utarā* (*utarā* = down, coming out). Afterwards, the groom leaves the altar for a while and reappears with a big yellow or reddish cross on the front and back of his shirt. This cross, drawn by the *suhāsen* with a mixture of *chunā*, brick powder, etc., is also applied to the basket and the small stool. The groom and bride now wear a crown of at least leaves. This symbolizes their higher status and from now on they will not have to show their respect to any elder relative, but only to the priest. The groom is now considered a king according to some Aghriā. The same crowns are also placed on top of the *kalyānī khuṇṭ*, on the *mahuā* branches, and the *kalaś* in the four corners of the altar as well as the pots symbolizing Lakṣmī and Nārāyaṇ.

In the final part of this sequence the *suhāsen* start applying turmeric mixed with castor oil not only to the whole body of the groom, but also to all other persons present, in particular to people with whom they can joke, as this applying of turmeric known as *haldi makhā* (*makhā* = to apply) is another form of joking during the wedding.

BATH

After completing the second *teilābhiṣek, suhāsen* accompany the bride and groom to the pond for a ritual bath. Neither groom nor bride should touch the ground before they return to the house later—so they are either carried in a vehicle, on a bike or leaves are simply placed on the ground, on which they are allowed to step. Ideally, a *bāṭo*, an elder sister's husband, should carry the bride or groom.[12] The *suhāsen* again carry the two *kalaś* and an umbrella for the bride or groom in this procession and the mother has to transport the *paralā ḍalā* on her head once more.

Near the pond, the groom or bride sit in the lower part of the basket (*paralā ḍalā*) while the *suhāsen* draw seven circles with differently coloured powders, as during the *Grām Śrī Pūjā*, but this time between the basket and the water of the pond. After this, they begin another *teilābhiṣek* for the groom or bride. Finally, seven *suhāsen* pull the basket collectively towards the water.

The *kalaś* with water is refilled and the procession returns home with the drummers in the lead. Before entering the house, the groom or bride waits in front still standing on a leaf plate and not touching the ground. The mother stands behind them holding the upper part of her *śaḍhi* over the head of her son or daughter—a custom known as *kāni ḍhapā*. A *suhāsen* then pours water from the *kalaś* just refilled over the head of groom or bride—a process regarded by some Aghriā as *abhihāri pāen utarā* (throwing out of the unmarried water), while others call it *pāen neuchā* (*pāen* = water; *neuchā* = taking).

PITRU PŪJĀ—RITUAL FOR THE ANCESTORS

The Aghriā are allowed to perform a *pitru pūjā* for the first time as a bride or groom. Both, the groom as well as the bride should fast until the *pūjā* is over. Some people are also of the opinion that the groom or bride should not speak from the bath until the end of the ritual.

The ancestors are invited to the marriage altar, sealed off by cloths in order to avoid any kind of disturbance for the ancestors. Apart from the bride and groom, the parents perform the ritual. In front of the *mahuā* branches, seven wicks (*soltā*) soaked in *ghī* are lit in remembrance of the previous seven generations on the father's side. Some leaf plates are prepared. Their number seems to differ from family to family. In one case, five big leaf plates, consisting of fifteen small leaves each, were prepared and offered to the father of the groom (who had died before the marriage), the father's elder brother, the father's father, great grandfather (FFF) and great great grandfather (FFFF). Additionally, smaller leaf plates consisting of two *phalśā* (Sambalpuri)/*phalās* (Oriya) leaves each were offered for the wives of these ancestors in the male line. Special cakes (*barā* and *mai muhuri*) as well as water in a *panas* (Sambalpuri)/*paṇas* (Oriya) leaf (jackfruit) were offered for each ancestor. Later some of the cakes were distributed among family members although some argue that it should be given only to one's own clan.

THĀḌA ŪCHCHĀ/THĀL DHARĀ—THE OFFERING OF GIFTS TO THE BRIDE AND GROOM AND FOLLOWING THE RITUALS

In his old clothes and decorated with the crown of palm leaves, the groom and bride accept gifts from relatives, neighbours and friends. Before the ritual, a sister of the groom's or bride's father ties a knot in the clothes of her brother and brother's wife. If there are no sisters of the father or if she is a widow, she can be replaced by her granddaughter (e.g. DD). This knot, in which a *haridā* is tied, is called the *ganṭhlā jurā* (*ganṭhlā* = knot; *jurā* = to join). The gift that the father's sister receives for her service in performing the ritual is also known by the same name.

While the bride or groom stands at the wedding altar with the father to the left and the mother to the right it is the responsibility or privilege (*kām*) of the groom's or bride's mother's brother to offer the first gift. This gift consists usually of money, sweets and some jewellery such as a golden ring placed on a brass plate. This gift-giving is also known as *thāl dharā* (*thāl* = plate; *dharā* = to give). Without this gift and the presence of a *māmu* (MB), who can also be a widower, a wedding cannot take place. It is also the mother's brother who feeds some sweets to his sister's son or sister's daughter and who has already offered the clothes that are worn by the bride, the mother and the father on this occasion.

After the *māmu,* other relatives, neighbours and friends offer gifts. In the case of a bride, relatives feel obliged to offer more than in to the groom. A *jāti* relative usually makes a list of all the people, who present gifts and also the exact amount of money. Each giver throws first some *haldi chāul* over groom or bride and the parents, and then offers some money for the plate carried by the mother's brother which the groom and bride are keeping and shows respect to the parents. Some close relatives may also offer a separate plate. While gifts are handed over, a barber stands opposite the groom or bride and circles a mirror to ward off the evil eye.

After all the gifts have been accepted, the groom and bride must sit in the big basket (*paralā ḍalā*) once again. The seven female *suhāsen* carry them around the *mahuā* branches counterclockwise seven times. While being circled, the groom and bride are supposed to sit under a *śaḍhi* or a long cloth with their eyes closed. A belief prevails among the Aghriā according to which the groom and bride have to keep their eyes closed while the ritual is being performed. If they fail to do so, their children will have only one eye. Afterwards, groom and bride, still sitting in the basket under the sari, are lifted up to the roof of the altar and their heads are made to touch the roof seven times. This is known as the *maduā chhiān* (*maduā* = altar; *chhiān* = to touch). Back on the ground but still sitting in the basket, the *suhāsen* bring seven small pots (*naharen kuṇṭhi* or *pāen palṭā*) filled with water sometimes called *bihāri pāen*. These pots are placed on the heads of the groom or bride and then turned upside down so that the head of bride or groom gets wet. Subsequently, they are thrown backwards by all seven *suhāsen*. This custom is known as *baḍ pāen utarā* (*baḍ* = big, here in the sense of 'grown up'; *pāen* = water; *utarā* = throw out) or *abhihāri pāen utarā* (throwing out of the unmarried water).

Before the cloth that has been used to cover the groom and bride is finally removed, one or two *ghī* lamps are lighted in front of them and this is the first thing they should see after the removal of the cloth. Next, the seven *suhāsen* stand with their backs to the groom and bride who are still sitting in the basket next to the *mahuā* branches. One of the *suhāsen* then ties a white thread seven times around the other *suhāsen* standing in circle. The thread is soaked in turmeric and finally knotted around the right wrists of the bride and groom ten times to remember the Goddess Lakṣmī, whose personal number is ten. The thread remains until the arrival of the couple in the groom's house later on, when bride and groom open their threads mutually. Additionally, a golden ring is tied in one of the ten knots.

After the completion of these rituals a barber shaves the groom and cuts the nails of bride and groom. It is considered a privilege for the barber to demand the clothes the groom has worn up to this stage, which some Aghriā regard as rather impure. The groom and bride then take another bath and receive new clothes.

After the *thāḍa ūchchā*, another feast for the *jāti* is served.

GĀL SENKĀ—FAREWELL OF THE GROOM, *BARĀT*—GROOM'S PARTY AND *BHOJI* (FEAST)

Before leaving his house the groom—now traditionally dressed in a new white *dhoti*, white shirt and wearing a new white crown—worships the gods and goddesses present in the house and the hearth, in which a fire should burn. Later at the altar he sits on a bed on which some sweets are placed. He worships the *kalyāṇī khuṇṭ*, the Gauri, and the four *kalaś* in each corner of the altar by offering a *ṭikā* guided by a *suhāsen*, preferably an elder brother's wife.

A farewell is given to the groom at the gate of his house. At the gate, the mother carrying the basket (*paralā ḍalā*) and two *suhāsen* with the two *kalaś* circle seven times around the groom standing next to a bigger *kalaś*. Afterwards, the mother takes some water from the *kalaś*, and others say some *ghī* into her hands and touches the crown of the groom with both her hands and arms crossed. In some cases she just holds her hands over the *kalaś* with the *ghī* lamp and then touches the crown. This is described as *gāl senkā* (*gāl* = cheek; *senkā* = to warm). It is followed by the elder women of the family bidding farewell to the groom by touching his chin with their hands and then touching their own mouths. Some Aghriā insist that this should be done by the women of the mother's generation only. Sometimes a *gāl senkā* also includes the washing of the feet of the groom by his mother—and afterwards vice versa—as well as the feeding of the groom.

After the departure, the groom should not return to his house without a bride. Together with his male relatives, friends, and at least one *jāti* member he proceeds to the bride's village—the groom is traditionally carried in a sedan (*dulhā, palinki*), but nowadays driven in a car. Arriving in the bride's village the groom's party should first contact the local landlord or Gauntiā, should offer some gifts to him—the so-called *gauntiā baraṇ* (*baraṇ* = to invite) and ask for his protection during their stay. On the way to the Gauntiā or to the *jāti* of the bride's family, where the groom's party spends some time and will be offered some Tiffin, the groom should not pass the house of the bride, which again would be considered inauspicious. It is equally inauspicious for a groom to see another *barāt* in the village of the bride.

After the bride's side has received the news of the groom's arrival, a picture is drawn in the kitchen of the bride's house—and roughly at the same time in the groom's kitchen as well—which is known as *maen* (*maen* = a mixture of *khai*: paddy heated on sand; *birhi*: a type of lentils and *maida*: wheat-flower) and the process of painting as *maen ḍhaḷā* (*ḍhalā* = to draw). The auspicious picture symbolizing a car of Jagannāth, as it is used in the *Rath Jātrā,* is drawn by the female *suhāsen.* In the lower part of the picture, three betel leaves are added, representing Jagannāth, Subhadra and Balabhadra, who are asked for their blessings. A white thread called the *kakan moer* is placed on the leaves. *Ghī* is also poured on the leaves and flows down the wall. The number of long *ghī* lines on the wall is said to indicate the number of children the couple can expect to have.

After some snacks, the groom's party finally heads towards the bride's house. This procession is led by drummers or a full wedding band followed by some members of the groom's party engaged in wild dancing and, finally, by the groom in a car at the end of the procession. In most cases, firecrackers and illuminations are essential parts of the *barāt*—a part called *bājā rośani* (*bājā* = music; *rośani* = light). At the same time a smaller procession starts from the bride's house.

The gathering of both processions is called *samdhi bheṭ*, in which the potential affinal relatives (HF and WF) meet, and in which a new relation is ritually enacted. However, in most cases, the fathers offer primacy during this ceremonial welcome to their brothers—often the younger brother—in order to make the relation among the brothers closer. A barber unfolds a cloth on the ground on which both step. The two exchange *ṭikās*, sweets, cigarettes and *pān*, they offer a cloth and hug or lift each other.

From this point, the procession of the bride's party returns slowly to their house and the groom's party proceeds further, accompanying the bride's people until the groom reaches the bride's house. This is known as *bar āgamana* (*bara* = groom; *āgamana* = to reach) from the perspective of the bride's side and as *bar ānugamana (ānugamana* = to have to go) from the groom's perspective. At the gate of the bride's house, the women of the house, who also sprinkle some water over his car and have placed a *kalaś* at the entrance, welcome the groom.

After reaching the bride's house a dinner is served for the groom's party and all the other guests. Again the groom should not walk after leaving the car, but rather should be carried by a *bāṭo* (eZH). Although the caste organization tries to implement rules prohibiting the consumption of meat during the reception at the bride's family's house, in most cases meat is served. The groom, for whom a comfortable seat is arranged, takes his dinner at the wedding altar and receives special brass dishes for washing his hands.

Third day

BIBĀHĀ PĀNI GRAHAṆA—ACCEPTING THE BRIDE

In most cases the main part of the wedding begins after midnight at the wedding altar, which is decorated as during *teilābhiṣek*. The Tihāri priest of the bride's family performs the ceremonies, assisted by a barber. An auspicious time is fixed for the *hāth lagan* ritual, but quite often the *barāt* is delayed and additional rituals are required if the auspicious time has already passed.

The bride appears at the *bedī* and is asked by the Tihāri about her clan (*gotra*) and offers a cloth to the priest after the gods present in a *kalas* have been invoked and invited. At this stage, a bride is constantly accompanied by sisters or friends. The latter—as in case of the groom—always carry a hand-fan with them. The bride leaves the altar before the groom appears. To him—contrary to the bride—a *pindhā* to sit on is offered by his potential father-in-law. It is interpreted as 'greeting the groom happily' demonstrating the high status of the groom at this time. Additionally, the groom receives a *ṭikā* from the bride's father, which is seen as an invitation. The Tihāri passes a mango leaf on to the groom to bite on—jokingly cleansing or purifying his teeth. Afterwards, the groom receives a small closed leaf bowl filled with honey and curd from the priest. Ideally there should be seven such bowls, but in practice it is usually only one. The groom must open it and is asked by the priest if the contents are ripe. As another form of teasing, the groom can deny this several times, but in most cases he answers it in the affirmative immediately. The little bowl with the curd symbolizes a river that he must cross, as purification. Subsequently, the groom throws the bowl over his right shoulder where usually some of the bride's *suhāsen* sit behind him. This part is known as the *madhu parko* or *dadhi parko* (*madhu* = honey; *dadhi* = curd). The groom then worships the gods, including the *kalyāṇī khuṇṭ*, as the bride did before and offers a cloth to the Tihāri as *Tihāri baraṇ*.

The bride returns to the altar and takes her seat on the groom's right side—now wearing a crown and a sari and jewellery given by the groom's side on *naḍiā phuṭa*. A cloth held by the barber separates the bride and groom, as they should not see each other prior to the *hāth lagan* ceremony. Both pay the barber some money for this service. The Tihāri then asks about the *gotra* and he receives gifts in form of paddy (*chāul*). After the cloth between them has been removed, the groom and bride hold a small leaf bowl with a betel nut and throw some *chāul* over each other.

As one of the most decisive steps during the wedding, the parents of the brid—their clothes tied with a knot by the bride's father's sister—sitting next to her usually weeping daughter, then offer her their hand. This part is known as the *hāth lagan*. For this step the groom has already placed his right hand on a small round-shaped brass pot (*gaḍu*), which stands in a larger brass bowl (*khuri*). Into the hand of the groom a betel leaf, a *buro*-leaf, a basil leaf, some *kusa* and *duba* grass are placed by the priest before the hand of the bride is given the groom by the bride's parents. The priest ties a white thread around both of their right hands.[13] Relatives now offer water from a small copper bowl (*pātri* or *pātul*) carried by the priest into the *khuri* while announcing the gifts they have offered. Symbolizing these gifts, called *daij* or *yautuka,* they throw coins into the *khuri*-pots. These gifts are meant for the couple. The first person in the line of relatives is the father of the bride who offers the daughter as a *kanyā dān*. Furthermore, he announces what he will offer as *upahār* (dowry). The bride's younger brother also offers a gift to the groom, such as a golden necklace, however it is traditionally a cow (*dhenu*) or calf (*bachhā*). Other relatives can offer something if they wish, but the *kanyā dān* must be offered. After each gift the groom must say *asti*, 'I accept'.

After a while the younger brother of the bride tears the thread apart. Traditionally he has the right to beat or to hit his elder sister's husband. He is younger than the groom and this hitting is seen as a kind of revenge for taking his sister. Today however it is practised only rarely, however well known. The groom must then present a gift—either money or a cloth—to the *śalā* for tearing the thread apart.

The groom's side then offers some jewellery to the bride before the groom applies vermilion to her forehead, particularly on the part, as a crucial new symbol for the bride as wife now. This ritual is known as the *sindhur makhā* (*sindhur* = vermilion; *makhā* = to apply) and seen as a prime symbol of marriage. Additionally, the bride now receives a red veil from the groom's elder brother whom she must avoid from this point on. The husband's mother's brother may also give this veil, if there is no husband's elder brother, as the bride has to avoid him equally. In one case the husband's mother's brother said the following words while offering the veil to the bride via her *suhāsen*, 'Oh, *suhāsen*, give the *uḍhni* to the *bhānjibaha* (ZSW).' The *suhāsen* then replied: 'What are you giving to your *bhānjibaha* (ZSW)?' implying that he should offer more. Subsequently, the husband's mother's brother presented an additional necklace.

The bride puts on the veil and receives another crown, which some Aghriā interpret as the sign of a queen. In another vital step, the bride and groom exchange garlands—a part known as *baraṇ mālā*. The garland for the groom should be made of *mālti*-flowers (a symbol of the God Viṣṇu) and basil (*tulsī*). The bride then worships her husband by kneeling down in front of him.

At the same time, the priest lights a small fire (*homa*). He then ties a knot between the cloth of the bride and groom. The barber brings a big flat grinding stone on which seven small piles of *chāul* are placed with a betel nut on top. The priest then guides the couple clockwise around the *mahuā* branches. The bride, walking in front of the groom, holds in her hands some paddy heated on the sand. At the end of each round the priest recites some verses while the bride must put her right foot on the stone. In every round the Tihāri gives a condition, and if the groom standing behind the bride agrees, he can remove her foot from the stone after the recitation has been completed and the *khai* has been thrown into the fire. The bride then receives a new handful of *khai* before the next round and the barber removes one pile from the stone that is known as *kundi meṭā* (*kundi* = small pot made of clay; *meṭā* = to remove). In this manner seven rounds are to be completed. Particularly this part of a wedding, but also the entire marriage, is seen as a *lajjyā homa* or as a sacrifice of the shame (*lāj*) of the bride offering her husband her chastity and virginity.[14]

Finally, some *daksina* has to be paid to the priest and the barber; a gift of money must be given to the *suhāsen* at the wedding altar. This gift—the *sanga chhaḍāni* (*sanga* = friends)—is essential because without the consent of the *suhāsen,* the bride is not allowed to leave the wedding altar. Ideally a bride cannot go anywhere without the *suhāsen.* In exchange for the money, the *suhāsen* hands over her rights over the bride to the groom.

After completing the *bedī* ceremony, the couple proceeds to the kitchen where they sit symbolically on the lap of the bride's mother. Here the mother feeds a mixture known as *pañchāmrut* seven times to the groom and then to her daughter, who sits between them.

BIDĀI BHEṬ—FAREWELL OF THE BRIDE; *BAR KANYĀ BIDĀYA*—DEPARTURE OF THE COUPLE; *GĀL SENKĀ* AND *BAR KANYĀ PRATYĀBARTAN*—RETURN OF THE GROOM'S WEDDING PARTY

Before the couple leaves the bride's home, the *āīmā* (father's mother) of the bride should present some of her own gold jewellery to her granddaughter. At the time of the couple's departure another *gāl senkā* is enacted—similar to the one before the groom leaves his house with his *barāt.* The couple, their clothes once more tied with a knot, stand in front of the bride's house—not cn the ground, but on leaf plates. The bride faces the entrance of her house while the groom stands behind her. The bride's mother and two *suhāsen* circle around the couple seven times as previously described in the case of the groom. Then, the mother gives a *ṭikā* of curd to the couple and touches the crowns of both of them with her hands dipped in the water of the *kalaś* carried by a *suhāsen*. Afterwards, the bride and groom touch the feet of the mother as a sign of respect known as *juhār*. In some cases, sad marriage songs are sung by friends during the departure of the bride and groom (*bar kanyā bidāya*), which aptly relates to the emotional farewell between the bride and her family known as *bidāi bheṭ*.

During the ceremonial *bar kanyā pratyābartan* (*bar* = groom; *kanyā* = bride; *pratyābartan* = to return) in the groom's village, the car of the couple is sprinkled with water by the groom's mother. A *kalas* is erected on a *jhoti*. Before leaving the car, the mother-in-law of the bride presents a brass plate with white paddy, whereupon the bride steps out of the car with her right foot. This is known as *ḍulā utrā* (*ḍulā* = sedan-chair; *utrā* = to get down). The mother-in-law presents a gift also known as *ḍulā utrā*—preferably something made of gold. As a respectful gesture the daughter-in-law then touches the feet of her mother-in-law and presents her a cloth which is called *śāś ulgan* (*śāś* = mother-in-law; *ulgan* derived from *ulagi* = to show respect). The bride also brings almost football-sized sweets known as *māikundā* (*māi* = main; *kundā* = earthen container). Several items would be given to the bride by her relatives in earthen containers, but the container with the sweets given by her parents was the biggest and most important. Still, without these sweets the couple is not allowed to enter the house. Once more, a *gāl senkā* is performed. The bride is still almost completely veiled. For showing her respect to the elders of the house, the bride receives a gift known as *juhār karā (juhār* = showing of respect*)*—which means that elder men and women pay small amounts of money to her. The mother then hugs the groom, her son, and then the bride before they enter the house.

In at least one clan of the Aghriā—the Leuniā—a special *rakta pūjā* (*rakta* = blood) has commonly been or is still performed before the bride enters the house. A goat is sacrificed and the bride must step on the blood or in other cases the mother gives her daughter-in-law a *ṭikā* of blood before being allowed inside. Some Aghriā say the uncastrated goat is sacrificed for Dulhā Devtā.[15] However, this custom is now in decline.

In some cases, sisters of the groom block the way to the kitchen with a symbolical rope. This blocking of the way is known as *bāṭ chhenkā* (*bāṭ* = way). After some bargaining between the groom and his sisters and after having given some money to the sisters, the new bride is finally allowed to enter. This shows some initial ritualized tension between the sisters of the groom on the one hand and the bride or wife on the other. The same tension is expressed occasionally even after the marriage in a joking manner, e.g. during dancing known as *huma* (see ritual cycle). In one case at that time distant sisters were singing: 'Our elder brother got married, and he did not ask us, and now the *bahu* (elder brother's wife) is in her home as a guest (*kunuān*), and we will beat her with a heavy stick (*bāḍi*)!'

Next, the bride and groom sit on a bed at the altar. Upon this bed sweets are placed. Both give—with their clothes still tied—a *ṭikā* each to the *kalyāṇī khuṇṭ,* to the *kalaś* in the four corners of the altar and to the pot used to boil rice in the kitchen. Both of them also visit the house shrine. Later the groom and bride open the threads around their wrist mutually. That same morning the gift exchange continues. The bride brings gifts for her husbands sisters—usually consisting of a sari for each of them. The bride is generally accompanied by sisters, younger brothers or friends, who are entitled to receive a full dress (two clothes) for bringing the bride. In the evening of the same day usually a *jeṭhen* (husband's elder brother's wife), a *nanand* (husband's younger sister) or the *śāś* introduces the bride to all of the elder relatives, and she receives a gift of money from each.[16] A *bāṭo* (elder sister's husband) of the groom should instruct him before the first night with his wife. Some also say, that the groom should offer another gift to his wife in the first night in return for showing her face, which until then has been veiled. The gift is known as *muhun dekhā* (*muhun* = face; *dekhā* = to show) and often a ring is presented on this occasion.

On this day the *upahār* (dowry) is displayed in the groom's house. It usually consists of the furniture for the couple's bedroom, cooking utensils, and luxury items such as a cooler and TV-set, depending on the wealth of the families. Although there have been endeavours by the caste organization to ban dowry, the custom is still prevalent in practice. However, many Aghriā maintain that compared to a dowry in former times *upahār* is given voluntarily and the groom's side is not demanding anything. The sending of a daughter at the time of her marriage is also known as *pathien* (*patheibā* = to send; the opposition of *leuṭen*). Often women say that certain household goods—particularly kitchen items—were brought by the bride, e.g. a *panki*, kitchen cutter, *belnā pidhā* to make *chapāti; jhāmpi*, a big basket; a broom (*barun*); a *kulā*, a winnowing fan; various dishes such as *khuri* (bowl), *kansā thāli* (plate), *tāsak* (bowl for watered rice/*pakhāla*); *ḍuā*, a round ladle; *chaṭu*, a flat ladle; *jharā*, a ladle with holes; *peḍi*, a round basket; and *haṇīlā*, big brass pots to store water. Additionally, a bed (*khat*), clothes (*śaḍhi*) and gold are given too.

As an Aghriā elder explained, there were more symbolic acts in former times such as the gift of salt from the groom to the bride signifying her new legal status after her acceptance; the playing with cowry shells, in which the bride is defeated and susequently claimed as a wife; the bride placing a basket on her head, in which some cowdung is thrown by her husband and thus symbolically accepting her domestic work and also the placement of rice into the hearth by the bride, before being taken to the household deities. However, I did not observe any of these customs.

PRITIBHOJAN—RECEPTION AND *LEUṬEN*—FIRST RETURN OF THE BRIDE

After the return of the groom, an elaborate lunch or dinner known as reception or *pritibhojan* (*priti* = love; *bhojan* = feast) is served for all the guests in the groom's house. The number of guests is seen as an indicator of the prestige and wealth of the family. A separate feast for the *jāti*—the caste members of the village—is prepared by the *jāti* themselves while a Brahmin is hired as a cook for all the other guests. As it is difficult to serve meals to all villagers in addition to the guests present, the ingredients for a meal called *kharchā* consisting of rice, vegetables, oil, turmeric, etc., are distributed among the villagers by a Narihā.

Formerly, the bride would be accompanied by a Gauḍen—a female member of the Gauḍ-caste, the caste responsible for cattle herding—who stayed in the groom's village until the first return of the bride, or *leuṭen* (to return), seven to ten days after the wedding. Usually the date for the first return to her parent's house is fixed during the wedding. For the return to her natal village, the bringing of a gift of sweets is essential. This gift is known as a *chipṭi* (*chipṭi* = big leaf bowl usually closed, in former times used for carrying sweets) and meant for the caste members and sometimes other villagers in the bride's village.

Later, the bride may occasionally visit her natal family—her *mā ghar* (mother's house) as opposed to her *śāś-ghar* (mother-in-law's house), where she is married. Her husband may also visit his *śaśur ghar* (house of the father-in-law).

The wedding altar should remain in the house for at least one year, before it can finally be dismantled. Otherwise problems are expected to arise between husband and wife.

After marriage, gift exchanges continue and all affinal relatives visiting the house of the other side for the first time are entitled to receive a gift of cloth. If any male relatives senior to the bride visit the bride's house for the first time after the wedding, they have to pay for the food they eat there—a gift known as *bhāt khiā* (*bhāt* = boiled rice; *khiā* = to eat).

TIJHĀ—RUTURN OF THE BRIDE HOME AFTER THE FIRST DAŚARĀ

On the first *Daśarā* after the wedding, the groom and his relatives such as elders sister's husband and younger brothers, etc.,—relatives whom the bride is not supposed to avoid—should visit their in-laws' house to spend some time and to bring the bride home, who is supposed to go to her brother's house during the Daśarā. Formerly, the groom's party spent up to seven days there, but nowadays it is a much shorter period. During this time the groom should visit the wife's mother's brother or should be invited by him. At the time of departure every member of the groom's side receives a gift of a cloth plus sweets, while the groom receives a full dress including a *dhoti*. A *tijhā* should also take place in the case of cross-cousin marriage.

BHĀGBAṆṬĀ—DIVISION OF THE HOUSEHOLD

Often after the marriage of all sons has been completed, the father divides the household and land among his sons. This formal division is known as *bhāgbaṇṭā*. It is an important step in the life cycle not only for the married sons, who become more responsible for their 'own' families after the separation from their brothers, but also for the father, because it is considered to be his responsibility to divide everything before his death. Some people say that a new generation (*pāṭ*) starts only after the separation—otherwise it is remembered as the generation of their father or eldest brother even after the death of the father. Younger brothers are subsumed under their elder brother as long as no separation has been arranged. Others say a new generation starts when the responsibility of cultivating the land is handed over from father to son or sons. However, brothers may remain together even after having been married for a long time.

The *māmu* (MB) should be present during the separation to make sure that all sisters' sons get a sufficient share of the property. Usually an auspicious date is chosen for the establishment of the new hearth (*chulā*) of the younger brothers, which is an essential part of the separation. Often the separation is done in the months of Asādha and Māgha. The eldest son usually receives a larger share, known as *jyeṣṭhi bhāg* (*jyeṣṭhi* = eldest), because it is his prime responsibility to organize and perform the funeral rituals of his parents.

1.3. MARRIAGE—HISTORICAL, STRUCTURAL AND REGIONAL VARIATIONS

There have been considerable changes in the last hundred years as far as marriage and wedding rituals are concerned. Some of the changes I will describe below.

Child marriage

It was expected that every girl should be married before puberty—usually at the age of six or seven. This was satisfy the ancestors, who would receive nothing to eat if grown up and unmarried women remained in the house. There were symbolic forms of marriage in case no groom was found before puberty.

In the case of child marriage, the wedding rituals were almost identical to the ones practised today, but the bride would remain in her native family after the wedding until she reached puberty, although in some cases the bride—in a sedan—was carried symbolically to the outskirts of her village at the end of the wedding ceremonies. After having reached puberty, the bride's parents sent a message to the groom's family to take the bride to their home.

PAHANA—THE DELIVERY OF THE BRIDE AND *BANDĀPANĀ*—SUBSEQUENT RITUALS

After the arrival of the news that the bride had reached maturity, the groom's side, as an elder Aghriā woman told me, sent five—others say seven—people to bring her home. This party consisted, for instance, of the head of the family or father-in-law of the bride, three *jāti* and a Gauḍ. The latter carried a *bhār* filled with *guḍ* and *chuḍā* to be distributed among the bride's relatives as during the wedding. The transfer of the bride in a procession in which she was carried in a sedan was known as a *pahana*. *Pahana* appears to be a Lariā word (Aghriā language) and signifies something similar to a *barāt*, but without the groom. The sedan was usually carried by labourers of the Aghriā, but this custom seems to have been abolished at Independence. According to some Aghriā, after the arrival of a bride in the groom's house, a small ceremony was performed, the *bandāpanā* or first entrance, with a fire ritual.

There have been cases in which a bride was never brought to her groom's family after the wedding. In one case, during a visit to the bride's family, the father-in-law discovered that the bride was able touch her nose with her tongue—a highly inauspicious sign—and therefore decided to not bring his daughter-in-law home. In another case, the groom's family explained to me that the bride's people had complained that although the bride was already mature, the same was not true about the groom. Disappointed about such comments, they decided to not take the bride home. In yet another family, the bride's kin cancelled the marriage relationship after the groom had already brought another wife into his house. The bride's side then opted for a divorce.

Symbolic forms of child marriage

Although formerly child marriage was generally the preferred form of marriage, often a proper husband could not be found in time. For this reason, girls married a symbolic groom before finding a 'real' or second husband, who then had the right to consummate the marriage. By marrying symbolically the parents had more time to search for a suitable groom. Some Aghriā argued that these symbolic marriages were also chosen in order to enable their children to become ancestors.

Only after the *tel chaḍā* ceremony would it have been possible for the child to join the ancestors in the case of a sudden death. Often the marriages of many children were combined to save money, in particular as far as the feasts were concerned. For every child a marriage altar was erected, but only for older children would a groom or bride have to be found. Additionally and simultaneously, younger children may have also been married. In their cases, at the time of the second marriage, only the delivery of the bride would be performed as described. I came across four symbolic forms of marriage substituting child marriage:

1. Marriage with a distant grandfather or *ajā-bihā*;
2. Marriage with an elder sister's husband (eZH) or *bāto-bihā*;
3. Marriage with a turban or *jhatā-bihā* and
4. Marriage with flowers or *phul bihā*.

1. *AJĀ-BIHĀ*

To give a daughter in marriage to a distant grandfather or *ajā* was one opportunity to marry off a daughter early. Although close grandfathers (FF, MF) were not eligible, it was possible to marry one's mother's mother's brother (MMB) or one's father's mother's brother (FMB) and more distant grandfathers. I came across some of these cases, e.g. I met an elder lady who had initially married her father's father's younger sister's husband's younger brother (FFyZHyB). This Aghriā woman married her classificatory grandfather at the age of four or five (around 1930) before marrying again thirteen years later. For the first marriage with a grandfather, most of the rituals, in particular the anointing with oil and turmeric, the *teilabhiṣek/tel chaḍā* and the circling around the *mahuā* branches and fire were performed. Later the grandfather had to sign the divorce papers. For the second marriage another *teilabhiṣek* was not required, but the circling was repeated before the bride was brought into the groom's household (see child marriage). The girl never stayed in the house of her distant grandfather as a wife would have stayed with her husband.

In another case, a woman remembered that her cousin-sister (father's sister's daughter—FZD) had married her distant grandfather too. The groom was the mother's father's younger brother (MFyB) of his wife. However, this custom seems to have been in decline already by the 1930s. One reason may be the caste organization or Aghriā Samāj, which tried to abolish this tradition. Nevertheless, there are still cases in which a marriage with a distant grandfather may be performed—although quite rarely. In one case in 1996 an Aghriā woman married her mother's father's mother's brother's son (MFMBS). The Aghriā I asked agreed that a marriage with a distant grandfather is more acceptable than marrying a distant niece or nephew such as a brother's daughter or marrying a distant uncle or aunt like a father's sister or mother's sister.

2. *BĀṬO-BIHĀ*—MARRIAGE WITH A BROTHER-IN-LAW OR ELDER SISTER'S HUSBAND

The idea behind marrying a *bāṭo* before puberty is similar to a marriage to a grandfather. However, the marriage with an elder sister's husband seems to have been more frequent than marriage with a grandfather and the Aghriā Samāj or caste organization did not try to discontinue this custom. In one case, an old Aghriā lady remembered that her father had married his wife's younger sister (*śālī*), but had to sign the divorce papers actually before marriage. The marriage customs were the same as usual. Like the distant *ajā*, the *bāṭo* is a relative with whom one has a joking relationship and often the jokes between the *bāṭo* and the *śālī* are sexually quite explicit, for example, a *bāṭo* may say to his *śālī* in a joking manner that he wants to marry her.

Marriage with a brother-in-law—or *bāṭo* to be precise—is still common among the Aghriā—although arranged for different reasons and nowadays after puberty. In the cases I recorded the reasons were barrenness or death of the first wife.

3. *JHATĀ-BIHĀ*—MARRIAGE WITH A TURBAN

In other cases the family may have preferred to marry a daughter first in a purely symbolic act without any groom present—even a 'fake groom'. This might have even been the case if there was a *bāṭo* that the daughter could potentially have married. However, the family may have opted for a marriage with a *jathā* or turban instead. In one case a young girl was married in this manner in the presence of her elder sister and elder sister's husband. She was then married to her *bāṭo* much later in a second marriage, because her sister was barren.

During this form of marriage a groom was symbolically represented by a *jathā*, which stood, on one hand, for a turban, e.g. sent by the king to his Jamindār in order to invite them for their marriage. On the other hand, *jathā* also signifies a cloth that the groom usually wears over his shoulder at the time of *thāḍa ūchchā* in which some *chāul* and *haridā*-fruits are put. Additionally, a towel was placed at the wedding altar to replace the groom. Both sets of clothes were stored and given later to the next or second husband.

4. *PHUL-BIHĀ* OR MARRIAGE WITH FLOWERS

According to some Aghriā, marriage with flowers has been a symbolic act for boys between the ages of five and ten in order to get married—a procedure comparable to a *jathā bihā* for girls. However, others argued that it was also possible for girls to marry in this way. I did not meet any Aghriā who had actually married in that manner, rather some who had only heard about the custom from parents or grandparents. A Brahmin was usually called for the ritual. The flowers offered during this ritual did not include red flowers favoured by Mother Goddesses like Durgā (in particular hibiscus-flowers), but rather yellow or white flowers such as marigolds, offered to Lakṣmī. Apparently, flower marriage was also practised in rare cases of a previously unmarried groom marrying a widow, that is to say that a groom was first married to the flowers and subsequently to a widow.

Changes in the gifting pattern

GIVING UP BRIDEWEALTH OR *SAGĀI*

Significant changes in the marriage pattern are visible in the transformation of gifting. Probably the most important change is an abolition of bridewealth or *sagāi*. The groom's father had to pay to the bride's father a gift of money known as *sagāi* either before the *lagan,* together with a *sari* or at least some time before the delivery of a bride. In Hindī, the word *sagāi* is used for engagement and it is quite possible that an early payment at the time of *lagan* had the legal status of an engagement. In the early scriptures of the Aghriā Samāj, the term *kanyā śulka* (*śulka* = tax) was used instead of *sagāi*. To give bridewealth was considered to be auspicious.

Elder Aghriā remember that the bridewealth amounted to about 20 to 30 rupees in their youth roughly 60 to 70 years ago—a substantial amount of money at the time. An uncastrated goat would cost less then one rupee, while it costs around Rs. 500 today. Others remembered that a bullock cart full of paddy was worth less than a rupee.

TENDENCY TOWARDS DOWRY OR FROM *YAUTUKA* TO *UPAHĀR*

There is a clear tendency towards dowry at the same time that bridewealth has been given up. However, in former times bridewealth and dowry were both presented at the same marriage, and there was no question of either bridewealth or dowry. The gifts offered in dowry—or *yautuka* as it was known in former times—included everything necessary for daily life, such as cooking utensils, food and basic furniture like a cot. It was not as lavish as it is today. Usually, a basket called a *jhampi* filled with sweets and clothes was handed over. If at all, a little gold was presented, but not furniture.

Additionally, a change is recognizable as far as the name of the gift is concerned. Nowadays the name *upahār* is used instead of *yautuka* and the Aghriā emphasize its voluntary nature. The state, in trying to eradicate the custom of dowry, is likely an influence behind this change from *yautuka* to *upahār*, which seems to be more of a change of labels than a real structural change.

LĀṬ—GIFTS FROM THE GROOM'S SIDE TO THE BRIDE'S SIDE

In former times several people who had performed services or *sebā* for the bride and bride's family were entitled to receive a gift from the groom's side—in most cases a *dhoti* or a sari. These gifts were known as *lāṭ* and given to: (1) a barber; (2) a washerman; (3) the sacrificer of the village goddess or *Kālo*; (4) the messenger of auspicious news and keeper of the cattle herd or *Narihā;* (5) the messenger for village meetings or *Beherā* and (6) for the woman who massaged the child in her first year known as *sūtrien*. In some cases the midwife or *Dāi* was also included, but often the *Dāi* and *Sūtrien* were identical. In all, seven to nine *lāṭ* were given. The *lāṭ* were handed over during a ceremony at the wedding altar after the arrival of the *barāt*. At the time of the arrival of the bride, no *lāṭ* was obligatory, but at the time of a secondary marriage, after a divorce or after the death of her first husband, *lāṭ* had to be given again.

GIFTS BETWEEN THE WEDDING AND THE DELIVERY OF THE BRIDE

In the case of child marriage there used to be considerable time between marriage and the delivery of the bride. During these years the groom's side was obliged to send certain gifts during major festivals. Every year on *Nuā Khāi*—the ceremonial eating of the first rice—the groom's side offered ingredients for a feast known as the *nuā khāi ke khaṇde*. At the time of the *Rath Jātrā,* a gift called the *jātrā dekhā* consisting of sweets, a *śaḍhi* and money had to be given. A similar gift was presented at the time of *Daśarā* also known as *Daśarā dekhā*. The bride's side usually offered something in return although for them it was not an obligation, only a sign of good intentions. Thus, the gift of a *dhoti* for the groom was described as a *bandhu māen* (*mānya* = good behaviour; *bandhu* = here affines).

Due to a change in the pattern of gifting, none of above described gifts except the dowry and the *jātrā dekhā* are presented nowadays. Other gifts, notably dowry, changed in character and a *jātrā dekhā* is offered to younger unmarried wife-giving affines even after marriage.

Other historical changes

TREE MARRIAGE—*GACHA BIBAHA*

In the case of remarriage, as a widow or widower, sometimes a *sāhāḍā* tree or a banana plant was married, although the *sāhāḍā* tree was probably much more common. It is not quite clear whether or not a woman could really marry a tree. While some Aghriā argue that it was possible others disagree, as they believe that the *sāhāḍā* tree is female. Similarly, it is not fully clear whether a tree marriage was performed only after the death of two wives, because the number three was considered to be inauspicious by some, or if it could be arranged in any case, if a wife died shortly after the marriage.

I tend to believe that it was done particularly in the case of widowers when two wives had already died and one was afraid that the third would die also. Thus, before marrying the next wife, a tree was married as the 'third wife'. This is confirmed by the story that an elder Aghriā told about his mother's brother, who married in this manner. The last such case I came to know about happened about fifteen years ago.

These rituals resembled the wedding customs to a large extent. Before the marriage an astrologer would be contacted. *Teilabhiṣek* was performed by *suhāsen* and a *homa* by a priest before the husband finally circled around the tree seven times. A *bedī* may have been erected, but was not obligatory—in contrast to a *kalyāṇī khuṇṭ*. The tree was addressed as wife and often the next 'human' wife was married immediately afterwards—a divorce from the tree was not necessary. This same custom was practised by tribal communities like the Muṇḍā[17] in the village.[18]

BAḌ PĀEN UTARĀ—GETTING RID OF THE GROWN UP WATER

In the case that the groom and bride reached puberty before being married—either in a child marriage or in any symbolical form of marriage—female *suhāsen* with the boy or the girl or potential bride or groom respectively went to the outskirts of the village (*gānmuṇḍ*). There, a pot of water mixed with turmeric was circled over the head of a boy or girl seven times by the *suhāsen*. Afterwards, they poured out the water—a symbolic pouring out of the youth or old time. This custom was not only practised by the Aghriā but also by many other communities in the village. In some cases a marriage may have started immediately after this ritual, but in others it was also seen as a partial substitute for child marriage. Nowadays the ritual is combined with the other ceremonies and done after the *thāḍa ūchchā*.

COMPOSITION OF THE *BARĀT*

In former times, certain relatives where excluded from joining a *barāt*. Girls were generally not allowed to join, and an elder brother's son (eBS) or *putrā* was also excluded. A *putrā* was regarded as a son and sons should never have accompanied the father on a *barāt*. This was confirmed by the fact that in the case that a man married for a second time, the sons of his first wife were equally excluded.[19] There are no such strict rules nowadays and girls as well as *putrā* may join a *barāt*.

Beyond arranged marriages

The vast majority of marriages are arranged and celebrated in the *kanyā dān* form, i.e. the parents of the bride offer their daughter ritually as a gift to the groom. This can be done as a child marriage or at a grown up stage. However, other forms have existed and may still exist, eventhough they are practised to a much lesser extent. Already in the Dharmashastra literature, e.g. in the *Manusmriti,* other marriage forms are described and hierarchically ordered. Two that I found among the Aghriā are seen today as types of 'love marriage' and will be described below.

ḌHUKU SAMLĀ—'TO ENTER FORCEFULLY'

A bride would enter the house of the groom and simply remain there. She may even enter the house by force and against the will of her potential husband, who may not be happy with her presence and who may also try to throw her out. Thus, the name of this form, *ḍhuku samlā, is* derived from *ḍhukibā* 'to enter' and *samibā* 'to stay voluntarily and intentionally'. I came across a case from about fifty years ago in which a woman tried to enter the house with this intention. The groom had to serve a feast for his *jāti*: if he managed to throw the bride out before the feast, no divorce was necessary. This was the reason why the lady failed in the just mentioned case. As some Aghriā argue, it was not as rare as it is today and women usually tried to enter the house of rich men. In a more recent incident, about ten or twelve years ago, a bride and daughter of a local landlord entered the house of a poor *parjā* in the same village. The parents of the groom obviously supported the relationship, while the parents of the bride were against it. Later, a priest performed a small fire ritual and the couple sat as the *karttā*/sacrifier during the ritual. A *jāti* feast also had to be served. In the case of a Gaṇḍ, this form is also known.

UDHULIĀ—WITHOUT PERMISSION

Strictly speaking, there are two forms of *udhuliā*, which must be distinguished. Firstly, the *udhuliā āni āsibā* in which the groom brings his bride into his house before any marriage ritual. Here, the order of traditional events is reversed. The arrival of the bride takes place before the priest performs any ritual. However, a feast for the *jāti* of both sides is given later. Slightly different is the second form or *udhuliā bhāgibā*, in which both the bride and groom run away together. In a recent case both then opted for a registered marriage in a nearby town and returned later to their families. The families, after coming to know of the marriage, arranged an additional traditional marriage at that time. But this of course is not always the case.

Nowadays these forms of marriage are considered déclassé and not proclaimed to the world.

Marriage as purification

A central element of marriage appears to be the purification of bride and groom. Both are elaborately purified in the rituals of *teilābhiṣek* in all forms such as the *tel chaḍā* and *tel utarā* in which particularly turmeric is used as purifying substance. Only in a pure state are the bride and groom able to marry. Both have to leave their relatively impure states behind. Marriage and wedding customs do involve impurity, although to a much lesser extent than do birth and death. This is implied by the fact that old clothes worn by a groom until the end of all *teilabhiṣek* or before the ritual for the ancestors are given to a barber, who then has the right to demand them. Equally, the barber takes the old clothes worn by the sons of a deceased until the tenth day after death. Compared to marriage, however, on the tenth day the clothes are left at a pond or river after a bath and they are never touched again by the sons or anyone else in the family. This is not the case after the initial marriage rituals when everyone can still touch the old clothes of a groom. The extent of impurity seems to differ considerably, but in both cases some impurity seems to be involved.

Furthermore, marriage stands as an idiom for purification. To purify a pond or mango trees is expressed essentially as a kind of marriage—as *bihā* or *bibāha*—, although there are other words for purification such as *pratiṣṭhā*. I will describe two such types of marriage: the pond marriage and the mango tree marriage.

POND MARRIAGE OR *BANDHA BIBĀHA*

After digging a new pond, a pond marriage is usually performed and is intended to purify the pond in order to be used for ritual purposes. However, in practice this does not mean that every pond used in rituals has already been purified.

An elder Aghriā lady, after observing the ritual three times—the last time about 45 years ago—described it in the following manner. Before the marriage a basil shrine or *tulsī chaur* is erected next to the pond. A pillar is built in the middle of the pond with a crown (*makuṭ*) or *trishul* on top. This pond marriage takes three days. On the evening of the first day a lamp (*dīpa*) is lit, which burns continuously until the end of the whole ritual. On the second day, under the guidance of a Brahmin, an altar is erected using four wooden posts connected by ropes with mango leafs. It also includes the *tulsī chaur*. There, gods are worshipped. The presence of a married couple—in most cases the owners of the pond—who act as the *karttā* or sacrifier is most essential. At the altar a fire ritual to include the reading of sacred texts is performed by a Brahmin. Afterwards, a little boat prepared before the ritual is set into the pond and the idols of the gods worshipped under the altar are put into the boat. Using some ropes the boat is then pulled by the married couple, who walks clockwise seven times around the pond followed by relatives and guests. In another case the couple itself was sitting in the boot or big tub (*karāh*) and moving forward using some sticks. After that the gods return to the altar and the fire ritual is completed. The priest usually brings the idol, but only the married couple is allowed to put it into the boat and take it out. On the third day a feast or reception is given for relatives and friends.

TREE MARRIAGE—*GACHA BIBĀHA*

There has been a tradition that the Aghriā coming into the region have planted a number of mango trees in the villages where they settled. Before eating the fruits, however, the trees should also have been purified. This purification has been celebrated as a marriage—here as mango tree marriage or *ām gacha bibāha*. But, because the planting often took place seventy to a hundred years ago, information on the matter is scarce. However, an Aghriā whose husband's uncle (HFyB) had planted some trees and purified them in her presence remembered the following details. A Brahmin was called for the ritual and all the necessary items for the *teilabhiṣek* were arranged. The obligatory married couple—the owner—in new clothes went to the newly planted trees. Their *suhāsen* performed a *teilabhiṣek* for the couple and a Brahmin conducted a fire ritual using the same *sāl* wood. *Ṭikā* were given to the tree by the couple and by the *suhāsen*. Afterwards, the *suhāsen* bound a white thread around the trunk of the tree and the couple circled around all the trees planted. Some musicians were invited as well—as for all weddings. After the ritual the couple went home and offered a feast for their *jāti*.

In both cases one finds important elements known from the weddings such as the circling, the *homa* and, particularly in case of tree marriage, the *suhāsen* and the *teilabhiṣek*. There is a greater similarity between the wedding rituals and the tree marriage, but both forms are actually described as marriage. However, in the case of mango tree marriage, rituals may have been mixed with the tree marriage for widowers, as I did not find many Aghriā who had actually seen a mango tree marriage themselves. But it seems clear that purification stands at the centre of the rituals—either to purify the fruits or the pond for rituals including ritual baths. Among the Orām described by S.C. Roy (1999 [1928]: 90ff), similar rituals are mentioned. Roy also noticed a marriage with early rice plants before actually transplanting them. This form, however, is unknown among the Aghriā.

Structural variations

LEVIRATE AND SORORATE

A junior-levirate, i.e. widow's a marriage with the husband's younger brother seems to have been frequent in former times, although rarely are concrete cases remembered. The Aghriā in Chhattisgarh argue that the status of the Aghriā in Orissa declined, because they regularly practised this custom. However, they also say that they have discontinued this custom. According to my interlocutors it is still possible to marry your *bahu/diar*. Very recently in a tragic accident the husband of a young pregnant Aghriā died. Since the deceased husband had a younger brother, people say, it was possible to marry him, but it was up to the wife's or widow's will. In another case, a widow denied marrying her *diar* by arguing that she regards him as a brother.

In contrast to this, no case of senior-levirate—marriage with the husband's elder brother after the death of one's husband—is known. Similarly, a junior-sororate—marriage with the wife's younger sister after the wife's death—is possible and I did find a recent case. Often, however, the wife's younger sister is married for other reasons. Opposingly, a marriage relationship with a wife's elder sister—a senior-sororate—is not known.

This pattern fully corresponds to the pattern of joking and avoidance relationships. Relatives with whom one can joke, such as a husband's younger brother and a wife's younger sister are potential marriage partners, while relatives one must avoid—here the husband's elder brother or the wife's elder sister—are not matches for a remarriage.

INTERCASTE-MARRIAGE

Although comparatively rare, there are cases of intercaste-marriages among the Aghriā. In most cases these are love marriages. Generally, one finds more intercaste marriages in an urban environment, and it seems that such marriages with castes of similar status like the Aghriā, e.g. with the Chasā, are more frequent. Marriages with a big difference in status such as a marriage between an Aghriā and very low community are very rare indeed. Aghriā opting for an intercaste-marriage are excluded from their caste and become *sarliā*.

As far as rituals are concerned, there are different possibilities. Either a court marriage is chosen, or a couple may opt for a temple marriage. In another case, the parents of a bride belonging to the Chasā community (Kandayat) supported their daughter and the wedding was celebrated in the house of the bride as usual, but by mixing the customs of both communities. In this case the wedding, performed by a Brahmin, included the *hāth lagan* and the circling around the fire, but the *teilabhiṣek* and *thāḍa ūchchā* were left out and there was no reception on the groom's side.

TEMPLE MARRIAGE

In case of temple marriage, one must distinguish between two kinds: (1) the love marriages, where lovers may run away from their homes to marry secretly without their relatives and (2) a method to reduce the costs of marriage.

In one wedding that I observed belonging to the latter category, before the marriage both sides agreed to opt for a temple marriage even though it was not as prestigious as a traditional wedding. Here, the first day was performed in the traditional manner. In the same way the second day was observed including the *thāḍa ūchchā*, but the groom did not leave with his *barāt* in the evening. Instead, he left the next morning with a considerably smaller *barāt*. For most relatives and friends—as I was told—it was not attractive to join a *barāt* in a temple marriage, as only some food, or rather a small vegetarian meal, was served next to the temple. Neither was it allowed to offer any meat nor was there any spectacular *barāt* with firecrackers, dancing and alcohol.

At the temple—often a Śiva-temple—the customs of the castes involved are often included and on the platform next to the temple three *mahuā*-twigs are placed and the ritual followed traditional Aghriā customs in the central aspects, such as the *hāth lagan, sindhur makhā*, circling, etc., although the performance depends to a large extent on the priest conducting the ritual. Arriving at the groom's house, the couple is welcomed exactly in the traditional manner including the *gāl senkā* and an expensive reception.

The temple marriage may help a family to save money—particularly, it can help the bride's side to avoid a reception in their village. However, in another case the marriage was performed in a temple in the bride's village, which did not reduce the costs in the same way. Furthermore, it helps to bring down the costs for the *barāt*, which the groom's side must bear.

WIDOWS AND WIDOWER: REMARRIAGE—WIDOW-MARRIAGE

Widows—known as *rāṇḍi* or formerly in the case of child widows as *bālya bidhabā* (*bālya* = child; *bidhabā* = widow/Oriya)—face certain restrictions—though not to the same extent as in other parts of India. For example, they are allowed to wear jewellery, but it should be decent and not flashy. They may use simple necklaces or a few flowers, but glass bangles are prohibited, because they are reserved for married women. Men sometimes say that women, after the death of their husbands, do not want to wear jewellery, as beauty does not matter after the husband's death. In practise, however, I often saw widows wearing gold necklaces and metal bangles.

The rituals in the case of a secondary marriage are simple. As a widower, a groom also has to go to the bride's house and, most importantly, has to offer glass bangles. The groom must also apply vermilion to the parting of his bride—a ritual known as *sindhur makhā*. Usually, the bride's side gives some gifts, although they are not obligatory—in contrast to a feast for the *jāti*.

In most cases widows were formerly married to widowers and only rarely were previously unmarried daughters given to widowers, because problems were anticipated in the latter's families. However, people say that rich widowers used to face fewer problems when arranging a secondary marriage compared to the situation today.

In the rare case of a previously unmarried groom marrying a widow a flower marriage would be performed before the actual wedding. Only one elderly Aghriā that I met had seen such a marriage once in her life. She narrated that the groom was first married to a *śaḍhi*, on which flowers were laid. The groom then offered five pairs of bangles and vermilion to it. Both—*śaḍhi* and bangles—were brought to the house of the bride or widow, where a Brahmin performed a ritual by putting the hand of the widow into the groom's hand.

Regional variations

While there are no major differences between the Aghriā in Sambalpur and the Sundargarh district, there have been significant changes if one compares these Aghriā to their caste-brethren in Chattisgarh region on the one hand and in Bolangir district on the other hand.

WEDDING RITUALS OF THE AGHRIĀ IN CHATTISGARH

The number of marriage relationships between the Aghriā in Sambalpur and the Sundargarh district on one side and in Chattisgarh on the other side is rather limited. I did not observe a wedding in Chattisgarh, but was able collect some information about a recent marriage there.

In the Chattisgarh tradition, there is no *naḍiā phuṭā*, but a ceremony about two months before the wedding known as the *sagāi* or engagement, and the *thāḍa ūchchā* is not performed. During the *samdhi bheṭ,* all elder relatives are involved and not only the father or father's elder brother on either side. At this time a coconut is exchanged between two relatives—one from each side—seven times. After the *barāt*, the groom and bride exchange their garlands immediately and not at the altar as in Sambalpur. For the rituals, two priests are required. There is no *madhu parko* and no cloth kept by the barber between the bride and groom. However, a cloth is held between the bride's mother and groom's father who should not see or touch each other. The circling around the *mahuā* sticks is similar, except for the circling itself. As usual, the bride steps on a stone after every of the seven rounds, but the small pile of rice on the stone is removed by a small dagger that the groom carries and not by the barber as in the Sambalpur district. This dagger is said to represent the martial tradition of the Aghriā as warriors or *kethriā*. Furthermore, younger sisters of the bride may try to steal the shoes of the groom, who then must pay something to them in order to get the shoes back.

WEDDING RITUALS IN THE BOLANGIR DISTRICT

In Bolangir district, in the first part of the wedding, a Kālo is not involved. Instead, a relative performs the same function. It is not the mother who goes to the outskirts of the village carrying the *paralā ḍalā* joined by the *suhāsen*, but rather an elder sister (eZ), a father's sister (FZ), an elder brother's wife (eBW) and a grandmother that go to a temple in order to bring back two—not three—*mahuā*-sticks (without a bullock-cart). Some soil is dug up by an elder sister's husband or a grandfather depending on who is carrying the *paralā ḍalā*—it should be the husband of whoever is carrying the *paralā ḍalā*. If an elder sister carries it, an elder sister's husband will dig the soil—if a grandmother carries it, it will be done by a grandfather, etc. The role of the mother is limited to the carrying of a *kalaś* at the time of the *gāl senkā*.

Furthermore, while erecting the *mahuā* sticks in the middle of the altar, there is no joking. The *kalyāṇī khuṇṭ* is equally important, but known here as the *karāli khuta*. The meaning of these words, however, is unknown. Seven male *suhāsen* are necessary to hold the *karāli khuta* while a *jāti* binds it to the *mahuā* sticks. The male *suhāsen* have to be married and widowers are excluded. In Bolangir, a sister instead of a sister-in-law (elder brother's wife—eBW), guides the groom to and around the altar by slightly pulling on his *dhoti* instead of holding his hand.

When a groom goes to take his bath, a bed sheet is kept above him instead of an umbrella.[20] Later, seven small pots called *patul* or *kānchi* are filled with water from the pond. A white thread is then tied around each pot and all of them are hung at the altar by the *suhāsen*. After the bride has arrived with the groom, this water is used to wash her. Before the *teilabhiṣek,* a priest—a Brahmin because there are no Tihāri in Bolangir—performs a little ritual. During the *thāḍa ūchchā* a barber is present, but does not circle a mirror.

In all corners of the altar, 14 or 21 pots should be erected. On top of each pot a special cake called an *arishā* is placed, which, at the end of the wedding, is given to the musicians. Before the departure of the *barāt,* the groom sits on the lap of his mother, and after the arrival of the couple, both sit on the lap of the groom's mother. Afterwards, seven pots are filled with rice and lentils in the kitchen and the couple is asked whether the pots are filled. They have to answer in the affirmative in order to show and to keep the wealth in the house. The return of the bride is known here as the *bandāpanā* and the *sindhur makhā* takes place only in the house of the groom, not in the bride's house. In addition to this a Brahmin is obliged to perform a small fire ritual in the groom's house after the arrival of the couple. In some cases, a male goat for the groom and a female goat for the bride are sacrificed. With the blood a *ṭikā* used to be given.

In former times the *barāt* would bring a sheep for the *jāti* of the bride and offer it in order to be allowed to enter the bride's village. The *barāt* had to ask whether it is permitted to enter, and usually the *jāti* of the bride denied asking for some money in addition to the sheep. Nowadays, only money known as *jāti tonkā* is given. It is also claimed that the dowry is considerably smaller compared to Sambalpur, and people believe that this is the reason why Aghriā men from Bolangir prefer to marry women from the Sambalpur district. In cases of marriage between the Bolangir and Sambalpur districts, the rituals are a mixture of both traditions.

1.4. DEATH AND FUNERARY RITES

Among the Aghriā there is no clear concept of a good death as opposed to a bad death as found among tribal communities like the Kisān. However, there are certain notions about a good death. Certain days such as every Thursday in the month, Mārgaśīra, the day of *Nuā Khāi*, *Panchaka* or *Gaṇeṣ Pūjā* are generally considered auspicious, but also for one's death and it is believed that the soul goes directly to heaven on these days. Every person who dies on an auspicious day is regarded as a *bhāgyabān*—lucky. Furthermore, a good time to die is after one's duties are over, after the marriages of all children have been arranged and the children are well settled financially. In contrast, an untimely death by accident, or if a life is unfulfilled, is considered a bad death. A 'good' life—a simple life, having land and earning enough for the family, having a son and children in general, being in harmony with one's relatives—does not automatically lead to a good death. Generally, a wife should die before her husband. If a father witnesses the death of his son or a grandfather of his grandson these elders are considered *pāpi*, sinners, who are punished by painfully watching their children die. If one suffers for a long time before death, e.g. by being paralysed, one is also seen as *pāpi* and as a *hatabhāgā* or unlucky person. Such strong punishments are also related to one's *karma* and determined by merits (*puniya*) or sins (*pāp*) in an earlier life (*purba-janma*). There is no particularly 'good' place to die, but people prefer to die at home and often dying people are brought out of their rooms to the veranda.

If death is seen as imminent, and if the Aghriā are afraid that their relative may not survive the next night, some Ganga-water mixed with sacred basil-leaves (*tulsī*) is placed in the mouth of the dying person. This is known as *dān debā*. After this, the person is otherwise considered to be dead. It is further believed that only with the Ganga-water can the person reach *mukti* (redemption) and leave the cycle of birth and rebirth. Some Aghriā also believe that the gifts to be given during the following rituals should be announced on this occasion. However, if the person survives and recovers—some say as a kind of mistake of Yama, the God of Death—it is seen as a birth again. Such a person, having survived after receiving *dān debā,* cannot eat boiled rice (*bhāt*) before a Brahmin has performed a small ritual and some gifts (*dān* such as paddy) have been given to that priest.[21]

To be present at the time of someone's death is seen as proof that there has been a relationship with that person's death in an earlier life.

The first day

On the day of death the body of the deceased is brought into the house and laid out usually in an inner yard on the ground with the feet pointing south. It is anointed with turmeric by the daughters or daughters-in-law, who may also write 'Ram' and 'Krishna' on the legs and '*Oum*' on the forehead. Small coins, preferably made of copper, are placed around the body and on the hands and are wrapped in a part of the new clothes. However, a small part of the cloth is kept to throw it together with the bones into the Ganga later. A basil twig is placed on the top of the body and little bit of the Ganga water and gold is put into the mouth. Furthermore, the head is decorated with several flower garlands.

Relatives and neighbours come to the house to bid farewell. People present at the time of the death are considered to be lucky. The Aghriā believe that in the case they are relatives, they were strongly emotionally related (*lāgithibā*) with the departed and in the case they are not related they must have had a relationship in a former life.

At the same time, the preparations for the cremation begin. Firewood must be arranged. If a family is not capable of providing the wood, a less expensive burial is also possible. However, the general tendency is towards cremation. The rituals prior to the cremation or burial are the same. A bed (cot) is prepared which is turned upside down and is decorated on the legs with banana leaves. Some Aghriā say that the dead should spend some time in the kitchen of the house before the procession. This, however, is not done in all cases.

A few hours after the death, a procession starts from the house to the cremation ground. The women of the house bid farewell either in the outer yard of the house or join the procession, but usually do not go to the cremation. During the procession, *Ram Nam Satya Hai* is uttered on the way to the cremation ground and sometimes a group of singers (*kirthan*) is arranged to sing devotional songs. The bed should be carried by the eldest son supported by other sons (including classificatory) or other relatives of the deceased such as the daughter's husbands, etc., who often do not wear shoes on the way. In front of the bed a light (*dīpa*) is carried if possible by a daughter's son. In the procession husked rice (*khai*) and coins are thrown, a gong (*ghaṇṭa*) and a shell (*śankha*) are used to produce additional sounds. During the procession the bed is placed on the ground seven times—six times on the way itself and a last time next to the cremation ground. Each time one relative circles around the bed once and puts cotton, raw rice (*dhān*) and husked rice in all four corners of the bed. Both the cotton and the raw rice are carried in a basket used for winnowing which is also burned during the cremation. The big pot used to boil rice in the family of the deceased is also carried during the procession by a *jati* member and is destroyed next to the pyre. This *jāti,* acting as a witness to almost all the ceremonies, is imperative among the Aghriā.

After reaching the cremation ground the bed is taken seven times counter-clockwise around the pyre, and the body is placed on top of it with the head in northern direction and the feet towards the south. On the ground and the lowest layer of the pyre there should be three logs crosswise to the deceased. In the same way on top of the grave three long stones are usually placed.[22] Sometimes relatives call the dead person one last time—as if they want to wake him up.[23] Relatives and friends usually throw some pieces of sandalwood dipped into clarified butter (*ghī*) on the pyre after all the knots of the clothes have been opened or, in many cases, the clothes of the deceased himself have been removed. The eldest son lights the fire using a lamp that was carried by the daughter's son. The lighting of the fire is also known as the *mukhāgni*. Some say that the eldest son should leave the pyre afterwards and should not look back. Very few relatives remain to observe the burning or to occasionally add salt to the fire to speed up the process. The bed of which one leg has to be broken after the arrival at the cremation ground is also burnt. At a later stage of the burning a relative breaks the skull.

The men participating in the burning are not allowed to enter the house before the corpse is completely burnt. From the cremation ground the men go to the pond (or river) to take a bath. A small plant (e.g. mango) is planted on the banks of the pond by the eldest son, and water is given (*pāen diyā*) to that plant on this and the following day. Before leaving the pond all the men stand in a row and the first man, sometimes a *jāti*, takes a stone and passes it over his shoulder to the man behind him, which is repeated till the last man throws the stone into the pond. Some Aghriā think that this is a precaution so that the death never occurs again. When entering the house further washings of the feet are necessary and some water is also sprinkled over one's head.

Immediately after returning home from the cremation the so-called *sītal khiā* (*sītal* = to cool down; *khiā* = to eat) takes place. It is prepared by the women of the house. Everyone who participated in the cremation should eat this cold dish. Some argue that it is given to cool the *pret* (the spirit/ghost), while others say that it is offered to cool the participants.

Later, the family after having changed their dress sits together and rice—boiled over and slightly salted (*miṭhi bhāt*)—is served. Certain restrictions have to be followed by the family from now on. Particularly, no oil (*tel*) should be used (including for oil lamps). Milk, onions, garlic and non-vegetarian foods are forbidden (however chilli, salt or turmeric is not prohibited). The family and to some extent the whole clan is not allowed to attend any rituals such as marriages or to visit any temple. No god should be worshipped inside the house either. For the eldest son additional restrictions are applied such that he should not sleep in a bed but on the ground instead.

The following day the eldest son, accompanied by other relatives, goes again to the cremation ground and collects seven small bones which are kept to be put into the tomb (*samādhi*) and later into the Ganga near Allahabad. Water is sprinkled on the ash, which is then immersed in a nearby river or pond. The participants must take another bath after which water is given to the recently planted plant again.

Invitations for the following rituals, particularly for the eleventh day, are sent to relatives and guests. The invitations should be thrown away after reading and should not be kept in the house, which would be inauspicious. In former times, Harijan or Ghansiā messengers carried this inauspicious news, but they refuse to do so nowadays. If an Aghriā brought this news for someone else from another community he could be excluded from his own community.

The third day: telghar/telkām

In the morning of the third day, the barber comes to shave all the men who participated in the cremation except the sons and to cut the nails of the women. The washerman collects one cloth from every Aghriā household, which is, however, a token, as the rest are washed in the home. Most of the restrictions regarding the food are lifted on this day and the family is allowed to eat oil again. Some *jāti* cook a simple meal for all the caste members in the village including the family of the deceased. However, the restrictions regarding oil, fish, meat or eggs remain for the eldest son and the whole family is not yet allowed to eat non-vegetarian food. In the following days the invitations for the funeral feasts are distributed and a *samādhi* is built.

The ninth day: naakiriyā /nabakriyā

With the ninth day, the funeral period called *kam ghar* lasting until the eleventh or twelfth day begins. For the rituals of this period the presence of a priest, usually one of the Aghriā's own priests called a Tihāri, is required. In a first *pūjā* in the evening the priest lights the *akhaṇḍa dīpa* —the continuous and unbreakable light, which should burn the whole night (to ensure the burning a second light is put in another place). Additionally, water (ideally a mixture from seven holy rivers) mixed with milk, curd, *jabdhān* (a kind of wheat), *kusa*-grass and flowers is placed in a special pot with little holes so that drops of water fall on the earth all night.

The tenth day: daśāh

On the tenth day a little hut is erected near the pond known as the *daśāh ghar* or *pret ghar*. The *akhaṇḍa dīpa* and the pot with the holes from the evening before are placed near it (the pot is destroyed after the *pūjā*). Sitting under the hut, the Tihāri faces north while the son sits facing south. The priest, the eldest son (or the other sons) and a *jāti* must be present. Next to the hut, a fireplace is prepared and unbroken pulses and half-boiled rice are cooked which is said to be the favourite dish of a *pret*. From the rice and pulses, 10 big balls (*piṇḍa*) are formed plus one additional ball for the ancestors (*pitru*). The number ten is related to the tenth day, but also seen as the recreation of a body, i.e. the ten *piṇḍa*: (1) for the head and forehead; (2) nose; (3) eyes; (4) neck (*golā*); (5) chest; (6) arms; (7) legs; (8) navel; (9) hair and (10) for the life or for everything (*sabu*).[24] After offering these 10 + 1 rice balls everything is placed in one big pot into which fruits and a cloth are also placed. The eldest son then immerses the pot in a western direction into the pond. Afterwards, the eldest son burns down the hut.

After that morning *pūjā*, the barber shaves the eldest son and other relatives but only in the case of the sons is a complete shaving (including the head) done. If the father dies, the moustache is of course shaved as well and occasionally never allowed to be grown again. Another bath follows and again the plant near the pond is watered. The sons receive new, white clothes, which are given to them by their father-in-law or mother's brother. The old and impure clothes are left behind of the pond or river. Nobody should touch these cloths or bring them back into the house. It is considered to be the right of the barber to take them. At the same time, the women of the family take their bath and, in the case of the widows, they take off their jewellery and bangles and receive a white *śāḍhi* from their brothers.

Later, a small *pūjā* takes place inside the house called a *ghar sanskār* to purify the house. It can be combined with another ritual *asthi sanskār* to purify the bones if one wishes to keep the bones inside the house instead of the *samādhi*. After this *pūjā* a procession to the *samādhi* follows. It is led by the priest and the eldest son, who carries the seven bones, and is followed by other relatives. Again, the gong and the shell are used in the procession. The *samādhi* erected during the last days is surrounded by four little trees (one in every corner). Between the trees, a line of mango leaves is placed. After a short *pūjā* the eldest son places a red flag on top of the *samādhi* and circles the *samādhi* seven times clockwise followed by all the relatives. Now the bones with some coins and gold[25] are placed inside the *samādhi* (if not kept in the house) and the *samādhi* is closed with bricks.

The eleventh day: kām ghar/antyeṣṭikriyā

On the eleventh day of the funeral the biggest number of relatives, friends and neighbours is present—usually everyone cleanly shaven. Outside, a gift of money called a *panmilā* is given by them and a member of the family carefully writes down every amount and every giver.

In the morning a longer *pūjā* takes place inside the house. Here, the relatives bring gifts (*dān*) for the deceased such as all kinds of food (fruits, vegetables, rice, *ghī*, curd, etc.), clothes, household goods (oil lamp, torch, etc.), umbrellas, and toilet articles (soap, hair oil, shampoo, etc.). A seat (*ābān*) is offered for the deceased where, if possible, also his photo is kept. Initially, the eldest son as the main sacrificer sits to the left of the priest, facing east. After the invocation of several gods, four leaf-plates (*khali*) are put in front of the priest. In the next step, the deceased on his chair with the photo is worshipped with flower garlands. The eldest son changes his seat—now facing south. The eldest son's wife brings a mixture of boiled rice, and fruits and sweets are added.

In one case, three rice balls were formed by the eldest son out of this mixture and placed on one leaf-plate each. Later, another ball was prepared and placed a slight distance from the other three. The eldest son then added Ganga-water, mixed with raw rice (*aruā chāul*), milk, *duba* and *kusa* grass, to all the leaf-plates. A *dhoti* was then given by the eldest son and placed around the three rice balls. The rice balls (*piṇda*) were worshipped by the eldest son by circling some incense and a *dīpa*. In another case only two *piṇda—ekādaśāha piṇda* and *mrutyu śajyā piṇda*—were offered, the first to feed the *pret* on the eleventh day, the second given on the cremation ground according to a Tihāri. However, the rice balls are then put together in a big bowl and the eldest son holds the bowl for a few minutes on his right shoulder and promises to bring the bones to the Ganga. The content of the bowl is later immersed in a nearby pond. A *homa* follows, which is fed with *ghī* by the priest.

The following sequence consists of eight gifts, known as *mrutāṣṭaka dān*, given to the *pret* symbolically and, practically, to eight Brahmins.[26] These gifts consist of items that the deceased needs for his well-being, are comprised of (1) oilseed (*tiḷ/rāśī*); (2) gold (*svarṇa*); (3) land (*bhūmi*); (4) rice (*arṇa*); (5) cloths (*kapḍā/basthra*); (6) water (*jaḷa*); (7) a light (*dīpa*) and (8) a cow (*gāī*).

Subsequently, ten leaf-bowls with raw rice (*aruā chāul*) are given by the eldest son to the priest. These ten gifts called *daśa dān* symbolize (1) a cow (*go dān*); (2) land (*bhūmi*); (3) gold (*hiraṇya*); (4) cloth (*basthra*); (5) water (*jaḷa*); (6) raw material for oil (*tiḷ*); (7) raw rice (*aruā chāul*); (8) mixture of milk and ghee (*prọpanaka*); (9) light (*dīpa*) and (10) bed (*śajyā*[27] *dān*). In the case that a real cow is given the priest and the eldest son may go to the cattle shed to worship the cow and her tail there. All of these gifts should be equally distributed among all present priests or Brahmins, because in wealthier families, sometimes in addition to the family priest (*purohit*), other priests are invited. At the same time, near the fire of sacrifice a new bed including bed cover, blanket, mosquito net, fruits and rice is prepared. A lower Brahmin takes his seat on the bed, which is considered to be the gift of the bed of death or the bed of the ghost. He gets his feet massaged and is fed by the eldest son. Afterwards, the lower Brahmin has to leave the house immediately, taking the gifts with him.[28]

After the *śajyā dān* the women of the family can give another gift of a cow (*go dān*), which, however, is usually substituted by money. Furthermore, the eldest son gives some money (*dakṣiṇa*) to the family priest. At the end of the ritual the priest distributes some *ghī* among the sons and the other people present—the so-called *homā ghī*—which is also used for the fire ritual and is said to have a purifying effect when eaten and applied to one's head.

The *pūjā,* done by the family priest, is followed by the *bhanjā dān*—a special gift for the sister's son (*bhanjā*) of the deceased (or in case of a woman, the sister's son of her husband). The *bhanjā* and sometimes the *bhanjā*'s wife are worshipped and fed by the family, e.g. the widow and usually receives some money and cloths.

Furthermore, one or two meals are served for the relatives and guests on that day. The Aghriā prefer to cook for themselves. This means that a *jāti* is engaged to cook for all caste members of the village while another Brahmin acts as a cook for all the guests including the Aghriā from other villages. Because it is practically impossible to invite the whole village and cook for them on such an occasion, food for one raw meal (*kharchā*) including raw rice, vegetables, oil and spices are distributed in the village for every family. In the evening of the eleventh day the family is allowed to eat non-vegetarian food for the first time again, which is served to the *jāti*, relatives and guests on that day. It is considered to be the responsibility of the married daughters to arrange the non-vegetarian food, usually fish,[29] called *bisar* (literally the smell of fish).

Sometimes—and in fact quite often—death occurs at a time favourable or auspicious for the deceased, but very inauspicious for the family of the dead. This time is called the *puṣkarā.* A *puṣkarā* necessitates further rituals to remove the danger or negative effect for the family. I will return to this point. If such a ritual is performed, it is usually done in the night of the eleventh day at a time fixed by the priest or astrologer according to the stars. In a special *homā,* nine kinds of wood, which resemble the nine stars, are burnt in the presence of the eldest son, the family priest (*purohit*) and a few family members. Afterwards, an earthen pot called a *dān pātra* is filled with rice, cloth, a little bit of gold, some money and two little iron nails which symbolize Yama and his brother Sama. The eldest son gives this pot to a lower Brahmin, who is called upon for this ritual. This transfer is known as the *puṣkarā ṭalā* (= to get rid off). Ideally, no one should see this moment and everyone should close his eyes while the pot is handed over. Immediately afterwards the Brahmin has to leave the house—even if it is in the middle of the night and the *homā* is completed. Some *dakṣiṇa* is given to the family priest, who then gives a pot with water (usually the lower part of a *kalaś*) whose water is sprinkled with the help of a mango leaf by the family members inside the house and also in the cowshed. This pot of water should be immersed in a pond or river on the following day.

The twelfth day/the ritual of six month: chhamāsi

Traditionally, this ritual should take place six months (six months = *chhamāsi*) after the *kām ghar*. However, nowadays it is usually done on the twelfth day. The *pūjā* in the morning is almost identical with the *pūjā* of the eleventh day. Again, the eldest son appears in the white clothes gifted to him by the father-in-law or mother's brother. In front of the priest three leaf-plates are arranged and the eldest son, facing south, puts a rice ball on each of them. Later he adds some water. However, only three rice balls, instead of four, are used on this day. The eldest son, the priest and other relatives recall the names of ancestors as far as they can remember. At the end, the rice is placed into a big bowl again and put on his shoulder by the eldest son.

Compared to the eleventh day, the recipient of the *śajyā dān* is different. This time the family priest himself accepts this gift after the eldest son has applied some oil to his feet. Now the bed is considered to be a 'happy' one (*sukha śajyā dān*) or a 'bed of the ancestors' (*pitru śajyā dān*).

After the main *pūjā* another ritual for the ancestors called the *śrāddha* is observed in the kitchen of the house—this time conducted by the eldest son and his wife. One big leaf plate for the deceased is placed in the middle, some smaller leaf plates for other ancestors around it and another small one for Vishma Deb is slightly separated. Raw rice, raw vegetables and pulses, and cloth are given. The eldest son then worships all the leaf plates made of *phalśā* leaves by circling with lights and incense. Afterwards, everyone leaves the room. The ancestors should not be disturbed while eating. In the second part of the *śrāddha,* boiled rice (*bhāt*) and cooked food (*dal*, curry, *khir*, etc.) are offered by the eldest son. On the big leaf plate six portions of food are served. At the end, water is served using a *paṇas*-leaf (jackfruit) for each plate with food, and, again, the room is left. After this, the raw food is given to a Brahmin. The family members eat the cooked food. Some Aghriā argue that the food of the main leaf should be eaten by the deceased's daughter's sons or by other grandchildren.

This *pūjā* is repeated exactly one year after the death and called *barṣika śrāddha* (the *śrāddha* of one year). The procedure is identical apart from the minor difference that twelve portions of food are now offered to the deceased. If no Brahmin is present at that time the obligatory *dān*—consisting of rice (*usnā-chāul*), lentils (*mug/birhi*), molasses (*guḍ*), some coins and flowers—may be given later.

At the end of a *kām ghar* of a woman, her gold jewellery should be distributed. All married daughters should receive at least one piece as a memory.

Variations

I have mentioned the existing variations generally as a result of different priests performing the rituals. In the case of death, differences could be found particularly in relation to the number of *piṇda* offered, to the time and number of certain gifts presented as well as the order of the ritual activities.

The rituals described are performed in the case of the death of a married or widowed adult. If a child dies before the rituals of the sixth/twenty-first day after birth are conducted or before the first rice has been fed, only a small feast must be served to the *jāti* (usually, only one member of every family—not all *jāti*) and the barber and washerman have to be called.[30] A Brahmin or priest is only required afterwards—if death occurs after the twenty-first day—as most Aghriā say. For all unmarried Aghriā dying later, a much smaller funeral is performed on the seventh day after death. In the case of small chiidren—before the age of one or two years or before five years according to others—no *samādhi* is built and they are usually buried. A burial is also done in the case of women dying during pregnancy or during delivery.

There is another option to shorten the funeral considerably, that includes bringing the bones to the river Ganga immediately after cremation. In this case only a *jāti bhoji* has to be served to the *jāti* and the relatives, which is known as *Ganga-bhoji*. No *kām ghar* and no other rituals are required.

1.5. BIRTH (*JANMA*), REBIRTH (*PUNRAJANMA*) AND THE ANCESTORS (*PITRU*)

Who becomes an ancestor? Not every Aghriā. Although there is no complete consensus among Aghriā, most see marriage as an essential condition to be met in order to become an ancestor.[31] One has to be married in order to be included among the forefathers. Only for married Aghriā are the complete funeral ceremonies performed. Unmarried Aghriā are not even allowed to worship the ancestors and only as brides or grooms are they allowed to perform a ritual for the ancestors for the first time. Some Aghriā argue explicitly that the *tel chaḍā* is the most important of all rituals in becoming an ancestor. Furthermore, there is the idea that if grown up women remain in the house, i.e. they are not married in time, the ancestors would receive nothing to eat. Therefore, early marriages, in particular child marriages or other forms of symbolical marriages, had to be arranged in former times in order to satisfy the ancestors. Unmarried men and women turn into evil spirits or *bhut* according to some.

However, even married Aghriā do not become ancestors automatically after death. Exceptions include people committing suicide, women dying during pregnancy or during confinement (until the sixth day after birth). In these cases, men or women become spirits or ghosts instead of ancestors—in the case of suicide they turn into *bhut*, in the latter cases, into *chirgin*. Particularly if nails and hair grow after death, some people believe that it is a clear indication of turning into a *chirgin*. Women who die during pregnancy or confinement are not burned, but buried. No *samādhi* is erected in these cases. In former times, in case of death during confinement, a *guniā* or local healer was consulted, who performed a special ritual to lock the evil soul in the cemetery—a ritual known as *bāndhi debā*. These Aghriā are never remembered in rituals as ancestors, however, in some cases it seems that some food (*piṇda*) is offered to all of them collectively, i.e. for the whole category separately from the proper ancestors. This food is later thrown away and remains uneaten by relatives such as the other *piṇda*. However, there is uncertainty about the fate of Aghriā who die before marriage. Some Aghriā maintain that they become *rākas*, another category of ghosts, or they turn into a *bhut*, an evil spirit, or they remain in the state of a *pret* (see death rituals).

Worshipping the ancestors

Apart from rituals for certain ancestors, and within a period of one year after their respective deaths, the main rituals for the ancestors take place in the dark side in the month of Āśbina or *Daśarā* (roughly September/October), when the ancestors temporarily return to their families. This entire time is known as the fortnight of the ancestors or *pitru pakṣ*. Some peculiar rules have to be observed during this period. The Aghriā are neither allowed to cut their hair and nails nor to shave. Furthermore, the house is cleaned only with a broom and is not properly cleaned.

The ancestors are constantly worshipped for half of the month (14–15 days). Every morning a woman of the house—it has to be a daughter-in-law—offers flowers, ground rice milk and green gram under the eaves of the house—in most cases the eaves of an inner yard—on a spot precisely between the veranda and the place where the raindrops fall down from the roof. Here, a place is erected for them in the form of a small platform (*pindhā*) on which cigarettes and tobacco are placed as well as small twigs as traditional tooth-brushes. A daughter-in-law then circles a *ghī*-lamp and some embers with incense in front of the platform. This procedure is repeated every morning for the whole fortnight.

Additionally, there are rituals for ancestors whose bones have not yet been brought to the river Ganga. A ritual should be performed for them on the lunar day (*tithi*) which they died, that is, if a relative died on the sixth day, no matter which month, he should be worshipped also on the very same day during the *pitru pakṣ*. For all female ancestors together a ritual should be performed on the ninth day while all male forefathers are remembered on the tenth day in a specific ritual. On these two days—the ninth and tenth—ploughing is not allowed and also the use of bullocks prohibited. No one should dig the earth, at least not with a plough, there is no consensus regarding other instruments. And, no one should use the agricultural instruments worshipped on Harli Uāns. Anyone ignoring these strict rules can become an outcaste (*ajātiā*).

Another important day is the last day of the fortnight—known as *mahāḷayā*. On this day, gifts of the category *dān* such as sweets, cloths and paddy should be given to the Brahmin, but not to the family priest (*purohit*), who should not accept it. In case that there is no Brahmin, it can be offered to a sister's son (ZS) or *bhanjā*. However, in a landlord's family I was told that this tradition of giving to a *bhanjā* was discontinued in the 1980s. Essentially, part of the ritual is the gift of food (*piṇda*) to the ancestors. Finally, a daughter-in-law brings a *ghī*-lamp into the field and requests the ancestors: 'Please, protect our fields'.

Another important occasion to worship the ancestors is at the time of marriage, when the bride and groom, together with their parents, perform a ritual for the ancestors for the first time—the so-called *pitru pūjā*. As some Aghriā told me explicitly, the blessings of the ancestors are sought after for the new marriage relationship.

In all these rituals special food, such as cakes prepared of *khuda*—the smallest pieces of grinded rice—is served to the ancestors. It is believed that the cake known as the *khuda piṭha,* offered once a year during the dark side of the month of Āśbina, remains in the stomach of the ancestors for a year. However, compared to tribal communities, no alcohol is served to the ancestors.

The ancestors in dreams

CASE 1: ANCESTORS TAKING CARE OF THEIR FAMILY

An elderly Aghriā—now about 65 to 70 years old—told me that he once dreamed of his father after he had passed away. The father had suffered from different illnesses before his death and went to Calcutta for a treatment. On the way, he met a childless man, who gave him Rs. 2,000 to sponsor a school in Kuchinda—a small town, where the father held the landlordship. The school should be opened in the name of this childless man. However, his father used the money to pay for his treatment in Calcutta and later died there. In coming to know of this, the donor wanted his money back. He even thought of taking the landlord to court. However, he decided to visit his sons first. On the day before his arrival at the village the son dreamed of his father, who asked him to pay Rs. 100 to the stranger as a first instalment. The next day, the donor turned up indeed and demanded Rs. 100. A case in court was avoided.

CASE 2: ANCESTORS TAKING CARE OF THEIR FAMILY AND FIELDS

After the death of her father-in-law, an Aghriā lady had a dream of him. In this dream he recommended to his daughter-in-law to contact another person because both—his son and his daughter-in-law—were not able to properly take care of the fields. At that time boars had started to destroy the paddy fields. The next morning, the person she was asked to contact appeared in their house and, as it turned out, this person himself had dreamed of this father-in-law as well. In his dream the father-in-law requested that the man help his family in order to save the harvest. They went together to the field, saw the damage the boars had caused and started cutting the paddy quickly. In this way, further damaged was avoided.

In a similar incident an ancestor appeared in the dream of his daughter-in-law and told her to take care of certain guests, who indeed arrived little later.

CASE 3: ANCESTORS COMPLAIN ABOUT BAD TREATMENT

Later the father-in-law (of case 2) appeared once more in a dream of the same woman and complained that she had forgotten to offer him tobacco during the rituals for all ancestors in the month of Āśbina (October). She replied in the dream that he would find tobacco in a box on the cupboard. The next morning she found the box half-empty which had been full the evening before.

In the same way other Aghriā remembered that their ancestors had told them about mistakes their descendants had committed in certain rituals. Receiving advise from their ancestors the concerned Aghriā could correct their mistakes. Thus, they were able to perform the rituals in the proper manner next time.

CASE 4: ANCESTORS ANNOUNCE THEIR REBIRTH

In another incident shortly after the death of her father-in-law, a woman had a dream of him. He told her about his wish to be reborn as a daughter in the family again and asked her what she thought. Shortly thereafter, she became pregnant and a second daughter was born in the family. However, in other cases, Aghriā may also announce their wish to be reborn within the family while still alive—saying, for example, that they will never leave the family.

In still another dream, the rebirth of a woman was announced. An aunt of the father of the girl had this dream. Because of this, the baby was considered to be the rebirth of her mother's father's mother (MFM), who at the same time was also the father's mother's mother (FMM). Additionally, an identity between ancestor and rebirth was indicated by the fact that both were seen as a bit egoistic and very similar in character.

What can be concluded from these dreams? First communication with the ancestors appears to be possible, although not via traditional mediums. Secondly, the ancestors appear to care about their families even after death. They try to ensure that the harvest is successful, the most essential thing in a rural society, that guests are served properly, and that problems can be solved—even if they have caused them, as in case 1. Finally, they tell of their wishes to return to the family, as in case 4, which leads to the question of rebirth.

Birth and rebirth

SIGNS OF A REBIRTH

Prior to a birth or during pregnancy, ancestors may already appear in dreams. In one case, a pregnant woman dreamed of her mother-in-law, who had recently passed away. In this dream, the mother-in-law walked up to the room of the pregnant daughter-in-law, but did not enter the room before disappearing again. At the same time, another son in the same house dreamed of his mother (the mother-in-law) and was equally convinced that if a daughter was to be born, it would be a rebirth of his mother.

Later, after the birth of a daughter, in January 2002, some family members observed the child in great detail in order to find similarities and an uncle (FeB) told me that, in his opinion, the mouth of the girl resembled that of his mother while sleeping. He argued that it was quite possible that his mother had been reborn into the family as his niece (yBD), but one can never be entirely sure. The examination of newly born babies in order to find characteristics of relatives earlier expired is quite common. If such similarities are found, the children are often considered to be rebirths of these relatives. In another case in the same family the dislike for hair oil was explained as circumstantial evidence that an uncle may have been the rebirth of his grandfather. Accordingly, they are addressed as such. The newly born girl already mentioned was therefore addressed as mother by the sisters of the baby's father and another child in the family was called 'father's elder brother' (*baḍa bāpā*) by his father's sisters, because he was also seen as a rebirth of his grandfather.

In the same family, in August 2002, another child was born. Several times before the birth the mother had dreamed of her grandfather (her father's father), who—as family members recalled—had been particularly fond of this grandchild. In one of these dreams, the grandfather asked for a glass of water mixed with *bel*. Some time later, the pregnant grandchild woke up and herself felt a big thirst for water and *bel* but did not find any. Her father's younger brother became angry after he heard about this dream. In his opinion, his father should return to his own house and should not be reborn in the house of his son's daughter in another village. He cracked jokes with his pregnant elder brother's daughter by saying that she should come into his house. Later, the potential mother again had a dream in which the grandfather complained about the behaviour of his son (the uncle of the mother), who would bar him from entering his own house. However, the father's younger brother of the potential mother acknowledged that his father had some problems in the latter stage of his life and was no longer interested in agriculture. Instead, the ancestor may have decided to join the family of his granddaughter, for which agriculture was not the main source of income.

APPEASEMENT OF UNHAPPY ANCESTORS

If newly born babies refuse to eat or drink it is believed that born-again ancestors are unhappy for some reason and must be appeased. A case in point is the birth of Binod Chandra Naik—a popular poet and writer, now about 70 years old—who was born in the house of his mother's brother. Immediately after the birth the baby refused to drink milk. The family was convinced that Binod was the rebirth of his father's father and denied to drink milk because he was not born in his 'own' house, that is, the house of the father of the child. Accordingly, the father's elder brother of the child arrived in the mother's brother's house in order to beg the pardon of his 'father' that he was born there and not in his village, as the baby was considered to be a rebirth of his father. An older horse bowing its head in front of the child was regarded as proof that Binod was the rebirth of his father's father. The British had presented the horse once to the grandfather. It is believed that animals can see the soul (*ātmān*) and the horse obviously must have recognized his old owner—now reborn. Also, the mother's father of the baby welcomed the baby as the rebirth of his *samdhi* or affinal relative (daughter's husband's father—DHF). Therefore, from his birth Binod took the nickname '*ajā*'—'grandfather'.

In another similar case, a girl—now about 26 years old and the mother of the baby in case 1—was born in the village of her mother but not in her father's house. In the same manner the child initially refused to drink the milk of her mother and continued to refuse it for a couple of days. A relative then dreamed of the girl as a rebirth of her father's father, that is, the girl was the grandfather, who claimed in this dream 'I'm going to your family once more in the stomach of my daughter-in-law'. When the girl still refused to drink, the mother's mother asked the baby: '*Samdhi*, why are you angry with us?' The mother's mother then worshipped the girl by washing her feet with milk. After this incident, the girl did not refuse the mother's milk any longer.

VARIATIONS

Quite often, it is assumed that a grandparent is reborn into the family and, in some cases; a person may also be a rebirth of another child of the family, for instance a brother. This is shown in the case of a small child, nicknamed Ghansiā, as he was sold to a so-called 'Untouchable' community in order to save him, but who later died at the age of one and a half years—about 45 years ago. The aunt of the child (the father's younger brother's wife) loved him very much and criticized the mother because, in her opinion, she did not care enough for him. At the funeral the aunt sat in a corner and cried. Her own son—at that time roughly four years old—saw his crying mother and asked 'Why are you crying?' and the mother replied 'I had hoped that you and Ghansiā would grow up together and both of you would go to school together, but now you are alone.' The son: 'Why are you crying? He will come back!' In the same month this aunt became pregnant and gave birth to another son, who showed similarities to Ghansiā, e.g. in the form of the ear. During the ritual of the sixth day, the mother of Ghansiā saw the newborn baby, held him in her arms and looked into his eyes for a long time. Then she said, 'Perhaps I have not loved you enough. I have beaten you. Your aunt loved you so much and now you have gone to her.' Another wife of the landlord, considered equally as a mother (although not a mother in biological terms), dreamed of a Bābā (an ascetic) after the death of Ghansiā.

This Bābā offered the child to her again (or her family) and said: 'You don't have to worry. The child will come once more to your family.' Later, this mother recognized a particular form of the neck of the newborn child to be characteristic of Ghansiā. The similarities found between Ghansiā and the later born son of the aunt might have been an important reason why Ghansiā's father subsequently adopted the son of his brother.

In other cases, even persons staying in a family, although not related, may be reborn into this family. The family of a wealthy landlord patronized the religious movement of Mahima Dharma at one point in time by inviting male or female ascetics—known as Bābā and Mātā respectively—to stay with the family. Thus, for several years a Bābā and a Mātā lived together with this family. A daughter of the landlord was particularly fond of the Bābā—and vice versa. They played together and spent much time together. In contrast, the daughter rather disturbed the Mātā. Later, this daughter had a son, who was known to be very patient, calm and supportive of his mother and her family was convinced that the Bābā was reborn in this son. Also, a daughter was born to this landlord's daughter. This newly born daughter was slightly mentally disturbed and very demanding the attention of her mother and some say, that she is the rebirth of this Mātā who now disturbs the landlord's daughter.

What is obvious from the three cases described above is that there is a keen interest in rebirth. Family members try to find out who may be reborn in the family. Historically, another way of identifying rebirths was to call the names of ancestors when the babies cried a lot. If the child kept quiet after having listened to the name of a certain ancestor, it was believed that the child could be the rebirth of this ancestor. Generally, there is an underlying assumption that—as one Aghriā had put it—'Ancestors wait in heaven for a rebirth. They are worshipped to come back to their family.' Although most ancestors seem to be reborn in an alternating generation—as grandchildren—there is no fixed rule. A forefather may appear in the same generation again as in the case of the death of a child or an ancestor may be reborn as a great grandchild. Additionally, a male forefather could reappear in the family as a girl. Compared to other communities in the village, there is, however, no standardized way to prove a rebirth.[32]

NOTES

1. With my male bias and men as my main interlocutors, it was rather difficult to learn about ideas of conception—not the domain of men. The only women with whom men could talk about the topic are their own wives or they may talk to rather distant grandfathers such as a mother's father (MF) or wife's mother's father (WMF) with whom they can joke and can drop veiled hints about sexuality. However, these elder male relatives of my interlocutors had already passed away. So my knowledge of this sensitive topic is rather limited.
2. Also explained as a lower part of the back or as the waist.
3. Also used for cleaning the face.
4. In one case, a small girl was decorated for the *Rath Jātrā* and was carried to the outer yard. Later on the child started vomiting and the parents were convinced that the beautiful child had attracted the evil eye of some elder women during the festival.
5. If women try new bangles, which break while someone is watching whose shadow falls on the bangles, this person is said to have a hard shadow. Furthermore, if something is fried in oil and miraculously more oil than usual is needed while someone is watching whose shadow falls on the pot with oil, this person is recognized as having a hard shadow. Men and women may have hard or soft shadows—people affected by evil spirits are generally said to have a soft shadow.
6. In one concrete case, a girl was named Suāti—a short form of her grandmother's name Satyabati of whom she was believed to be a reincarnation.
7. In this specific case the hair was not cut completely, because a child of the family had died shortly after the first haircut and the family feared the effects of a complete shaving. However, other family members saw this as a particular superstition in the family.
8. In the local hierarchy Gosain are considered to be low Brahmin, but higher than Gauḍ.
9. It corresponds to what is known in Hindi as *dābat*.
10. It is also the elder brother's wife who should instruct the groom as far as the first night after the wedding is concerned.
11. In one case out of two brothers the younger brother married first. Later, during the marriage of the elder brother, the younger brother's wife could not act as a *suhāsen* for her husband's elder brother, whom she has to avoid, although she belongs to the same generation.
12. Some Aghriā speculated that this custom might be a legacy of child marriages.
13. Traditionally, the 'younger brother' of the Aghriā and the custodian of the sacred thread—the Dossondhi—is invited to the wedding and recites a blessing during the *hāth lagan*. However in recent times this does not occur.

14. Henceforth husband and wife share one *lāj*.
15. It is believed by some Aghriā that Dulhā Devta should be represented by a small silver or golden plough. Furthermore, others say, that during the arrival two goats (*bukā*) are sacrificed—one for Dulhā Devtā in the kitchen and one for the Bhanjāri in the cattle stable (*guhāl*). However, I did not observe these rituals.
16. In a case observed by me the bride received Rs. 2,500.
17. An elder Muṇḍā told me that it was possible either as a wife or husband to marry a tree after two husbands or wives had passed away respectively. An astrologer was asked to find the cause of deaths and to select a tree—either *sāl*, *mahuā* or *sāhāḍā*. The *suhāsen* performed the *teila bhiṣek* and the husband or wife circled around the tree—a *bedī* was not necessary. After the tree marriage the divorce followed immediately. The husband or wife could proceed to their next marriage partner. As in the case of all divorces, a *jāti bhoji* was obligatory.
18. A similar custom is also described in the *Mahābhārat*.
19. Others argued that a *putrā* should not join the *barāt* because the bride as his *kāki* or father's younger brother's wife (FyBW) had to avoid her *putrā*. This, however, is not fully convincing because the husband's elder brother or husband's mother's brother can join the *barāt* even though the bride has to avoid them.
20. This custom is also prevalent in the region around the village Kuanrmāl.
21. The first serving of rice in this case should not be given by any concrete person (like the the *māmu* in case of a child), but it should be a close relative or *ātmiya lok*—a person, who is related to the soul, who shares all the joy and pain, e.g. the eldest son. If there is no Brahmin to perform the ritual, one can also mix Ganga-water and preboiled rice (*chāul*) in a pot and hold it towards the sky thus giving it symbolically to a Brahmin and Dharma Devta. This gift (*dān*) is considered to be rather inauspicious and impure and should be given to a lower Brahmin (*dānuā* Brahmin). The family priest or *purohit* would refuse to accept it. It should not be given to a *bhanjā* (ZS) either, because it resembles the *mrutyu sajjā dān*.
22. Stones are placed on top of the grave to avoid wild animals or straying dogs digging there. However, if a dog, wolf or any other animal manages to eat the deceased, which happens very rarely, it is believed that the departed was a good person (*bal lok*), a person living according to the religious laws (*armik lok*) and a pure person (*pabitra lok*), who even at the time of death was useful for others and therefore will reach *mukti* (*mokṣa*).
23. An Aghriā from Bargarh claimed that next to the pyre rice is boiled. A little bit of the freshly prepared rice is offered into the mouth of the departed, who is then called for a last time: 'When you are alive, please come!'.
24. The priests I interviewed sometimes named only a few of these parts or had to think a long time before remembering or naming certain parts. The

list presented here was given by one of the priests—the only complete list I recorded.

25. The coins and the little bit gold offered here often lead to the defiling of graves, by people searching for money and throwing away the bones. This is the reason why bones are also kept in the house nowadays in order to be protected.
26. According to a Tihari and my observations, these gifts have to be presented on the eleventh day. However, a Brahmin, who also performs rituals for the Aghriā insisted on giving these gifts on the twelfth day only. According to him they are offered only among the Aghriā. This shows a general and possible inherent variation in all rituals.
27. The spelling differs sometimes and some Aghriā prefer to write it as *sajjā dān* instead of *śajyā dān*.
28. According to some priests, the recipient of the *mrutyu śajyā dān* should not even enter the house, but should accept it near a pond or river, but I have never seen it done in this manner.
29. In most cases that I observed fresh fish was offered, traditionally however small dried fish (*henduā*) should be and in some cases are indeed served to guests as some Aghriā told me. However, there seems to be a clear tendency towards fresh fish—particularly in richer families.
30. There is an interesting belief, that women whose children have died should not eat in darkness. Thus, an older lady whose son had died always kept an oil lamp next to her while eating her dinner in case there would be a power cut.
31. Not all priests of the Aghriā shared this opinion and in one case an Aghriā argued that unmarried Aghriā also become ancestors (*pitru*), but are not remembered during the rituals for the ancestors, i.e. they do not become full ancestors.
32. Case of the Kisān.

APPENDIX 2

The Ritual and Agricultural Cycle— A Description

2.1. CLASSIFICATIONS OF RICE AND LAND

The soil, land and associated qualities

Local peasants differentiate between three types of soil (*māet*) as shown in Table 33.

TABLE 33: VARIETIES OF SOIL

balyā māet	*māet*	*khalya māet*
• sandy (= *balyā*) soil • no cracks when dry • *guḍā* land (see below) • *dihi* land (for houses)	• mixed soil • *māl*- and *bernā*-land	• sticky (= *khalya*) soil • cracks when dry • capacity to keep rain-water • *bāhāl*-land
worst quality	←————→	best quality

In contrast to soil, there are basically four categories of land—known as *jamin* or *māl*—as distinguished by peasants:

Guḍā: the lowest quality of land[1]—dry fields and the highest altitude—land after rain, it is usually dry after a day—used for early varieties of paddy, but also chilli and mustard, if there is an additional water supply:- present price: around Rs. 10,000 per acre (or less).

Māl: medium quality land (*māl* is also used as super-category for all kinds of land), i.e. it can remain wet after a rain for three to four days—present price: Rs. 15,000 per acre.

Bernā: also medium quality land, but more valuable than *māl*, it usually stays wet until October if there are occasional showers—present price: Rs. 15,000 per acre.

Bāhāl: the highest quality of land—the lowest land in terms of the general elevation and usually wet until April (hot season)—therefore, standing water for the longest period after the monsoon and the most suitable for late varieties of paddy—maximum profit—present price: Rs. 20,000 per acre.[2]

The quality of land is to some extent relative. If there is a flood or heavy rain it may be an advantage to have some *guḍā*-land, where one can also grow chilli and mustard. However, *bernā* and *bāhāl* are the best types of land for rice cultivation. The prices are given here for cultivable land in villages, but not for towns, where *guḍā*-land—perfect for building houses—can get a much higher price when sold. However, in general the most valuable land is *bāhāl* compared to the least profitable *guḍā* land. As a landlord told me, while one can expect around 20 bags of 75 kg each of paddy per acre of *māl* land, on *bāhāl* land one can expect between 30 and 35 bags.

There is another category known as *khāri*-land, one to two acres of land on each side of the village road, which is naturally irrigated via the road at the time of the monsoon. The monsoon water thus supplied and mixed with cow dung is regarded as especially fertile (*khāri* = fertile). Furthermore, the land known as *panku māti* near the hills and mountains is particularly fertile because the water from the hills carries humus and naturally fertilizes the field.

Categories of rice

There is an impressive number of categories of rice—primary or secondary products of paddy—which shows the great significance rice maintains in this regional culture. The main categories are introduced here briefly:

1. *dhān*: paddy/raw rice.
2. *chāul*: term for pared paddy (*aruā*, *uṣnā* and *balkā*).
3. *aluā* (S)/*aruā* (O): relatively pure variety of *chāul*, because it is not parboiled. Two sub-categories can be distinguished: (a) a smaller one for rituals, ancestors, *khiri* (sweet rice) and fried rice and (b) a bigger one for cakes such as *dosā*, *chakel* (S) and *babrā* (S) (similar to *uttapam*). *Aruā* is traditionally produced in a *ḍhenki*, but nowadays in modern mills. It has the disadvantage

that *aruā* rice breaks easily without parboiling and tends to become sticky while boiling.

4. *uṣnā* (S)/*uṣunā* (O): another variety of *chāul*, whose name is derived from the term *uṣuneibā* (= to bake). It is also called *khāibā-chāul* (*khāibā* = to eat) in landlords' families, as it is the rice eaten daily. *Uṣnā* is produced by parboiling paddy with little water or rather in steam and drying it in the shadow, before it is pared like *aluā*. The traditional preparation of *uṣnā* takes up to six or seven days depending on the outside temperature. Due to parboiling, *uṣnā* does not break easily while paring it.
5. *balkā*: the lowest variety of *chāul*. Its name is derived from *balkeibā* (= to boil) indicating that it is produced by parboiling paddy with more water than *uṣnā*. It is dried in direct sunlight (8-10 hours) and pared (like *aluā*). The advantage of *balkā* is that it can be produced relatively quickly within one day. It is the staple of poorer people.
6. *kudha*: the smallest remains of *aruā* after paring. It is offered to the ancestors in the form of cakes, but also used to prepare *papad.*[3]
7. *bhāt*: or boiled rice. In the case of *aluā,* it is rice boiled for the first time, while in the case of *uṣnā* or *balkā,* it is boiled for the second time.
8. *pakhāḷa*: *bhāt* with water—and perhaps spices—offered as a main dish.
9. *phaklo-liā* (S)/*khai* (O): rice produced by heating paddy (usually *moṭā-dhān*) in a pot already half filled with sand and by subsequently sevening the rice with a special sieve-basket (*ghari*).
10. *murhi* (S), *liā* (S), *muḍhi* (O): *balkā-chāul* instead of paddy heated on sand as described above.
11. *chūna*: rice-powder, which is produced from *aruā-chāul* ground traditionally in a *ḍhenki* (S)/*ḍhinki* (O) or a modern mill.
12. *chuḍa*: flattened rice. It is boiled ribe flattened in a *ḍhenki*.

Paddy or *dhān* as a central category can be further differentiated into: *atimoṭā* (over-fat), *moṭā* (fat), *saru* (small) und *atisaru* (over-small—sometimes also called *aruā*). Most common in the region are *moṭā* and *saru*. Each category in turn can be separated further into as sub-categories.

TABLE 34: VARIETIES OF PADDY (*DHĀN*)

Dhān	Size	Price and Quality
atimoṭā	biggest	lowest (Rs. 310 per bag/75 kg)
moṭā		
saru		
atisaru	smallest	highest (Rs. 330 per bag/75 kg)

Another line can be drawn between 'white *dhān*' (white = *saphā* or *dhob*—but often even the farmers use the term 'white'), paddy with a light brown shade rather than being completely white, and *bagrā dhān* (*bagrā* = red-layered, with red stripes), darker paddy or paddy with dark spots. In ritual contexts *white dhān* is clearly preferred.

The labourers are usually paid in *moṭā dhān* or *atimoṭā dhān*—although the latter is rarely found in the region. If there is a good harvest, *saru* may be given as well. However, labourers never receive *atisaru* as payment, which would be expansive for the landlords. Asked about why the labourers are paid in *moṭā dhān* the usual answer of the landlords is: the labourers prefer it.

TABLE 35: RELATIONSHIP BETWEEN QUALITIES OF LAND AND CULTIVATION OF PADDY

Quality of land	Category of paddy (*dhān*)	Sorts/varieties of paddy
guḍā	only *moṭā*	early sorts (60-90 days)
bernā	*moṭā/saru*	middle sorts (125 days)
māl	*moṭā/saru*	middle sorts (125-35 days)
bāhāl	*atimoṭā, moṭā, saru, atisaru*	late sorts (150-60 days)

TABLE 36: RELATIONSHIP BETWEEN CATEGORIES OF *DHĀN* AND THEIR UTILIZATION AS *CHĀUL*

		chāul	
dhān	*balkā*	*uṣnā*	*aruā*
atimoṭā	yes	no	Rarely (or not)
moṭā	yes (rarely)	yes	yes (only white *dhān*)
saru	no	yes (very common)	yes (only white *dhān*)
atisaru	no	yes	yes (for rituals)

TABLE 37: SECONDARY PRODUCTS OF RICE AND CATEGORIES OF *DHĀN* OR *CHĀUL* USED

Secondary products	Categories of *dhān/chāul*[4] used
khai	*motā/atimotā-dhān* and often *bagrā-dhān* (big rice corns are necessary)
murhi	*saru*—white *dhān*
chunā (rice-powder)	*aruā*
chuḍa	all categories of *dhān*—except *atisaru* (too expansive)
kusnā (rice-beer[5])	*balkā-chāul*
tarpan (rice-beer for ancestors)	*aruā-chāul* (in case of Muṇḍā also balkā)

TABLE 38: CATEGORIES OF *DHĀN* AND RELATED SORTS (EARLY, LATE ETC.)

Category of *dhān*	Sorts
atimoṭā	1009/*sābitri*, *sariā*[6] *dhān* (earliest variety)
moṭā	*anna purṇa*
saru	1030/*utkāl prabhā*, *kalmā dhān*
atisaru	*bādhsā bhog*, *gagan ahuiel*

No distinction is made between types of rice produced for consumption in one's own family and the rice produced for the market. Such a differentiation may exist in some cases in Chhattisgarh or Madhya Pradesh, where certain varieties of paddy are grown in order to be eaten by the peasant families exclusively, while higher yielding varieties are produced to be sold. In this context, certain varieties, such as the *utkāl prabhā*, are valued because of their taste, while others, like *sarnā,* are considered to be higher-yielding, but less tasty. However, *sarnā-dhān* is also eaten occasionally.

Among the types of rice used there are traditional older or *desi* varieties and the modern varieties produced and improved in laboratories. *Desi* or local varieties are *kalmā, bhujni, geel-singh, agni-sāl, mayurbhanj, butiā,* 141, *kalā-butā, sariā, liṭi-sariā, bādhsā bhog* or *luhuṇi*. Modern varieties commonly used are *sābitri* (1009), *utkāl prabhā* (1030), 1001, *svarnā* (7029), *jagannāth, bijay lakṣmi, lalāt, konārka, khandagiri, hirā, jāyā, pādmā,* IR 36, *surendra, mahānādi*. In the family with whom I stayed the production has completely changed from *desi* to modern varieties within the past five or six years.

TABLE 39: VARIETIES OF PADDY AND THEIR HARVEST

Variety	Name	Harvest after
Early varieties	*sariā*	60 days
	hirā	60 days
	anna purṇā	90 days
Late varieties	*sābitri*	160 days

Late varieties are more difficult to thresh when compared to early varieties, that is, the separation of paddy and chaff is more problematic and more time-consuming.

Seeds

The seeds available on the market today are classified by the Seed Corporation—a government company. Seeds produced in modern laboratories are specially protected against fungus and insects and are particularly high-yielding varieties. If paddy produced from such seeds is used again as seeds the following year, these characteristics, it is said, are slowly lost. Accordingly, 'nuclear' seeds are the best protected offering the maximum harvest, while 'Certified' seeds are less protected and yield less. Seeds are sold in different 'modern' varieties such as '*Sābitri*' in all four categories. In some cases, the Seed Corporation also sells seeds of the 'Foundation' category to peasants and repurchases them a year later in order to sell them again as 'Certified' seeds the following year. In the area of my research, 'Foundation' and 'Certified' seeds are the most common, as the categories of higher quality are too expensive. Poorer villagers may not even be able to afford 'Certified' and simply use their traditional older *desi* seeds. Accordingly, their harvest is usually less.

TABLE 40: VARIETIES OF SEEDS

Seeds	Age	Price per 30 kg
1. Nuclear	directly from the laboratory	Rs. 3000
2. Breeder	after 1 year	Rs. 900
3. Foundation	after 2 years	Rs. 600-700
4. Certified	after 3 years	Rs. 300 (former times: Rs. 400-500)

2.2. THE AGRICULTURAL CYCLE: CULTIVATION OF RICE AND OTHER WORKS

The Hindu calendar begins in the month of Cheitr according to the *pāñjji* (horoscope), but the agricultural cycle begins with the month of Baiśākh according to the peasants. A third relevant beginning is the month of Pouṣ, when yearly contracts with labourers (*guti*) are settled or renewed.

The agricultural calendar

---

1. Baiśākh (mid April–mid May)[7]

Marriage season

Agricultural tasks:	1. Collecting cow dung and taking it to the field as fertilizer 2. Beginning to plough (if the rain starts) 3. Harvesting groundnuts
Additional food-products:	mango, lichu, *chāra*,[8] melon (*tarabhuj*), cauliflowers, cucumber (*kānker*), pumpkin (*mākhan*)
Additional activities:	1. Collecting fire wood 2. Collecting kendu leaves 3. Collecting tamarind fruits 4. Government-works (road construction, etc.)

2. Jyeṣṭha (mid May–mid June)

Agricultural tasks:	1. Collecting cow dung and taking it to the field as fertilizer 2. Drying of Seeds before sowing (*bunā*) 3. Ploughing (with the beginning of rain) 4. Dry sowing (before the rain—always after ploughing)—first sowing on *Akshya Trutīyā* (see below)
Additional food-products:	mango, litchi, *chāra*, melon (*tarabhuj*), cucumber (*kānker*), pumpkin (*mākhan*)
Additional activities:	1. Collecting jackfruit (*panas*)[9] 2. Collecting tamarind

3. Government works (works with the tractor)
4. Repairing the roof before the rain

3. Āṣāḍh (mid June–mid July)

Heavy rain

Agricultural works:

1. Collecting cow dung and taking it to the field as fertilizer
2. Ploughing and paddling (*kādo*) with tractor/bullocks in the field
3. Wet sowing (after the beginning of the monsoon rain)
4. Growing of small rice plants for transplanting (*palhā ghāri*)
5. Planting (*jageibā*) groundnuts (*muphuli*/S., *bādam*/O.)
6. Cleaning sidewalls (*pāer*) of the rice fields
7. Repairing cuts (*ghāi*) in the sidewalls
8. Bihuḍā work (ploughing after the sowing)

Additional food-products: mango, *kurlu*,[10] guava (*mayā*), cucumber (*kānker*), pumpkin (*mākhan*), jackfruit (*panas*), mushrooms (*bihiden chhati*), *munga sarg*[11]

Additional activities:

1. Narihā start to grazing the cattle
2. Planting turmeric (*haldi*)
3. Collecting jackfruit
4. Repairing the roof before the rain

4. Śrābaṇ (mid July–mid August)

Agricultural work:

1. Fertilizing the land after paddling and before transplanting
2. Transplanting (*palhā jageibā*) small rice plants (after paddling and after *Bihuḍā-Pūjā*)

	3. Pulling up grass in the fields
	4. Bihuḍā work
	5. Putting rice plants into an order after Bihuḍā
Additional food-products:	Mushrooms[12] (*chhati*), small fish (*jhuri*) in the fields, *kurlu*, guava (*mayā*), cucumber (*kānker*), pumpkin (*mākhan*), late jackfruit

5. Bhādraba (mid August–mid September)

Nuā Khāi

Agricultural work:	1. Transplanting—if late
	2. Checking the water level in the fields
	3. Checking the rice for fungus and insects
	4. Pulling grass (*laṭā ghichā*)
	5. Fertilizing the fields
	6. Harvesting the first paddy
	7. Planting the Chilli seedlings
	8. Sowing oilseeds/til (*rāeś*) on dry fields
	9. Sowing pulses (*birhi, kuluth, mug*)
Additional food-products:	small fish (*jhuri*) in the fields, mushrooms (*chhati*), lemon, *masumi* (like oranges), *carambola/karamangā*,[13] bamboo
Additional activities:	Collecting bamboo (*heṇḍuā*) in small forests and drying it

6. Āśbina (mid September–mid October)

Agricultural work:	1. Checking the water level in the fields
	2. Checking the rice for fungus and insects—applying fungicides and pesticides
	3. Fertilizing the fields
	4. End of ploughing and paddling (as *chitālāgi*)

5. Preparing/Watering the chilli and mustard fields (on dry land)
6. Harvesting paddy (beginning—early varieties)
7. Transplanting chilli (beginning)
8. Loosening the soil around the chilli plants
9. Sowing mustard (beginning)
10. Sowing pulses
11. Planting tomato, castor, sweet corn, garlic, red beet, radish, carrots, tobacco,[14] onion
12. Sowing wheat
13. Transplanting sugarcane

Additional food-products: small fish (*jhuri*) in the fields, mushrooms (*chhati*), tomato (in the garden), custard-apple (*baḍhel* (S)/*baḍhiāḷ* (O)), lemon, guava (*mayā*), *masumi* (like oranges), *carambola/karamangā*, cauliflowers

Additional activities: Binding brooms (*bāḍhun*)

7. Kārttika (mid October–mid November)

puniya māsa (month to earn religious merits)

Agricultural works:

1. Harvesting/Cutting paddy
2. Checking the water level for late varieties
3. Transplanting chilli (sometimes combined with tomato)
4. Loosening the soil around the chilli plants
5. Sowing mustard (late)
6. Watering the chilli and mustard fields (if necessary)
7. Planting potatos in the garden
8. Harvesting pulses
9. Harvesting groundnuts
10. Sowing wheat

	11. Planting tomato, castor, sweet corn, garlic, red beet, radish, carrots, tobacco,[15] radish and transplanting cabbage and onion
	12. Transplanting sugar cane
Additional food-products:	Guava (*mayā*), cauliflowers
Additional activities:	Collecting *haridā* (for medical purposes)

8. Mārgaśīrṣa (mid November–mid December)

Agricultural works:	1. Harvesting paddy
	2. Threshing paddy
	3. Watering paddy fields (if necessary)
	4. Harvesting til
	5. Loosening the soil for chilli plants (loosening as *kudāli*)
	6. Harvesting cabbage (beginning) and onion
	7. Planting potato
	8. Harvesting groundnuts
Additional food-products:	*Chingri* (shrimps), cauliflowers, radish (*mulā*)
Additional activities:	1. Catching rats and digging for the rice rats that have bunkered in the fields[15]
	2. Collecting the bark of the *bāghlāl* tree for selling (only by poorer communities)[16]

9. Pouṣ (mid December–mid January)

Renewing contracts with labourers (Guti) on Pouṣ Pūni; impossible to earn religious merits in this month

Agricultural work:	1. Harvesting paddy (last month)
	2. Threshing paddy
	3. Parboiling paddy to produce *chāul* (*uṣnā/balkā*)
	4. Harvesting potato, cabbage, onion, red beet (*biṭ*), carrots (*gājar*) and sweet corn

	5. Harvesting mustard (beginning)
	6. Harvesting, threshing and drying of pulses (*kuluth*, *birhi*)
	7. Harvest sugar cane
	8. Ploughing and sowing pulses (*mug*)
Additional food-products:	*Chingri* (shrimps), radish (*mulā*), *patar kandā* (roots similar to potato)[18]
Additional activities:	1. Collecting *sāl* and bamboo branches
	2. Building fences with the branches (for chilli and mustard fields)[19]
	3. Catching rats and digging for rice rats that have bunkered in the fields

10. Māgha (mid January–mid February)

Agricultural work:	1. Parboiling paddy to produce *chāul* (*uṣnā/balkā*)
	2. Harvesting chilli (first month/dry land)
	3. Harvesting mustard
	4. Harvest sugar cane
Additional food-products:	Radish (*mulā*)
Additional activities:	Building fences (for chilli and mustard fields)

11. Phalgun (mid February–mid March)

Agricultural work:	1. Harvesting chilli (main season)
	2. Planting groundnuts
	3. Harvesting mustard (end)
	4. Ploughing (if there is rain)
	5. Harvest of wheat
	6. Harvest sugar cane
	7. Harvest tobacco and turmeric
	8. Selling paddy
Additional activities:	1. Collecting *mahuā*
	2. Government works (road construction etc.)

12. Chaitra (mid March–mid April)

Agricultural work:	1. Harvest of chilli (end)
	2. Harvest of wheat
	3. Harvest of tobacco
	4. Planting groundnuts
	5. Ploughing (if there is some rain)
Additional food-products:	Lemon, cauliflowers
Additional activities:	1. Collecting *mahuā*
	2. Collecting *kendu* leaves
	3. Government works

In addition to the food grown or collected at certain times of the year, other food, not mentioned in the tables, is available the whole year round in from the gardens: bananas, coconuts, pomegranates (*dālim*), papaya (*amrutabhandā*), aubergine (*baigana*), *karlā*[20] (S)/*kalarā* (O). From the ponds, varieties of fish can be caught: *rohu*/*ruhi* (fish); *bilati fuhi* (fish); breeding fish (*bhakur*); *mrigal/mrikal* (fish); shrimps (*chingri*). Furthermore, one should also note that apples, oranges, and grapes are also available at nearby markets.

In order to catch small fish, often bamboo constructions are used. A house-like construction of bamboo known as a *dhaer* is placed in the pond, where small fish swim into the lower entrances. The small fish in the fields can be caught in the months of Bhādraba and Āśbina.

Apart from fishing instruments such as this there are various forms of nets. One type is known as the 'throwing net' or *phikā jāl* (*phikā* = to throw; *jāl* = net). In this case, one man stands in the pond or river and throws the round-shaped net with a span of one to two meters. It can be closed on one side by pulling a line and the fish are caught. Another type is called the *ṭanā jāl* (*ṭanā* = to pull at once), a kind of permanent fish trap. Still another way to catch the fish is by using a simple square-shaped net with a bamboo-stick on either side known as a *ghichā jāl* (*ghichā* = to pull continuously). Usually two men—each one of them handling a stick—walk through the pond pulling the net. This method is popular in the warmer season—between March and June—when the water level in the pond is rather low, but can generally be applied from Pouṣ to Āṣāḍha.

Rain and monsoon calendar

Various forms of rain are distinguished between: *jhanker* or continuous, but not so heavy, rain for two to three days; *baī barṣā* or heavy rain; *achharā* or a short, but heavy shower; *bhurbhuri* as drizzling, light rain and *chāer muṇḍi jhanker* (*chāer* = four; *muṇḍi* = direction) as a weather condition, in which heavy and light showers follow one another quickly and there are black clouds, literally rain comes from four directions.

In general, there are certain signs of the coming rain or monsoon peasants know such as the ants (*chāṇṭī*) carrying eggs, the singing of a certain bird (*ḍāhuka*) or the flight of glow-worms on the veranda of the house. Every year the family priest (*purohit*) offers a particular monsoon calendar for the peasants known as a *bāhāna patrikā*. In this the beginning of the monsoon is predicted (last year: 25th of May). *Bāhāna* signifies the carriers of the gods such as Garuda for Viṣṇu or Nandi for Śiva, while *patrikā* means journal. In a detailed description, the priest predicts the rain—listed for every fortnight and every constellation. Certain constellations like the elephant and the cobra promise a lot of rain, while with the constellations of the horse or lion only a little rain can be expected. However, not every constellation is present every year. The peasants know the constellations, but to my knowledge do not take these predictions very seriously. For example, last year I was told that there had heavy rains and parts of the region were flooded, but the constellation of the elephant, promising the most rain, did not even occur that year. Additionally, the family priest recommends the planting of certain varieties of paddy according to this calendar—last year it was white *dhān*. However, the peasants follow their own experience and plant the varieties they trust.

Ploughing, agricultural instruments and gender

Generally, ploughing is known as *hala dharibā* (*hala* = pair, meant is a pair of bullocks; *dharibā* = catch); occasionally it is called *hala phāndichhe* (*phāndichhe* = to join) or *nangala dharibā*. Several kinds of ploughing are distinguished at different times. If rice is sown, ploughing is necessary at least three times. The first, after the first rain of the month in Phalgun or Cheitr (rarely up to Āṣāḍh), is called *uār*. The date of the first ploughing is often decided by an astrologer according to the *pāñjji*. The second, to loosen the fields before sowing as well as to destroy the grass, in the month of Jyeṣṭha and Āṣāḍh—15 to 20 days after *uār*—is known as *dun*.[21] Furthermore, the field is ploughed once more after sowing in the months of Jyeṣṭha, Āṣāḍh or Śrābaṇ—a ploughing called *bun* or *tinpuriā*, which corresponds to the *bihuḍā*. Occasionally, the field can be ploughed a fourth time, which is known as *batar* (or *charpuriā*). This is done for the early varieties (up to 100 days) on *guḍā*- and *māl*-land, two to three days after the wet sowing (*batri bunā*). The same is true for loosening the soil—a kind of ploughing known as *bihuḍā*—and is necessary for the late varieties of paddy and optional for early varieties. Until the *Bihuḍā* ritual for the village goddess has been performed, no loosening (*bihuḍā*), ploughing, or transplanting is allowed. Formerly, the number of ploughs and pairs of bullocks used for ploughing was an indicator of the wealth of a family—in the same way that owning a tractor is today.

Corresponding to the animals used for ploughing and to the purpose and work in the field, different types of ploughs exist. The normal plough (*nangala*) varies in size—a bigger one for the extremely tall bullocks and a smaller one for ordinary bullocks. A third type of plough is known as a *bihuḍā nangala* or *khuni nangala* (*khuni* = murderer). It is the smallest type used to loosen (*bihuḍā*) the soil. All items necessary to plough—the plough itself, the yoke, the iron share (*luhā*), and the connecting wooden part between plough and yoke (either called *danḍhā* or subsumed as part of the plough) are considered to be male. The instruments necessary for levelling the ground before paddling and after ploughing—*kural* and *kapar*[22]—are also clearly regarded as male and women should not use them. Slightly different is the case of the hoe (*koeī*), which is also seen as male. However, women are allowed to use it to carry sand from the river, to cleanse thick forest around *kendu* plants, or to build or repair the irrigation system for the fields, but they should not use it in the fields in general. Even if some locals are not sure of this rule, they had never seen a woman using one in the fields. Another firm restriction regulates the use of wooden sticks or *bhār*—the traditional mode to carry goods on the shoulder—the use of which is forbidden for women.[23]

In contrast to all other communities in the village, there is no restriction for Aghriā women as such to touch the plough (*nangala*). On the contrary, during the ritual of *Harli Uāns*, women worship the plough and have to touch it at that time. Significantly, the plough is only worshipped among the Aghriā. No other community does so, on *Harli Uāns* or *Akshya Trutiyā*. However, while the touching of the plough is possible for Aghriā women in the ritual context, it is forbidden for these women to tie the bullocks to the yoke and thus to connect the plough to the yoke. There are no such restrictions for a tractor, although no one that I asked had ever seen a woman driving one.

Apart from certain restrictions according to gender, ploughing is limited to certain time periods. Another time, during which ploughing is taboo is Raja Sankrānti on the thirteenth and fourteenth of June. The menstruation (*raja* = menstruation;[24] not to be confused with *rājā* or king) of Mother Earth or *Dharati Mātā* is said to happen on these days. While the earth is menstruating (*bhuin raja*) ploughing would be a crime and punished by the villagers collectively. Still another period in which ploughing is prohibited is the fortnight of the ancestors, particularly on the ninth and tenth day—the days on which all female and male ancestors are remembered—on *uāns* (new moon day) and on the days of the death of recently departed ancestors. The reasons for these taboos are difficult to come by. In only one case was it explained by telling the story of King Janaka, who, while ploughing the land and preparing it for a ritual, discovered Sita below the surface. This indicates that the soil was conceived of as female, which was further substantiated by the association of village land with Grām Śrī.

Sowing and bihudā

In the case of sowing and transplanting, the small walls (*pāer*) dividing the fields have to be cleaned—particularly on the sides. This is known as *pāer chhanchā*. If the walls have been damaged due to heavy rain, new cuts (*ghāi*) have to be repaired in order to keep the water in the field.

There are different kinds of sowing. All these kinds are generally regarded as 'throwing' or *bunbār*. In the case of paddy sowing is also known as *dhān bunā*. On the one hand, paddy can be sown before the rain, and this is called 'dry throwing' or *kharli bunā*. On the other hand, it can also be done after the beginning of the monsoon and is then called 'wet throwing' or *batri bunā*. Dry sowing can be done on every type of land but for wet sowing higher lands are preferred (*guḍā*, *māl*, *bernā*). Dry sowing is more risky because the rain could be very late. In any case, the first sowing, also called *muiṭh nebār* (S) or *muthi nebā* (O), should be done on an auspicious day—a Wednesday.

A transplanted field can be distinguished from a field on which the rice has been sown by the furrows of the plough that are still visible after sowing. In the case of transplanting, however, the ground is levelled before transplanting. The seeds for both kinds of sowing are often dried once more in the month of Jyeṣṭha in order to prepare them for the sowing. Sometimes, a third type of sowing is practised—the so-called *achharā*, which is a form of late sowing. *Achharā*—meaning shower—hints at the connection to the rain. If it is raining too heavily, *batri bunā* is impossible, because the seeds would be washed away. In this case, a paddling of the field is required first to reduce the water level or to diminish water standing in the field. Simultaneously, the seeds are soaked in the house for two days for better germination. Only after germination has begun is the sowing done.

After sowing, when the water is still standing in the field, there is an additional ploughing or loosening of the soil required known as *bihuḍā* (loosening). This is intended to reduce the density of the rice plants. For *bihuḍā* work the water level in the field must be high enough to not see the soil. It takes about six hours to plough an acre of land with a small *bihuḍā*-plough. If the water level is still high enough after the *bihuḍā*, a peasant may use the *kapar* to break or to destroy some varieties of grass, which subsequently decompose in the water and act as a natural fertilizer. Using a *kapar* does not damage the rice plants.

After the *bihuḍā*-work, when the soil is loose, another important step known as *baṭiā khelā* (*baṭiā* = big clay clods; *khelā* = to play, but here rather to distribute) is essential for the cultivation of rice fields after sowing. Clods with the already grown rice plants are distributed from the middle of the field, where usually too many plants have grown, to the corners. In practice, the peasants, while standing in the water of the field, take the loose rice plants with their hand from below—the rice plants are not pulled—and throw the rice plants including the clods into the corners. Thus, there is also an aspect of play. *Baṭiā khela* is done only in *māl-*, *bernā* or *bāhāl*-fields, in which rice is sown. This is sometimes combined with the cleansing of grass known as *laṭā ghichā* (*laṭā* = grass; *ghichā* = to pull). The grass pulled in this manner is often used to feed the cattle.

Transplanting

Transplanting is generally higher yielding than sowing. However, it is also more expensive, as more labour is required—not only for the transplanting itself, but also for the obligitory ploughing necessary more often than in the case of sowing. While one has to plough a field three times in the case of sowing, one must plough it six to seven times in the case of transplanting. Transplanting—but also sowing—should be finished as early as possible. In the case of transplanting, people say that it should be completed by the beginning of August, but in practise this is not always possible. The later transplantation is done, the lesser will be the harvest due to insects and fungus, etc.

Transplantation, called *jagābār* in the case of rice or *rupā* (S)/*ruā* (O) for any transplanting, can be done only after the *Bihuḍā*-ritual. Until then the small paddy seedlings (*palhā*) have to remain in the nursery field known as the *palhā ghāri* (*ghāri* = small field)—quite often in the garden. Afterwards, seedlings, which are also regarded as Lakṣmī, can be picked—a process considered to be the same as killing (*palhā marā*) —and subsequently transplanted.[25] After sowing, it takes from 15 to 21 days for the seedlings to grow sufficiently in order to be transplanted. To transplant around 10 acres, 0.2 acres *palhā ghāri* and roughly 3.5 bags (75 kg each) of seeds are needed—given almost 100 per cent germination.

While pulling rice seedlings women usually sing improvized songs, in which they crack jokes as during the *huma* dances.[25] In one such song, women[27] were singing: 'under the tree there is a shop. A new shopkeeper has prepared betel. There is much lime in the betel. *Pilā chahatiā* (handsome, naughty boy, searching for girls) is selling betel. Friends, I desire him.'

Often *guḍā*-land is preferred for a *palhā ghāri*, because due to the higher percentage of sand seedlings can be pulled easily. Also, land next to the village road—known as *gān khari* and believed to be particularly fertile—is often chosen for a *palhā ghāri*. Fertilizers may also be applied. After pulling the seedlings from the *palhā ghāri* they must be transported to the pond in order to be washed, a process known as *palhā duā* (*duā* = to wash) or *palhā saphā* (*saphā* = to clean).

The seedlings are usually pulled and packed in bundles. Each bundle consisting of roughly 60 seedlings is bound with the leaf of a date palm tree (*tal*). In some villages, labourers are paid according to the bundles they have packed, while in other villages they are paid a daily wage, for packing around 80 such bundles per day.

Generally, the sowing of seeds for transplantation can be done before or after the rain. In the first case it is known as 'dry planting' or *kharli palhā*, while the latter, it is called 'wet planting' or *batri palhā*. In the *ghāri*, paddy is sown as in bigger fields—the sowing is known here as *palhā pakā*. *Kharli palhā* has an advantage for the landlord in terms of an existing labour problem. Often it is easier to find labourers for the earlier period of transplantation, as many people prefer the *batri palhā*—which is less risky when compared to 'dry planting'. Like dry sowing, dry planting entails the risk of withering if the rain does not start in time or if one does not have additional water supplies. Early transplantation brings about another risk: weeds. The little rice seedlings of *kharli palhā* can be overgrown by weeds, while the latter and bigger seedlings of the *batri palhā* are more resistant. If the weed grasses grow too quickly in comparison to the rice, they must be picked by hand, which means, for a landlord, that additional labour is required. Labourers are difficult to find in this high season of agricultural work and must be brought in from other districts. That in turn means that the rice—due to the extra labour costs—is less profitable in the end.

The cleansing of grass is called *laṭā bachhā*. One can use a big rake known as *kaṇṭā kapar* (*kaṇṭā* = big nail or prong). The *kaṇṭā kapar* can be pulled by a tractor or by the bullocks and is used against the grass as well as to destroy remaining the clods of soil—thus, levelling the field—before sowing and during paddling.

Before actually transplanting the seedlings, the soil has to be paddled to produce the mud necessary for transplantation. Various instruments, such as a scraper connected to a tractor, can be used.[28] Between ploughing and paddling, on one hand, and transplanting on the other, there should be one or two days, in which the grass destroyed by plough starts to decompose below the surface and fertilizes the field in a natural way. Thus, mud after two days in the field, called *bāsi kādo* (*bāsi* = fallen; *kādo* = mud), is preferred to the mud immediately after paddling known as *rukā* (fresh) *kādo*. The paddling is done with a tractor to which *kej*-wheels (metal wheels) have been fitted. Since driving with these *kej*-wheels is dangerous, sometimes a small ritual is performed.

In the process of transplantation, two to three rice plants are placed together into the mud. At the distance between the thumb and forefinger, say, another two to three plants are placed. Often, seasonal labourers from Bolangir or Bargarh district are hired and occasionally landlords complain that they are trying to increase the distance between the rice plants and thus cheat the owner.

At the end of the transplantation, labourers usually give each other a *ṭikā* of mud as a kind of joke. The Landlord or Sahu was included in former times. Furthermore, a feast is offered to the labourers—particularly the seasonal labourers—known as the *kādo chheḍ* (*kādo* = mud; *chheḍ* = end), which should include meat or chicken and, in many cases, liquor.

Harvesting and threshing

In order to start cutting, a small ritual is performed known as the *guras dhāre* (*guras* = milk; *dhār* = flowing of liquid) in which some milk is offered, together with incense—ideally by a daughter-in-law of the house, who also worships Lakṣmī on this occasion. It is also done for an auspicious start or *subh karibā* on an auspicious day—in this case a Friday. A precise auspicious moment may be fixed according to the *pāñjji*. A family member, not a labourer, cuts the first rice. Preferably, a daughter-in-law should do this as well, but a son can also perform it. Similarly, the last paddy should be cut on an auspicious day, a Tuesday or Saturday.

Before actually cutting the paddy sometimes the plants are pressed (to press = *marā*) to one side with a big bamboo-stick (*lāeṭh*) in order to simplify cutting. This is especially necessary if the paddy has fallen to different sides naturally. Cutting with a sickle (*dā*) is known as *dhān duā*, and afterwards, the paddy is bound (to bind = *bandhibā*) with a rope of straw called *beṇṭiā* and the bundles of paddy or *dhān muṭhiā* are transported to the threshing floor. The transport or *dhān kaḍhā* may be managed by simply carrying (*buhā*) two bundles over one's shoulder using wooden sticks (*suil*—similar to a *bhār*), or by placing them on a bullock-cart or the trailer of a tractor.

After having carried away the bundles, the remains of paddy, i.e. spikes left on the ground, are collected by hand in a process known as *dhān kuljā* (*kuljā* = to collect). This may either be done for the landlord, if he hires some labourers for this task, or labourers may do it for themselves, if the landlord allows them to do so. Sometimes, the landlord pays his wage labourers (*butiyā*) to pick up the remains after cutting—at least for a day—however, sometimes the owner of the fields just leaves the rest for his workers to be picked up in their spare time. Often children and old people, particularly Kol or Kisān, collect the remaining spikes. In this manner one can get up to two *tāmi* (say 1.7 kg) paddy by working half a day. It is not a particular a privilege for wage labourers: everyone is free to collect what he can find, but usually only the families of the labourers of a particular landlord are found in his fields. For some landlords it is important to collect the rest also, because it would be regarded as disrespectful to leave paddy, symbolically Lakṣmī, in the field. The rice should be brought completely into one's house. Spikes fallen down while transporting the paddy should also be collected, which is also known as *kuljā*.

On the last day of cutting the paddy, simply called *chheḍ* (end)—a Tuesday or Friday is considered auspicious to complete the cutting—the labourers receive a bonus known as a *chuḍā chitkā* which consists of flattened rice (*chuḍā*), *khai* and *guḍ*. Some people consider it to be *praśād*, though there is no ritual. However, the last of the cutting of paddy is usually done in a particularly vivid and joyful atmosphere with labourers oalling out the names of gods, such as Jagannāth, while bringing the last paddy to the threshing floor.

Threshing and winnowing

At the threshing place, the paddy is first piled up (*khari karibā* = to pile up; pile = *khari*)—of course, differentiated according to various sorts.

Usually in the morning, paddy is spread on the threshing floor (*khalā*). The quantity to be threshed in one turn is known as a *paer*. Before the threshing can start some water, mixed with basil (*tulsī*) and often with a little piece of gold placed in it, is sprinkled (*paer jhiṭā, jhiṭibā* = to sprinkle) in order to purify the threshing floor. A young daughter of the family should do this task preferably. However, it is meant not only as a measure to purify, but also—together with a line of coal powder drawn around the *paer*—to get rid of the evil eye and the *motiā* (small supernatural beings who are supposed to steal paddy).

Next, the paddy is loosened (to loosen = *tali dharā*), before the tractor rolls over it or before bullocks or buffalos thresh it by circling continuously around the wooden *merkhuṇṭ* at the centre. Occasionally, also a wooden roller (*ghuḍ ghuḍi*) tied to and pulled by the bullocks is used to thresh. Generally, threshing is called *dhān maḍā* (*maḍā* = to put the foot on) or *madāibā*.

In-between, the rice is loosened again and turned around (*dhān jhāribā* = to turn around)—either by hand or using an instrument called a *karālī* —looking like a small blunt sickle with a long stick. Often the paddy is threshed again and subsequently, the straw (*puāl*) is separated from the paddy and bundled (straw-bundle = *puāl biḍā*). Sometimes the straw—collected on a separate pile (*puāl bhāḍī*)—is carried there with two wooden sticks or ladders (*ṭikāsi*).

To filter the remaining straw from the grain it is swept with special brooms (broom = *bāḍhun*; to sweep = *banḍheibā*). In another context the sweeping would be an insult to the Goddess Lakṣmī, but on the threshing floor (*khalā*) it is allowed. In some cases the labourers also just walk barefoot through the grain on the floor to turn it around for extra drying, if necessary. In the next step, the paddy is piled up using a board (*paṭā*)—a process called *gadā* or *dhān ranpā paṭā* (*ranpā* = to collect; *rampibā* = to comb, to scratch). The remaining blades are sorted out by pressing the paddy through a *khaṭ* (a wooden structure with ropes functioning as a sieve). The grain and chaff fall through (to fall through = *galābār*) in this process of *dhān galābār*, while the blades and straw remain.

Then in the afternoon the winnowing or *dhān dhukā* or *dhukibā* starts, to separate the chaff from paddy. A winnowing basket (*kulā*) is used, though in recent years fans[29] have replaced them, if people can afford them. Often the paddy is winnowed twice to get rid of all the chaff. There are two types of chaff, *cherpeṭiā,* a mixture of chaff with little remaining paddy, which is usually given to the cattle, and *pol*[30] as the chaff used for constructing mud-houses—it is added to the clay—or stored on the compost heap. *Cherpeṭiā* consists basically of the lower part of a spike—a part without liquid or very little food grains, which, if boiled would be black in colour, but is usually not boiled, rather just fed to the animals. It has a little more value than *pol,* which is totally without grains. While winnowing, rice grains fall almost directly to the ground; *cherpeṭiā*—not as heavy as paddy—falls at a slight distance; and *pol,* lighter than *dhān* and *cherpeṭiā,* is blown even further away.

Finally, the paddy is measured and weighed (to weigh = *nāpibā*) using special baskets (= *napā ṭupā*; basket = *ṭupā*). In a smaller basket known as a *dasmaniā*[31] the paddy is brought into the house for storage until it is sold. In bigger houses there are special storerooms called *dhān kuṭhi.*

Measuring and storing rice

The smallest unit to measure paddy or *chāul* is known as the *pā*—although sometimes also ½ *pā* is used. A *pā* consists of roughly ¼ kg. Two *pā* fit into one *mān* and two *mān,* in turn, form a *tāmi*—a little less than a kg or about 800 g. However, sometimes different *mān* are used for measuring rice and for ritual purposes—the latter being slightly smaller. A *tāmi* is usually of brass or bell metal (*pital/ kansā*), while a *kaṭhā* has the same size as a *tāmi*, but is made of tin. *Tāmi* is sometimes also called *ser*. 20 *tāmi* form a *khandi* or 12.5 kg.

On the threshing floor *dhān* is measured after threshing using a basket known as a *ṭupā*. There are various types of *ṭupā,* e.g. measuring three *khandi* or 4.8 *khandi.* The *ṭupā* is a rectangular basket that has four leather applications on the lower 'corners' of the basket. These are produced by Chamār, who receive some paddy for their service. The next unit in size to the *purug*, but again one finds *purug* of different sizes. A small *purug* measures 8 *khandi*, while a larger one consists of 24 *khandi* (= 8 small *ṭupā*) and the biggest one consists of 34-5 *khandi*. Such a big *purug* then comprises eight big *ṭupā*.

A *purug* is not only used to measure rice, but also to store it. It is usually built by taking ropes made of straw and forming a round container. This container stands on a wooden platform to protect the paddy against rats. The straw ropes, having all in all a height of up to 2 meters, are stabilized by clay. The *purug*—ritually important in case of selling children—may contain in its biggest version 4 quintal, each quintal being 100 kg. Finally, another way to measure and store paddy is by using bags—each one containing around 75 kg (in the case of a small *ṭupā*: two *ṭupā* = one bag). Roughly six bags fill a purug.

Apart from *purug*, paddy is kept in the house in *kuṭhi* (Oriya: *koṭhi*). Often a *dhān ghar*—a room, where paddy is stored in the house—is subdivided into smaller chambers, the *kuṭhi*. Different varieties of paddy are kept in different *kuṭhi*.

TABLE 41: UNITS TO MEASURE PADDY

Unit	Weight in g/kg
pā	~ 220 g
mān	~ 450 g
tāmi, kaṭhā, ser	~ 850 g
khandi	~ 12.5 kg
ṭupā	~ 37.5 kg (= 3 *khandi*); ~ 60 kg (= 4.8 *khandi*)
bag	~ 75 kg
purug	~ 100 kg (= 8 *khandi*); ~ 300 kg (= 24 *khandi*)
	~ 425 kg (= 34 *khandi*)

In former times, more paddy was kept in the house. The paddy was sold only after the next year's harvest—nowadays it is sold immediately after the harvest. The reasons to keep it longer in the house in former times were inspired by the fear of droughts and fewer opportunities to market the paddy.

2.3. THE RITUAL CYCLE OF THE YEAR

The festivals and rituals described below are common among all Aghriā. Apart from that, however, there are local festivals celebrated in a few villages or only one village, such as the *Danantāri Pūjā* which is a purely local festival. The Aghriā may also attend big festivities such as the *Dhānu Jātrā* in Bargarh celebrated on *Pouṣ Pūni*.

Rituals of the village goddess have been described in Chapter 4.

TABLE 42: MAIN RITUALS OF THE YEAR

Hindu Calendar	European Calendar[32]	Ritual	Comments
Baiṣākh	April-May	*Akshya Trutīyā*	
Jyeṣtha	May/June	*Sābitri Brata, Raja Sankrānti*	
Āṣāḍh	June/July	*Rath Jātrā*	
Śrābaṇ	July/August	*Harli Uāns, Rākhī Pūni*	
Bhādraba	August/September	*Bhādraba Uāns, Gaṇeṣ Pūjā, Nuā Khāi, Janmāṣṭami*	
Āśbina	September/October	*Pua Jiūntiā, Pitru Pakṣ, Bhāi Jiūntiā, Daśarā, Boil*	
Kārttika	October/November	*De Uthā, Pānchaka, Anlā Navarmi, Diāli*	puniya māsa—month to earn religious merits
Mārgaśirṣa	November/December	*Lakṣmī Pūjā, Pratamastami*	—
Pouṣ	December/January		month without religious merits
Māgha	January/February	*Makrā, Sarasvati Pūjā*	
Phalgun	February/March	*Śibrātrī, Holi*	
Cheitr	March/April	*Danīa Nrutya, Manglā Pūjā*	

HARLI UĀNS (S), *HARIĀLI AMĀBASYĀ* (O)/
CHITĀLĀGI/NANGALA PŪJĀ

Celebrated in the month of Śrābaṇ (August), *Harli/Hariāli* literally means green in the sense of prosperity, while *uāns/amābasyā* means new moon. Chita signifies a picture drawn like a *jhoti*. Three rituals take place on this day: the first in the *guhāl duār* (the cattle yard); the second in an inner yard of the house in which agricultural instruments are worshipped; and the last a ritual in the kitchen. All are performed by a *baha* (daughter-in-law). The doors of the house are decorated with castor leaves (leaves—*patar*), which are said to protect against blood-sucking *tandhei* (witches) and against the *bhut-pret* who are supposed to be particularly active on this day.

Cattle and bullocks are not used for any work on this day—except milking. Symbolically for all cattle, one cow is worshipped at the cattle yard first by washing her legs and feet with haldi-pāen (water with turmeric) then offering a vermilion-*ṭikā,* and then a flower garland. Additionally, *dhūpa* (incense) and *dīpa* (light) are offered before the *chipti* are fed. *Chipti* are *sāl*-leaves in which dried *mahuā* fruits and salt are wrapped. The stomach of the bullocks and the cattle, as the Aghriā say, should be full on this day. The horns of the cow are massaged with oil, e.g. caster oil (*jaḍā*) or *duri*-oil (made of *mahuā* seeds). Feeding and massaging is done for all the other cattle and bullocks subsequently. Generally the Narihā should feed the cattle and bullocks with *chipti*, but family members can also do it.

During the second ritual in a south-east corner of the inner yard under the eaves (*ulchcha tal*) of the house, the daughter-in-law worships agricultural instruments—plough (*nangala* with an iron ploughshare/*luhā*), *kapar* and *kural* (two types of planks to level the land after paddling and ploughing), *jueḍ* (yoke) and *koeḍ* (hoe)—by touching them with her hands using a mixture of rice powder, water and turmeric leaving seven handprints on them. All of these instruments are thought to be male (only the *koeḍ* might be used by women to carry soil, etc.). Furthermore, a cake known as an *upkā babrā* is offered, which is eaten later as *praśād* by the men only. This cake is made of *aruā chāul* and *khai* grounded together, and mixed with *guḍ* and fried. The ancestors are then offered water (*pāen chhaḍā*) and asked for their blessings.

Additionally, in the kitchen another ritual is performed by a *baha*. Initially, pictures of cattle, bullocks and oxen as well as of the already mentioned agricultural instruments are drawn preferably on the eastern wall of the kitchen, which is, however, in practise not always possible. The pictures, which include Saha Deb—the keeper of the cattle drawn in the form of a Gauḍ with a stick—, are painted with red colour known as *altā*.[33] The number of cattle thus drawn is not decisive. Some of the cattle, bullocks, and persons drawn are named as well, e.g. Pujākarā, a brother of the Pandavas in charge of the cattle; *rangī*, the coloured one; *chitari*, the one with spots; *kāliā*, the black one or *ṭikiri*, the name of the latest calf of the family. Afterwards, *ṭikā* are given to all pictures, at with incense and lights. Little pieces of cake are practically pasted the mouths of each animal in the picture. The cake offered in this ritual in the kitchen may be eaten by everyone as *praśād*. Later, the gods of the house shrine, the *tulsī-chaur*, are worshipped.

Hariāli Āmābāsyā is said to mark the end of the work with bullocks, but in practice there is no strict rule against working with bullocks afterwards.[34] *Harli Uāns* is also the appropriate day for transplanting beans (*śemi*).

AKSHYA TRUTĪYĀ

This ritual has to be celebrated on the *trutīyā,* the third day of the light side of Baiśākha. *Akshya* means 'never ending' which hints at the permanent character of the ritual and the agricultural cycle in general, because the first sowing is performed on this day. The seeds—given by the village goddess after the Grām Śrī ritual—are brought to the field before sunrise. Ideally, no one should see this act. An astrologer is consulted to decide about the exact time and the auspicious direction to walk into the fields. After consulting the *pāñjji* he also decides which family member should perform the ritual. The ritual is also known as the *Dhān Muthi* or throwing of seeds (*dhān* = paddy, *muthi* = fist—hinting at the seven handfuls of paddy in the fist in the act of throwing).

On the evening before going into the fields a ritual is performed inside the house, in an inner yard or inside the kitchen—facing east. During the ritual a plough with an iron ploughshare (*luhā*), a yoke (*jueḍ*), a hoe (*koeḍ*) as well as a *mān* and a *tāmi* measure are worshipped. The *mān* and *tāmi* are filled with paddy and regarded as Lakṣmī. They are painted with flowers. Additionally, seven handprints are made inside the kitchen with the same mixture on the eastern wall. Afterwards, the paddy is brought into the field.

Ritual items necessary for the *pūjā* include: (1) a plough (*nangala*) and a yoke (*jueḍ*); (2) a ploughshare (*luhā*); (3) a hoe (*koeḍ*); (4) *tāmi* and *mān*; (5) a new *burni* (basket for sowing); (6) white *dhān* (of the *Grām Śrī Pūjā*); (7) a *kalas*; (8) flowers; (9) *aruā chāul*; (10) milk; (11) *pañchāmrut* (see *Niśā Pūjā*); (12) *soltā* (long cotton lamps); (13) *dhūp kāthi* (incense); (14) *chandan* (sandalwood); (15) vermilion (*sindhur*); (16) incense (*dhūp*); (17) *niyā* (fire); (18) *hantā* (*hatili*), i.e. *aruā chāul* grinded for the 7 handprints.

RATH JĀTRĀ

This festival is celebrated for Jagannāth, Lord of the Universe, starting on the second day of Āṣāḍh. After a ritual for Jagannāth, his white idol—often together with the black idol of his elder brother Balabhadra and the yellow idol of his sister Subhadra—is carried on a special car known as a *rath* to the temple of his mother's younger sister or *māusī* (MyZ) named Gundicha. This first procession is known as the Pahuḍa.

There, the god stays for nine days before he returns to his own temple. The return procession is called the *Bāhuḍa Jātrā*.

In one case, a temporary temple was installed in the house of the local Gauntiā—in the formal representative room at the entrance known as the *baiṭhak*—, while the house of a Gaṇḍ or a community centre at the other end of the village was turned into a temple of Gundicha. The entrances were purified with cow dung prior to the rituals. A Gosain who was the *pujāri* of a Jagannāth temple in a neighbouring village acted as a priest for the festival and also brought the idol of Jagannāth[35] to be installed in front of peacock feathers. A car for the god had been made by local carpenters and had been painted red, blue, green, and yellow.[36]

On the day of the *Pahuḍā Jātrā*, villagers worshiped the installed god from the morning on—offering flowers (white ones/*tagar* or long yellow ones/*kaniar* are popular), fruits, vegetables, *dīpa*, *dhūpa*, rice, money and *dhoti*. In exchange, the *pujāri* applied sandal paste on their foreheads and put flowers behind their right ears. Devotees received *mahāpraśād* (*chāul*)—which consisted of rice (*aruā chāul*), molasses (*guḍ*), milk, *ghī*, pulses (*mug-dāl*), coconuts, cardamom, gloves, raisins, cashew-nuts and rice-powder (*chunā*)—depending on the financial condition of the concerned Gauntiā. It was prepared earlier by the *pujāri*. In the afternoon a *Mandli* Party[37] was dancing and singing. At sunset—the ritual should be completed before dark—the villagers formed a procession. It was led by the *Mandli* Party. One *Baḍ Parjā*—a Māḷi—carried the idol, another *Baḍ Parjā* the feathers, a third (member of the Gauntiā family) fulfilled the royal function of sweeping the road for Lord Jagannāth on his way from his temporary temple to the car (*rath*), which had been pulled to the entrance of the village. During the cleaning of the road with a new broom is known as *chhera pahanra* (*chhera* = broom; *pahanra* = to clean). The Gauntiā himself sprinkled *tulsī-pāen* (water with basil-leaves) on the road—slightly behind the 'Sweeper'—as a part of purifying the way for the god. The procession circled around the car seven times. After every round the god was placed on a cloth in front of the car before he was eventually installed on top. On the way, the Gosain-*pujāri* sat on the car—in some other villages the Gauntiā did as well. Everyone was allowed to pull or push the car—including the so-called 'Untouchables' and women. In one village there was a convention that only women could pull the car using special ropes. The car was then moved to the temporary Gundicha-temple, where Lord Jagannāth was symbolically placed, but in practise it is usually not left there, but in its temple. Newly born children are brought to Jagannāth during the procession to touch his idol in order to get his blessings. Khai was thrown from the car during and at the end of the procession and many people tried to keep pieces of the rope as they were believed to have a healing capacity.

On the day of the *Bāhudā Jātrā* the programme was repeated. The route of the procession was, however, different, leading from the Gauntiā house as a symbolic Jagannāth temple to the symbolic Gundicha temple and back. Before Jagannāth was actually allowed into his temple, he had to pacify his wife Lakṣmī, who was sulking due to the long absence of her husband (nine days). Symbolically, the argument between Lakṣmī and Jagannāth was read and re-enacted by the *pujāri*[38] and an Aghariā man. Lakṣmī closed the door at the arrival of her husband leaving him outside. Jagannāth had to appease Lakṣmī by offering her a *sari* before being finally allowed inside. The Jātrā usually ends with an *ārthi*.

In former times, vulgar words like 'penis' were used by some participants to speed up the pulling of the car. The belief behind that is that Jagannāth, listening to such words in the presence of his sister Subhadra, would prefer to move quickly. However, such words were forbidden some years ago. Furthermore, the village decided to ban alcohol on this day. Gifts of money, known as *jātrā dekhā*, should be given to relatives younger than oneself and to servants.

RĀKHĪ PŪNI OR *RAKSHĀ BANDHĀ*

The day resembles *Harli Uāns* to a large extent. In the morning, the same ritual for the cattle as well as the ritual in the kitchen performed on *Harli Uāns* is repeated. However, the worship of a cow by a daughter-in-law of the family has an important extra element—the binding of a *rākhī* to the horn of the cow—and to all cattle, bullocks and even goats, subsequently. The *rākhīs* are also bound to all important technical devices such as TV-sets, cars, water pumps, to guns and rifles, and to the doors of the house particularly of the Mahapru Ghar (room of the house-shrine), the Bhandār Ghar (general store room) and the Dhān Ghar (store room for paddy). Furthermore, it is tied to the ancestors and to all gods and goddesses residing in the house-shrine. Generally, the Aghriā argue that it should be tied to everyone or everything, on whom or on which you depend.

Later, another ritual is performed in the kitchen, in which the pictures drawn on *Harli Uāns* are worshipped again in the same manner as already described for *Harli Uāns*. Afterwards, in still another ritual the sisters, who usually have returned to their natal families for this occasion bind a thread around the wrist of their brothers similar to *Bhāi Jiunṭiā*. This is considered to be the responsibility (*kām*) of a sister—sister here understood in the wider sense of generation-set including alternating generations. If it is not possible to bring a *rākhī* personally, they are at least sent. Compared to *Bhāi Jiūntiā*, the worship of brothers takes place outside the kitchen—on a veranda—and is simpler; the brother does not stand on any platform (*pindhā*). The sister applies some sandalwood paste and a vermilion to the forehead of the brother, places flowers behind the ear, circles a light in front of him, binds a *rākhī*, feeds him with sweets and finally bows down or touches his feet. In exchange, the brother offers money to his sister. It is a privilege of unmarried sisters to demand some money.

In the same way as sisters bind a *rākhī* to their brothers villagers, the *pujāri* of the local temple, the Kālo, *Guti*, and young boys do the same. After having received a *rākhī*, a Gauntiā offers money or *kharchā* in return. The Kālo also ties a *rākhī* to the village goddess. Here, a relationship of superiority is symbolized—one offers a *rākhī* to the one on whom one depends. It is also meant to show one's respect and loyalty—particularly to the Gauntiā as the *sab karanu baī*—the biggest of all in the village context.

Rākhī Pūni, as an important ritual between brother and sister, seems to be a more recent phenomenon among the Aghriā, because elderly Aghriā women do not remember to have done it in their young age. Thus, *Bhāi Jiūntiā* seems to be the older tradition.

The relationship may be extended to a *dharam bhāi* or *dharam dadā* that is, a new relationship can be established by binding the thread, which ideally continues until death. Like a sister asks for the help of their brother, villagers come to the Gauntiā for her safety. Another aspect of the *Rākhī Pūni*, people say, is to maintain the good relations between brother and sister, Gauntiā and villagers, etc.

BHĀDRABA ĀMĀBĀSYĀ (OR *SAPTA PURĪ ĀMĀBĀSYĀ*)

Celebrated on the new moon of the month of Bhādraba, a month after *Harli Uāns*, a figure of a cow or bullock is made of clay and worshipped. The pictures of the cattle and bullocks drawn on *Harli Uāns* in the kitchen are fed *ghī* and *guḍ* again, and then removed—the walls of the kitchen are white-washed.

It is not permitted to use the bullocks and cattle for any work on this day. According to the Aghriā Samāj, young Aghriā should begin to take care of the cattle and bullocks on this day.

GAṆEṢ PŪJĀ

Performed a day before Nuā Khāi, this festival for the son of Śiva is to be celebrated at colleges or schools, but rarely among common villagers.

NABĀNNA (S)/*NUĀ KHĀI* (O)

Nabānna—the Sambalpuri name—literally means 'new rice' (*naba* = new; *anna* = rice), while the Oriya-name *nuā khāi* means 'new eating' (implicit of new rice). Usually the house is painted or at least cleaned before the festival and all family members should wear new clothes. On this day the first rice of the season is eaten. It is the time when the harvest begins and the first, the earliest variety is ripe. *Nabānna* is celebrated on the fifth day of the light side of the month of Bhādraba—a day after *Gaṇeṣ Pūjā*. It can be performed only after the *Bihuḍā Pūjā*. Invitations have to be sent to family members—even if the day is fixed and well known. Two to three days before *Nuā Khāi* the first rice is collected. The earliest variety eaten on this occasion is known as *sariā dhān.*[39] It is not necessary for every family to produce its own *sariā.*[40] The *sariā*-rice should traditionally be ground in a grinder known as *ḍhenki* (not in an electric mill), which should be cleaned with cow dung before use. The *sariā dhān* is only pared, not parboiled. It is mixed with curd, sugar, honey, *ghī* and milk—a mixture known as *nabānna*.

The women perform a ritual for Lakṣmī and also worship Brahma, Viṣṇu, Śiva, Samlei, a banyan tree, a *pipal* tree, the rice fields, the *tulsī-chaur* and the cattle shed (*guhāl*). The temple servant performs a ritual in the Śiva temple and the Kālo at the Grām Śrī shrine. The whole family should be present on this day—including the servants (in particular the *Guti*). To all *barttaniā*—barber, washerman, etc.—*kharchā* should be offered. If someone is unable to come, the ritual eating of the first rice may be delayed until *Daśarā*. Before beginning to eat, everyone gives himself a *ṭikā* with the rice mixture. After eating the new rice, the blessings of the elders are asked for by juniors, who show their respect by doing *namaskar*—not only in the family, but the whole village.

At least a day or a night before *Nuā Khāi* the Kālo should bring *śiśā*, spikes of rice, for the doors of the houses. *Śiśā* consists of a spike (*kheḍ/dhān keṇṭā*) of paddy wrapped in a *bheluān* leaf and is placed in a corner of the doors. It is offered to the village goddess and then distributed among villagers. It is interpreted by some Aghriā to be a sign that the goddess has accepted the new rice and received her share. The Kālo gets some sweets in exchange for *śiśā* on the day after *Nuā Khāi*.

Nuā Khāi is a very auspicious day to feed the first rice to a newborn child.

The preparation of two cakes known as *upkā babrā* (made of *maidā*/wheat, *chunā*, cardamom, bananas, gloves and fried in *ghī*—similar to *arisa*) and as *sisiri*-cake was a must in former times on this day. In the evening, usually fish is served. There is a belief among the Aghriā that one becomes a stark in one's next life, if one does not eat fish on *Nuā Khāi*.

GUHĀL PŪJĀ—RITUAL IN THE CATTLE SHED

According to some Aghriā, on the day of *Nuā Khāi* a ritual is performed by the head of the family in the cattle shed. However, most Aghriā do not perform this ritual. Some say that during this ritual the gods and goddesses, Rakasbuddha, a giant, who eats people, Cuttack Chandi (a form of Samlei) and Nandu Gauḍ are worshipped. The *praśād* of this ritual is only eaten by men—women are not allowed to eat it. One family told the following story about Rakasbuddha and why they performed the ritual for him. The father of the storyteller was a trader. Once, on his way from Kusmi to Kuchinḍa he met an old man sitting there and asked him, who he was. The old man replied: 'It's me'. Later, the other three men travelling with him told him that this must have been Rakasbuddha. After returning home, the trader thought that it would be better to perform a little ritual for Rakasbuddha and offer him some marijuana (*ganjā*). All of the other three men travelling that night died within a week mysteriously. The trader was convinced that he only survived due to the ritual. Since this event, he does the *Guhāl Pūjā*.

Another family also perform the ritual on *Nuā Khāi*, but offers some *chāul* (three piles), flowers, milk and a cake (*suhāli* or *sijhari pitha*) to Jagannāth, Subhadhra and Balabhadra on this day. In still another family, on *Nuā Khāi* a ritual is performed in the cattle shed that women are not allowed to see. It is prohibited for female family members to eat any part of the goat sacrificed during the ritual, which is reserved for the men. The consumption of the head is further restricted to the men of one's own clan (*banśa*) plus the daughter's husband. On the same day, another goat is sacrificed in the kitchen by the men of the house. The head is again reserved for the men of the clan, but women may eat the rest.

However, not all families perform the ritual and another family claimed that a *Guhāl Pūjā* is performed only every three years for Mauli Mā in their home. In that case, only men of their own clan are allowed to see the ritual. In former times this ritual was performed by a Gaud in this family.

HUMA

Between *Nuā Khāi* and *Bhāi Jiuntiā*, dancing and singing known as *huma* takes place every evening—performed by women of the village. The dances are often performed in groups—resembling, in form, friendly competitions. Women used to joke in their improvized singing and dancing with men, with whom they maintain joking relationships, e.g. sisters make fun of their brothers. Every woman—including widows and unmarried women—can participate. Only the so-called 'Untouchables' are excluded.

VISHWAKARMA PŪJĀ

This festival for the god of machines and all technical equipment and architecture is performed every year on the 16, 17 September by a male member of the house. All machines are cleaned and decorated with flowers (except the hibiscus).

PUA JIŪNTIĀ OR *DUTIBHĀN OSĀ*

The name is derived from *pua* or 'son' and *jiuntā*—a thread tied around the wrist. Particularly women wishing to have children perform it. Mothers and childless women fast for one day on the eighth day of the dark side of the month of *Daśarā*/Āśbina. A small hole is dug in the street and small fishes (*jiān*) and water are placed into it. The hole may be one to two square *hāth* (length according to one hand). The women sit in front of the hole with their *saris* unfolded in the hope that the fish jump into it. This is seen as proof that the wish to have children will be fulfilled. Afterwards, the fish are thrown into a pond or river. Sugar cane may be offered as a *praśād*.

PITRU PAKṢ/ŚRĀDDHA/MAHĀLAYĀ

In the dark half of month of Āśbina (October), recently deceased ancestors are worshipped on the lunar day (*tithi*) of their death, if their bones have not yet been brought to the river Ganga. Leaves are spread in the kitchen and raw rice and raw vegetables as well as cloth are offered. This food is known as *piṇda*. Afterwards, on new *phalśā* leaves, cooked food (rice, curry) is given, known as *pani*. At the end of the dark fortnight, a ritual for all ancestors—at least of the last three generations until *paenbaḍu*—is performed. In the case that individual names are not remembered, the names of Jagannāth (for men) and Lakṣmī (for women) may be used as substitutes. The clothes and the raw food should be given to a Brahmin, while the cooked food should be eaten by the family (B, ZS, Z, M, S) except by the eldest son who performed the ritual. If there is no Brahmin, this auspicious *dān* may be given to a *bhanjā*.

GARBHAṆA SANKRĀNTI

There is no special significance assigned to *Garbhaṇa Sankrānti* apart from the abstinence with regard to non-vegetarian food.

There is one *sankrānti* in each month of the Hindu calendar. Every *sankrānti* occurs between the thirteenth and the eighteenth of the month of the English calendar and is fixed in the *pāñjji*. Only *Makar Sankrānti*, *Panā Sankrānti*, and *Raja Sankrānti* appear to be of wider importance.

BHĀI JIŪNTIĀ

The name of the ritual is derived from *bhāi* 'younger brother' and *jiuntiā*, which may be translated with 'to live long', but it is also the name of the thread that sisters bind around the wrist of their brothers. In the ritual sisters pray for the well-being of their brothers. Though *bhāi* denotes younger brother in the terminology, the sisters perform it also for elder brothers. They even include grandchildren—terminologically also considered as *bhāi*—if present. It is performed on the seventh and eighth day of the light side of the month of Āśbina. The sisters should be invited by their brothers personally and should return to the house, in which they were born. Thus, all sisters return—as if marriages had never taken place.[41] This invitation is also known as the *upās karā*, which means 'to fast'. It hints at the fasting of the sisters for their brothers during the day. The fasting usually starts a little before midnight on the sixth day after a meal of the sisters, called *uṭhmen* or *uṭhgan* (*uṭh* = to stand up) consisting of bananas, flattened rice, curd, milk, and sugar. The fasting continues for a whole day and is broken only in the morning of the next day.

In the afternoon of the seventh day (*saptami*), the sisters go to a nearby river or pond and—facing east—they build a so-called *bālukāliṅgā*. There are two explanations of the name: Firstly, *bālukā* means sand and *lingā* as symbol of Śiva means together 'sand-*lingā*'. Secondly, *bālu* means sand, but *kālingā*, as temple, mean together 'sand temple'. After taking a bath, the sisters form two half globes of sand for every brother they have. The 'sand' itself is a mixture of turmeric, *anlā*, *gandhā*, and sand. Usually, in the left hemisphere three small wooden sticks (each about 10 cm long) are placed forming a pyramid, in the right one, four sticks form a similar structure (the order is sometimes reversed). On top of the 'pyramids' some turmeric is put mixed with *gandhā-anlā*.[42] Before leaving the place, the nearby *pipal* tree, seat of Viṣṇu, is watered.

On the morning of the eighth day (*aṣtami*) the sisters go to the pond before sunrise to worship the sand *lingā* they erected the afternoon before. They throw some *chāul* and flowers around them. Standing in the pond and facing east, they eat eight pieces of *mug dāl* and *chāul* they received the evening before during the ritual for Durgā (eight pieces are swallowed in total, not eight for every brother)—mixed with some curd, *ghī*, honey and sugar cane juice. Afterwards, they bind the *jiūntiā* themselves. Before leaving, the *bālukā-lingā* are thrown into the river or pond and some water poured in front of the *pipal* tree.

Back in the house they perform a small ritual for Durgā in the kitchen using *dīpa* and flowers. Afterwards, a cake (*piṭhā*) is prepared from of the *lingā bharāni*—*chāul* mixed in a ritual the evening before. The cake is known as '*pāen chhaḍā piṭhā* (*pāen* = water, brought from the pond after taking the bath; *chhāḍeibā* = to take forcefully—but in the sense of offering to the gods). Only women who have prepared the cake can distribute it. The cake must be eaten completely—nothing can be wasted.

Later, brothers, after having taken their bath, stand on a *pindhā* under which a *jhoti* is drawn, and their sisters apply a *ṭikā* and sandal paste on their foreheads, throw some *chāul* with turmeric over them, make an auspicious *hulhuli*-sound, put some flowers behind the right ear, and, finally, bind a thread (*jiūntiā*) around the right wrist. This thread is a symbolic protection. Before that they also move a bunch of 108 *duba*-grass-blades seven times up and down on the body of the brother—three times on the left side and four times on the right side. This movement is called *dub chaḍā* (similar to the *tel chaḍā* during the wedding). The bunch with *duba*-grass is wrapped in a *sāl* leaf (or mango leaf), in which also 108 corns of *aruā-chāul* are placed (the 108 corns are not part of the *lingā bharāni*). Some say that the sisters pray for the long life of their brothers—ideally 108 years. The sisters also offer some sweets or feed the brother directly, e.g. with pieces of the *pāen chhaḍā piṭhā* - and offer clothes to their brothers. In exchange, they receive a *sari*. The gift of a *sari* or money is known as *Daśarā māsiā* (*māsa* = month). The women, however, are not allowed to eat anything, not even *praśād* until the next morning, when they break their fast by eating *pāen chhaḍā piṭhā*. The end of the ritual is described as *utjāpan* (= finishing ritual). Old *jiūntiā* of former years might be thrown into a river or pond on this day. For newly married sisters in the first year after marriage, it is important to offer dress material to all her brothers including the 'cousin-brothers' (MBS, FZS, FBS, MZS).

There is a difference in significance between *Bhāi Jiūntiā* and *Rākhī Pūni*, although many symbolic elements are similar. On *Rākhī Pūni*, the sister begs for protection, while on *Bhāi Jiūntiā* the sister prays for the long life of her brother in front of Durgā. As a *pujāri* claimed, *Bhāi Jiūntiā* is performed in memory of Subhadra binding a *jiūntiā* to her brother Jagannāth.

On the day of *Bhāi Jiūntiā*, the eighth day of the light side, but sometimes a day later—the women and sisters, who fast for their brothers, perform a ritual for Durgā. Men hardly participate in this, unless they are invited to perform it or in order to read the sacred text. Most people agree that a Brahmin should conduct it, although some argue that it should be the work of a Kālo. If there is no Brahmin in the village a high caste villager may perform it.

In a one case that I observed, the ritual took place on the outer veranda of the house of the local landlord, where a picture of Durgā had been placed. Flowers, mango leaves, *anlā*, *phaklo-liā* in form of *muān*, *dīpa*, incense, *chāul* and vermilion, were offered. In addition to that, a mixture of *chāul*, *pañchāmrut*, *muān* and *mug dāl* was brought to the altar known as *lingā bharāni*, which was later distributed among the participants to prepare a special cake (*piṭhā*) to be eaten by the brothers on the next day of *Bhāi Jiuntiā*. Afterwards, a sacred text—the *Bhāi Jiūntiā/Durgāṣṭami Bratā* (*Durgā Mālashree*) was read. A pumpkin (*mākhan* or *kumbhdā*) in the form of a goat was symbolically beheaded. Initially, the symbolic 'goat' was cleaned like an ordinary goat before it was sacrificed. Usually, women are allowed to touch the axe or sword, but are not allowed to sacrifice a goat (*bukā*). The pumpkin is later distributed as *praśād* and used for a curry.[43] Men are also allowed to eat this curry. After the sacrifice an *arthi*—a fire ritual—was performed. Every woman warmed her hands over the fire and applied the heat symbolically to her head. Money was offered and collected. Later, it was given to the *pujāri* together with some *chāul*. Apart from the pumpkin, *muān* was distributed as *prasād*.

The women also take eight pieces of *mug dāl* and *aruā chāul* from the altar to be eaten the next morning near a pond for *Bhāi Jiūntiā* and to be given to their brothers.

When asked if women are also allowed to sacrifice the pumpkin, the *pujāri* told me that the women also sacrificed in former times, but not today. As a reason, the following story was told. Once, the men challenged the women, whether or not they knew where the *jiban* (life energy) of a he-goat was situated. A test was arranged by covering the goat with a cloth. The women saw the moving tail and thought that the *jiban* was where something was moving. Subsequently, they decided to cut the tail and not the head. Since this failure, the men sacrifice the goats. Implicitly, it means that jiban is situated in the head. Some Aghriā also argue that women have never done the sacrificing themselves and this story only describes an attempt to do so.

BOIL/BALI JĀTRĀ

This is celebrated on the full moon after *Daśarā*—the *purnimā* of the month of Āśbina to honour the Goddess Samlei.[44]

DE UTHĀ

This ritual is celebrated on the eleventh day of the light side of the month of Kārttika. All temples and all gods in the house are worshipped and blackberries are offered to them. In former times, this day marked the beginning of the marriage season, which ended with the coming of the monsoon rain. The day is not particularly celebrated in the Kuchinda block.

KĀRTTIKA

The month of Kārttika is known as *puniya māsa*—as a month to earn religious merits. The month is generally considered to be holy, because, as some say, *tulsī*, *anlā*, *pipal* and banyan were born in this month. Particularly *tulsī* is worshipped during the month. It is believed that Ganga is present in the roots of the sacred basil plant, while Viṣṇu stays in its leaves.

Every Monday a *Śiva Pūjā* or *Mahadev Pūjā* is performed at the local temple. For the ritual, a flower garland (*māli*) is usually prepared consisting of 108 bel-leaves. In addition to that, hibiscus flowers are given and the shrine of Mā Bhainro opposite the temple is worshipped.

Some people maintian a vegetarian diet for the whole month. Therefore, the first day of the following month of Mārgaśirṣa is also called *chhāḍ khāī*, which means literally 'to give up eating', but is meant in the sense of 'the break the diet'. Among some communities, widows light a lamp called the *ākāsh dīpa* (light of the sky) every evening—a custom not observed among the Aghriā.

BHAGBAD

In the month of Kārttika the performance of *Bhagbad* seems to be very popular, though it can be performed the whole year round. Bhagbad means the singing of devotional songs of a *Kirthan* party. The patron has to arrange something to smoke including cigarettes (*biḍi*) and marijuana smoked in small pipes (*chillum*) and *prasād* (*khai* mixed with *guḍ*). Usually, one man reads passages from the *Śrīmad Bhāgbad Gītā*, which the other men start to sing afterwards. Some men also play drums (*mrudunga*) or small cymbals (*gini*). The intensity of the singing rises until the next passage of the text is read or the procedure is interrupted to smoke. At the end, a little ritual is performed in front of a Tulsī shrine for Brundabati by placing the text on a small stool (*pindhā*) and offering some *chāul*, marigold flowers, *dīpa*, *dhūpa* and *bhog* (bananas).

ANLĀ-NAVAMI

On the ninth day of the light side of the month of Kārttika a ritual for an *anlā* tree associated with Durgā is performed. Some red bangles and a red cloth are tied on the tree after the women have taken their bath. Furthermore, *dhūpa* and *dīpa* are offered. According to some Aghriā, the ritual is conducted for the well being of the husbands.

PAÑCHAKA

This ritual is celebrated in some Aghriā families for five (*pañch*) days beginning the tenth day of the light side of the month of Kārttika and continuing until the full moon night (*purnimā*), while other families only observe the ritual on the most important day—the day of the full moon. The rituals are performed remembering the name of Kārtikeshwar—the son of Śiva.

A bath should be taken before sunrise. There is also a belief that after taking these baths for five days sins are washed away. Some Aghriā say that all sins are washed away, while others argue that all sins are removed only by bathing in the river Ganga, rather by taking the bath in an ordinary river only five sins are washed away. Non-vegetarian food (meat, fish, eggs) should be avoided. In the morning only *aruā-chāul*, in the evening only *roti* or a cake made of wheat and prepared not directly in the fire, but in a *pan* should be eaten. This kind of diet is known as *habiṣ*, while the food eaten is known as *habiṣyānna*. The *Kārttika Mahatmiya* is read during the whole month.

If the ritual is performed for five days usually after the bath near the pond or river, a so-called *bālukā-pūjā* is conducted for Śiva, in which a sand *lingā* is formed. On this spot *bel* leaves, hibiscus flowers, *pān*, *pañchāmrut*, vermilion, and coconut are offered. A *rath* used by Śiva and Krishna is drawn on the ground occasionally as a temporary decoration. This is repeated in front of the *tulsī* shrine in the yard of one's house. Inside the car drawn with coloured powders Krishna and Balaram have a seat. On the left and right sides of the car Atisila and Susila, below Rai and Bijay and on the top Jaya are present as guardians.

In the morning of the full moon of Kārttika, women go again to the river or pond to take a bath before sunrise. This bath is called *kārttik buḍ* (*buḍ* = complete dip into the water). Often women take several *buḍ* at this time on behalf of different family members. Afterwards, lights and small boats (*ḍungā*) with lights inside are let into the water. They are made of a special plant called kaunriā. In one case, water was later poured in front of a *pipal* tree near the pond. A garland made of marigold flowers was offered to the tree. Subsequently, an *anlā* tree was worshipped in a similar way including the pouring of water, but bangles were also offered. Inside the house a ritual was performed at the Tulsī shrine, which had been previously washed. A garland was given and the shrine was decorated with coloured powders (white rice powder/*chuna*; red *sindhur*/vermilion; black and green powder/*phagu* and yellow turmeric/*haldi*). On all four sides a symbolic man representing the mythological figures of Jaya, Bijay, Sula and Atisula were drawn to act as guardians. The women circled around the shrine seven times—the circling was called *beḍhā*. With using a gong and a shell, before the *Kārttika Mahatmiā*, a sacred text already placed in front of the *tulsī chaur* was read.

DIĀLI/DIPĀVALI—FESTIVAL OF LIGHTS

There are actually two *Diāli*—the *Baḍ Diāli* celebrated on the day before the new moon (*uāns*) and the so-called 'small *Diāli*' (*choṭ diāli/sān diāli*) a day later. No particular ritual is performed on that day, but, at sunset, little lights are placed everywhere in the house—in the inner yards, the entrances to the rooms, even in the cattle shed and on the threshing floor. Apart from the lights, firecrackers are very popular. Additionally, a light is offered in the fields for the ancestors to guard and to protect the field.

MAKAR SĀNKRĀNTI

This is traditionally celebrated on 14 January and a bath should be taken before sunrise. *Makar Sankrānti* is generally regarded as the end of the cold season—from this day onwards the temperature rises. Sometimes, it is performed a few days later in order to attract a bigger crowd in the case that there is competition among neighbouring villages. The festival is opened by a ritual for Jagannāth and Śiva who—as some people claim—have been *makrā*-friends or at least met on this day. In remembrance of this meeting, two different altars are constructed and two rituals performed for them. In one case, I saw a Gauntiā and his wife who acted as the *karttā* (or *jajmān*/ sacrificer) patronizing the ritual. Later, a priest was sitting on a carriage (*rath*) for the respective god—similar to the ones used in the *Rath Jātrā*. The two cars placed at different ends of the village were pulled by a crowd each and finally met between the two altars. People from different communities can become *makrā* on this day and, ideally, only potential friends should pull the cars. To all devotees, *makrā chāul* is offered as *praśād*, which is prepared like the chāul for *Nuā Khāi*.

ŚIVRĀTRĪ

This is celebrated on the fourteenth day of the dark side of the month of Phalgun. Usually, a meeting of the villagers takes place before the festival—often on the veranda of the Gauntiā house—to decide about different tasks related to the *Jātrā* such as the building of an altar (*maduā*) and inviting dancing groups. A *maduā* is usually erected, if there is no permanent altar in the village. Such an altar is identical with the ones used for *Nām Jagya*, and *Makar Sankrānti.* If a temporary *maduā* is constructed, *jām* branches and leafs are used for the roof, since a cooling effect is ascribed to them. As instruments, *kastel* or big cymbals are used in addition to drums. Before entering the *maduā*, dancers of the *Mandli* groups sprinkle some water standing in pots at the entrance over their heads and then touch the soil of the *maduā*. All the male dancers must wear the traditional *dhoti* or, in the rare case of female dancers, they wear *shalwar kameez*. The dancing usually starts around sunset and continues all night. However, it is allowed to interrupt the music. Additionally, there is fair in the village that attracts big crowds.

As in any other ritual where a *maduā*—particularly a temporary one—is used, the altar cannot be dismantled immediately afterwards, because it is still considered to be hot. Only a few days later, after another small ritual known as *maduā śītal* has been performed by the villagers, can it be dismantled. Until then, the gods such as Śiva and Krishna are still present and leave only after the *Mandli* groups have performed once again. In the small ritual a *Kirthan* or *Mandli* group sings and dances for a short time before Krishna is worshipped. For the god, the platform (*pindhā*) is arranged as a seat. Apart from this a coconut, roses, bananas, incense, vermilion, and sugar cane juice mixed with flattened rice are offered. The latter is distributed as *praśād*. *Dīpa* and *dhūpa* are also given; the shell and gong are used for auspicious sounds. At the end a male member of the *Kirthan*-group performing the ritual announces that 'Everything will go right in the village and all wishes of the donors will be fulfilled. The blessings of the gods will always be with the villagers and everyone will lead a good life!' and a coconut is subsequently broken.

In one case, the Gauntiā sponsored rice for the dancers and police guards present. The contributions collected in the village were used to pay for the food except the rice and for the payment of the *Kirthan* groups.

GUNDI CHAḌHĀ/ĀM GUNDI

The name is derived from *gundi* or small pieces of mango and *chaḍhā*, 'to offer for Gods'. Some say that small flowers and fruits of mango trees, of *mahuā* trees and of *chāṛ* tree are brought and distributed among family members during the full moon night of the month of Phalgun. According to others, the day is not fixed. However, the ritual eating of the first mango (*ām*) is central and therefore the ritual is also known as *ām pūjā* or *ām gundi khiā*. Mangos are first offered to the gods and are then eaten by the family. Mangos should not be eaten before the ritual offering to the gods—quite similar to rice. Usually in the morning small pieces of mango are mixed with curd and honey before being offered to Viṣṇu and Lakṣmī.

POUṢ PUNI

There is no significant ritual celebrated on the full moon day of the month of Pouṣ, but contracts with labourers such as the *Guti* and the *Kāmkarā* end on this day and may be renewed subsequently. In some regards it is seen as the beginning of the new year. Often a special cake is prepared similar to a *mandā* cake, but with a filling of *guḍ* and *raeś*. Instead of frying the cake in oil, steam (*bhāp*) is used for the preparation. *Guḍ* and *raeś* are easily available at this time after the harvest of sugar cane and *raeś*-plants.

MANGALĀ PŪJĀ

The ritual for *Mangalā* is celebrated every Tuesday during the month of Cheitr. Tuesday is also known as *Māngalbār*—the day of *Mangalā*. Some Aghriā regard Mangalā as another name of the Goddess Parvati. *Mangalā* is further associated with pox. A daughter-in-law—usually the eldest—performs the ritual. She conducts it at the entrance of the house, but still on the road in the late morning. The spot for the ritual is purified with cow dung before the ritual and is cleaned once more immediately before the ritual. A half circle of 13 *ṭikā* is applied to the road. The number 13 is intimately related to *Mangalā*. On each *ṭikā* a *bel* leaf resembling a *triśul* is placed as well as a hibiscus flower. Additionally, *bel* leaves and hibiscus flowers are put in the middle. In the centre, as in most rituals, incense or *dhūpa*—produced with a paste of the *sāl* tree and mixed with sugar cane juice—is offered. Furthermore, a lamp and food—fruits, curd, milk, and raw rice are given as the other two central elements of every ritual. The latter is offered in a small pile on each of the 13 leaves. *Dīpa* and *dhūpa* are circled (*dīpa* in the right hand), while the arms of the daughter-in-law are crossed. After about 15 minutes the ritual on the road is completed and the offerings to the Goddess are left there.

A small ritual in the cattle shed is performed afterwards. In a case I observed, the daughter-in-law selected a place at the centre in front of a wooden post (*khuṇṭ*). There, she offered the same items—in particular *bel* leaves and hibiscus flowers—but without any order compared to the first ritual. Again, she faces east. A *chanda bindu* is drawn on the *khuṇṭ*. Later, the daughter-in-law explained that she performed the ritual wishing for the well-being of the cattle. Compared to the *Lakṣmī Pūjā*, which is intimately linked to paddy, the *Mangalā Pūjā* is apparently related to the cattle.

TĀRINĪ BRATA (AS PART OF THE *MANGALĀ PŪJĀ*)

This ritual is performed on a Tuesday in the month of Chaitra, but only once. As some Aghriā say, it should be done during the light part of the month. The goddess Tārinī, for whom the ritual is performed, has her central shrine near Keonjhar on a hill. However, there is no temple there, because, according to a legend, the goddess told the king of Keonjhar that she did not wish to reside in a temple. Her idol in the form of a red stone resembles the one of Samlei.

In another observed case, a daughter-in-law, after having taken her bath, performed the ritual inside the house on a wall in a south-east corner of an inner yard. The ritual for Tārinī was combined with a ritual for Mangalā and Durgā. Accordingly, there were three altars for the three goddesses. Facing east, the altars for Mangalā and Tārinī were prepared. The former prepared with 13 handprints on the wall, the latter with 7 handprints. Both handprints were arranged in the form of a pyramid. On every handprint a *ṭikā* was added and at the centre of each pyramid a bunch of *duba* grass—13 and 7 blades each. This kind of altar is known as a *hantā*. Below the 13 handprints a *jhoti* was drawn having 13 symbolic rooms. On top of it and in front of the other altars a *kalaś*, different kinds of flowers such as hibiscus (*mandār*) and leaves (13 mango leaves, 13 pieces of *nīm* tree, 13 betel-leaves/*pān*, *phalsā*-leaves, etc.) are put on banana leaves. Apart from that, 13 blue or black[45] bangles and 13 *harida* fruits are offered for Mangalā.

Additionally, fruits such as oranges, melons, guava, bananas, grapes, two coconuts, vermilion, turmeric, *muān* (a mixture of *khai* and *guḍ* formed into pyramids), *tikhur* (black sweet jelly produced of *pālo* and said to have a cooling effect) and *mohan bhog* (sweet, black/dark brown balls made of wheat) are offered. The fruits and sweets are distributed in 13 small bowls and given later as *praśād*. Another addition is a small *kansā* bowl with two sacred texts—the *Tārinī Brata* and the *Cheitr Mangalā Osā*—as well as a small red thread, which is later used as a *brata* to be worn on the upper arm of the woman who performs the *pūjā* and who fasts during the day. The thread ideally should have a length of 13 hands of a 13-year-old boy and 13 knots should be tied in it. Later, during the ritual, two bowls with 13 and 7 rice corns are offered for Mangalā and Tārinī respectively. On the much smaller altar in a southern direction a bowl with *tikhur* and some fruits were offered.

Everything was sprinkled with sandal paste and both texts were given a *ṭikā*. *Dīpa* as well as *dhūpa* were offered. With a shell and a gong auspicious sounds were produced. The gods present in the *kalaś* were invoked and afterwards the texts read. In the *Tārinī Brata*, the story of a barren Ghansiā woman was described. After having bought all the necessary ritual items at a bazaar, she worshipped Mangalā and subsequently became pregnant.

After reading the texts, flowers were circled 13 and 7 times respectively and a coconut was sacrificed. Some pieces of the coconut were given as *praśād* after the coconut milk had been sprinkled over the altars, and some money was offered. The 13 bowls of *praśād* were distributed and the daughter-in-law who had performed the *pūjā* took the *brata*, consisting not only of the red thread, but also of 13 blades of *duba*-grass and 13 rice corns wrapped within. The *brata,* bound for the well-being of the house, should not become lost, as it would imply that the property would also become lost. The old *brata* of the last year's ritual may be immersed into a pond or river.

Afterwards, a *Mangalā* ritual was performed on the road as described above.

SU DASĀ BRATA

This ritual is celebrated if the tenth day (*daśami*) of the light side (*ujwala pakṣ*) happens to be on a Thursday (*Gurubār*). This combination usually occurs up to three times a year. On this day a strict vegetarian diet should be kept, and no one should cut their hair or shave.

In the morning, a ritual for Lakṣmī is performed at the house shrine by a daughter-in-law. At the altar a *kalas*, fruits such as melons, bananas, oranges, grapes, *ghī*-lamps, flowers (no hibiscus) and also the book *Su Dasā Brata* are placed. Additionally, a shell and a gong are used to produce auspicious sounds. The women sometimes produce an auspicious sound known as a *hulhuli*. A *baha* (SW) performing the ritual, binds a saffron-coloured thread around her right upper arm with some *duba* grass wrapped in a mango leaf with eight rice corns. She fasts the whole day. The ritual is especially meant for the women of house. The *praśād* is given only to close family members, i.e. not to cousin-brothers (FBS, etc.), to uncles (FB), to married daughters or married sisters. The latter may perform a separate ritual in the house, if they are present.

PANĀ SANKRĀNTI—HANUMAN JAYANTI (HANUMAN'S BIRTHDAY)

This is celebrated always on the 13th or 14th of April according to the *pa-jji* (astrological calendar). A special drink is offered to Mangalā—*Panā Sankrānti* is seen as a part of the *Mangalā Pūjā*—the other Gods and the family on this day known as *panā*—a mixture of curd, water and grains. Sometimes, it is also called *jharā panā*. *Jharā* signifies a ladle with small holes through it through which a mixture of rice powder and boiled rice known as *maḍiā* is pressed.

Panā is said to cool the body (*sītal heba*). It is seen as the beginning of the coming heat. The *panā* should stand below a black berry tree (*jām*). However, in the case that there is no such tree close by, a twig may be brought into the house and placed there as substitute. From this day onwards free water is served in the bazaar.

SĀBITRĪ BRATA/SĀBITRĪ UĀNS

The ritual is performed by wives for their husbands on the new moon day of the month of Jyeṣṭha (May/June). Every wife worships her husband and prays for his long life. The wife takes a bunch of *duba* grass and moves with it over the body of the husband up and down seven times. She also throws some flowers and *aruā* rice over him while he stands on a small stool (*pindhā*). The wife anoints the forehead of the husband with a sandal paste and she offers 12 or 13 kinds of fruits. Furthermore, a wife pours some milk and/or water over the feet of her husband and subsequently drinks some of it. This milk/water is called *pādukā* and considered to be *praśād*. *Dīpa* and *dhūpa* are circled in front of the husband. Finally, the wife, who fasts the whole day or eats only *roti* with *ghī* in the evening, offers new cloths to her husband who is considered to be a god. Every wife binds a thread or *brata* on her right upper arm. The *brata* is not bound to her husband's arm, as wife and husband see each other as one anyway.

A king had a single son, Satyaban. At the time of his birth there was a prophecy that he would die young. Later, he married Sābitrī, who knew the prophecy. (She had met the unmarried Satyaban in the jungle.) Later the king became blind and another occupied the kingdom. The family of the king had to flee. Sābitrī and Satyaban escaped into the forest. One day Satyaban went to fetch wood, and was bitten by a snake. He died on the spot. Sābitrī searched for her husband and found him dead under a tree. She took Satyaban's head in her lap. The servants of Yama came to take the soul of Satyaban, but did not succeed, because Sābitrī loved him so much. Yama had to come personally. Sābitrī followed Yama to his kingdom, but Yama, disapproving, granted her a wish in order to stop her. Sābitrī said: 'Let my father-in-law be able to see again and return his kingdom to him!' Yama agreed and said: 'I will grant you this wish, but do not follow me anymore!' However, Sābitrī followed him even after having been granted the wish. Yama built some barricades and blockages to stop her, but she managed to follow. Yama asked: 'Why are you still following me? The soul of your husband cannot come back. His time is over!' To stop her, Yama offered another wish and Sābitrī demanded: 'Give me 100 sons!' Yama agreed. Still Sābitrī followed and Yama asked: 'Why are you still following?' Sābitrī said: 'You have promised me 100 sons, but without a husband it will be impossible!'. Yama noticed his mistake, but had to keep his promise and decided to send back the soul of Satyaban. The love of Sābitrī was stronger than death.

According to some Aghriā, *Sābitrī Brata* in former times was not as popular as it is today.

PRATHAMAṢṬAMI

This ritual is celebrated on the eighth day of the light side of the month Mārgaśirṣa by a mother (or parents) for the first-born child, but some argue only for the first-born son. The name is derived from *pratham* or 'first' hinting at the first-born and from *aṣṭami* or the eighth day of the month, on which the ritual is performed. The ritual itself resembles *Bhāi Jiūntiā*. The mother moves with *duba* grass ten times over the body of the eldest son or daughter, which is known as *dub chaḍā* and then binds the *duba* grass to the wrist of her firstborn. It is performed only in some Aghriā families.

NĀM JAGYA

The date for this festival is not exactly fixed. It is often combined with *Makar Sankrānti*, but may also be held at any other date. The Gauntiā or any interested and financially sound party may act as the patron here. The length of the ritual depends on the sponsor: either 24 hours, known as *aṣṭa praharī* (*aṣṭa* = eight; *praharī* = three hours), or 48 hours, known as *solā praharī* (*solā* = 16). The dancers should not eat onion or garlic, they should eat only *aruā chāul,* as far as rice is concerned, and should not drink alcohol. The *mantra* 'Hare Krishna, Hare Rama' is continuously sung throughout the time of the ritual without any interruption. *Kirthan* groups as well as the Gauntiā or patron earn religious merits (*puniya*) for acting in their respective roles. The Brahmin performs the rituals for Krishna, Cheitanya and his followers.

In Mundaloi, the Gauntiā sponsored the festival by paying for the dancers or *Kirthan* or *Mandli* groups as well as for the paddy as a payment for the priest—all in all about Rs. 2,000, according to the Gauntiā. In another village, the money for the meals was shared by the Gauntiā and three other financially capable villagers, for whom it was probably also a sign of prestige to contribute.

At the end of the ritual a pot with curd known as *dadhi bhaṇda,* is carried by the Gauntiā's wife around the altar and then smashed in front of the altar. However, the Gauntiā in Mundaloi did not take part in the rolling in the mud mixed with curd that the villagers practised to show their joy. For instruments, *gini* or small cymbals were used. On the final day the *Kirthan* groups walked in a procession through the village to collect money from the households, which was then brought to the Gauntiā or patron, who counted it and distributed it among the *Kirthan* groups. According to a local Brahmin, only villagers initiated by a Kān Guru should enter the *maduā* during the *Nām Jagya.*

JANMĀṢṬAMI

This festival is celebrated for the memory of the birth of Lord Krishna. Women fast during the day to show their respect for Krishna. The *Sapukhaṇḍa Haribanśa* text is read during the day. All ritual items necessary for the ritual are often provided by the local landlord, in whose house—the representative outer room or *baiṭhak*—the ritual may take place. A temporary altar is built with a small idol of Krishna as young boy decorated with flowers. After a first ritual in the morning with *dīpa*, *dhūpa*, flowers, *aruā chāul*, bananas, and sandalwood paste the reading starts and continues throughout the day. Villagers may come to listen. The main ritual starts around sunset. All villagers bring *muān*, coconuts, flower garlands, *sindhur*, *dīpa*, and *dhūpa*. Again, parts of the text are read. Garlands are presented to Krishna and, later, milk is poured over the idol. The ritual is completed with an *arthi*. *Praśād* consisting of *muān,* and coconuts are distributed. The money offered during *arthi* and the *chāul* are taken by the *pujāri.* On the next day, Kirthan Parties and Krishna Guru Parties move around in the villages in a process known as *dahi kādo* (*dahi* = curd; *kādo* = mud). Formerly on this occasion, curd was thrown on the ground and the group would dance upon it—thus, turning the soil into mud. Often the group would first visit the house of the local Gauntiā.

Additional rituals not fixed in the calendar

TRINĀTH MELĀ

A *Trināth Melā* may be performed the whole year round, but the time of *Pañchaka* seems to be particularly popular. Trināth is regarded as a combination of the three gods: Viṣṇu, Brahma and Śiva. If a child is ill, if someone has to pass an important exam, etc., the mother or someone else may promise to arrange a *Trināth Melā* in order to secure the recovery of child, the successful passing of exams, etc., with the help of these three gods. In another case, a cow had two stillbirths and the mother of the house promised in the case of a successful birth to organise the *melā*. In yet another case, the promise was given during a flood in the hope it would stop.

There are various versions of the *melā*. A simple type is the *tri-melā* offering everything three times, i.e. once for Viṣṇu, Brahma and Śiva each. However, more prestigious is a *pañch-melā* (five *melā*) offering everything five times for each god, i.e.15 times in all. Usually, a picture of the three Gods stands on top of a small altar—symbolically erected on a small stool (*pindhā*). For a simple *melā*, at least three betel leaves, three betel nuts and three flowers are placed on the *pindhā*. In front of it, three lights and three small pipes (*chillum*) with marijuana (*ganjā*) are placed for the gods, who like marijuana. Additionally, bananas, *chāul*, *khai*, *guī*, a *kalas*, an extra *dīpa* and vermilion may be offered. The people conducting the ritual face east. The main part of the ritual is the reading of the book *Trināth Melā*. If celebrated in the landlord's house, other people may be invited to read the book. Afterwards, *murhi* (*chāul* heated on sand), *khai* and some betel leaves mixed with nuts are distributed in the house or sometimes even the whole village as *prasād*.

INDRA PŪJĀ—RAIN RITUAL

This ritual is sometimes performed in the month of Bhādraba (or Śrābaṇ) if there is not sufficient rain or an imminent drought. The Gauntiā then acts on behalf of the village—occasionally being asked to do so by the village community. Here, other villagers could do it as well, but no case was known where this had actually happened.

For the ritual performed by a Brahmin as sacrificer and the head-man and his wife as sacrifiers, four small copper bowls (*pātul*) are obligatory, which are said to symbolise clouds. Furthermore, a boat (*daṅgā*), a statue of the saint Rusya Srunga as well as two statues of the female dancers Urbasi and Menakā are required. The latter two have to call the saint, it is believed. The boat is essential, because the dancers have to cross a river on their way in order to bring the saint. The rain, it is believed, comes together with the saint. It is said, that the saint once brought the rain to the kingdom Lomapāda after a heavy drought and the ritual is performed in remembrance of this incident.

NOTES

1. Often Landlords decided to give up *guḍā*-land, if forced to do so in a land reform.
2. *Bernā* and *bāhāl* are occasionally subsumed in one category.
3. *Papad* is prepared by over-boiling *khuda*, adding spices, drying it in the sun and frying it.
4. I describe here the categories used in practice—theoretically, of course, every category of paddy would be possible.
5. Also called *hāṇḍiā*.
6. In Koraput *sariā* stands for the land where the paddy seedlings are planted.
7. The calculation between Hindu and Western calendars is rough and may differ slightly.
8. *Chāra* are collected in the small forest near the village. The taste of these small black fruits is sweet and sour. Particularly the tasty seeds inside are eaten.
9. Occasionally also jackfruit trees are planted in the same period, but it takes some years before the fruits can be collected.
10. Small green fruits collected in the small forests/bushes, sweet in taste.
11. Vegetables from a tree planted in the garden.
12. The mushrooms grow on the straw.
13. A sour fruit from the garden.
14. The seeds are planted not thrown.
15. The seeds are planted not thrown.
16. Only by poorer people of communities such as the Muṇḍā or Māḷi. The digging for rats in the fields or rather the small boundaries between the fields where rats are not disturbed by ploughing is known as *musā kuḍā* (*musā* = rat). Another way to catch the rats and to get the rice they have bunkered is to smoke them out—a process called *musā dhungā*. In this way a fire is prepared for a short period. Afterwards the smoke is channelled into the rat holes. Both ways are dangerous in the sense that you may find not only rats, but also snakes. The landlord tolerates these activities in his fields as long as the boundary walls are not heavily damaged.
17. The bark is said to be sold for medical purposes. The collection, however, causes damage to the trees.
18. *Kandā* means root. The taste is very similar to potato, but the form resembles rather carrots than potato. *Patar kandā* are collected by Malār and exchanged for *chāul* in the village (e.g. 6 pieces for ½ *tāmi* of *chāul*).

19. After 31st of January or traditionally with the month of Pouṣ, the Narihā do not take of the cattle any more (till May/June). After completing the paddy harvest the cattle and goats can graze alone in the paddy fields. However, to avoid any damage for the chilli and mustard, these fields have to be fenced, i.e. old fences (*ghuran*/S.; *bāḍā*/O.) have to be repaired or new ones erected. The same is true for the garden in general. The local Forest Guard usually collects a fine (for being caught red-handed—*dharā paḍi jibā*) according to the estimated length of the fences, because the cutting of these little trees particularly in the Reserved Forest is forbidden.
20. A small green vegetable, bitter in taste.
21. It is not necessary in the case of sandy soil (*balya jami*).
22. While the *kural* is used to level the ground by pulling or rather to reduce unevenness in the field in general, the *kapar* is necessary to make the mud plain and to destroy clods of soil.
23. In the case of the Muṇḍā, I was told that the same restrictions exist except for the *bhār*, which women may use. However, I was also told that they do not do so in practise because they are too weak to use a *bhār*.
24. Menstruation is also known as *rutu* (= season) or *māsakiā* (= monthly).
25. The *palhā marā* is also continued during the rain—the labourers protect themselves with umbrellas or plastic bags—in former times, raincoats known as *ghango* were produced of *siāl* leaves.
26. In former times, I was told such songs were also sang on *Raja Sankrānti*, when a swing (*duli*) was erected, where people used to joke.
27. In the presence of men, the women certainly did not feel totally comfortable. Thus, I only recorded a short part of a usually longer song.
28. In one case, a Landlord had created a new instrument by adding very small ploughs known as *kaṣnā* to the scraper and called that new instrument a *phandel*.
29. There are various types of fans—electric, pushed by hand, or as a special function of a power tiller (using diesel).
30. The share of the labourers of the harvest or of the *dhān* is also called *pol*. Similar to chaff, this share is without value for the landlord.
31. A *dasmaniā* consists of 10 *mān* (1 *mān* ~ 450 g).
32. The European calendar corresponds roughly to the Hindu calendar.
33. *Altā* is purchased in the market.
34. Some elders argued that in former times the Narihā and children used to to walk on stilts on this day.
35. The idol is made of the wood of the mahalimb tree and is renewed every four years in a ritual known as *nabakalebara*.
36. The colours used resemble those used in Puri.
37. A *Mandli* party performing during the *Rath Jātrā* or *Śibrātri* is characterized by using big brass bells known as *kastel*, big drums known as *mrudunga* and the singing of devotional songs of different rhythms while dancing. In

contrast, a *Kirthan* party performing during the *Nām Jagya* uses small brass bells (*gini*) and medium-sized drums (*nāḍiā-mrudunga*) and usually only sings the name of God (apart from the end of the *Nām Jagya*). A *Mandli* party should be present during the *Rath Jātrā*, but that does not mean that a *Kirthan* party will not come.

38. The texts are known as the *Lakṣmī Jagannāth Khotap Kathan* (conversation) or the *Lakṣmī Jagannāth Bachchanikā* (argument).
39. In Koraput the word *sariā* is used for the land, where the small seedlings grow before being transplanted.
40. In one case, the family received it from a married sister staying in a small town nearby. In another case, a very distant relative—a FyBW—had given the *sariā*.
41. The sisters usually stop returning to their brothers at the time of *bhāi jiūntiā*, when their own daughters, after their marriage, return to their mother's house. However, in some cases the sister may visit her brother together with her married daughters.
42. Before leaving, the sisters sometimes cover the 'pyramids' with little bowls made of leaves (*chakni*) to protect them against straying dogs. However, it happens occasionally that they are destroyed the next morning by dogs or kids and have to be repaired.
43. Other castes like the Kisān use the pumpkin for a cake to be offered on *bhāi jiūntiā*.
44. I intend to write a separate article on this festival.
45. Red bangles would also be possible, but black are preferred.

APPENDIX 3

Rituals Performed by the Different Communities

Legend: A—all families (or vast majority); S—some families; N—no families (or almost none)

Rituals[1] \ Community	Brahmin	Gauḍ	Ganḍ	Kandh	Bhuyān	Aghria	Chaṣā	Māli	Keunṭ
Akshya Trutīyā	A	S	A	A	A	A	A	A	A
Sābitrī Brata	A	S	S	S	S	S	S	S	S
Harli Uāns[2]	N	N	N	N	N	A	N	N	N
Pua Jiūntiā	A	S	S	S	S	S	S	S	S
Mahālayā	A	N	N	N	N	A	N	N	N
Garbhaṇā Sankrānti	A	N	N	N	S	A	A	S	N
Huma	S	S	S	S	S	S	N	S	S
Anlā Navarmi	A	N	N	N	N	S	N	N	S
Pañchaka	A	S	S	S	S	S	S	S	S
Lakṣmī Pūjā	A	A	A	S	A	A	A	A	A
Prathamastami	S	N	N	N	N	S	S	S	N
Tārinī Brata	A	S	S	N	S	S	S	S	S
Mangalā Pūjā	A	N	S	N	S	S	S	S	A
Panā Sankrānti	A	N	A	N	S	S	A	N	S
Vishvakārmā[3]	S	S	S	S	S	S	S	S	S
Su Dasā Brata	A	S	A	S	S	S	S	S	S
Guhāl Pūjā	N	A	A	N	N	S	A	N	N
Pitru Pūjā[4]	A	A	S	S	A	A	S	S	S
Dharma Pūjā	N	N	S	N	N	N	A	N	N

(contd.)

TABLE (contd.)

Rituals	Kisān	Kolhā/Muṇḍā	Luhurā	Tūrī	Khaḍiā	Orām	Malār	Gandā/Harijām	Chamār
Akshya Trutīyā[5]	A	S	S	A	N[6]	N	N	A	A
Sābitr Brata	S	N	N	N	N	N	S	S	S
Harli Uāns[7]	N	N	N	N	N	N	N	N	N
Pua Jiūntiā	S	S	N	S	N	N	N	S	S
Mahālayā	N	N	N	A	N	N	N	N	A
Garbhaṇā Sankrānti	N	N	N	N	N	N	N	S	S
Huma	S	S	S	S	N	N	S	S	S
Anlā Navami	N	N	N	N	N	N	N	S	S
Pañchaka	S	S	S	S	N	N	S	S	S
Lakṣmī Pūjā	A	S	S	A	N	N	N	A	A
Prathamaṣtami	N	N	N	N	N	N	N	N	S
Tārin Brata	N	N	N	N	N	N	N	S	N
Mangalā Pūjā	N	S	S	A	N	N	N	A	S[8]
Panā Sankrānti	S	N	S	A	N	N	N	N	N
Vishwakarmā[9]	S	S	A[10]	S	S	N	N	S	S
Su Dasā Brata	N	N	N	N	N	N	N	S	S
Guhāl Pūjā[11]	A	A	N	A	S	N	N	S	N
Pitru Pūjā[12]	S	S	S	A	A	S	A	A	A
Dharam Pūjā	A	A	A	N	N	N	A[13]	N	N

In the table, certain rituals which are celebrated in the village, such as the *Rath Jātrā*, *Śibrātri*, *Makar Sankrānti*, *Holi*, *Grām Śri Pūjā* are not listed, as more or less everyone participates in them—even the Christians (Orām and Khaḍiā), although they insist, they are not worshipping the respective god or goddess. In other ritual performances, such as the Dana Nrutya, all villagers except the Christians may particpate, but in the case of a Brahmin joining the group, a purification is needed afterwards from his side. In other cases, such as *Makar Sankrānti*, all non-Christian communities may celebrate it, but are perhaps separated by space—not using the same altar, etc.

NOTES

1. There are several rituals not listed here, because they are specific or unique to certain communities. Nevertheless, some of these rituals should be mentioned here. An initiation ritual is obligatory for young Brahmin men known as *baru*. The Gaṇḍ worship Jangā Lingā particularly and celebrate the so-called *Pāṭ Pūjā* as the start of a new generation, while only the Māḷi worship Bansa Devtā Muṇḍ Kaṭā in Chaitra. Samlei is of special importance to the Keuṇṭ, who worship her every Tuesday in the months of Chaitra and Āśbina. The Luhurā celebrate a ritual named *Kuthi Pūjā* resembling the Uṣā of the Gothiā Gaṇḍ.
2. Although other communities other than the Aghriā do not celebrate it, they nevertheless do not use bullocks and cattle on this day.
3. Only families, who use machines, technical instruments, etc., considered.
4. Often combined with *Nuā Khāi*, *Pouṣ Pūnī* or *Rākhī Pūnī.*
5. The ritual relates only to families having their own land. The sowing is usually started after this day. In some cases also small rituals in the field might take place, but no plough ritual if N is written.
6. In 'pure' Khaḍiā-villages the bullocks are used on this day. There is no such restriction.
7. Although other communities except the Aghriā do not celebrate it, they nevertheless do not use bullocks and cattle on this day. In case of the Kisān additionally the horns of the bullocks, etc., are anointed with oil and according to a legende a Chamār died on this very day and since then no ritual is performed among them.
8. Combined with Dussehra.
9. Only families, who also machines, technical instruments, etc., considered.
10. Particularly important for the machines, which have replaced the traditional bellows.
11. The Muṇḍā celebrate it in Chaitra, Māgha or Bhādraba, while the Khaḍiā perform it in Chaitra and Phalgun. In case of the Harijan it is combined with *Nuā Khāi*.
12. Often combined with *Nuā Khāi*, *Pouṣ Pūnī* or *Rākhī Pūnī*. In case of the Tūrī celebrated in the month of Phalgun. The Khaḍā offer sacred rice beer (*tarpan*) on *Nuā Khāi*, *Guhāl Pūjā* and *Diāli.* The Ḥarijan combine it with *Nuā Khāi*, while the Malār celebrate it on *Rākhī Puni*. In case of the Chamār it is performed in Chaitra and on *Nuā Khāi.*
13. Celebrated on *Rākhī Pūnī* and *Nuā Khāi*. On *Pouṣ Pūnī* in the jungle.

APPENDIX 4

Acceptance of Food and Water—A Comparison

In Chapter 3 a hierarchy of purity has been introduced, which is intrinsically linked to the acceptance of water and food, i.e. various categories of rice (raw, parboiled, boiled). The pattern of the Aghriā and their rules of acceptance have already been depicted. In the following the other communities of the village will be listed and it will be indicated from whom food or water is accepted. Since some communities like the Tūrī are very small the given pattern could not be cross-checked; this data may be less reliable than the lists for the Muṇḍā and other larger communities, which have been confirmed by several interlocutors. However, the data given below only indicate a certain situation in a restricted context and may not be applicable for the same communities elsewhere.

The following abbreviations have been used in the lists:

Legend

U♂	unmarried men
M♂	married men
U♀	unmarried women
M♀	married women
X	accepted in front of *jāti*
Y	accepted in front of *jāti*—in former times and nowadays (acceptance in former times more restricted)
O	accepted if produced by others
S	accepted only secretly (not in the presence of one's own *jāti*)
D	disputed acceptance (no consent)

As far as the consumption of alcohol is concerned, the Aghriā,

Brahmin, and Māḷi having strict rules against its production and consumption. Therefore the communities do not figure in the parts on alcohol. Thus, in most cases it is not non-acceptance, but rather non-giving.

Caste

BRAHMIN	Water accepted from				*Dhān* accepted from				*Chāul*[1] accepted from				*Bhāt* accepted from				Alcohol accepted from			
	U ♂	M ♂	U ♀	M ♀	U ♂	M ♂	U ♀	M ♀	U ♂	M ♂	U ♀	M ♀	U ♂	M ♂	U ♀	M ♀	U ♂	M ♂	U ♀	M ♀
Brahmin	X	X	X	X	X	X	X	X	X	X	X	X	X	X	X	X				
Gauḍ	X	X	X	X	X	X	X	X	X	X	X	X								
Aghriā					X	X	X	X	X	X	X	X								
Chaṣā					X	X	X	X	X	X	X	X								
Ganḍ					X	X	X	X	X	X	X	X								
Kandh					X	X	X	X	X	X	X	X								
Bhuyān					X	X	X	X	X	X	X	X								
Māḷi					X	X	X	X	X	X	X	X								
Keunṭ					X	X	X	X	X	X	X	X								
Kisān					X	X	X	X	O	O	O	O								
Munḍā					X	X	X	X	O	O	O	O								
Luhurā					X	X	X	X	O	O	O	O								
Khaḍiā					X	X	X	X	O	O	O	O								
Orām					X	X	X	X	O	O	O	O								
Tūrī					X	X	X	X	O	O	O	O								
Malār					X	X	X	X	O	O	O	O								
Harijan					X	X	X	X	O	O	O	O								
Chamār					X	X	X	X	O	O	O	O								

[1] If produced by a *bal lok* community.

Caste

GAUḌ	Water[1] accepted from				*Dhān* accepted from				*Chāul* accepted from				*Bhāt* accepted from				Alcohol accepted from			
	U ♂	M ♂	U ♀	M ♀	U ♂	M ♂	U ♀	M ♀	U ♂	M ♂	U ♀	M ♀	U ♂	M ♂	U ♀	M ♀	U ♂	M ♂	U ♀	M ♀
Brahmin	Y	Y	Y	Y	X	X	X	X	X	X	X	X	X	X	X	X				
Gauḍ	Y	Y	Y	Y	X	X	X	X	X	X	X	X	X	X	X	X	X	X	X	D
Aghriā	X	X	X	D	X	X	X	X	X	X	X	X	X	X	X	D				
Chaṣā	X	X	X	D	X	X	X	X	X	X	X	X	X	X	X	D	X	X	X	D
Gaṇḍ	X	X	X	D	X	X	X	X	X	X	X	X	X	X	X	D	X	X	X	D
Kandh	X	X	X	D	X	X	X	X	X	X	X	X	X	X	X	D	X	X	X	D
Bhuyān	X	X	X	D	X	X	X	X	X	X	X	X	X	X	X	D	X	X	X	D
Māḷi	X	X	X	D	X	X	X	X	X	X	X	X	X	X	X	D				
Keunṭ	X	X	X	D	X	X	X	X	X	X	X	X	X	X	X	D	X	X	X	D
Kisān	D				X	X	X	X	O	O	O	O	D							
Muṇḍā	D				X	X	X	X	O	O	O	O	D				X			
Luhurā	D				X	X	X	X	O	O	O	O								
Khaḍiā					X	X	X	X	O	O	O	O								
Orām					X	X	X	X	O	O	O	O								
Tūrī					X	X	X	X	O	O	O	O								
Malār					X	X	X	X	O	O	O	O								
Harijan					X	X	X	X	O	O	O	O								
Chamār					X	X	X	X	O	O	O	O								

[1] Some Gauḍ also argued that in former times they were not allowed to take water from any other caste in the village, because they would have lost their job as water carriers.

Caste

AGHRIĀ	Water accepted from				*Dhān* accepted from				*Chāul*[1] accepted from				*Bhāt* accepted from				Alcohol accepted from			
	U ♂	M ♂	U ♀	M ♀	U ♂	M ♂	U ♀	M ♀	U ♂	M ♂	U ♀	M ♀	U ♂	M ♂	U ♀	M ♀	U ♂	M ♂	U ♀	M ♀
Brahmin	X	X	Y	X	X	X	X	X	X	X	X	X	X	X	Y	X				
Gauḍ	X	X	Y	X	X	X	X	X	X	X	X	X	X	X	Y	X				
Aghriā	X	X	Y	X	X	X	X	X	X	X	X	X	X	X	Y	X				
Chaṣā	X	X	X		X	X	X	X	X	X	X	X	X		X					
Gaṇḍ	X	X	X		X	X	X	X	X	X	X	X	X		X					
Kandh	X	X	X		X	X	X	X	X	X	X	X	X		X					
Bhuyān	X	X	X		X	X	X	X	X	X	X	X	X		X					
Māḷi	X	X	X		X	X	X	X	X	X	X	X	X		X					
Keunṭ	X	X	X		X	X	X	X	X	X	X	X	X		X					
Kisān	X		X		X	X	X	X	X	X	X	X	X		X					
Muṇḍā	X		X		X	X	X	X	X	X	X	X	X		X					
Luhurā	X		X		X	X	X	X	X	X	X	X	X		X					
Khaḍiā	X		X		X	X	X	X	X	X	X	X	X		X					
Orām	X		X		X	X	X	X	X	X	X	X	X		X					
Tūrī	X		X		X	X	X	X	X	X	X	X	X		X					
Malār	X		X		X	X	X	X	X	X	X	X	X		X					
Harijan					X	X	X	X	X	X	X	X								
Chamār					X	X	X	X	X	X	X	X								

[1] *Chāul* is produced for the landlords by their Muṇḍā, Kisān and Luhurā labourers. Theoretically it can be produced by any community except the 'Untouchables'.

It can be accepted at the time of *kām ghar* or funeral from any community, but is usually returned with some money during the same *kām ghar*.

Caste CHAṢĀ	Water accepted from				*Dhān* accepted from				*Chāul* accepted from				*Bhāt*[1] accepted from				Alcohol[2] accepted from			
	U ♂	M ♂	U ♀	M ♀	U ♂	M ♂	U ♀	M ♀	U ♂	M ♂	U ♀	M ♀	U ♂	M ♂	U ♀	M ♀	U ♂	M ♂	U ♀	M ♀
Brahmin	X	X	X	X	X	X	X	X	X	X	X	X	X	X	X	X				
Gauḍ	X	X	X	X	X	X	X	X	X	X	X	X	X	X	X	X				
Aghriā	X	D	X	D	X	X	X	X	X	X	X	X	X	D	X					
Chaṣā	X	X	X	X	X	X	X	X	X	X	X	X	X	D	X					
Gaṇḍ	X	X	X	X	X	X	X	X	X	X	X	X	X	D	X					
Kandh	X	X	X	X	X	X	X	X	X	X	X	X	X	D	X					
Bhuyān[3]	X	X	X	X	X	X	X	X	X	X	X	X	X	D	X					
Māḷi	X	X	X	X	X	X	X	X	X	X	X	X	X	D	X					
Keunṭ	X	D	X	D	X	X	X	X	X	X	X	X	X	D	D					
Kisān	X				X	X	X	X	O	O	O	O	D				S			
Muṇḍā	X				X	X	X	X	O	O	O	O	D							
Luhurā	X				X	X	X	X	O	O	O	O	D							
Khaḍiā	X				X	X	X	X	O	O	O	O	D							
Orām	X				X	X	X	X	O	O	O	O	D							
Tūrī	X				X	X	X	X	O	O	O	O	D							
Malār	X				X	X	X	X	O	O	O	O	D							
Harijan	X				X	X	X	X	O	O	O	O	D							
Chamār	X				X	X	X	X	O	O	O	O	D							

[1] Food prepared by a Gauḍ is acceptable for married men only outside the Gauḍ-house and for married women only if prepared exclusively for Chaṣā.

[2] Chaṣā should neither produce alcohol nor consume it. If the *jāti* come to know about a violation of the rule, a feast has to be given, barber and washerman have to be called and a complete shaving of the head of the offender is obligatory.

[3] The acceptance of water from the Bhuyān is restricted for married men and women to the Rajwari Bhuyān.

Caste

GAṆḌ	Water accepted from				*Dhān* accepted from				*Chāul*[1] accepted from				*Bhāt* accepted from				Alcohol accepted from			
	U ♂	M ♂	U ♀	M ♀	U ♂	M ♂	U ♀	M ♀	U ♂	M ♂	U ♀	M ♀	U ♂	M ♂	U ♀	M ♀	U ♂	M ♂	U ♀	M ♀
Brahmin	Y	X	X		X	X	X	X	X	X	X	X	X		X					
Gauḍ	Y	X	X		X	X	X	X	X	X	X	X	X		X		S			
Aghriā	Y	X	X		X	X	X	X	X	X	X	X	X		X					
Chaṣā	Y	X	X		X	X	X	X	X	X	X	X	X		X					
Gaṇḍ	X	X	X		X	X	X	X	X	X	X	X	X		X		S			
Kandh	Y	X	X		X	X	X	X	X	X	X	X	X		X		S			
Bhuyān	Y	X	X		X	X	X	X	X	X	X	X	X		X		S			
Māḷi	Y	X	X		X	X	X	X	X	X	X	X	X		X					
Keunṭ	Y	X	X		X	X	X	X	X	X	X	X	X		X		S			
Kisān	X				X	X	X	X	X	X	X	X					S			
Muṇḍā					X	X	X	X	X	X	X	X					S			
Luhurā					X	X	X	X	X	X	X	X					S			
Khaḍiā					X	X	X	X	X		X						S			
Orām					X	X	X	X	X		X						S			
Tūrī					X	X	X	X	X		X						S			
Malār					X	X	X	X	X		X						S			
Harijan					X	X	X	X												
Chamār					X	X	X	X												

[1] Some Gaṇḍ argued that in case of a *kām ghar chāul* is acceptable from any community, but it is returned immediately if given by 'Untouchables' (often with extra coins). In case the Khaḍiā, Orām, Tūrī or Malār give *chāul* on such an occasion—although usually the prefer to give money—it is accepted, but not eaten by married household members.

Caste KANDH	Water accepted from				*Dhān* accepted from				*Chāul* accepted from				*Bhāt*[1] accepted from				Alcohol accepted from			
	U ♂	M ♂	U ♀	M ♀	U ♂	M ♂	U ♀	M ♀	U ♂	M ♂	U ♀	M ♀	U ♂	M ♂	U ♀	M ♀	U ♂	M ♂	U ♀	M ♀
Brahmin	X	X	X	X	X	X	X	X	X	X	X	X	X	X	X	X				
Gauḍ	X	X	X	X	X	X	X	X	X	X	X	X	X	X	X		X	X		
Aghriā	X	X	X	X	X	X	X	X	X	X	X	X	X	X	X					
Chaṣā	X	X	X	X	X	X	X	X	X	X	X	X	X	X	X					
Gaṇḍ	X	X	X	X	X	X	X	X	X	X	X	X	X	X	X		X	X		
Kandh	X	X	X	X	X	X	X	X	X	X	X	X	X	X	X		X	X		
Bhuyān	X	X	X	X	X	X	X	X	X	X	X	X	X	X	X		X	X		
Māḷi	X	X	X	X	X	X	X	X	X	X	X	X	X	X	X					
Keunṭ	X	X	X	X	X	X	X	X	X	X	X	X	X	X	X		X			
Kisān					X	X	X	X	O	O	O	O	D				X			
Muṇḍā					X	X	X	X	O	O	O	O	D				X			
Ḻuhurā					X	X	X	X	O	O	O	O					X			
Khaḍiā					X	X	X	X	O	O	O	O								
Orām					X	X	X	X	O	O	O	O								
Tūrī					X	X	X	X	O	O	O	O								
Malār					X	X	X	X	O	O	O	O								
Harijan					X	X	X	X	O	O	O	O								
Chamār					X	X	X	X	O	O	O	O								

[1] Boiled food is also acceptable from Gosain.

Caste BHUYĀN	Water accepted from				*Dhān* accepted from				*Chāul* accepted from				*Bhāt*[1] accepted from				Alcohol accepted from			
	U ♂	M ♂	U ♀	M ♀	U ♂	M ♂	U ♀	M ♀	U ♂	M ♂	U ♀	M ♀	U ♂	M ♂	U ♀	M ♀	U ♂	M ♂	U ♀	M ♀
Brahmin	X	X	X	X	X	X	X	X	X	X	X	X	Y	X	X	X				
Gauḍ	X	X	X	X	X	X	X	X	X	X	X	X	Y	X	X	X				
Aghriā	X	D	X	D	X	X	X	X	X	X	X	X	X		X					
Chaṣā	X	D	X	D	X	X	X	X	X	X	X	X	Y		X					
Gaṇḍ	X	D	X	D	X	X	X	X	X	X	X	X	Y		X					
Kandh	X	D	X	D	X	X	X	X	X	X	X	X	Y		X					
Bhuyān	X	X	X	X	X	X	X	X	X	X	X	X	X		X					
Māḷi	X	D	X	D	X	X	X	X	X	X	X	X	X		X					
Keunṭ	X	D	X	D	X	X	X	X	X	X	X	X	X		X					
Kisān					X	X	X	X	O	O	O	O								
Muṇḍā					X	X	X	X	O	O	O	O								
Luhurā					X	X	X	X	O	O	O	O								
Khaḍiā					X	X	X	X	O	O	O	O								
Orām					X	X	X	X	O	O	O	O								
Tūrī					X	X	X	X	O	O	O	O								
Malār					X	X	X	X	O	O	O	O								
Harijan									O	O	O	O								
Chamār									O	O	O	O								

Additionally *bāt* is acceptable from the Gosain.

Caste

MĀḶI	Water[1] accepted from				*Dhān* accepted from				*Chāul* accepted from				*Bhāt* accepted from				Alcohol accepted from			
	U ♂	M ♂	U ♀	M ♀	U ♂	M ♂	U ♀	M ♀	U ♂	M ♂	U ♀	M ♀	U[2] ♂	M ♂	U ♀	M ♀	U ♂	M ♂	U ♀	M ♀
Brahmin	Y	Y	Y	Y	X	X	X	X	Y	X	Y	X	X	X	X	X				
Gauḍ	Y	Y	Y	Y	X	X	X	X	Y	X	Y	X	X	S	S					
Aghriā	X	X	X	X	X	X	X	X	Y	X	Y	X	X	S	S					
Chaṣā	X	X	X	X	X	X	X	X	Y	X	Y	X	X	S	S					
Gaṇḍ	X	X	X	X	X	X	X	X	Y	X	Y	X	X	S	S					
Kandh	X	X	X	X	X	X	X	X	Y	X	Y	X	X	S	S					
Bhuyān	X	X	X	X	X	X	X	X	Y	X	Y	X	X	S	S					
Māḷi	X	X	X	X	X	X	X	X	Y	X	Y	X	X	S	S					
Keunṭ	X	X	X	X	X	X	X	X	Y	X	Y	X	X	S	S					
Kisān	D				X	X	X	X	X	X	X	X	D							
Muṇḍā	D				X	X	X	X	X	X	X	X	D							
Luhurā	D				X	X	X	X	X	X	X	X	D							
Khaḍiā	D				X	X	X	X	X	X	X	X	D							
Orām	D				X	X	X	X	X	X	X	X	D							
Tūrī	D				X	X	X	X	X	X	X	X	D							
Malār	D				X	X	X	X	X	X	X	X	D							
Harijan					X[3]	X	X	X												
Chamār					X[4]	X	X	X												

[1] Additionally water might be accepted from Teli, Gosain or Maradi (a trader caste).

[2] Most people maintain that it is acceptable for boys below sixteen.

[3] Some Māḷi argued that they do not like to take it. They further said, in such a case they would not store it inside the house and would not eat it, but sell it. However, other Māḷi also said, that they can eat it.

[4] See Harijan.

Caste KEUNṬ	Water accepted from				*Dhān* accepted from				*Chāul*[1] accepted from				*Bhāt* accepted from				Alcohol accepted from			
	U ♂	M ♂	U ♀	M ♀	U ♂	M ♂	U ♀	M ♀	U ♂	M ♂	U ♀	M ♀	U ♂	M ♂	U ♀	M ♀	U ♂	M ♂	U ♀	M ♀
Brahmin	X	X	X	X	X	X	X	X	X	X	X	X	X	X	X	X				
Gauḍ	X	X	X	X	X	X	X	X	X	X	X	X	D	S	S	S	S	S	S	S
Aghriā	X	X	X	X	X	X	X	X	X	X	X	X	D	S	S	S				
Chaṣā	X	X	X	X	X	X	X	X	X	X	X	X	D	S	S	S				
Gaṇḍ	X	X	X	X	X	X	X	X	X	X	X	X	D	S	S	S	S	S	S	S
Kandh	X	X	X	X	X	X	X	X	X	X	X	X	D	S	S	S	S	S	S	S
Bhuyān	X	X	X	X	X	X	X	X	X	X	X	X	D	S	S	S	S	S	S	S
Māḷi	X	X	X	X	X	X	X	X	X	X	X	X	D	S	S	S	S	S	S	S
Keunṭ	X	X	X	X	X	X	X	X	X	X	X	X	X	X	X	X	X	X	X	X
Kisān	S	S			X	X	X	X	O	O	O	O								
Muṇḍā					X	X	X	X	O	O	O	O								
Luhurā					X	X	X	X	O	O	O	O								
Khaḍiā					X	X	X	X	O	O	O	O								
Orām					X	X	X	X	O	O	O	O								
Tūrī					X	X	X	X	O	O	O	O								
Malār					X	X	X	X	O	O	O	O								
Harijan					X	X	X	X												
Chamār					X	X	X	X												

[1] Accepted from the lower castes only if produced by a Gauḍ.

Caste

KISĀN	Water accepted from				*Dhān* accepted from				*Chāul*[1] accepted from				*Bhāt* accepted from				Alcohol accepted from			
	U ♂	M ♂	U ♀	M ♀	U ♂	M ♂	U ♀	M ♀	U ♂	M ♂	U ♀	M ♀	U ♂	M ♂	U ♀	M ♀	U ♂	M ♂	U ♀	M ♀
Brahmin	X	X	X	X	X	X	X	X	X	X	X	X	X	X	X	D				
Gauḍ	X	D	X	D	X	X	X	X	X	X	X	X	X	X	X	D	X		X	
Aghriā	X	D	X	D	X	X	X	X	X	X	X	X	X	S	X					
Chaṣā	X	D	X	D	X	X	X	X	X	X	X	X	X	S	X					
Gaṇḍ	X	D	X	D	X	X	X	X	X	X	X	X	X	S	X		X		X	
Kandh	X	D	X	D	X	X	X	X	X	X	X	X	X	S	X		X		X	
Bhuyān	X	D	X	D	X	X	X	X	X	X	X	X	X	S	X		X		X	
Māḷi	X	D	X	D	X	X	X	X	X	X	X	X	X	S	X					
Keunṭ	X	D	X	D	X	X	X	X	X	X	X	X	X	S	X		X		X	
Kisān	X	X	X	X	X	X	X	X	X	X	X	X	X	X	X	X	X	X	X	X
Muṇḍā	X		X		X	X	X	X	O	O	O	O	D		D					
Luhurā[2]	D		D		X	X	X	X	O	O	O	O	D		D					
Khaḍiā	D		D		X	X	X	X	O	O	O	O	D		D					
Orām	D		D		X	X	X	X	O	O	O	O	D		D					
Tūrī	D		D		X	X	X	X	O	O	O	O	D		D					
Malār	D		D		X	X	X	X	O	O	O	O	D		D					
Harijan	D		D		X	X	X	X	O	O	O	O								
Chamār	D		D		X	X	X	X	O	O	O	O								

[1] Accepted if produced by a Gauḍ outside the houses of the communities. However, not eaten, but returned on other occasions or given to beggars.

[2] In former times water of the Luhurā was not acceptable, but nowadays it is without problems.

Caste MUṆḌĀ	Water accepted from				*Dhān* accepted from				*Chāul*[1] accepted from				*Bhāt* accepted from				Alcohol accepted from			
	U ♂	M ♂	U ♀	M ♀	U ♂	M ♂	U ♀	M ♀	U ♂	M ♂	U ♀	M ♀	U ♂	M ♂	U ♀	M ♀	U ♂	M ♂	U ♀	M ♀
Brahmin	X	X	X	X	X	X	X	X	X	X	X	X	X	X	X	X				
Gauḍ	X	X	X	X	X	X	X	X	X	X	X	X	X	X	X	X	X	X	X	S
Aghriā	X	X	X	X	X	X	X	X	X	X	X	X	X	X	X	X				
Chaṣā	X	X	X	X	X	X	X	X	X	X	X	X	X	X	X	X				
Gaṇḍ	X	X	X	X	X	X	X	X	X	X	X	X	X	X	X	X	X	X	X	S
Kandh	X	X	X	X	X	X	X	X	X	X	X	X	X	X	X	X	X	X	X	S
Bhuyān	X	X	X	X	X	X	X	X	X	X	X	X	X	X	X	X	X	X	X	S
Māḷi	X	X	X	X	X	X	X	X	X	X	X	X	X	X	X	X				
Keunṭ	X	X	X	X	X	X	X	X	X	X	X	X	X	X	X	X				
Kisān	X	X	X	X	X	X	X	X	X	X	X	X	X	X	X		X	X	X	S
Muṇḍā	X	X	X	X	X	X	X	X	X	X	X	X	X	X	X	X	X	X	X	X
Luhurā	D	D			X	X	X	X	O	O	O	O	S		S					
Khaḍiā	D	D			X	X	X	X	O	O	O	O					X		X	
Orām	D	D			X	X	X	X	O	O	O	O					X		X	
Tūrī	D	D			X	X	X	X	O	O	O	O					X		X	
Malār	D	D			X	X	X	X	O	O	O	O								
Harijan					X	X	X	X	O	O	O	O								
Chamār					X	X	X	X	O	O	O	O								

[1] Accepted from lower communities if produced by a Gauḍ. However, some Muṇḍā also argued that some Harijans give it to Kisāns for preboiling/grinding, which is acceptable too. If not produced by these communities, it would be accepted, but sold and not eaten.

Caste	Water accepted from				*Dhān* accepted from				*Chāul*[1] accepted from				*Bhāt* accepted from				Alcohol accepted from			
LUHURĀ	U	M	U	M	U	M	U	M	U	M	U	M	U	M	U	M	U	M	U	M
	♂	♂	♀	♀	♂	♂	♀	♀	♂	♂	♀	♀	♂	♂	♀	♀	♂	♂	♀	♀
Brahmin	X	X	X	X	X	X	X	X	X	X	X	X	X	X	X	X				
Gauḍ	X	X	X	X	X	X	X	X	X	X	X	X	X	X	X	X	X	X	X	X
Aghriā	X	X	X	X	X	X	X	X	X	X	X	X	X	X	X	X				
Chaṣā	X	X	X	X	X	X	X	X	X	X	X	X	X	X	X	X				
Gaṇḍ	X	X	X	X	X	X	X	X	X	X	X	X	X	X	X	X	X	X	X	X
Kandh	X	X	X	X	X	X	X	X	X	X	X	X	X	X	X	X	X	X	X	X
Bhuyān	X	X	X	X	X	X	X	X	X	X	X	X	X	X	X	X	X	X	X	X
Māḷi	X	X	X	X	X	X	X	X	X	X	X	X	X	X	X	X				
Keunṭ	X	X	X	X	X	X	X	X	X	X	X	X	X	X	X	X	X	X	X	X
Kisān					X	X	X	X	X	X	X	X	S				S	S	S	S
Muṇḍā					X	X	X	X	X	X	X	X								
Luhurā	X	X	X	X	X	X	X	X	X	X	X	X	X	X	X	X				
Khaḍiā					X	X	X	X	O	O	O	O								
Orām					X	X	X	X	O	O	O	O								
Tūrī					X	X	X	X	O	O	O	O								
Malār					X	X	X	X	O	O	O	O								
Harijan					X	X	X	X												
Chamār					X	X	X	X												

[1] *Chāul* from the Khaḍiā, Orām, Tūrī or Malār is acceptable if produced by Gauḍ.

Caste

KHAḌIĀ	Water accepted from				*Dhān* accepted from				*Chāul* accepted from				*Bhāt*[1] accepted from				Alcohol[2] accepted from			
	U ♂	M ♂	U ♀	M ♀	U ♂	M ♂	U ♀	M ♀	U ♂	M ♂	U ♀	M ♀	U ♂	M ♂	U ♀	M ♀	U ♂	M ♂	U ♀	M ♀
Brahmin	X	X	X	X	X	X	X	X	X	X	X	X	X	X	X	X				
Gauḍ	X	X	X	X	X	X	X	X	X	X	X	X	X	X	X	X	X	X	X	X
Aghriā	X	X	X	X	X	X	X	X	X	X	X	X	X	X	X	X				
Chaṣā	X	X	X	X	X	X	X	X	X	X	X	X	X	X	X	X				
Gaṇḍ	X	X	X	X	X	X	X	X	X	X	X	X	X	X	X	X	X	X	X	X
Kandh	X	X	X	X	X	X	X	X	X	X	X	X	X	X	X	X	X	X	X	X
Bhuyān	X	X	X	X	X	X	X	X	X	X	X	X	X	X	X	X	X	X	X	X
Māḷi	X	X	X	X	X	X	X	X	X	X	X	X	X	X	X	X				
Keunṭ	X	X	X	X	X	X	X	X	X	X	X	X	X	X	X	X	X	X	X	X
Kisān	X	X	X	X	X	X	X	X	X	X	X	X	X	X	X	X	X	X	X	X
Muṇḍā	X	X	X	X	X	X	X	X	X	X	X	X	X	X	X	X	X	X	X	X
Luhurā[2]					X	X	X	X	D	D	D	D								
Khaḍiā	X	X	X	X	X	X	X	X	X	X	X	X	X	X	X	X	X	X	X	X
Orām[3]	X	X	X	X	X	X	X	X	X	X	X	X	X	X	X	X	X	X	X	X
Tūrī	D	D	D	D	X	X	X	X	D	D	D	D	D	D	D	D				
Malār					X	X	X	X	D	D	D	D								
Harijan					X	X	X	X	D	D	D	D								
Chamār					X	X	X	X	D	D	D	D								

[1] In former times not accepted from any other community.

[2] Luhurā are regarded by some Khaḍiā as similar to the Ghansiā.

[3] In former times alcohol was not accepted from the Orām because it was suspected that they eat beef occasionally.

Caste

ORĀM	Water accepted from				*Dhān* accepted from				*Chāul* accepted from				*Bhāt* accepted from				Alcohol accepted from			
	U ♂	M ♂	U ♀	M ♀	U ♂	M ♂	U ♀	M ♀	U ♂	M ♂	U ♀	M ♀	U ♂	M ♂	U ♀	M ♀	U ♂	M ♂	U ♀	M ♀
Brahmin	X	X	X	X	X	X	X	X	X	X	X	X	X	X	X	X				
Gauḍ	X	X	X	X	X	X	X	X	X	X	X	X	X	X	X	X	X	X	X	X
Aghriā	X	X	X	X	X	X	X	X	X	X	X	X	X	X	X	X				
Chaṣā	X	X	X	X	X	X	X	X	X	X	X	X	X	X	X	X				
Gaṇḍ	X	X	X	X	X	X	X	X	X	X	X	X	X	X	X	X	X	X	X	X
Kandh	X	X	X	X	X	X	X	X	X	X	X	X	X	X	X	X	X	X	X	X
Bhuyān	X	X	X	X	X	X	X	X	X	X	X	X	X	X	X	X	X	X	X	X
Māḷi	X	X	X	X	X	X	X	X	X	X	X	X	X	X	X	X	X	X	X	X
Keunṭ	X	X	X	X	X	X	X	X	X	X	X	X	X	X	X	X	X	X	X	X
Kisān	X	X	X	X	X	X	X	X	X	X	X	X	X	X	X	X	X	X	X	X
Muṇḍā	X	X	X	X	X	X	X	X	X	X	X	X	X	X	X	X	X	X	X	X
Luhurā					X	X	X	X	X	X	X	X					X[1]	X	X	X
Khaḍiā	X	X	X	X	X	X	X	X	X	X	X	X	X	X	X	X	X	X	X	X
Orām	X	X	X	X	X	X	X	X	X	X	X	X	X	X	X	X	X	X	X	X
Tūrī					X	X	X	X	X				D		D[2]		D			
Malār					X	X	X	X	X				D		D		D			
Harijan					X	X	X	X												
Chamār					X	X	X	X												

[1] Not in former times from the Luhurā.

[2] From Tūrī and Malār only before puberty.

Caste

TURĪ	Water[1] accepted from				*Dhān* accepted from				*Chāul* accepted from				*Bhāt* accepted from				Alcohol accepted from			
	U	M	U	M	U	M	U	M	U	M	U	M	U	M	U	M[2]	U	M	U	M
	♂	♂	♀	♀	♂	♂	♀	♀	♂	♂	♀	♀	♂	♂	♀	♀	♂	♂	♀	♀
Brahmin	X	X	X	X	X	X	X	X	X	X	X	X	X	X	X	X				
Gauḍ	X	X	X	X	X	X	X	X	X	X	X	X	X	X	X	X	X		X	
Aghriā	X	X	X	X	X	X	X	X	X	X	X	X	X	X	X	X				
Chaṣā	X	X	X	X	X	X	X	X	X	X	X	X	X	X	X	X				
Gaṇḍ	X	X	X	X	X	X	X	X	X	X	X	X	X	X	X	X	X		X	
Kandh	X	X	X	X	X	X	X	X	X	X	X	X	X	X	X	X	X		X	
Bhuyān	X	X	X	X	X	X	X	X	X	X	X	X	X	X	X	X	X		X	
Māḷi	X	X	X	X	X	X	X	X	X	X	X	X	X	X	X	X	X		X	
Keunṭ	X	X	X	X	X	X	X	X	X	X	X	X	X	X	X	X	X		X	
Kisān	D	D	D	D	X	X	X	X	X	X	X	X	D	D	D		D	S	D	
Muṇḍā	D	D	D	D	X	X	X	X	O	O	O	O	D	D	D		D	S	D	
Luhurā	D	D	D	D	X	X	X	X	O	O	O	O	D	D	D		D		D	
Khaḍiā	D		D		X	X	X	X	O	O	O	O	D		D		D		D	
Orām	D		D		X	X	X	X	O	O	O	O	D		D		D		D	
Tūrī	X	X	X	X	X	X	X	X	O	O	O	O	X	X	X	X	X		X	
Malār	D		D		X	X	X	X	O	O	O	O	D		D		D		D	
Harijan	D		D		X	X	X	X	O	O	O	O	D		D		D		D	
Chamār	D		D		X	X	X	X	O	O	O	O	D		D		D		D	

[1] Some Tūrī argued that in former times no water at all was acceptable.
[2] Married women should accept it only in a case of emergency.

Caste

MALĀR	Water accepted from				*Dhān* accepted from				*Chāul* accepted from				*Bhāt* accepted from				Alcohol accepted from			
	U ♂	M ♂	U ♀	M ♀	U ♂	M ♂	U ♀	M ♀	U ♂	M ♂	U ♀	M ♀	U ♂	M ♂	U ♀	M ♀	U ♂	M ♂	U ♀	M ♀
Brahmin	X	X	X	X	X	X	X	X	X	X	X	X	X	X	X	X				
Gauḍ	X	X	X	X	X	X	X	X	X	X	X	X	X	X	X	X	X	X	X	X
Aghriā	X	X	X	X	X	X	X	X	X	X	X	X	X	X	X	X				
Chaṣā	X	X	X	X	X	X	X	X	X	X	X	X	X	X	X	X				
Gaṇḍ	X	X	X	X	X	X	X	X	X	X	X	X	X	X	X	X	X	X	X	X
Kandh	X	X	X	X	X	X	X	X	X	X	X	X	X	X	X	X	X	X	X	X
Bhuyān	X	X	X	X	X	X	X	X	X	X	X	X	X	X	X	X	X	X	X	X
Māḷi	X	X	X	X	X	X	X	X	X	X	X	X	X	X	X	X				
Keunṭ	X	X	X	X	X	X	X	X	X	X	X	X	X	X	X	X	X	X	X	X
Kisān	X[1]	D	D	D	X	X	X	X	X	X	X	X	D	D	D	D	X	X	X	X
Muṇḍā	X	D	D	D	X	X	X	X	X	X	X	X					X	D	D	D
Luhurā	X	D	D	D	X	X	X	X	X	X	X	X								
Khaḍiā	X		D		X	X	X	X	O	O	O	O								
Orām					X	X	X	X	O	O	O	O								
Tūrī	D		D		X	X	X	X	O	O	O	O								
Malār	X	X	X	X	X	X	X	X	X	X	X	X	X	X	X	X	X	X	X	X
Harijan					X	X	X	X	O	O	O	O								
Chamār					X	X	X	X	O	O	O	O								

[1] Some argued, it was not acceptable in former times and is still not acceptable for ritual purposes.

Caste

HARIJAN	Water[1] accepted from				*Dhān* accepted from				*Chāul* accepted from				*Bhāt*[2] accepted from				Alcohol[3] accepted from			
	U ♂	M ♂	U ♀	M ♀	U ♂	M ♂	U ♀	M ♀	U ♂	M ♂	U ♀	M ♀	U ♂	M ♂	U ♀	M ♀	U ♂	M ♂	U ♀	M ♀
Brahmin	X	X	X	X	X	X	X	X	X	X	X	X	X	X	X	X				
Gauḍ	X	X	X	X	X	X	X	X	X	X	X	X	X	X	X		X	X		
Aghriā	X	X	X	X	X	X	X	X	X	X	X	X	X	X	X					
Chaṣā	X	X	X	X	X	X	X	X	X	X	X	X	X	X	X					
Gaṇḍ	X	X	X	X	X	X	X	X	X	X	X	X	X	X	X		X	X		
Kandh	X	X	X	X	X	X	X	X	X	X	X	X	X	X	X		X	X		
Bhuyān	X	X	X	X	X	X	X	X	X	X	X	X	X	X	X		X	X		
Māḷi	X	X	X	X	X	X	X	X	X	X	X	X	X	X	X					
Keunṭ	X	X	X	X	X	X	X	X	X	X	X	X	X	X	X		X	X		
Kisān					X	X	X	X	O	O	O	O					S	S		
Muṇḍā					X	X	X	X	O	O	O	O					S	S		
Luhurā					X	X	X	X	O	O	O	O								
Khaḍiā					X	X	X	X	O	O	O	O								
Orām					X	X	X	X	O	O	O	O								
Tūrī					X	X	X	X	O	O	O	O								
Malār					X	X	X	X	O	O	O	O								
Harijan					X	X	X	X	X	X	X	X								
Chamār					X	X	X	X												

[1] Only children may accept the water.

[2] See n. 1.

[3] Any alcohol produced by Gauḍ is acceptable.

Caste

CHAMĀR	Water[1] accepted from				*Dhān* accepted from				*Chāul*[2] accepted from				*Bhāt* accepted from				Alcohol accepted from			
	U ♂	M ♂	U ♀	M ♀	U ♂	M ♂	U ♀	M ♀	U ♂	M ♂	U ♀	M ♀	U ♂	M ♂	U ♀	M ♀	U ♂	M ♂	U ♀	M ♀
Brahmin	X	X	X	X	X	X	X	X	X	X	X	X	X	X	X	X				
Gauḍ	X	X	X	X	X	X	X	X	X	X	X	X	X	X	X	X	D	D	D	D
Aghriā	X	X	X	X	X	X	X	X	X	X	X	X	X	X	X	X				
Chaṣā	X	X	X	X	X	X	X	X	X	X	X	X	X	X	X	X				
Gaṇḍ	X	X	X	X	X	X	X	X	X	X	X	X	X	X	X	X	D	D	D	D
Kandh	X	X	X	X	X	X	X	X	X	X	X	X	X	X	X	X	D	D	D	D
Bhuyān	X	X	X	X	X	X	X	X	X	X	X	X	X	X	X	X	D	D	D	D
Māḷi	X	X	X	X	X	X	X	X	X	X	X	X	X	X	X	X				
Keunṭ	X	X	X	X	X	X	X	X	X	X	X	X	X	X	X	X	D	D	D	D
Kisān	X	X	D		X	X	X	X	X	X	X	X					D	D	D	D
Muṇḍā	X	X			X	X	X	X	X	X	X	X					D	D	D	D
Luhurā	X	X			X	X	X	X	X	X	X	X								
Khaḍiā					X	X	X	X	X	X	X	X								
Orām					X	X	X	X	X	X	X	X								
Tūrī					X	X	X	X	X	X	X	X								
Malār					X	X	X	X	X	X	X	X								
Harijan					X	X	X	X	O	O	O	O								
Chamār	X	X	X	X	X	X	X	X	X	X	X	X	X	X	X	X				

[1] Water is not accepted from the barber, washerman or *khajuriā* (palm-wine seller).

[2] *Chāul* is accepted from the Harijan only if produced by a *bal lok* community or by a Kisān or Muṇḍā.

APPENDIX 5

Kinship Terminologies in a Converging Tribal and Caste Society

In Chapter 5 the kinship terminology of the Aghriā has been presented. In order to get a better idea about variations—structural as well as lexical—within a converging tribal and caste society other terminologies have been collected for comparison. These terminologies are obviously not as inclusive as the Aghriā terminology for which a permanent stay in a community and a constant process of cross-checking data is certainly required. However, these additional terminologies may also demonstrate the high degree of common features within this societies—for example as far as the principle of alternation is concerned. Apart from lexical differences a difference in semantic distinction is striking: the merging of FZH and MB in a common category among the Gaṇḍ and Orām, is absent among the Aghriā.

Orām Terminology

Terms of reference	Relation	Terms of address
Generation +3		
baḍu	all men	*bāḍā*
bāḍi	all women	*bāḍi*
Generation +2		
ājā	FF, MF	*ājā*
āji	FM, MM	*āji, iyāyā*
Generation +1		
ābā	F	*ābā*
āya	M	*āya*
bāḍā/babā	FeB	*bāḍā, babā*

baḍu	FeB, MeZH, (MZHB)e>F	*baḍu*
bāḍi	MeZ, FeBW, (FBWZ)e>M	*bāḍi*
kakā	FyB, (MZHB)y<F	*kākā*
kāki	FyBW, (FBWZ)y<M	*kāki, mi*
phuphu	FZ, MeZHZ, MBWZ	*phuphu*
māmo	MB, FZH, FBWB, MBWB	*māmo*
māmi	MBW	*māmi*
mausi	MyZ, MyZHZ	*mausi*
mausā/masā/musā	MyZH	*mausā*
sasur	HF, WF, BWF, ZHF	*ābā*
sais	HM, WM, BWM, ZHM	*sāis-āyo*
sāmdho	SWF, DHF	*sāmdho*
samdhi	SWM, DHM	*samdhi*
Generation 0		
dādā	eB, WeZH, HeZH, (MBS)e, etc.	*dādā*
bhāi	yB, HyZH, (MBS)y, etc.	*bābu*, by name
didi	eZ, HeBW	*didi*
bāhin	yZ, HyBW	*nani*, by name
bhāuji	eBW	*bhāuji*
bhaibohu/bhaiputo	yBW	*bhaibohu/bhaiputo*
yāār	BWB, ZHB	*yāār*
goyā/goi	BWZ, ZHZ	*goi*
bātu	eZH	*bātu*
dāmād (bāhin-dāmād)	yZH	*dāmād*, by name, *juen*
jāni	W	by village, 'our' ChM
dulhā	H	*gharlok*
deḍsais	WeZ, HeZ	*didi*
sāri	WyZ	*sāri*, by name
sāḍhu	WyZH	*sāḍhu*
baḍsārā	WeB	*dādā*
sārā	WyB	*sārā*
nānād	HyZ	*nānād*, by name
nānādsia	HZH	*dādā* (HZHe), *bhāi* (HZHy)
deḍsasur/bhāisur	HeB	*dādā*
debār	HyB	by name
deoren	HyBW	*bāhin*, by name
Generation -1		
bābu/betā	S	*betā, bābu*, by name
beti	D	*beti, nani*, by name
puto	SW	by name, *beti*
dāmād (beti-dāmād)	DH	by name
bhāgni	SWZ, DHZ, HZD, WBD, ZD (ms), BD (f.s.)	*bhāgni*, by name
bhegnā (bhānjā)	SWB, DHB, HZS, WBS, ZS (ms), BS (f.s.)	*bhegnā*, by name

bāḍā (baḍu-beta)	WyZS, HyBS, yZS (fs), yBS (ms)	*bāḍā*, by name
baḍi (baḍi-beti)	WyZD, HyBD, yZD (fs), yBD (ms)	*bāḍi*, by name, *baḍamā*
musā (musā-betā)	WeZS, eZS (fs)	*musā*, by name
musi (musi-beti)	WeZD, eZD (fs)	*musi*, by name
bhāijtā-betā	eBS (ms), HeBS	*betā*, by name
bhājtin-beti	eBD (ms), HeBD	*beti*, by name
Generation -2		
nāti	SS, DS	by name, *bhāi*
nātin	SD, DD	by name, *bahin*
Generation -3		
baḍu	all men	*bāḍu*, by name
baḍi	all women	*bāḍi*, by name

Ganḍ Terminology

Terms of reference	Relation	Terms of address	F/Inf address
Generation +4			
ajā	all men	*dadā, ajā*	a
āi	all women	*āi, āimā, bāi*	a
Generation +3			
baḍu	all men	*babā, baḍabāpā*	a
baḍi	all women	*baḍamā, baḍkāmā*	a
Generation +2			
ajā	FF, MF	*dadā, ajā*	a
āi	FM, MM	*āi, āima, bāi*	a
Generation +1			
bāpā	F	*bāpā, buā, bapā*	a
mā	M	*mā*	a
babā	FeB, MeZH	*babā, baḍabāpā*	a
baḍamā, baḍkāmā	MeZ, FeBW, (FZHZ)e>M	*baḍamā, baḍkāmā*	a
kakā	FyB	*kakā, sānbāpā*	a
kāki	FyBW	*kāki, sānmā*	aso
mausi	MyZ, (FZHZ)y<M	*mausi, munomā*	a
mausā	MyZH	*mauṣā*	aso
māmu	MB, FZH, FBWB, MBWB, sangat's/sangi's F	*mamā, māmu*	aso
māi	MBW, sangat's/sangi's M	*māi, nanā*	aso
phuphu, jhi	FZ	*phuphu, jhi*	a
sasur	WF, HF	*bapā*	aso
sas	WM, HM	*mā*	aso

Generation 0			
dadā	eB, WeZH, HeZH, MBSe, etc.	*dadā*	a
bhāi	yB, HyZH, MBSy, etc.	*bhāi, bābu*, by name	a
bāi	eZ, WeBW, MBDe, etc.	*bāi*	a
nani, bahin	yZ, WyBW, HyBW, MBDy, etc.	*nani, bahin*, by name	a
bhenei/bāto	eZH	*bhenei (bāto)*	a/aso
bahinjuien	yZH	by name, *bābu*	aso
bohu	eBW	*bohu*	aso
bhaibohu	yBW	♂: by village; ♀: by name	aso
sangāt	ZHZ, BWZ	*sangāt*	aso
sangi	ZHB, BWB	*sangi*	aso
salā	WyB	by name	a
baḍsala	WeB	*dadā*	aso
deḍsas	WeZ, HeZ	*bāi*	aso
sāli	WyZ	by name	aso
saḍhu	WyZH	*saḍhu*	aso
deḍsasur	HeB	rarely: ChF[1]	aso
diar	HyB	*bābu*	aso
jethen	HeBW	*bāi*	aso
nanand	HyZ	*nani*	aso
samdhi	SWF, DHF	*samdhi*	aso
samdhen	SWM, DHM	*samdhen*	aso
Generation -1			
betā/bābu	S	*betā, bābu*, by name	a
beti/jhi	D	*beti, nani*, by name	a
mausāpu	eZS (fs), WeZS	*mausā, bābu*, by name	a
mausijhi	eZD (fs), WeZD	*mausi, nani*, by name	a
baḍupu/baḍu	yZS (fs), yBS (ms), WyZS, HyBS	*babā, bābu*, by name	a
baḍuji/baḍi	yZD (fs), yBD (ms), WyZD, HyBD	*baḍi, nani*, by name	a
bhanjā	ZS (ms), BS (fs), WBS, HZS, DHB, SWB	*bhanjā*	aso
bhanji	ZD (ms), BD (fs), WBD, HZD, DHZ, SWZ	*bhanji*	aso
putrā	eBS (ms), HeBS	♂: *putrā, bābu*, by name; ♀: *bābu*	♂: a; ♀: aso
jhiāri	eBD (ms), HeBD	♂: *jhiāri, nani*, by name; ♀: *nani*	♂: a; ♀: aso
bhanjibaha	bhanja's W	*bhanji*	aso
baha	SW	by name	a/aso
juien	DH	*bābu*, by name	a/aso

[1] A *deḍsasur* has to be avoided and should not be addressed. However, in urgent cases he might be addressed as father of his children using the specific names of his children.

Generation -2			
nati	SS, DS	*bābu, nati, natiā, bhāi*, by name	a
naten	SD, DD	*nani, naten, bahin,* by name	a
Generation -3			
baḍu (baḍupu)	nati's S, etc.	see *baḍu*	a
baḍi (baḍuji)	nati's D, etc.	see *baḍi*	a
Generation -4			
nati	all men	see *nati*	a
naten	all women	see *naten*	a

Muṇḍā Terminology

Generation +4			
ajā	all men (FFFF, FMFF, etc.)	*ajā, dadā*	a
āi	all women (FMMM, etc.)	*āi, bāi*	a
Generation +3			
babā	all men (FFF, FMF, etc.)	*babā*	a
baḍi	all women (MMM, MFM, etc.)	*baḍi, baḍamā, baḍkāmā*	a
Generation +2			
ajā	all men (FF, MF, etc.)	*ajā, dadā*	a
āi	all women (MM, FM etc.)	*āi, bāi*	a
Generation +1			
buā	F	*buā*	a
mā	M	*mā*	a
babā	FeB, MeZH	*babā*	a
kakā	FyB	*kakā, sānbāpā*	a
baḍkāmā	MeZ, FeBW, (MZHZ)e>M	*baḍi, baḍamā, baḍkāmā*	a
kāki	FyBW	*kāki*	aso
mausi	MyZ, FBWZ, FZHZ, MBWZ, (MZHZ)y>M[2]	*mausi*	a
phuphu, jhi	FZ, MZHZ[3]	*jhi*	a
mausā	MyZH	*mausā*	aso
māmo	MB, FZH, FZHB, MBWB, FBWB	*māmo*	aso
māi	MBW, MBWZ	*māi*	aso
sasur	WF, HF	*buā*	aso
sas	WM, HM	*mā*	aso

[2] There is no agreement.

[3] Ibid.

Generation 0			
dadā	eB, (FBS)e, (MBS)e, (FZS)e, (MZS)e	*dadā*	a
majla bābu, majla bhāi	mB		a
bābu, bhāi	yB, (FBS)y, (MBS)y, (FZS)y, (MZS)y, HyZH, yZHB, HyZH	*bābu*, by name (for HyZH only *bhāi*, no name)	a
bāi	eZ, (FBD)e, (MBD)e, (FZD)e, (MZD)e, (WBW)e	*bāi, nāni*	a
majla bāi, majla bahin	mZ		a
chot bāi, chot bahin, bahin	yZ, (FBD)y, (MBD)y, (FZD)y, (MZD)y, (WBW)y, yZHZ	*nani*, by name	a
bāto	eZH, eZHB, eZHZH	*bāto*	a
bahinjuien	yZH, yZHB, yZHZH	*bābu*, by name	aso
sangat	eZHZ, BWZ	*sangāt*	aso
sangi	eZHB, BWB	*sangi*	aso
bohu	eBW	*bohu*	aso
bhāibohu	yBW	[4]	aso
bor	H	no term, sounds like 'a'	aso
kania	W	by name, SM, *bābu*'s M	a
deḍsas	HeZ, WeZ	*bāi*	aso
nanand	HyZ	*nani*	aso
deḍsasur	HeB, HeZH	[5]	aso
diār	HyB	*bābu*	aso
jethen	HeBW	*bāi*	aso
derien	HyBW	by name, by village	aso
baḍsalā	WeB	*dadā*	aso
sālā	WyB	*bābu*, by name	a
sāli	WyZ	*nani*, by name	a
saḍhu	WZH	*saḍhu*	aso
samdhi	SWF, DHF	*samdhi*	aso
samdhen	SWM, DHM	*samdhen*	aso
Generation -1			
pu (eS: *baḍa pu*, yS: *sān pu*)	S, ZS (fs)	*buā, pu*	a

[4] The *bhāibohu* should be avoided too and might only be addressed in cases of emergency. In such a case she might be called as 'yBChM'.

[5] Similar like the *bhāibohu* a *deḍsasur* might only be addressed in urgent cases and then only from a distance, e.g. as 'HeBChF'.

jhi (eD: *baḍa jhi*, yD: *sān jhi*)	D, ZD (fs)	*mā, jhi*	a
bhanjā	BS (fs), ZS (ms), WBS, HZS, SWB, DHB	♂: *bhanjā, mamo*, by name; ♀: *bhanjā*	aso - for BS (fs): a
bhanji	BD (fs), ZD (ms), WBD, HZD, SWZ, DHZ	♂: *bhanji*, by name; ♀: *bhanji*	aso - for BD (fs): a
putrāpu, putrā	eBS (ms), HeBS	♂: *putrā, bābu*, by name; ♀: *putrā, bābu* (not by name)	♂: a; ♀: aso
putrājhi, jhiāri	eBD (ms), HeBD	♂: *nani*, by name; ♀: *nani*	♂: a; ♀: aso
baḍupu, babā	yBS (ms), HyBS, WyZS	*baḍupu, babā*, by name	a
baḍi	yBD (ms), WyZD, HyBD	*baḍi*, by name	a
mausijhi	WeZD	*mausi, nani*, by name	aso
mausāpu	WeZS	*mausā, bābu*, by name	aso
bhanjibaha	BSW (fs), ZSW (ms), HZSW	*bhanji*, by name (for HMB, HMBW only *bhanji*, no name)	aso
bhanjājuien	BDH (fs), ZDH (ms), HZDH	*bhanjā*, by name; for ♀: only *bhanjā*	aso
juien	DH, ZDH (fs), DHB	*bābu*, by name	a/aso
baha	SW, ZSW (fs), SWZ	by village[6] (not by name)	a
Generation -2			
nāti	all men (SS, DS, WBSS, etc.)	*nāti, bābu, ajā, bhāi*, by name	a
nāten	all women (SD, DD, HZDD etc.)	*nāten, nani, bahin*, by name (not *āi*)	a
Generation -3			
baḍu (*babā*)	all men (SSS, SDS, DDS, etc.)	see *baḍu*	a
baḍi	all women (DDD, SSD, DSD, etc.)	see *baḍi*	a
Generation -4			
nāti, bhāi	all men (SSSS, etc.)	see *nāti*	a
nāten, bahin	all women (DDDD, etc.)	see *nāten*	a

[6] Usually the name of her village of origin is used in a form for women such as *Kuntlāmālian* for a woman from Kuntlāmāl, or *Kondhbondian* for a woman from Kondhobolonda.

Kandh Terminology

Generation +3			
baḍu	all men	*baḍu*	a/aso
baḍi	all women	*baḍi*	a/aso
Generation +2			
ajā/dadā	all men - FF, MF, etc.	*ajā/dadā*	a
ai/bai	all women - FM, MM, etc.	*ai/bai*	a
Generation +1			
bapā/buā	F	*bapā/buā*	a
mā	M	*mā*	a
jhi/phuphu	FZ, MBWZ, MZHZ, FyBWZ, *sangi*'s/ *sangāt*'s M	*jhi*	a
māmo	MB, FZH, *sangi*'s/ *sangāt*'s F	*māmo*	aso
māin	MBW, MBWZ	*māin*	aso
babā/baḍu	FeB, MeZH	*babā, baḍu*	a
baḍi	MeZ, FeBW, (FeBWZ)e>M	*baḍi, baḍkāmā*	a
māusi	MyZ, (FeBWZ)y<M	*mausi, munomā*	a
mausā	MyZH	*mausā*	aso
kakā	FyB	*kakā*	a
kāki	FyBW	*kāki*	aso
samdhi	SWF, DHF	*samdhi*	aso
samdhen	SWM, DHM	*samdhen*	aso
sāsur	HF, WF	*bapā, buā*	aso
sās	HM, WM	*mā*	aso
Generation 0			
dadā	eB, HeZH	*dadā*	a
bhāi/bābu	yB	*bhāi, bābu,* by name	a
bāi	eZ, WeBW	*bāi*	a
nani/bahin	yZ, WyBW	*nani, bahin,* by name	a
kamiān	W	sounds like 'a', by village	a
deḍsās	WeZ, HeZ	*bāi*	aso
sāli	WyZ	*nani*, by name	a
saḍhu	WZH	*saḍhu*	aso
deḍsasur	HeB	no term, 'ChF'	aso
diar	HyB	*bābu*	aso
nānand	HyZ	*nani*	aso
jethen	HeBW	*bāi*	aso
derian	HyBW	by name, *nani*	a
nandia-diar	HyZH	*bābu, bhāi*	a/aso
salā	WyB	by name	a

basalā	WeB	*dadā*	aso
bar/swami	H	sounds like 'a', 'ChF'	aso
bāto	eZH	*bāto*	a
bahinjuien	yZH	*bābu*	aso
bohu	eBW	*bohu*	aso
bhāibohu	yBW	by village	aso
sangāt	ZHZ, BWZ	*sangāt*	aso
sangi	ZHB, BWB	*sangi*	aso
Generation -1			
po (pu)	S	*bābu, buā,* by name	a
jhi	D	*nani, mā,* by name	a
baḍi (baḍijhi)	yBD (ms), yZD (fs), WyZD, HyBD	*nani, jhi,* by name	a
baḍu (baḍupu/ babā)	yBS (ms), yZS (fs), WyZS, HyBS	*bābu, pu,* by name	a
bhanji	ZD (ms), BD (fs), HZD, SWZ, DHZ, WBD	*bhanji, nani,* by name- for BD (fs): *nani*, by name; for HZD: only *bhanji*	for HZD: aso, for BD (fs): a
bhanjā	ZS (ms), BS (fs), HZS, SWB, DHB, WBS	*bhanjā, bābu,* by name - for BS (fs): only *bābu,* by name; for HZS: only *bhanjā*	for HZS: aso; BS (fs): a
putrā	eBS (ms), HeBS	*bābu, buā, betā* (name) - *putrā* for distant relatives - *kāki*: only *bābu, buā*	♀:aso; ♂:a
jhiāri	eBD (ms), HeBD	*nani, mā, beti* (name) - *jhiari* for distant relatives - *kāki*: only *nani, mā*	♀:aso; ♂:a
mausā (mausāpu)	eZS (fs), WeZS	*bābu*, by name	a
mausi (mausājhi)	eZD (fs), WeZD	*nani*, by name	a
baha	SW	by name (not *nani*)	a
juen	DH	*bābu*, by name	a
bhanjājuen	ZDH (ms), HZDH	*bhanjā*	aso
bhanjibaha	ZSW (ms), HZSW	*bhanji*	aso
Generation -2			
nāti	SS, DS, etc.	*nāti, bhāi, bābu,* by name	a
nāten	SD, DD, etc.	*nāten, bahin, nani,* by name	a
Generation -3			
baḍu/baḍi	all men/all women	*baḍu/baḍi*	a

Kisān Terminology

Generation +4			
ājo	all men	*ājo*	a
ājji	all women	*ājji*	a
Generation +3			
bāḍu/baḍu	all men	*bāḍu/baḍu*	a
bāḍi/baḍi	all women	*bāi/baḍi*	a
Generation +2			
ājo	all men	*ājo, dadā*	a
ājji	all women	*ājji, bāi, buḍhi, buḍhimā*	a
Generation +1			
buā/bāng	F	*buāye*	a
māyo/āyāng	M	*māyo*	a
jhi	FZ	*nānāyo, jhi, nānā*	a
māmu	MB, FZH, MZHB, FeBWB, sāngha's/sānghi's F	*māmuye*	aso
nanā	MBW, MBWZ, FZHZ, sāngha's/sānghi's M	*nānā, māiyo*	aso
baḍi	MeZ, FeBW, FyBWeZ	*baḍkāmā*	a
baḍu	FeB, MeZH	*baḍu, babā*	a
mausi	MyZ, FyBWyZ	*mausi, munomā*	a
māsā	MyZH	*māsāyo*	aso
kākā	FyB	*kākā, sānbāpā*	a
kāki	FyBW	*kāki*	aso
sasur	HF, WF	*buāye*	aso
tāchi	HM, WM	*māyo*	aso
Generation 0			
dadā/dādā	eB, HeZH	*dādā*	a
bābu	yB	*bābu*, by name	a
dāi	eZ	*dāi*	a
hāi/bhuni	yZ	*hāi*, by name	a
bheta	eZH	*bheta*	a
bhunijuen	yZH	*bhunijuen* (no name)	aso
sāngha	ZHZ, BWZ	*sāngha*, by name if y<ego	aso
sānghi	BWB, ZHB	*sānghi*, by name, if y<ego	aso
mehatā	H	'ChF'	aso
kāniāt	W	'ChM', by name	a
deḍsasur	HeB	*emekahā*	aso
erkha	HyB, HyZ	*erkha, bābu*, by name (old usage)	aso

deḍsas	HeZ, WeZ	*dāi, bāi*	aso
jādā	HeBW	*dāi, bāi*	aso
deren	HyBW	*hāi*	aso
nandia bhai	HyZH	*dadā*	a
sāhḍi	WyZ	by name	a
nāska	eBW	*nāska,* bohu	aso
bhāibohu	yBW	*hāi,* by name	aso
sāmdi	SWF, DHF, SWFB	*sāmdi*	aso
sāmdho	SWM, DHM	*sāmdho*	aso
Generation -1			
engdās, kukko	S	*bābu,* by name	a
hāi, kukāe	D	*nani,* by name, hāi	a
māsā	eZS (fs)	*māsā,* by name	aso
mausi	eZD (fs)	*mausike,* by name	a
baḍu	yZS (fs), yBS (ms), HyBS	*bāḍu,* by name	a
baḍi	yZD (fs), yBD (ms), HyBD	*bāḍi,* by name	a
bhānājā	BS (fs), ZS (ms), HZS, SWB, DHB	*bhānājā,* by name	aso
bhānāji	BD (fs), ZS (ms), HZD, SWZ, DHZ	*bhānāji,* by name	aso
putrā (putrapoas)	eBS (ms), HeBS	*putrā, bābu,* by name	aso
jhi, jhiāri, jhiārikukai	eBD (ms), HeBD	*jhiāri, hāi, nani,* by name	aso
hea	SW	*heḍa*	aso
jaens	DH	*jaens*	aso
Generation -2			
natti	all	*natti, bābu,* by name	a
Generation -3			
baḍu	all men	see above	a
baḍi	all women	see above	a
Generation -4			
natti	all	see above	a

Khaḍiā Terminology

Generation +4			
ājā	all men	distant: *ājā*; close: *buddhā*	a
yāyā	all women	distant: *yāyā*; close: *buddhi*	a

Generation +3			
bāḍā	all men	*bāḍā*	a
bāḍi	all women	*bāḍi*	a
Generation +2			
ājā	all men	distant: *ājā*; close: *buddhā*	a
yāyā	all women	distant: *yāyā*; close: *buddhi*	a
Generation +1			
ābā	F	*ābā*	a
āya	M	*āya*	a
māmi	FZ, MBW, MZHZ	*māmi*	F-side: a; M-side:aso
māmo	MB, FZH	*māmo*	F-side: a; M-side;aso
bāḍā	FeB, MeZH	*bāḍā*	a
bāḍi	MeZ, FeBW	*bāḍi*	a
masi	MyZ, FyBWZ	*masi*	a
masā	MyZH	*masā*	a
kākā	FyB	*kākā*	a
miij	FyBW	*miij, kāki*	a
sāsur	HF, WF, ZHF, BWF	*abā*	aso
kinkār	HM, WM, ZHM, BWM	*mā, āya*	aso
Generation 0			
dadā	eB, HeZH, MBSe, etc.	*dadā*	a
bhāi/bhaya	yB, HyZH, MBSy, etc.	*bābu*, by name	a
didi	eZ, WeBW, HeBW, MBDe, etc.	*didi*	a
bāhin	yZ, WyBW, HyBW, MBDy, etc.	by name	a
bāathi	eZH	*bāathi*	a
ārām	yZH	*ārām*	aso
eaar	ZHB (ms), BWB (ms)	*eaar*	aso
goi	ZHB (fs), ZHZ, BWZ, BWB (fs)	*goi*	aso
āji	eBW	*āji*	a
kimin	yBW	*kimin, bahariā,* by name	aso
sauḍai	W	*nani's* M, *bābu's* M (not by name)	a
lebunai	H	no term, 'eh', *nani's* F, *bābu's* F	aso
bāutāng	WeB	*dadā*	aso
bāo	HeB	in emergency: *dadā*	aso
baker (salā, sārā)	WyB, HyB	by name	a

aijkār	WeZ, HeZ	*didi*	aso
baksel	WyZ, HyZ	by name	a
sāhu	WZH	*sāḍhu*	aso
samdhi	SWF, DHF	*samdhi*	aso
samdhen (samdhi-dai)	SWM, DHM	*samdhen (samdhi-dai)*	aso
Generation -1			
betā	S	*betā, bābu,* by name	a
beti	D	*beti, nani,* by name	a
kimin	SW, SWZ, DHZ	*kimin, bahariā,* by name	a
ārām	DH, DHB, SWB	*ārām,* by name	a
bhetiā, bhegtā-betā	eBS (ms), HeBS	*bābu,* by name	a
bhāgtin	eBD (ms), HeBD	by name	a
bāḍā (bāḍā-betā)	yBS (ms), yZS (fs), WyZS	*bāḍā (bāḍā-betā)*	a
bāḍi (bāḍi-beti)	yBD (ms), yZD (fs), WyZD	*bāḍi (bāḍi-beti)*	a
bhegnā	ZS (ms), BS (fs), HZS, WBS	*bhegnā,* by name	a
bhāgni	ZD (ms), BD (fs), HZD, WBD	*bhāgni,* by name	a
masā (masā-betā)	eZS (fs), WeZS	*masā (masā-betā)*	a
masi (masi-beti)	eZD (fs), WeZD	*masi (masi-beti)*	a
Generation -2			
nati, bakḍu	all men	*nati, bakḍu, bābu,* by name	a
naten, bakḍu	all women	*naten, bakḍu,* by name	a
Generation -3			
bāḍā	all men	see Gen +3	a
bāḍi	all women	see Gen +3	a
Generation -4			
nati	all men	*nati, bakḍu, bābu,* by name	a
naten	all women	*naten, bakḍu,* by name	a

Bibliography

Ahuja, R., forthcoming, '"Captain Kittoe's road": Early colonialism and the politics of road construction in peripheral Orissa', in: G. Pfeffer, *Centre and Periphery*, Delhi: Manohar.

Allen, N.J., 1986, 'Tetradic Theory: An Approach to Kinship', *Journal of the Anthropological Society of Oxford*, vol. 17, no. 2, pp. 87-109.

———, 2000, *Categories and Classifications: Maussian Reflections on the Social*, New York.

Alvi, A., 1999, 'Bearers of Grief: Death, Women, Gifts, and Kinship in Muslim Punjab', Ph.D. thesis, Free University of Berlin.

Assmann, J., 1999, *Das kulturelle Gedächtnis: Schrift, Erinnerung und politische Identität in frühen Hochkulturen*, München: beck'sche reihe.

Babb, L.A., 1975, *The Divine Hierarchy: Popular Hinduism in Central India*, New York: Columbia University Press.

Bailey, F.G., 1957, *Caste and the Economic Frontier: A Village in Highland Orissa*, Manchester: Manchester University Press.

———, 1959, 'Correspondence "For a Sociology of India?"', *Contributions to Indian Sociology*, vol. III, pp. 88-101.

———, 1960, *Tribe, Caste and Nation*, Manchester: Manchester University Press.

———, 1961, '"Tribe" and "Caste" in India', *Contributions to Indian Sociology*, no. V, Oct., pp. 7-19.

Barnard, A., A. Good, 1984, *Research Practices in the Study of Kinship*, London: Academic Press.

Basu, H., 1994, *Habshi-Sklaven, Sidi-Fakire: Muslimische Heiligenverehrung im westlichen Indien*, Berlin: Das Arabische Buch.

———, 2000, 'Die Göttin und die Chāraṇ. Das Gedächtnis des Königtums, Verwandtschaft und Askese in Kacch (westl. Indien)', unpublished Habilitation, Free University of Berlin.

Béteille, A., 1991, 'The concept of tribe with special reference to India' in: A. Beteille, *Society and Politics in India: Essays in a Comparative Perspective*, London: The Athlone Press.

Bennett, L., 1983, *Dangerous Wives and Sacred Sisters*, New York.

Berger, P., 2000, 'Gesellschaft, Ritual und Ideologie: Eine relationale

Betrachtung der Gadaba des Koraput Distriktes, Orissa', *Mitteilungen der Berliner Gesellschaft für Anthropologie, Ethnologie und Urgeschichte*, Band 21, Berlin.

Berger, P., 2001, 'Feeding the Dead: Rituals of Transformation among the Gadaba of Koraput', *ADIBASI* 40/41, Bhubaneswar: Government of Orissa Press.

———, 2002, 'The Gadaba and the Non-ST Desia of Koraput, Orissa', in: G. Pfeffer and D. Behera, *Contemporary Society: Tribal Studies*, vol. 5 *Concept of Tribal Society*, Delhi: Concept, pp. 57-90.

Berkemer, G., 1993, *Little Kingdoms in Kalinga: Ideologie, Legitimation und Politik Regionaler Eliten*, Stuttgart: Franz Steiner.

Biardeau, M., 1994 [1981], *Hinduism: The Anthropology of a Civilisation*, Delhi: OUP.

Bloch, M. and J.P. Parry, 1982, 'Introduction: death and the regeneration of life', *Death and the Regenration of Life*, Cambridge: Cambridge University Press.

Boas, F., 1911, *The Mind of Primitive Man*, New York: MacMillan.

Bodding, P.O., 1935, *A Santal Dictionary*, vol. III (H-Kh), Oslo.

Bouglé, C., 1997 [1957], 'The Essence and Reality of the Caste System', in: D. Gupta (ed.), *Social Stratification*, Delhi: OUP.

Burke, P., 1993, 'Geschichte als soziales Gedächtnis', in: A. Assmann and D. Harth (eds.), *Mnemosyne: Formen und Funktionen der kulturellen Erinnerung*, Frankfurt/M.: Fischer.

Burridge, K.O.L., 1988 [1968], 'Lévi-Strauss and Myth', in: *The Structural Study of Myth and Totemism*, A.S.A. Monographs 5, ed. E. Leach, London: Tavistock, pp. 91-118.

Cambridge History of India, 1958, vol. III, *Turks and Afghans*, Delhi: S. Chand.

Census of India, 1971, Series 16—*Orissa*, Part IX-A.

Choudhury, N.C., 1977, *Munda Social Structure*, Calcutta: KLM Private.

Cohn, B.S., 1995 [1983], 'Representing Authority in Victorian India', in: E. Hobsbawm and T. Ranger, *The Invention of Tradition*, Cambridge: Canto.

———, 2001 [1959], 'Some Notes on Law and Change in North India' in: ibid., *An Anthropologist among the Historians and other Essays*, Delhi: OUP, pp. 554-74 .

———, 2001 [1962], 'Political Systems in Eighteenth-Century India: The Banares Region', in: *An Anthropologist among the Historians and other Essays*, Delhi: Oxford, pp. 483-499.

Conzelmann, E., 1996, *Heirat, Gabe, Status. Kaste und Gesellschaft in Mandi*, Berlin: Arabisches Buch.

Dalton, G., 1968, 'Economic Theory and Primitive Society', in: E.E. LeClair Jr. and H.K. Scheider (eds.), *Economic Anthropology: Readings in Theory and Analysis*, New York: Holt Rinehart and Winston.

Das, V., 1997 [1982], *Structure and Cognition: Aspects of Hindu Caste and Ritual*, Delhi: OUP.

Demmer, U., 1999, 'How to Make the Spirit of the Dead Happy: The Rhetoric of Words and Deeds in a Jenu Kurumba Death Ritual', in: E. Schömbucher, and C.P. Zoller, *Ways of Dying: Death and its Meanings in South Asia*, New Delhi.

Dey, A., 1997, 'Sickle cell gene: its pattern of distribution and association with natural selection' (unpublished Ph.D. thesis, Sambalpur University), Sambalpur.

Dirks, N.B., 1979, 'The structure and meaning of political relations in a south Indian little kingdom', *Contributions to Indian Sociology* (NS), vol. 13, no. 2, pp. 169-206.

———, 1987, *The Hollow Crown. Ethnohistory of an Indian Kingdom*, Cambridge: University Press.

Doniger, W., 2002, *Splitting the Difference. Gender and Myth in Ancient Greece and India*, Delhi: OUP.

Douglas, M., 1988 [1968], 'The Meaning of Myth. With special reference to 'La Geste d' Asdiwal', in: *The Structural Study of Myth and Totemism*, A.S.A. Monographs 5, ed. E. Leach, London: Tavistock, pp. 49-70.

Dubashi, J., 1992, *The Road to Ayodhya*, Delhi: Voice of India.

Dumont, L., 1983 [1953], 'The Dravidian Kinship Terminology as an Expression of Marriage,' in: idem, *Affinity as a Value,* Delhi: OUP, pp. 3-17.

———, 1957, 'Hierarchy and Marriage Alliance in South Indian Kinship' in: Occasional Papers of the Royal Anthropological Institute of Great Britain and Ireland, no. 12.

———, 2000 [1957], *A South Indian Subcaste: Social Organisation and Religion of the Pramalai Kallar*, Delhi: OUP.

———, 1962, Correspondence '"Tribe" and "Caste" in India', *Contributions to Indian Sociology*, vol. VI, pp.120-2.

———, 1966, 'Marriage in India: The Present State of the Question (III). North India in Relation to South India', *Contributions to Indian Sociology*, 9: pp. 90-114.

———, 1980 [1966], *Homo Hierarchicus: The Caste System and Its Implications*, Chicago: Chicago University Press.

———, 1998 [1966], 'North India in Relation to South India', in: P.P. Uberoi, *Family, Kinship and Marriage in India*, Delhi: OUP.

———, 1983 [1970], 'The Kariera Kinship Vocabulary: An Analysis', in: idem, *Affinity as a Value*, Delhi: OUP.

Dumont, L. and D.F. Pocock, 1957, 'For a Sociology of India', *Contributions to Indian Sociology*, vol.1, pp. 7-22.

———, 1959, Review of Verrier Elwin 'The Religion of an Indian Tribe' *Contributions to Indian Sociology*, vol. III, pp. 60-74.

———, 1960, Correspondence 'For a Sociology of India: A Rejoinder to Dr. Bailey', *Contributions to Indian Sociology*, vol. IV, pp. 82-9.

Durkheim, E., 1977 [1930], *Über die Teilung der sozialen Arbeit*, Frankfurt/ M.: Suhrkamp.

Eggan, F., 1950, *Social Organisation of the Western Pueblos*, Chicago: University of Chicago Press.

Elwin, V., 2000 [1936], *Leaves from the Jungle: Life in a Gond Village*, Delhi: OUP.

———, 1939, *The Baiga*, London: Murray.

———, 1991 [1942], *The Agaria*, Delhi: Vanya Oxford.

———, 1945, 'Funerary customs in Bastar State', *Man in India*, vol. XXV, no. 2.

———, 1998 [1964], *The Tribal World of Verrier Elwin: An Autobiography*, Delhi: OUP.

Eschmann, A., 1994 [1975], 'Sign and Icon: Symbolism in the Indian Folk Religion', in: G.C. Tripathi and H. Kulke, *Religion and Society in Eastern India*, Delhi: Manohar.

———, 1986a, 'Hinduization of Tribal Deities in Orissa: The Śākta and Śaiva Typology', in: A. Eschmann, H. Kulke and G.C. Tṛipathi (eds.), *The Cult of Jagannath and the Regional Tradition of Orissa*, New Delhi: Manohar.

———, 1986b, 'The Vaiṣṇava Typology of Hinduization and the Origin of Jagannātha', in: A. Eschmann, H. Kulke, and G.C. Tripathi (eds.), *The Cult of Jagannath and the Regional Tradition of Orissa*, Delhi: Manohar.

Evans-Pritchard, E.E., 1940, *The Nuer: A Description of the Modes of Livelihood and Political Institutions of a Nilotic People*, Oxford: Clarendon.

Falk, N.E., 1973, 'Wilderness and Kingship in Ancient South Asia', in: *History of Religions*, vol. 13, no. 1, August.

Fortes, M., 1987 [1950], 'Kinship and Marriage among the Ashanti', in: A.R. Radcliffe-Brown and D. Forde (eds.), *African Systems of Kinship and Marriage*, London.

———, 1969a, *Kinship and the Social Order: The Legacy of Lewis Henry Morgan*, London: Routledge.

———, 1969b, *The Web of Kinship among the Tallensi*, London: Oxford University Press.

———, 1970, *Time and Social Structure, And Other Essay*, London: The Athlone Press.

Fried, M., 1968, 'On the Concepts of "Tribe" and "Tribal Society"', in: J. Helm (ed.), *Essays on the Problem of Tribe*, Seattle: Washington University Press.

Fuchs, S., 1960, *The Gond and Bhumia of Eastern Mandla*, London: Asia Publishing House.

Fürer-Haimendorf, C.V., 1979, *The Gonds of Andhra Pradesh: Tradition and Change in an Indian Tribe*, Delhi: Vikas.

Gaenszle, M., 1999, 'The Making of Good Ancestors. Separation, Transformation and Exchange in Mewahang Rai Funerary Rites', in: E. Schömbucher, C.P. Zoller, *Ways of Dying: Death and its Meanings in South Asia*, Delhi: Manohar.

Galey, J.-C., 1990, 'Reconsidering Kingship in India: An Ethnological Perspective', in: ibid. (ed.), *Kingship and the Kings*, Chur: Harwood Academic Publishers.

Gausdal, J., 1960, *The Santal Khuts. Contribution to Animistic Research*, Oslo (Aschehoug).

Gazetteers of India, Orissa (1971/1975), Sundargarh District, ed. N. Senapati and D.C. Kuanr.

Gell, S.M.S., 1992, *The Ghotul in Muria Society*, Chur: Harwood Academic Publishers.

Gellner, E., 1993 [1988], *Pflug, Schwert und Buch. Grundlinien der Menschheitsgeschichte*, München: dtv.

Ghurye, G.S., 1963, *The Scheduled Tribes*, Bombay: Popular Prakashan.

Godelier, M., 1977, 'The concept of the 'Tribe': a crisis involving merely a concept or the empirical foundations of anthropology itself?', in: ibid., *Perspectives in Marxist Anthropology*, Cambridge: Cambridge University Press.

Good, A., 1991, *The Female Bridegroom: A Comparative Study of Life-Crisis Rituals in South India and Sri Lanka*, Oxford: Clarendon.

Goody, J. and I. Watt, 1986 [1968], 'Konsequenzen der Literalität', in: J. Goody, I. Watt and K. Gough, *Entstehung und Folgen der Schriftkultur*, Frankfurt/M.: suhrkamp.

Gough, K., 1986 [1968], 'Implikationen der Literalität im traditionellen China und Indien', in: J. Goody, I. Watt and K. Gough, *Entstehung und Folgen der Schriftkultur*, Frankfurt/M.: suhrkamp.

Gregory, C.A., 2003 'The Oral Epics of the Women of the Dandakaranya Plateau: A Preliminary Mapping' in: *Journal of Social Sciences (JSS)*, July 2003, (Special Issue: 'Orissan Studies', ed. C. Mallebrein and L. Guzy).

Griffiths, W.G., 1993 [1946], *The Kol Tribe of Central India*, Calcutta: The Asiatic Society.

Grigson, W., 1991 [1938], *The Maria Gonds of Bastar*, Delhi: Vanya Prakashan.

Guha, R., 2000, *Savaging the Civilized. Verrier Elwin, His Tribals, and India*, Delhi: OUP.

Gupta, M. and K. Voll, 1999, 'Child Labour in India: An Exemplary Case Study', in: K. Voll, *Against Child Labour. Indian and International Dimensions and Strategies*, Delhi: Mosaic.

Guzy, L. 2002, '*Baba-s und Alekh-s—Askese und Ekstase einer Religion im Werden*', Berlin: Weißensee.

Hardenberg, R., 1999, '*Die Wiedergeburt der Götter. Ritual und Gesellschaft in Orissa*', Hamburg: Kovac.

———, 2000, *Die Ideologie eines Hindu-Königtums. Struktur und Bedeutung der Rituale des Königs von Puri, Orissa/Indien*, Berlin: Arabisches Buch.

———, 2002a, 'Dongria Kond: Youth between Aggression and Friendship', paper presented at Inter-Congress of IUAES, Tokyo.

———, 2002b, 'Caste as Tribe: an analysis of social relations in the Niamgiris of Orissa', paper presented at the 17th European Conference on Modern South Asian Studies, Heidelberg.

Hardenberg, R. and S.K. Panda, 1999, *Oriya-German-English: Basic Vocabulary*, Berlin: Institut für Ethnologie der Freien Universität.

Heesterman, J.C., 1998, 'The Conundrum of the King's Authority', in: J.F. Richards, *Kingship and Authority in South Asia*, Delhi: OUP.

Helm, J. (ed.), 1968, *Essays on the Problem of Tribe*, Seattle: University of Washington Press.

Hertz, R., 1960 [1907], *Death and the right hand*, Aberdeen.

Hocart, A.M., 1927, '*Kingship*', Oxford: OUP.

———, 1987 [1935], 'The Basis of Caste', in: *Imagination and Proof: Selected Essays of A.M. Hocart*, ed. R. Needham, Tuscon: University of Arizona Press.

Iteanu, A., 1999, 'Synchronisations among the Orokaiva', in: *Social Anthropology*, 7. 3, pp. 265-78.

Jamous, R., 1992, 'The brother-married-sister relationship and marriage ceremonies as sacrificial rites: a case study from northern India', in D. de Coppet (ed.), *Understanding Rituals*, London: Routledge, pp. 52-73.

Jeffrey, P., 2000, 'Identifying differences: gender politics and religious community in rural Uttar Pradesh', in: J. Leslie and M. McGee, *Invented Identities: The Interplay of Gender, Religion and Politics in India*, Oxford: OUP.

Jena, M.K. et al., 2002, '*Forest Tribes of Orissa*, vol. 1: The Dongria Kondh', New Delhi: DK Printworld.

Jensen, J., 1992 [1983], 'Wirtschaftsethnologie', in: H. Fischer (ed.), *Ethnologie. Einführung und Überblick*, Berlin: Reimer.

Kantorowicz, E.H., 1994 [1957], *Die zwei Körper des Königs. Eine Studie zur politischen Theologie des Mittelalters*, München: dtv.

Kapadia, K., 1996, *Siva and her Sisters: Gender, Caste, and Class in Rural South India*, Delhi: OUP.

Karve, I., 1998 [1953], 'The Kinship Map of India', in: P. Uberoi (ed.), *Family, Kinship and Marriage in India*, Delhi: OUP, pp. 50-73.

Kaushik, M., 1976, 'The symbolic representation of death', in: *Contributions to Indian Sociology* (NS), vol. 10, no. 2.

———, 1999, 'The Idea of Shakti', in: '*Woman/Goddess: an exhibition of photographs*', ed. G. Sinha, New Delhi.

Khare, R.S., 1976, *The Hindu Home and Hearth*, New Delhi.

Kinsley, D., 1987, '*Hindu Goddesses: Vision of the Divine Feminine in the Hindu Religious Tradition*', Delhi: Motilal Banarsidass.

Kochar, V., 1970, *Social Organisation among the Santal*, Calcutta: Temple Press.

Kolenda, PP. , 1990, 'Untouchable Churas through their Humor', in O.M. Lynch (ed.), *Divine Passions: The Social Construction of Emotion in India*, Berkeley, pp. 116-53.

Kroeber, A.L., 1948 [1923], *Ánthropology: Race, Language, Culture, Psychology, Prehistory*, New York: Harcourt, Brace and Co.

Kulke, H., 2001 [1976], 'Kṣatriyaization and Social Change: A Study in the Orissan Setting', in: idem, *Kings and Cults: State Formation and Legitimation in India and Southeast Asia*, Delhi: Manohar.

———, 2001 [1978], 'Royal Temple Policy and the Structure of Medieval Hindu Kingdoms', in: idem, *Kings and Cults: State Formation and Legitimation in India and Southeast Asia*, Delhi: Manohar.

———, 1979, '*Jagannātha-Kult und Gajapati-Königtum: Ein Beitrag zur Geschichte religiöser Legitimation hinduistischer Herrscher*', Wiesbaden: Franz Steiner.

———, 2001 [1987a], 'The Chronicles and the Temple Records of the Mādaḷā Pānji of Puri: A Reassessment of the Evidence', in: idem, *Kings and Cults: State Formation and Legitimation in India and Southeast Asia*, Delhi: Manohar.

———, 2001 [1987b], 'Reflections on the Sources of the Temple Chronicles of the Mādaḷā Pāñji of Puri', in: idem, *Kings and Cults: State Formation and Legitimation in India and Southeast Asia*, Delhi: Manohar.

———, 2001 [1993], 'Tribal Deities at Princely Courts: The Feudatory Rajas of Central Orissa and their Tutelary Deities (istadevatas)' in: idem, *Kings and Cults: State Formation and Legitimation in India and Southeast Asia*, Delhi: Manohar.

Kulke, H. and D. Rothermund, 1999 [1986], '*A History of India*', London: Routledge.

Kurin, R., 1990, 'Turbans, Skirts and Spirit: Folk Models of a Punjabi Muslim Brotherhood', in: *Social Analysis*, 28: pp. 97-113.

Langulesvara Itihasa, Translation of a Telugu manuscript of S.N. Rajguru (Local Records, vol. 37, pp. 409-98), GOML (Government Oriental Manuscripts Library), ORP. MS 457.

Leach, E., 1991, '*Lévi-Strauss—Zur Einführung*', Hamburg: Junius.

Lévi-Strauss, C., 1992 [1973], 'Die Geschichte des Asdiwal', in: ibid., '*Strukturale Anthropologie II*', Frankfurt/M.: Suhrkamp: pp. 169-224.

———, 1997 [1958], 'Die Struktur der Mythen', in: ibid., '*Strukturale Anthropologie I*', Frankfurt/M.: Suhrkamp: pp. 226-54.

———, 1996 [1980], '*Mythos und Bedeutung*', Frankfurt/M.: Suhrkamp.

———, 1985, '*Der Blick aus der Ferne*', München: Fink.

Lindquist, G., 1995, 'Travelling by the Other's Cognitive Maps or Going Native and Coming Back', in: *Ethos*, nos. 1-2, pp. 5-40.

Ludden, D., 1996, *Making India Hindu: Religion, Community, and the Politics of Democracy in India*, Delhi: OUP.

MacDougall, J., 1977, 'Agrarian reform vs. religious revitalization: collective resistance to peasantization among the Mundas, Oraons and Santals, 1858-95', in: *Contributions to Indian Sociology* (NS), vol. 11, no. 2.

Madan, T.N., 1989 [1965], *Family and Kinship: A Study of the Pandits of Rural Kashmir*, Delhi: OUP.

———, 1998 [1975], 'The Structural Implications of Marriage in North India: Wife-givers and Wife-takers among the Pandits of Kashmir,' in P. Uberoi (ed.), *Family, Kinship and Marriage in India*, Delhi: OUP, pp. 287-306.

———, 1985, 'Concerning the Categories subha and suddha in Hindu Culture: an Exploratory Essay', in: J.B. Carman and F. Apffel Marglin (eds.), *Purity and Auspiciousness in Indian Society*, Leiden.

———, 2001 [1987], *Non-Renunciation. Themes and Interpretations of Hindu Culture*, Delhi: OUP.

Mahapatra, L.K., 1987, 'Ex-Princely States of Orissa: Mayurbhanj, Keonjhar and Bonai', in: S. Sinha, *Tribal Polities and State Systems in Pre-Colonial Eastern and North Eastern India*, Calcutta: Bagchi.

Malamoud, C., 1992, 'Brothers and Sisters in Brahmanic India', in: D. de Coppet (ed.), *Understanding Rituals*, London: Routledge.

Malinowski, B., 1984 [1922], *Argonauten des westlichen Pazifik*, Frankfurt/M.: Suhrkamp.

Mallebrein, C., 1993 '*Die Anderen Götter: Volks- und Stammesbronzen aus Indien*', Köln: Edition Braus.

———, 2001a, 'When the buffalo becomes a pumpkin—The animal sacrifice contested', paper presented at Salzau Conference of the Orissa Research Project.

———, 2001b, 'Tribal Art: Continuity and Change', in: *Orissa Revisited* (ed. Pratapaditya Pal), Mumbai, vol. 52, no. 3, pp. 142-61.

———, 2004, 'Entering the Realm of Durga: Patkhanda, a Hinduized Tribal Deity', in: A. Malinar, H. Frese and J. Beltz (eds.), *Text and Context in Orissa (and beyond)*, Delhi: Manohar.

Mamoria, C.B., 1957, '*Tribal Demography in India*', Allahabad: Kitab Mahal.

Marglin, F.A., 1989 [1985], '*Wives of the God-King: The Rituals of the Devadasis of Puri*', Delhi: OUP.

Marglin, F.A., 1985, 'Types of Opposition in Hindu Culture', in: J.B. Carman, and F. Apffel-Marglin (eds.), *Purity and Auspiciousness in Indian Society*, Leiden.

Marriott, M., 1955, 'Little Communities in an Indigenous Civilization', in: ibid., *Village India*, Chicago: University of Chicago Press.

———, 1959, 'Interactional and Attributional Theories of Caste Ranking', in: *Man in India*, no. 39, pp. 92-107.

———, 1968, 'Caste Ranking and Food Transactions: A Matrix Analysis', in: N. Singer and B.S. Cohn, '*Structure and Change in Indian Society*', Chicago.

———, 1976, 'Hindu Transactions: Diversity without dualism', in: B. Kapferer, *Transaction and meaning*, Philadelphia.

Mauss, M., 1994 [1950], '*Die Gabe. Form und Funktion des Austauschs in archaischen Gesellschaften*', Frankfurt/M.: suhrkamp.

Mayer, A., 1978 [1966], 'The Significance of Quasi-Groups in the Study of Complex Societies', in: *The Social Anthropology of Complex Societies*, A.S.A. Monographs (ed. M. Banton), London: Tavistock.

McDougal, C.W., 1963, 'The Social Structure of the Hill Juang', Ph.D. thesis, The University of New Mexico.

Michaels, A., 1998, *Der Hinduismus*, München: Beck.

———, 1999, 'Ancestors, Demons and the Ritual Impossibility of Death in Brahmanical Hinduism: Bala's Fourteenth in Deopatan (Nepal)', in: E. Schömbucher and C.P. Zoller, *Ways of dying: Death and its Meanings in South Asia*, Delhi: Manohar.

Middleton, J. and D. Tait, 1970, *Tribes without Rulers: Studies in African Segmentary Systems*, London.

Mitchell, A.G., 1995 [1982], *Hindu Gods and Goddesses*, Delhi: UBSPD.

Moffatt, M., 1979, *An Untouchable Community in South India. Structure and Consensus*, Princeton: Princeton University Press.

Mohanty, U.C., 1973-4, 'Bond-Friendship among the Gadaba', in: *Man in Society*, vol. 1.

———, 1963-4, 'Traditional Officials in the Kisan Society', in: *Adibasi*, no.1.

Mukherjea, C., 1962 [1939], *The Santal*, Calcutta.

Nag, M., 1968, 'The Concept of Tribe in the Contemporary Socio-Political Context of India', in: J. Helm (ed.), *Essays on the Problem of Tribe*, Seattle: Washington University Press.

Nanda, S., 1994, 'Study on secular Growth Trend in Orissa', unpublished Ph.D. thesis, Sambalpur University, Sambalpur.

Narayanan, V., 1985, 'The Two Levels of Auspiciousness in Śrīvaiṣṇava Ritual and Literature', in: J.B. Carman and F.A. Marglin (eds.), *Purity and Auspiciousness in Indian Society*, Leiden: E.J. Brill, pp. 55-64.

Nayak, B.B., 1987-8, 'The Agharias of Western Orissa and their Socio-Economic Life', unpublished M.A. thesis, Sambalpur University, Sambalpur.

Nayak, P.K., 1989, *Blood, Women and Territory: An analysis of Clan Feuds of the Dongria Kondhs*, Delhi: Reliance.

———, 2001, 'Jagannath and the Adivasis: Reconsidering the Cult and its Traditions', in: H. Kulke and B. Schnepel (eds), *Jagannath Revisited. Studying Society, Religion and the State in Orissa*, Delhi: Manohar.

Needham, R., 1973, 'Prescription', *Oceania*, 42, pp. 166-81.

O'Flaherty, W.D., 1988 [1976], '*The Origins of Evil in Hindu Mythology*', Delhi: Motilal Banarsidass.

Oppitz, M., 1991, '*Onkels Tochter, keine sonst. Heiratsbündnis und Denkweise in einer Lokalkultur des Himalaya*', Frankfurt/M.

Otten, T., 2000, 'In a Remote Area: Categories of the Person and Illness among the *Desia* of Koraput, Orissa', in: *Journal of Social Sciences*, vol. 4, no. 4, Oct., 'Asian World Views: Context and Structure' by R. Hardenberg.

———, forthcoming (a), '"Given by God" and "Come on its own": Concepts of Illness among the Rona in Highland Orissa', in: G. Pfeffer (ed.) *Periphery and Centre*, Delhi: Manohar.

———, forthcoming (b) 'People of the Hills: How the Rona deal with Social Change' in: M. Carrin and H. Tambs-Lyche, *People of the Jungle*, Copenhagen: Curzon Press.

Padel, F., 1995, *The Sacrifice of Human Being. British Rule and the Konds of Orissa*, Delhi: OUP.

Panda, S.K., 1999, *Political and Cultural History of Orissa*, New Delhi: New Age International Publishers.

Pandey, R., 1993 [1969], *Hindu Samskaras: Socio-Religious Study of the Hindu Sacraments*, Delhi.

———, 2000, 'Proving "Indigenity", Exploiting Modernity: Modalities of Identity Construction in Middle India', in: *Anthropos* 95, pp. 49-63.

———, 1992, *The Munda of Central India: An Account of their Social Organization*, Delhi.

Parry, J., 1979, '*Caste and Kinship in Kangra*', Delhi: Vikas.

———, 1994, *Death in Benares*, Cambridge.

Pasayat, C., 1998, *Tribe, Caste and Folk Culture*, Jaipur: Rawat.

Patel, P.K., undated manuscript, 'The Agharias of Orissa: A brief Synoptic View'.

Patel, S. and D.K. Behera, 1999, 'Cultural Construction of Womanhood among the Agharias of rural western Orissa', in: R. Indira and D.K. Behera (eds.), *Gender and Society in India*, vol. 2, Delhi: Manak Publication.

Patel, S.K., 1995, 'Origin of the Agarias', in: Orissa History Congress, Proceedings of 1995 session, pp. 103-5.

Pattanaik, N., 1952, 'Offering to the Manes (Sraddha) among the Agrias of Sundargarh, Orissa', in: *Man in India*, vol. 32, no. 3, July-Sept., pp. 143-6.

Pattnaik, B.K., 1997, 'Tribe-Caste Interaction: A Process of Acculturation Among the Sabaras in an Oriya Village', in: G. Pfeffer and D. Behera, *Contemporary Society: Tribal Studies*, vol. 2: *Development Issues, Transition and Change*, Delhi: Concept.

Pfeffer, G., 1978, 'Puri's Vedic Brahmins: Continuity and Change in their traditional institutions,' in: A. Eschmann, H. Kulke and G.C Tripathi, *The Cult of Jagannath*, Delhi: Manohar.

———, 1982a, *Status and Affinity in Middle India*, Wiesbaden: F. Steiner.

———, 1982b, '"Indien und die Dualorganization": Eine Kritik an W. Koppers', in: *Anthropos* 77, pp. 134-50.

———, 1983, 'Generation and marriage in Middle India: the evolutionary potential of "restricted exchange"', in: *Contributions to Indian Sociology* 17 (1), pp. 87-121.

———, 1994, 'The Dualistic Culture of the Juang', in G.C. Tripathi and H. Kulke (eds), *Religion and Society in Eastern India*, Delhi: Manohar.

———, 1996, 'The Young and the Junior Set in Tribal Middle India', in: G. Pfeffer and D.K. Behera, *Contemporary Society: Childhood and Complex Order*, Delhi: Manak.

———, 1997, 'The Scheduled Tribes of Middle India as a Unit: Problems of Internal and External Comparison', in: G. Pfeffer and D. Behera, *Contemporary Society: Tribal Studies*, vol. 1: *Structure and Process*, Delhi: Concept, pp. 3-27.

———, 1999, 'Gadaba and the Bondo Kinship Vocabularies versus Marriage, Descent and Production', in: G. Pfeffer and D. Behera, *Contemporary Society: Tribal Studies*, vol. 4: *Social Realities*, Delhi: Concept.

———, 2000, 'Tribal Ideas' in: *Journal of Social Sciences (JSS)*, vol. 4, no. 4 (Oct.), (Special Issue: 'Asian World Views: Context and Structure', ed. R. Hardenberg), pp. 331-46.

———, 2001, 'A Ritual of Revival among the Gadaba of Koraput', in: H. Kulke, and B. Schnepel (eds.), *Jagannath Revisited: Studying Society, Religion and the State in Orissa*, Delhi: Manohar.

———, 2002, 'The Structure of Middle Indian Tribal Society Compared', in: G. Pfeffer and D. Behera, *Contemporary Society: Tribal Studies*, vol. 5 *Concept of Tribal Society*, Delhi: Concept.

———, 2003, Review of 'Verrier Elwin Philanthropologist: Selected Writings' by N. Rustomji, in: *Journal of Anthropological Reserach*.

———, forthcoming (a), 'Bondo Violence', in: M. Carrin and H. Tambs-Lyche, (eds.), *People of the the Jungle*, Copenhagen: Curzon Press.

———, forthcoming (b), 'Tribal Society of Highland Orissa, Highland Burma, and Elsewhere', in: A. Malinar, H. Frese and J. Beltz, *Text and Context*, Delhi: Manohar.

———, unpublished (c), 'Sahlins' Tribesmen reconsidered: Highland Orissa in eastern India'.

Pocock, D.F., 1957, 'Inclusion and Exclusion: A Process in the Caste System of Gujerat', in: *Southwestern Journal of Anthropology*, vol. 13, pp. 19-31.

———, 1962, 'Notes on *Jajmani* Relationships', in: *Contributions to Indian Sociology*, pp. 78-95.

———, 1972, *Kanbi and Patidar*, Oxford: Clarendon.

Polanyi, K., 1968 [1957], 'The Economy as Instituted Process', in: E.E. LeClair Jr. and H.K. Scheider (eds.), *Economic Anthropology: Reading in Theory and Analysis*, New York: Holt Rinehart and Winston.

Radcliffe-Brown, A.R., 1978 [1924], 'Der Mutterbruder in Südafrika', in: F. Kramer and C. Sigrist, *Gesellschaften ohne Staat, Band 2: Genealogie und Solidarität*, Frankfurt/M.: Syndikat.

———, 1931, *The Social Organization of Australian Tribes*, Melbourne: Macmillan.

———, 1952 [1940], 'On Joking Relationships', in: idem, *Structure and Function in Primitive Society*, London: Cohen & West, pp. 90-104.

Raheja, G.G., 1988, *The Poison in the Gift. Ritual, Prestation, and the Dominant Caste in a North Indian Village*, Chicago: University of Chicago Press.

Randeria, S., 1999, 'Mourning, Mortuary Exchange and Memorialization: The Creation of Local Communities among Dalits in Gujarat', in: E. Schömbucher and C.P. Zoller, *Ways of dying: Death and its Meanings in South Asia*, Delhi: Manohar.

Redfield, R., 1956, *Peasant Society and Culture*, Chicago: Chicago University Press (published in combination with R. Redfield, 'The Little Community').

Richards, J.F., 1998, 'Introduction' in: idem. (ed.), *Kingship and Authority in South Asia*, Delhi: OUP.

Risley, H.H., 1981 [1891], *Tribes and Castes of Bengal: Ethnographic Glossary*, vol. I, Calcutta: Mukhopadhyay.

Roseberry, W., 1989, 'Peasants and the World', in: S. Plattner (ed.), *Economic Anthropology*, Stanford: Stanford University Press.

Rothermund, D., 1978, *Government, Landlord, and Peasant in India: Agrarian relations under British rule 1865-1935*, Wiesbaden: Steiner.

Rowe, W.L., 1968(a), 'The New Cauhāns: A Caste Mobility Movement in North India', in: J. Silverberg, *Social Mobility in the Caste System in India*, The Hague: Mouton.

———, 1968(b), 'Mobility in the Nineteenth Century Caste System', in: M. Singer and B. Cohn (eds.), *Structure and Change in Indian Society*, Chicago: Aldine.

Roy, S.C., 1970 [1912], *The Mundas and their Country*, London: Asia Publishing House.

———, 1925, *The Birhors. A little known Jungle Tribe of Chota Nagpur*, Ranchi: The G.E.L. Mission Press.

———, 1999 [1928], *Oraon Religion and Customs*, Delhi: Gyan Publishing House.

Roy, S.C. and R.C. Roy, 1937, *The Khāṛiās*, 2 vols., Ranchi: 'Man in India' Office.

Russell, R.V. and Hiralal, 1975 [1916], *Tribes and Castes of the Central Provinces of India*, vol. II, Delhi.

Sahlins, M.D., 1963, 'Poor Man, Rich Man, Big Man, Chief: Political Types in Melanesia and Polynesia', in: *Society and History*, 5, pp. 285-303.

———, 1965 'On the Sociology of Primitive Exchange', in: *The Relevance of Models for Social Anthropology*, ASA Monographs, London: Tavistock.

———, 1968, *Tribesmen*, Englewood Cliffs: Foundations of Modern Anthropology Series.

Schnepel, B., 1997, '*Die Dschungelkönige. Ethnohistorische Aspekte von Politik und Ritual in Südorissa/Indien*', Stuttgart: Franz Steiner.

———, 2001, 'Kings and Rebel Kings: Rituals of Incorporation and Dissent in South Asia', in: H. Kulke and B. Schnepel, *Jagannath Revisited: Studying Society, Religion and the State in Orissa*, Delhi: Manohar.

———, 2002, *Jungle Kings: Ethnohistorical Aspects of Politics and Ritual in Orissa*, Delhi: Manohar.

Schwerin, D., 1977, *Von Armut zu Elend. Kolonialherrschaft und Agrarverfassung in Chota Nagpur, 1858-1908*, Wiesbaden: Steiner.

Sengupta, S., 1997, 'Tribe-Caste Transformation on Biological Plane: A Study among the Koch Population of Kamrup District, Assam', in: G. Pfeffer, and D. Behera, *Contemporary Society: Tribal Studies*, vol. 2: *Development Issues, Transition and Change*, Delhi: Concept.

Shanin, T., 1990, *Defining Peasants. Essays concerning rural societies, Explorary Economies, and Learning from them in the contemporary world*, Oxford: Basil Blackwell.

Sharma, A., 1988, *Sati: Historical and Phenomenological Essays*, Delhi.

Sinha, S., 1957, 'Tribal Cultures of Peninsular India as a Dimension of Little Tradition in the Study of Indian Civilisation: A Preliminary Statement' in: *Man in India*, vol. 37, no. 2, pp. 93-118.

Skoda, U., 2000, 'The Kinship System of the Aghria', in: *Journal of Social Sciences*, vol. 4, no. 4, Oct., 'Asian World Views: Context and Structure' by R. Hardenberg.

———, 2002, *Forever Yours: Mobility and Equilibrium in Indian Marriage*, Delhi: Mosaic.

Sontheimer, G.-D., 1994, 'The Vana and the Kṣetra: The Tribal Background of Some Famous Cults', in: G.C. Tripathi and H. Kulke, *Religion and Society in Eastern India*, Delhi: Manohar.

Sörensen, S., 1978 [1904], *An index of Names in the Mahabharat*, Delhi: Motilal Banarsidass.

Southall, A.W., 1970, 'The Illusion of Tribe', in: *Journal of Asian and African Studies*, 5/1-2: 28-50.

Spradley, J., 1979, *The Ethnographic Interview*, Manchester.

Stein, B., 1975, 'The State and the Agrarian Order in Medieval South Asia: A Historiographical Critique', in: idem, *Essays on South India*, Hawaii: University Press of Hawaii, pp. 64-91.

Strümpell, C., 2003, 'Industrial Centres in the Eastern Ghats', paper to be presented at the annual conference of the Orissa Research Project, Salzau.

Tambs-Lyche, H., 1997, *Power, Profit and Poetry: Traditional Society in Kathiawar, Western India*, Delhi: Manohar.

Tanabe, A., 1996, 'Indigenous Power, Hierarchy and Dominance: State Formation in Orissa, India', in: H.J.M. Claessen and J.G. Oosten, *Ideology and the Formation of Early States*, Leiden: Brill.

Tandon, J.S., 1966, 'Lakshmi Puja in Tribal Bastar', in: *Folklore* 7/1, pp. 96-9.

Thapar, R., 2002 [1978], 'Origin Myths and the Early Indian Historical Tradition' in: idem., *Cultural Pasts*, Delhi: OUP, pp. 754-81.

———, 2002 [1992], 'Clan, Caste and Origin Myths in Early India', in: idem, *Cultural Pasts*, Delhi: OUP, pp. 782-96.

Thapar, R. and M.H. Siddiqi, 1997 [1979], 'Tribals in History: The Case of Chota Nagpur', in: D. Gupta, *Social Stratification*, Delhi: Oxford University Press.

Trautmann, T.R., 1995 [1981], *Dravidian Kinship*, Delhi: Vistaar.

Trawick, M., 1992, *Notes on Love in a Tamil Family*, Berkeley: University of California.

Tripathi, N., 1972 [1936], 'A few Feasts, Festivities and Observances in Orissa: The Maha-Lakshmi Puja', in: *Man in India*, vol. 16, Amsterdam.

Trivedi, H.R., 1969 [1961], *The Mers of Saurashtra: An Exposition of their Social Structure and Organisation*, Baroda: Baroda University.

Troisi, J. 2000 [1979], *Tribal Religion: Religious Beliefs and Practices among the Santals*', Delhi: Manohar.

Turner, V., 1995, [1969], *The Ritual Process. Structure and Anti-Structure*, New York: Aldine De Gruyter.

Urhahn, M., 1985, 'Grenzen und Übergänge von Kasten- und Stammesgesellschaft in Indien', unpublished Ph.D. thesis, Heidelberg University.

van der Veen, K., 1973, 'Marriage and Hierarchy among Anavil Brahmins of South Gujarat', in: *Contributions to Indian Sociology*, NS 7, pp. 36-52.

Vatuk, S., 1969, 'A Structural Analysis of the Hindi Kinship Terminology', in: *Contributions to Indian Sociology*, 3 (NS), pp. 94-115.

———, 1975, 'Gifts and Affines in North India', in: *Contributions to Indian Sociology*, 9 (NS): pp. 155-96.

Vitebsky, P.P., 1993, *Dialogues with the Dead*, Cambridge.

Waterstone, R., 1995, *Indien. Religion und Riten, Götter und Kosmos, Meditation und die Kunst des Yoga*, Gütersloh.

Weber, M., 1988 [1921], *Gesammelte Aufsätze zur Religionssoziologie II*, Tübingen: UTB.

———, 1985 [1922], *Wirtschaft und Gesellschaft*, Tübingen.

Wiser, W.H., 1988 [1936], *The Hindu Jajmani System: A socio-economic system interrelating members of a Hindu Village community in services*, Delhi: Munshiram Manoharlal.

Wolf, E.R., 1966, *Peasants*, Englewood Cliffs: Foundations of Modern Anthropology.

Zimmer, H., 1947, *Myths and Symbols of Indian Art and Civilization*, New York: Pantheon.

Zimmermann, F., 1987, *The Jungle and the Aroma of Meats*, Berkeley: University of California Press.

Index